# DACEY
# ON
# MUTUAL
# FUNDS

*Other Books by* NORMAN F. DACEY

How to Avoid Probate!
What's Wrong with Your Life Insurance

# DACEY ON MUTUAL FUNDS

by Norman F. Dacey

Foreword by
The Honorable JOHN E. MOSS

Chairman
Subcommittee on Commerce and Finance
United States House of Representatives

CROWN PUBLISHERS, INC., NEW YORK

# ACKNOWLEDGMENTS

The author gratefully acknowledges his indebtedness to his friend and counsel Arthur Stephen Penn, of the New York Bar, whose instinct for doing what is right and whose capacity for rooting out what is wrong was of invaluable assistance in researching many of the investment practices here discussed. His keen insights into mutual fund management practices have contributed materially to this volume.

The author also acknowledges with thanks the important assistance of his friend and associate Richard L. Breault, who created the charts for this book.

SECOND PRINTING BEFORE PUBLICATION

# CONTENTS

# FOREWORD

Although the public associates Norman F. Dacey with his best seller of a few years ago, *How to Avoid Probate!,* he is equally well known to the mutual fund industry and its regulators as a gadfly of the mutual fund establishment. Mr. Dacey's professional involvement with mutual funds goes back over thirty years, and there are few who can match the fervor of his conviction when it comes to mutual funds, their pros and cons, their management, and their regulation.

My own professional experience with mutual funds is of a somewhat more recent vintage. In 1966 I assumed the chairmanship of the House Subcommittee on Commerce and Finance, which has jurisdiction over mutual funds as well as all other securities matters and the Securities and Exchange Commission. One of the first items of business that came before the Subcommittee under my chairmanship was a bill designed to bring about reforms in a number of mutual fund practices. The bill had the solid backing of the S.E.C. and its chairman, and the reforms it proposed to bring about had been so thoroughly studied and were of such a relatively mild nature that it did not seem at the time that its passage would involve anything out of the ordinary in the way of hearings or debate.

That was not the first error in judgment I have committed in twenty-two years as a legislator, but it was certainly one of the most grievous. At this writing, almost four years after the introduction of the original Mutual Fund Reform Bill, the matter is still pending in the House Commerce Committee. At least ten different Mutual Fund Bills have been introduced in both the 90th and the 91st Congresses and a bill has twice passed the Senate with virtually no dissenting votes. I stepped on a merry-go-round when the Subcommittee first began considering mutual fund reform four years ago and I have yet to get off.

It still seems incredible to me that mutual fund advisers, who will admit to you privately that they owe a fiduciary obligation to the shareholders of the funds they organize and advise, have nevertheless bitterly resisted being held to a fiduciary duty standard under the law. Nor can I understand how mutual fund salesmen can object to giving their own self-regulatory organization, the National Association of Securities Dealers, the authority to prevent them from charging "excessive" sales loads.

But they have objected, and very vigorously at that. They have expended enormous sums of money for Washington lobbying efforts to bring about the kind of legislation they feel they can live with. I am not aware of even one penny that has been spent in a similar endeavor to assure the public shareholder of mutual funds that the legislation will reflect his legitimate interests as well. Because of this situation the mutual fund lobby, though certainly not the most reliable nor the most experienced, has achieved some very effective results to date.

I would hesitate to put the entire blame on the shoulders of the mutual fund industry and its representatives, however. A substantial portion of it must, in my opinion, be placed directly at the doorstep of you, the public shareholder. Time and again during the course of our efforts to bring about mutual fund reform we have heard the argument that no legislation is needed because there is no public outcry, as evidenced by the meager volume of letters of complaint to Members of Congress and to the Securities and Exchange Commission.

I have a basic philosophical disagreement with this position, but philosophical arguments are a good deal less convincing to most Members than constituent mail. The fact is that our laws relating to mutual funds were written thirty years ago, when the industry was but a fraction of its present size, and they have not been updated since. As surely as I sit here today I know that mutual fund reform will come to pass and I only hope that it does not take place in an atmosphere of confusion and haste brought on by a major public scandal.

I do not by these remarks mean to impugn the motives or the character of the majority of men in the mutual fund industry. They are, for the most part, honorable men who are entrusted with the stewardship of the financial security of millions of investors. But this fact should not be used to excuse them from up-to-date and reasoned regulation.

I know from personal experience how difficult it is for a layman to read the average prospectus or to understand the sometimes tangled interrelationships of a mutual fund complex. If Norman Dacey's book serves no other purpose than to assist in this understanding, it will be a most valuable addition to the literature of the subject. I hope it will serve one other purpose as well. I hope it will make you, the public shareholder, not only understand the industry better but also want to do something about those aspects of it that, in your opinion, need improvement. I hope you will, at a minimum, give the Congress and the S.E.C. the benefits of your experiences and thoughts along these lines so that we can all be better servants of the public interest.

John E. Moss
Chairman
Subcommittee on Commerce and Finance
United States House of Representatives

Washington, D.C.
June 18, 1970

# PREFACE

What you are about to read represents one man's point of view.

We all have our prejudices and the individual point of view we express understandably reflects those prejudices. Henny Youngman tells the story of one of those Ben Hur-type movies playing in New York which pictured a band of early martyrs cowering before a pride of savage lions in the Roman Coliseum. A Jewish lady left her seat and made her way to the box office where she demanded her money back.

"What's the trouble, lady?" the manager inquired, to which the patron replied, "Those lions in there are eating up all the Jews."

"Oh, lady, you've made a mistake!" exclaimed the theater man. "Those people aren't Jews—they're Christians." At this, a look of relief spread over the lady's face, and, mollified, she returned to her seat, only to come hurrying back a moment later to again demand her money.

Wearily, the manager asked, "What's the trouble now, lady?" Came the reply, "Some of those lions in there ain't eating."

It is quite possible that many persons will disagree with the views expressed in this book which, I frankly acknowledge, reflect *my* prejudices. Such disagreement, in some instances, simply may be a reflection of *their* prejudices. Many stockbrokers, some mutual fund people, and certain government officials will take offense in varying degrees. One cannot criticize without offending someone. Having made a few contributions to the fund industry over the years, I hope that I may criticize it in the loving spirit in which a father criticizes his child, even the child of whom he is proud.

Very few things in this world are perfect. From a close identification with the organization, administration, and distribution of mutual funds for more than a third of a century, I can say that the mutual fund industry is not perfect. What follows—avoiding the mere cataloging of facts and figures readily available elsewhere—is the essence of what I have learned in those years about its good points and its imperfections, set down in the earnest hope that it may help separate the wheat from the chaff.

After publication of a book of mine on life insurance some years ago, insurance men were furious with me. Other people thought it was splendid. A lot of lawyers said, "Good stuff! Give it to them; they deserve it!" Then I wrote *How to Avoid Probate,* which made the lawyers furious—but the insurance men liked it. "Good stuff!" they said. "Give it to them; they deserve it!" Perhaps now both the insurance men and the lawyers will come saying, "Good stuff," etc. On the other hand, I just might end up with nobody speaking to me.

I expect, though, that it will be said that I have praised the fund industry with faint damns.

In any case, here are the mutual funds, warts and all.

N. F. D.

50 Sailors Lane
Bridgeport, Connecticut

# Chapter 1

# WHY INVEST?

In today's affluent America, fully emerged from that economic Dark Age when the average man earned scarcely enough to feed, clothe, and shelter his family, millions of people are able to save and invest a substantial part of what they earn.

Earlier generations generally did not "save and invest." They just "saved." Knowing little about inflation and caring less, the average man hoarded dollars in a savings account or in the cash value of a life insurance policy. He was content to turn his money over to others who paid him rent for it in the form of interest—while they put it to work and built fortunes in which he did not share.

He did not ask to be an "owner." He was satisfied to be a "lender." Possessed of a blind faith in the value of the dollar he was saving, he asked only for an assurance that the borrower would return the exact number of dollars, plus the agreed interest that had been lent. He "invested" in the dollar.

Arnold Toynbee, the British historian, reports no recorded instance where a nation's currency did not gradually lose its value. Historically, then, money has been a bad investment, and it is unrealistic to assume that our currency will do something no currency in history has ever been able to do—that is, retain its real value, its purchasing power.

The American dollar has been declining steadily in value since its first issuance nearly two hundred years ago. During most of that period we lived within our income as a nation. Yet the dollar went down steadily. Living within our income is now old fashioned; there is no year in the foreseeable future when as a country we will spend less than we've earned. We would do well to consider thoughtfully the effect of this trend upon the future value of the dollar and upon our financial security in the years ahead.

Since 1900, the decline in the purchasing power of the dollar has averaged slightly more than 1 percent per year. Since 1939, the decline has averaged slightly more than 2 percent per year. In 1968, it was just over 4½ percent; in 1969 it was 6.1 percent. In a word, inflation is picking up speed. Nothing can *stop* inflation, but we *could* slow it down by living within our income as a nation. We can be forgiven if we view with pessimism the likelihood of any significantly successful effort in that direction in the foreseeable future.

Think back to the conditions in Germany between the two World Wars. When a man died, his family immediately made application for the proceeds of the life insurance for which he had paid premiums all his life. Those premiums had been hard to meet at times but he had never begrudged them; they would give his family financial security when he was gone.

However, when the money came, it was just enough to pay for the wreath to hang on his door. Many beneficiaries did not even bother filing claims under insurance policies carried by the head of the family; the stamp to mail the claim papers would have cost more than they would get back. Inflation had made the currency nearly worthless.

We have all seen those Phoenix Mutual Life Insurance Company advertisements picturing a man sitting in a boat fishing. In the "balloon" above his head, it originally read, "How I retired on $100 per month." Later, the figure became $150, $200, $250, and now $300. These advertisements tell us as dramatically as possible the story of inflation and its effect upon the millions who placed their confidence in someone's promise to deliver a fixed number of dollars at some date in the future. Ironically, the advertisements are the most effective argument against the insurance policies they offer. What has become of the early purchasers who struggled for years to meet the premiums on a policy that would pay them $100 per month? For certain they're not sitting in that Phoenix rowboat in carefree retirement—they are working at odd jobs trying to keep going. We can see them in the supermarket check-out line, staring in numb disbelief at the register total and wondering what went wrong.

We must see to it that this never happens to us.

In France, between the two World Wars, they had a controlled inflation, as distinguished from Germany's uncontrolled, printing-press inflation. The cost of living rose 700 percent. An American Army captain in France during World War I earned $200 per month, which was paid to him in 1,000 French francs. If the same Army captain had gone back to France in World War II, and had been paid the same $200, he would have received 84,000 French francs. Under controlled inflation, the currency had wasted away to one eighty-fourth of its initial value.

Stop for a moment to consider the possibility of that happening here. If, in the next twenty-five years, we experience the same degree of inflation that France experienced, the average medium-priced automobile will sell for $250,000. One hundred dollars will buy enough meat for one meal for two adults. If you leave your wife $100,000 in life insurance, it will provide her with room and board for one year.

I can hear someone saying, "It can't happen here."

Forget it. It *is* happening here.

Just glance at the old *New York Times* advertisement for a new Chevrolet below. The price: $495. Today the cost of the *extras* would exceed that.

Nothing so dramatically discloses the flight from the American dollar as the portfolios of the life insurance companies which twenty-five years ago had 45 percent of their assets invested in U.S. government bonds and today have less than 2 percent so invested.

Many years ago, the Carnegie Foundation for the Advancement of Teaching created the Teachers Insurance and Annuity Association, which was intended to function on a nonprofit basis as an insurance company for educators. But in 1951, the TIAA reached this conclusion:

"Security in retirement poses a difficult problem when it means not only a sufficient annuity income in dollars, but also a reasonable income in purchasing power. Traditional methods of saving have fallen short of the goal of providing suitable purchasing power income."

As a result, the College Equities Fund was organized in the summer of 1952. Its purpose was to give teachers a chance to protect their surplus dollars from inflation through a participation in a broad list of securities.

Said the sponsors: "Business activity has its ups and downs—the investor in common stocks must expect them—but in the long run an accumulating share in the growth and earnings of the major American industries seems a good way to assure a healthy retirement income, much as industrial growth helps assure the economic well-being of the nation as a whole."

Lately, we have been hearing a lot of talk from so-called economists about stopping inflation. Such talk is drivel. We have already noted that inflation cannot be stopped. Inflation is a "natural" law, like gravity. It has gone on for all recorded time and will continue to do so. It *can* be slowed down, but any serious attempt to slow it down must always necessarily create a recession—the recession is evidence that the medicine is working. The Federal Reserve Board's current restraints upon the supply of money and credit have put us into a recession.

But will the public stand for such bitter medicine?

However unpopular inflation may seem to be, there is one thing that is less popular—deflation—as the Eisenhower Administration soon learned when it instituted a "hard money" policy. While inflation may be inveighed against publicly, privately it is like good perfume—no one wants to be doused with it, but a little of it is very pleasant.

The jobless have no patience with economic theories, however well intentioned. No generation like ours will ever be willing to pay the price to slow down inflation significantly. We continue to give our votes to the politicians who promise us the most, seemingly unaware that we are being bribed with our own money. We smack our lips at the multimillion-dollar "redevelopment projects" that abound in our communities, apparently under the impression that they are to be paid for with some new, mysterious kind of money that does not have to be worked for, but which emerges endlessly like link sausage from some kind of machine in Washington.

As wages rise abroad, there is less pressure upon American industry to hold the line on wages here. As the threat of pricing ourselves out of foreign markets evaporates, American labor will be even more demanding. The wage spiral will continue to swirl upward. Unless wages are controlled, inflation cannot be controlled. All governments have found it impossible to maintain wage controls successfully for any period of time. Britain, pressing wage and price curbs for the past five years, has dismantled the machinery for enforcing such unpopular controls. The distinguished economist of the Fidelity Bank of Philadelphia, Dr. E. Sherman Adams, has observed that "once upon a time we used to say that what goes up must come down. But today, when industrial prices or wages go up, we know they will not come down. They are geared to a ratchet, which my dictionary defines as a mechanism which allows motion in one direction only. The old saying needs to be updated to read: What goes up goes higher."

I shall not detail here the unparalleled financial drain of defense in the atomic age and of exploration in the space age, nor recite the enormous burden of expense we have assumed in pursuit of our well-intentioned goal of raising the living standards of the rest of the world, nor shall I make more than passing reference to the mounting cost of our "social progress." Suffice it to say that these all add up to one thing: we will spend more than we make in the decade ahead—which is simply another way of spelling "i-n-f-l-a-t-i-o-n."

The last decade has seen the most prosperous years in our country's history. Yet there has been a succession of penetrations of the steadily expanding legal limit of our national debt. It is obvious that if we cannot pay some of our back bills in the prosperous years, we shall certainly never be able to pay them in less prosperous ones. This inability to lower or even to keep our national debt level is an unfailing signal of inflation. A nation mired deeply in debt can meet its obligations and extricate itself temporarily from insolvency only by cheapening its currency. Everybody makes more money, everybody pays more taxes. In just this fashion, successive generations of Frenchmen were robbed legally of their financial security by their government. However shamelessly it may abdicate its moral obligations by this inflationary process, the government maintains the fiction that it is meeting its obligation and thus preserves its "integrity."

The nation seems committed to a course that must end inevitably in the bankruptcy of the dollar. It is too late to change—we have passed the point of no return.

A thousand gravy trains are running a busy schedule, filled to capacity. A railroad can cancel a run that has only a few passengers. It cannot do it with a packed train. The flow of money expended in the name of "welfare" or "social progress" can never be cut off; its recipients have acquired a vested interest in it.

Taking into account the current efforts to stem inflation, what is the outlook for the future? Will its pace continue to accelerate, or will it be harnessed?

The prospects are not good. There are many reasons why we are likely to have increased inflation, why the dollar seems destined inexorably to continue its long slide into eventual worthlessness.

One reason is our Social Security system. Social Security is a fine thing. It is an insurance company, though, and as such, should be operated on a businesslike basis like any other insurance company. If the Social Security Administration were a private insurance company with outstanding obligations equal to those it now bears, it would be required by law to have policy reserves in excess of $400 billion. It claims reserves of $34 billion. Actually, it has no reserves. As fast as the money came in, it was handed over to the Treasury to help meet the everyday expenses of government. Government bonds and treasury notes—Uncle Sam's IOUs —were placed in the box. Over the years, outgo has exceeded income. Since each year more people cross over from the paying side of Social Security to the receiving side, the outlook is hardly encouraging.

The premiums that we pay in now, which are supposed to be put away to provide our retirement benefits at age sixty-five, are instead being used to pay Social Security benefits to those who came before us. As fast as they were received, *their* payments were siphoned off for other expenses of government, leaving their accounts empty.

The people who run Social Security are sensitive about the charge that the box is full of IOUs and not cash. They reply that other insurance companies own government bonds and no one accuses *them* of holding IOUs. The difference, of course, is that when a private insurance company sells a government bond, it collects from *somebody else*. When the Old Age and Survivors Insurance Trust redeems a government bond, the government—for this agency *is* the government—is simply collecting from itself. To put cash in one pocket, it must take it out of another pocket.

This is an adaptation of the old Rooseveltian economic theory exemplified by his remark "After all, we owe it to ourselves."

But what about the claimed reserves of $34 billion in the face of policy obligations calling for reserves of $400 billion? Their explanation for this is a lulu. Let me quote in verbatim from their booklet, *Facts About the Old Age and Survivors Insurance Trust Fund*:

Private life insurance companies must have reserves equal to the present value of all benefits less the present value of future premiums. These reserves are required by law because the private insurance company must be prepared to pay benefit liabilities or cash surrender values even if it should cease writing new business. The Federal program, on the other hand, since it is compulsory under Federal law, can count on continuing participation in the program and the continuing payment of contributions.

Doesn't this seem familiar? Haven't you heard of that system before?

Yes, you have. A generation ago in Boston, a man named Charlie Ponzi devised an investment scheme guaranteeing people 10 percent per month on their savings. From the money paid in by investors this month, he paid the "interest" due those who had invested last month. Uncle Sam stepped in, branded Ponzi a thief and clapped him into jail for twenty years—the same Uncle Sam who is today operating the greatest Ponzi scheme of all time, Social Security. If the people who are running it were operating a private insurance company, they would long since have been clapped into jail for failing to maintain the assets required by law. The Keynesian socialists who designed our Social Security system figured that it wouldn't collapse so long as the government has the right to tax us endlessly to raise the money. It is a fact, though, that no nation can go on indefinitely spending money it doesn't have.

Each successive Congress vies with its predecessors in extending Social Security benefits. No one seems to worry about where the money is coming from. In 1969, the Congress approved a 15 percent increase in benefits without any increase in taxes. What matter, though? If the taxes were increased they wouldn't be put away in a reserve to pay the increased obligation. They would just be spent like all the other tax receipts. An increase in the tax rate of 5.2 percent and an increase in the wage base to $9,000 is now planned.

Technically, the Social Security trust and other trust funds are distinguished from revenue raised through other taxes. Under the new budget concept, though, both trust funds and taxes are lumped together under revenue. Thus, the government's revenue picture would improve through higher Social Security taxes.

The early Communists predicted that they would take the world without a fight. Capitalism would collapse of its own weight, they said, and the capitalist world would fall into their hands like a ripe plum.

If we continue as we are doing with the Social Security system, we will surely end up bankrupt and the Communists will be proved right.

Another economic time bomb ticking away in our closet—and completely ignored—relates to our military manpower, specifically to the tremendous liability the taxpayer faces in the future of paying for past service and for disability. Almost one third of each manpower dollar is now going for past service alone—or saying it another way, for each two men on duty, the military payroll now must compensate a man who has no further obligation for service. The most unrealistically conservative projections indicate that this will increase to two retirees for each two and one half men on duty in the year 2000. The budgetary implications are staggering. We shall then be obligated to pay to military retirees alone an annual sum greater than our present total annual manpower costs. Military disability pensions now total $10 billion annually. With a continuation of "undeclared war," they will rocket into the financial stratosphere.

A corporation that had such an obligation would long since have begun to fund it in advance. Institutions that have pension obligations *always* put aside the money that actuaries tell them will be required to meet the obligation. We are not putting aside a dime toward this enormous future annual obligation. Each year the money paid to such retirees will have to come out of taxes collected that year.

An era of endless deficit financing lies ahead. Successive increases will be voted in the limits on the national debt. Our children will see that debt reach one trillion dollars. It now stands at one third of that figure, and 11 percent of the federal taxes collected is applied toward interest on that public debt. The government must take in more and more money. To do that, it must see to it that we earn more and more money from which we will pay more and more taxes. The dollars we earn and pay to the government won't be worth much—they will be what Al Smith called "boloney dollars"—but the government's obligation is in dollars, and it will maintain its "honor" if it pays off the dollars it owes, no matter how depreciated they may be.

Our forefathers, who bequeathed us a pleasant country in good financial condition, must be turning over in their graves at what we are doing to it and to our children and our children's children.

Increasingly, the wage contracts being negotiated by labor today contain acceleration clauses tied to the cost of living. In other words, inflation is *built into* our future. Try as we may, we cannot escape it.

While still other factors will contribute to the certain continuation of inflation, I have mentioned these few to suggest how inevitably we shall one day see the dollar driven to its knees.

In the circumstances, the prudent person will not hoard dollars. He will recognize the grave danger to his financial security inherent in inflation and he will take steps to hedge against it.

### HOW CAN ONE HEDGE AGAINST INFLATION?

There are three principal hedges against inflation:

### Real Estate

Real estate values generally reflect the rising tide of inflation. Of course, if someone builds a glue factory across the street from you, the value of *your* real estate may not rise as fast as some other real estate. More importantly, real estate lacks the prime characteristic of a good investment: liquidity. You can put up a FOR SALE sign and wait, or if you need your money in a hurry, you can sacrifice it for a quick sale. Also, it is doubly taxed: the community taxes you simply because you own it and Uncle Sam taxes any income it produces. If it is only land, there is probably no income, only outgo in the form of taxes.

### Commodities

Commodities also rise in value with inflation. Anyone can, for example, fill a warehouse with wheat or corn or lead. This is a highly technical field, though, with great risks, and is best left to the experts.

### Common Stocks

These are probably the most easily used hedge against inflation. Indirectly, they offer the hedge characteristics of both real estate and commodities. When inflation pushes real estate prices upward, the vast real estate holdings of the nation's corporations appreciate in value and a share of stock in those corporations becomes worth more. Similarly, when commodity prices soar, the millions of dollars of raw materials owned by America's corporations go up in value, and again their stock becomes more valuable. If, as a result of rising prices for its product, a company's stock that formerly earned $5.00 per share now earns $10.00, as an income-producing piece of property, it is now worth twice as much.

There have been periods, generally brief, when stock prices went down while the cost of living kept rising. But over the last thirty years, while the dollar has been losing 60 percent of its value, common stocks increased in value by more than 800 percent. Not all common stocks rise in value at the same rate—some are a poor investment, inflation or no inflation. On balance, though, stock prices have gone up as the purchasing power of the dollar has declined. Each individual must decide for himself whether to accept the risks of investment in exchange for the possible rewards. A flow of capital is essential to our free enterprise system, and that capital must come from investors, though inevitably some ventures must fail and some investors lose. But there is another risk which must be taken into account—the risk of not investing.

Marcus Nadler, the noted economist, wrote:

> The willingness to take the risk of equity ownership goes hand in hand with progress. Where people refuse these risks and prefer to invest only in high-grade fixed-income-bearing securities, the economy of the country is bound to stagnate.

The great fortunes in America were not built through accumulation of money in savings accounts, in life insurance endowments, or in savings bonds. They were built by people who invested their money where they received earnings, not interest.

Inflation is an economic disease to which all of us are subject. We must vaccinate ourselves against its effects. We must build up financial "antibodies" which will fight the disease. We do this by putting our dollars to work where they will grow, where they will multiply. We must invest. Note that I said "invest." I did not say "speculate."

Investment is a hedge against inflation.

# Chapter 2

# WAYS TO INVEST

Are you convinced of the importance of investment as a hedge against inflation? If so, let us review the eight principal avenues of investment that are available to you.

**Do-it-yourself**

You can read *The Wall Street Journal, Barron's,* and *The New York Times* every morning and make your own decisions about which securities to buy. There are thirty-eight major industries, each with its own group of trade journals. You are going to have to wade through all of them before you decide in which industries to invest. You must then select the individual companies within each industry to which you will commit your money. This is a huge task, and an endless one. Some people consider it a hobby without realizing what an expensive one it can be.

Remember, it is your financial security that is involved. If you tinker with the hall clock and botch the job, you can always take it to a clock repairman. But if you tinker with your financial security and botch the job, you can't take it anywhere to have it put right; your security may be gone, and there may not be time to rebuild it.

Investment is a job for professionals. It requires special education, training, and experience. Granted, you may know of an individual who has reportedly been very successful investing on his own, but you may not know the whole story—it is human to boast of one's successes and to hide one's reverses. I have known many persons who claimed to be successful investors but who, when we got to the facts, actually had done a dismal job of it. The oft-quoted Bernard Baruch once said of do-it-yourself investors:

It never would occur to anyone to open a department store in competition with Macy's or

Gimbel's or to make motor cars against Ford and General Motors without prior training or preparation. Yet the same man will cheerfully toss his savings into a market dominated by men who are as expert in their line as Macy's and the auto makers are in theirs.

It is strange how people think investing is so easy. A man will spend forty years in the hardware manufacturing business and will cheerfully acknowledge that he still has something to learn about it. But that same man after reading the financial pages of *The New York Times* for fifteen minutes in the morning becomes a financial expert. Many men give no more thought to the making of a substantial investment than they give to the purchase of a pair of shoes. How often has an investor gone into the market on a tip from a cabdriver or elevator operator?

Investment is competition. It is your judgment against someone else's. When you buy 100 shares of General Motors, someone somewhere must decide to sell 100 shares of that stock in order for the transaction to be consummated. You have decided that General Motors is a good investment, while the other person has decided that it is not. Six months from now, you can both look back and decide who was right. The point is that you are competing with another person in a matter of investment judgment.

Actually, you are competing with millions of other investors, including thousands of professionals who make their living at it. Banks, insurance companies, endowment funds and foundations, mutual funds, and a hundred other types of financial institutions are paying these professionals to outsmart you when it comes to investment decisions.

You and I can go out into the park and throw a football around and think we are pretty good at it. But the Kansas City Chiefs would murder us. They are pros. In just the same way, we can invest on our own and, enjoying a few successes, get the idea that we are pretty good. But eventually the investment pros will murder us.

Investment is not a do-it-yourself job.

## Brokers

The majority of individual investors deal with a broker to whom they look for advice in the selection of securities. A broker is like a pharmacist who knows how to fill prescriptions but not how to write them. If you go to your pharmacist friend and say, "Joe, I've got a bad throat. Can you suggest something for it?" Joe will be glad to make a recommendation. He has filled thousands of prescriptions for sore-throat remedies and he has a shelfful of patent medicines. He will be glad to suggest something if you are willing to put your throat in his care. But you would be smarter to go to a doctor of medicine, have him look at your throat, and write a prescription which you can then take to Joe to be filled.

The broker is the pharmacist of the financial world. He knows *how* to buy and sell securities but he does not know *which* to buy and sell. Like your friend Joe, he is willing to suggest something if you are willing to put your financial throat in his care. You will be much better off, though, if you arrange to have a "doctor of economy" write you a prescription and let your broker friend simply fill it.

Much of what we are told by Wall Street tea-leaf readers" about the outlook for business and the stock market is pure rubbish, conjured up by people with a purpose. Most of us know that the cyclical raising and lowering of the hemline by Paris dress designers is simply a cunning scheme to make that closetful of clothes upstairs obsolete. Not so well known is that many of the "They're going up!" "They're going down!" warnings we get from the community characterized collectively as Wall Street cloak an ulterior purpose of getting us to move. Actually, they do not know any more about it than any of us, but if their warning of a sharp decline ahead can induce us to sell everything we own—only to be told next week that a new "buy signal" has suddenly and unexpectedly appeared among their tea leaves— their cash registers will tinkle merrily and the commissions will pour in both ways.

Investing is an emotional experience for most people, and even old-timers know occasional moments of panic, however much they may publicly deny it. It is easy, then, for the financial world's crystal gazers to prey on the emotional majority of investors.

It is important that you understand that a broker does not make money because you make money. He makes money because you move your assets around. Whenever you have movement, you have friction. When you have friction, you have wear, and if you move your money around long enough, you will wear it out. Brokers generally move your money around quite a bit. During the past few years, some of the biggest and most highly respected brokerage firms in America have been fined and otherwise disciplined because they "churned" accounts.

A retired New Jersey tool manufacturer sued Merrill Lynch, the largest brokerage firm in the world, for $1,300,000, claiming that he had invested $125,000 over a thirty-day period as a result of "coercion" on the part of the firm's salesman. During the next thirty months, he charged, they turned his portfolio over fourteen times, with commissions of more than $30,000 to the firm. The irony of it is that Merrill Lynch has always displayed a holier-than-thou attitude toward mutual funds, declining to sell them on the ground that their sales cost was higher than stock exchange commissions. According to the tool manufacturer's lawyer, the case was settled out of court to his client's full satisfaction.

After denouncing mutual funds for twenty years, in 1969 Merrill Lynch decided to sell them. Its salesmen now offer a dozen or so funds on an "approved list" established by the firm. I have not been able to determine whether the approved list is based upon the quality of the managements involved or upon the volume of brokerage commissions they direct to Merrill Lynch.

When brokers participate in underwritings, a group of them purchase an entire issue of securities; marked up in price, the shares are then resold to the public. Perhaps the issue may turn out to be less desirable than when the underwriting group agreed to buy it. No matter; they own it, and their registered representatives will be told to go out and get rid of it.

Such a one with whom you may deal may honestly want to recommend something else to you. But he has no choice. The word has come down that he is to leave no stone unturned to unload the shares sitting on his firm's shelves. The conflict of interest is further emphasized by the fact that the salesman receives a higher commission for selling securities in the firm's inventory than securities for which the firm simply acts as agent.

There are numerous circumstances in which a broker might pick up a substantial number of shares of an over-the-counter stock, that is, one not listed on any securities exchange. Not infrequently, the purposes for which the stock was acquired do not materialize. The natural reaction is for the firm to divest itself of the holding. Happily, it can turn loose its sales force to unload the stock. The firm calls a meeting of its salesmen, gives them some information about the stock, omits reference to the unfavorable facts that have led to the decision to dispose of it, and asks the salesmen to recommend the stocks to clients. The reward is a higher rate of compensation than if they had sold listed stocks to the client. Sometimes the salesmen themselves know of the unfavorable facts affecting the stock or they simply sense that something is wrong with the offering. What do the salesmen do in such circumstances? At one end of their tug-of-war is their loyalty to the firm; at the other end, their regard for their clients, many of whom are also friends. If a man repeatedly declines to recommend such stocks, he will surely find himself out of a job. On the other hand, if he follows instructions and peddles the stock, he will lose a few clients including friends. Generally, the law of self-preservation prevails. He sacrifices his scruples.

The action of the broker in such circumstances is not unlike that of a used-car dealer who sells a defective used car knowing that the defect exists.

In the case of an over-the-counter issue for which only a thin market exists, the broker will frequently accompany his pitch with an assurance that he will find another buyer for it whenever you want to unload. If you call him a few months later and tell him that you are disenchanted with it and ask him to keep his promise, he will get busy on it. The very next person who walks in will be told that Widget, Inc., is a real sizzler, a once-in-a-lifetime opportunity, etc. Your broker has no choice. He promised you he would get rid of the lemon and he is keeping his promise. You have nothing to complain about unless it was *someone else* who bought Widget, Inc., from him three months ago and who is now dissatisfied, and *you* are the "next person" who has just walked in the door. You, trusting soul that you are, are about to become the proud owner of 250 shares of Widget, Inc.

You cannot blame the broker for doing his best to sell his wares, but you *can* blame yourself for thinking you are obtaining unbiased advice. You may wish to bear in mind that over half of all active brokerage firm representatives came into the business after the 1961–1962 bear market. What you are hearing, then, is not exactly the "voice of experience." However much some brokers may strive, therefore, to provide adequate research facilities and competent advice, too often it does not work out to the advantage of the customer.

The story is told of a visitor to New York being shown the sights—which included an impressive row of palatial yachts moored off the financial district and identified as the property of various prominent stock-brokers—innocently inquiring, "But where are the customers' yachts?"

## Tipster Services

The financial pages of the leading newspapers offer an endless variety of advertisements for tipster services available at prices ranging from a lowly $5.00 trial subscription to $200 or $300 per year. These have approximately the same validity as the "scratch sheet" sold outside racetracks. Generally speaking, they tell everyone to do the same thing at the same time. Actually, successful investing frequently consists in doing just the opposite of what a lot of people are doing. When they are buying furiously, you sell at the high prices then prevailing; when they are unloading, you buy back at a bargain.

It is not uncommon for the sponsors of such touting services to load up on a stock two or three weeks before the services enthusiastically recommend it. After the gullible subscribers have run the market up, these sponsors quietly unload their holdings at a handsome profit. It is astonishing how many people will fall for this trick over and over again in their financial meandering from tipster to tipster.

I knew a famous-name "economist" who operated a Boston advisory service. His nephew was in the same racket. They used to trade subscription lists. When one had exhausted the gullibility of his subscribers, he would turn his names over to the other, who would go to work to prove the maxim that there is a sucker born every minute.

My advice is to stay away from all of them.

## Investment Counsel

All professional investment counsel firms are registered under the Investment Advisers Act of 1940. Many such firms have a long and excellent record. They gather together a group of experts in the various fields of investment and apply the knowledge and judgment of that staff to the solution of the investment problems of individual clients.

They display varying degrees of competence, of course. The number of a firm's clients generally may be taken as a measure of its competence—assuming that a firm with many clients came to enjoy that happy state by delivering the goods. If a firm is long established and has only a few clients, it is a reasonable assumption that its investment performance has not been distinguished.

While this may not seem to be a completely dependable way of judging the skill of an investment counsel firm, there is actually no other way. Their accounts are private and confidential, and such firms properly do not make it a practice to open their records to examination by prospective clients. Actually, such records would be misleading anyway. Accounts have a variety of investment objectives and, reflecting those objectives, some accounts may be invested heavily in stocks while others are in bonds. If it were the practice to display performance records, a counsel firm could, in a bear market, easily produce an account concentrated in bonds that eloquently testified to the firm's sagacity in going into senior securities just before a market decline. On the other hand, the firm's farsightedness in a bull market could be proven by the display of an account heavily in stocks. In any case, the records are not available, and one must hire the firm pretty much on the strength of its reputation.

Regarding the successful firms, because they have more accounts, it is important to realize that each account must compete with the others for the attention of the managers. Also, the larger the account, the more fees it generates and, consequently, the greater the attention it gets.

A study by the S.E.C. revealed that the average investment counsel account was $795,000. A firm of real standing seldom accepts accounts under $100,000, which eliminates the great bulk of the population.

*Forbes* magazine has an investment counsel affiliate specializing in small accounts: $10,000–$25,000. These are the people who would ordinarily invest in a mutual fund. The magazine has for some years published a semi-annual "exposé" of mutual fund performance. In its early years, fund presidents used to write regularly to the editor, patiently explaining the errors in the figures given for their funds. They were ignored, and eventually they wearied of writing. *Forbes,* by offering its semi-annual issue about mutual funds as a come-on to new subscribers, persuades quite a number of people who are interested in mutual funds to identify themselves. Subscribe and you will be bombarded with junk mail from the investment advisory service affiliate. I have never known anyone who used the advisory service, but, on the basis of the magazine's general reputation, I would avoid it.

## Bank Trust Department

The trust department of a bank attempts to provide the same skilled professional management offered by an investment counsel firm. However, the bank performs two additional services. It accepts physical custody of the assets, whereas the investment counsel firm will simply instruct you (or your custodian) on what changes are to be made in your investments from time to time, and undertakes the after-death distribution of the assets in accordance with your prearranged instructions. Bank trusteeship has made a substantial contribution to the preservation of large estates in America. Our concern here, however, is solely with investment skill.

If one is to judge by the average performance of the two groups, there is not the slightest question but that the quality of the investment management provided by a bank is not nearly as good as that provided by an investment-counsel firm.

An investment-counsel firm exists because some individual or group of individuals feels that he or they have skill at money management. A trust department, on the other hand, frequently exists for no other reason than that such a department is traditionally a part of a bank. The charter of the bank entitles it to exercise trust powers. It exercises them not because it is skilled at the job but simply because it is entitled to do so.

Some banks have a trust department and encourage trust business even though they know that they are not qualified to perform the work. (The money was made in Smithville, and it should stay in Smithville. They would rather botch the job themselves than let it be done by a big-city bank.)

The last such survey showed that 74 percent of the banks in New York State with trust powers had not even one full-time trust officer. In the smaller cities, banks ordinarily do not have enough trust business to warrant the employment of the topnotch investment brains needed to put the money to work.

However, big-city banks frequently have so many accounts that they cannot watch them all often enough. New York banks, for example, have thousands of accounts each, but certainly not thousands of trust officers. It is obvious that each trust officer has a very large number of accounts for which he is responsible. No account enjoys continuous supervision. The best one can hope for is a monthly review—the As are checked on the first of the month, Bs on the second, and so on.

*New York Times* financial columnist Robert Metz stirred up a hornet's nest recently when he set out to explore the adequacy of the service provided by New York trust companies. His award-winning series featured complaints from many owners of accounts, and admissions from bank officers that some accounts were reviewed as infrequently as once a year.

But you have a choice: your account can suffer from incompetence in a bank in the boondocks or from neglect in a big-city bank.

As in the investment-counsel firm, bank trust accounts compete with each other for the attention of the managers, and size dictates attention.

Again, as in the investment counsel firm, the bank will not open its books to allow inspection of its performance record. Its services are hired solely on the basis of faith and hope.

Big-city banks seek accounts of $250,000 or more. Some will accept $100,000. In the smaller towns, they will take a smaller amount, perhaps as little as $25,000, but generally the quality of their service is similarly reduced.

A few years ago, the Trust Division of the American Bankers Association stated that an account of less than $35,000 could not properly be diversified. To solve the problem of inadequate diversification in small accounts, many banks long ago adopted the policy of maintaining a "common trust fund," a catchall account into which they dump all of their small, nuisance accounts.

A while ago, *Trusts and Estates* magazine, the professional journal in the trust field, published the results of a nationwide study that compared the ten-year performance of bank trust departments and a group of nine leading balanced mutual funds on the basis of an assumed investment of $100,000. The study was conducted by bankers, not by fund men, and since it reflected reports from a full 60 percent of the nation's trust companies, was the most significant report of its kind ever undertaken.

Income results before deducting trustee fees were:

(a) Bank trusts individually invested in a balanced portfolio of bonds and stocks: 4.48 percent,

(b) Bank trusts pooled with other trusts in a "common trust fund" under bank administration: 4.22 percent,

(c) Average of nine leading balanced mutual funds: 4.23 percent.

Note that trustee fees would reduce the bank income figures by perhaps 10 percent, whereas the mutual fund income figure reflects the net dividends paid by the funds after deduction of management fees and overhead expenses. Naturally, these results represent an average and some bank trusts did better than others, but this was equally true of the mutual funds.

In capital appreciation, an even more significant factor in these inflationary times when capital must grow so that there will be more money working to produce a larger income to keep up with the rising cost of living, here is what the $100,000 in each account was worth after ten years:

(a) Bank trusts individually invested in a balanced portfolio of bonds and stocks: $124,500,

(b) Bank common trust funds: $128,400,

(c) Average of nine leading balanced mutual funds: $145,200.

In capital appreciation, the bank common trust fund outperformed the individually managed accounts. This greater performance of the catch-all funds at first may be difficult to understand. The fact is that as the common trust funds have grown in size, they have begun to assume more importance in the banks, and for no other reason than that these funds represent the combined financial interests of hundreds of beneficiaries, they probably now receive a more careful, watchful supervision than any individual trust account.

Therefore, in seeking investment management via a bank trust, one must pick one's way carefully between the Scylla of incompetence and the Charybdis of neglect.

## Closed-End Investment Companies

Let us pretend that we have created a new corporation of which we are the directors, and we have issued one million shares of stock at $10.00 per share. As directors, we then invest the $10 million proceeds of the sale in a diversified portfolio of securities. Our company does not engage in any other business—it is simply an investment company.

We have created a "closed-end investment company."

"Closed-end" means that we will not issue any more shares after the original issue is sold. The absence of a continuous or regular sale of securities is this medium's chief characteristic. If someone wants to buy some of our shares, he will have to find an investor who owns some and who is willing to sell. On the other hand, if someone wants to sell some of his shares, we have no obligation to buy them back from him—he has to find a buyer elsewhere. Since buyers and sellers seldom find each other on their own, the transaction is effected through a broker who charges a regular stock exchange commission for his services.

The price a new buyer pays for the shares bought through the broker, or which a seller gets for shares sold through the broker, bears no relationship to their real value. The company issues a periodic report to shareholders which discloses the net asset value per share, but this figure is purely academic, for the company will not redeem the shares at that price and the broker disregards it in handling transactions in the stock. The market value is subject to the same forces operating on individual stocks or bonds. The price at which the shares are traded depends upon the public's interest in them and its appraisal of the skill of the company directors supervising the investment of the company's assets.

For many years, the shares of most closed-end investment companies have been selling at an appreciable discount from net asset value. The net asset value of the share may be $50.00 but the stock may be selling at $25.00 or $30.00. If the shareholders decided to wind up the company, they could sell all its assets, divide up the proceeds and go out of business. If they did that, they could collect the $50.00 each share is actually worth.

In the Great Depression years of 1931–1934, when shares of closed-end investment companies were selling at a huge discount, financier Floyd Odlum bought sufficient shares of one such company to gain control. He promptly voted to liquidate it—and collected the $50.00 per share. With the proceeds of this operation, he turned his attention to a second company where he repeated the process. From a series of such moves, Odlum accumulated a huge fortune. The average investor, of course, would lack the resources, the knowledge, and the shrewdness to carry out such an operation.

In 1929 there were hundreds of closed-end investment companies and only a handful of open-end investment companies (mutual funds). Today, the situation is reversed. There are hundreds of mutual funds and fewer than twenty closed-end companies. These figures reflect the investor's awareness that when he buys a mutual fund, whose daily computed actual asset value is the determining price, he pays exactly what it is worth; and when he sells it, he gets exactly what it is worth. Two or three closed-end investment companies' shares today sell at a premium, which means that an investor pays more for them than they are worth. However, the majority of closed-end company shares continue to sell at a discount, which means that when the investor sells them, he receives less than they are worth.

In one particular market period, the averages fluctuated narrowly, closing at almost the exact level at which they had begun the month. Despite the relative stability of the market, the price of the shares of one of the largest and best-known closed-end investment companies fell 10 percent. A substantial shareholder had died, and it was anticipated that his shares would be thrown upon the market to raise money to pay death taxes. I would never permit my estate to be invested in a manner in which, despite its diversification, it could lose 10 percent of its value because some stranger's heart stopped beating.

If the managers of a closed-end investment company decide that a shift in investment balance is desirable, they must sell some of the company's assets in order to accomplish the shift. If the nature of their operation was such that they had a regular flow of new money, they could change the investment balance from, say, stocks to bonds simply by directing all new money into bonds. The closed-end company managers have no such flow of new money, however. In order to buy bonds, they must obtain the money by first selling stocks.

In a sharp market decline, when bargains abound, a flow of new money could provide the wherewithal to take advantage of the bargains. There again, however, the closed-end company has no such flow of new money. It can raise money only by selling some of what it already owns, which obviously isn't very practical. One

commentator has compared this "dead end" characteristic of closed-end companies to a stagnant pool.

During the past year, some new closed-end investment companies have been organized by groups intending to pursue aggressive high-risk—and sometimes exotic—investment practices which, after the original sale of these shares, are not subject to the full-disclosure requirements of mutual funds. The shares of such companies appear to have found a ready market. However, closed-end investment companies, popular in the twenties, are financial dinosaurs, relics of a bygone age, and as a medium of investment for the public are far from ideal.

## Stock Life Insurance Companies

Quite often, one hears stock life insurance companies touted as a suitable medium for acquiring an interest in a diversified portfolio of securities. Certainly insurance companies do have such holdings, but their principal business is insurance, not investment.

Regulation of life insurance in this country is so negligible as to be practically nonexistent, and its securities reflect a degree of risk no sensible investor would want to take.

For years, Senator Thomas J. Dodd successfully prevented the Senate Antitrust and Monopoly Subcommittee from conducting an appropriate investigation into the industry's improprieties. Hearings conducted by the committee's chairman, Senator Philip A. Hart, revealed the sorry state of the automobile insurance segment of the industry. More recently, Senator Hart's hearings disclosed activities in the credit life insurance field that would make the Mafia green with envy.

If Senator Hart can overcome the apparent conflict of interest in Mrs. Hart's substantial holdings in stock life insurance companies, we may yet see the long-overdue Senate investigation of life insurance. It should come soon. Until then, I would not invest ten cents in the stock of any life insurance company.

Thousands of people in 1962 bought a book called *Life Insurance Stocks—The Modern Gold Rush* and followed its advice only to lose their shirts. It was written by Arthur Milton, a New York stockbroker/insurance man. He recently revised and reissued the book under a similar-sounding title. Anyone who ends up a sourdough in the new gold rush can't say he wasn't warned.

# Chapter 3

# WHY INVEST IN A
# MUTUAL FUND?

We have considered seven possible ways to invest. Let us now consider the eighth way: mutual funds.

Suppose we get together with a group of people twice a month, at which times we each pay in $25.00. We discuss what we have read about the stock market since our last meeting, review the tips we have been given and our hunches about individual issues, and decide collectively how to put the kitty to work. Perhaps we invite a stockbroker to our meetings to explain how the stock market works and to make investment suggestions.

What we would have, of course, is an investment club. There are now more than a hundred thousand such clubs across the country. There is even a National Association of Investment Clubs.

For many men, the investment club has supplanted the poker game. If the money we pay in at each meeting is money we might otherwise put into a poker game—money we can afford to lose—we might have some fun with our investment club. (The poker game has one advantage, though: The money stays in the crowd.)

Actually, as laymen, we know nothing about investing. We might just as sensibly get together twice a month and talk about how to take out an appendix. We are individually ignorant of just how the operation is done; if we get together and talk about it, we remain collectively ignorant. Even if we get a salesman from a surgical supply house to come and show us some scalpels, we still will not know how to take out an appendix.

Investment is a job for professionals. People who know nothing about it can get together and discuss it until the cows come home—but they will end by still knowing nothing about it.

If the money we are investing in the club is "serious money"—if it represents our financial security—we are going to be smart and go one step further. We are going to hire professionals to tell us how to put the money to work. When we do that, we will have created a mutual fund.

In a mutual fund, many individual investors get together, pool their money, and hire professionals to manage it. They share the cost of the management and they share the profits.

Mutual funds do not spring full blown from a rocky cleft in the earth. Someone has to start them. Mostly, they are started by people who want to make money. There is nothing wrong with the profit motive. The Carnegie Foundation, the Ford Foundation, the Rockefeller Foundation all exist today—and do a lot of good—because a long time ago someone wanted to make money. At least one mutual fund was organized because a man needed a sensible way to have his own money invested. He figured that as long as he was doing it, he might just as well set it up so that other people could benefit from it, too. But most funds are set up by people who hope to enjoy a reward for doing a good job. In other words, they are privately sponsored for profit.

In essence, then, a mutual fund is an investment club with professional management which has been set up by the managers or others in the hope or belief that it will be a successful business operation, not simply a fraternal group.

When I observe an individual investing on his own, I am invariably reminded of a small rowboat bobbing about in the Atlantic with a single passenger pulling frantically on the oars and with huge waves threatening to engulf him at any moment. When I think of a mutual fund, I envision the *Queen Elizabeth II* overtaking the tiny boat. While thousands of passengers line the railings, the deck officer calls out with a bullhorn to the rowboat's passenger: "Ahoy, you in the little boat! Come aboard! There are storms ahead. You'll be much safer in this big ship with an experienced crew. Come aboard, I say!"

We hear it said that if you cannot afford to diversify, you cannot afford to invest. Certainly, diversification is the bedrock of sound investing. The eggs-in-many-baskets principle of risk spreading must be observed. But many people cannot obtain adequate diversification investing on their own: trust bankers agreed, you will recall, that one cannot adequately diversify a fund under $35,000.

In a mutual fund, an investor pools his assets with those of thousands of other persons and becomes a proportionate shareholder in a portfolio that may contain anywhere from fifty to four hundred different securities. Whether his investment be $100, $1,000, or $1,000,000, he enjoys exactly the same diversification.

The securities owned by the fund have been chosen by experts for whom the selection of securities is a full-time job. Moreover, those same experts provide continuing full-time supervision. It is not enough to have begun with a good list; keeping it good is equally important. The professional fund manager looks far ahead and takes careful note of matters that are barely discernible on the financial horizon. He looks at a security in his portfolio and asks himself: "What could make that security go down?" Having determined what circumstances would be likely to have an unfavorable effect on his holding, he carries his reasoning a step further: He attempts to establish what events could produce the unfavorable circumstances, makes a note of those possible events, and sets up a warning system to alert him. When his warning signal flashes, the event may be far off on the horizon, but his job demands that he not wait until the unfavorable event is this morning's news. His "early-warning system" is intended to get him out when the first domino falls, not when the last one tumbles on the stock he is holding.

When you examine a mutual fund's investment policy and objectives—no other investment medium makes such complete disclosure of its operations—and decide that it suits your desires, you can go ahead with your investment secure in the knowledge that once you have invested, the fund can never change its policy or objectives without first notifying you. Not so the character of individual stocks, which can change without your knowledge. A mutual fund's performance can change, of course, if its management falters or there are personnel changes, but it must maintain its originally stated objective.

One large mutual fund has 222 securities in its portfolio. If you bought one share of each of those securities, you would have 222 certificates to be safeguarded, about 800 dividend checks to cash or deposit each year, and a steady flow of statements on proxies, rights, etc., to study and act upon. The bookkeeping Uncle Sam re-

quires of the investor-on-his-own for tax-accounting purposes is a chore in itself. Assuming that you would be unwilling to take on such a huge accounting job, how large a portfolio *are* you willing to tackle? One hundred securities? Fifty? Twenty-five? It is still a chore—one you can eliminate by owning a mutual fund. The mutual fund solves the tax-accounting problem by sending you one simple tax-information form at the end of the year.

When you own a portfolio of individual stocks which you have acquired carefully and which you feel is well balanced and distributed among industries and companies, you may suddenly be called upon to raise some money, and the decision on which security to sell may present problems and upset your carefully planned balance. When you own a mutual fund, you do not have to decide which stock to sell. You can sell a small or large portion of your shareholdings, and your remaining shareholdings reflect exactly the same investment balance as you had before you sold.

Mutual fund shares are good collateral. Banks recognize that a single security accepted as collateral may move downward, contrary to the long-term upward trend of the market, whereas a cross section of 75 to 200 different securities combined in a mutual fund is unlikely to move contrary to the market as a whole.

Radio commercials that feature an announcer braying that "the New York Bank for Savings has paid dividends uninterruptedly for 150 years!" bore me to death. For 150 years, the public has been lending its money to banks in consideration of their agreement to pay rent for it regularly in the form of interest. What is so wonderful about the fact that the banks paid the rent? In a way, a mutual fund investment is just the opposite of a savings bank account. In the one instance, you turn your own money over to the bank, which pays you a fee for the use of it. It puts it to work and keeps the profit. In the other instance, you turn your money over to the mutual fund, you pay the fund managers a fee for putting it to work for you, and they turn all the profits over to you. In one case, *you get the fee and the bank gets the profit,* in the other, *the fund gets the fee and you get the profit*. When you open a savings account, it costs the bank something to set it up on its books and to pay for the advertising that brought you in. It cheerfully pays that cost because it knows that it is going to get the profit on your money. When you buy a mutual fund, you pay the cost because you are going to get the profit. Since the amount of interest anyone will pay you for the use of your money is always considerably less than what they expect to make by putting it to work, it follows that invariably you will be better off if you arrange simply to pay someone a fee for his services with the understanding that he will turn the profit over to you.

The wide diversification of investment has given mutual funds a dividend-producing consistency worthy of note. Like the savings bank, they have paid dividends consistently over the years, but those dividends represent earnings, not mere interest.

All funds except for straight growth funds tend to produce a fairly regular dividend. An individual corporation may fall upon evil days and be forced to suspend dividends on its stock, but a broadly diversified portfolio of securities held by a mutual fund is far less likely to have its dividend flow dry up completely even in a period of extreme recession.

Banks, insurance companies, and endowment funds traditionally have been niggardly with their employee compensation. The result has been that the best investment minds in America are employed by the mutual funds. It is simple mathematics—the mutual funds have been willing to pay them.

That is not to deny the existence of incompetents in the mutual fund business. There are incompetents in all businesses and professions. But the performance record of a mutual fund is an open book, and it is a simple matter to check on the competency of a fund under consideration—far simpler, indeed, than checking on the past performance of a particular bank or investment counsel firm. Also, a careful watch can be kept on its comparative performance after it is bought.

When you own individual securities, there is no easy or convenient way to reinvest dividends. They come in dribs and drabs, and either you endorse the check and spend it or accumulate the money in idleness in a bank account until you have enough to reinvest. Then you return to the broker and pay more brokerage fees. With mutual funds, it is so simple: you instruct the fund automatically to reinvest all dividends in additional shares. The great majority of funds let you reinvest dividends without any brokerage fee. That is a big saving. If dividends are 4 percent, in ten years without any compounding you will be reinvesting 40 percent of what you invested in the first place, and, if instead of funds you bought individual stocks, you will pay again at least 40 percent of what you paid to put the money to work in the first place. With the fund, you save all that.

You can arrange to be paid a convenient monthly retirement check (from dividends and principal) through a withdrawal plan.

Mutual funds can help you save on taxes through participation in the Keogh plan for self-employed people.

Fund ownership vastly simplifies the settlement of an estate. Your executor or trustee is not called upon to deal with a myriad of transfer agents with multiple demands for documents of one kind or another, or face the problem of which securities to sell to raise money to pay taxes, and so on. He simply sells enough shares to provide the needed funds; the investment balance of the remainder of the estate is undisturbed. Inter vivos trusts to avoid probate may be set up very easily to cover mutual fund shares.

# Chapter 4

# THE INCREASINGLY IMPORTANT
# ROLE OF MUTUAL FUNDS

In 1950, after twenty-six years of operations, American mutual funds held assets totaling $2.5 billion. In 1960, assets had climbed to $17 billion. Today, the mutual fund money managers have the awesome responsibility for handling more than $50 billion, which represents a significant proportion of the financial security of more than five million people. Of the twenty-five largest American corporations in number of shareholders, ten are mutual funds.

Many major corporations have plans similar to Mobil Oil's which matches an employee's investment in a mutual fund up to a specified percentage of his salary or wages.

It is said that the poor followed the rich into the stock market. Now the rich have followed the poor into mutual funds. Funds—begun ostensibly as a means of investment for persons in modest circumstances who could not obtain professional supervision and adequate diversification on their own—by becoming top bidder for the country's best investment brains, have increasingly won the attention and respect of substantial investors, both individual and institutional.

As more and more of the wealth of the country gravitated toward mutual funds, more and more of the top investment brains in the country gravitated in the same direction. Whether in a bank, insurance company, or investment counsel firm, as fast as an investment man shows his head above his fellows', some fund grabs him.

As their assets have grown, the funds increasingly have become a stabilizing influence upon the securities markets. When prices are falling, professionals do not dump securities on the market in a panic-stricken effort to unload as individual investors are prone to do.

In the past, some critics claimed to see a great danger: in a market decline, mutual fund shareholders would panic and rush to redeem their holdings.

Prophets of doom predicted that under forced selling by the funds, securities prices would snowball downward to disaster. Louis Engel, a decade ago in *How to Buy Stocks,* wrung his hands in despair:

> The big worry about mutual funds today is . . . a matter of economics. How stable would they prove to be in another period of economic stress? Would the big bubble burst again? This is a legitimate worry, because in the structure of most mutual funds there is one contradiction that can spell trouble.
>
> This trouble lies in the dangerous . . . situation that might exist if the market went into a tailspin. That's the time when people who owned shares in a mutual fund would be most tempted to cash them in, for that is when they as individuals of generally modest means would be most likely to need their savings. And yet that is precisely the time when it would be most difficult for a mutual fund to redeem its shares, because to raise cash, it would probably have to sell stocks from its portfolio . . . if there were a heavy run on a fund it would have to sell off sizable blocks of stock to raise cash and it might very well have to take a loss on those forced sales. Additionally, those very sales might further depress the market.

Engel was Merrill Lynch's publicity man, and the book was part of the brokerage firm's continuing campaign to downgrade mutual funds and promote individual brokerage accounts.

While acknowledging that the funds had "performed creditably" during the market declines of 1946, 1950, 1957, and 1960, Engel failed to mention the fact that in all those years, sales ran ahead of redemptions, and he persisted in maintaining that the periods involved "were not really severe tests" of the snowball principle.

But then, in 1962, a combination of factors, capped by a confrontation in Cuba in October, caused the market to suffer a real shake-out. On a single day, May 28, the Dow-Jones Industrial Average tumbled 34.95 points, the sharpest decline since October 28, 1929.

Worried investors jammed brokerage offices as $20.8 billion melted before their eyes. Newspapers, radio, and television nervously reported the financial disaster and speculated upon its extent.

Here was a real test of the mutual funds and of the people who invested in them. Would they panic? Would they demand their money? How much of the $23 billion in assets then held by the funds would be liquidated to pay off frightened investors? Would fund redemptions send the reeling market into a crash which would make 1929 pale?

To all of these questions, the mutual fund shareholders of the country gave a resounding "No!"

An article in one of the popular magazines observed: "The role of the hero was filled, surprisingly, by the most frightening of untested forces—the mutual funds." Analyzing the events of the crucial week, the New York Stock Exchange reported that on the fateful Monday when prices were tumbling sickeningly, the funds actually purchased 530,000 more shares than they sold. By Thursday, when the market had turned upward again, the funds sold 375,000 shares. Or, as the magazine article put it, ". . . far from increasing the market's fluctuations, the funds actually served as a stabilizing force."

In the moment of crisis, when thousands upon thousands of individual investors all over the country were panicking, the unemotional professional money managers at the helm of the mutual funds were coolly buying on behalf of their shareholders. A few days later, when prices were rising, they sold. The steady hand of the professional manager was at work, not only taking advantage of the situation for his shareholders but also —by the very act—restoring some sense of order and control to the market place.

During all this time, what were the mutual fund shareholders doing? While the boardrooms were jammed with do-it-yourself investors nervously chewing their nails and trying to make up their minds whether to go home and hang themselves in the attic, for fund investors exactly the reverse was happening: They were licking their chops. To them, it was bargain day. In the month of the dramatic break in the market, more than 40,000 individuals opened new accumulation plans with mutual funds. True, they redeemed $122 million of shares in the crucial month of October—but they bought $292 million of new shares! Those new pur-

chases provided the funds with more than enough money to meet the redemptions and the funds were not forced to unload portfolio stocks.

A contemporary report summed it up:

> Apparently the mutual funds had so much cash on hand that in most cases they could pay off their shareholders without selling substantial amounts of stock. Taken as a group, the funds proved to be so rich and so conservatively managed that they not only could weather the storm but, by happy inadvertence, could do something to decrease its violence.

A somewhat similar pattern marked the stock market decline of 1966. Again the funds performed well. Seventeen of the twenty largest funds showed smaller losses than the market as a whole.

Although the market declines of 1962 and 1966 were comparatively short-lived, that of 1969–1970 imposed quite different conditions upon the funds. It is one thing to move decisively to take advantage of a brief downturn, but quite another to measure the likely duration of a protracted decline and withhold new equity commitments until it has run its course. While the 1969–1970 decline astonished nearly all professional managers with its staying power, many funds shrewdly accumulated large cash reserves with which they took advantage of the successive lows.

Mutual funds, along with other institutional investors, are increasingly a factor in the market, accounting today for more than 50 percent of all trading. Their purchases and sales are in multi-thousand lots, giving a new depth and stability to the market.

One particular fund development is worth special note. For two decades, the life insurance industry has fought to stem the inroads into its business by the mutual funds. But as inflation has grown steadily more menacing, the public has shown an increasing disenchantment with the life insurance product as an investment medium. The cash-value policy, with its guarantee of a specific number of dollars at a date in the future without any assurance of what those dollars will buy when they are paid by the insurance company, has lost its charm. More and more people are rejecting such policies (on which the companies make their greatest profit) and are turning instead to the pure protection of term insurance. After years of denouncing the mutual fund salesman, there are now over two hundred insurance companies in the fund business, with the likelihood that the majority of the sixteen hundred remaining companies will soon follow.

Collectively, these companies employ more than 450,000 of the most skillful salesmen in America. The impact is breathtaking. These persuasive salesmen will bring out of hiding billions of dollars from savings accounts, savings bonds, and insurance policy cash values. With normal growth plus this influx of new money, mutual fund assets are quite likely to double in the next five years. In what is this huge accumulation to be invested? We are literally going to run out of securities. There will not be enough stocks to go around; certainly, new issues are not going to come on the market at a rate equal to this incredible demand, and prices are bound to be bid up to astronomical heights, completely out of proportion to the intrinsic value of the shares.

The banking industry is quietly watching the efforts of the First National City Bank of New York to set up its own mutual fund. The Securities and Exchange Commission took the position that it had no objection so long as the fund was properly registered and conformed to the various securities laws. The National Association of Securities Dealers has bitterly opposed this development on the grounds that the Glass-Steagall Act precludes banks from engaging in the securities business. In July 1969 the United States Court of Appeals for the District of Columbia handed down a decision—which the Supreme Court has since agreed to review—allowing banks to go into the fund business. If the lower court is sustained, we may see an additional five hundred new mutual funds sponsored by banks.

The entry of the life companies and banks into the fund field may give funds a little better standing than they presently enjoy in an area where they have been considered "second-class" securities. If a broker recommends that you acquire a portfolio of twenty-five stocks and agrees to lend you part of the purchase price (via a margin account) or arranges for you to borrow the needed money elsewhere, he will meet no official objection whatever to such a course of action. But if the same twenty-five stocks are represented by the portfolio of a mutual fund, and the broker lends you the money or arranges for you to borrow it elsewhere, he may be suspended from business for from three months to one year or even have his registration permanently revoked. The law insists that no broker may arrange for credit for the purchase of mutual fund shares.

Ten years ago, William McChesney Martin, then Chairman of the Federal Reserve Board, admitted that this ruling did not make much sense and that the Board's staff was working on a revision of the law. To date nothing has been done.

# Chapter 5

# TYPES OF FUNDS

Mutual fund literature emphasizes that funds come in a variety of shapes and sizes "to suit the varying needs of individuals."

Mutual fund advertising frequently invites the reader to check a coupon to indicate whether his interest lies in "conservation of capital," "reasonable income," "long-term capital appreciation," and so on.

However, basically, all investors have the same objective: maximum profit with as little risk as possible. The "maximum profit" can be ordinary income, long-term capital gains, or unrealized appreciation (increase in the value of the shares). Investors do not care what the profit is called, so long as they get it.

As for risk, it is common to differentiate between an investment for a widow and a businessman, but I have known businessmen who bellowed louder than widows when their holdings went down. We will cover risk more fully in Chapter 6.

Sixteen types of funds are available, each with its special appeal. However, funds do not always fall precisely within these categories. Frequently, they will blend the characteristics of two or more broad types. But this listing will serve to alert the reader to some of the opportunities—and problems:

## 1. BOND FUNDS

The bond fund places almost all of its emphasis on safety of principal. A bond is a promissory note. You lend $1,000 to a corporation, to a municipality or state, or to the federal government. The issuer of the bond agrees to pay you interest, say, 4½ percent, over a period generally ranging from fifteen to fifty years, at which time such issuer repays the principal. It is a secured loan: that is, the bondholders have a lien on the bricks, mortar, and machinery of the issuer. (An unsecured bond is a debenture, having no specific lien on any asset.)

You are not required to hold a bond until maturity, of course. If you need the money or simply decide you no longer wish to lend your $1,000 to the ABC Corporation, you go to a broker, who, for a very modest commission, will sell your bond to someone else who is willing to lend the money to the corporation.

Theoretically, the bond for which you paid $1,000 is always worth that amount. Actually, two things can happen to it. First, if the issuer defaults in the payment of the interest, or if the issuer's credit deteriorates and there is some question of whether the money will be available to pay off the bond at maturity, you may find it difficult to sell it for $1,000 because the market will reflect this change of circumstances.

Second, its fixed rate of interest may become unfashionable—a major problem to bondholders today as interest rates zoomed in recent years. Savings banks and others are paying 6 percent or more. The largest corporations are paying 7 percent and 8 percent on their newly issued bonds. Nobody wants your 4½ percent bond. Someone might pay $750 for it. The $45.00 interest it pays each year will be 6 percent on his $750 investment—and on maturity he will pick up another $250 profit. He offers you $750—take it or leave it.

You are not going to run into anyone who will spell it out in just those words, but actually, the market is that blunt.

As an individual, you have the option to hold on to your $1,000 bond loan. But if you are a mutual fund, required to value your portfolio at the close of business each day, you are going to have to put that bond in at $750. That is all the market says it is worth today in an era when savings media offer instant withdrawal of the face amount without risk of any loss of principal.

Of course, managers of bond funds have not been paying $1,000 for many of the bonds they have bought lately. They have been buying bonds that were selling at a discount, hoping that these would recover some of their value. They have been hoping, too, that the high-interest rate trend would reverse itself. When interest rates fall, the interest paid on the bonds they hold will not look quite so unattractive, and the bonds would rise in price.

Aside from the trend of interest rates, another consideration has affected the price of bonds. Years ago, trust companies, big endowment funds, pension funds, and other aggregations of wealth followed a more conservative course than today. Their investments were largely in bonds. As more and more of them have become aware of the inroads of inflation and of the necessity of hedging against it, increasingly they have been turning to common stocks. The withdrawal of their support from the bond market contributed substantially to the decline in price of that type of security.

Some issuers are so shaky that their bonds fluctuate in the market every bit as much as common stock. Conversely, some common stocks may be considered a safer investment than some bonds.

Generally speaking, though, bonds have been associated with safety of principal, and investors have bought bond funds with the objective of acquiring an interest in a diversified portfolio of senior securities selected and supervised by professionals.

To simplify selection, bonds are given a rating (AAA, AA, A, BBB, and so on) which reflects the credit standing of the issuer and the general desirability of the security as an investment. Some bond funds concentrate in holdings of a specified rating. Thus, one fund may hold all prime bonds whereas another will hold issues rated far down the list.

Some bond funds specialize in tax exempt bonds (state, county, municipal, and territorial bonds or bonds guaranteed by a state), thus providing tax-free income to the fund's shareholders. However, interest rates on such bonds are substantially lower than other classes and mostly appeal to the very rich.

Because inflation must be taken into account in all our investing and since an investment in a bond is an investment in the dollar, I do not regard bond funds as a desirable investment medium.

*Examples of bond funds:*
Keystone Custodian Funds
    B–1 Series
    B–2 Series
    B–3 Series
National Securities Bond Series

*Examples of tax-exempt bond funds:*
Municipal Investment Trust Fund
Nuveen Tax Exempt Bond Series

## 2. BALANCED FUNDS

As the name implies, funds of this type "balance" their investments among the various types of securities —stocks, both common and preferred, and bonds. This long was an established investment policy of fiduciaries. The Carnegie Foundation, the Rockefeller Foundation, the Yale and Harvard endowment funds—indeed, most of the great aggregations of wealth which were professionally managed—employed the principle of balanced investment.

Wellington Fund, the first balanced fund, was organized in 1928, and over most of the years since, this group of funds enjoyed the solid respect of the investment community. A decade ago, for example, Wellington had more than twenty-five thousand bank and individual trustees and insurance companies among its shareholders, an indication of its high standing among professional investors.

Like Wellington, the Scudder, Stevens & Clark Balanced Fund, the Eaton & Howard Balanced Fund, the Boston Fund, and the George Putnam Fund all typified a conservative approach to investment management, and their sponsors and managers exemplified a sense of fiduciary integrity and responsibility we can look back upon with nostalgia.

The balanced funds performed well until 1963, when their huge bond holdings became a liability. Locked into them by a stated policy that they would at all times maintain approximately 35 percent of their assets in bonds and preferred stocks, the balanced funds fell far, far behind in the performance derby. At one point, Wellington, with half a billion dollars in bonds, had a loss on every bond, including U.S. government securities.

Of the hundreds of funds organized during the past ten years, not one has been a balanced fund. The trend away from "balance" has been noted everywhere. This has been reflected in the reduced sale of new shares of such funds, and in the rising redemption rate of the relatively small group of funds of this type. The result has been a steady shrinking in the total assets of balanced funds.

The bond market is close to a forty-year low. Some might wish to gamble that it has reached rock bottom. Not I.

I would not invest in a balanced fund.

*Examples of balanced funds:*
American Business Shares
American Express Investment
Axe-Houghton Fund A
Axe-Houghton Fund B
Balanced Income Fund
Boston Foundation Fund
Boston Fund
Channing Balanced Fund
Composite Bond & Stock Fund
Diversified Investment Fund

Dodge & Cox Balanced Fund
Eaton & Howard Balanced Fund
Group Securities—Fully Administered Fund
Investors Mutual
Loomis-Sayles Mutual Fund
Massachusetts Fund
Mutual Shares
Nation-Wide Securities Company
National Securities—Balanced Fund
George Putnam Fund of Boston
Scudder, Stevens & Clark Balanced Fund
Security Diversified Shares
Shareholders Trust of Boston
Sigma Trust Shares
Stein Roe & Farnham Balanced Fund
Wellington Fund
Whitehall Fund

### 3. INCOME FUNDS

The overriding concern of income funds is maximum yield. Some income funds resemble balanced funds in that they hold bonds as well as preferred and common stocks. High-yield preferreds and blue chip commons with a consistent dividend record are most popular with such investment companies. A study of performance over a long period of time suggests that not infrequently, high yield is achieved at the expense of capital growth. Exceptions like Puritan Fund in the Fidelity group in Boston (which has a way-above-average long-term record of capital increase) and Provident Fund for Income in Philadelphia (which has done remarkably well in rising markets) are exceptions that prove the rule.

It is an investment maxim that "the higher the yield, the greater the risk." However, the high interest paid by some corporate and municipal borrowers merely reflects their poor credit standing, and managers of income funds display varying degrees of willingness to accept undue risk. Some reveal an increasing tendency to invest substantially in low-grade bonds and convertible securities. Because of the differing approaches of income fund managers, it is becoming increasingly difficult to maintain the identity of an income fund classification. Certainly the designation no longer tells us as much about a fund's portfolio as it once did.

The necessity for consistently producing a high yield imposes pressure upon a fund manager that is generally undesirable and a handicap to him. Though he may be willing to accept the handicap, you should not. Investing for income is shortsighted. Invest for total overall gain and, if necessary, spend a part of your principal each year.

*Examples of income funds:*
American Investment Income Fund
Associated Trust Fund

Channing Income Fund
Decatur Income Fund
Income Fund of Boston
Keystone K–1 Income Fund
Lexington Income Fund
Liberty Fund
Morton (B.C.) Income Series
National Securities Dividend Fund
National Securities Income Fund
Northeast Investors Trust
Provident Fund for Income
Puritan Fund
Putnam Income Fund
Value Line Income Fund

### 4. BLUE CHIP COMMON STOCK FUNDS

In the early years of the mutual fund industry, there were only two types of funds: balanced funds and blue chip common stock funds. In those days, of course, a blue chip remained a blue chip. But today we live in an age of obsolescence. (Consider the impact upon the coal and oil industries and the gas and electric utility companies when a recently perfected device the size of a grapefruit, capable of heating a house, is made economically feasible.) No blue chip is safe. This points up the increasingly difficult job of investment management faced by professionals—and the almost hopeless odds against the amateur. Maintaining a portfolio of blue chip securities was not too difficult in the days when one could "buy a few good stocks and put them away and forget them." If they were good when bought, there was reasonable assurance they would stay good.

Blue chip common stock funds attempt to maintain holdings of seasoned stocks and one hallmark of a seasoned stock is a good, steady dividend record. But long-time dividend payers ordinarily are not growth situations. It follows that while blue chip common stock funds do invest in equities and are therefore a viable hedge against inflation, they do not provide the maximum protection available, that is, maximum opportunity for long-term capital growth. I am not saying that you should not invest in such a fund; I merely observe that your dollars will not be invested at their maximum potential. On the other hand, these funds suffer minimum fluctuation in price. Some blue chip common stock funds have exhibited greater stability than some balanced funds, which simply is a reflection of superior management ability and/or timing.

*Examples of blue chip common stock funds:*
Affiliated Fund
American Express Stock Fund
Broad Street Investing Corporation
Bullock Fund
Commonwealth Fund—Plan C

Crown Western Diversified Fund
Dividend Shares
Eaton & Howard Stock Fund
Fidelity Fund
Founders Mutual Fund
Fundamental Investors
Group Securities—Common Stock Fund
Investment Company of America
Investment Trust of Boston
Keystone S–1 High Grade Common
Keystone S–2 Income Common
Massachusetts Investors Trust
National Securities Stock Fund
Pioneer Fund
Scudder, Stevens & Clark Common Stock
Selected American Shares
Wall Street Investing Corporation
Washington Mutual Investors Fund
Wisconsin Fund

## 5. GROWTH AND INCOME FUNDS

The managers of this type of fund are interested in maintaining reasonable income but they recognize that blue chips offer reduced growth possibilities. In making their investment selections, then, they try to avoid commitments in companies whose growth pattern has leveled off. The total overall gain should be greater with this type of fund than with the blue chip funds.

*Examples of growth and income funds:*
Aberdeen Fund
AMCAP Fund
Babson (David L.) Investment Fund, Inc.
Boston Common Stock Fund
Consumers Investment Fund
Eberstadt Fund
Federated Growth Fund
Growth Industry Shares
Johnston Mutual Fund
Keystone S–3 Growth Common
National Securities Growth Stock Fund
Putnam Investors Fund
Steadman Fiduciary Investment Fund
Windsor Fund

## 6. GROWTH FUNDS

A growth fund does not concern itself at all with earnings. It invests in growth companies. Ordinarily such companies do not pay much in dividends—they plow all their profits back into research and development. When you buy a growth stock, you look to long-term increase in the price of the stock for your profit. It is the same with a growth fund.

Without engaging in any of the exotic practices dis-

cussed elsewhere in this book, an orthodox growth fund will easily outperform all of the balanced funds, income funds, and blue chip common stock funds. The problem is that the kind of people who gravitate toward running growth funds also include a class of "swingers" who are not content with producing marvelous results for their investors; their results have to be incredible. In their struggle to gild the investment lily, they frequently overreach and are therefore more vulnerable to market declines.

*Examples of growth funds:*

*Large:*
American Investors Fund
Channing Growth Fund
Chemical Fund
Delaware Fund
Diversified Growth Stock Fund
Dreyfus Fund
Enterprise Fund
Fidelity Capital Fund
Fidelity Trend Fund
Ivest Fund
Keystone S–4 Low Priced Common
Manhattan Fund
Massachusetts Investors Growth Stock Fund
National Investors Corporation
T. Rowe Price Growth Stock Fund
Putnam Growth Fund
Technology Fund
United Accumulative Fund
Value Line Special Situations Fund

*Small:*
Axe-Houghton Stock Fund
Axe Science Corporation
Blair Fund
Channing Special Fund
Chase Fund of Boston
Colonial Equities
Crown Western Dallas Fund
Drexel Equity Fund
Fairfield Fund
First Investors Fund for Growth
Gibraltar Growth Fund
Hartwell & Campbell Fund
Ivy Fund
Mathers Fund
Neuwirth Fund
Oppenheimer Fund
Pennsylvania Mutual Fund
Rowe Price New Horizons Fund
Putnam Equities Fund
Security Equity Fund
Steadman American Industry Fund

Supervised Investors Growth Stock Fund
Winfield Growth Fund

## 7. SPECIALIZED COMMON STOCK FUNDS

Where once there were many funds specializing in a single industry, the list has dwindled to a very few. As corporations have diversified in this age of conglomerates, it is no longer possible to identify a particular company with a particular industry. Many specialized funds have voted a change of name and policy to remove the restrictions which hampered their effective operation and have thus lost some of their significance.

*Examples of specialized funds:*
Capital Life Insurance & Growth Stock Fund
Century Shares Trust
Energy Fund
Insurance Investors Fund
Life and Growth Stock Fund
Life Insurance Investors
Morton (B.C.)—Insurance Series
Ocean Technology Fund
Oceanographic Fund

## 8. CANADIAN AND INTERNATIONAL FUNDS

A few funds specialize in foreign securities but not all are available to American investors. Investment abroad must take into account the additional hazards of currency devaluation, expropriation of property, unstable governments, death tax problems, etc.

*Examples of Canadian and international funds:*
Canadian Fund
Loomis-Sayles Canadian and International Fund
Scudder International Investments
Stein Roe & Farnham Capital Opportunities Fund
Templeton Growth Fund

## 9. GEOGRAPHIC FUNDS

Where once there were several, only one such fund of any significance remains: Florida Growth Fund, restricting its investments to Florida and the South. There seems little to be gained by restricting one's investments geographically.

## 10. COMPETITIVE CAPITAL FUND'S CONCEPT

Competitive Capital Fund, unique in form, divides its assets into five parts and hires five different management groups to put the money to work. Periodically, the performance of the respective managers is appraised and the new money—generated by the continuing sale of the fund's shares—for the next operations period is directed to the two or three managers who are currently pro-

ducing the best results. The poor performers thus get to manage a decreasing percentage of the fund and can even be replaced by the sponsors. A fund of this type makes good sense. Similar funds have since been started or are in registration. The theory, of course, is that the sponsors are selecting a group of superior performers from among the existing fund or investment counsel managements. This does not necessarily mean that they get the five best managements. Many investment counsel firms, operating in the noncompetitive world of their craft, shrink from exposing themselves to the unfavorable publicity that could attend the disclosure that they were in last place in the fund's performance derby. The fifth-place management might actually be very good—it is just that the other four managements are better.

In any event, the idea of hiring the cream of the management crop is very sound. (It is strange that it has not been more rewarding for investors in Competitive Capital Fund.)

## 11. LEVERAGE FUNDS

Leverage funds adopt investment policies that permit them to borrow money, usually from banks, for investment purposes. If the market goes up, they enjoy the profit on the borrowed money as well as on their own. If the market declines, they lose on the borrowed money as well as on their own money. The "leverage" makes them go up or down more pronouncedly than the market.

They may also seek to obtain leverage via the purchase or sale of put and call options, which are a debatedly effective means of seeking profits and protecting against losses. Actually, many of the out-and-out growth funds use leverage to some degree. Thus, there are many leveraged funds in the list given above for growth funds.

*Examples of leverage funds:*
Affiliated Fund
Axe-Houghton Stock Fund
Chase Capital Fund
Colonial Fund
Dreyfus Leverage Fund
Fairfield Fund
Gibraltar Growth Fund
Hedge Fund of America
Imperial Growth Fund
Income Fund of Boston
Investment/Indicator Fund
Investment Trust of Boston
Neuwirth Fund
Ocean Technology Fund
Omega Fund
O'Neil Fund
Oppenheimer Fund
Pennsylvania Mutual Fund
Putnam Voyager Fund

Revere Fund
Sherman Dean Fund
Sigma Capital Fund
Tower Fund
WinCap Fund

## 12. CONVERTIBLE FUNDS

A fund of this type specializes in investments in "convertible securities," that is, bonds, debentures, or preferred stocks which contain an option giving the holder the right to convert at any time to a specified number of shares of common stock of the issuer. There is only one to rate. This type of investment is discussed in Chapter 13.

*Example of convertible funds:*
Harbor Fund, Inc.

## 13. EXCHANGE OR SWITCH FUNDS

While these funds are not presently being offered and none is in prospect, they are included here because a dozen or so are in existence.

Let us say that you have a block of ABC Corporation common stock which that corporation made available to you at a discount price of $1.00 per share as an inducement to you to leave your old employer and go with ABC. Since you bought it, the market price of the stock has climbed to $100 per share. You and ABC are parting company, or perhaps you just think that you have too much of your estate tied up in that one stock. But you feel locked into it by the capital gains tax liability of nearly 25 percent of the sales price. Otherwise you would sell it.

A "switch fund" will exchange your shares of ABC common for shares of its fund and you will have no capital gains tax liability: the fund assumes your cost basis, and if it ever sells the shares, it will be liable for the capital gains tax. However, not the fund but shareholders collectively will pay the tax through the fund's dividends and distributions.

What many people who went into switch funds did not know was that these funds were loaded with wealthy gents with huge capital gains tax problems, and that in joining the fund they came to share the *average* liability of all the participants. They did not realize that their own tax liability was far below the average of all the shareholders in the fund and that it was therefore very disadvantageous to them to enter into the arrangement.

Some switch fund shares may be bought over-the-counter, but they are not a good buy considering the enormous tax liability hanging over them. Actually, it was a pretty silly idea.

A few years ago, the Internal Revenue Service stopped approving switch funds, which is why no new ones are being set up. If they ever become available again, be careful.

*Examples of switch funds:*
Capital Exchange Fund, Inc.
Congress Street Fund, Inc.
Constitution Exchange Fund, Inc.
Devonshire Street Fund, Inc.
Diversification Fund, Inc.
Empire Fund, Inc.
Exchange Fund of Boston, Inc.
Exeter Fund, Inc.

## 14. DUAL FUNDS

These are not true funds but closed-end investment companies that offer two classes of shares: "income" and "capital." The income shares resemble preferred stock in that they have a stated minimum dividend, which is cumulative. Actually, the income shares receive all of the income earned by the fund, while all realized profits are reinvested. If you buy income shares and I buy capital shares, you are getting the income on my money as well as your own. In effect, I benefit from the capital gains on your money as well as my own. The capital shareholders have the use of the income shareholders' money without paying interest, except for the income dividends, which they agree to forgo. The income shares are callable at a stated date in the future. By 1985, the last of them will be retired, and each such shareholder will be paid exactly what he invested, provided they achieve their investment objective. There is no guarantee. What is left will be divided among the capital shareholders.

Dual funds are a new concept. They have not as yet had an opportunity to demonstrate their soundness, though their performance thus far has not been distinguished. An example of what can happen as a result of the "leverage" built into such funds is American Dual Vest's performance: a 1969 high of $19.50 versus a low of $8.75 on the capital shares, more than a 50 percent decline, while the income shares were yielding a generous 8.8 percent.

*Examples of dual funds:*
American Dual Vest Fund, Inc.
Gemini Fund, Inc.
Hemisphere Fund, Inc.
Income and Capital Shares, Inc.
Leverage Fund of Boston, Inc.
Putnam Duofund, Inc.
Scudder Duo-Vest, Inc.

## 15. PUBLIC HEDGE FUNDS

funds. If indeed they were made, it was in private
Fortunes are alleged to have been made in hedge

funds with less than 100 shareholders. Many public hedge funds are not true mutual funds but closed-end investment companies organized to pool assets and invest them under a variety of highly speculative techniques. Principal among these is short selling: on the assumption that the market for a particular security is about to decline, shares are borrowed from an investment broker only to sell them. By the time the borrowed shares are returnable, the borrower expects to be able to buy them on the market cheaper.

Hedge funds have not done very well and are for people who can afford to live dangerously. The 1969–1970 market decline took the measure of a lot of young geniuses who were masterminding them.

*Examples of hedge funds:*
Blair Fund
Drexel Hedge Fund
Dreyfus Leverage Fund
Hedge Fund of America
Heritage Fund
Imperial Growth Fund
Incentive Fund
Index Fund
Ling Fund
Naess & Thomas Special Fund
Revere Fund
State Farm Growth Fund
State Farm Income Fund
Tower Fund
Tudor Hedge Fund
Washington Investment Network

## 16. LETTER FUNDS

These, too, are in practice closed-end investment companies. They have no occasion to value their assets from day to day, since their price is whatever the public is willing to pay for them. They specialize in investment letter (restricted) stocks, which are an acceptable form of investment for this type of company. See Chapter 12 on this subject.

*Examples of letter funds:*
Diebold Technology Venture Fund
Fund of Letters
SMC Investment Company
Value Line Development Capital Corporation

## 17. SAVINGS BANK MUTUAL FUNDS

An interesting development in the mutual fund field is (in addition to the First National City Bank of New York interest mentioned earlier) the Fund for Mutual Depositors, Inc., sponsored by the National Association of Mutual Savings Banks "in order to provide at minimum expense a managed medium for depositors in mu-

tual savings banks to invest their funds in common stock." This curious venture, the legality of which has not yet been clearly established, claims that its "organization has been encouraged by individual savings bank officers and trustees for the purpose of making available a low-cost mutual fund to people who already have the primary financial protection of savings bank deposits. The organizers earn no profits from the management of the Fund."

Why are they going to all this trouble? Shares are made available to the public through forty-two savings banks in Alaska, Connecticut, Maine, Massachusetts, New Jersey, and New York. The fund is managed by its own directors, most of whom are officers of savings banks, but a member firm of the New York Stock Exchange, Smith, Barney & Co., Inc., is retained as investment adviser. It is the policy of the fund to invest "primarily" in common stocks of companies listed on the New York Stock Exchange—not too surprising a coincidence. While the fee paid Smith, Barney for its services is quite modest, the fund is committed to effect all of its securities transactions through that brokerage firm. In addition, a "Mutual Depositors Service Corporation" receives an annual fee for paying the fund's expenses. The prospectus notes that the organizers earn no profits from the management of the fund. It does not say that they make no profits from the *administration* of the fund. The prospectus states: "In addition to certifying the status of depositors, certifying banks have been requested by the Fund to post advertisements on their premises containing certain limited information about the Fund and to consent to the publication of similar newspaper advertisements by the Fund listing the banks' names. The banks will also make available upon request copies of the Fund's prospectus containing purchase order forms, and related literature. Upon request the banks will also forward purchase orders and remittances to the Fund's custodian, and guarantee the depositor's signature on a transfer or redemption order form for any depositor who desires to redeem shares of the Fund."

Note that the bank employees are here called upon to do exactly what the employees of a broker-dealer are required to do. But the broker-dealer is required to be federally registered under the Securities Exchange Act of 1934 and licensed as a broker in the state in which he operates, while the savings bank is granted an incredible exemption from such requirements. The employees of the broker-dealer are required to pass an extremely difficult examination given by either the Securities and Exchange Commission or the National Association of Securities Dealers, while the bank employees are not required to take any examination or to know anything at all about mutual funds. Every state in the Union licenses mutual fund salesmen; the bank employees are not required to have any such license. The Glass-

Steagall Act prohibits banking institutions from engaging in the business of underwriting securities. Here, an amalgam of savings banks is clearly underwriting a security in brazen defiance of the law. Surely, someone is going to challenge this fund's operation. What was the Securities and Exchange Commission thinking of when it approved something designed to operate in obvious violation of both federal and state law?

The fund got off to an unfortunate start. An error in the printing of its prospectus resulted in the duplication of one page and the omission of another. As a result, the prospectus failed to comply with the requirements of the Securities Act of 1933. Every person who received that prospectus and purchased shares is now entitled to ask for his money back, with interest. Since everyone who bought shares has a loss at the time of this writing, a substantial liability accrues to the fund, which claims that it will hold the unfortunate printer responsible. Some of the sponsors probably are beginning to wonder if they should not have stayed in the savings-bank business.

Now that we have some idea of the characteristics of varying types of funds, here is a hypothetical typical year's performance of four types of funds that fairly reflects contemporary comparative investment results:

| Fund Type | Income Dividend (%) | Increase in Value of Shares (%) | Total Overall Gain (%) |
|---|---|---|---|
| Income Fund | 5 | 3 | 8 |
| Balanced Fund | 3 | 8 | 11 |
| Blue Chip Common Stock Fund | 2½ | 13 | 15½ |
| Growth Fund | 1 | 19 | 20 |

Assuming that you are investing for long-term capital growth as a hedge against inflation, isn't it obvious which you should choose?

Should you invest in the income fund simply because it pays a much larger dividend than the others? If you require income, wouldn't you be far better off to select the growth fund, take its 1 percent cash dividend and liquidate sufficient shares each year to provide the other 4 percent that the income fund would have given you? In other words, invest for growth and spend a part of your capital each year. If you spend 4 percent of the 19 percent increase in value provided by the growth fund, you will still have a net increase of 15 percent in the value of your investment, and you will have had your 5 percent "dividend." Isn't that better than getting 5 percent from the income fund and having your shares increase only 3 percent in value?

As your estate grows by reason of the gain in principal value, you will have more money working for you. The more money you have working, the more income it will produce. You may well find after a period of years that you are drawing as much ordinary income from the growth fund as you were originally scheduled to draw from the income fund.

Remember, you don't care what profit is called so long as you get it. Taxwise, too, you are better off with this arrangement. The entire 5 percent from the income fund is taxable to you, whereas the portion of the growth fund shares that you have liquidated to spend is a return of your own principal and thus not taxable.

The National Securities and Research Corporation, which sponsors the National Securities Series of funds, has for years invited potential investors to select a combination of three of its funds that pay dividends in monthly sequence—the first fund paying quarterly beginning in January, the second quarterly beginning in February, the third quarterly beginning in March. In this way, the company points out, one can enjoy a "check-a-month." I have seen some financial columnists suggest this sort of arrangement.

This must surely be the silliest investment idea of all time. Imagine choosing a fund not because its objective is your objective, not because its performance is outstanding, but simply because it pays a dividend in January, April, July and October!

Canny Buffalo fundman Hugh A. Johnson, whose *Johnson's Charts* has chronicled the good and the bad of mutual fund performance for the past quarter of a century, suggests that the potential mutual fund investor ask himself three questions:

*Objective:* Does the fund do what I want done?
*Policy:* Do I approve of the methods it uses to attain its objective?
*Record:* What success has it had doing it that way?

I don't know of a better way to put it.

# Chapter 6

# THE FLUCTUATION FACTOR

Risk is present in all investment. However, its applicability to mutual funds requires clarification. When you buy an individual stock, there is always the chance that you may lose all that you have invested. Individual securities can go counter to the general market trend. If you have bought heavily into a buggy-whip company, your investment may be headed for the cellar even though the market as a whole is rising. When you buy individual stocks, there is always the chance that you may get into a decadent industry or company. It may be a well-intentioned promotion of a new product, or a new version of an old product that never gets off the ground. Or it may simply be a stock promotion.

In my own community, a group of promoters moved in, got the Chamber of Commerce all starry-eyed over the idea of turning the city into a new Pittsburgh, sold 4,000 people $5,000,000 worth of stock in something called the Northeastern Steel Company, and set up shop with some tired old furnaces that were relics of a bygone day. Everyone smiled happily at the smoke pouring out of the old stacks, not realizing that it was coming from the $5,000,000 that was being burned up. The investors lost every nickel.

It is not possible to lose all of your investment in a mutual fund. In that respect, there is a sharp difference between investing in an individual stock and investing in a mutual fund. If your investment is spread over a broad cross-section of the market, as with a mutual fund, you reduce substantially the likelihood that your investment will go contrary to the trend of the market as a whole. Risk, then, has a different application when applied to a mutual fund.

The risk you run in a mutual fund is the risk of fluctuation. It is just not possible to avoid fluctuation; everything in the world fluctuates in value. In bank accounts, life insurance cash values, United States savings bonds, and mortgages, which represent constant dollars, fluctuation is measured in terms of purchasing power.

Fluctuating from year to year and day to day, such dollars buy a greater or lesser provision of butter and pork chops.

All investments fluctuate in value. Therefore, resign yourself to the fact that your investment in a mutual fund is going to fluctuate. But the fluctuation in a mutual fund is measured in dollars, rather than purchasing power. Obviously we are better off with a fluctuating dollar rather than a fluctuating purchasing power: in the historic market decline of 1929–1932, a man with $50,000 in 1929 who had only $25,000 in 1932, lost nothing—he could buy more with $25,000 in 1932. A $10.00 basket of groceries was $3.00, a $15,000 house, $6,500.

Fluctuation is the single most significant difference between funds, not size or investment policy, which are simply elements to help determine the degree of price fluctuations. It is upon the fluctuation factor that

### DEGREE OF FLUCTUATION OF VARIOUS TYPES OF FUNDS

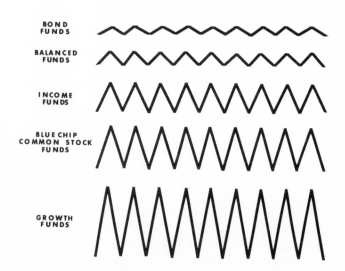

34

you should base your choice of funds. "How much fluctuation am I willing to take?" is the key. In short, become aware of and give proper consideration to the *degree* of fluctuation that may characterize your choice of investment.

The preceding graph illustrates the comparative degree of fluctuation likely to be experienced by the various types of funds.

It will be immediately obvious that the growth fund is the more volatile vehicle on both the upside and the downside. In other words, those things that go up the most also go down the most.

Actually, the graph is a little deceptive because it suggests that the mean between the extremes of fluctuation remains level, that each high point of the market coincides exactly with the level of the previous high point, and that each low point coincides with the previous low. Of course, this is not so. We have already established that inflation induces a long-term upward trend of the market reflecting the long-term upward trend of all prices. However, it is not an uninterrupted path upward but rather is marked by the fluctuations indicated by the chart. Someone has suggested the analogy of a boy playing with a yo-yo as he walks upstairs. The yo-yo moves up and down, just as the market does, but it keeps getting higher and higher as the boy ascends the stairs, just as the market keeps going higher and higher under the influence of inflation. The important thing to remember is that after every major decline, the market climbs out to a new high. That long-term upward trend of the market is working inexorably in your favor. Given time, any investment in a broad cross-section of the market must increase in value.

As for the fluctuation factor of each type of fund, let us look at the record for the last few years and observe the dollars and cents significance:

### Value on January 1, 1968, of $100 invested

|  | One year earlier |
| --- | --- |
| In growth funds | $144.37 |
| In growth and income funds | 125.19 |
| In income funds | 123.05 |
| In balanced funds | 120.85 |

### Value on January 1, 1969, of $100 invested

|  | One year earlier | Two years earlier |
| --- | --- | --- |
| In growth funds | $117.71 | $169.93 |
| In growth and income funds | 117.55 | 147.16 |
| In income funds | 119.89 | 147.52 |
| In balanced funds | 115.78 | 139.92 |

### Value on January 1, 1970, of $100 invested

|  | One year earlier | Two years earlier | Three years earlier |
| --- | --- | --- | --- |
| In growth funds | $ 83.10 | $ 91.81 | $141.00 |
| In growth and income funds | 86.10 | 101.32 | 126.00 |
| In income funds | 84.30 | 101.06 | 124.00 |
| In balanced funds | 87.60 | 101.42 | 122.00 |

In the bull market of 1967, the growth funds raced ahead of all other categories, while the balanced funds trailed the pack as might be expected. In the not-quite-so ebullient market of 1968, the income funds moved ahead but the gap between best performer and poorest performer narrowed. In the disaster year of 1969, the maxim that those that rise the most decline the most was proven. It is interesting to note that in a three-year period that included a vigorous up-market, a reasonably successful up-market, and a vigorous down-market, the growth fund investment would have proven best. Apparently, a package of two good years and one poor one is decidedly profitable, even when the poor one comes last.

Because no single fund necessarily reflects the group performance of all funds of its type, it isn't enough for us to know the fluctuation factor of a group. Following is a table disclosing the fluctuation factor of each of the principal funds for recent significant market periods, based on the New York Stock Exchange (composite) Average, which we will call 1.00. If the fluctuation factor of a fund is 1.25 in a rising market, it indicates that the fund rose 25 percent more than the market as a whole as evidenced by the NYSE index. Conversely, if a fund has a fluctuation factor of .50 in a falling market, it indicates that percentagewise it went down only half as much as the market as a whole. Bearing always in mind that one type of fund is bound to fluctuate more widely than another type, the fluctuation factor shown here indicates the real comparative skill of the respective investment managements. In this respect, I disagree with Wiesenberger (a fund-performance authority) who holds that volatility is not a measure of management performance. My feeling is that a fund that consistently displays a fluctuation factor of substantially more than 1.00 in rising markets and substantially less

than 1.00 in falling markets is performing ideally, and that a fund can easily stand a downside fluctuation factor of 1.25 if it delivers a factor of 2.25 in a rising market.

In the periods here illustrated, the performance of the New York Stock Exchange (composite) Index was as follows:

June 28, 1965, to February 9, 1966
  (7½ months):                              +17.0%
February 9, 1966, to October 7, 1966
  (8 months):                               −22.9%
October 7, 1966, to January 12, 1968
  (15 months):                              +37.6%
January 12, 1968, to March 5, 1968
  (2 months):                               −10.9%
March 5, 1968, to November 29, 1968
  (8½ months):                              +25.8%
November 29, 1968, to February 10,
  1970 (14½ months):                        −16.5%

The first fund, Aberdeen Fund, which began the last period at $3.50 per share, ended it with $2.51, declining 28.5 percent or 72 percent more than the Index. Thereby it earned a fluctuation factor of 1.7.

These figures show how the funds perform in bad as well as good markets.

| Fund | Rising Market 6/28/65 to 2/9/66 | Falling Market 2/9/66 to 10/7/66 | Rising Market 10/7/66 to 1/12/68 | Falling Market 1/12/68 to 3/5/68 | Rising Market 3/5/68 to 11/29/68 | Falling Market 11/29/68 to 2/10/70 |
|---|---|---|---|---|---|---|
| Aberdeen Fund | 1.28 | 0.95 | 0.99 | 0.87 | 0.95 | 1.7 |
| Admiralty Growth Fund | 3.27 | 1.00 | 3.13 | 2.09 | 1.61 | 2.92 |
| Admiralty Income Fund | 0.81 | 0.88 | 0.85 | 0.45 | 1.02 | .57 |
| Admiralty Insurance Fund | 0.58 | 1.21 | 0.84 | 1.78 | 2.08 | 1.21 |
| Affiliated Fund | 1.04 | 0.83 | 0.83 | 0.78 | 0.68 | 1.55 |
| AMCAP Fund | — | — | — | 0.84 | 1.32 | .95 |
| American Business Shares | 0.49 | 0.52 | 0.37 | 0.26 | 0.57 | 1.32 |
| American Express Capital Fund | — | 1.13 | 2.65 | 1.46 | 1.73 | 1.64 |
| American Express Income Fund | 0.80 | 0.81 | 0.67 | 0.65 | 1.03 | 1.32 |
| American Express Investment Fund | 0.88 | 0.92 | 0.83 | 0.83 | 0.86 | 1.50 |
| American Express Stock Fund | 1.63 | 1.05 | 1.27 | 1.00 | 1.24 | 1.46 |
| American Growth Fund | 1.36 | 0.92 | 1.28 | 0.60 | 0.72 | 1.65 |
| American Investors | 4.18 | 1.24 | 2.31 | 1.85 | 1.69 | 2.58 |
| American Mutual | 1.08 | 0.74 | 0.84 | 0.77 | 0.97 | 1.67 |
| American National Growth | 0.80 | 1.11 | 2.18 | 1.42 | 1.71 | 1.34 |
| Anchor Fundamental | 1.69 | 1.13 | 1.08 | 1.17 | 1.00 | 1.74 |
| Anchor Growth | 3.26 | 0.99 | 2.04 | 1.67 | 1.21 | 1.93 |
| Anchor Income | — | — | — | — | — | 1.68 |
| Axe-Houghton A | 1.65 | 1.04 | 2.64 | 1.78 | 1.43 | 1.56 |
| Axe-Houghton B | 1.27 | 1.02 | 1.64 | 1.17 | 1.00 | 1.95 |
| Axe-Houghton Stock | 3.52 | 1.32 | 3.59 | 1.78 | 1.41 | 1.74 |
| Axe Science Corporation | 2.90 | 1.03 | 3.42 | 1.82 | 1.05 | 2.11 |

| Fund | Rising Market 6/28/65 to 2/9/66 | Falling Market 2/9/66 to 10/7/66 | Rising Market 10/7/66 to 1/12/68 | Falling Market 1/12/68 to 3/5/68 | Rising Market 3/5/68 to 11/29/68 | Falling Market 11/29/68 to 2/10/70 |
|---|---|---|---|---|---|---|
| Babson (David L.) Investment | 1.21 | 0.93 | 0.99 | 0.92 | 1.31 | .57 |
| Bondstock Corporation | 2.16 | 0.82 | 0.85 | 0.88 | 1.40 | 1.10 |
| Boston Common Stock Fund | 0.27 | 0.89 | 0.43 | 1.17 | 1.38 | .22 |
| Boston Foundation Fund | 1.34 | 0.80 | 0.88 | 0.63 | 0.88 | 1.33 |
| Boston Fund | 0.16 | 0.71 | 0.31 | 0.61 | 0.66 | 1.15 |
| Broad Street Investing | 0.75 | 0.92 | 0.73 | 0.84 | 1.06 | .80 |
| Bullock Fund | 1.12 | 0.92 | 0.93 | 0.92 | 1.12 | 1.10 |
| CG Fund | — | — | — | — | — | 1.41 |
| Canadian Fund | 0.36 | 0.66 | 0.53 | 1.05 | 1.01 | .02 |
| Capital Investors | — | — | — | — | — | 3.48 |
| Capital Shares | 0.34 | 1.48 | 0.69 | 1.09 | 1.73 | 1.64 |
| Century Shares Trust | 0.39 | 1.28 | 0.32 | 0.95 | 1.96 | 1.30 |
| Channing Balanced Fund | 1.02 | 0.77 | 0.71 | 0.90 | 0.86 | 1.54 |
| Channing Common Stock Fund | 1.46 | 0.96 | 0.91 | 1.20 | 1.22 | 1.87 |
| Channing Growth Fund | 3.59 | 0.61 | 1.42 | 1.98 | 1.32 | 2.66 |
| Channing Income Fund | 1.05 | 0.76 | 0.57 | 0.37 | 0.99 | 1.52 |
| Channing Special Fund | 4.89 | 1.21 | 2.87 | 2.14 | 2.14 | 1.93 |
| Chase Fund of Boston | 3.49 | 1.27 | 3.16 | 1.60 | 1.96 | 1.77 |
| Chase Frontier Fund | — | — | — | — | — | 1.40 |
| Chemical Fund | 1.67 | 0.94 | 1.25 | 0.98 | 0.97 | .59 |
| Colonial Equities | — | — | — | 1.87 | 1.51 | 2.01 |
| Colonial Fund | 1.05 | 0.91 | 1.06 | 1.03 | 0.92 | 1.46 |
| Colonial Growth Shares | 1.87 | 0.93 | 2.47 | 1.59 | 1.31 | 1.34 |
| Common Stock Fund | 1.53 | 0.79 | 1.37 | 1.15 | 1.56 | 1.51 |
| Competitive Capital Fund | — | — | — | — | — | 1.97 |
| Composite Fund | 1.33 | 0.85 | 1.41 | 0.85 | 1.25 | 1.62 |
| Concord Fund | — | — | — | — | — | 1.68 |
| Consumers Investment Fund | 2.18 | 1.16 | 2.42 | 0.73 | 1.64 | 2.09 |
| Corporate Leaders | 0.72 | 1.01 | 0.45 | 0.55 | 0.76 | 1.38 |
| Country Capital Investment | — | — | — | — | — | 1.08 |
| Crown Western Dallas Fund | 1.58 | 0.94 | 1.76 | 1.05 | 2.59 | 2.43 |
| Crown Western Diversified | 1.13 | 0.87 | 1.09 | 0.50 | 1.53 | 2.31 |
| Decatur Income Fund | 1.15 | 0.79 | 1.05 | 0.46 | 1.10 | 1.24 |
| de Vegh Mutual Fund | 2.18 | 0.64 | 1.52 | 0.82 | 1.40 | 1.33 |
| Dividend Shares | 0.67 | 0.87 | 0.80 | 0.65 | 0.91 | 1.03 |
| Drexel Equity Fund | 2.96 | 1.16 | 2.07 | 1.30 | 1.82 | 2.01 |
| Dreyfus Fund | 2.38 | 0.90 | 1.18 | 1.11 | 1.13 | 1.32 |
| Eaton & Howard Balanced | 0.26 | 0.62 | 0.31 | 0.50 | 0.78 | 1.46 |
| Eaton & Howard Growth | — | — | — | — | — | .86 |
| Eaton & Howard Income | 0.48 | 0.70 | 0.56 | 0.52 | 1.00 | 1.88 |
| Eaton & Howard Special | — | — | — | — | — | 2.34 |
| Eaton & Howard Stock | 1.17 | 0.93 | 0.86 | 1.07 | 1.11 | 1.64 |
| Eberstadt Fund | — | — | — | * | 1.20 | .83 |
| Energy Fund | 2.34 | 0.94 | 1.72 | 0.93 | 0.74 | 1.47 |
| Enterprise Fund | 3.19 | 1.24 | 5.28 | 1.45 | 2.56 | 1.91 |
| Equity Fund | 0.96 | 0.97 | 0.92 | 0.68 | 1.07 | 1.40 |
| Equity Growth Fund | — | — | 2.07 | 1.79 | 1.88 | .82 |
| Everest Fund | — | — | — | — | — | 2.01 |
| Explorer Fund | — | — | — | 0.41 | 0.77 | 1.05 |
| Fairfield Fund | 3.78 | 0.95 | 3.03 | 2.08 | 1.56 | 2.23 |
| Farm Bureau Mutual Fund | 0.90 | 1.09 | 1.09 | 1.01 | 1.00 | 1.38 |
| Federated Growth Fund | 1.91 | 0.49 | 1.23 | 1.06 | 1.21 | 1.36 |

* Fund moved contrary to the market

| Fund | Rising Market 6/28/65 to 2/9/66 | Falling Market 2/9/66 to 10/7/66 | Rising Market 10/7/66 to 1/12/68 | Falling Market 1/12/68 to 3/5/68 | Rising Market 3/5/68 to 11/29/68 | Falling Market 11/29/68 to 2/10/70 |
|---|---|---|---|---|---|---|
| Fidelity Capital Fund | 4.00 | 0.78 | 1.35 | 1.46 | 0.94 | 1.83 |
| Fidelity Fund | 1.63 | 0.83 | 1.18 | 1.00 | 1.18 | 1.03 |
| Fidelity Trend Fund | 4.32 | 1.03 | 1.29 | 1.26 | 1.02 | 1.49 |
| Financial Dynamics Fund | — | — | — | 1.47 | 2.35 | 1.50 |
| Financial Industrial Fund | 1.69 | 1.09 | 1.15 | 1.20 | 1.13 | 1.47 |
| Financial Industrial Income | 1.32 | 0.93 | 1.33 | 0.43 | 1.67 | 1.48 |
| First Investors Fund | 1.22 | 0.93 | 0.77 | 1.06 | 0.95 | 1.81 |
| First Investors Growth | — | — | 1.48 | 0.26 | 0.54 | 1.48 |
| Fletcher Capital Fund | — | — | — | — | — | 2.35 |
| Fletcher Fund | — | — | — | 1.72 | 1.92 | 3.94 |
| Florida Growth Fund | 0.88 | 1.00 | 1.47 | 1.00 | 1.73 | .92 |
| Founders Mutual Fund | 1.34 | 1.14 | 0.82 | 0.95 | 0.88 | 1.34 |
| Foursquare Fund | 2.95 | 1.19 | 1.13 | 1.42 | 1.09 | 1.71 |
| Franklin Common Stock Fund | 1.76 | 0.95 | 1.24 | 0.98 | 0.93 | .90 |
| Franklin Dynatech Fund | — | — | — | — | — | 2.16 |
| Franklin Utilities Fund | * | 0.72 | 0.44 | 1.04 | 0.64 | 1.52 |
| Fund of America | 3.79 | 1.20 | 1.55 | 1.96 | 1.38 | 1.85 |
| Gibraltar Growth Fund | — | — | — | — | 3.38 | 1.41 |
| Group Sec.—Aerospace Science | 3.75 | 1.03 | 1.67 | 1.56 | 0.88 | 1.76 |
| Group Sec.—Common Stock | 1.02 | 0.96 | 0.68 | 0.78 | 0.92 | 1.27 |
| Group Sec.—Fully Administered | 0.69 | 0.79 | 0.38 | 0.48 | 0.63 | .92 |
| Growth Industry Shares | 1.26 | 0.84 | 0.98 | 1.07 | 0.84 | .80 |
| Gryphon Fund | 2.78 | 1.24 | 2.36 | 1.05 | 1.30 | 2.45 |
| Guardian Mutual Fund | 1.14 | 0.88 | 1.18 | 0.94 | 0.97 | 1.18 |
| Hamilton Fund | 1.24 | 1.26 | 1.22 | 1.00 | 1.11 | 2.14 |
| Harbor Fund | 1.01 | 0.52 | 1.73 | 0.92 | 0.93 | 2.22 |
| Hartwell & Campbell Fund | — | — | — | 2.09 | 2.09 | 2.28 |
| Hartwell & Campbell Leverage | — | — | — | — | — | 1.17 |
| Hedge Fund of America | — | — | — | — | — | 1.65 |
| Hubshman Fund | — | — | — | 1.98 | 1.33 | 3.29 |
| IDS New Dimensions Fund | — | — | — | — | — | 2.27 |
| Imperial Capital Fund | 1.26 | 1.00 | 1.10 | 0.97 | 1.12 | .98 |
| Imperial Growth Fund | 2.57 | 0.88 | 2.43 | 1.67 | 1.69 | 1.65 |
| Income Fund of Boston | 0.52 | 0.65 | 0.30 | 0.31 | 0.60 | 1.20 |
| Independence Fund | — | 0.93 | 2.46 | 2.04 | 1.41 | 2.13 |
| Industries Trend Fund | 3.31 | 1.01 | 1.53 | 1.21 | 1.45 | 1.58 |
| Industry Fund of America | — | — | — | — | — | 1.03 |
| Investment Co. of America | 1.94 | 0.94 | 1.34 | 1.02 | 1.21 | 1.26 |
| Investment Indicators Fund | — | — | — | — | — | 1.89 |
| Investment Trust of Boston | 1.11 | 1.13 | 1.09 | 1.06 | 1.02 | 1.12 |
| Investors Mutual | 0.33 | 0.73 | 0.40 | 0.50 | 0.53 | .98 |
| Investors Stock Fund | 0.75 | 0.94 | 0.83 | 1.00 | 0.92 | 1.14 |
| Investors Variable Payment | 1.51 | 1.11 | 1.45 | 1.50 | 1.24 | 1.68 |
| ISI Growth Fund | — | — | — | — | — | 1.55 |
| Istel Fund | 1.59 | 0.93 | 2.24 | 1.00 | 1.41 | 1.55 |
| Ivest Fund | 3.39 | 1.04 | 1.82 | 1.76 | 1.50 | 1.07 |
| Ivy Fund | 2.51 | 1.10 | 3.93 | 1.24 | 2.33 | 2.04 |
| Johnston Mutual Fund | 1.83 | 0.86 | 1.42 | 1.22 | 1.11 | .68 |
| Keystone K-1 Income Fund | 0.48 | 0.59 | 0.40 | 0.76 | 0.58 | 1.35 |
| Keystone K-2 Growth Fund | 2.51 | 1.07 | 1.88 | 1.73 | 1.46 | 1.85 |
| Keystone S-1 High Grade Common | 0.06 | 0.82 | 0.69 | 0.69 | 0.97 | 1.00 |
| Keystone S-2 Income Common | 1.23 | 1.10 | 0.82 | 0.74 | 1.26 | 1.46 |

\* Fund moved contrary to the market

| Fund | Rising Market 6/28/65 to 2/9/66 | Falling Market 2/9/66 to 10/7/66 | Rising Market 10/7/66 to 1/12/68 | Falling Market 1/12/68 to 3/5/68 | Rising Market 3/5/68 to 11/29/68 | Falling Market 11/29/68 to 2/10/70 |
|---|---|---|---|---|---|---|
| Keystone S–3 Growth Common | 2.95 | 1.11 | 1.64 | 0.98 | 0.52 | 1.42 |
| Keystone S–4 Low Priced Common | 2.68 | 1.36 | 2.90 | 2.02 | 2.29 | 1.88 |
| Knickerbocker Fund | 1.39 | 1.01 | 0.89 | 0.78 | 1.24 | 1.52 |
| Knickerbocker Growth Fund | 3.22 | 0.91 | 2.53 | 1.86 | 1.62 | 1.63 |
| Lexington Research Fund | 1.71 | 1.17 | 1.73 | 1.14 | 1.48 | .96 |
| Liberty Fund | 0.71 | 0.89 | 1.45 | 0.98 | 1.00 | 1.73 |
| Life and Growth Stock Fund | 0.14 | 1.55 | 0.29 | 0.81 | 1.42 | .75 |
| Life Insurance Investors | 0.32 | 1.58 | 0.66 | 1.24 | 1.76 | 1.08 |
| Loomis-Sayles Canadian & International | 0.51 | 0.70 | 1.15 | 0.82 | 1.13 | * |
| Loomis-Sayles Capital Development | 2.02 | 0.70 | 1.57 | 1.53 | 1.41 | 1.40 |
| Loomis-Sayles Mutual Fund | 0.58 | 0.66 | 0.55 | 0.52 | 0.86 | 1.00 |
| Magna Income Trust | — | — | — | — | — | .54 |
| Manhattan Fund | — | 0.94 | 1.66 | 1.77 | 0.84 | 1.32 |
| Massachusetts Fund | 0.56 | 0.66 | 0.70 | 0.82 | 1.04 | 1.34 |
| Massachusetts Investors Growth Stock | 1.63 | 0.90 | 1.33 | 1.35 | 0.95 | .56 |
| Massachusetts Investors Trust | 0.68 | 0.79 | 0.69 | 0.90 | 0.90 | 1.16 |
| Mathers Fund | — | 1.04 | 4.20 | 1.76 | 2.22 | 3.36 |
| MidAmerica Mutual Fund | 1.57 | 0.86 | 1.20 | 1.07 | 0.97 | 1.52 |
| Moody's Capital Fund | 0.75 | 0.79 | 0.85 | 0.91 | 1.45 | 1.83 |
| MIF Fund | 1.06 | 0.89 | 0.92 | 0.83 | 1.22 | 3.72 |
| Nation-Wide Securities Co. | 0.45 | 0.70 | 0.39 | 0.34 | 0.62 | 1.03 |
| National Industries Fund | 2.68 | 1.10 | 1.58 | 1.29 | 0.99 | 1.95 |
| National Investors | 1.54 | 0.85 | 1.30 | 0.98 | 1.07 | .44 |
| National Securities—Balanced | 0.39 | 0.82 | 0.34 | 0.38 | 0.90 | 1.29 |
| National Securities—Dividend | 1.28 | 0.96 | 0.95 | 0.64 | 1.08 | 1.46 |
| National Securities—Growth Stocks | 1.77 | 0.92 | 1.93 | 1.11 | 1.21 | 1.22 |
| National Securities—Income | 0.77 | 0.79 | 0.59 | 0.64 | 0.73 | 1.11 |
| National Securities—Stock | 1.09 | 0.90 | 0.90 | 0.83 | 1.21 | 1.56 |
| NEA Mutual Fund | 1.29 | 1.02 | 0.89 | 0.89 | 0.68 | 1.04 |
| Neuwirth Fund | — | — | — | 0.28 | 3.50 | 1.78 |
| Newton Fund | 0.88 | 0.89 | 1.52 | 0.90 | 1.65 | 1.26 |
| Northeast Investors Trust | 0.34 | 0.57 | 0.27 | 0.28 | 0.39 | .92 |
| Oceanographic Fund | — | — | — | — | — | 2.17 |
| Omega Fund | — | — | — | — | — | 1.74 |
| One Hundred Fund | — | — | — | 1.03 | 1.79 | 1.65 |
| One William Street Fund | 1.09 | 0.85 | 1.21 | 1.37 | 0.88 | .94 |
| Oppenheimer Fund | 3.26 | 1.06 | 1.81 | 1.80 | 2.10 | 1.41 |
| Penn Square Mutual Fund | 1.56 | 1.14 | 0.78 | 0.61 | 1.11 | 1.43 |
| Pennsylvania Mutual Fund | — | — | — | 2.22 | 5.03 | 2.56 |
| Philadelphia Fund | 1.45 | 0.89 | 0.90 | 1.12 | 1.03 | 1.00 |
| Pilgrim Fund | — | — | 2.73 | 1.81 | 1.39 | 1.05 |
| Pilot Fund | — | — | 2.60 | 1.62 | 2.07 | 1.61 |
| Pine Street Fund | 0.92 | 0.83 | 0.83 | 0.89 | 1.08 | 1.12 |
| Pioneer Fund | 1.48 | 0.81 | 1.32 | 0.33 | 1.14 | 1.00 |
| Planned Investment Fund | — | — | — | — | — | 1.59 |
| T. Rowe Price Growth Stock Fund | 1.51 | 0.82 | 1.15 | 1.11 | 1.05 | .45 |
| Rowe Price New Horizons Fund | 3.06 | 0.48 | 3.63 | 1.55 | 1.83 | 1.02 |
| Pro Fund | — | — | — | — | 1.09 | .69 |
| Provident Fund for Income | 1.49 | 0.88 | 1.34 | 0.53 | 1.44 | 1.43 |
| Puritan Fund | 1.45 | 0.91 | 0.99 | 0.82 | 0.89 | 1.41 |
| Putnam Equities Fund | — | — | — | 1.78 | 2.91 | 2.74 |
| George Putnam Fund | 0.88 | 0.79 | 0.70 | 0.79 | 0.89 | .88 |

* Fund moved contrary to the market

| Fund | Rising Market 6/28/65 to 2/9/66 | Falling Market 2/9/66 to 10/7/66 | Rising Market 10/7/66 to 1/12/68 | Falling Market 1/12/68 to 3/5/68 | Rising Market 3/5/68 to 11/29/68 | Falling Market 11/29/68 to 2/10/70 |
|---|---|---|---|---|---|---|
| Putnam Growth Fund | 2.32 | 1.11 | 1.69 | 1.51 | 1.47 | 1.45 |
| Putnam Income Fund | 0.42 | 0.77 | 0.56 | 0.92 | 0.86 | 1.74 |
| Putnam Investors Fund | 1.12 | 0.91 | 1.24 | 1.02 | 1.28 | .61 |
| Putnam Vista Fund | — | — | — | — | — | 2.24 |
| Republic Technology Fund | 1.70 | 1.14 | 2.74 | 0.45 | 0.79 | 1.81 |
| Revere Fund | 3.48 | 1.41 | 3.41 | 2.32 | 2.03 | 1.83 |
| Schuster Fund | — | — | — | 1.41 | 2.22 | 1.01 |
| Scudder International Investments | 0.45 | 0.81 | 0.69 | 0.43 | 0.98 | * |
| Scudder Special Fund | — | — | 2.55 | 1.27 | 1.57 | 1.47 |
| Scudder, Stevens & Clark Balanced | 0.72 | 0.97 | 0.46 | 0.79 | 0.70 | .97 |
| Scudder, Stevens & Clark Common | 1.31 | 1.08 | 0.78 | 1.28 | 0.96 | 1.06 |
| Security Equity Fund | 5.25 | 1.04 | 3.00 | 1.72 | 1.68 | 1.88 |
| Selected American Shares | 1.89 | 0.99 | 1.19 | 0.96 | 0.96 | 1.52 |
| Selected Special Shares | — | — | — | — | 3.03 | 1.07 |
| Shareholders Trust of Boston | 1.15 | 1.02 | 1.33 | 0.74 | 1.54 | 2.09 |
| Sigma Capital Shares | — | — | — | 1.21 | 2.02 | 1.55 |
| Sigma Investment Shares | 1.38 | 0.96 | 1.10 | 1.16 | 1.04 | 2.40 |
| Sigma Trust Shares | 0.65 | 0.68 | 0.51 | 0.89 | 0.74 | 1.33 |
| Smith Barney Fund | — | — | — | — | — | .57 |
| Southwestern Investors | 0.98 | 0.85 | 0.97 | 0.57 | 1.07 | 1.49 |
| Sovereign Investors | 1.11 | 1.06 | 0.81 | 0.97 | 0.79 | 1.34 |
| State Farm Growth Fund | — | — | — | — | — | 1.65 |
| Steadman American Industry | — | — | — | 1.58 | 1.88 | 1.44 |
| Steadman Fiduciary Investment | — | — | — | 1.27 | 1.22 | .65 |
| Steadman Science & Growth | 2.19 | 1.09 | 2.39 | 2.03 | 1.13 | 2.19 |
| Stein Roe & Farnham Balanced | 0.72 | 0.97 | 0.46 | 0.79 | 0.70 | 1.06 |
| Stein Roe & Farnham Capital Oppor. | — | — | — | — | — | .66 |
| Stein Roe & Farnham Stock | 1.34 | 0.90 | 1.06 | 1.11 | 1.39 | 1.12 |
| Supervised Investors Growth | — | — | 2.69 | 1.55 | 2.02 | 1.38 |
| TMR Appreciation Fund | — | — | — | — | — | .44 |
| Teachers Association Mutual | 2.11 | 1.08 | 1.31 | 1.36 | 0.85 | 1.84 |
| Technology Fund | 2.19 | 1.13 | 1.41 | 1.29 | 1.09 | 1.09 |
| Templeton Growth Fund | 1.33 | 0.48 | 0.38 | * | 1.10 | * |
| Transamerica Capital Fund | — | — | — | — | — | 2.02 |
| Twentieth Century Growth Investors | 3.45 | 1.18 | 2.48 | 2.81 | 1.41 | 2.00 |
| United Accumulative Fund | 1.06 | 0.83 | 0.53 | 1.50 | 1.33 | 1.75 |
| United Income Fund | 1.00 | 0.92 | 0.94 | 1.13 | 1.35 | 1.40 |
| United Science Fund | 2.29 | 1.22 | 1.32 | 1.60 | 1.21 | 1.26 |
| Value Line Fund | 2.01 | 1.01 | 2.82 | 1.31 | 1.46 | 1.78 |
| Value Line Income Fund | 1.21 | 0.87 | 1.17 | 0.92 | 0.83 | 1.64 |
| Value Line Special Situations | 3.62 | 1.10 | 4.38 | 1.41 | 1.86 | 2.43 |
| Varied Industry Plan | 1.70 | 0.98 | 0.84 | 0.83 | 0.96 | 1.58 |
| Wall Street Investing | 0.75 | 0.71 | 0.78 | 0.81 | 0.87 | 1.21 |
| Washington Mutual Investors | 1.14 | 0.94 | 1.02 | 0.88 | 1.22 | 1.39 |
| Wellington Fund | 0.28 | 0.72 | 0.32 | 0.69 | 0.64 | 1.09 |
| Western Industrial Shares | 2.51 | 1.28 | 2.01 | 1.42 | 1.82 | 1.78 |
| Whitehall Fund | 0.47 | 0.78 | 1.01 | 0.72 | 1.02 | .61 |
| Windsor Fund | 1.94 | 0.90 | 1.30 | 0.75 | 1.22 | 0.67 |
| Winfield Growth Fund | 3.28 | 1.04 | 4.23 | 2.15 | 1.86 | 2.40 |
| Wisconsin Fund | 1.31 | 0.85 | 1.00 | 1.04 | 0.95 | .90 |
| Worth Fund | — | — | — | — | — | 2.14 |

* Fund moved contrary to the market

# Chapter 7

# HOW FUNDS ARE SOLD

There are several principal types of mutual fund salesmen, and it is important to identify them in order to measure properly the quality of the advice given and to determine whether that advice is both expert and unbiased.

First, there is the salesman who is employed by a mutual fund sponsor that sells direct to the public and limits its representatives to offering only the company fund or funds. Investors Diversified Services, the world's largest mutual fund organization, illustrates this type. Once known as Investors Syndicate, for more than half a century this company sold "face amount certificates," a simple form of long-term savings account upon which the saver received a quite modest rate of interest. He paid an agreed sum per month over a ten- to fifteen-year period, at the end of which time the company was obligated to pay him a specified sum equal to his principal plus interest. In 1940 or thereabouts, the Securities and Exchange Commission issued a stop-order against the company on sixteen counts of fraud. Actually, it is difficult to understand how anyone could have bought the product—considering the sales charge; you had to be in it eight or nine years before you could get out what you put in, much less a profit. Before its recent abandonment, countless millions of dollars of such certificates were sold, a measure of the public's gullibility. The company changed its name and like a phoenix rose from the ashes of the stop-order, creating several new mutual funds, including Investors Mutual, now the world's largest. IDS has done a magnificent job of selling its product. Over the years, the company has developed probably the finest financial sales organization in America and has sold more financial services than any other company.

Its men are well trained. However, its investment management has been mediocre. If you are solicited by one of its men, you will be advised to buy one or the other of the company's funds because the salesman is not permitted to sell other funds, and his recommendations cannot embrace the whole field of fund possibilities. Understand the limitations placed upon the salesman, and look up the record of the funds.

With the entry into the mutual fund field of such mass marketers as Sears, Roebuck, and the development of their own sales organizations by a number of fund sponsors, we are likely to see marked increase in the activities of salesmen restricted to the offering of a single fund or group of funds under common management.

The first thing to say to the salesman who approaches you to buy funds is, "Let's begin by making a list of the funds you sell, and another list of the funds you don't sell." You will find out immediately if he is part of a "kept" sales organization and you will take that fact into account in evaluating his recommendations.

The second type of sales organization is one which, though it sponsors a fund or funds of its own, allows its salesmen to sell any fund. It is worth remembering that although salesmen for these companies can sell almost any fund, they generally are paid a higher commission for selling a "house" fund. Examples of companies of this type are First Investors Corporation, Investors Planning Corporation, and Provident Management Corporation. These firms have large retail sales organizations and many offices, and they make a genuine effort to train their men properly. (Investors Planning trained Bernie Cornfield, who was until recently the fantastically successful head of Investors Overseas Services. They must be doing something right!)

Unfortunately many men who tackle mutual fund selling are not particularly suited for the work. A good fund salesman must first be intelligent and understand financial planning. Second, he must have a genuine concern for the financial well-being of his clients. Finally, he must have a pleasant approach, which makes him a welcome visitor. Many large fund-selling organizations put on anyone who can be trained to pass the difficult written examination. Many, perhaps the majority, of such men do not make a living at their work, but collectively they make a living for the sales manager and a profit for the company. The life insurance industry, with one half of its sales organization just coming into the business or about to get out of it, has demonstrated that transient salesmen do not serve the public well. They are the fund industry's greatest sales problem. Proselytizing is another problem. Because examination requirements are stiff, some companies prefer not to spend time and money recruiting new people; instead, they try to steal other companies' successful salesmen—not without success. Some such companies do not employ "salesmen," only "regional managers"—all chiefs and no Indians.

The third type of sales organization is the independent dealer. Occasionally, one of these firms handles over-the-counter securities, but mostly they specialize in mutual funds. Sometimes a "firm" is one man in business for himself. Mostly though, the firms have five to twenty-five salesmen, although some companies have prospered and built very large sales groups. The independents' training facilities are generally not as efficient as those of the other two types of companies described. However, the dealer himself is generally very knowledgeable about funds.

The great majority of mutual funds do not retail their own shares. They employ a group of "wholesalers" who periodically call upon all dealers in their assigned territory, giving the salesmen a pep talk on behalf of their fund or group of funds. The wholesalers are energetic and persuasive fellows, and their activities give rise to a curious sales phenomenon: immediately after the wholesaler for ABC Fund has been around lecturing the dealer's sales organization on the splendid investment quality of his fund, the salesmen will sally forth with attaché cases loaded with the fund's prospectus, and everyone they talk to will be given a glowing story about ABC. This continues until the wholesaler for XYZ Fund shows up. He goes to work and soon erases all thought of ABC Fund from their collective minds. The attaché cases are emptied of the dog-eared ABC literature and refilled with bright new material from XYZ Fund, and the group sallies forth to spread the good word.

The point of all this is that the fund that is recommended to you tonight stands a good chance of being the one whose wholesaler called upon the dealer most recently. That does not mean that it is not a good fund. We are not discussing fund quality here. We are talking about the recommendation you get from the man who is selling you a fund and the extent to which that recommendation may be distorted by factors unknown to you. It is entirely possible that the wholesaler for XYZ Fund triumphed over his business adversary and captured the interest of the local sales force simply by displaying a superior performance record.

The last type of mutual fund salesman you may encounter is not really a mutual fund salesman at all. He is a broker, a customer's man, a registered representative, a salesman of stocks and bonds who spends his business day sitting at a telephone calling people to tell them, "They're up!" or "They're down!" Actually he does not like mutual funds. He makes money because you trade, you move your money around. In a mutual fund, your money stops moving around and goes to work. As more and more do-it-yourselfers have decided to get smart and hire professionals to manage their money via a mutual fund, your friend on the telephone has had to face up to the fact that if he does not sell his people mutual funds, they will go somewhere else to buy them. Like the life insurance companies, rather than let the money go elsewhere, he has reluctantly begun to sell mutual funds. But his heart is not in it.

Some brokerage firms which for years were sharply critical of mutual funds now advertise themselves as specialists in funds.

Brokerage firms have observed that non-investors are more easily led to buy mutual funds than to launch upon a program of buying individual stocks. Many of them have set up a mutual fund department merely to coax skittish non-investors into investing in a conservative mutual fund. Once they taste the investment profits, it isn't long before the customer's man calls them with a hot tip on an over-the-counter stock which just can't help but be a winner. They fall for it—and they are caught.

Another sales bias involves the amount of the commissions. How much does the dealer (or broker) make when he sells you shares of a particular fund? A typical schedule of sales charges follows, which allows for discounts for quantity purchases:

| | |
|---|---|
| Under $25,000: | 8% |
| $25,000–$49,999: | 6% |
| $50,000–$99,999: | 4% |
| $100,000–$249,000: | 2½% |
| $250,000 or more: | 1½% |

(If you are about to invest $22,000, it will cost you 8 percent, or $1,760. You could invest $25,000 for only 6 percent, or $1,500: go to the bank and borrow the $3,000 for two or three weeks until your share account can be opened. Then sell $3,000 worth of shares and repay the bank. Total interest charges will be about $10.00, while total saving on sales charge will be $260. You might decide to continue the loan, with the bank holding the fund share certificate as collateral, and an arrangement to pay it off at the rate of a few dollars per month—in which case you have in effect bought the additional $3,000 worth of shares without any sales charge.)

The fund generally pays 75 percent of this sales charge to the dealer, and the dealer generally pays 65 percent of what he gets to the salesman. Most salesmen end up with 3½ to 4 percent of the principal invested. In fairness to the many fine investment dealers and salesmen I have known during thirty-five years in the fund business, most of them sell the fund they honestly believe will do the best job, and they pay small attention to the commission rate, on the theory that if they do a good job, they will end up not only being amply paid, but with the full confidence and trust of those whom they have served to the best of their ability.

Below are the amounts principal load funds pay dealers who sell their shares (from which dealers pay their salesmen approximately 65 percent). Commissions shown are on sales of minimum amounts, which in most cases means less than $25,000. Do not confuse these figures with the fund's established sales charge, which is higher. This is simply what the fund pays to the dealer who sells you the shares.

| | | | |
|---|---|---|---|
| Aberdeen | 7.0% | Consumers Investment | 6.375% |
| Admiralty Growth | 7.75% | Corporate Leaders | 7.53% |
| Admiralty Income | 7.75% | Country Capital Investment | 7.5% |
| Admiralty Insurance | 7.75% | Crown Western Dallas | 8.0% |
| Affiliated | 6.0% | Crown Western Diversified | 8.0% |
| AMCAP | 7.0% | Decatur Income | 6.5% |
| American Business Shares | 7.25% | Dividend Shares | 7.0% |
| American Express Capital | 7.0% | Dreyfus | 8.25% |
| American Express Income | 7.0% | Dreyfus Leverage | 8.25% |
| American Express Investment | 7.0% | Eaton & Howard Balanced | 7.0% |
| American Express Stock | 7.0% | Eaton & Howard Growth | 7.0% |
| American Growth | 7.0% | Eaton & Howard Income | 7.0% |
| American Mutual | 7.0% | Eaton & Howard Special | 7.0% |
| American National Growth | 7.0% | Eaton & Howard Stock | 7.0% |
| Anchor Fundamental | 7.0% | Eberstadt | 6.5% |
| Anchor Growth | 7.0% | Enterprise | 6.5% |
| Anchor Income | 7.0% | Equity | 7.0% |
| Axe-Houghton A | 7.0% | Equity Growth | 7.0% |
| Axe-Houghton B | 7.0% | Everest | 7.0% |
| Axe-Houghton Stock | 7.0% | Explorer | 4.5% |
| Axe Science | 7.0% | Fairfield | 6.0% |
| Bondstock | 7.5% | Federated Growth | 7.0% |
| Boston Common Stock | 6.0% | Fidelity | 7.0% |
| Boston Foundation | 7.0% | Fidelity Capital | 7.0% |
| Boston Fund | 6.0% | Fidelity Trend | 7.0% |
| Broad Street Investing | 6.0% | Financial Dynamics | 7.0% |
| Bullock | 7.0% | Financial Industrial | 7.0% |
| CG | 5.0% | Financial Industrial Income | 7.0% |
| Canadian | 6.0% | First Investors | 6.5% |
| Capital Investors | 7.0% | First Investors Fund for Growth | 6.5% |
| Capital Shares, Inc. | 7.0% | Florida Growth | 7.0% |
| Century Shares Trust | 6.0% | Founders Mutual | 7.395% |
| Channing Balanced | 6.0% | Foursquare | 7.0% |
| Channing Common Stock | 6.0% | Franklin Common Stock | 7.5% |
| Channing Growth | 6.0% | Franklin Dynatech | 7.5% |
| Channing Special | 6.0% | Franklin Income | 7.5% |
| Chase Fund of Boston | 6.75% | Franklin Utilities | 7.5% |
| Chemical | 6.5% | Fund of America | 7.0% |
| Colonial Equities | 6.5% | Group Aerospace Science | 7.0% |
| Colonial | 6.5% | Group Securities Common Stock | 7.0% |
| Colonial Growth Shares | 6.5% | Group Securities Fully Administered | 7.0% |
| Common Stock | 6.0% | Growth Industry Shares | 7.0% |
| Competitive Capital | 7.5% | Gryphon | 7.395% |
| Composite | 6.5% | Hamilton | 8.5% |

| | | | |
|---|---|---|---|
| Harbor | 6.5% | Oppenheimer | 8.0% |
| Hartwell & Campbell Leverage | 6.0% | Philadelphia | 8.0% |
| Hedge Fund of America | 6.5% | Pilgrim | 7.5% |
| Hubshman | 8.0% | Pilot | 6.8% |
| IDS New Dimensions | 7.0% | Pioneer | 7.0% |
| Imperial Capital | 7.6% | Planned Investment | 7.0% |
| Imperial Growth | 7.6% | Provident | 8.0% |
| Income Fund of Boston | 7.75% | Puritan | 6.0% |
| Independence | 6.50% | Putnam Equities | 6.25% |
| Industries Trend | 6.8% | George Putnam | 6.25% |
| Industry Fund of America | 7.4% | Putnam Growth | 6.25% |
| Investment Company of America | 7.0% | Putnam Income | 6.25% |
| Investment Trust of Boston | 6.5% | Putnam Investors | 6.25% |
| Investors Mutual | 7.0%* | Putnam Vista | 6.25% |
| Investors Stock | 7.0%* | Republic Technology | 7.0% |
| Investors Variable Payment | 7.0%* | Revere | 7.65% |
| Investors Research | 7.0% | Schuster | 8.0% |
| ISI Growth | 7.0% | Security Equity | 7.0% |
| Istel | 3.0% | Selected American Shares | 6.0% |
| Ivest | 6.5% | Selected Special Shares | 7.0% |
| Keystone K–1 Income | 6.0% | Shareholders Trust of Boston | 6.75% |
| Keystone K–2 Growth | 6.0% | Sigma Capital Shares | 7.0% |
| Keystone S–1 High Grade Common | 6.0% | Sigma Investment Shares | 7.0% |
| Keystone S–2 Income Common | 6.0% | Sigma Trust Shares | 7.0% |
| Keystone S–3 Growth Common | 6.0% | Southwestern Investors | 6.0% |
| Keystone S–4 Low Priced Common | 6.0% | Sovereign Investors | 7.0% |
| Knickerbocker | 7.0% | Steadman American Industry | 7.0% |
| Knickerbocker Growth | 7.0% | Steadman Fiduciary Investment | 7.0% |
| Lexington Research | 7.0% | Steadman Science and Growth | 7.0% |
| Liberty | 8.0% | Supervised Investors Growth | 7.0% |
| Life Insurance Investors | 7.0% | TMR Appreciation | 8.0% |
| Life and Growth Stock | 7.0% | Technology | 7.0% |
| Manhattan | 8.0% | Templeton Growth | 7.0% |
| Massachusetts | 6.5% | Twentieth Century Growth Investors | 8.5% |
| Massachusetts Investors Growth Stock | 6.0% | United Accumulative | 6.0% |
| Massachusetts Investors Trust | 6.0% | United Income | 6.0% |
| MidAmerica Mutual | 7.0% | United Science | 6.0% |
| Moody's Capital | 6.5% | Value Line | 8.0% |
| MIF | 7.5% | Value Line Income | 8.0% |
| Mutual of Omaha Growth | 7.0% | Value Line Special Situations | 8.0% |
| Nation-Wide Securities | 6.0% | Varied Industry Plan | 6.0% |
| National Investors | 6.0% | Wall Street Investing | 7.0% |
| National Securities Balanced | 6.0% | Washington Mutual Investors | 7.0% |
| National Securities Dividend | 6.0% | Wellington | 6.0% |
| National Securities Growth Stock | 6.0% | Western Industrial Shares | 7.0% |
| National Securities Income | 6.0% | Whitehall | 7.0% |
| National Securities Stock | 6.0% | Windsor | 6.5% |
| Newton | 7.0% | Winfield Growth | 8.25% |
| One Hundred | 8.0% | Wisconsin | 7.0% |
| | | Worth | 7.1% |

Of course, the figures above cover only those funds that make a sales charge. As for the quantity purchase

*No dealers. This amount paid to own sales organization.*

sales charge, the structure has been contested but only once, to my knowledge. Two holders of Investors Mutual brought a class action charging the sponsor, Investors Diversified Services, Inc., with price discrimination under the Robinson-Patman Act, alleging that the price discounts granted for quantity purchases of shares were discriminatory. The Act states: "It shall be unlawful for any person engaged in commerce, in the course of such commerce, either directly or indirectly, to discriminate in price between different purchasers of commodities of like grade and quality." The court decided against the shareholders on the ground that mutual fund shares are intangibles, not commodities. The ruling held that a mutual fund share "is not merely a piece of paper which happens to be a tangible thing. It is a representation of a fractional ownership in a large investment account. The rights which are owned—investment services and redemption rights—are intangible and not commodities."

Recently, the S.E.C. imposed sanctions upon a mutual fund dealer who granted commission rebates to customers. Interestingly, the same ruling that mutual funds are intangibles and not commodities also eliminates any claim that they can be price-protected by a fair trade law. I anticipate that someone soon will make a legal test of the question of price fixing by funds.

Some funds, starting with a sales charge, later have become no-load funds. In 1958, the prestigious investment banking firm of Lehman Brothers brought out the One William Street Fund. During the initial three-week underwriting period, the sponsors agreed to pay investment dealers the entire 8½ percent sales charge instead of the 6 percent usually paid the selling agent. This is an old ploy now for many funds who want the assurance of a sizable amount in the kitty at the start of operations. But in 1958, it was electrifying news. All the big NYSE member firms which had up to then scorned the fund business, turned loose their army of customers' men to sell One William Street Fund with its outsized commission. The Lehman name was magic and everyone knew that the partnership was privy to most of the big financial deals in the country. The results were phenomenal: in twenty days, $183,000,000 flowed into the new fund. Its personnel accepted it gracefully as a personal tribute, becoming quite insuf-

ferable to the point where veteran fundmen began muttering to each other: "Who do they think they are?" The frowns turned to broad grins a few months later, however, when all the leading brokerages decided that a decent interval of time had elapsed and began selling their fund customers out of it. Despite the Lehman name, One William's performance was inferior from the start and these Stock Exchange firms had no trouble talking their customers out of the shares. The fund panicked as redemptions mounted and it began soliciting the regular mutual fund dealers it had just previously been upstaging. Everywhere across the country the answer came rolling back: "Get lost!"

One William maintained its dreary investment record and redemptions continued. The Lehman people spent a fortune trying to pump life back into the carcass. At the annual mutual fund conferences, One William's medicine men, decked out in bright red vests and straw hats (in October) scurried around, buttonholing dealers and chattering a bright sales talk. Dealers responded with an uh-huh and winked at each other. The funereal scene was repeated annually until 1964 when One William threw in the sponge. About this time, someone in the august crowd at fund headquarters reasoned that if no one was willing to sell the fund, no matter how much he was paid, maybe the public would buy it direct— for nothing. "Let's wipe out the sales charge," he said.

That is how they became a no-load fund.

Incidentally, when One William had a sales charge, it was precluded from buying its securities through Lehman Brothers. When the sales charge ended, this provision also was abandoned. Last year Lehman collected $642,992 in brokerage fees on the fund's portfolio transactions.

We will see in the following chapter that the fund that makes no sales charge requires you to do much of the work which the salesman would otherwise be doing for you. You must consider the advantages and disadvantages involved in investing in a no-load fund and decide for yourself whether the sales charge is worth paying.

# Chapter 8

# LOAD VS. NO-LOAD

In mutual fund parlance, the sales charge made by a fund is the "load." Perhaps the term was invented by someone selling funds without a sales charge who wanted to saddle the competition with a psychological handicap. (No one wants to carry a "load.")

Conversely, no-load funds carry no sales charges; they sell at the net asset value. This is made possible because no-load funds are offered without salesmen. Shares are purchased directly from the fund, the investor contacting the fund of his choice in person or by mail or telephone. In contrast, the great majority of funds that make a sales charge do not deal directly with the public—that is, they do not "retail" their shares but sell them through investment dealers who solicit the public.

The first no-loads were started over forty years ago by investment counsel firms as a depository for small, nuisance accounts. A wealthy client would send his cook in to the counsel firm with a note to put her savings to work where she would enjoy earnings rather than just interest. Her assets were too meager to be invested on their own, so the firm maintained a fund into which it dumped all such accounts, investing them collectively.

Later, brokerage firms set up their own no-load funds for much the same reason, seeing in them a vehicle that would provide a steady flow of brokerage business for the sponsor. Also, they did not have to wait for the customer to give them an order to buy or sell as with individual accounts; the firm exercised discretionary power in its management of the money.

No-load funds have come a long way from those early days when they were only a handful and generally scorned by the industry. They were second-class funds. They are that no longer, and for one reason: they have delivered the goods.

Today, a million Americans (61 percent more than a year ago) have nearly $4 billion invested in more than 100 no-load funds. In 1969's disastrous market, sales of load funds rose 11 percent against the no-loads' 58 percent. Of all the new funds whose registrations became effective during the past year (or are still in registration), an astounding 30 percent are no-load funds.

To one who remembers when you could count all such funds on the fingers of one hand, this remarkable explosion of no-load funds suggests that they must be doing something right. We are witnessing only the dawning of the age of no-loads. By 1975 there may well be twice as many, with their assets climbing to $15 billion.

The New York Stock Exchange has recently established new, higher minimum commissions for small-amount purchases, while reducing the rates for big-ticket purchases by mutual funds and other institutional investors. This should cause some investors to take their modest sums to mutual funds, since the spread between the cost of buying individual stocks and the cost of funds is thus reduced. No-load funds, on the other hand, will be made that much more attractive.

It is a paradox that these funds, employing no salesmen, nevertheless owe their success to salesmen. Nothing happens until someone sells something, and it was mutual fund salesmen who made it possible for the no-load funds to take root. They educated the investing public to the mutual fund concept and, in so doing, carried the gospel to millions of people who otherwise would not have been exposed to the many, many advantages of asset management by professionals and all the other conveniences offered by mutual funds.

Like life insurance men who sell their clients expensive cash-value policies while they themselves buy low-cost term insurance, many mutual fund salesmen sell load funds and buy no-load funds.

What kind of people buy no-load funds? The investing public generally has become increasingly sophisticated. Ten years ago, the average mutual fund prospect was visited by a mutual fund salesman who told him about a single fund—and he bought it. He did not do any comparison shopping. Today the number of salesmen has increased tenfold and the sophistication of the buyer one hundredfold. Increasingly, the prospect is not "sold"—he "buys." No longer can a fund salesman with only a smattering of knowledge of his subject impress a prospect. In all likelihood the prospect will startle him with statistics on comparative performance. People have become knowledgeable; they are looking into mutual funds on their own.

It is interesting to note that it is in this climate of investor initiative, and without the benefit of any salesmen, that the no-load funds have begun to set sales records. It takes a little digging to get the facts and figures on no-loads, but prospective investors appear willing to do that work. Notwithstanding, there will always be a need for salesmen, for there will always be people too immersed in their business with no time to explore the intricacies of mutual funds. Also, many people feel shy and inadequate when it comes to investment, and they want—and need—the assistance of a professional salesman.

Those who buy no-load funds, on average, tend to be more sophisticated than those who buy funds with a sales charge. The latter's thinking has been formed as a result of a certain amount of sales pressure. Conservatively, 75 percent of the people who own load funds bought them because they were sold the idea. The no-load buyers, on the other hand, explored the subject of mutual funds on their own initiative. A few months ago, Irving L. Straus Associates, Inc., reported that a study by the firm of both types of investors suggested that no-load fund owners are better educated and are in higher income brackets and better job positions. A recent *National Observer* analysis of respondents to comparable advertisements—half of them promoting load funds and half no-loads—showed that 50 percent of those inquiring about no-load funds had liquid assets of $25,000 or more—double that of those who replied to the load fund ads. Also, four no-load respondents were subsequently converted to purchasers for every three who had inquired about load funds. Put another way, purchasers of no-load funds tend to be smarter investors, as we shall see.

It is frequently claimed that the new-cash flow of no-load funds tends to dry up in a market decline, whereas the thousands of salesmen out beating the bushes tend to keep a steady flow of new money directed into a load fund. But is not this theory disproved by the disclosure that during the 1969 market decline, load fund sales were up only 11 percent while no-load funds boosted new share sales by 58 percent? The no-load fund buyers recognized a bargain day when they saw it, without urging from sales representatives of funds. Perhaps more importantly, redemption figures appear to confirm that no-load fund owners are a different breed of cat. While load fund redemptions were climbing to 50 percent of sales in 1969, the no-load redemption rate actually shrank to 35 percent of sales. This is a curious phenomenon: anyone paying a sales charge to get into a fund should be loath to sell out and lose the investment advantage he paid for. The no-loaders, on the other hand, having paid nothing to get in, might be expected to have no qualms about getting out. That they did not redeem suggests that no-load fund shares are in strong hands, a high confidence factor no doubt resulting from these no-load fund owners having bought after a thorough analysis and not under sales pressure.

We often are told that we pretty much get what we pay for. Many people think that if they pay an 8½ percent sales charge to get into one fund, and nothing to get into another, they must be getting short-changed on the latter. They should remember that the sales charge has nothing to do with management ability. The sales charge goes solely to compensating the salesman, and for promotion. Not a cent of this pays for fund management's investment advice or otherwise benefits the fund itself in any way. By not paying the 8½ percent, then, the only thing you are missing is the salesman.

In the rare event that a stockbroker recommends a no-load fund, he is not necessarily doing it out of the kindness of his heart. A number of no-load funds recruit dealers almost as vigorously as do load funds, compensating them with brokerage business from the fund.

Some people argue that there are so few no-load funds that there is not the same wide choice that exists among load funds. That isn't true, either. With over one hundred such funds in existence now and many more in registration, there is every bit as wide a choice as among load funds.

Another argument is that the expense ratios of no-load funds are larger than those of load funds, including management fees. Actually, comparing funds of similar size will generally disclose similar expense ratios. Expenses tend to reduce proportionately as fund size increases. In this regard, because of the obvious commitment of investment dealers who make a living selling load funds, these tend to grow faster than no-load funds. The result is more very large load funds than no-load funds. Therefore, with no-load funds smaller on average, their expense ratios tend to be higher. Even so, the dollar impact on the individual investor is minuscule. A recent industry survey turned up the fact that whereas the median expense ratio of load funds was only $6.00 per year per $1,000 of assets, that of no-load funds was $7.40 per year per $1,000 of assets. It would take a long time for $1.40 per year to offset the $85.00 per $1,000 cost of getting into the load fund in the first place.

Many mutual fund salesmen insist that no-load investment results are inferior to results obtained by load funds but there is no foundation for this claim. Syndicated columnist J. A. Livingston observed that "studies indicate that investors will do better on the average in no-load funds. In terms of managerial performance in 1969, no-load funds outperformed the loads in eight instances out of fifteen. But on the basis of how the investor fared, the no-load funds outperformed the load funds in all fifteen instances."

In the same survey of performance results of leading funds over the past five years, the top-performing 10 percent included nineteen funds of which six were no-loads, the number of no-loads being disproportionately high.

Detractors say that no-load funds try to save money by not reporting as fully or frequently to their shareholders. Actually, the contrary is true. Lacking contact through salespeople, the no-load funds tend to compensate by reporting more fully and elaborately than do many load funds.

Others believe that the minimum investment requirements of no-load funds are higher than those of load funds. Not so. Some no-loads permit the purchase of a single share.

Automatic dividend reinvestment is common to both types of funds, and while many load funds apply a full sales charge to the reinvestment of dividends, all no-load fund reinvestments are free. To discourage "hot money" (one such investor in Hartwell & Campbell Fund deposited $3 million and sold out two days later), some no-load funds charge a 1 percent or 2 percent redemption fee, but you pay that only if and when you get out, which is a lot different from paying 8½ percent when you get in.

No-load funds range in size from very large (T. Rowe Price Growth Fund, twenty years old, with over $550 million of assets) to small and obscure funds with only a million or two.

In recent years, mutual funds have widened their range of special services they supply to shareholders. While a few no-load funds, particularly the smaller ones, do not offer every possible service, in general it may be said that the same convenient shareholder services are available with either type of fund.

One problem experienced by no-load funds involves bad checks. One fund manager reported that at times up to 8 percent of the checks received by his fund were worthless. Obviously, what these "investors" were doing was betting that in a volatile rising market, the shares they purchased would appreciate in value before the check they gave in payment for them was processed.

Attempts are under way to set up a clearinghouse of information about such bad check artists. A subscriber to the service would submit the name of a previously unknown prospective purchaser and would be advised whether or not the name appeared on the black list.

Dealers also have had experiences with buyers who place an order for shares and then decline to pay for them because the market has gone down. This leaves the dealer on the spot with the fund. In effect, he has bought the shares from the fund and is reselling them to the customer. Some funds will cancel an order in such circumstances, but many others will hold the dealer to it, selling the shares, and requiring him to make good the loss. Their position is that in doing so they are protecting the existing shareholders. Never place an order for any mutual fund unless you are prepared to pay for it within the required five days.

For people concerned about death taxes, no-load funds offer an important advantage. Uncle Sam has always insisted that mutual funds left as part of an estate must be valued for death tax purposes at the asked price set by the fund, which includes the sales commission. The Tax Court and the Court of Appeals of the Sixth and Seventh Circuits lately have supported the IRS on this. With no-load funds, there is no such problem—they are valued at the bid price. For death tax purposes, then, a holding of load fund shares can be valued at 9 percent more than a holding of no-load shares.

All this notwithstanding, whether a fund makes a sales charge or not is of secondary importance. Investment results are the only important thing. If you require an appendectomy, you don't go shopping all over town trying to find a surgeon who will do the job cheaper. When it comes to your health, nothing but the best is good enough.

Similarly, when it comes to your financial health, nothing but the best is good enough. All investment managers make mistakes. Your job is to find the one who will make the fewest mistakes. It does not matter what he charges. Get the best.

But when you have narrowed your choice to two or three who seem equal in ability, that is when you look at the sales charge.

Do not begrudge the fee you pay for financial service. You do not begrudge it elsewhere. You put money into a savings account on which you are paid interest of 5 percent per annum. The bank lends your money out on personal loans or installment loans and gets 13 percent. It gives you 5 percent and keeps 8 percent. You are paying the bank a fee of 8 percent.

A $1,000 U.S. government bond, Series G, held for five years, returns $949. You paid a net "sales charge" or "load" of 5.1 percent.

It would be a mistake for you to limit your choice of

mutual funds to those that make no sales charge. Pay whatever is required to obtain the best results.

No-load funds do have advantages, and they have been demonstrated in the 1969–1970 market decline. The minute you buy a load fund, you are behind 8½ percent. If, in a subsequent market decline, your shares go down 9 percent, the worth of your holdings is actually 17½ percent less than your purchase price. If you bought no-load shares, the value of your shares is off 9 percent, and no more. However, remember that the absence of a selling commission will not make up for a mediocre performance record.

Below are the names and addresses of leading no-load mutual funds compiled by the Wiesenberger people.

Afuture Fund
8 Pennell Road
Village of Lima, Pa. 19060

American Investment Counseling Fund
615 S. Flower Street
Los Angeles, Calif. 90017

American Investors Fund, Inc.
88 Field Point Road
Greenwich, Conn. 06830

David L. Babson Investment Fund
301 West Eleventh Street
Kansas City, Mo. 64105

Columbia Growth Fund, Inc.
621 S. W. Morrison
Portland, Ore. 97205

Consultant's Mutual Investment, Inc.
211 South Broad Street
Philadelphia, Pa. 19107

Dodge & Cox Balanced Fund
200 Bush Street
San Francisco, Calif. 94104

Dodge & Cox Stock Fund
200 Bush Street
San Francisco, Calif. 94104

Drexel Investment Fund, Inc.
1500 Walnut Street
Philadelphia, Pa. 19101

Energy Fund, Inc.
55 Broad Street
New York, New York 10005

Gibraltar Growth Fund
P.O. Box 7171
2455 East Sunrise Blvd.,
Fort Lauderdale, Fla. 33304

Guardian Mutual Fund
120 Broadway
New York, New York 10005

Hedberg & Gordon Fund, Inc.
1 Station Square
Paoli, Pa. 19301

Herold Fund
35 Mason Street
Greenwich, Conn. 06830

Investment Indicators Fund
Albert Building
San Rafael, Calif. 94902

Johnston Mutual Fund
230 Park Avenue
New York, New York

Mathers Fund
1 First National Plaza
Chicago, Ill. 60670

Mutual Shares Corp.
200 East 42nd Street
New York, New York 10017

Mutual Trust Fund
4901 Main Street
Kansas City, Missouri 64112

Naess & Thomas Special Fund, Inc.
Arlington Building
201 N. Charles Street
Baltimore, Md. 21201

Neuwirth Fund, Inc.
Middletown Bank Bldg.
Middletown, New Jersey 07748

Northeast Investors Trust Fund
50 Congress Street
Boston, Mass. 02109

The One William Street Fund, Inc.
One William Street
New York, New York 10004

Penn Square Mutual Fund
451 Penn Square
Reading, Pa. 19603

Pennsylvania Mutual Fund, Inc.
111 Broadway
New York, New York 10006

Pine Street Fund, Inc.
20 Exchange Place
New York, New York 10005

T. Rowe Price Growth Stock Fund, Inc.
1 Charles Center
Baltimore, Md. 21201

Rowe Price New Era Fund
1 Charles Center
Baltimore, Md. 21201

Rowe Price New Horizons Fund, Inc.
1 Charles Center
Baltimore, Md. 21201

Pro Fund
1107 Bethlehem Pike
Flourtown, Pa. 19031

Rittenhouse Fund
2 Penn Center Plaza
Philadelphia, Pa. 19102

Scudder Special Fund, Inc.
10 Post Office Square
Boston, Mass. 02109

Scudder, Stevens & Clark Balanced Fund
10 Post Office Square
Boston, Mass. 02109

Scudder, Stevens & Clark Common Stock
10 Post Office Square
Boston, Mass. 02109

Smith, Barney Equity Fund
42 Broadway
New York, New York 10005

Stein Roe & Farnham Balanced Fund
135 South LaSalle Street
Chicago, Ill. 60603

Stein Roe & Farnham Capital Opportunities Fund
135 South LaSalle Street
Chicago, Ill. 60603

Stein Roe & Farnham Stock Fund
135 South LaSalle Street
Chicago, Ill. 60603

# Chapter 9

## TYPES OF PLANS OFFERED
## BY MUTUAL FUNDS

Mutual funds provide for investments of small or large sums of money. While we have noted that some mutual funds permit the purchase of a single share, others set a minimum of ten shares, or some such dollar amount as $250. Some funds will accept round sums such as $1,000 or $5,000, crediting purchasers with fractions of a share out to the third decimal place. Still others require that purchase orders be for even shares. (With rare exception, mutual funds will issue certificates for full shares only.) Most funds have what is called an "open account," which may be opened with a nominal investment and any sums invested thereafter are simply added to the account. Most funds will accept telephone orders; a few insist that payment accompany the order. Of course, if you are buying through an investment dealer, he will attend to all such details. It is only when buying a no-load fund that you must accept the responsibility for contacting the sponsor, giving registration instructions and paying for the order.

Shares are purchased at a price computed at the time of the next closing of the New York Stock Exchange, although some funds require that the order be in their hands before twelve noon of that day in order to get the day's closing price—otherwise, it is bought at the next day's closing price.

Only a small minority of shareholders take certificates. They can be lost, stolen, burned, or otherwise difficult to produce, and to replace them will require the payment of a bond premium of approximately 6 percent of the value of the missing share certificate. It is much more sensible to take advantage of the fund's facilities for leaving certificates on deposit with the custodian bank, particularly if you are reinvesting dividends and capital gains distributions. Such reinvestment results in having your shares on deposit with the bank, anyway. In the circumstances, you might just as well have all of your shares in one place. If you require a certificate for all or a part of your shares for some special reason (e.g., to use as collateral for a bank loan), you may have it issued at the time you purchase or on any later date. If you find that you no longer need the certificate as collateral, return it for safekeeping by the custodian bank. Do not confuse this arrangement with leaving individual securities on deposit with a broker. The broker has the use of such shares and registers them in his name. If he gets into financial difficulties, you may have problems. The New York Stock Exchange has exhausted its $25 million trust fund over the past five years making good customer losses resulting from brokerage firm failures. When mutual fund shares are left on deposit, nobody has the use of them —they are secure in the custodian bank's vaults at all times.

Funds provide two principal types of monthly investment plans, "voluntary" and "contractual." The voluntary plan requirements vary: one fund may require an initial investment of $250 or $500 while another will permit a $25.00-per-month initial investment. One very important difference between the two types is that with the voluntary plan the burden rests upon the investor to remember when a payment is due, whereas the contractual-plan sponsor will probably mail the investor a reminder ten days before the due date and an overdue notice twenty days beyond that. With the voluntary plan, the fund's custodian bank sends a receipt for payment which may go out anywhere from five to twenty-five days after the date of investment.

I do not know what the figures are lately, but at one time, 65 percent of all voluntary plans established were going off the books within three years. They are just too voluntary. Promise yourself that you will do something, and it is easy to backslide. Promise someone else

| Equal Share Purchase | | SHARE PRICE | Equal Dollar Purchase | |
|---|---|---|---|---|
| **Shares** | **Cost** | | **Cost** | **Shares** |
| 100 | $100 | $1 | $300 | 300 |
| 100 | $200 | 2 | $300 | 150 |
| 100 | $300 | 3 | $300 | 100 |
| 100 | $400 | 4 | $300 | 75 |
| 100 | $500 | 5 | $300 | 60 |
| 500 | $1,500 | | $1,500 | 685 |

| 500 at $5 = $2,500 | 685 at $5 = $3,425 |
|---|---|
| (A profit of $1,000) | (A profit of $1,925) |

# DOLLAR COST AVERAGING

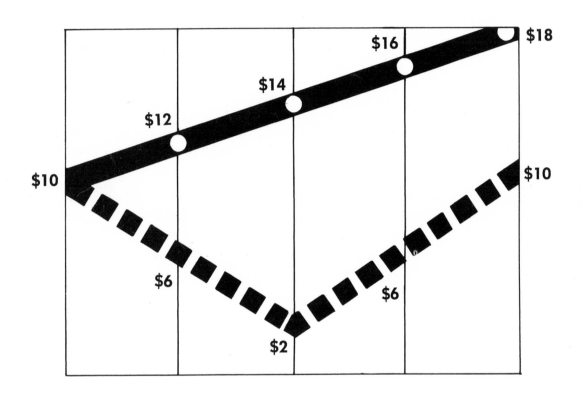

Price Shares

$30 at $10 = 3.
$30 at $12 = 2.5
$30 at $14 = 2.14
$30 at $16 = 1.87
$30 at $18 = 1.67

TOTAL SHARES 11.18
at $18
Total value $201.24

Price Shares

$30 at $10 = 3
$30 at $6 = 5
$30 at $2 = 15
$30 at $6 = 5
$30 at $10 = 3

TOTAL SHARES 31
at $10
Total value $310.00

that you will do it, and if he reminds you periodically, there is a greater chance that you will follow through.

One or two voluntary plans include a reducing-term life insurance feature, notably the Putnam Plan, but generally this arrangement is available only with contractual plans, the subject of the next chapter.

Voluntary, as well as contractual, plans permit the employment of a simple scientific investment principle called "dollar-cost averaging." This is not as complicated as it sounds. It simply involves the investment of equal amounts of money at equal intervals over a period of time. Ordinarily, an individual who has bought 100 shares of stock, noting that it has declined in price, might elect to "average" his cost downward by buying another 100 shares at the lower price. He is averaging shares instead of averaging dollars. The trick is always to invest the same amount of money.

Suppose you have $12,000 to invest, and you are uncertain as to whether the market is going up or down in the immediate future. You might elect to invest $4,000 of it now, another $4,000 of it in thirty days and the remaining $4,000 in sixty days. You would have used dollar-cost averaging on the simplest possible scale.

The classic employment of the principle of dollar-cost averaging involves investment on a monthly basis over a period of several years. Mutual funds offer an ideal medium for such investment. It is not easy to dollar-cost average otherwise. New York Stock Exchange member firms offer a monthly investment plan but with it you are buying the stock of a single company. You have a diversification of one in place of the hundred or more securities that you can own through a mutual fund. The in-and-out cost averages about 10 percent versus the 8 to 8½ percent to get in and out of a mutual fund.

The preceding Equal Share Purchase/Equal Dollar Purchase chart illustrates the substantial benefits obtainable through systematic investment under a program of dollar-cost averaging. The left half of the chart displays the results of making five equal-share purchases. Individual purchases of 100 shares each were made at five price levels ranging from $1.00 to $5.00 per share. Altogether, 500 shares were purchased at a total cost of $1,500. If all holdings were then sold at the $5.00 per share price then prevailing, the $2,500 proceeds would reflect a $1,000 profit.

The right-hand side of the chart illustrates the different results that would have been obtained from dollar-cost averaging. The same $1,500 total was invested over the same period of time, but it was divided into five equal investments of $300 each. Observe the phenomenon that equal-dollar investment has produced: the $1,500 invested in this manner has resulted in the acquisition of 685 shares instead of the 500 obtained via equal-share purchases. If the shareholdings are sold out at the end of the program when the share price is $5.00, the proceeds of $3,425 will represent a profit of $1,925 over cost.

Market declines find those who practice dollar-cost averaging rejoicing. Indeed, such declines play a very important role in the employment of this investment principle. This is revealed in the preceding Dollar-Cost Averaging chart. The solid line illustrates a series of equal-dollar investments of $30.00 each made in a steadily rising market, with per-share prices starting at $10.00 and going successively to $12.00, $14.00, $16.00, and $18.00. At the end of the period, the purchaser has accumulated a total of 11.18 shares which (at $18.00 each) would bring proceeds of $201.24 if sold. Note that these results were achieved during a period when the market rose steadily, closing at a level 80 percent higher than at the start. The broken line illustrates the results of a similar series of $30.00 investments made during what most persons would regard as a very upsetting market. Opening at the same $10.00 as in the first case, the share price sagged to $6.00 and then to $2.00, after which it recovered to $6.00 and closed the period at the same level at which it had started. In these seemingly far less desirable circumstances, a total of thirty-one shares were acquired with the same outlay, and such shares were worth $310 when the last purchase was made. Dollar-cost averaging produced a nice profit in the rising market, but it produced a considerably greater profit in the market that declined sharply and then recovered only to its original starting point.

What all this proves is that when you are investing equal sums of money at equal intervals over a period of time—that is, when you are dollar-cost averaging—market declines cease to hold any terrors for you. You come to look forward to market declines as bargain days, as unexpected opportunities to put money to work on a more favorable basis than you had anticipated. People who invest worry constantly about the timing of their investments. With dollar-cost averaging, your "timing" worries are over. You put market fluctuation to work *for* you, not against you. One of the greatest services the mutual fund industry offers you is the opportunity to conveniently employ dollar-cost averaging.

Increasingly, institutions are coming to appreciate the advantages of dollar-cost averaging. The Equitable Life Assurance Society, explaining its investment procedures, noted: "We are continuing our policy of buying common stocks on a dollar-averaging basis."

All mutual funds offer a dividend payment plan, paying dividends quarterly from ordinary income, although many growth funds pay them semiannually or even annually. Such dividends may be taken in cash or reinvested in additional shares. Your election has nothing to do with the taxability of the dividends, of course. If they are reinvested, it is considered to be a "constructive distribution," that is, they are paid to the custodian bank as your agent and the bank reinvests them.

Capital gains distributions, too, may be taken in cash or reinvested in additional shares. Many investors take their ordinary income dividends in cash and reinvest their capital gains on the theory that capital gains are a part of their principal.

Another service available from mutual funds is called a "systematic withdrawal plan." In 1938, I designed for Commonwealth Fund of Boston what I believe was the first such plan. Investors deposited a lump sum of $500 or more and received a regular quarterly distribution of 6 percent per annum. The idea came from a $55 million trust fund that Charles Hayden had set up for his family, in which he provided that the beneficiaries were to be paid 6 percent in good years and bad. Any earnings or profits above that figure were to be reinvested in the good years, and principal was to be drawn on in lean years. The theory was that the good years outnumbered and outweighed the poor years. Commonwealth Fund operated only within Massachusetts during the first three years of its existence and did not require registration with the Securities and Exchange Commission. When the fund became registered, the Commission required me to discontinue the plan with its 6 percent distribution on the grounds that someone might get the impression that it guaranteed a 6 percent return. Now, practically every fund has a systematic withdrawal plan under which you may instruct the fund exactly how much to pay you, stating it in dollars (a fixed amount) or in percent (a variable amount), and the Commission has no objection. You can terminate at any time. (We had to discontinue a $5.00-per-month plan, too, when the Commission ruled that a person could not accumulate any worthwhile sum investing only $5.00 per month.)

The systematic withdrawal plan is a very sensible arrangement. It is unfortunate that most funds require a $10,000 minimum holding of their shares (a few will settle for $5,000) in order to have a systematic withdrawal plan. The minimum should be reduced to $1,000 with the proviso that no payment under such a plan shall be less than $25.00. The withdrawal most commonly requested is 6 percent, but in a well-managed fund, a larger percentage could be taken without fear of substantially diminishing capital. This larger percent withdrawal would be particularly appropriate in the case of persons who do not desire to leave a substantial estate when they are gone. The systematic withdrawal plan is also a great convenience to those who have occasion to send a regular check to an elderly relative, a youngster at college, or in payment of a mortgage or other obligation.

Just about every fund makes available a tax-sheltered retirement plan for self-employed individuals. Such plans, called "Keogh" plans (named after Congressman Keogh) may be set up using insurance policies, United States savings bonds, or bank trust accounts, but nothing is as suitable for a Keogh plan as a mutual fund. First, such plans are easy to set up through a simple form of application. Second, the mutual fund gives the dollars a fighting chance against inflation, unlike the fixed-dollar insurance policy or savings bond plans. Third, the mutual fund provides a managed investment.

Under a Keogh plan, a self-employed person may put aside up to 10 percent of his income (maximum contribution $2,500), with the full amount currently deductible for income tax purposes, the tax being deferred until the funds are withdrawn at retirement age. All earnings from the investment, be they ordinary income or capital gains, likewise are tax deferred. In addition, he may deposit up to another 10 percent of his taxable income on a voluntary basis. There is no immediate deduction on that but there is the same tax shelter for the earnings. And tax shelter is important these days. Keogh plans must include every employee who works a 20-hour week, temporary employees excepted.

It would pay a doctor earning $30,000, or anyone in similar circumstances, to find something for his wife to do in his practice. He can pay her a salary of $5,000. This reduces his income to $25,000 but leaves their combined income the same. Since they file a joint return, there is no tax change. He deposits $2,500 in a Keogh plan for himself, fully tax deductible, and another $500 for his wife, also tax deductible. Then he and she can put in an additional $2,500 and $500 respectively as a voluntary contribution. Of course, the doctor must take into account Social Security taxes on his wife's salary.

There is even a tax-free way to get the money out of Keogh at age 70½. Uncle Sam has a U.S. Government Retirement Plan Bond. Any money taken out of the Keogh plan and invested in these bonds is tax free. They pay tax-free interest of 3¾ percent, and the interest is compounded. No tax is payable until the owner or his beneficiary cashes in the bonds. They stop paying interest five years after the death of the Keogh planholder.

It is worth noting, too, that Keogh assets are beyond reach of creditors and not subject to bankruptcy or divorce proceedings.

One thing that many Keogh planholders do not understand is that they are free to change from one Keogh plan to another. If you were sold one of those dreary plans which use insurance or savings bonds as the medium of investment, despair not. Pick yourself out a good mutual fund Keogh plan, execute all the papers, write a letter to your old Keogh plan custodian bank telling them to forward a check for the present value of the plan to the bank that is the custodian of the mutual fund Keogh plan, and send a carbon of it with the new application plan to the new custodian. It is very important that you not ask them to send the money to you. Once you take possession of it, it is taxable. Be sure, then, that you have one bank send it direct to the other.

Fund plans also include the privilege of switching from fund to fund within a group without the payment of any charges other than a nominal $5.00. Some groups restrict this to switching *types* of funds. That is, they will let you switch from a growth fund to a balanced fund or vice versa, but they will not let you change from growth fund to growth fund.

If you do not have all of your money available at one time to take advantage of a reduced sales charge for quantity purchases, you may sign a "letter of intention" indicating that you plan to invest within thirteen months a total sum that would entitle you to a discount. When you invest $15,000 under a $25,000 letter of intention, you buy at the first discount price which, lower than the regular asked price, reflects the discount to which the execution of the letter entitles you. Your $15,000 thus buys more shares than are obtained by someone else investing $15,000 without a letter of intention. The extra shares are put into an escrow account in your name which you cannot claim until you have completed your letter of intention.

For a period varying between thirty and ninety days from the date of purchase, most load funds will allow the execution of a letter of intention retroactively. This can be helpful to an investor who has made a minimum purchase and who then concludes that he will make an additional purchase which, taken with his original order, would entitle him to a discount. Once the period arbitrarily set by the fund (and not disclosed in the prospectus) has expired, the discount opportunity is lost, however. My firm once invested $85,000 in a fund for a woman client, thereby entitling her to a 4 percent sales charge. Eighty-seven days later, she called to report that she had available an additional $15,000. With three days left in which to do it, we hurriedly processed a retroactive $100,000 letter of intention entitling her to a 2½ percent sales charge. Her dollar cost to invest the $85,000 had been $3,400. The cost of the $100,000 investment was only $2,500. The fund credited her with additional shares representing a $900 refund, and when we sent in her $15,000, we had to enclose our own check for $675. Not only had we not made anything on her last $15,000 investment—it had cost us $675 for commission adjustment.

Even if there is only the slightest possibility that you may have additional funds during the next thirteen months, sign a letter of intention, for you have nothing to lose.

For example, consider the case of an investor con-templating the purchase of $10,000 of shares at a low point in the market. He signs a $100,000 letter of intention. This will entitle him to an immediate discount on the price of the shares, and his $10,000 will therefore buy a larger number. Assuming that he makes no additional investments, at the end of the thirteen months the fund will notify him that since he has not completed the $100,000 investment contemplated by the letter of intention, he must remit to them the difference between what he paid for his shares and what he would have paid for them if he had not been given the discount. He can send them a check for it or he can write them to sell enough of his shares to pay what he owes. The amount involved will be about $600. In effect, he has borrowed $600 for thirteen months at no interest to invest in the fund's shares. He can sell them and keep the profit, represented by the dividends and distributions paid on them during the thirteen months, plus any appreciation in their value. Such an arrangement could produce a modest profit if initiated at a historically low point in the market when a period of recovery appeared to lie ahead.

Bear in mind, too, that a letter of intention can be increased in amount at any time during its term.

One technical point should be noted regarding a letter of intention. If they can get away with it, some funds will take the position that you lose credit toward the purchase of such shares if you sell them before the letter expires. To illustrate: you invest $15,000 under a $25,000 letter of intention. Four months later, you have an emergency need for $5,000 and you liquidate shares to obtain it. Shortly before the expiration of the letter, you send in the $10,000 difference between your $15,000 purchase and the $25,000 total you agreed to invest. The fund advises you that you are in effect using $5,000 of your money twice, that it not only will not give you the discount on the new $10,000 but it is also going to take back the shares in the escrow account. If this happens, scream as loudly as you can. Write to the president of the fund and to the Securities and Exchange Commission. It does not matter how many times you use your money—if the fund has received the fee for $25,000 worth of purchases, you are entitled to the discount. Once you have purchased a block of shares and paid the sales charge, they are your property absolutely and you are entitled to do what you will with them—and that includes redeeming them.

Another mutual fund arrangement worth mentioning is called "rights of accumulation." One form provides for the granting of a discounted sales charge on new purchases made by a shareholder whose holdings are above the fund's regular breakpoints. To illustrate: assume your investment of $15,000 in ABC Fund increases in value to $20,000. If you make a new $5,000 investment in the fund, you will pay the reduced sales charge applicable to a $25,000 purchase. The second form of "rights of accumulation" is not as favorable: it disregards the *value* of your holdings and takes into account only the amount you actually have paid into the fund. Under this form, in the circumstances described above, you would not be entitled to the discount.

An interesting plan, which is still in prospect, is sponsored by the Harleysville Insurance Company of Harleysville, Pennsylvania It provides "loss insurance" on mutual fund purchases. For a premium of 6 percent, the company will guarantee that your investment, after a ten- or fifteen-year period, will not be worth less than you paid for it. It is required that all dividends and capital gains be reinvested. If you invest $12,000 in a lump sum with "no-loss" insurance for ten years, the premium would be $720, and this would take the form of a deduction of $72 per year from income or capital gains distributions over the ten-year period. If the insurance is to cover fifteen years, the same $720 total will be deducted at the rate of $48 per year. Since the $720 is considered to reduce your net investment to $11,280, this is the amount actually insured against loss. With dividends and capital gains reinvested, it would be difficult to imagine how the investment could possibly not have increased in value. (I recall, though, that after the market break of 1929, it took thirty years for Massachusetts Investors Trust shares to recover to their 1929 peak.) The Harleysville plan will also cover monthly investment programs. If you invest $100 per month for ten years, insurance on the $12,000 total investment will still cost $720 (6 percent) or $72 per year deducted from earnings or, if these are not sufficient, from principal. In proportion to the amount of money invested in the early years, the insurance premium is obviously higher with the monthly plan, but so is the company's risk. About ten years ago, a British mutual fund (they call them "unit trusts" there) offered a somewhat similar insurance coverage on its shares at a 4 percent premium, but the investor paid 4 percent more for the shares at the outset, thus paying the ten years' premium in advance. The offering was sold out overnight, but even more significant was a marked increase in the purchase of the fund's uninsured shares. The investors evidently decided that if the insurance company felt that it could safely take the risk, they could gamble on it themselves and save the premium. The Harleysville coverage will be obtained pursuant to an agreement between the company and interested mutual funds. You cannot obtain it unless the fund you buy has signed for it. One significant aspect: the insurance company must approve the investment policy of an insured fund. That will cut out many "go-go" funds.

# Chapter 10

# CONTRACTUAL PLANS

The contractual plan for monthly investment in mutual funds is probably the fund industry's single most controversial subject.

Harry J. Simonson in 1929 invented the contractual plan for his Independence Fund of North America. It had a "double-load": you paid 9 percent to get into it, and your money was then invested in trust shares, which themselves were purchased with a 9 percent sales charge. That made the sales charge 18 percent. Six months later, Jack Thomas, another financial figure of that era, brought out the second contractual plan. Simonson's original company, now National Securities & Research Corporation, though prominent in the mutual fund industry, has ceased to promote its contractual plan. Thomas's company, First Investors Corporation, headed by David Grayson, one of the most upright men in the investment field, remains one of the largest and most successful companies in the plan business.

The first $10.00-per-month contractual plan called for an initial payment of $100, of which $90.00 was the sales charge and $10.00 was the first payment into the plan. Many people found it inconvenient to get up the $100 to start the plan, so it was altered to provide for a payment of $20.00 for the first nine months—in effect, paying the $90 sales charge in installments at the rate of $10 per month. When the Securities and Exchange Commission designed the Investment Company Act of 1940, it insisted that the concept of the sales charge as a separate payment be dropped. The sales charge must be deducted from the investment, it decreed.

It is curious that the industry that began by taking nothing from the investor's payment, and was then forced into a policy of deducting its sales costs from the investment itself, now is under fire because it is deducting too much from that payment. It is that method of deduction that has stirred up all the controversy. More than one meeting of the Investment Companies Institute has broken up in a row because of differences among members over the propriety of contractual plans.

My own investment firm has sold many thousands of such plans for over thirty-five years, and I have written a great many articles extolling their virtues. Contractuals once had important advantages which it seemed to me should weigh heavily in the selection of an investment medium. Many of these advantages no longer are available. Moreover, the character of the mutual fund industry has so changed over the years that contractual plans no longer are a desirable investment.

A contractual plan provides for regular investment in a specific mutual fund over a period of ten or fifteen years. The weakness of the plan lies in the fact that few funds are likely to stay topnotch that long. It can be stated another way: you should invest for long-term capital appreciation. If you require income, spend 6 percent of your principal each year rather than seeking investments that yield 6 percent. What you want, then, is the most spectacular growth performance you can find, because that is what is going to provide the maximum hedge, the maximum protection, against inflation, your No. 1 economic enemy.

Note that I am not saying you should speculate with your money. I am saying that your major objective should be capital growth and not income.

But no one growth fund is going to deliver a spectacular performance for ten or fifteen years. It may produce an adequate performance, even a good performance. But nothing is just "good" or "poor." It is "better" or "poorer" than something else.

More than 750 open-end investment companies are now in an active status. Of these, about 500 are of significant size. About a dozen turn in a spectacular performance each year, though not the same twelve each year, of course. These spectacular performers almost invariably are smaller funds, because only a small fund has the flexibility and liquidity to produce a spectacular investment result. The small fund owns 1,000 shares of ABC Common. If the fund's managers decide that ABC Common is no longer a good investment, they can pick up the telephone and sell out their holding in three minutes. But the large fund owns 50,000 shares of ABC Common. Deciding that it is no longer suitable, the managers may spend weeks, even months, working it off piecemeal so as not to disturb the market.

The spectacular performance of each of the top dozen funds contains the seeds of its own destruction because in this day and age, the performance of funds is widely publicized. I can remember when a fund's size and the number of Boston Brahmins on its board of directors were an important determinant in the amount of publicity given it. But, today, performance is the payoff, and the small fund that delivers it is given wide publicity. Where once the financial editors scorned the little funds, now they seek eagerly to find the small fund that is hiding its investment light under a bushel. They trumpet its praises, the new money pours in, the small fund begins to swell—until one day it is no longer small. Like a 300-pound man, it begins to waddle. It has lost its flexibility, its nimbleness. Soon, performancewise, it begins its gradual slide downward into the pack.

The Fidelity Trend Fund serves as an example. Started in 1958, it did very well for a number of years. It began 1965 with $200 million of assets and ended the year as the No. 1 performing fund in the country, with a record gain of 57 percent. That record was widely publicized, and in the next twenty-four months the fund took in $1 billion of new money. It finished 1967 with $1.4 billion of assets—but out-performed by eighty-four other funds. The managers simply could not do with $1.4 billion what they had been able to do with $200 million. Fund president Edward Johnson issued a somewhat gloomy annual report in which he acknowledged sadly that the Fund had grown to unwieldy proportions and was unlikely ever again to duplicate its early successes. The managers presumably were just as smart as they had been in 1965, but $1.4 billion was just too great a weight to handle—for them, at least.

Use a growth fund as you would use an escalator to get to the fifth floor of a department store. Pick a fund among the top dozen quality performers and ride it up until you see that it is leveling off. Then step off and onto another growth fund that will carry you up another financial flight. Or regard the investment managers who serve you as members of a relay team. One runner carries the baton at his top speed. When he is tired, another takes it from him and starts afresh from there. In much the same fashion, mutual fund managements can become winded and paunchy and unable to run as fast. At that point, you should thank them for the good job they have done for you, and find a new manager without a paunch. If you wish to obtain maximum

benefit from mutual fund investment, you must be prepared to switch funds now and again.

Obviously, then, an investment plan that requires you to purchase shares of the same fund month in and month out for ten or fifteen years is not likely to prove of maximum benefit in the long run. Investors feel locked in by their payment of the front-end load. That remains my principal objection to the contractual plan. Contractual plans favor fund managers whose performance is slipping.

But the method by which sales charges are deducted from payments is still central to the controversy. The Investment Company Act of 1940 limits deductions to one half of each of the first twelve payments, with the balance of the sales charge being spread equally among the remaining payments contemplated to be made under the plan. Ordinarily, then, on a $50.00-per-month account, the investor would pay in $600 during the first year, of which up to $300 could properly be deducted by the sponsor. But sponsors have a small gimmick which increases the first year cost: they require that the first payment be double the regular monthly amount. On a $50.00-per-month plan, then, you would make an initial investment of $100 and eleven additional investments of $50.00, for a total of $650 the first year. Out of this, the sponsor could deduct 50 percent, or $325.

The net effect of the contractual plan is to require the investor to pay more in fees during the first year than he would pay if he simply invested in shares of the same fund under a voluntary plan. It is true that he pays less during each of the remaining contractual nine or fourteen years the plan has to run than he would if he were continuing regular monthly investments in a voluntary plan. In the long run, though, his costs will be greater under a contractual plan than under a voluntary plan, especially if the custodian bank's fees on the contractual plan are taken into account.

For many years, these somewhat higher costs were worth paying. In some instances, the sales charge was a slightly lower percentage under the contractual plan. Later, we will see that, contrary to what I have said of most funds, some reinvest ordinary income dividends at the asked price, that is, with a full sales charge. However, the Investment Company Act required them to reinvest at net asset value all such dividends paid on their shares held under a contractual plan. For many years, contractual plans were taxed as associations, entitling them to a substantial tax exemption on their income. Indeed, for quite a period, most contractual plan investors paid no tax at all on the income from their plans. All such tax benefits have now been removed. Contractual plans permit partial withdrawals of up to 80 percent or 90 percent of their value, and subsequent redeposit of the sum so withdrawn with no sales charge. They also permit the investor to name a beneficiary.

# DREYFUS FUND RESULTS

## Voluntary Plans vs. Contractual Plans

During 15 years ending 12/31/68

*(All figures reproduced from Dreyfus Fund sales literature)*

---

### ASSUMED INITIAL INVESTMENT OF $50 AND SUBSEQUENT INVESTMENTS OF $50 PER MONTH

- Initial and Subsequent Investments . . $9,000
- Income Dividends Reinvested . . . 3,146
- Total Cost (Payments Plus Income Dividends Reinvested) . . **$12,146**
- Total Value December 31, 1968 (1,974 Shares)* . . . . . . **$32,471**

*Includes 389 shares acquired through reinvestment of $3,691 in capital gain distributions.

---

### $50 SYSTEMATIC PROGRAM: TOTAL $9,000 ASSUMED $100 INITIAL INVESTMENT AND $50 MONTHLY

- Total Monthly Payments . . . . $ 9,000
- Income Dividends Reinvested . . 2,854
- Total Cost (Payments Plus Income Dividends Reinvested) . **$11,854**
- Total Value December 31, 1968 (1,824 Shares)* . . . . . . **$30,003**

*Includes 343 shares acquired through reinvestment of $3,328 in capital gain distributions.

---

### ASSUMED INITIAL INVESTMENT OF $100 AND SUBSEQUENT INVESTMENTS OF $100 PER MONTH

- Initial and Subsequent Investments . . $18,000
- Income Dividends Reinvested . . . 6,304
- Total Cost (Payments Plus Income Dividends Reinvested) . . **$24,304**
- Total Value December 31, 1968 (3,964 Shares)* . . . . . . **$65,207**

*Includes 779 shares acquired through reinvestment of $7,396 in capital gain distributions.

---

### $100 SYSTEMATIC PROGRAM: TOTAL $18,000 ASSUMED $200 INITIAL INVESTMENT AND $100 MONTHLY

- Total Monthly Payments . . . . $18,000
- Income Dividends Reinvested . . 5,761
- Total Cost (Payments Plus Income Dividends Reinvested) . **$23,761**
- Total Value December 31, 1968 (3,681 Shares)* . . . . . . **$60,547**

*Includes 692 shares acquired through reinvestment of $6,718 in capital gain distributions.

---

### ASSUMED INITIAL INVESTMENT OF $250 AND SUBSEQUENT INVESTMENTS OF $250 PER MONTH

- Initial and Subsequent Investments . . $45,000
- Income Dividends Reinvested . . . 15,901
- Total Cost (Payments Plus Income Dividends Reinvested) . . **$60,901**
- Total Value December 31, 1968 (10,027 Shares)* . . . . . . **$164,949**

*Includes 1,961 shares acquired through reinvestment of $18,658 in capital gain distributions.

---

### $250 SYSTEMATIC PROGRAM: TOTAL $45,000 ASSUMED $250 INITIAL INVESTMENT AND $250 MONTHLY

- Total Monthly Payments . . . . $ 45,000
- Income Dividends Reinvested . . 14,577
- Total Cost (Payments Plus Income Dividends Reinvested) . **$ 59,577**
- Total Value December 31, 1968 (9,358 Shares)* . . . . . . **$153,936**

*Includes 1,743 shares acquired through reinvestment of $16,985 in capital gain distributions.

# HOW LONG DID IT TAKE TO GET EVEN?

## IT TOOK ONLY ONE YEAR WITH THIS DREYFUS FUND VOLUNTARY PLAN...

### (All figures reproduced from Dreyfus Fund sales literature)

## ASSUMED INITIAL INVESTMENT OF $25 AND SUBSEQUENT INVESTMENTS OF $25 PER MONTH

| | COST OF SHARES | | | | | VALUE OF SHARES ACQUIRED | | | | | |
|---|---|---|---|---|---|---|---|---|---|---|---|
| Dec. 31 | Total of Initial and Monthly Investments | Dividends Reinvested (Annual) | Dividends Reinvested (Cumulative) | Total Cost Including Dividends Reinvested | Capital Gain Distributions Reinvested | Through Initial and Monthly Investments | As Capital Gain Distributions (Cumulative) | Sub Total | Through Reinvestment of Dividends | Total Value | Total Shares |
| 1954 | $ 300 | $ 6 | $ 6 | $ 306 | $ 7 | $ 363 | $ 8 | $ 371 | $ 8 | $ 379 | 98 |
| 1955 | 600 | 8 | 14 | 614 | 27 | 733 | 40 | 773 | 18 | 791 | 174 |
| 1956 | 900 | 22 | 36 | 936 | 66 | 1,057 | 116 | 1,173 | 43 | 1,216 | 258 |
| 1957 | 1,200 | 29 | 65 | 1,265 | 45 | 1,212 | 148 | 1,360 | 66 | 1,426 | 336 |
| 1958 | 1,500 | 45 | 110 | 1,610 | 29 | 2,144 | 253 | 2,397 | 157 | 2,554 | 406 |
| 1959 | 1,800 | 65 | 175 | 1,975 | 63 | 2,871 | 376 | 3,247 | 260 | 3,507 | 464 |
| 1960 | 2,100 | 85 | 260 | 2,360 | 134 | 3,159 | 525 | 3,684 | 352 | 4,036 | 534 |
| 1961 | 2,400 | 92 | 352 | 2,752 | 41 | 4,175 | 692 | 4,867 | 531 | 5,398 | 582 |
| 1962 | 2,700 | 98 | 450 | 3,150 | 85 | 3,744 | 650 | 4,394 | 545 | 4,939 | 641 |
| 1963 | 3,000 | 121 | 571 | 3,571 | 11 | 4,878 | 808 | 5,686 | 800 | 6,486 | 689 |
| 1964 | 3,300 | 137 | 708 | 4,008 | 152 | 5,753 | 1,074 | 6,827 | 1,039 | 7,866 | 745 |
| 1965 | 3,600 | 160 | 868 | 4,468 | 291 | 7,403 | 1,680 | 9,083 | 1,467 | 10,550 | 812 |
| 1966 | 3,900 | 200 | 1,068 | 4,968 | 283 | 7,478 | 1,903 | 9,381 | 1,625 | 11,006 | 870 |
| 1967 | 4,200 | 250 | 1,318 | 5,518 | 201 | 9,427 | 2,557 | 11,984 | 2,254 | 14,238 | 922 |
| 1968 | 4,500 | 253 | 1,571 | 6,071 | 411 | 10,337 | 3,197 | 13,534 | 2,680 | 16,214 | 986 |
| | | | | | $1,846 | | | | | | |
| Number of shares acquired | | | | | | 628 | 194 | 822 | 164 | 986 | |

Total cost represents the initial investment of $25, plus the cumulative total of monthly investments of $25 per month, plus the cumulative amount of income dividends reinvested and includes an 8¾% sales charge on initial and monthly investments only.

## ... BUT IT TOOK FIVE YEARS WITH THIS DREYFUS FUND CONTRACTUAL PLAN!

## $30 (MINIMUM) SYSTEMATIC PROGRAM: TOTAL $5,400
### ASSUMED $60 INITIAL INVESTMENT AND $30 MONTHLY UNTIL COMPLETION

| | MONTHLY PAYMENTS | | Income Dividends Reinvested | Total Cost (a) | DEDUCTIONS | | BALANCE INVESTED AFTER DEDUCTIONS | | Capital Gain Distributions Reinvested | TOTAL | |
|---|---|---|---|---|---|---|---|---|---|---|---|
| Dec. 31 | Annual | Cumulative | | | Sales and Creation Charge | Custodian Fee | Annual | Cumulative | | Value | Shares |
| 1954 | $390* | $ 390 | $ 4.58 | $ 394.58 | $195.00* | $ 11.31* | $188.27 | $ 188.27 | $ 4.68 | $ 257 | 66 |
| 1955 | 360 | 750 | 6.77 | 761.35 | 20.64 | 10.44 | 335.69 | 523.96 | 20.50 | 702 | 154 |
| 1956 | 360 | 1,110 | 20.09 | 1,141.44 | 20.64 | 10.44 | 349.01 | 872.97 | 59.86 | 1,175 | 249 |
| 1957 | 360 | 1,470 | 28.53 | 1,529.97 | 20.64 | 10.44 | 357.45 | 1,230.42 | 44.46 | 1,440 | 339 |
| 1958 | 360 | 1,830 | 46.38 | 1,936.35 | 20.64 | 10.44 | 375.30 | 1,605.72 | 29.54 | 2,647 | 421 |
| 1959 | 360 | 2,190 | 67.63 | 2,363.98 | 20.64 | 10.44 | 396.55 | 2,002.27 | 65.61 | 3,684 | 488 |
| 1960 | 360 | 2,550 | 89.72 | 2,813.70 | 20.64 | 10.44 | 418.64 | 2,420.91 | 141.31 | 4,284 | 567 |
| 1961 | 360 | 2,910 | 98.21 | 3,271.91 | 20.64 | 10.44 | 427.13 | 2,848.04 | 43.25 | 5,772 | 623 |
| 1962 | 360 | 3,270 | 105.45 | 3,737.36 | 20.64 | 10.44 | 434.37 | 3,282.41 | 90.72 | 5,318 | 690 |
| 1963 | 360 | 3,630 | 130.81 | 4,228.17 | 20.64 | 10.44 | 459.73 | 3,742.14 | 12.13 | 7,022 | 745 |
| 1964 | 360 | 3,990 | 148.27 | 4,736.44 | 20.64 | 10.44 | 477.19 | 4,219.33 | 164.62 | 8,550 | 810 |
| 1965 | 360 | 4,350 | 174.51 | 5,270.95 | 20.64 | 10.44 | 503.43 | 4,722.76 | 316.79 | 11,504 | 885 |
| 1966 | 360 | 4,710 | 217.90 | 5,848.85 | 20.64 | 10.44 | 546.82 | 5,269.58 | 308.26 | 12,033 | 951 |
| 1967 | 360 | 5,070 | 274.00 | 6,482.85 | 20.64 | 10.44 | 602.92 | 5,872.50 | 219.29 | 15,598 | 1,010 |
| 1968 | 330 | 5,400 | 277.62 | 7,090.47 | 18.92 | 9.57 | 579.13 | 6,451.63 | 450.05 | 17,770 | 1,080 |
| | | | $1,690.47 | | $482.24 | $156.60 | | | $1,971.07 | | |

(a) Monthly payments plus cumulative amount of income dividends reinvested.

* From the initial payment of $60.00, $30.00 is deducted as a Sales and Creation Charge, with $15.00 deducted as a Sales and Creation Charge from each of the next 11 payments. Other deductions include $1.74 from the initial payment, and $.87 from each of the next 11 payments for Custodian Fees. A Delegated Service Charge which cannot exceed $2.00 per year for the first 15 years and $3.00 per year thereafter, is not included. Total deductions from the first 13 Monthly Payment Units equal to $206.31, or 52.9% of the Total of the first 13 payment units. After all 180 payments are completed, total charges amount to 11.8% of the total agreed payments.

For insurable persons, most such plans offer life insurance coverage guaranteeing the immediate completion of the contemplated payments in the event of the death of the planholder during the period of accumulation. This is low-cost decreasing term group life insurance. Available at premiums varying between $3.60 and $9.00 per year per $1,000, it is a bargain for a man over age fifty because of the system of averaging the age of all plan participants to determine cost. Actually, a man under age thirty-five can buy term insurance cheaper on his own. Senator Philip Hart's Antitrust and Monopoly Subcommittee has held extensive hearings on the subject of creditor's insurance and has uncovered facts that suggest the return of enormous profits.

Some years ago, my investment firm introduced disability coverage on contractual plans, underwritten by the Monarch Life Insurance Company. Under it, the insurance company made the monthly investment for the planholder if he became disabled. After ten years of operation, we noted that the premiums collected were thirty-three times the claims paid, and we asked the insurance company to reduce the premiums. When it declined to do so, we eliminated the coverage. We felt that premiums should be determined by actuarial considerations, not by how much the traffic would bear.

For years, First Investors Corporation stressed in its contractual plan prospectus that while it had arranged for life insurance coverage on its plans to be provided by three major companies, it derived no profit of any kind from the coverage. Many persons were influenced to go into the plan because of the low life insurance rate. Because of the obvious sales advantage, the sponsor maintained a continuing gentle pressure upon the insurers to continue to reflect the favorable mortality experience in a lower premium rate. This was to the advantage of the participants, of course. But then the plan sponsor began to lust after some of the huge profits that it knew the life insurance companies were making on the credit coverage. It ended by forming the First Investors Life Insurance Company and it required of the three insurers that they reinsure a substantial part of their coverage with First Investors Life. This was a device to force the insurers to share their profits with the plan sponsor. From that point on, there were no further reductions in the premium rate. With the plan sponsor getting a cut from the premium income running into substantial six figures each year, it no longer had any interest in reducing the premiums. Having gotten thousands of people into the plan by assuring them in the prospectus that the sponsor derived no profit from the insurance, it blandly carved itself a chunk of the profits, without notice. These matters were brought to the attention of the Securities and Exchange Commission and it was pointed out that the profits made by plan sponsors through the operation of the life insurance provision

were a "material fact" that was not being disclosed in the prospectus. The Commission did nothing and the impropriety continues to this day. (The subject of life insurance has a curiously disturbing effect upon the Commission. Whenever it is mentioned, the Commission begins to perspire heavily and it invariably claims that it has a headache and must go lie down.)

I testified on these matters in December, 1969, before a House committee. Afterward, representatives of the Commission were invited to come in and answer a few questions. Solomon Freedman, director of the Division of Corporate Regulation, was asked if the Commission had taken any steps to cause life insurance profits to be disclosed in plan prospectuses. He acknowledged that it had not but indicated that the Commission expected to get around to the matter soon. He observed that there was a limit to the information that could be given in a prospectus. Considering the extent of the truly extraneous information Freedman's division requires of registrants, it might surely have included informing the public of so obvious a conflict of interest as with First Investors, especially when such disclosure has for years been urged upon the Commission.

Many persons whose estate planning has been insurance oriented conclude that they will terminate their existing life insurance policies, replacing the coverage in whole or in part with the protection afforded through the contractual plan that they purchase as part of the reorientation of their estate planning with greater emphasis upon investment. Such persons quite sensibly conclude that the fruits of their investment should inure to their benefit rather than to the benefit of an insurance company. They purchase the insured contractual plan in the belief that, once issued, it will be there, providing the agreed protection at the agreed rate, for the full term that the plan is to run. Such is not always the case.

National Securities and Research Corporation in connection with its sponsorship of the National Growth Stock Series has offered a contractual plan with insurance at sixty cents per month per $1,000 covered by an insurance consortium headed by the John Hancock Life. Last year, the planholders were given sudden notice that the monthly rate was being increased 260 percent to $2.00 per month per $1,000. This increase was allegedly made necessary by the failure of the sponsor to promote new sales of the plan, with the result that the average age of the group had increased to the point where the insurance company had arbitrarily increased the rate. Inevitably, some participants will quit. They will be the younger and healthier men who know that they can get the coverage cheaper elsewhere. This leaves the older, unhealthier participants holding the bag as the insurance company, aware of what is happening, boosts the rates again, forcing still more younger men to quit, and so on. Recalling the disclosures by the Hart committee in the credit insurance area (and my own experience with Monarch Life Insurance), I attempted to obtain figures of claims paid versus premium income on the group policy. The New York Insurance Department, which freely approved the increase (as it has all of the group credit life policies discredited by the Hart committee), declined to disclose the figures. As for the sponsor, after first claiming it did not have them, it finally took refuge in silence. Mutual fund planholders who are influenced by low-cost credit life insurance to buy contractuals, and who pay a front-end load, must be protected against such arbitrary huge cost increases.

(Come to think of it, it is not as bad as a voluntary plan with life insurance which the Axe-Houghton people arranged some years ago with the Prudential as the insurer. No evidence of insurability was required, and a lot of enterprising mutual fund salesmen appeared to be setting up shop just outside the doors of hospital operating rooms, selling the plan to eager buyers who jumped at the chance to buy life insurance for 75 cents per month per $1,000. After only one year of operation, the Prudential executive who had signed the company onto this time bomb was led before a firing squad, and the company raised the rate to $3.60 per month per $1,000.)

Two principal sales arguments are advanced in favor of the contractual plan. First, it is offered as a device by which persons of modest means may put to work at regular intervals small sums which would otherwise not be investable. There was a time when this was substantially true. The only monthly investment plans available at one time were contractual plans. But in the late 1940s Commonwealth Investment Company, a balanced mutual fund, introduced the first voluntary plan, making it possible for investors to set aside sums of as little as $25.00 without committing themselves to the long-term investment or front-end load that was characteristic of the contractual plan. In time, other funds followed Commonwealth's lead and today virtually every fund offers a voluntary plan. Increasingly, then, the strong sales argument for contractual plans has lost much of its validity.

The second argument (which is a response to the rejection of the first) advanced in favor of the contractual plan was that it forced a savings discipline which many, if not most, people needed. It is a fact that many people cannot save without some pressure, some discipline. I have heard people say that the only money they ever saved was the money the life insurance company took away from them. Millions of Americans join Christmas Clubs and hand over their money to a savings bank at no interest just to give their weekly savings the authority of an obligation to someone else.

Advocates of the contractual plan, attacking the voluntary plan, make much of the argument that their plan imposes an obligation upon people who might not otherwise put money aside regularly.

Contractual-plan people readily acknowledge that the front-end load will result in a loss to the investor who remains in the plan for only two or three years. But, they point out, if the investor faithfully makes his payments for seven, eight, nine, or ten years, he will surely end up with a very satisfactory profit, which will justify the fees.

In a sense, the contractual plan is claimed to be an arrangement by which a few people who lack the financial fortitude to save beyond the critical first two or three years are sacrificed in the interests of the long-term benefits to the consistent savers who can persist with their payments through seven, eight, nine, or ten years. If so, then let us at least establish the fact of the claimed long-term benefits.

While there have been many examples shown of the results of a hypothetical contractual plan carried to completion, I have never seen a published study of the actual investment results of a cross section of active contractual plans from inception to liquidation. From the records of the accounts on its books, my company has therefore compiled such a study. The plans are those sponsored by David Grayson's company, First Investors Corporation, which I have identified as the oldest, and quite likely the most successful, plan company. Some of the plans represent an investment in Wellington Fund, a conservative balanced fund with assets of more than $1.5 billion. Other plans were invested in Fundamental Investors, a highly successful blue chip common stock fund of the Anchor Group, with assets of $1.2 billion.

The study discloses the account number; the fund whose shares were purchased; the date the account was begun; the amount of the monthly payment and the number of payments made prior to the termination of the account; the amount of ordinary income dividends and capital gains distributions received and reinvested, which became a part of the cost of the plan for tax purposes; the total "cost" to the investor; the amount received upon liquidation; the net loss to the investor, which is tax deductible; and the number of years the plan actually ran. Accounts into which less than three years' payments had been made have been excluded because such plans would be bound to show a loss. One more point: the computer-stored information, on which we based our study, did not record dividends and capital gains received and reinvested prior to 1961. Accordingly, on all accounts established prior to 1961 (the listing is chronological), the investor's cost was in fact greater than shown here, and his loss correspondingly higher.

| Account No. | Fund* | Date Established | Monthly Payment | Payments Made | Total Paid In | Div. & Dist. Reinvested | Total Invested | Liquidated For | Loss | After Years |
|---|---|---|---|---|---|---|---|---|---|---|
| **1952** | | | | | | | | | | |
| DW–15604 | W | 10–1–52 | $ 50 | 120 | $ 6,000 | $ 4,247 | $10,247 | $10,055 | $ 192 | 15$\frac{1}{2}$ |
| DW–15605 | W | 10–1–52 | 50 | 120 | 6,000 | 4,247 | 10,247 | 10,055 | 192 | 15$\frac{1}{2}$ |
| DW–16164 | W | 11–18–52 | 50 | 120 | 6,000 | 4,197 | 10,197 | 9,868 | 329 | 15$\frac{1}{3}$ |
| DW–16166 | W | 11–18–52 | 50 | 120 | 6,000 | 4,197 | 10,197 | 9,868 | 329 | 15$\frac{1}{3}$ |
| DW–16292 | W | 11–24–52 | 50 | 120 | 6,000 | 4,164 | 10,164 | 9,857 | 307 | 15$\frac{1}{3}$ |
| **1953** | | | | | | | | | | |
| DW–19668 | W | 7–15–53 | 50 | 120 | 6,000 | 3,797 | 9,797 | 9,377 | 420 | 14$\frac{1}{2}$ |
| DW–19671 | W | 7–15–53 | 50 | 120 | 6,000 | 3,797 | 9,797 | 9,317 | 480 | 14$\frac{1}{2}$ |
| DW–20513 | W | 10–1–53 | 50 | 120 | 6,000 | 3,652 | 9,652 | 9,376 | 276 | 14 |
| **1954** | | | | | | | | | | |
| DW–22259 | W | 2–1–54 | 30 | 120 | 3,600 | 2,133 | 5,733 | 5,391 | 342 | 14 |
| DW–22574 | W | 2–15–54 | 50 | 120 | 6,000 | 2,467 | 8,467 | 8,134 | 333 | 12$\frac{1}{2}$ |
| DW–24051 | W | 5–7–54 | 50 | 120 | 6,000 | 3,461 | 9,461 | 8,471 | 990 | 14 |
| DW–24292 | W | 5–8–54 | 75 | 120 | 9,000 | 6,380 | 15,380 | 14,790 | 590 | 14$\frac{2}{3}$ |
| DW–24661 | W | 6–15–54 | 100 | 120 | 12,000 | 5,587 | 17,587 | 16,803 | 784 | 12$\frac{1}{2}$ |
| DW–24649 | W | 6–16–54 | 50 | 120 | 6,000 | 4,325 | 10,325 | 9,140 | 1,185 | 15 |
| DW–24735 | W | 6–21–54 | 20 | 120 | 2,400 | 1,339 | 3,739 | 3,480 | 259 | 14 |
| DW–24791 | W | 6–24–54 | 25 | 120 | 3,000 | 1,663 | 4,663 | 4,402 | 261 | 14 |
| DW–25136 | W | 7–19–54 | 100 | 120 | 12,000 | 5,794 | 17,794 | 17,578 | 216 | 13 |
| DW–25305 | W | 7–27–54 | 50 | 120 | 6,000 | 3,296 | 9,296 | 8,457 | 839 | 13$\frac{1}{2}$ |
| **1955** | | | | | | | | | | |
| DW–29019 | W | 1–28–55 | 15 | 119 | 1,785 | 655 | 2,440 | 2,130 | 310 | 11$\frac{3}{4}$ |
| DW–36122 | W | 2–7–55 | 50 | 120 | 6,000 | 2,346 | 8,346 | 7,844 | 502 | 11$\frac{1}{3}$ |
| DW–29625 | W | 2–17–55 | 100 | 120 | 12,000 | 4,458 | 16,458 | 14,556 | 1,902 | 11$\frac{2}{3}$ |
| DW–30574 | W | 3–24–55 | 50 | 120 | 6,000 | 3,131 | 9,131 | 7,818 | 1,313 | 13 |
| DW–31403 | W | 5–2–55 | 100 | 120 | 12,000 | 4,972 | 16,972 | 16,313 | 659 | 11$\frac{3}{4}$ |
| DW–31895 | W | 5–25–55 | 25 | 120 | 3,000 | 1,255 | 4,255 | 4,017 | 238 | 12 |
| DW–31933 | W | 5–27–55 | 15 | 119 | 1,785 | 772 | 2,557 | 2,312 | 245 | 12$\frac{1}{2}$ |
| DW–32443 | W | 6–3–55 | 150 | 120 | 18,000 | 7,978 | 25,978 | 24,849 | 1,129 | 12$\frac{1}{4}$ |
| DW–32209 | W | 6–13–55 | 50 | 120 | 6,000 | 3,557 | 9,557 | 9,191 | 366 | 13 |
| DW–32436 | W | 6–23–55 | 75 | 120 | 9,000 | 4,565 | 13,565 | 12,436 | 1,129 | 12$\frac{5}{6}$ |
| DW–32963 | W | 7–18–55 | 50 | 120 | 6,000 | 2,577 | 8,577 | 8,208 | 369 | 12$\frac{1}{6}$ |
| DW–37761 | W | 8–26–55 | 150 | 120 | 18,000 | 7,607 | 25,607 | 24,569 | 1,038 | 12 |
| DWN–34320 | W | 8–30–55 | 25 | 45 | 1,125 | 187 | 1,312 | 1,128 | 184 | 13 |
| DWN–34311 | W | 8–30–55 | 25 | 71 | 1,775 | 492 | 2,267 | 2,103 | 164 | 11$\frac{2}{3}$ |
| DW–33852 | W | 9–1–55 | 20 | 74 | 1,480 | 725 | 2,205 | 2,108 | 97 | 12 |
| DW–33833 | W | 9–1–55 | 15 | 119 | 1,785 | 726 | 2,511 | 2,331 | 180 | 12 |
| DW–33834 | W | 9–1–55 | 20 | 120 | 2,400 | 990 | 3,390 | 3,159 | 231 | 12 |
| DW–34043 | W | 9–13–55 | 100 | 108 | 10,800 | 3,998 | 14,798 | 13,190 | 1,608 | 11 |
| DW–34548 | W | 10–4–55 | 25 | 120 | 3,000 | 1,682 | 4,682 | 4,203 | 479 | 13$\frac{1}{2}$ |
| DW–34640 | W | 10–17–55 | 50 | 120 | 6,000 | 2,501 | 8,501 | 8,064 | 437 | 12 |
| DW–34800 | W | 10–21–55 | 50 | 120 | 6,000 | 2,434 | 8,434 | 7,891 | 543 | 12 |
| DW–37285 | W | 11–9–55 | 100 | 120 | 12,000 | 3,402 | 15,402 | 14,767 | 635 | 10$\frac{1}{3}$ |
| DW–86886 | W | 11–17–55 | 30 | 110 | 3,300 | 1,485 | 4,785 | 4,287 | 498 | 10$\frac{1}{4}$ |
| **1956** | | | | | | | | | | |
| DW–50524 | W | 1–26–56 | 40 | 120 | 4,800 | 1,467 | 6,267 | 5,556 | 711 | 10$\frac{3}{4}$ |
| DW–50661 | W | 2–1–56 | 25 | 120 | 3,000 | 926 | 3,926 | 3,231 | 695 | 10$\frac{2}{3}$ |
| DW–51079 | W | 2–14–56 | 50 | 120 | 6,000 | 1,758 | 7,758 | 7,385 | 373 | 10 |
| DW–51084 | W | 2–14–56 | 25 | 120 | 3,000 | 1,150 | 4,150 | 3,723 | 427 | 11$\frac{3}{4}$ |
| DW–51256 | W | 2–20–56 | 100 | 120 | 12,000 | 5,625 | 17,625 | 14,705 | 2,920 | 12 |
| DW–51485 | W | 3–1–56 | 225 | 120 | 27,000 | 11,921 | 38,921 | 35,164 | 3,757 | 12 |
| DW–51733 | W | 3–7–56 | 50 | 120 | 6,000 | 2,217 | 8,217 | 7,646 | 571 | 11 |
| DW–52572 | W | 4–5–56 | 20 | 120 | 2,400 | 981 | 3,381 | 3,134 | 247 | 11$\frac{1}{2}$ |

* W = Wellington Fund

| Account No. | Fund* | Date Established | Monthly Payment | Payments Made | Total Paid In | Div. & Dist. Reinvested | Total Invested | Liquidated For | Loss | After Years |
|---|---|---|---|---|---|---|---|---|---|---|
| **1956** *Cont.* | | | | | | | | | | |
| DW–52706 | W | 4–11–56 | $100 | 120 | $12,000 | $ 6,079 | $18,079 | $16,467 | $1,612 | 11½ |
| DW–53339 | W | 5–2–56 | 20 | 120 | 2,400 | 718 | 3,118 | 2,644 | 474 | 10½ |
| DWN–53821 | W | 5–17–56 | 25 | 120 | 3,000 | 1,079 | 4,079 | 3,785 | 294 | 10½ |
| DW–53866 | W | 5–21–56 | 50 | 120 | 6,000 | 2,147 | 8,147 | 7,438 | 709 | 10⅚ |
| DW–54759 | W | 6–22–56 | 100 | 120 | 12,000 | 5,231 | 17,231 | 15,123 | 2,108 | 11½ |
| DW–54976 | W | 7–5–56 | 15 | 119 | 1,785 | 522 | 2,307 | 1,976 | 331 | 10⅙ |
| DW–55123 | W | 7–11–56 | 50 | 120 | 6,000 | 1,724 | 7,724 | 7,098 | 626 | 10 |
| DW–55183 | W | 7–12–56 | 50 | 120 | 6,000 | 3,078 | 9,078 | 7,771 | 1,307 | 12½ |
| DW–55332 | W | 7–17–56 | 100 | 120 | 12,000 | 5,467 | 17,467 | 15,859 | 1,608 | 12 |
| DW–56512 | W | 9–5–56 | 100 | 88 | 8,800 | 3,230 | 12,030 | 10,440 | 1,590 | 10 |
| DW–56617 | W | 9–12–56 | 50 | 120 | 6,000 | 1,756 | 7,756 | 6,643 | 1,113 | 10 |
| DW–56752 | W | 9–20–56 | 15 | 119 | 1,785 | 749 | 2,534 | 2,191 | 343 | 11½ |
| DW–56819 | W | 9–24–56 | 15 | 119 | 1,785 | 622 | 2,407 | 2,184 | 223 | 11 |
| DWN–57572 | W | 10–19–56 | 100 | 90 | 9,000 | 3,965 | 12,965 | 12,434 | 531 | 11 |
| **1957** | | | | | | | | | | |
| DW–72450 | W | 1–18–57 | 25 | 120 | 3,000 | 1,411 | 4,411 | 3,869 | 542 | 11 |
| DW–60143 | W | 1–29–57 | 100 | 120 | 12,000 | 5,427 | 17,427 | 16,528 | 899 | 11½ |
| DW–60499 | W | 2–7–57 | 120 | 120 | 14,400 | 4,920 | 19,320 | 17,763 | 1,557 | 10½ |
| DW–60569 | W | 2–11–57 | 100 | 120 | 12,000 | 3,890 | 15,890 | 14,599 | 1,291 | 9½ |
| DW–61746 | W | 3–8–57 | 50 | 120 | 6,000 | 1,995 | 7,995 | 6,757 | 1,238 | 10½ |
| DW–61475 | W | 3–8–57 | 25 | 120 | 3,000 | 868 | 3,868 | 3,419 | 449 | 10 |
| DW–61934 | W | 3–21–57 | 100 | 64 | 6,400 | 2,912 | 9,312 | 8,405 | 907 | 10½ |
| DW–62082 | W | 3–27–57 | 30 | 120 | 3,600 | 1,135 | 4,735 | 4,122 | 613 | 10 |
| DW–62490 | W | 4–9–57 | 50 | 120 | 6,000 | 2,269 | 8,269 | 6,877 | 1,392 | 10⅚ |
| DW–63146 | W | 5–1–57 | 50 | 120 | 6,000 | 1,827 | 7,827 | 7,209 | 618 | 10 |
| DW–64055 | W | 5–27–57 | 50 | 120 | 6,000 | 1,876 | 7,876 | 7,021 | 855 | 10 |
| DW–64980 | W | 6–25–57 | 15 | 105 | 1,575 | 397 | 1,972 | 1,765 | 207 | 8¾ |
| DWN–63768 | W | 7–2–57 | 100 | 112 | 11,200 | 4,464 | 15,664 | 13,814 | 1,850 | 10¼ |
| DW–65667 | W | 7–19–57 | 50 | 119 | 5,950 | 1,806 | 7,756 | 6,831 | 925 | 10 |
| DW–66628 | W | 8–27–57 | 50 | 113 | 5,650 | 1,676 | 7,326 | 6,490 | 836 | 9½ |
| DW–66798 | W | 8–30–57 | 75 | 120 | 9,000 | 2,742 | 11,742 | 10,542 | 1,200 | 11 |
| DW–66809 | W | 9–1–57 | 25 | 120 | 3,000 | 857 | 3,857 | 3,381 | 476 | 10 |
| DW–67669 | W | 10–2–57 | 25 | 120 | 3,000 | 849 | 3,849 | 3,384 | 465 | 10 |
| DW–67732 | W | 10–4–57 | 100 | 95 | 9,500 | 1,969 | 11,469 | 11,173 | 296 | 8 |
| DW–67757 | W | 10–7–57 | 25 | 120 | 3,000 | 781 | 3,781 | 3,244 | 537 | 9¼ |
| DWN–65844 | W | 10–18–57 | 40 | 120 | 4,800 | 1,784 | 6,584 | 5,888 | 696 | 10¾ |
| DW–68113 | W | 10–21–57 | 25 | 107 | 2,675 | 686 | 3,361 | 3,138 | 223 | 8⅓ |
| DW–68126 | W | 10–21–57 | 150 | 120 | 18,000 | 5,403 | 23,403 | 20,678 | 2,725 | 10 |
| DW–68216 | W | 10–23–57 | 40 | 65 | 2,600 | 1,063 | 3,663 | 3,217 | 446 | 10 |
| DW–68654 | W | 11–6–57 | 15 | 119 | 1,785 | 650 | 2,435 | 2,257 | 178 | 10 |
| DW–68706 | W | 11–7–57 | 50 | 120 | 6,000 | 2,623 | 8,623 | 6,980 | 1,643 | 11⅔ |
| W–106172 | W | 11–8–57 | 25 | 44 | 1,100 | 279 | 1,379 | 1,074 | 305 | 11 |
| DW–68874 | W | 11–12–57 | 25 | 120 | 3,000 | 984 | 3,984 | 3,304 | 680 | 10⅓ |
| DW–69000 | W | 11–15–57 | 50 | 120 | 6,000 | 2,033 | 8,033 | 6,711 | 1,322 | 10 |
| DW–69302 | W | 11–25–57 | 20 | 110 | 2,200 | 591 | 2,791 | 2,543 | 248 | 8⅓ |
| DWN–66794 | W | 11–26–57 | 225 | 112 | 25,200 | 8,033 | 33,233 | 31,035 | 2,198 | 9¼ |
| DW–69648 | W | 12–5–57 | 15 | 119 | 1,785 | 501 | 2,286 | 1,933 | 353 | 10 |
| **1958** | | | | | | | | | | |
| DW–70779 | W | 1–17–58 | 50 | 120 | 6,000 | 1,689 | 7,689 | 6,858 | 831 | 9¾ |
| DW–70873 | W | 1–21–58 | 25 | 117 | 2,925 | 999 | 3,924 | 3,289 | 635 | 9¾ |
| DW–70875 | W | 1–21–58 | 40 | 120 | 4,800 | 2,241 | 7,041 | 6,476 | 565 | 9½ |
| DW–71178 | W | 1–30–58 | 20 | 120 | 2,400 | 991 | 3,391 | 3,046 | 345 | 10½ |
| DWN–68522 | W | 2–17–58 | 100 | 117 | 11,700 | 3,477 | 15,177 | 13,148 | 2,029 | 9¾ |

\* W = Wellington Fund

| Account No. | Fund* | Date Established | Monthly Payment | Payments Made | Total Paid In | Div. & Dist. Reinvested | Total Invested | Liquidated For | Loss | After Years |
|---|---|---|---|---|---|---|---|---|---|---|
| **1958** *Cont.* | | | | | | | | | | |
| DW–14531 | W | 2–28–58 | $ 50 | 120 | $ 6,000 | $ 1,815 | $ 7,815 | $ 6,831 | $ 984 | 10 |
| DW–72090 | W | 3–5–58 | 25 | 114 | 2,850 | 796 | 3,646 | 3,127 | 519 | 9 |
| DW–72117 | W | 3–5–58 | 150 | 120 | 18,000 | 5,995 | 23,995 | 19,313 | 4,682 | 11 |
| DWN–68934 | W | 3–10–58 | 50 | 111 | 5,550 | 1,488 | 7,038 | 5,903 | 1,135 | $8\frac{1}{2}$ |
| DW–72612 | W | 3–24–58 | 250 | 114 | 28,500 | 8,369 | 36,869 | 33,324 | 3,545 | $9\frac{1}{2}$ |
| DW–72832 | W | 3–30–58 | 100 | 76 | 7,600 | 3,279 | 10,879 | 9,070 | 1,809 | 10 |
| DW–73050 | W | 4–9–58 | 15 | 119 | 1,785 | 858 | 2,643 | 2,501 | 142 | 9 |
| DW–73225 | W | 4–15–58 | 50 | 98 | 4,900 | 1,167 | 6,067 | 5,235 | 832 | $8\frac{1}{6}$ |
| DW–73698 | W | 5–5–58 | 20 | 118 | 2,360 | 736 | 3,096 | 2,386 | 710 | 10 |
| DW–74354 | W | 5–27–58 | 100 | 111 | 11,100 | 3,056 | 14,156 | 12,404 | 1,752 | $9\frac{1}{4}$ |
| DW–74893 | W | 6–17–58 | 100 | 108 | 10,800 | 2,951 | 13,751 | 12,056 | 1,695 | 9 |
| DWN–70924 | W | 6–24–58 | 10 | 119 | 1,190 | 689 | 1,879 | 1,723 | 156 | $9\frac{1}{2}$ |
| DW–75161 | W | 6–25–58 | 120 | 106 | 12,720 | 3,396 | 16,116 | 14,340 | 1,776 | $8\frac{5}{6}$ |
| DWN–70981 | W | 6–26–58 | 15 | 101 | 1,515 | 420 | 1,935 | 1,657 | 278 | $8\frac{1}{2}$ |
| DW–75480 | W | 7–9–58 | 100 | 113 | 11,300 | 3,058 | 14,358 | 11,790 | 2,568 | $9\frac{1}{4}$ |
| DW–75511 | W | 7–10–58 | 20 | 120 | 2,400 | 833 | 3,233 | 2,632 | 601 | $9\frac{1}{2}$ |
| DW–76140 | W | 8–1–58 | 20 | 37 | 740 | 315 | 1,055 | 823 | 232 | $9\frac{3}{4}$ |
| DW–71811 | W | 8–7–58 | 20 | 70 | 1,400 | 276 | 1,676 | 1,577 | 99 | 7 |
| DW–76562 | W | 8–20–58 | 250 | 85 | 21,250 | 11,684 | 32,934 | 24,417 | 8,517 | $11\frac{1}{3}$ |
| DW–79650 | W | 8–27–58 | 120 | 110 | 13,200 | 3,878 | 17,078 | 13,416 | 3,662 | $9\frac{1}{2}$ |
| DW–76813 | W | 9–5–58 | 25 | 108 | 2,700 | 667 | 3,367 | 2,794 | 573 | 9 |
| DW–76899 | W | 9–10–58 | 30 | 93 | 2,790 | 636 | 3,426 | 2,775 | 651 | $8\frac{1}{6}$ |
| DW–77086 | W | 9–17–58 | 50 | 59 | 2,950 | 1,083 | 4,033 | 3,231 | 802 | $9\frac{1}{4}$ |
| DW–77263 | W | 9–29–58 | 50 | 112 | 5,600 | 1,710 | 7,310 | 5,725 | 1,585 | 10 |
| DW–77874 | W | 10–27–58 | 100 | 118 | 11,800 | 3,645 | 15,445 | 13,721 | 1,724 | 10 |
| DW–77940 | W | 10–29–58 | 150 | 43 | 6,450 | 2,901 | 9,351 | 7,466 | 1,885 | $9\frac{1}{2}$ |
| DW–78032 | W | 11–3–58 | 25 | 114 | 2,850 | 819 | 3,669 | 2,808 | 861 | $9\frac{1}{2}$ |
| DW–78572 | W | 11–20–58 | 120 | 90 | 10,800 | 2,355 | 13,155 | 11,619 | 1,536 | $7\frac{1}{2}$ |
| DW–78690 | W | 11–24–58 | 75 | 112 | 8,400 | 2,517 | 10,917 | 8,550 | 2,367 | $9\frac{1}{2}$ |
| DW–78838 | W | 12–1–58 | 50 | 109 | 5,450 | 2,162 | 7,612 | 5,741 | 1,871 | 11 |
| DW–78862 | W | 12–2–58 | 225 | 91 | 17,985 | 4,670 | 22,655 | 19,650 | 3,005 | $8\frac{1}{2}$ |
| DW–79450 | W | 12–22–58 | 20 | 105 | 2,100 | 505 | 2,605 | 2,183 | 422 | $8\frac{3}{4}$ |
| **1959** | | | | | | | | | | |
| DW–80465 | W | 1–21–59 | 50 | 103 | 5,150 | 1,289 | 6,439 | 5,428 | 1,011 | $8\frac{1}{2}$ |
| DW–80702 | W | 1–29–59 | 50 | 105 | 5,250 | 1,302 | 6,552 | 5,248 | 1,304 | $8\frac{3}{4}$ |
| DW–80910 | W | 2–5–59 | 25 | 102 | 2,550 | 613 | 3,163 | 2,642 | 521 | $8\frac{1}{2}$ |
| FN–3608 | F.I. | 2–11–59 | 20 | 120 | 2,400 | 934 | 3,334 | 3,311 | 23 | $9\frac{1}{2}$ |
| DWN–75827 | W | 2–15–59 | 100 | 105 | 10,500 | 2,765 | 13,265 | 11,228 | 2,037 | $8\frac{3}{4}$ |
| DW–81577 | W | 3–2–59 | 40 | 119 | 4,760 | 1,535 | 6,295 | 5,087 | 1,208 | 10 |
| DW–81644 | W | 3–3–59 | 75 | 120 | 9,000 | 3,121 | 12,121 | 9,612 | 2,509 | $10\frac{1}{3}$ |
| DW–81884 | W | 3–11–59 | 25 | 120 | 3,000 | 1,311 | 4,311 | 3,889 | 422 | 8 |
| DW–82012 | W | 3–17–59 | 25 | 120 | 3,000 | 1,165 | 4,165 | 3,673 | 492 | 8 |
| W–85362 | W | 3–22–59 | 50 | 81 | 4,050 | 1,205 | 5,255 | 4,190 | 1,065 | $8\frac{1}{2}$ |
| DW–82401 | W | 4–1–59 | 30 | 120 | 3,600 | 917 | 4,517 | 3,522 | 995 | 9 |
| DW–82505 | W | 4–6–59 | 20 | 120 | 2,400 | 665 | 3,065 | 2,579 | 486 | $8\frac{1}{2}$ |
| DW–82618 | W | 4–8–59 | 25 | 97 | 2,425 | 582 | 3,007 | 2,472 | 535 | $8\frac{1}{4}$ |
| DW–82622 | W | 4–8–59 | 30 | 120 | 3,600 | 940 | 4,540 | 3,920 | 620 | 7 |
| DWN–76779 | W | 4–8–59 | 40 | 108 | 4,320 | 1,115 | 5,435 | 4,607 | 828 | $8\frac{1}{2}$ |
| DWN–77070 | W | 4–23–59 | 25 | 120 | 3,000 | 1,217 | 4,217 | 3,723 | 494 | 8 |
| DW–83114 | W | 4–28–59 | 25 | 106 | 2,650 | 718 | 3,368 | 2,592 | 776 | 9 |
| W–84080 | W | 5–5–59 | 120 | 103 | 12,360 | 3,729 | 16,089 | 15,567 | 2,522 | 9 |
| W–84106 | W | 5–7–59 | 20 | 120 | 2,400 | 909 | 3,309 | 2,972 | 337 | $8\frac{1}{2}$ |
| FN–5032 | F.I. | 5–11–59 | 250 | 91 | 22,750 | 11,813 | 34,563 | 33,549 | 1,014 | 9 |

\* W = Wellington Fund, F.I. = Fundamental Investors

| Account No. | Fund* | Date Established | Monthly Payment | Payments Made | Total Paid In | Div. & Dist. Reinvested | Total Invested | Liquidated For | Loss | After Years |
|---|---|---|---|---|---|---|---|---|---|---|
| **1959** *Cont.* | | | | | | | | | | |
| WN–79578 | W | 5–29–59 | $ 50 | 120 | $ 6,000 | $ 2,109 | $ 8,109 | $ 6,294 | $1,815 | 10½ |
| WN–79736 | W | 6–8–59 | 25 | 120 | 3,000 | 1,306 | 4,306 | 3,893 | 413 | 9⅓ |
| WN–80139 | W | 6–29–59 | 30 | 104 | 3,120 | 877 | 3,997 | 3,134 | 863 | 8¾ |
| WN–82928 | W | 6–30–59 | 25 | 104 | 2,600 | 675 | 3,275 | 2,850 | 425 | 8¼ |
| W–85629 | W | 7–2–59 | 40 | 120 | 4,800 | 1,640 | 6,440 | 5,084 | 1,356 | 8½ |
| WN–80312 | W | 7–9–59 | 15 | 56 | 840 | 280 | 1,120 | 953 | 167 | 9 |
| WN–80319 | W | 7–9–59 | 25 | 51 | 1,275 | 533 | 1,808 | 1,539 | 269 | 9¼ |
| W–86029 | W | 7–20–59 | 50 | 103 | 5,150 | 1,400 | 6,550 | 5,152 | 1,398 | 9 |
| W–87018 | W | 8–20–59 | 20 | 120 | 2,400 | 717 | 3,117 | 2,719 | 398 | 9 |
| W–87098 | W | 8–26–59 | 30 | 100 | 3,000 | 782 | 3,782 | 2,971 | 811 | 9 |
| WN–81439 | W | 9–9–59 | 75 | 120 | 9,000 | 2,741 | 11,741 | 10,070 | 1,671 | 9⅓ |
| W–87595 | W | 9–23–59 | 25 | 95 | 2,375 | 542 | 2,917 | 2,375 | 542 | 7¾ |
| W–87643 | W | 9–25–59 | 50 | 109 | 5,450 | 1,666 | 7,116 | 6,061 | 1,055 | 7¾ |
| W–87706 | W | 9–28–59 | 100 | 120 | 12,000 | 2,548 | 14,548 | 12,408 | 2,140 | 8 |
| WN–81771 | W | 9–30–59 | 20 | 116 | 2,320 | 581 | 2,901 | 2,244 | 657 | 8½ |
| W–87761 | W | 10–1–59 | 25 | 37 | 925 | 302 | 1,227 | 927 | 300 | 8 |
| W–88016 | W | 10–13–59 | 25 | 95 | 2,375 | 732 | 3,107 | 2,690 | 417 | 7½ |
| W–88129 | W | 10–16–59 | 15 | 91 | 1,365 | 306 | 1,671 | 1,383 | 288 | 7¾ |
| WN–82111 | W | 10–20–59 | 50 | 97 | 4,850 | 1,186 | 6,036 | 5,295 | 741 | 9 |
| W–88199 | W | 10–20–59 | 25 | 96 | 2,400 | 522 | 2,922 | 2,386 | 536 | 8 |
| WN–82128 | W | 10–21–59 | 20 | 97 | 1,940 | 464 | 2,404 | 2,082 | 322 | 8 |
| W–92715 | W | 10–26–59 | 50 | 90 | 4,500 | 969 | 5,469 | 4,557 | 912 | 8 |
| WN–82302 | W | 10–29–59 | 100 | 101 | 10,100 | 2,535 | 12,635 | 10,414 | 2,221 | 8 |
| W–88447 | W | 10–29–59 | 30 | 120 | 3,600 | 867 | 4,467 | 3,896 | 571 | 6½ |
| W–88577 | W | 11–4–59 | 20 | 91 | 1,820 | 385 | 2,205 | 1,830 | 375 | 7½ |
| WN–82558 | W | 11–12–59 | 50 | 75 | 3,750 | 741 | 4,491 | 4,086 | 405 | 6¼ |
| W–88964 | W | 11–18–59 | 20 | 120 | 2,400 | 374 | 2,774 | 1,863 | 911 | 6½ |
| WN–82806 | W | 11–23–59 | 40 | 120 | 4,800 | 1,455 | 6,255 | 5,566 | 689 | 9 |
| WN–83022 | W | 12–3–59 | 50 | 99 | 4,950 | 1,331 | 6,281 | 4,996 | 1,285 | 9⅙ |
| W–89595 | W | 12–10–59 | 250 | 91 | 22,750 | 5,223 | 27,973 | 23,903 | 4,070 | 7¾ |
| WN–83249 | W | 12–11–59 | 15 | 107 | 1,605 | 477 | 2,082 | 1,710 | 372 | 8 |
| W–89832 | W | 12–16–59 | 50 | 52 | 2,600 | 799 | 3,399 | 2,757 | 642 | 7¾ |
| **1960** | | | | | | | | | | |
| WN–83551 | W | 1–14–60 | 25 | 110 | 2,750 | 834 | 3,584 | 2,895 | 689 | 9⅙ |
| W–90224 | W | 1–15–60 | 15 | 98 | 1,470 | 369 | 1,839 | 1,382 | 457 | 8 |
| W–90296 | W | 1–18–60 | 50 | 78 | 3,900 | 719 | 4,619 | 3,783 | 836 | 6½ |
| W–90475 | W | 1–25–60 | 100 | 99 | 9,900 | 2,538 | 12,438 | 10,239 | 2,199 | 8¼ |
| W–90553 | W | 1–27–60 | 25 | 89 | 2,225 | 465 | 2,690 | 2,180 | 510 | 7½ |
| WN–83848 | W | 1–28–60 | 50 | 76 | 3,800 | 711 | 4,511 | 3,853 | 658 | 6⅓ |
| W–90683 | W | 2–1–60 | 30 | 98 | 2,940 | 896 | 3,836 | 3,103 | 733 | 9 |
| W–108013 | W | 2–3–60 | 25 | 93 | 2,325 | 590 | 2,915 | 2,302 | 613 | 7¾ |
| WN–83989 | W | 2–4–60 | 50 | 102 | 5,100 | 1,794 | 6,894 | 5,541 | 1,353 | 8½ |
| W–90895 | W | 2–9–60 | 50 | 77 | 3,850 | 698 | 4,548 | 3,716 | 832 | 6⅓ |
| W–90896 | W | 2–9–60 | 50 | 92 | 4,600 | 997 | 5,597 | 4,736 | 861 | 7½ |
| W–91034 | W | 2–15–60 | 25 | 89 | 2,225 | 460 | 2,685 | 2,180 | 505 | 7½ |
| W–91056 | W | 2–15–60 | 250 | 74 | 18,500 | 3,535 | 22,035 | 18,546 | 3,489 | 6⅓ |
| W–91321 | W | 2–25–60 | 50 | 100 | 5,000 | 1,235 | 6,235 | 5,211 | 1,024 | 8⅓ |
| WN–84661 | W | 3–10–60 | 40 | 68 | 2,720 | 723 | 3,443 | 2,837 | 606 | 7¼ |
| W–91885 | W | 3–21–60 | 25 | 91 | 2,275 | 466 | 2,741 | 2,207 | 534 | 7½ |
| W–91892 | W | 3–21–60 | 30 | 120 | 3,600 | 889 | 4,489 | 3,695 | 794 | 7½ |
| W–91964 | W | 3–23–60 | 50 | 93 | 4,650 | 1,074 | 5,724 | 4,718 | 1,006 | 8 |
| W–92075 | W | 3–28–60 | 40 | 88 | 3,520 | 740 | 4,260 | 3,491 | 769 | 7½ |
| W–92063 | W | 3–28–60 | 30 | 87 | 2,610 | 522 | 3,132 | 2,037 | 1,095 | 7½ |

* W = Wellington Fund

| Account No. | Fund* | Date Established | Monthly Payment | Payments Made | Total Paid In | Div. & Dist. Reinvested | Total Invested | Liquidated For | Loss | After Years |
|---|---|---|---|---|---|---|---|---|---|---|
| **1960** *Cont.* | | | | | | | | | | |
| W–92143 | W | 3–30–60 | $ 40 | 95 | $ 3,800 | $ 964 | $ 4,764 | $ 3,696 | $1,068 | 8 |
| W–92190 | W | 4–1–60 | 25 | 88 | 2,200 | 439 | 2,639 | 2,132 | 507 | 7¼ |
| W–92896 | W | 5–5–60 | 20 | 120 | 2,400 | 712 | 3,112 | 2,320 | 792 | 8 |
| W–93050 | W | 5–11–60 | 50 | 93 | 4,650 | 983 | 5,633 | 4,553 | 1,080 | 7½ |
| W–93144 | W | 5–13–60 | 50 | 46 | 2,300 | 539 | 2,839 | 2,153 | 686 | 6½ |
| W–100310 | W | 5–13–60 | 50 | 120 | 6,000 | 1,999 | 7,999 | 6,829 | 1,170 | 6 |
| WN–85846 | W | 5–19–60 | 20 | 88 | 1,760 | 376 | 2,136 | 1,812 | 324 | 7¼ |
| WN–85904 | W | 5–23–60 | 100 | 71 | 7,100 | 1,367 | 8,467 | 7,014 | 1,453 | 6⅙ |
| F–10694 | F.I. | 5–27–60 | 20 | 63 | 1,260 | 387 | 1,647 | 1,522 | 125 | 7 |
| W–93506 | W | 5–30–60 | 100 | 51 | 5,100 | 1,177 | 6,277 | 4,657 | 1,620 | 6⅓ |
| W–93625 | W | 6–3–60 | 250 | 71 | 17,750 | 3,256 | 21,006 | 17,549 | 3,457 | 6 |
| WN–86126 | W | 6–7–60 | 50 | 84 | 4,200 | 956 | 5,156 | 4,386 | 770 | 7¼ |
| W–94339 | W | 7–11–60 | 30 | 77 | 2,310 | 451 | 2,761 | 2,095 | 666 | 6½ |
| W–94459 | W | 7–15–60 | 50 | 93 | 4,650 | 1,106 | 5,756 | 4,297 | 1,459 | 7½ |
| W–94641 | W | 7–22–60 | 50 | 75 | 3,750 | 763 | 4,513 | 3,581 | 932 | 6½ |
| WN–86843 | W | 7–27–60 | 50 | 106 | 5,300 | 1,536 | 6,836 | 2,774 | 4,062 | 9 |
| W–94869 | W | 8–2–60 | 20 | 120 | 2,400 | 391 | 2,791 | 2,394 | 397 | 6½ |
| W–95065 | W | 8–9–60 | 50 | 68 | 3,400 | 1,256 | 4,656 | 3,307 | 1,349 | 9 |
| FN–11668 | F.I. | 8–10–60 | 25 | 57 | 1,425 | 582 | 2,007 | 1,750 | 257 | 8⅚ |
| W–95109 | W | 8–12–60 | 25 | 60 | 1,500 | 248 | 1,748 | 1,422 | 326 | 5½ |
| W–95137 | W | 8–15–60 | 25 | 63 | 1,575 | 397 | 1,972 | 1,574 | 398 | 7 |
| WN–87196 | W | 8–19–60 | 30 | 86 | 2,580 | 637 | 3,217 | 2,578 | 639 | 7¼ |
| WN–87270 | W | 8–26–60 | 20 | 87 | 1,740 | 346 | 2,086 | 1,706 | 380 | 7 |
| W–95326 | W | 8–26–60 | 25 | 84 | 2,100 | 391 | 2,491 | 2,035 | 456 | 7 |
| W–95575 | W | 9–13–60 | 25 | 81 | 2,025 | 374 | 2,399 | 1,903 | 496 | 6¾ |
| WN–87728 | W | 10–5–60 | 25 | 52 | 1,300 | 235 | 1,535 | 1,347 | 188 | 5 |
| W–98790 | W | 10–7–60 | 25 | 90 | 2,250 | 570 | 2,820 | 2,293 | 527 | 7⅔ |
| WN–87806 | W | 10–10–60 | 50 | 120 | 6,000 | 1,581 | 7,581 | 6,659 | 922 | 5¾ |
| W–96226 | W | 10–18–60 | 25 | 65 | 1,625 | 240 | 1,865 | 1,539 | 326 | 5⅓ |
| W–96783 | W | 11–10–60 | 30 | 81 | 2,430 | 448 | 2,878 | 2,286 | 592 | 6½ |
| W–97298 | W | 11–30–60 | 50 | 93 | 4,650 | 1,048 | 5,698 | 4,749 | 949 | 7 |
| WN–88892 | W | 12–15–60 | 50 | 54 | 2,700 | 546 | 3,246 | 2,592 | 654 | 7 |
| W–97651 | W | 12–15–60 | 50 | 41 | 2,050 | 398 | 2,448 | 2,013 | 435 | 5⅙ |
| W–97997 | W | 12–28–60 | 25 | 93 | 2,325 | 503 | 2,838 | 2,336 | 492 | 7¾ |
| **1961** | | | | | | | | | | |
| W–98243 | W | 1–16–61 | 150 | 78 | 11,700 | 2,170 | 13,870 | 11,571 | 2,299 | 8½ |
| F–14855 | F.I. | 1–20–61 | 50 | 97 | 4,850 | 1,991 | 6,841 | 5,869 | 972 | 8½ |
| W–98436 | W | 1–24–61 | 50 | 81 | 4,050 | 750 | 4,800 | 3,992 | 808 | 6½ |
| W–98648 | W | 2–1–61 | 20 | 70 | 1,400 | 214 | 1,614 | 1,257 | 357 | 5⅓ |
| W–98661 | W | 2–1–61 | 20 | 90 | 1,800 | 376 | 2,176 | 1,752 | 424 | 7½ |
| W–99123 | W | 2–23–61 | 20 | 71 | 1,420 | 241 | 1,661 | 1,322 | 339 | 6⅙ |
| W–99362 | W | 3–3–61 | 50 | 62 | 3,100 | 468 | 3,568 | 2,874 | 694 | 5 |
| W–99569 | W | 3–13–61 | 30 | 80 | 2,400 | 405 | 2,805 | 2,170 | 635 | 6½ |
| W–99653 | W | 3–15–61 | 50 | 60 | 3,000 | 419 | 3,419 | 2,779 | 640 | 5 |
| W–99663 | W | 3–15–61 | 100 | 42 | 4,200 | 1,538 | 5,738 | 4,498 | 1,240 | 7¼ |
| W–99745 | W | 3–20–61 | 20 | 40 | 800 | 213 | 1,013 | 753 | 260 | 7¼ |
| FN–14657 | F.I. | 3–22–61 | 30 | 120 | 3,600 | 1,522 | 5,122 | 3,780 | 1,342 | 9 |
| W–100425 | W | 4–18–61 | 50 | 84 | 4,200 | 881 | 5,081 | 4,052 | 1,029 | 7 |
| W–100516 | W | 4–21–61 | 50 | 44 | 2,200 | 516 | 2,716 | 2,150 | 566 | 6½ |
| F–16662 | F.I. | 4–21–61 | 50 | 79 | 3,950 | 868 | 4,818 | 4,567 | 251 | 6½ |
| W–100541 | W | 4–24–61 | 15 | 78 | 1,170 | 195 | 1,365 | 1,092 | 273 | 6½ |
| W–90923 | W | 4–27–61 | 50 | 77 | 3,850 | 711 | 4,561 | 3,856 | 705 | 6½ |
| WN–91225 | W | 5–17–61 | 20 | 53 | 1,060 | 228 | 1,288 | 1,005 | 283 | 6½ |

* W = Wellington Fund, F.I. = Fundamental Investors

| Account No. | Fund* | Date Established | Monthly Payment | Payments Made | Total Paid In | Div. & Dist. Reinvested | Total Invested | Liquidated For | Loss | After Years |
|---|---|---|---|---|---|---|---|---|---|---|
| **1961** *Cont.* | | | | | | | | | | |
| W–101197 | W | 5–19–61 | $ 30 | 76 | $ 2,280 | $ 418 | $ 2,698 | $ 2,154 | $ 544 | $6\tfrac{1}{4}$ |
| W–101223 | W | 5–22–61 | 15 | 78 | 1,170 | 265 | 1,435 | 1,083 | 352 | $6\tfrac{3}{4}$ |
| W–101240 | W | 5–22–61 | 50 | 73 | 3,650 | 634 | 4,284 | 3,470 | 814 | 6 |
| WN–91333 | W | 5–24–61 | 25 | 75 | 1,875 | 522 | 2,397 | 2,029 | 368 | $7\tfrac{1}{2}$ |
| WN–91332 | W | 5–24–61 | 25 | 72 | 1,800 | 321 | 2,121 | 1,773 | 348 | 7 |
| WN–91376 | W | 5–25–61 | 75 | 73 | 5,475 | 1,012 | 6,487 | 5,471 | 1,016 | 6 |
| W–101314 | W | 5–25–61 | 25 | 120 | 3,000 | 350 | 3,350 | 2,826 | 524 | 6 |
| W–101460 | W | 6–1–61 | 50 | 120 | 6,000 | 3,459 | 9,459 | 7,670 | 1,789 | 8 |
| W–101564 | W | 6–7–61 | 15 | 58 | 870 | 115 | 985 | 768 | 217 | $4\tfrac{3}{4}$ |
| W–101830 | W | 6–21–61 | 20 | 58 | 1,160 | 150 | 1,310 | 1,018 | 292 | $4\tfrac{3}{4}$ |
| WN–91712 | W | 6–22–61 | 20 | 82 | 1,640 | 337 | 1,977 | 1,582 | 395 | $6\tfrac{1}{2}$ |
| W–101906 | W | 6–23–61 | 50 | 76 | 3,800 | 637 | 4,437 | 3,647 | 790 | 7 |
| WN–91976 | W | 7–11–61 | 20 | 103 | 2,060 | 442 | 2,502 | 2,100 | 402 | $6\tfrac{1}{4}$ |
| W–102298 | W | 7–13–61 | 25 | 69 | 1,725 | 630 | 2,355 | 1,841 | 514 | $6\tfrac{1}{4}$ |
| W–102329 | W | 7–14–61 | 20 | 61 | 1,220 | 168 | 1,388 | 1,144 | 244 | $4\tfrac{1}{2}$ |
| W–102363 | W | 7–17–61 | 25 | 64 | 1,600 | 227 | 1,827 | 1,395 | 432 | 5 |
| W–102609 | W | 7–26–61 | 50 | 76 | 3,800 | 754 | 4,554 | 3,499 | 1,055 | $6\tfrac{1}{2}$ |
| W–102971 | W | 8–4–61 | 15 | 75 | 1,125 | 176 | 1,301 | 1,029 | 272 | 6 |
| W–102844 | W | 8–7–61 | 25 | 56 | 1,400 | 173 | 1,573 | 1,237 | 336 | $4\tfrac{2}{3}$ |
| W–102951 | W | 8–10–61 | 25 | 71 | 1,775 | 275 | 2,050 | 1,588 | 462 | 6 |
| W–103153 | W | 8–23–61 | 20 | 61 | 1,220 | 151 | 1,371 | 981 | 390 | 5 |
| W–103249 | W | 8–29–61 | 50 | 81 | 4,050 | 809 | 4,859 | 4,070 | 789 | 7 |
| WN–92817 | W | 9–19–61 | 20 | 34 | 680 | 74 | 754 | 615 | 139 | 4 |
| W–103602 | W | 9–25–61 | 15 | 72 | 1,080 | 165 | 1,245 | 1,002 | 243 | 6 |
| W–103757 | W | 10–3–61 | 20 | 44 | 880 | 221 | 1,101 | 798 | 303 | $6\tfrac{1}{2}$ |
| W–103932 | W | 10–17–61 | 15 | 76 | 1,140 | 207 | 1,347 | 1,005 | 342 | $6\tfrac{1}{2}$ |
| W–104032 | W | 10–20–61 | 20 | 43 | 860 | 110 | 970 | 713 | 257 | $4\tfrac{3}{4}$ |
| F–20051 | F.I. | 10–24–61 | 50 | 37 | 1,850 | 530 | 2,380 | 2,351 | 29 | $6\tfrac{1}{6}$ |
| W–104249 | W | 10–30–61 | 100 | 120 | 12,000 | 3,637 | 15,637 | 13,369 | 2,268 | $7\tfrac{1}{2}$ |
| W–104405 | W | 11–6–61 | 50 | 66 | 3,300 | 540 | 3,840 | 3,111 | 729 | 6 |
| W–104502 | W | 11–10–61 | 25 | 45 | 1,125 | 89 | 1,214 | 954 | 260 | $3\tfrac{3}{4}$ |
| F–21057 | F.I. | 12–5–61 | 25 | 47 | 1,175 | 247 | 1,422 | 1,101 | 321 | 6 |
| W–105042 | W | 12–5–61 | 20 | 90 | 1,800 | 374 | 2,174 | 1,752 | 422 | $7\tfrac{1}{2}$ |
| FN–18395 | F.I. | 12–6–61 | 50 | 120 | 6,000 | 3,389 | 9,389 | 8,857 | 532 | $5\tfrac{1}{2}$ |
| W–105408 | W | 12–20–61 | 40 | 61 | 2,440 | 348 | 2,788 | 2,152 | 636 | 6 |
| W–105842 | W | 12–28–61 | 25 | 120 | 3,000 | 462 | 3,462 | 2,807 | 655 | 6 |
| **1962** | | | | | | | | | | |
| WN–94222 | W | 1–2–62 | 50 | 61 | 3,050 | 490 | 3,540 | 2,926 | 614 | $5\tfrac{1}{6}$ |
| W–105526 | W | 1–2–62 | 100 | 45 | 4,500 | 377 | 4,877 | 4,128 | 749 | $3\tfrac{3}{4}$ |
| W–105577 | W | 1–9–62 | 30 | 84 | 2,520 | 646 | 3,166 | 2,619 | 547 | 6 |
| W–105584 | W | 1–9–62 | 100 | 80 | 8,000 | 1,428 | 9,428 | 7,962 | 1,466 | $4\tfrac{1}{6}$ |
| F–21677 | F.I. | 1–9–62 | 30 | 84 | 2,520 | 715 | 3,235 | 3,190 | 45 | 6 |
| W–105714 | W | 1–17–62 | 50 | 51 | 2,550 | 296 | 2,846 | 2,267 | 579 | $4\tfrac{1}{4}$ |
| W–105757 | W | 1–19–62 | 100 | 66 | 6,600 | 975 | 7,575 | 6,093 | 1,482 | $5\tfrac{1}{2}$ |
| W–105825 | W | 1–23–62 | 100 | 44 | 4,400 | 1,212 | 5,612 | 4,275 | 1,337 | 6 |
| F–22081 | F.I. | 2–1–62 | 20 | 56 | 1,120 | 233 | 1,353 | 1,207 | 146 | $5\tfrac{1}{4}$ |
| W–106157 | W | 2–7–62 | 30 | 120 | 3,600 | 1,361 | 4,961 | 3,778 | 1,183 | $7\tfrac{1}{2}$ |
| W–106568 | W | 2–28–62 | 30 | 72 | 2,160 | 418 | 2,578 | 1,981 | 597 | 6 |
| WN–95019 | W | 3–1–62 | 20 | 51 | 1,020 | 183 | 1,203 | 907 | 296 | $5\tfrac{3}{4}$ |
| F–22633 | F.I. | 3–1–62 | 50 | 88 | 4,400 | 1,519 | 5,919 | 5,087 | 832 | $7\tfrac{1}{4}$ |
| WN–95373 | W | 3–27–62 | 20 | 72 | 1,440 | 255 | 1,695 | 1,265 | 430 | 6 |
| W–107269 | W | 4–5–62 | 50 | 61 | 3,050 | 411 | 3,461 | 2,781 | 680 | $5\tfrac{1}{4}$ |
| W–107379 | W | 4–11–62 | 25 | 63 | 1,575 | 208 | 1,783 | 1,381 | 402 | $5\tfrac{1}{4}$ |

\* W = Wellington Fund, F.I. = Fundamental Investors

| Account No. | Fund* | Date Established | Monthly Payment | Payments Made | Total Paid In | Div. & Dist. Reinvested | Total Invested | Liquidated For | Loss | After Years |
|---|---|---|---|---|---|---|---|---|---|---|
| **1962** *Cont.* | | | | | | | | | | |
| W–107486 | W | 4–17–62 | $ 20 | 63 | $ 1,260 | $ 165 | $ 1,425 | $ 1,109 | $ 316 | $5\frac{1}{4}$ |
| F–23665 | F.I. | 4–27–62 | 40 | 80 | 3,200 | 950 | 4,150 | 3,581 | 569 | 7 |
| FN–20088 | F.I. | 5–1–62 | 25 | 57 | 1,425 | 274 | 1,699 | 1,470 | 229 | $4\frac{3}{4}$ |
| FN–20122 | F.I. | 5–2–62 | 50 | 69 | 3,450 | 952 | 4,402 | 3,725 | 677 | 6 |
| W–107906 | W | 5–16–62 | 100 | 41 | 4,100 | 698 | 4,798 | 3,682 | 1,116 | 5 |
| W–107914 | W | 5–17–62 | 100 | 55 | 5,500 | 579 | 6,079 | 4,314 | 1,765 | $4\frac{1}{2}$ |
| W–150046 | W | 5–22–62 | 50 | 67 | 3,350 | 468 | 3,818 | 3,030 | 788 | $5\frac{1}{2}$ |
| W–107939 | W | 5–28–62 | 100 | 67 | 6,700 | 1,160 | 7,860 | 6,082 | 1,778 | $5\frac{1}{2}$ |
| W–150065 | W | 5–28–62 | 100 | 62 | 6,200 | · 834 | 7,034 | 5,520 | 1,514 | 5 |
| W–150179 | W | 6–22–62 | 100 | 50 | 5,000 | 1,121 | 6,121 | 4,690 | 1,431 | $6\frac{1}{6}$ |
| W–400378 | W | 6–22–62 | 50 | 54 | 2,700 | 323 | 3,023 | 2,197 | 826 | $4\frac{2}{3}$ |
| WN–400253 | W | 6–28–62 | 15 | 47 | 705 | 76 | 781 | 608 | 173 | 4 |
| F–150224 | F.I. | 7–17–62 | 20 | 68 | 1,360 | 333 | 1,693 | 1,447 | 246 | $5\frac{1}{2}$ |
| WN–400431 | W | 7–24–62 | 100 | 55 | 5,500 | 789 | 6,289 | 5,073 | 1,216 | 5 |
| FN–150314 | F.I. | 8–3–62 | 20 | 73 | 1,460 | 350 | 1,810 | 1,689 | 121 | 6 |
| WN–150360 | W | 8–3–62 | 20 | 59 | 1,180 | 153 | 1,333 | 1,063 | 270 | 5 |
| F–150304 | F.I. | 8–10–62 | 20 | 120 | 2,400 | 1,061 | 3,461 | 2,567 | 894 | $7\frac{1}{2}$ |
| W–400960 | W | 8–13–62 | 15 | 62 | 930 | 106 | 1,036 | 731 | 305 | $5\frac{1}{4}$ |
| WN–400675 | W | 8–30–62 | 25 | 63 | 1,575 | 253 | 1,828 | 1,412 | 416 | $5\frac{1}{2}$ |
| WN–150486 | W | 9–6–62 | 50 | 116 | 5,800 | 766 | 6,566 | 5,538 | 1,028 | $4\frac{1}{2}$ |
| F–40191 | F.I. | 9–10–62 | 50 | 69 | 3,450 | 1,023 | 4,473 | 3,641 | 832 | $6\frac{1}{3}$ |
| WN–150545 | W | 9–25–62 | 15 | 57 | 855 | 164 | 1,019 | 822 | 197 | $5\frac{3}{4}$ |
| W–150552 | W | 10–19–62 | 50 | 60 | 3,000 | 343 | 3,343 | 2,594 | 749 | $5\frac{3}{4}$ |
| W–150599 | W | 11–5–62 | 20 | 120 | 2,400 | 812 | 3,212 | 2,523 | 689 | $6\frac{1}{3}$ |
| F–401777 | F.I. | 11–20–62 | 150 | 70 | 10,500 | 2,183 | 12,683 | 11,181 | 1,502 | $5\frac{5}{6}$ |
| W–150668 | W | 12–3–62 | 20 | 73 | 1,460 | 251 | 1,711 | 1,292 | 419 | $6\frac{1}{6}$ |
| WN–150747 | W | 12–4–62 | 20 | 75 | 1,500 | 282 | 1,781 | 1,315 | 466 | 7 |
| WN–150748 | W | 12–4–62 | 40 | 76 | 3,040 | 646 | 3,686 | 2,966 | 720 | 7 |
| F–401966 | F.I. | 12–12–62 | 150 | 77 | 11,550 | 3,023 | 14,573 | 12,075 | 2,498 | $6\frac{1}{2}$ |
| F–150612 | F.I. | 12–17–62 | 50 | 43 | 2,150 | 175 | 2,325 | 1,695 | 630 | $3\frac{3}{4}$ |
| **1963** | | | | | | | | | | |
| F–402514 | F.I. | 2–27–63 | 20 | 65 | 1,300 | 239 | 1,539 | 1,199 | 340 | $5\frac{1}{2}$ |
| W–150942 | W | 3–5–63 | 20 | 52 | 1,040 | 118 | 1,158 | 879 | 279 | $4\frac{1}{4}$ |
| W–150949 | W | 3–5–63 | 100 | 54 | 5,400 | 544 | 5,944 | 4,658 | 1,286 | $4\frac{1}{2}$ |
| FN–401631 | F.I. | 3–6–63 | 50 | 46 | 2,300 | 769 | 3,069 | 2,659 | 410 | $5\frac{5}{6}$ |
| FN–401643 | F.I. | 3–11–63 | 20 | 62 | 1,240 | 270 | 1,510 | 1,279 | 231 | 5 |
| W–403196 | W | 4–8–63 | 15 | 62 | 930 | 115 | 1,045 | 777 | 268 | $5\frac{1}{6}$ |
| F–402948 | F.I. | 5–2–63 | 150 | 40 | 6,000 | 395 | 6,395 | 4,929 | 1,466 | $3\frac{1}{4}$ |
| FN–402044 | F.I. | 5–21–63 | 50 | 67 | 3,350 | 678 | 4,028 | 3,577 | 451 | $5\frac{1}{6}$ |
| W–151282 | W | 6–17–63 | 20 | 60 | 1,200 | 116 | 1,316 | 998 | 318 | 4 |
| F–151085 | F.I. | 6–28–63 | 100 | 71 | 7,100 | 1,794 | 8,894 | 6,940 | 1,954 | 6 |
| F–404011 | F.I. | 9–30–63 | 100 | 64 | 6,400 | 1,413 | 7,813 | 6,128 | 1,685 | $5\frac{1}{2}$ |
| F–404226 | F.I. | 10–29–63 | 100 | 59 | 5,900 | 927 | 6,827 | 5,577 | 1,250 | 5 |
| F–404322 | F.I. | 11–7–63 | 50 | 48 | 2,400 | 245 | 2,645 | 2,032 | 613 | 4 |
| F–151401 | F.I. | 11–12–63 | 40 | 72 | 2,880 | 721 | 3,601 | 2,489 | 1,112 | $6\frac{1}{3}$ |
| **1964** | | | | | | | | | | |
| FN–151419 | F.I. | 1–21–64 | 20 | 58 | 1,160 | 271 | 1,431 | 1,120 | 311 | $4\frac{3}{4}$ |
| F–404928 | F.I. | 1–24–64 | 20 | 56 | 1,120 | 171 | 1,291 | 1,032 | 259 | $4\frac{2}{3}$ |
| F–404944 | F.I. | 1–27–64 | 100 | 50 | 5,000 | 797 | 5,797 | 3,952 | 1,845 | $4\frac{1}{6}$ |
| F–405072 | F.I. | 2–13–64 | 50 | 55 | 2,750 | 587 | 3,337 | 2,020 | 1,317 | 6 |
| W–151829 | W | 2–14–64 | 30 | 46 | 1,380 | 138 | 1,518 | 1,139 | 379 | $4\frac{1}{2}$ |
| F–405192 | F.I. | 2–28–64 | 20 | 55 | 1,100 | 216 | 1,316 | 982 | 334 | $5\frac{1}{4}$ |
| F–151699 | F.I. | 3–13–64 | 25 | 49 | 1,225 | 191 | 1,416 | 1,124 | 292 | $4\frac{1}{6}$ |

\* W = Wellington Fund, F.I. = Fundamental Investors

| Account No. | Fund* | Date Established | Monthly Payment | Payments Made | Total Paid In | Div. & Dist. Reinvested | Total Invested | Liquidated For | Loss | After Years |
|---|---|---|---|---|---|---|---|---|---|---|
| **1964** *Cont.* | | | | | | | | | | |
| F-415596 | F.I. | 3-23-64 | $ 25 | 84 | $ 2,100 | $ 335 | $ 2,435 | $ 1,834 | $ 601 | 4½ |
| F-405570 | F.I. | 4-10-64 | 20 | 43 | 860 | 73 | 933 | 696 | 237 | 3½ |
| F-407107 | F.I. | 5-1-64 | 100 | 69 | 6,900 | 1,423 | 8,323 | 5,128 | 3,195 | 5¾ |
| F-405809 | F.I. | 5-6-64 | 20 | 57 | 1,140 | 213 | 1,353 | 951 | 402 | 4¾ |
| F-406008 | F.I. | 5-25-64 | 50 | 54 | 2,700 | 354 | 3,054 | 2,420 | 634 | 4½ |
| FN-151752 | F.I. | 5-28-64 | 50 | 46 | 2,300 | 380 | 2,680 | 2,045 | 635 | 3⅚ |
| F-151953 | F.I. | 6-10-64 | 25 | 50 | 1,250 | 146 | 1,396 | 1,173 | 223 | 3¼ |
| F-151968 | F.I. | 6-18-64 | 30 | 55 | 1,650 | 326 | 1,976 | 1,536 | 440 | 4½ |
| F-406480 | F.I. | 7-10-64 | 150 | 39 | 5,850 | 489 | 6,339 | 4,890 | 1,449 | 3¼ |
| F-406465 | F.I. | 7-16-64 | 20 | 41 | 820 | 65 | 885 | 672 | 213 | 3½ |
| F-152383 | F.I. | 11-17-64 | 40 | 120 | 4,800 | 1,576 | 6,376 | 4,956 | 1,420 | 4⅔ |

\* F.I. = Fundamental Investors

The disheartening statistics disclosed by the survey accurately represent the investment results of the First Investors contractual plans we have handled. We do have accounts on our books that show a profit, but these have run for from fifteen to twenty years. But the question to be answered is not "Do a few people show a profit?" but rather "Do an overwhelming majority of people show a loss?"

The investors who initiated these plans did so in the hope and belief that they would enjoy income and profits. The layman who deposits his money in a riskless investment—a savings bank, a savings and loan association or in a certificate of deposit in a commercial bank—is paid the earnings on it. On the other hand, when a person invests in equities via a mutual fund, he accepts the risks that go with the hazarding of his capital in the hope of a greater reward—profits. The mutual fund pays him earnings periodically which are generally comparable to those he would obtain from "riskless" depositories, but these earnings he generally puts back into additional investment in the contractual plan. The average dividend and capital gains distributions for all of the accounts shown in our study is a quite satisfactory 5.9 percent, not dissimilar to what the investors would have earned in a riskless deposit account. That leads to an analysis of the profit reward which the investor enjoyed for having taken the risk of equity investment, and here we make the disconcerting discovery that there was no profit—everyone who bought these contractual plans lost money. The amount of the tax-deductible loss is shown in the second-to-last column of the foregoing tables.

When we consider that mutual funds are offered as an investment hedge against inflation, and that the years covered by this survey were the most inflationary in our history, it is difficult to reconcile the contractual plan performance with Grayson's statement to a House subcommittee considering mutual fund legislation that such plans are "the only effective method of meeting the needs of the investor who has not yet accumulated his 'nest egg.'"

Wellington and Fundamental Investors are not obscure funds, unsuccessful funds, or "go-go" funds, nor are the results distorted by our recent troubled market. These are two huge funds, each with assets of over a billion dollars, and over 150,000 active accounts remain on the books of Grayson's First Investors Corporation which no doubt reflect results comparable to our study. Perhaps contractual plans offered by other sponsors show happier results. However, the burden of proof should be on the seller to confirm that what he is offering is not a financial trap for the unwary. The theory of the contractual plan may be sound but the results are what count.

Efforts are being made in Congress to spread the front-end load over a greater number of years. In considering the desirability of such a move, it is worth examining the following computation on the terminated accounts covered by our survey (note that the heaviest terminations occurred between the fifth and tenth years):

Percentage of Terminations Experienced in Each Plan Year

| Year | Percent |
|---|---|
| 3 | 2.48 |
| 4 | 7.46 |
| 5 | 10.50 |
| 6 | 15.76 |
| 7 | 13.26 |
| 8 | 12.43 |
| 9 | 11.60 |
| 10 | 10.77 |
| 11 | 5.52 |
| 12 | 4.70 |
| 13 | 1.66 |
| 14 | 2.21 |
| 15 | 1.66 |

On contractuals, my advice is: Don't.

71

# Chapter 11

# PROBLEMS AND PRACTICES

In this chapter, I shall touch briefly on some of the principal problems and more damaging practices that are a blemish on the fund industry. I do so in the hope that disclosure will not only make the fund buyer wary but may also encourage him to become vocally critical himself. The industry, sensitive to his displeasure, may then take steps to end the abuses. The regulatory authorities, too, may find this checklist a reminder that there is work to be done.

Though I have already mentioned churning by brokers, it is worth noting its application to funds. Varying degrees of portfolio churning are too frequently employed by many mutual funds for the purpose of generating brokerage commissions, the objectives being (a) to channel such commissions back into the pockets of insiders (the sponsors, managers, or underwriters), (b) to provide a steady flow of "reciprocal business" to dealers who have vigorously promoted the sale of the fund's shares, or (c) to produce realized profits solely for sales promotional purposes.

Sometimes the brokerage commissions flow openly to the sponsor. Dreyfus is typical of large funds and Energy Fund of small funds whose sponsors are member firms of the New York Stock Exchange and who direct a substantial proportion of the funds' portfolio transactions through themselves. Such funds insist that the obvious self-interest involved does not influence their investment decisions but I have never seen a fund whose sponsor handled the brokerage transactions which did not have a high portfolio turnover rate. However much the sponsors may protest that they are impartial, the fact remains that if they face a decision on whether to sell 50,000 shares of ABC Common and buy 50,000 shares of XYZ Preferred, the fact that there is a brokerage commission of thousands of dollars in it for them simply means that they are no longer unbiased. There should be legislation to remove such self-interest from mutual fund management decisions, perhaps by reducing management fees

by the amount of brokerage commissions thus received.

Many sponsor-managers note in their prospectus that portfolio transactions are directed to certain brokerage firms in exchange for technical or statistical information supplied to the manager by such firms. They hasten to add that it is impossible to place a dollar value upon such information or services. Actually, their management advisory contract states that they stand ready, willing, and able to provide all managerial services and that their facilities are adequate. However, if managers are able to obtain valuable assistance from brokers or others, it is they, not the shareholders, who should pay for those services. Management fees are adequate. Accordingly, any benefits that may accrue from the directing of portfolio transactions to certain firms should be applied to reduce the cost of the management services to the shareholders collectively. The managers of one small fund with a 1½ percent load collected $250,000 in sales charges on the fund shares sold in 1969, but they also received an additional $250,000 in management fees and a further $250,000 in compensation from the purchase of portfolio securities. It takes a little digging to assemble this information from the prospectus. I have no objection to any of the fees themselves, but they should be stated together and prominently, since they reveal where the managers' interests lie.

The Anchor Group of funds long had a special list of about eighty mutual fund dealers among whom it distributed all of its reciprocal commission business. In addition to the normal 6 percent dealer allowance, these dealers collected another 5 percent or more in reciprocal commissions. While I have no knowledge that it was done in the case of Anchor, it is a fact that many funds have churned their portfolios unnecessarily to generate the brokerage commissions with which they reward those brokers who push their shares to the exclusion of others. Merrill Lynch, which for years payrolled a publicist to plant discouraging articles about mutual funds (while cheerfully—and profitably—executing securities trades for those same funds) and forbade its salespeople to process an order from a customer for fund shares, has taken off its ermine robes and now is out contesting for the mutual fund commission dollar.

It is reported that only a certain dozen funds may be sold by the Merrill Lynchers—which raises a question of propriety. What determines whether a fund is on the firm's "approved list"? There are far more than twelve fine funds. Why are some of the others not eligible for recommendation by Merrill Lynch salesmen? Is investment quality the sole factor in the assignment of a spot on the "approved list," or are brokerage fees the real determinant? Does a fund, in effect, "buy" a spot on the list with a gentleman's agreement to favor the brokerage firm with a steady volume of brokerage business in connection with the investment of the fund's assets? In addition to the regular dealer commissions payable to Merrill Lynch for its sale of the fund's shares, is it also collecting millions of dollars in brokerage commissions from the funds on its approved list? If that is so, is not the receipt of such special compensation a "material fact" which reveals the special interest of the company's salesman who recommends Fund A, which generates the brokerage fees, rather than Fund B, which does not? Should not the funds on the approved list be required to disclose in their prospectuses the exact dollars-and-cents extent of this special interest of the firm and its sales people?

The Securities and Exchange Commission, which has long made a fetish of the disclosure of special interest, has not seen fit to make, much less enforce, any rules in this reciprocal commission area. Only if the broker-recipient of such commissions is a subsidiary of the sponsor, manager, or underwriter of the fund, or if an "affiliated person" of the fund is connected with the broker-recipient, is the fund required to disclose the fact of the commissions paid.

In the operation of a system of undisclosed considerations of the type discussed here, what chance is there that the mutual fund investor will get an unbiased recommendation of which fund to buy? Implicit in such an arrangement is an obligation for the fund to generate brokerage commissions to permit it to continue to enjoy "favored fund" status with the field force of the brokerage firm. The maintenance of such an approved list is contrary to the best interests of the shareholders of the fund and should therefore be regarded as an unfair trade practice. Strong sanctions should be applied against those who engage in it.

In addition to giving brokerage business directly to New York Stock Exchange member firms who have pushed their shares (about 70 percent of all fund sales are made by member firms), funds may direct the business to such a firm and require the recipient to give up

60 percent of the commission to another member. Sometimes a financial daisy chain is created as the commission is sent through for credit to the account of a particular salesman. A housewife residing in some splendor on Paradise Island in the Bahamas doubled as a registered representative of the member firm of Delafield & Delafield in New York. Through the kindness of Investors Planning Corporation, then owned by Investors Overseas Services, the registered representative (a friend of the head of IOS) received more than $3 million in "give-up" commissions in a single year.

In December, 1968, the New York Stock Exchange ruled that such commissions could not be given up to anyone other than another member firm. This eliminated thousands of nonmember firms, principally small broker-dealers; it has not benefited the shareholders, however, since the commissions paid by the funds remain concentrated in the hands of the member firms.

Some funds see a necessity for maintaining a steady record for payment of capital gains distributions year after year. In pursuit of this objective, they sell whatever securities are necessary to produce a minimum dollar amount per share of realized profits. One fund has for many years paid ordinary income dividends and capital gains distributions ranging between $.90 and $1.00 per share. Its chairman of the board, one of the oldest, most conservative and most highly respected figures in the fund industry, once asked me if I thought the fund's public image would suffer if it were to pay a substantially reduced capital gains distribution that year. He disliked doing it, he explained, but he was prepared to realize whatever profits were necessary to maintain the fund's payment record. This unjustified portfolio turnover not only wasted the shareholders' money in unnecessary brokerage commissions but it also subjected those shareholders to an unnecessary tax liability on the capital gains distributions thus forced upon them. Since the Securities and Exchange Commission has not seen fit to establish regulations outlawing this practice, perhaps Congress should legislate the abuse out of existence.

In the area of portfolio management, something should be done to raise ethical standards. Fund managers are profiting privately from their positions. A short while ago, the vice-president and portfolio manager of the highly respected Puritan Fund, one of the Fidelity group of funds in Boston, pleaded guilty to charges of improper dealings in connection with portfolio purchases for the fund. Evidence disclosed that in negotiating for the fund's purchase of a block of securities from a corporate issuer, he had received a $195,000 kickback. Obviously, had he chosen to do so, he could have negotiated a $195,000 better deal for the fund shareholders. His action in not doing so simply robbed the investors. The judge who levied a $7,500 fine told him that only his age saved him from a jail sentence. Noting that the fundman had been on the executive committees of funds controlling billions of dollars, the judge charged that "money managers today have violated their fiduciary relationship to the poor people who have put their money in mutual funds . . . and are being taken by the mutual funds." The court's action was made the basis for a New York *Daily News* headline: Mutual Funds Called Swindle by U.S. Judge. This incident serves to illustrate the bad faith which has characterized the operations of some fund managers. In this instance, the chairman of the fund's investment committee was disclosed to be a director of the company giving the kickback.

These activities may not necessarily do direct harm to the fund they manage but such private profits cannot fail to have an influence upon their decisions—and no such influence should be permitted to exist. Acting in a fiduciary capacity, they should be like Caesar's wife. In the letter-stock area, discussed in detail in the next chapter, abuses are particularly common. Such negotiated transactions present special opportunities for the development of a financial quid pro quo for the portfolio manager.

Too many portfolio managers are buying stock privately for themselves today which they intend to begin buying for the fund tomorrow. They know that in the course of building the fund's position in the stock, they will run its price up to their own advantage. A fund portfolio manager should be required to file with the S.E.C. a monthly report of his own investment holdings. Indeed, why not require that a portfolio manager maintain at least 50 percent of his own personal investments in the fund he is managing? Why should not his investment interests and those of the shareholders who are depending upon his judgment be made identical?

Incidentally, do not think that mutual fund portfolio managers have a monopoly on brokerage commission kickbacks. Many a bank man who buys securities for the institution's trust department is riding around in a Cadillac paid for by a local securities dealer.

The banks themselves quietly promote a profitable form of "reciprocal" business which compromises their integrity and not infrequently leads to portfolio churning with trust accounts: they require brokers who are favored with the institution's security trades to maintain substantial non-interest-paying balances. The money thus obtained rent free is loaned out at 8½ percent or better, with no disclosure that the bank is thus secretly profiting from the securities transactions in its trust department.

We cannot legislate honesty and morality, but we *can* make dishonesty unprofitable. A man caught transgressing should be punished. We could, for example, classify the principal abuses as Class A, Class B, or Class C of-

fenses and provide that a man found guilty of a Class C offense be banned from an investment management association for five years, a Class B offense would carry ten years, while a Class A offender would be banned from professional investment management permanently. Considering that these men collectively hold in their hands the financial security of millions of Americans, we need not hesitate to impose strict standards of business morality upon them.

The majority of investment managers are honest. They voluntarily meet these standards and will have no occasion to be offended by our imposed rules. Do we offend bankers when we require them to be bonded? Does a bank display a lack of confidence in its trust officers when it requires them to go into the vault in pairs? It simply recognizes that it has an enormous responsibility to its customers, and it meets that responsibility appropriately. Have mutual funds a lesser responsibility? As our laws are presently written, they do not spell out all of what fund people must not do. The law assumes that they will recognize dishonest practices and outlaw them. Obviously, that assumption is not enough. The rules should be made crystal clear.

Managing a successful mutual fund is highly profitable. Presumably, the fee earned is for doing a full-time job. In the case of many managers, each of several funds is paying them the same substantial fee for doing that full-time job. If a firm is managing six funds, it is giving one sixth of its time to each fund, but it is collecting pay for doing six full-time jobs. The Securities and Exchange Commission appears to compartment each individual fund and to judge the adequacy of the fee paid by the fund to its managers. It never adds up the total fees being collected by the managers from all of the funds under their control and says: "Hold on, fellows. You're collecting too much, considering the total amount of money you are handling and the total time you are giving to the job." The Commission does exert pressure upon funds to reduce their fees proportionately as their assets grow, but it does not take into account the total of the fees received by the managers from all of the funds in their care. Many funds have management fees that reduce proportionately as the size of the fund increases. To avoid such fee reduction, some managers organize a new sister fund upon which management fees will start from the beginning again at the maximum rate.

When does size become a handicap? My own observation has been that funds with assets of less than $50 million are far more likely to perform outstandingly. Many funds pass that mark and continue to do well. Somewhere in the area of $400 million to $500 million, nearly all funds begin to stumble. Enterprise Fund tried to stave off the inevitable by dividing itself into four parts, with a different portfolio manager for each segment. It wasn't very successful.

Size *is* a handicap. It would seem proper to compensate shareholders in a huge fund for the disadvantage of that size by providing for sharply reduced management fees. There is some compensation now—the ratio of expenses to assets is invariably substantially lower with the giant funds. But even funds with a billion dollars or more of assets disclose a curious dissimilarity in their expense ratios—as the figures below comparing funds of like size show.

Granted that Dreyfus Fund, in the first group, has done an excellent management job, why should its expense ratio be nearly three times that of Massachusetts Investors Trust? The Dreyfus people received $11,873,449 in management fees alone in 1969, plus another $2,956,541 in brokerage commissions, for a total "take" of $14,829,990, while Massachusetts Investors Trust, with comparable assets, paid $3,280,976. A later chap-

| Fund | Assets | Expense Ratio |
| --- | --- | --- |
| Dreyfus Fund | $2,398,200,000 | .55 |
| Investors Mutual | 2,681,100,000 | .29 |
| Investors Stock Fund | 2,221,400,000 | .30 |
| Massachusetts Investors Trust | 2,118,400,000 | .20 |
| Affiliated Fund | 1,595,000,000 | .31 |
| Wellington Fund | 1,421,800,000 | .55 |
| Investment Company of America | 1,065,100,000 | .48 |
| Massachusetts Investors Growth Stock Fund | 1,252,400,000 | .32 |
| United Accumulative Fund | 1,256,000,000 | .39 |
| Fidelity Trend Fund | 1,096,100,000 | .49 |
| Fundamental Investors | 1,166,900,000 | .49 |
| Investors Variable Payment Fund | 1,050,700,000 | .34 |

ter will discuss a frustrated attempt by some of Dreyfus Fund's shareholders to reduce management fees and thus the expense ratio of the fund, which is inordinately high. Investors Mutual that same year paid its sponsor manager $8,179,547. In the second group, why should Wellington Fund's expense ratio be 80 percent higher than that of the larger Affiliated Fund? Wellington is too big and has been around too long (1928) to have an expense ratio of .55. Wellington Fund shareholders in 1969 paid $4,000,166 in management fees. The Wellington management has been paid $31,437,671 for doing a drearily unsatisfactory job over the past seven years. (To illustrate how confused the investment picture has

become, in the disastrous first quarter of 1970, conservative old Wellington went down 1 percent while its supposedly racy growth fund sister, Windsor Fund, went up 3.5 percent. As a disillusioned bridegroom once remarked, "Things ain't what they seemed.") Perhaps management fees should be reduced for continuously unsatisfactory performance.

Since there are incompetents in every field, there are bound to be some in the fund business. The public should be protected against them when so much of its financial security is at stake. Perhaps, therefore, we should rate the performance of all funds carefully and anyone that for three consecutive years finishes in the bottom 5 percent on the list should be required to merge with another fund among the top 10 percent. In other words, if they don't deliver the goods, they should be required to turn the job over to someone else who will perform it well.

In the third group, how does one justify that United Accumulative Fund's expense ratio is 22 percent greater, and Investment Company of America's is 50 percent greater than that of Massachusetts Investors Growth Stock Fund?

Among three funds of approximately the same size in the fourth group, why should Fidelity Trend Fund and Fundamental Investors each display expenses ratios 45 percent higher than that of Investors Variable Payment Fund? Are some fund administrations less efficient than others—or just greedier? Both the Massachusetts Investors funds and those sponsored by Investors Diversified Services deserve commendation for their low expense ratios.

Mutual funds do not come into being through spontaneous combustion or a "big bang." Someone has to organize them and promote them—and it is the sponsor-manager who does it. However, the term "mutual fund" implies that the entity is owned by its shareholders. That means that it should be operated for their benefit, not for the benefit of the managers. Perhaps when fund assets or management fees reach a certain size, the fund should be completely mutualized, with all personnel thereafter being compensated on a salary basis. I am not saying that after all of their effort, investment, and risk in creating the fund, the sponsors should be dumped simply because their creation turned out to be a howling success. I do think, though, that there should be some sort of ceiling on the total dollar amount of management fees. They should not be permitted to take off into the stratosphere.

The idea of management control needs rethinking. A mutual life insurance company does not have a "management company" that controls it, a separate entity whose stock is publicly traded and valued at millions of dollars. Why should a mutual fund be in the position of not owning its own soul? Why can't mutual funds be truly democratic institutions controlled only by their own shareholders? Why not a formula for a fund gradually to buy out its own management company over the years? This would compensate the sponsors for their initiative, their work, and their risk-taking. Perhaps we could arbitrarily set a price/earnings ratio of 20 to 1 and capitalize the management company at twenty times the annual management fee, with a built-in agreement that the fund would buy 5 percent of the management company's stock each year for twenty years. The managers could go right on working for the fund, but on a salary basis.

Changes recently introduced in the New York Stock Exchange commission structure have had the effect of increasing the cost of securities trading for the small investor and decreasing it for the large institutional buyer. Obviously, the bookkeeping costs on a 1,000-share trade are not exactly ten times those on a 100-share trade, and the commissions should not be ten times as great.

The position taken by some of the large mutual funds, though, is difficult to understand. Curiously, John C. Bogle, president of Wellington Fund, opposed the reduction in commissions for large institutional buyers— such as Wellington Fund—on the grounds that the financial health of the brokers processing such trades would be adversely affected by such reductions. While it is true that during the market decline of 1969–1970 many brokerage firms experienced a sharp diminution of income, it is also a fact that they had a field day during the three years prior to the decline. (It is worth noting where their profits went: between 1958 and 1968, a period of sharply rising volume, the dollar amount of salesmen's compensation increased 91 percent, while profit to brokerage firm owners rose only 29 percent.) In any case, I disagree with my good friend Jack Bogle's stand that institutional buyers are not entitled to a discount. The broker does not have to hold the hand of the institutional buyer and answer endless questions as he does with small individual investors.

To reduce the costs of securities trading, some mutual funds have sought direct access to the market through the purchase of a seat on one or more of the stock exchanges. Oddly, other mutual funds have opposed this effort. Howard Stein, president of Dreyfus Fund, has been particularly vocal in his opposition. Remembering that his management company, which has a seat on the New York Stock Exchange, in 1969 enjoyed brokerage fees of $2,956,541 from portfolio transactions for Dreyfus Fund, it all seems clearer.

In this area of management, during most of its lifetime the fund industry practically without exception displayed a proper fiduciary respect for the assets entrusted to it. Its operations were conditioned by its recognition of the fact that its first obligation was not to lose the money entrusted to it. Some funds adopted a more aggressive stance than others. (In an age when "balanced" investment was a standard policy among those charged with handling other people's money, "aggressiveness" consisted of putting all of the assets into blue chip common stocks.) But their approach to investing remained conservatively professional, and at no time did they operate in the spirit of an individual investor sitting in a boardroom playing the market.

Now, however, we have the cult of "performance." To some extent, the blame rests upon the nation's financial journals which have given freely of their space to publicize the exploits of the speculators while ignoring the respectable element among fund managers. In April 1967, *Barron's* ran an adulatory piece about Fred Carr, of Enterprise Fund, which could not have been better if Carr had written it himself. It helped create the hero-worship which sent a tide of new money flooding through the Enterprise doors. Perhaps the financial journals felt that they were simply printing what their subscribers wanted to read. Carr found himself the owner of stock of Shareholders Capital Corporation, Enterprise Fund sponsor's holding company, comfortably valued at more than $50 million. However, he became too busy to concern himself any longer with the day-to-day management of the fund and, in a later chapter, we shall see how it got into serious difficulties. The principals had a falling out, as a result of which Carr resigned, leaving behind thousands of bewildered investors who had invested in either the fund or the management company on the strength of Carr's association with it.

Gerald Tsai, Jr., then portfolio manager of Fidelity Capital Fund in Boston, is a parallel. He achieved an outstanding performance record and became the subject of widespread publicity in the financial press. Rumor had it that the head of the Fidelity group was chafing at the attention given his employee; Fidelity declined to distribute reprints of the laudatory articles. In any case, Tsai electrified the financial world with an announcement that he would resign his post at Fidelity and start his own fund, which he did. The third-of-a-billion dollars paid into his Manhattan Fund by investors remains the largest sum ever invested in any mutual fund during its initial underwriting period. It was a remarkable expression of faith and confidence in one man: Gerry Tsai.

The results were disappointing. The fund's performance was mediocre right from the start. Many investors resented the fact that Tsai's interest in the fund wandered as he concerned himself with the establishment and merchandising of three other funds instead of making Manhattan Fund the investment success that Fidelity Capital had been. The resentment boiled over when Tsai disclosed that he had sold his management company to a huge insurance combine for $35 million. While he continued to be identified with the operation, he ceased to be responsible for the day-to-day investment management of Manhattan Fund. The thousands of shareholders who had invested their money upon the representation that it would be personally managed by Gerry Tsai were left holding the bag while he went seeking greater fortunes elsewhere, carrying with him the multimillion dollar fruits of this exercise in personal hero worship.

The objects of investor hero worship obviously do not regard the loyalty of their fans as something necessarily to be reciprocated, which raises the question: At what point does a successful portfolio manager cease to have an obligation to the investors who have made him wealthy?

Mutual funds were never intended to be devices for playing the market. Implicit in the term "mutual fund" is an implication that the people running it are professionals who seek profits without undue risk. Mutual fund shareholders think that is what they are buying. Increasingly, however, they are turning their money over to men, frequently quite young, who are simply playing the market with it.

Recently, examining the prospectus of a young fund with many millions of dollars of assets, I noted that the oldest man among its officers and directors was twenty-seven years of age. I have nothing against bright young men with fresh, young ideas. However, investment management competence is compounded of more than brightness—it needs experience. Judgment comes with experience, so I am somewhat uneasy when I see vast sums representing the combined financial security of thousands of people riding on the judgment of a young man who was still sucking his thumb at the time of the postwar market decline in 1946. We hear some of our national problems today credited to a too-permissive attitude toward youth. We are being too permissive also with our youthful money managers. The fund industry should return to its earlier policy of entrusting men with the responsibility for managing millions of dollars of other people's money only after they have demonstrated that they are up to the task. Let us stop sending boys to do a man's job.

Mutual fund managements used to consist of investment committees. There was group judgment. If one of the members got a foolish idea, the others undoubtedly knocked it down. It is fashionable now to deprecate the committee form of management, and increasingly the committee has been replaced by a single portfolio manager. In many cases, there are no analysts, there is no research staff.

The job of investing money is far more difficult and complex today than it was ten or twenty years ago. In the circumstances, how do we justify entrusting to one man the responsibility once shared by five men? Traditionally, a successful mutual fund had several men who traveled constantly, investigating investment candidates. They interviewed the presidents, treasurers, sales managers, and research directors of corporations and re-

ported back to the investment committee, which studied the facts thoughtfully and arrived at its decisions. The "New Day" portfolio manager, on the other hand, depends upon the facilities of brokerage firms—described in an article in *The Institutional Investor,* the journal of professional managers, as "outhouse research" carried out by analysts "half of whom can't even read a balance sheet." The portfolio manager has a coterie of broker friends who tip him off to situations, to "deals." He has no time to investigate each investment suggested to him, and so he comes to rely upon brokers and other "finders," many of them pushers of letter stock, whose standing with him depends directly upon the past record of successful deals they have brought to his attention.

The old-time investment committee bought facts. Its brash young successors buy stories. They have no interest in interviewing the knowledgeable principals of corporations. The eventual profitability of their investment does not hinge upon the basic soundness of a company but rather upon the "bigger fool" theory that they will find someone even more gullible than themselves on whom to unload the prize package being offered.

Some interesting observations on the buying of stories from the Wall Street rumor mill were offered by Curran W. Harvey, president of the Rowe Price New Horizons Fund, in a *New York Times* interview. Said Harvey:

> One of the biggest problems with the performance funds is that they buy stories. Let me give you an example of what I mean. A friend of mine went to a hot performance fund to do research. But he quickly learned that checking out a story didn't mean visiting management, etc., to find out if the story was true. What it meant was to find out how many people on the street had heard it because if too many people had acted on the story already, the stock's price would have discounted it. A lot of people have ended up as long-term investors in companies with good stories but lousy fundamentals. There may be bad management, a lousy product or just no substance to the story in the first place. When people lose interest in the story, there may be nothing left. That's a damned expensive way to invest.

In its December 1969 issue, *Fortune* magazine analyzed the gyrations of Parvin/Dohrmann, a onetime hotel kitchen equipment and furnishings company that was manipulated into a big-time conglomerate with holdings of hotels and gambling casinos in Las Vegas and elsewhere. The magazine recounted how Tsai Management Company was suckered into making repeated large purchases of the company's stock for its Manhattan Fund, Fundex, and TMR Appreciation Fund, and how J. M. Hartwell & Co. bought thousands of shares for the mutual funds it managed and for its other client accounts. It was a classic example of supposedly professional investment people buying a story. There was little to support the purchase. A pusher whispered in the ear of a portfolio manager, who bought the story. The best way to make certain that such a purchase turns out well is to get other people to buy, too, thus helping to run the price up. So the portfolio manager told another portfolio manager who also took the bait. This is an example of the follow-the-leader syndrome that has infected part of the fund industry's investment management. When it became obvious that the stock was being manipulated, the Securities and Exchange Commission suspended trading in it. But Nathan Voloshen, friend of Speaker of the House John McCormack, arranged for the president of Parvin/Dohrmann to meet with Commission Chairman Hamer Budge, and within a week the suspension was lifted. Concluded *Fortune:*

> Doubtless everyone who follows this long and still unfinished tale will draw his own moral from it. But one almost irresistible inference concerns the proclivities of the big institutional buyers, which are so ardent for instant performance. When they believe that they are among the first to learn about a company's ambitious and attractive plans, they may buy in—not so much because they have strong convictions that the plans will work out, but because they think others will respond to the spreading news the same way they do.

> Just as disturbing is the irrelevance of actual corporate performance in all this. It doesn't matter very much whether what the fund manager hears is accurate or not—as long as he is right in his assumption about the behavior of the competitive institutions. After all, he figures, he can always sell out before the hard and sometimes disappointing facts about corporate earnings are in.

> When they are caught up in a wave of enthusiasm, the big institutional buyers don't seem to be any wiser than ordinary mortals. If even part of the SEC's narrative is correct, the fund managers ignored some pretty obvious danger signals. Most of the funds mentioned in the SEC's complaint still have large positions in Parvin/Dohrmann and they are now virtually locked in. Some of the funds have huge paper losses, as well as considerable assets that are immobilized. A quick loss, of course, can be considered instant performance, too. But, like the judgment of the portfolio managers, it isn't the kind that some people have been led to expect.

A highly respected investment counselor and fund manager, David L. Babson, has taken note of the trend of fund management. Citing the almost daily disclosures by the S.E.C. of a disturbing increase in conflicts of interest and in illicit, unethical, or unhealthy practices of virtually every kind throughout the securities industry, Babson concluded:

> By far the greatest difference between today and past periods of excess is the degree of participation by institutional investors. Never before has this group speculated on such a huge scale with such vast amounts of money. And because so many professionals have taken the in-and-out, short-term approach, millions of individual investors assume that this is what they should do, too. Future observers may well credit the new type of aggressive mutual funds with getting this tidal wave of speculation under way. In order to sell shares and attract assets to manage, the primary objective of this band of fund plungers, and the brokers allied with them, is to seek "instant performance." To them, the methods used are secondary. A portfolio manager with a dynamic short-term record can become a multi-millionaire in short order. This holds out a powerful temptation for fund executives to take big risks with shareholders' money, a sort of "heads I win, tails you lose" proposition. The advent of this new breed of funds and the extravagant publicity focused on them has been the most unhealthy development in the industry's history. Their mushrooming growth brought about a virtual revolution in the attitudes of fund managers. With the sales emphasis tied to instant results, the short-term trading approach supplanted long-range investment considerations.

The intensity of the competition among funds has put tremendous pressure upon portfolio managers. They are buying new issues, warrants, and investment letter stock. In speculative markets, new issues can double or triple overnight. Individual investors generally find it hard to get such shares—the broker allots them to the favored few who are his best customers. Mutual funds, with their huge volume of brokerage business, are indeed "favored customers." Securities salesmen have been known to suggest to a customer, when they could not obtain for him shares of a popular new issue, that he purchase a mutual fund that had been successful in getting a big block of the stock. It is quite possible for a fund to buy such shares, sell them the very next day for double the price and immediately buy another issue. The underwriters of such issues are glad to take care of the mutual funds that agree to direct substantial brokerage business to them.

The purchase of thinly held issues has been another avenue to profit for some funds. By undertaking a program of regular purchases of 100-share or 200-share lots of such stock, the fund can push the price up. But is the valuation which it places on such stock a valid one? The trouble with being the market-maker in a stock is that if one is called upon to sell it, there is no other market. When a fund has a holding for which no ready market exists, it loses some of its flexibility. In any case, the contrived price inflation creates a false impression of the skill of the managers and deceives prospective purchasers who are led to buy the shares at a price higher than their true value Conversely, shareholders who choose to redeem are paid more than the shares would be worth if the underlying assets had not been manipulated upward in price.

The American Stock Exchange is a gold mine of candidates for such manipulation. That exchange listed 103 speculative securities which it forbade its own members to trade in for their own accounts. Virtually every one of the stocks on the list was held in the portfolio of one or more mutual funds. Some funds held up to 10 percent of the individual issues. This is not investment; it is speculation.

Ralph S. Saul, president of the American Stock Exchange, has called attention to the numerous situations in recent years where rumors surround two companies allegedly involved in merger talks, their market prices climb, and eventually a tender offer results: "It is interesting to speculate how often portfolio managers who hold large blocks of the companies involved are part of the action," he said, "and what kind of roles they play and what their public responsibilities should be." (A tender offer is a public offer by a corporation to buy up outstanding shares of a take-over prospect at a price above the going market.)

University Computing, Volt Technical, and AITS are typical of the stocks that have been successfully manipulated upward. The part that fund portfolio managers played in the schemes to inflate their prices to the extent of many millions of dollars bears investigation.

Nothing so encourages the development of a speculative approach to investment management as the "incentive" or "performance" fee, which directly links the compensation of the managers to the fund's investment performance. Some fund managers can be paid annual fees of as much as 4 percent of fund assets. Of course, such compensation would be paid out of profits, the reasoning being that no one should grumble about paying managers a whopping big fee if they produce whopping big profits.

Such fees are paid in addition to regular management fees. Some, but not all, funds employing this compensation plan have a penalty fee: if the fund displays a poor performance, the managers not only do not qualify for the incentive compensation, they must forfeit a part of their regular fee. The penalty for poor performance is not nearly as great as the incentive for superior results.

Henry Ansbacher Long, astute mutual fund editor of *Trusts and Estates,* has pointed out that the performance fee arrangement suggests that a greater incentive is needed above the normal compensation to obtain better management. As Long observed: "An adviser managing several funds, the contracts of some of which might incorporate incentive fees, would be tempted to favor those mutuals with the more lucrative fee arrangements. Further, the investors in these performance funds might well expect preferential treatment."

The Canadian Committee on Mutual Funds and Investment Contracts, a governmental group, reported in December 1969:

> Performance bonuses [arrangements whereby the mutual fund investment manager benefits from obtaining an above-average rate of return for the fund] cannot be fairly calculated and charged. Therefore, management fees should be required to be calculated as fixed percentages of average total net assets and the percentage should not be affected by performance of the mutual fund.

Our own Senate Banking Committee concluded in July 1969 that a similar prohibition against performance fees "would insulate investment company shareholders from arrangements that give investment managers a direct pecuniary interest in pursuing high risk investment policies."

The S.E.C., however, has gone on record concluding that "sustained investment performance of a company would be an appropriate consideration in evaluating the reasonableness of its adviser's compensation." Whose side is the Commission on?

Another devious practice of fund managers involves "parking." An individual or group bent upon taking over a company via a tender offer will quietly advise several portfolio managers of the take-over plan. The funds will begin a program of accumulation of that company's shares, being assured of a nice profit by going along with the tender offer. For example in the second and third quarters of 1968, Enterprise Fund accumulated 352,800 shares, worth $28 million, in Great American Holding Corporation, a company reportedly with close connections with Fred Carr, Enterprise's portfolio manager. In December of that year, Great American was taken over by Los Angeles-based National General Corporation; Enterprise holdings were now worth $38.6

million. But by the end of 1969, what Enterprise wound up holding was "the bag"—its National General package declined to $17.5 million.

These are not the high standards of investment professionalism which the industry describes so fulsomely in its sales literature. These unhealthy practices are not universal but they are common enough so that the mutual fund buyer can no longer blindly buy any fund.

I have mentioned "unaffiliated persons" in discussing special interest and its disclosure in broker-fund relationships. The Investment Company Act of 1940 specifies that at least 40 percent of the directors of a mutual fund that makes a sales charge must be "unaffiliated persons," that is, individuals who are not otherwise connected with the sponsor, manager, or distributor of the fund. The Act further provides that periodic renewals of the contract with the investment manager, the custodian, and the independent auditors must be approved either by the holders of a majority of the shares or by a majority of the directors, including a majority of the unaffiliated directors. In theory, these directors are the representatives of the public on the board of directors. In actuality, they are invariably the creatures of the sponsor, and it is difficult for them not to be so. They are selected and appointed by the sponsor.

Obviously, sponsors do not approach total strangers and invite them to become directors of a new fund. It is understandable that they first approach close personal friends. They say to them, "Take a comfortable seat," and, like Greyhound, "leave the driving to us." Most unaffiliated directors are not knowledgeable about fund matters; if they were, they would be in the fund business. The people who are supposedly on the board of directors to protect the investing public are actually in no position to protect the public's interest. They are there as window-dressing or simply to fill the quota of unaffiliated directors required by law.

Perhaps the solution might be to create a formal panel of persons knowledgeable on the subject, but with no specific connection in the fund business. From among these, all funds would be required to select their "unaffiliated" directors. This arrangement would ensure that the shareholders were represented by an independent voice on the board. Limiting such directors to a single three-year term would reduce the likelihood of their developing too close a relationship with the sponsor. All such directors should perhaps receive the same rate of compensation, being paid by the panel itself, which in turn would assess the funds on the basis of a percentage of the assets for which the directors were responsible. This would eliminate any competition among the independent directors for choice posts with larger funds. If having 40 percent of a board so constituted might prove burdensome, at the very least every fund might be re-

quired to have at least one such independent director. Unless and until some such system is established, the term "unaffiliated director" will remain meaningless and deceptive.

We have considered the problem of multiple fees accruing to managers who handle several funds. But what of the conflict in interest inherent in such multiple fund management? When an attractive investment opportunity presents itself, to which fund is a multiple-fund manager going to assign it? Large, well-established funds tend to grow larger even when they do not receive a lot of tender, loving care. Most fund shareholders reinvest dividends, and this simple procedure can add millions to an established fund's assets each year. Once a fund has grown to $250 million, the managers have it made: the fund will grow by itself without an outstanding performance record. In this situation, there is a tendency for fund managers to give their newer, smaller funds the cream of the investment opportunities to help them build the performance record so essential to their successful merchandising. This is obviously disadvantageous to the shareholders of the older fund who are paying the same management fee per $1,000 and are equally entitled to share in the goodies. They are already contributing indirectly to the growth of the small fund by the sponsor's lavishing the big fund's brokerage business on investment dealers who are pushing the sale of shares of the small fund. Ideally, each fund should have its own separate management which works to develop good investment opportunities for the fund and does not assign them to a sibling fund.

In another area, a layman investor, Robert M. Neirman of Baltimore, suggested to the House Interstate and Foreign Commerce Subcommittee considering new mutual fund legislation that a fund be required to disclose in its periodic reports to shareholders the purchase and sale price of any securities it has disposed of since the last such report. Commenting upon the suggestion, *New York Times* financial columnist Robert Metz observed:

> When a mutual fund sells shares, it does so in secret to protect the management from any possible criticism for a bad job on the stock in question. There is no requirement that the fund say what price it got for the shares or that it mention the price it paid for the shares. Besides that, the mutual fund does not have to say on what date it bought the shares or identify the date the shares were sold. What's more, when a stock has been acting badly, the mutual fund may sell before the end of the current quarter and avoid the inference that it has been lax in holding the investment—the shares will not, under current reporting rules, show up in the portfolio. If a

mutual fund buys and sells shares within a given quarter and takes a heavy loss in the process, the shareholders will not be aware that the mutual fund owned the shares.

If funds lived up to the accounting requirements— and if the Securities and Exchange Commission enforced such requirements—the information would be partially disclosed. Investment companies are supposed to list by name all portfolio additions or deletions since the last report. However, they are not required to disclose the number of shares or the amount of money involved. Neirman contended that shareholders had a right to decide how good their management was and suggested that fund managers would think twice before dumping depressed stocks primarily for window-dressing purposes.

In reply to Mr. Neirman, counsel to the House Subcommittee stated that the S.E.C. already had the authority to require the funds to supply the information he sought, but Chief Counsel Alan Rosenblat of the Commission's Division of Corporate Regulation disagreed. Section 30 (d) (3) of the Investment Company Act of 1940 provides that funds must disclose their income, but Rosenblat questioned the Commission's authority to require that profits or losses be clearly revealed. Since the Commission seems unsure of itself, it should not be too difficult to amend the 1940 Act to provide for this healthy disclosure.

# Chapter 12

# LETTER STOCK

On December 20, 1968, a bomb exploded within the mutual fund industry.

The force of the blast shattered the industry's proudest record and demolished its most cherished sales argument: guaranteed redeemability. More important, it tore aside a curtain of secrecy that had shrouded two years of spectacular performance by some of the funds, and exposed the gravest shareholder abuse chargeable to mutual funds today.

It incidentally disclosed the incredible ineptitude of a federal regulatory agency, the Securities and Exchange Commission.

Earlier that day the Commission had announced that it was suspending trading in the shares of Omega Equities Corporation, a nondescript over-the-counter real estate firm that yearned to become a conglomerate. Its stock had begun life humbly, but between April and December 1968, undergoing skillful manipulation by a bevy of promoters, it had zoomed from 60 cents to $35.00 per share, despite an operating deficit of $14 million and a current mortgage debt of $3 million.

Later in the same day that the Commission announced the suspension of trading in Omega Equities, the Mates Investment Fund asked for and received permission to suspend redemption of its shares on the grounds that more than 20 percent of its assets consisted of Omega Equities stock, which it could not sell and which could not be valued because of the suspension of trading.

The Omega stock could not be sold because it was "investment letter," or restricted stock. Mates was locked in. That day marked the end of an era in the mutual fund industry.

The very reputable ABC Corporation wants to raise $5 million. If it elects to issue bonds, it must face the fact that this type of financing does not have much appeal to investors right now. In competition with the giants, it probably will have to pay 8 percent or more for the money it borrows.

If it registers $5 million worth of additional stock, its underwriting costs and the legal fees to the "specialist in securities matters," whom it will need to hire to clear the issue with the S.E.C., will total quite a sum. The delay may be deadly. It needs the money now.

The answer is letter stock. The ABC Corporation arranges a "private placement" of a block of its shares subject to the endorsement reprinted below or to an equivalent "letter of investment" from the buyer certifying that the purchase is made for the long term and agreeing that the stock may not be resold publicly for a specified period, generally two or three years.

> Notice is hereby given that this certificate and the shares evidenced hereby have been acquired for investment, and not with a view to, or for resale in connection with, any distribution within the meaning of the Securities Act of 1933, as amended, and may not be transferred until the Company has been furnished with an opinion of counsel, satisfactory to it, to the effect that such transfer will not involve any violation of the Securities Act of 1933, as amended, or other applicable securities laws.

The private placement does not have to be registered with the Securities and Exchange Commission. It is quick and easy. Some such transactions have been consummated in forty-eight hours. If a corporation needs money in a hurry, this is the quickest way to obtain it.

It pays a price for the convenience, though. If its regular shares are currently trading on the market for, say, $10.00, it may sell the letter stock at $7.00 or $8.00 per share. Until two or three years ago, investment letter stock generally sold at a discount of 10 to 15 percent from the market price of the company's regular shares.

In contrast, the XYZ Corporation's situation is quite different. It is one of the hundreds of ventures begun each year that struggle to find and keep a place in what we call our "free enterprise system." A few make it big, the majority fall by the wayside. Its capital nearly exhausted, the XYZ Corporation must raise money somehow. If it attempts to register additional shares with the Securities and Exchange Commission for public sale, the details of its dreary history and unhappy financial condition are required to be spelled out in the prospectus— and no one will buy the stock.

So the XYZ Corporation travels the letter stock route. The price may be high; it may have to sell its shares at a discount of 50 to 60 percent from market. It has no choice, though, and no price is too high for survival. Perhaps the infusion of new money will give it that one last needed shove that will carry it into the big time. Traditionally, the promoters of such companies are optimistic right up until the day the firm's creditors file an involuntary petition in bankruptcy.

The requirement that securities be registered and that their public offering be accompanied by a prospectus disclosing the material facts concerning the true financial condition of the issuer and the proposed application of the proceeds of the sale is intended to protect the public from inadvertently becoming the owner of securities it would not deliberately and knowingly buy.

Letter stock defeats that objective. The XYZ Corporation has sold a block of securities to raise additional capital, but it has not made the disclosures required for registration. The solution had been simple: through a "pusher," contact was made with the Climax Mutual Fund's portfolio manager who agreed to buy a block of unregistered stock at a discount.

Restricted securities are not new. Traditionally, the most significant use of the private placement exemption has been the sale of bonds to insurance companies. In the past decade, too, insurance companies, foundations, and pension funds also have accepted private placements of stock from companies like the ABC Corporation. They knew the company and its principals. They made certain that it was not survival money they were providing, but additional needed financing. It was not a question of risk. If there were a risk element, they would not have gone into it. They bought the shares at a modest discount from the current market price of the existing shares in exchange for a promise not to sell it publicly for a specified period. The restriction did not hamper the insurance company or the pension fund. All their investments were made for the long haul and they probably had no thought of disposing of the stock during the next ten years. Moreover, there was no requirement that they value their holdings from day to day.

Until recent years, most such private placements were made by reputable companies like the ABC Corporation. In connection with its short-term financing, Ling-Temco-Vought issued restricted stock warrants. Talley Industries, Inc., Husky Oil Canada Ltd., Standard Products Company, Transcontinental Investing Corporation, Pioneer Systems, and Unexcelled, Inc., have issued letter stock to the principals of companies or properties they were acquiring. Today, more than $100 billion in restricted securities are outstanding.

Increasingly, the underwriters of so-called "hot issues" are accepting compensation in the form of restricted stock or warrants, opting for the potential capital gain rather than commission income taxable at the regular rate.

Legitimate placements leave everybody happy. The issuer has raised the needed capital quickly, while avoiding the expense and detailed disclosures that would attend a public offering. The purchaser has picked up an investment bargain that outweighs the temporary loss of marketability. Marketability is the last thing an insurance company or pension fund has to worry about. There is no question about the usefulness and propriety of letter stock as a vehicle for legitimate companies to obtain financing. Lately, though, it has come into increasing popularity as a device by which speculative business ventures obtain capital and promoters make a fast buck.

In 1961, some mutual fund managers, puzzled by the nature of letter stock and unsure of its suitability as an investment for mutual funds, approached the Securities and Exchange Commission and asked for guidance. The Commission, with astonishing naïveté, told them that it had no objections to letter stock purchase so long as it did not exceed 15 percent of the assets of a fund. It did not make clear whether it meant 15 percent at cost or 15 per cent at market. The guidance was oral. It refused to put anything in writing.

Recently, the president of the Value Line Development Capital Corporation disclosed the purchase by his company of a block of letter stock at a 90 percent discount from market. What determines this discount of course is the desperation of the issuer and the guillibility of the portfolio manager. What is the investment quality of a company in a position where it is forced to sell a block of its stock for ten cents on the dollar? What kind of an investment manager would *buy* that kind of stock? In the case of Climax Fund's acquisition of the XYZ Corporation's letter stock, it spreads its ownership among its hundred thousand shareholders. If the issuer had registered the stock and distributed it to the public in the customary way through an underwriter, the stock might have been peddled to two or three thousand people at most. As it is, the corporation has succeeded in palming it off on a hundred thousand innocents who had entrusted their money to "professional managers."

The reason they sought out the professional manager in the first place was because they were afraid that if they attempted to invest on their own, some unscrupulous securities salesman might sell them just such a dog as XYZ Corporation.

The Investment Company Act of 1940 specifically prohibits mutual funds from acting as underwriters of securities other than their own shares. Since an underwriter is the channel by which securities pass from an issuer to the public, clearly the mutual fund that buys an issue of letter stock and proceeds to parcel out interests in it among its own shareholders—the public—is acting as an underwriter in contravention of the securities laws.

Mutual funds commonly issue a portfolio breakdown that shows—in a representative $10,000 investment—just how much of the investor's commitment is invested in each security in its portfolio. When such a portfolio illustration is applied to the holdings of a fund owning letter stock, it is abundantly clear that the mutual fund is simply a device by which the investor's assets are channeled into an unregistered security.

How does one distinguish a private placement from a distribution to the public generally? Here, again we have an example of the S.E.C.'s vacuity. A private placement does not have to be restricted to one buyer. At a New York public seminar on restricted securities early in 1970, two attorneys on the panel of "experts" with vast experience in the letter stock field, reported that they had each been identified with placements where more than 125 purchasers were involved. It is ridiculous to claim that any such distribution is not a public offering. The Commission has said that it is not alone the number of purchasers that determines whether or not it is a public offering—it is the number of *offerees*. Add to that the likelihood that for everyone who bought into the "deal," three others declined. That would make 500 persons altogether who were solicited to buy the restricted stock that ended up in the hands of 125 of them. If that isn't a public offering, "then it don't rain in Indianapolis in the summertime!"

If so, why does the Securities and Exchange Commission allow the practice to continue? It holds that the prospectus requirements are intended to protect small, unsophisticated investors, whereas the managers of mutual funds are hardened professionals who require no such protection. In bringing charges against Winfield Growth Fund, discussed in a later chapter, the Commission accused the managers of failing to look carefully into some of the letter stock deals they accepted. If one is to judge by what some of the "professionals" have fallen for in the past two years, one must conclude that some of them, at least, share the layman's need to be handed a prospectus.

The term "go-go fund" is not entirely lacking in appropriateness so far as many of the new breed of funds are concerned. They operate on the golden rule of "Profit at Any Price," and the very hallmark of their operation is their ownership of letter stock.

The S.E.C. case against Omega Equities Corporation illustrates the letter stock evil and especially the inappropriateness of the holding of such securities by mutual funds.

The Securities and Exchange Commission charged that Omega Equities engaged in a "deceptive and manipulative course of conduct" in its attempt to raise new capital with which to finance the purchase of other companies in pursuit of its objective of becoming a conglomerate.

As a part of this scheme, the Commission charged, the company paid several individuals and investment firms a commission of 25 cents per share to find buyers for blocks of unregistered shares of its stock. At 25 cents per share, such finder's fees aggregated more than half a million dollars.

The "pushers" were identified by the Commission as Theodore M. Lakos, who was paid $324,650; Meyerson & Co., which received $29,948; Leonard Cohen and Erwin Bernstein who together earned $10,000; Kleiner, Bell & Co., which was paid $75,000; and John B. Licata & Co., which received $78,125.

The Commission charged that at the time these salesmen and investment firms were engaged in the "underwriting and distribution" of the Omega letter stock, they also traded in the stock for themselves and "recommended and effected" trades for their customers and others at "increasingly higher market prices."

Five mutual funds, including the Mates Investment Fund, purchased collectively 513,000 shares of the stock at an aggregate price of $1,705,500.

Two of the five funds that bought Omega purchased their stock for $3.25 per share. Another paid $3.34 per share. Ocean Technology Fund and the Golden Gate Fund both paid $5.50 per share. While the discount price on the date of the signing of the agreements to purchase was approximately 50 percent of the current market price of the free stock of the company, the subsequent manipulation of the free stock ran its price up with the result that its purchase price on the date the letter stock was actually acquired was approximately 25 percent of the market value of the free stock.

The Commission's files also disclosed that the same John B. Licata & Co. that made a killing pushing the letter stock received a further $76,500 in commissions for placing 306,000 shares of Omega Equities letter stock with the JBL Investment Company at $8.00 per share. A general partner of the JBL Investment Company is John B. Licata. John B. Licata is also the investment manager of the Golden Gate Fund, one of the five that bought the stock. Mr. Licata filed a report with the Commission claiming that no finder's fee was paid to him on the stock he sold to his own fund. How far can some elements in the mutual fund industry stray from the original fiduciary concept of the fund business? How can a firm be both the manager of a fund and a vendor to it?

It is bad enough when Big Board members profit by supplying seasoned listed securities to their funds. If we accept their protestations that their decision to sell a big block of something the fund owns and replace it with a big block of something else is unbiased, they are nevertheless compromised by the big commission they earn in the transaction. The obvious conflict of interest persists. At least, they are dealing in seasoned securities, but when they are paid to fob off a piece of financial junk upon unsuspecting investors, in the absence of applicable standards of morality, effective securities legislation should prohibit their peddling such junk to their own funds.

The five mutual funds, which paid an aggregate of $1,705,500, subsequently revalued the Omega letter stock in their portfolio at more than ten million dollars! This raises the fundamental question of how letter stock should be valued.

A mutual fund is required to value its assets at the close of the New York Stock Exchange each business day and to make a public announcement of what a share is worth. If a buyer has signed an agreement that prevents him from selling a block of shares for two or three years, how does he value those shares? If he can't sell it, how much is it worth?

Accounting firms provide a variety of answers. Some are extreme, holding that an asset has value only if it can be sold; if it can't, it is worth nothing. True, it can acquire a value at some date in the future, but who knows what may happen to a company in the meantime, especially the kind that finds it necessary or desirable to go the letter stock route for financing?

Other accountants contend that letter stock can be valued at its cost price. What if the market for the free stock goes down? Must not the value of the letter stock be reduced? What of the inconsistency in a policy that prevents an increase in the value of letter stock if the market price of the free stock rises but requires revaluation downward if the market price of the free stock falls?

Value Line Special Situations Fund recently bought 74,000 shares of Waitt & Bond at the current market price—but under an investment letter. In the interest of acquiring a reasonable position without "chasing" the stock up, Value Line apparently had been willing to pay the going market price, that is, with no discount. But the stock is financially disabled: it cannot be sold until the two- or three-year period covered by the investment letter has expired and the stock has been registered. In this instance, is the fund entitled to value its financially disabled stock at cost? Advocates of valuation-at-cost really scratched their heads over that one.

Another accounting group holds that letter stock purchased at a discount of, say, 50 percent from market, can always be carried at 50 percent of the current market price. Such advocates might well consider the advantage to be gained by insiders who know in advance the maturity date of a large holding of letter stock—which means a release from discount status and automatic valuation at market. A timely purchase of the fund's shares obviously could prove profitable to persons acting upon such inside information. Curiously, the S.E.C., which has always been sensitive about "insider information," completely overlooks this aspect of fund letter stock holdings.

What about the effect of the maturity of letter stock on the free stock market? If the dumping of freed letter stock on the market depresses the price—a very real danger with thinly capitalized issues (the favorite vehicle for letter stock)—might not insiders, aware of the possibility and the exact date of the intended dumping, unload or sell short free shares in advance of an action that is bound to have an untoward effect upon the free shares?

An important reason why letter stock must be discounted in its valuation is the cost of registration. Part of the arrangement that some funds make with the issuer involves a commitment by the issuer to pay all or part of the registration costs. The commitment is unenforceable, at least without the expenditure of legal fees that may well equal the costs of registration. How can a proper valuation thus be placed on the stock? And what of the cost of a future underwriting if the letter stock is to be disposed of in a public offering? How can the fund arrive at a correct valuation in advance?

Many issuers refuse to pay the costs of registration. Curiously, some of these firms are the very ones who protest that the principal reason for offering letter stock is to get money in a hurry.

On March 6, 1970, flip Lawrence Hurwitz, thirty-year-old president of Sprayregen & Co., a New York brokerage firm that has been one of the principal pushers in the letter stock field, told a New York public seminar: "Our clients sell letter stock for three reasons: speed, speed and speed."

After raising the money in a hurry, they should have no objection to underwriting the costs of registration—unless they cannot afford the disclosure of registration.

Some accountants contend that as the expiry date of the investment letter approaches, an owner can reduce his discount. Thus, if a letter has thirty-six months to run, the stock could be valued at a 36 percent discount from market; if the letter expires in three months, it could be carried at a 3 percent discount. James Flanigan in *The Los Angeles Times* likened such a holding to wine in a cask, increasing in value as it ages.

Actually, the criterion by which letter stock is judged is not whether it is to remain restricted for two, three, or five years. The stock must have been purchased for investment, that is, it is bought to be retained, not for resale at any future date. Technically then, the passage of years does not automatically free the stock for sale. Rather, it establishes a period of time in which conceivably there might have been an untoward change in the circumstances of the buyer, which might make the retention of the restricted securities no longer suitable or feasible. Any purchase made with the intention of resale after a specific period is invalid. The "amortizing" principle of pricing letter stock—reducing the discount at a fixed rate per month over a period of years—obviously indicates an intention of freeing the stock for sale at a specific date in the future, in itself enough to disqualify the purchase as having been properly made without formal registration.

Frederick M. Werblow, a partner in Price, Waterhouse, prominent among accounting firms, disclosed that the firm's survey of valuation methods followed in 1968 by funds owning letter stock revealed that 39 percent of the funds valued the restricted securities at the market for unrestricted stock, 37 percent "at fair market value by the board of directors," 12 percent made no disclosure of how they valued the securities, 9 percent valued them at the same discount from market at which they had bought them, and 3 percent valued them at cost.

At least 39 percent of the surveyed funds with letter stocks deceived their shareholders by valuing at market. Valuation "at fair market value by the board of directors" invariably has meant overvaluation, and therefore another 37 percent most likely deceived their shareholders. Of all the funds owning letter stocks, then, at least 75 percent overvalued them—a damning record of breach of fiduciary trust. Werblow concluded: "Maybe letter stock doesn't belong in the portfolio of an open-end investment company."

An accountant is supposed to confirm the financial facts shown by a balance sheet. He counts the shares of stock. He counts the cash. If a client claims to have $1 million in assets, the accountant certifies that he has checked the facts and confirms that his client does have the million dollars.

Dozens of accounting firms have certified the financial statements of funds owning letter stock. They have seen stock purchased at $5.00 per share valued the next day at $10.00 per share. They have counted at market value shares of restricted stock they knew to be financially disabled. They were, alas, among the greatest names in accounting in America, and by not taking a stand, they prostituted their professional honor and integrity.

Their actions generally, with respect to some mutual fund financial statements, have been no less reprehensible than that of one of their number—Lybrand, Ross Bros. & Montgomery—in the case of Mill Factors (not a fund). *The New York Times* reported that the big C.P.A. firm for years certified Mill Factors as being in good financial condition when in fact it was insolvent. In the light of this a mutual fund purchaser might be justified in viewing with distrust a fund whose financial statement was certified by that firm.

Defending his and other accounting firms against the charge that they had failed in their trust when they certified the financial statements of such funds without first making an effort to establish that the value placed upon the security was reasonable, Werblow denied that certified public accounting firms have any obligation to look into the valuations.

But of what real value is a "certified" statement if no independent third party has confirmed that the claimed assets do in fact exist?

Valuation abuses are greater even than they appear because of the application of the doctrine of fungibility, which holds that the presence of tainted securities prejudices the value of like securities which are otherwise untainted. Many funds have held both free and restricted securities of the same company. Accordingly, if a fund holds the free securities of a corporation and thereafter acquires through private placement a block of restricted stock of the same class, the free securities must thereafter be valued at the same price as the restricted securities. Conversely, if a fund acquires a block of restricted securities, and then begins a program of market purchases of the free stock of the same company (quite possibly as part of a scheme to run up the price of the free stock to justify increasing the valuation of its restricted holdings), it must value all such free stock so acquired at exactly the same price as it values the restricted stock.

Many funds do have such dual holdings, and not a single one of them has observed the fungibility doctrine in their valuation. The Securities and Exchange Commission, which as long as twenty years ago adopted the fungibility rule, has done nothing whatever to enforce it with respect to these funds. Indeed, the Commission's position on fungibility wavers so that it has become the subject of jokes. At a public seminar, when the general counsel of the Commission's Division of Corporation Finance was asked what is the present rule of fungibility, he replied: "I can't tell you. I left Washington yesterday. I can tell you what it was yesterday, but I can't tell you what it is today."

Anything about which so much question exists has no place among the investments of a mutual fund.

An S.E.C. regulation requires that securities for which market quotes are available shall be carried at the latest quoted market price, while any for which no quotes are available shall be carried "at fair market value as determined in good faith by the board of directors."

While mutual fund shares must be valued daily, the board of directors of a fund does not meet daily. In actual practice, it is the portfolio manager who is responsible for the daily valuation of the restricted holdings for which no market quotes are available.

There appears to be a substantial divergence between what fund managers do and what they *say* they do. For example, Arnold Bernhard of the Value Line funds issued a bulletin "for dealer distribution only" in which he stated:

> Our funds do buy restricted securities from time to time below the market. In this way, our funds are able to buy large blocks without driving prices up. They buy these blocks with investment letters at substantial discounts from market. Each restricted security in the Value Line Funds is carried at the same discount from market value as existed at the time of its purchase. For instance, if a restricted security was bought 40% below market, our policy is to value it daily at 40% below current market until such time as it has been registered or has otherwise ceased to be restricted. If there is no public market for the security at all (a rare occurrence), the fund values the security at cost until circumstances clearly dictate otherwise.

We will not labor Mr. Bernhard's disclosure that his mutual funds, which are required by law to make an accurate valuation of their holdings at the close of each business day, manage somehow to justify an occasional purchase of a security for which there is no public market at all.

Let us instead examine the financial reports of Mr. Bernhard's Value Line Special Situations Fund and see at what percentage of market he carried certain restricted securities. (The cost price of these securities is not available, and I cannot therefore determine the discount from market at which the fund purchased them.) Bearing in mind Mr. Bernhard's statement that "each restricted security is carried at the same discount from market value as existed at the time of its purchase," consider the following:

The fund's holdings of All Tech Industries, Inc. was carried at 90.6 percent of market in the fund's December 31, 1967, report, at 87 percent of market in the June 30, 1968, report, and at 89 percent of market in the September 30, 1968, report.

A holding of 100,000 shares of General Gilbert Corporation was carried at 80.4 percent of market in the fund's December 31, 1967, report, at 78.2 percent of market in the June 30, 1968, report, and at 86.8 percent of market in the September 30, 1968, report.

Dero Research and Development Corporation was carried at 87.9 percent of market in the December 31, 1967, report and at 91.7 percent of market in the June 30, 1968, report.

Pacific Plantronics, Inc., was shown at 99.3 percent of market in the December 31, 1967, report. It did not show up at all in the June 30, 1968, report but was back in the September 30, 1968, report at 101.4 percent of market!

Radiation Dynamics, Inc., was carried at 98.8 percent of market on December 31, 1967, at 85 percent of market on June 30, 1968, and at only 79.3 percent of market on September 30, 1968.

Ormont Drug & Chemical Ltd. showed up at 64.7 percent of market on December 31, 1967, at 60 percent of market on June 30, 1968, and at 61 percent of market on September 30, 1968. Value Line paid $625,000 for this, but promptly carried it at $1.1 million—instant performance.

Mauchly Associates, Inc. was carried at 88.8 percent of market on December 31, 1967, at 85 percent of market on June 30, 1968, and at only 81.5 percent of market on September 30, 1968.

The standby of letter funds, University Computing Company, was carried in the June 30, 1968, report at 90 percent of market but only three months later, on September 30, 1968, it had climbed to a valuation of 98.5 percent of market.

How much credence should we place in the statement of a mutual fund manager that he is valuing his letter stocks at the same discount from market at which he purchased them?

What shall we say of the valuation of a stock at 98.8 percent of market in December, at 85 percent of market the following June, and at 79.3 percent of market three months later in September? Is there not the impression of an investment manager frightened by his own brashness in valuing restricted stock practically at market and deciding that he had better take advantage of the rising market to cut back his valuation percentage in succeeding periods?

And what shall we say of a fund manager who values letter stock at 101.4 percent of the market price of the free stock? Unfortunately, it is not a rare occurrence.

In June 1970, the S.E.C. charged that Arnold Bernhard had accepted cash fees from the sale of unregistered securities to his Special Situations Fund. As of this writing, Mr. Bernhard has not responded.

Any fund management obviously profits from overvaluation in the course of making its "good faith" determination of the market value of its restricted securities. Management fees are always calculated as a percentage of the fund assets. If a billion dollar fund values restricted stocks at $100 million which should properly have been valued at $60 million, and its management fee is one half of 1 percent per annum, it receives an overpayment of $200,000 in management fees that year.

Overvaluation may benefit a redeeming shareholder: the higher a stock is valued, the more a redeeming shareholder will get for his shares. But it disadvantages the shareholders remaining in the fund, and though individual losses may be small, the collective harvest to the investment manager can be very substantial.

Inflating the value of a fund's letter stock holdings obviously improves the fund's record in the performance derby, which is the basis for attracting new investors. The display of a superior record inevitably attracts a flow of new money—on which managers build their fees.

Obviously, there is a conflict of interest. Arbitrary valuations of letter stock holdings can produce widely differing results in comparative performance records. On June 30, 1968, the market price for one particular stock was 110 bid, 120 asked. Enterprise Fund owned shares in the company and valued them at $100.53 per share. Winfield Growth Fund owned identical letter stock in the same company but its June 30, 1968, valuation was $108 per share.

When the assets of a fund may be declining in value, reflecting a general market decline, the simple device of reducing the discount it carries its letter stock at can manipulate an apparent increase in the fund's net asset value per share. Will it not mistakenly encourage people to turn to it as a refuge from a declining market?

Actually, the designated value does not depend on the discount or on the current market value. It depends on the gall of the portfolio manager making the valuation.

The impact of letter stock overvaluation upon total fund performance can be demonstrated best by citing the recent example of a fund with $55 million in unrestricted shares. During the year reported, this part of the portfolio appreciated to $86 million. By contrast, the same fund had $1,686,000 in restricted shares on January 1, which by year-end had grown to $17,446,000 in reported value!

A second mutual fund with $144 million in unrestricted securities reported in the same period that this portion of its portfolio had grown to $191 million in value. Its restricted holdings, valued at $9.3 million at the beginning of the year, at year-end were up-valued to $19.3 million!

Where would these funds be in the performance derby without their letter stock and their concurrent juggling of the books?

Small, thinly capitalized companies are especially susceptible to such manipulation. Giffen Industries is one example. Prior to a recent public offering, they had well over 2.2 million of their 2.8 million shares in letter stock. How easy it would be to manipulate the free stock upward, increase the valuation and management fees, and create an illusion of spectacular management ability, which in turn would bring new investors into the fold, further enhancing management fees.

Documented instances show how fund managers who also operated investment counsel accounts used the assets in those private accounts to trade up the price of the free stock of companies whose letter stock they had bought for their fund.

If the Securities and Exchange Commission does not know that all this is going on, it is incredibly incompetent. If it does know, and is doing nothing to protect the investing public, it is violating its trust.

In a scholarly dissertation on "Mutual Funds, Letter Stock and Instant Appreciation," Edward T. O'Donnell noted that few, if any, mutual funds made adequate disclosure in their prospectuses of their intention to buy letter stock. Said he:

> This isn't just an instance in which a few unwary souls suffer because they don't pay attention to what is spelled out in the prospectus. If the prospectus is the only guide, few but Wall Street professionals are likely to be alerted to the distinction between "instant appreciation" and the sort of growth the investor normally hopes for—that is, a non-recurring gain from a discount purchase, the proportionate effect of which will become more difficult to duplicate once the fund grows, as opposed to appreciation in value of fully marketable securities which have been chosen by management for their investment value.

> For example, the only warning which Enterprise Fund gives is a "2" after some of its investments and an explanatory note which says, cryptically enough, "private placement."

> It seems doubtful that the ordinary citizen approached by a salesman would know what a private placement was, even if he chanced to read the footnote, let alone appreciate the possible significance in this context.

> The securities designated in the Enterprise Fund prospectus as privately placed have a total unrealized appreciation of $16,631,857, a considerable amount when contrasted to the net realized gain on investment for the preceding year [1967] of $19,660,402 and the total increase in unrealized appreciation on all securities in the same period of $52,883,846. The latter gave the fund its spectacular growth record in 1967.

But the only indication to the reader that almost one-third of the gain claimed could not be measured objectively but instead existed in the subjective "fair judgment" of the fund's management (which stood to gain by exaggeration) is a footnote saying "private placements have been valued at fair value as determined by the Board of Directors of the fund." The fact that Enterprise is said to have reached the billion dollar mark this year suggests that the possibility that the public may not understand what it is buying deserves the Commission's close attention.

Section 1 of the Investment Company Act of 1940 states that the public interest is:

> . . . adversely affected (1) when investors purchase, pay for, exchange . . . sell or surrender securities issued by investment companies without adequate, accurate and explicit information, fairly represented, asserting the character of such securities and the circumstances, policies and financial responsibility of such companies in their management [and] (2) . . . where investment companies are organized, operated, managed . . . [or] where their portfolio securities are selected, in the interest of the directors, officers, investment advisers . . . rather than in the interest of all classes of such companies' security holders.

Has the policy of investing in letter stock been *accurately* and *explicitly* stated in the prospectuses distributed by funds employing that policy? It has not. They have deliberately omitted or failed to state that the fund would invest in restricted securities. More specifically, they have failed to note the following special factors which should be considered by prospective investors in the fund:

1. Fund purchasers of securities having no public market face the problem of eventually attempting to sell the securities where no public market exists.
2. Investment in restricted securities presents the following risk factors, which do not usually affect diversified investment companies:

  (a) The investment company will not be able to sell its restricted securities without first registering them under the Securities Act of 1933.
  (b) To realize the benefit from the difference between the purchase price of restricted securities and the market price of freely marketable securities of the same class, such restricted securities must be sold to the public after registration under the Securities Act of 1933.
  (c) The process of preparing a registration statement for restricted securities and having it become effective under the Securities Act of 1933 may involve a considerable period of time.
  (d) A considerable period of time may elapse between the time a decision is made to sell the restricted securities and the time when the sale may actually be made.
  (e) The fund may be unable to sell restricted securities to the public when it wishes to do so because registration under the Securities Act of 1933 may not have become effective.
  (f) The decision to sell the restricted securities may be based on factors other than strictly investment considerations and the fund may be precluded from selling its securities at the most opportune time.
  (g) The fund is likely to incur higher costs in the sale of restricted securities than would be incurred if such securities had been readily marketable.
  (h) The sale of restricted securities usually will require the services of an underwriter. As a result, in most cases the fund will receive from the sale of restricted securities a net price below the market price of unrestricted securities in the same class.
  (i) Investment in restricted securities involves greater risk than investment in other securities.
  (j) No known and accepted formula for valuing restricted securities exists, and the process of valuation presents so many variables as to make it impossible for a fund to make such accurate determination of its per share net asset value as required by the provisions of the Investment Company Act of 1940.

All of the above facts are material, and their statement in the fund prospectuses is necessary in order to make the fund's description of its policies not misleading.

As Edward O'Donnell noted in the case of Enterprise Fund, most funds have simply placed an unobtrusive asterisk after items of letter stock in their prospectuses and financial reports, keyed to a footnote which merely mentions "private placement." Others have buried away in a long list of "fundamental policies" set forth in the prospectus only the barest mention of the fact that they would not invest more than 15 percent of their assets in securities that were restricted for resale.

Obviously, there has not been adequate disclosure. The front of every prospectus bears a legend that the Securities and Exchange Commission has not passed upon the accuracy or adequacy of the prospectus. In fact, the Commission will not allow a fund's registration to become effective until it has passed upon the "adequacy" of every word in it. The funds' failure to disclose may therefore properly be laid at the door of the Commission.

In an appearance last year before the House Interstate and Foreign Commerce Committee, S.E.C. Chairman Budge was asked what the S.E.C. required with respect to the disclosure of letter stock purchases by the funds. The Chairman called upon an aid, Solomon Freedman, Director of the Commission's Division of Corporate Regulation, which supervises the operation of mutual funds, to supply the answer. In tortured syntax, Mr. Freedman replied: "We have said that in any presentation of the portfolio of an investment company, each security held in the portfolio that is restricted must be identified by some kind of symbol, and then attach a footnote which, among other things, would state how the directors of the fund have valued that security and what factors the board took into consideration."

I have before me the November 30, 1969, annual report of the $170 million Supervised Investors Growth Fund, Inc. Its list of investment holdings contains absolutely no indication that any of its assets are in letter stock or are otherwise restricted for resale. Five pages later, at the very end of a section headed "Supplementary Information," is a statement that "eleven securities included in the statement of investments at an aggregate market value of $15,847,650, as determined by the Board of Directors of the Fund, may require registration under the Securities Act of 1933 in order to effect sale in the ordinary course of business."

There are no "symbols," no indication whatever of *which* holdings are restricted, nor does the footnote disclose "how the directors of the fund have valued that security and what factors the board took into consideration."

How could the Securities and Exchange Commission approve an annual report to shareholders that does not identify any of its letter stock holdings? Examining Supervised Investors' holdings of Ford Motor Company of Canada or Connecticut General Insurance Corporation and noting its valuation of those shares, I can check the market prices at the close on November 30, 1969, and easily confirm their valuation of the stock. But if I want to check their letter stock holdings to see at what discount, if any, they have been valued, I must check their entire portfolio against the November 30 closing prices and by elimination identify the letter stock. More than 9 percent of Supervised Investors' assets are invested in securities for which no public market exists, but they will not disclose which stocks they are. The report states that such securities "may require registration." Don't they know whether or not

registration will be required? Of course they do, but they are afraid to state that registration *will* be required. It is hardly likely that the S.E.C. would issue a no-action letter to a mutual fund. If the S.E.C. does not act responsibly on such statements, maybe the Federal Trade Commission could be urged to move under the "truth in packaging" legislation! Supervised Investors is part of a group that collectively involves nearly a billion dollars of the public's money. The public is entitled to a report that clearly discloses what is being done with the money.

The 1969 annual report of Oppenheimer Fund, Inc., is not much of an improvement. Scattered here and there through their list of securities in such manner as to make them difficult to find are tiny asterisks. At the end of the list, in equally tiny type, appears this footnote: "These securities were acquired under investment letters with certain restrictions on transfer or resale and are valued by the Board of Directors of the Fund." Does this disclose, as Mr. Freedman specified, "how the directors of the Fund have valued that security and what factors the board took into consideration?"

Is it not clear that what the Commission requires and what it *says* it requires are quite different things, and that the testimony of this top regulatory official described Commisson policies that are more apparent than real?

The Investment Companies Institute, a fund-sponsors' group and the nearest thing to an industry trade association, in *The Money Managers,* their competent if somewhat dull promotional book, state in part:

> What determines the price of a mutual fund share? The answer is the value of the fund's portfolio. As the fund receives money from its shareholders, it buys the securities of other corporations for its portfolio. At the close of business each day, the typical fund calculates *the exact value* of each of the securities in its portfolio. Adding all this plus other assets (cash, etc.)—minus liabilities, of course—gives the fund the aggregate worth of its holdings, called its "net asset value." This figure is then divided by the number of shares of the fund held by its own stockholders. The result is the net asset value per share. [Italics added.]

We know that this is not so because the nature of letter stocks precludes a determination of their "exact value." And so does the S.E.C. but they do nothing about it.

In the case of most of the funds that own letter stock, the board of directors has absolutely nothing to do with the valuation of such securities and the representation in the prospectus and in the periodic financial statements that the valuation is determined "in good faith by the board of directors" is a complete and utter fraud.

When I instituted a shareholders' derivative suit against one fund for improprieties in the purchase and valuation of letter stock, the suit also named the directors. I did not discover until three days after filing the suit that one of the directors involved was a university chancellor with whom I had lunched one week earlier. When I telephoned him to apologize for the trouble I was causing him, he explained that at no time had he ever been called upon to value anything, "in good faith" or otherwise.

When the Mates Investment Fund redemptions were suspended, it was of great concern to the rest of the industry, but the Investment Companies Institute held no meetings of its officers or directors to discuss the situation and took no public notice of it. It was a time when the public needed to be reassured that Mates was an exception and that suspension was not likely to recur. In the face of this threat to the public's faith in the guaranteed redeemability which is one of the industry's key sales arguments, the Institute stood mute. Few industries are so poorly organized or so ineffectively represented.

In the meantime, public criticism of the letter stock racket has mounted, both within and without the industry. George Pratt, president of Diebold Technology Venture Fund, observed that "one of the biggest reasons for issuing letter stock is to cover up bad management. Some of the deals floating around today are obscene."

Oscar Lasdon, senior editor of *The Bankers Magazine* and associate editor of the *Banking Law Journal,* editorialized:

> Letter stock purchases do not conform with the fundamental precept of the Securities Act of 1933. The registration requirement . . . was designed to protect the public, particularly the small rank-and-file shareholder. Today, investment companies . . . bypass the registration requirements of the Act via the letter route. Can one contend that the spirit of the 1933 Act is not being seriously negated?
>
> The SEC should be prepared to remedy the situation by outlawing further open-end purchases of letter stock.

John M. Hartwell, whose firm manages the Hartwell-Campbell Fund and the Hartwell & Campbell Leverage Fund, became disenchanted with letter stock, saying: "We have some letter stock but so far we have never made any money on it. Usually it gets registered much later than you think. One company promised to get us out in six months and it was closer to a year, and another said one year and it turned out to be two years. All that for the sake of a 25% discount. It's not worthwhile to be locked up that way."

*The Wall Street Journal* reported: "Getting rid of letter stock can be a frustrating—and often hopeless—struggle.

" 'No more letter stock for us,' says Ramsey Joslin, treasurer of National Distillers & Chemical Corporation. When Mr. Joslin took over management of the company's pension fund a year ago, he inherited an assortment of unregistered securities—in this case, bonds and warrants purchased with an investment letter rather than stocks. 'We've been showing the stuff around for more than a year for resale on a letter basis, but we can't get rid of it,' Mr. Joslin complains."

Continued the *Journal:* "One investor, a professional investment adviser, tells of buying $250,000 of letter stock at a 15% discount from the American Stock Exchange price. Fifteen months later, with the company doing well and the stock up, the investor needed cash. He went back to the investment banker who had found him the stock to ask him to locate a buyer.

" 'We tried for three months with no success,' he relates. 'Finally, we rounded up the other people who had bought the letter stock and persuaded the company to register it. The registration process has dragged on for another five months, and I still can't sell. The stock is down now, and when it's finally registered, who knows where the price will be.' "

Financial columnist Sylvia Porter counseled readers to beware of mutual funds which purchased "highly speculative—and to a great extent—unmarketable securities."

In February 1969, impressed with the management approach and investment performance of Gibraltar Growth Fund, and finding no mention whatever of letter stock in the sections on investment policy and restrictions in the prospectus, I telephoned David Ehlers, its president, to ask about its policy with respect to restricted securities. Mr. Ehlers explained that the fund held only one such stock, Standard-Pacific Corporation, that he was personally acquainted with the principals of that company and knew it to be a sound purchase. However, the furor engendered by the Mates mess had led his management group to make a careful reappraisal of the whole question of letter stock and it had been decided that they would make no more such purchases.

I decided that before proceeding further, it would be well to get Ehlers' assurances in writing so I wrote him asking him to confirm the statements he had made on the telephone. On March 31, 1969, I received a reply from Phillip D. Anderson, vice-president and general counsel of Gibraltar Growth Fund, acknowledging my letter and saying: "In February 1969 we sent a letter to our shareholders concerning our Investment Letter stock. I believe that this letter is self-explanatory in answer to your inquiry."

The letter to shareholders was to the point. It acknowledged the recent "substantial publicity" in the financial press given to the purchase of investment letter stock by mutual funds and also disclosed that Gibraltar had received inquiries from some of its shareholders "concerning our policy on this type of security." It explained the nature of letter stock and noted that it was generally purchased at a considerable discount from the market price of registered shares. Observing that generally provision was made for registration with the S.E.C. at a specified future date, it acknowledged that prior to such registration, marketability was limited. It then continued that "Gibraltar Growth Fund holds only one block of 'letter' stock" and explained that it was purchased at an "approximately 30% discount from the market value, that it was being carried on their books at 30 percent discount, and would continue to be so valued until the stock became fully registered. As a final assurance to shareholders, the letter then stated: *"We have no present intention of purchasing 'letter' stock in the future."* [Italics added.]

On the strength of the fund's letter to its shareholders and my telephone conversation with Ehlers, I made substantial personal investments in the fund and directed large amounts of client funds to it.

In the circumstances, you can imagine my surprise when the fund's 1969 annual report disclosed that it had made another purchase of letter stock, this one being three times the size of the first one. I immediately called them for an explanation of the management's deliberate variation of its investment policy. In reply, they asserted that (a) they had not said "positively," (b) they had concluded that letter stock was a suitable investment for an open-end fund, and (c) they were counting on the Wheat Report to make an honest woman out of the fund. They concluded by inviting me to meet with their directors to explain my views. Meeting to exchange views with someone who tells you one thing and then does the opposite is an exercise in futility, as Neville Chamberlain once discovered. I filed a vigorous protest with the Securities and Exchange Commission which, from all I can learn, accorded it its usual decent burial. I was left to pursue the matter on my own, which I am doing.

Gibraltar has other troubles. Shareholders have filed suit, not yet heard, charging that the fund sold 3,378,621 shares with a prospectus containing financial information more than sixteen months old, in violation of Section 5 of the Securities Act of 1933. If this is true, purchasers of such shares (those people who bought Gibraltar between October 6, 1968, and March 28, 1969) are entitled to demand their money back with interest. In the sharply declining market, the fund's liability could be spectacular. Gibraltar shareholders who disagree with the fund's letter stock practices may wish to join the lawsuit.

Despite the obvious impropriety of letter stock ownership, American mutual funds now hold $3.2 billion in letter stock or other restricted securities, most of which is being mishandled by their managers. But the greatest blame must lie with the Securities and Exchange Commission. Its incomprehensible action in 1961, giving mutual funds permission to invest in securities which could not be sold or properly valued must rank as the greatest goof in the history of securities regulation in America.

After studying the Mates mess and the disclosures of widespread improper purchase and valuation of letter stock, the Commission announced in August 1969 that within two weeks it would issue a new pronouncement on the subject of fund purchase of letter stock. The respectable element in the mutual fund industry breathed a sigh of relief. At last, the Commission was going to do its job and "ban the bomb," the financial bomb called letter stock.

Nationally syndicated financial columnist Bill Doyle reported:

> The days are dwindling down to a precious few for those go-go mutual funds who have engaged in the highly questionable practice of dealing in restricted stocks. At long last, the Securities and Exchange Commission has set a sort of deadline for speaking its mind on the controversial subject.
>
> Holdings of restricted stocks by mutual funds can cause a host of problems which are expected to be spelled out when the SEC makes its long-awaited statement on the subject. Basically, the Commission has two courses of action. It can insist that a fund holding restricted stock value it at the same discount from free stock that existed when the deal was made. Or the agency can ban all future purchases of restricted stocks by mutual funds.

Alas, the mountain labored and brought forth a mouse. After two months of stalling, the Commission spoke, not with the thunderous roar which the financial community had expected but in a piping squeak. From now on, it said, funds must not put more than 10 percent of their assets into letter stock, and the stock had to be valued "in good faith."

In the face of this sorry display of regulatory namby-pambyism, Commission Chairman Hamer H. Budge appeared before the House Committee on Interstate and Foreign Commerce two months later and, when asked about letter stock, testified: "Speaking for myself only, it just does not seem to me to be consistent with the operation of an open-end mutual fund, which supposedly guarantees that it will at any moment redeem the shares which it has sold, that it have in its portfolio securities which are not liquid."

Of interest is that he was "speaking for myself only." But had he not been called in his official capacity as Chairman of the Securities and Exchange Commission? Privately, it was his opinion that mutual funds should not own letter stock—officially he did not have an opinion.

It seems that Chairman Budge has one opinion while private citizen Budge has another. Does this suggest that the members of the Commission cannot agree upon a policy? Has Chairman Budge simply been outvoted? On March 6, 1970, former Chairman Manuel Cohen addressed a seminar on the subject of restricted securities. Asked if he considered letter stock a suitable investment for an open-end mutual fund, he replied in the affirmative. Are the Cohen holdovers still running the Commission? Is it not embarrassing to see the present chairman of this important regulatory agency placed in the humiliating position of having to qualify his statement as being his private opinion and not that of the Commission he heads?

The day after the Commission's announcement of the 10 percent restriction on letter stock, the New York brokerage firm of Gregory & Sons was suspended by the New York and the American Stock exchanges on the grounds that the firm had improperly valued its assets. Newspaper accounts disclosed that the firm was holding huge amounts of restricted stock. Under its Rule 325:15, the New York Stock Exchange will not allow a member to include in its assets any amount representing the value of letter stock it owns. Unlike the S.E.C., the Exchange recognizes the serious disability under which such stock exists. It knows that there is no reasonable and consistent formula under which such stock may properly be valued. It therefore insists that no value be assigned to it.

The "Wheat Report," prepared in 1969 by a small group of S.E.C. personnel working under the general supervision of Commissioner Francis Wheat, who has since resigned, contains an assortment of proposals to alter the securities laws. With respect to letter stock, it proposes that all restrictions on its sale be removed after it had been held for one year, good news to many fringe operators who shudder at the thought of registering their offering and making a public disclosure of their operations. Now, all they need do is find someone who will put up the money for one year, much as a bank might make a construction loan to a building contractor. At the end of the year, the private placement will become "free" and they can palm it off on the suckers without having to show them a prospectus. No one will register any securities any more when they can "park" their dubious package somewhere for a year and have it become public without registration. No wonder Wheat resigned!

Restricted securities are all right for insurance companies or pension funds that are investing for the long haul. These groups have no obligation to their participants to maintain liquidity and have no occasion to arrive at day-to-day valuations of their assets which form the basis upon which participants enter or leave the fund. A mutual fund, however, has no business owning letter stock.

While many large funds have refused to put restricted securities into their portfolios, here are the facts concerning the stockholdings of certain large growth funds:

| Fund | as of | Restricted Securities Held |
|---|---|---|
| American Express Capital Fund | 5/31/69 | 11 |
| American Investors Fund | 12/31/69 | 5 |
| Colonial Equities Fund | 3/31/70 | 4 |
| Competitive Capital Fund | 12/31/68 | 2 |
| Energy Fund | 12/31/69 | 4 |
| Enterprise Fund | 12/31/69 | 18 |
| Fidelity Capital Fund | 2/28/70 | 1 |
| Fidelity Trend Fund | 12/31/69 | 5 |
| Fletcher Capital Fund | 12/31/69 | 3 |
| Fund of America | 2/28/70 | 6 |
| Investors Variable Payment Fund | 11/30/69 | 20 |
| Keystone S-4 | 11/30/69 | 4 |
| Manhattan Fund | 12/31/69 | 14 |
| Massachusetts Investors Growth Fund | 2/28/70 | 2 |
| Oppenheimer Fund | 3/31/70 | 3 |
| Rowe Price New Horizons Fund | 3/31/70 | 1 |
| Salem Fund | 2/28/70 | 2 |
| Scudder Special Fund | 3/31/70 | 6 |
| Security Equity Fund | 3/31/70 | 1 |
| Supervised Investors Growth Fund | 11/30/69 | 11 |
| Technology Fund | 10/30/69 | 7 |
| Value Line Special Situations Fund | 12/31/69 | 49 |
| Winfield Fund | 12/31/69 | 9 |

Winfield's holdings exceed the limitations imposed by the S.E.C.'s "guidelines"; American Express Capital Fund, Manhattan Fund, and Supervised Investors Growth Fund are all close to the limit.

# Chapter 13

# CONVERTIBLES

This is the Age of Aquarius.

It is also the age of convertibles, securities that may be exchanged upon demand for the common stock of the issuer.

In its most popular form, the convertible security is a debenture, which was discussed earlier. Traditionally, debentures were issued by corporations that already had bonds outstanding but whose credit was so good that lenders did not require of them that they mortgage their physical plant when they sought to borrow more money.

Individual investors have not altered materially their thinking with respect to debentures, but institutional investors have gone on a debenture binge and some of the deals they make are pretty appalling. What has given great impetus to the peddling of debentures is the introduction of a convertibility clause into this type of security. Such a clause gives the purchaser the right to exchange his $1,000 debenture for, say, 100 shares of the common stock of the PDQ Corporation, which has issued the debenture. This "sweetener" has made debenture buying a whole new ball game.

Assume that at the time you buy the PDQ debenture, the company's stock is selling for $10.00 per share. If you wish, you can immediately convert the $1,000 loan just made to the corporation into an equity holding of 100 shares, which happen also to be worth $1,000.

But why should you convert it? Knowing that it is convertible to the 100 shares, you will always value it at 100 times whatever the stock is selling for. If the stock goes up to $30.00 per share, you will consider your piece of paper worth $3,000, whether you actually convert it or not. On the other hand, if the bottom falls out of the market for the company's common stock and it becomes worth only $5.00 per share, you will simply forget the stock and value the piece of paper as evidence of a $1,000 loan made to the company.

Let us assume that you are one of the "New Day" portfolio managers of a zippy young mutual fund hotly contesting for a top spot in the performance derby. A beady-eyed character sidles into your domain and, with the manner of someone about to sell you some dirty French postcards, explains that he has something real good in the form of a debenture issued by Florence Nightingale Nursing Homes, Ltd., a tidy little operation that is expanding the financial frontiers of Medicare in Dogpatch, Arkansas. It is a profitable business, he explains, and the promoters intend to keep it that way. The company would like to raise some money but it does not want to put out additional stock and share the control with a lot of total strangers who think only of money and who do not share the promoters' dreams of making it possible for every American over the age of sixty-five to spend his golden years in the snug security of a Nightingale Nursing Home. Accordingly, the nursing-home entrepreneurs propose to make available $1 million of 6 percent convertible debentures to some worthy mutual fund portfolio manager who will enter into a gentleman's agreement with them that the debentures will never be converted.

It is a good deal. The mutual fund man buys it. Thereafter, in valuing his fund each day, he puts the investment in at 100,000 times the current price of the stock. The market for the stock is rather thin, of course. A few shares trickle into the listing in the over-the-counter market's pink sheets (published privately for brokers) each week. Someone somewhere keeps interested in the stock and the price edges up steadily. The portfolio manager is delighted. Each day, he values his Nightingale paper at 100,000 times the price of a share. *A hundred thousand shares?* That is twice as much as the company has outstanding! Meanwhile, the boys at Nightingale are sending copies of the mutual fund's latest financial report to all their friends. After all, if a large mutual fund run by highly skilled professional managers is a big holder of Nightingale securities, they must be pretty solid.

If we have a year like 1969 and the market drops sharply, with Nightingale listed at only $5.00 per share, the portfolio manager forgets about the convertibility business. He loaned Nightingale $1,000,000. Their credit is good and they are paying interest. He quite properly carries the paper at the $1,000,000 he paid for it. There he sits, enjoying the best of both worlds.

Raising money through this device is very desirable from the standpoint of the issuer. Only a small amount of stock is involved in the corporation's capitalization, the rest is debt certificates.. The holders of the stock are thus enabled to retain control of the company. Of course, if the debentures were presented for conversion, the issuance of new common shares would water the company's stock and seriously undermine its value per share. In effect, then, when the mutual fund carries the debenture at a price based on the market value of the stock, that valuation is a false one which could never be realized. If the debenture holders did convert, the actual price of the stock would tumble. What we have, then, in the portfolios of mutual funds are billions of dollars of securities carried at a completely fictitious value—convertible securities which will never be converted.

A longshoreman, pointing to cases of sardines stacked on a pier, asked a fellow worker why they had been sitting there for over a year. "What's the matter with those sardines?" he inquired. "Doesn't anyone want to eat them?" "Oh, they're not for eating," came the response. "They're for buying and selling."

In the same way, these convertible "sardines" are not for converting—they are for buying and selling. But how honest is all this? These contrived profits make no contribution to our economy. As with all unethical investment values, in the end someone must be hurt.

# Chapter 14

# THE COST OF REINVESTMENT

It is said that the man who invented compound interest was a genius. Compound earnings are even better —they generally run more than interest. The great majority of mutual fund investors reinvest all dividends and distributions, which is a smart thing to do.

We have seen how in investing in individual securities, it is difficult to compound earnings because of the small returns during the year, and because the broker charges a fee for selling you additional shares. Also, the cost of investing small sums continues to rise. We also noted that mutual funds provide a convenient means by which all earnings may be converted automatically into additional shares.

The great majority of funds of course reinvest dividends free. That is, the additional shares are purchased at net asset value with no sales charge. On the other hand, quite a number of funds reinvest ordinary income dividends at the asked price, which includes the full sales charge. Capital gains distributions, however, are always reinvested at net asset value. The rationale is that they represent an increase in the capital value of your present share of the underlying portfolio investments of the fund, while ordinary income dividends are regarded as new money generated from the dividends and interest which the fund collected on its securities holdings.

If you have narrowed your choice of funds down to two, and one of them reinvests at the asked price, if other things are equal it will obviously pay you to select the fund that will let you plow back all earnings without a further charge.

Let us assume that you have invested $10,000 in a fund with an 8½ percent sales charge. It has therefore cost you $850 to put your money to work in the first place. If ordinary income dividends ran 4 percent per year, you would be reinvesting over a ten-year period a sum equal to 40 percent of what you had invested in

the first place—which would cost you an additional $340. Actually, since the earnings would be compounding and, in addition, you could reasonably expect your principal to climb over the years with consequent increase in earnings from the increased capital at work, the total involved would probably be much larger. There is a good chance, then, that if you reinvest at the asked price, you may pay in further fees an additional amount equal to or greater than your original sales cost.

Also, when it comes to reinvesting the earnings at the asked price, most funds forget to take into account the discount to which the shareholder became entitled under the rights of accumulation. They assess him the full sales charge. Few shareholders think to check such costs. Some funds do not have rights of accumulation: if you have obtained a discount by investing $200,000 initially, or some lesser figure, it will still cost you the maximum sales charge to reinvest your dividends each year.

Mutual funds should not charge anything to reinvest dividends, but if you like a fund's policies and objectives, and its record is a good one, you may feel that the extra cost is something you are willing to pay. However, one good reason why you should take the trouble to learn what the fund's reinvestment policy is, is that the salesman shares in the commissions derived from that dividend reinvestment, although he performs absolutely no service in connection with the reinvestment of dividends. However, it could influence his recommendations.

For years, Affiliated Fund stressed in its dealer bulletins the many thousands of dollars that were going out to dealers and salesmen as a result of the reinvestment of the current dividend. Many fund salesmen have built up an impressive continuing income by carefully selecting for recommendation those funds that reinvested all earnings at the asked price. Unfortunately, this has been easy to justify when many, though by no means most, of the best-managed funds make such a charge.

Funds that reinvest dividends with a sales charge are listed below.

Affiliated Fund
Alpha Fund
American Business Shares
American Growth Fund
Boston Common Stock Fund
Boston Fund
Broad Street Investing Corporation
Brown Fund of Hawaii
Bullock Fund
Canadian Fund
Century Shares Trust
Commerce Stock Fund of State Bond & Mortgage
Composite Bond and Stock Fund
Composite Fund
Diversified Fund of State Bond & Mortgage
Diversified Growth Stock Fund
Diversified Investment Fund
Dividend Shares
Dow Theory Investment Fund
Eaton & Howard Balanced Fund
Eaton & Howard Growth Fund
Eaton & Howard Special Fund
Eaton & Howard Stock Fund
Equity Growth Fund of America
Everest Fund
Fidelity Capital Fund
Fidelity Fund
Fidelity Trend Fund
Financial Fund
First National Fund
Franklin Common Stock Series
Franklin Dynatech Series
Franklin Income Series
Franklin Utilities Series
Fundamental Investors
Index Fund of Boston

Industries Trend Fund
International Investments
Investment Trust of Boston
Keystone B–1 Investment Bond
Keystone B–2 Medium Grade Bond
Keystone B–4 Discount Bond
Keystone K–1 Income Fund
Keystone K–2 Growth Fund
Keystone S–1 High Grade
Keystone S–2 Income
Keystone S–3 Growth
Keystone S–4 Low Price Common
Massachusetts Investors Growth Stock Fund
Massachusetts Investors Trust
Nation-Wide Securities
National Investors Corporation
National Securities Balanced
National Securities Bond
National Securities Dividend
National Securities Growth Stocks
National Securities Income
National Securities Preferred Stock
National Securities Stock
Old Dominion Investors' Trust
One Hundred Fund
One Hundred and One Fund
Pioneer Enterprise Fund
Pioneer Fund
Provident Fund for Income
Puerto Rican Investors Trust
Puritan Fund
Putnam Equities Fund Inc.
Putnam Growth Fund
Putnam Income Fund
Putnam Investors Fund
Putnam Vista Fund
Security Investment Fund
Selected American Shares
Sovereign Investors
Technology Fund
Vance, Sanders Special Fund
Whitehall Fund
Wisconsin Fund

# Chapter 15

# REDEMPTIONS

Father James W———— is a hard-working member of a mission order. His parish, spread out over the back country of one of our Southern states, is one of the largest—and poorest—in the country. All of his waking hours are spent amidst poverty of the worst sort.

Father W. asked to be transferred to his present post. When he left a teaching assignment in New England, a prosperous businessman who admired his priestly devotion to his work handed him a check for many thousands of dollars to be used in any way he saw fit. Father W. decided he would invest it carefully until he became settled in his new post and had concluded how best to use the money.

He invested it in the Fletcher Capital Fund.

After nine months in the back country, Father W. had accumulated a long list of worthy projects in his parish. On February 11, 1969, he wrote to the Bank of New York, custodian of Fletcher Capital Fund, and requested the redemption of his shares. The dealer who sold him the shares had assured him that he could liquidate his investment on one week's notice. He timed his withdrawal carefully. In two weeks, he would have to pay for the pump he bought for one family, the shingles he'd bought to fix the ramshackle home of another, purchases of agricultural tools, seeds, and several cases of children's shoes in assorted sizes for others, and so on. The list was long, and so was the list of bills.

He was anxious to receive the money. Each morning he made the long trip to the nearest post office. No check.

He wrote a second letter, and then a third. Then he telephoned the investment dealer through whom he bought the shares. The dealer wrote in his behalf and again two weeks later.

Finally, on May 5, 1969, seventy-seven days beyond the statutory time set by the Investment Company Act of 1940 for the redemption of mutual fund shares, the custodian bank mailed him a check.

Violation of the provisions of the Investment Company Act of 1940 relating to the redemption of shares is widespread. Section 22 (e) of the Act specifies that "no registered investment company shall . . . postpone the date of payment upon redemption of any redeemable security in accordance with its terms for more than seven days after the tender of such security to the company or its agent designated for that purpose for redemption." Most prospectuses specify that payment will be made within seven days. Note that the law and the prospectuses do not say "seven business days"; they say "seven days." At least half of the people who redeem mutual fund shares are not being paid their proceeds within that period.

An important factor in a bank's custodianship of a fund is the "float," which consists of the cash included among the fund's assets, the payments received from new shareholders and not yet processed, and the payments due redeeming shareholders. Collectively, these total a very substantial sum which the custodian bank has the use of interest free and which it can lend out at the prime rate or better—at a handsome profit. If a fund sponsor approaches a bank about serving as custodian, one of the first questions the bank will ask is, "What sort of float do you expect you'll have?"

There is nothing wrong with the bank's using these sums, but it is certainly wrong for the bank to increase the float, and thus increase its profits, by deliberately delaying payment of redemptions. Cynics might point out that there is no incentive for the bank to maintain a high standard of efficiency aimed at prompt delivery of redemption proceeds when (a) slovenly practice makes a bigger float, and (b) the shareholder raises no objection. Some principal custodian banks make it a regular practice to forward redemption proceeds well beyond the time set by the statute and the prospectus. For example, my firm has filed repeated complaints with the S.E.C. against the State Street Bank and Trust Company in Boston and the Bank of New York, both prominent custodians, for redemption delays. In no way is this the fault of the fund, unless the fund has received repeated complaints from redeeming shareholders and has not taken steps to correct the improper practice. The two above-mentioned banks are custodians for 91 and 51 funds respectively, apparently more than they can handle.

My firm makes it a practice to keep careful track of redemption requests and we have demanded that the custodian pay interest, at the prime rate, when in default of a timely payment of redemption proceeds.

Unfortunately, funds and their custodian banks are applying different rules to mutual fund redemptions from those that apply to regular securities transactions. Required by law to remit redemption proceeds within seven days of the date upon which the shares are "tendered," funds are taking the position that the shares are not "tendered" until the custodian bank has the certificates in its possession. By telephoning the fund, your mutual fund dealer can redeem your shares as of the next closing of the New York Stock Exchange, but the countdown on the delivery of the proceeds won't begin until your shares reach the bank.

The dictionary defines "tender" as "to offer or proffer." When the dealer calls the fund on your behalf, he certainly "proffers" the shares. The Investment Company Act of 1940 contains no definition of "tender," however, and Alan Rosenblat, Chief Counsel of the Division of Corporate Regulation, has issued a ruling that it is permissible for the bank to hold onto your money for seven days from the date it receives the share certificate. This is improper, but as Charles Evans Hughes once said, "The law is what the judges say it is," and in this case, the law is what Mr. Rosenblat says it is.

If I sell 100 shares of General Motors through a broker, I am entitled to collect on the fifth day following the trade date. I can choose to deliver the certificate on the first, second, third, fourth or even the fifth day, and still be entitled to my money on the fifth day. If I deliver the certificate on the fifth day, the broker is not entitled to withhold my check for an additional five days. Of course, the mail being what it is these days, the bank may not receive the certificate promptly. Sometimes the certificate gets onto the wrong desk or gets mislaid in the shuffle; I have seen countless examples of banks blandly insisting that the certificate never reached them at all.

Bearing all this in mind, let us review the procedures for collecting the proceeds of the redemption of your fund shares with a minimum of difficulties.

*If it is a load fund:*

You bought it through an investment dealer, and your best bet is to go back to him. He told you that the sales charge was to cover getting in and getting out, so let him do the work of getting you out. If you have the share certificate in your possession deliver it to him or call him and tell him you are bringing it in. (Of course, you can mail it but this will only cause further delay.) Ask him to telephone the fund sponsor (not the custodian bank) and redeem the shares. Tell him to ask the fund to give him the number of the confirmation. If the broker is a member of the New York Stock Exchange, you have no further problems; when you come in, he will ask you to sign either the back of the certificate or a "stock power"—simply a piece of paper with the same printed matter that is on the back of your certificate—and he will guarantee your signature. If your broker is not a member of the New York Stock Exchange, then you will have to attend to the signature guarantee. Take the certificate to the bank where you have a checking account, that is, a commercial bank (savings banks are not acceptable), and ask an officer to guarantee your signature. He will rubber-stamp it and sign his name. Deliver the certificate to the broker and tell him to mail it out that day to the fund's custodian bank, identifying it as the shares redeemed on the telephone with the fund, giving the confirmation number he obtained from the fund, and enclosing a copy of his own confirmation of the sale which he was required by the rules to send to the fund. Most funds tell the dealer not to send in the certificate until he receives their actual confirmation. Rarely do they send the confirmation out the same day, however, and frequently it takes three or four days. If the dealer waits until he gets it, you will wait that much longer for your money, so tell him to rush it to the bank.

If your shares are unissued, that is, you have left them on deposit with the fund's custodian bank, do not try to liquidate them by telephone. Telephone redemptions are only for people with a certificate in their hands. Actually, the telephone liquidation is not a "redemption," it is a "repurchase" of the shares by the sponsor. Sponsors repurchase, custodians redeem. The sponsor will not repurchase unissued shares. If you try it, it will be necessary for the custodian bank actually to issue a share certificate (which will take upwards of a week) and send it to you for forwarding to the sponsor. This is a very traumatic experience for the custodian's computer. It will shudder and groan and very likely burst. If you have unissued shares, then, simply write a letter addressed to the fund in care of the custodian bank, saying: "I am the registered owner of shares of ABC Fund held in Account No. ———. I direct that you liquidate all such shares and remit a check for the proceeds to me within the statutory period. Enclosed is a signed stock power with signature guaranteed."

Your broker could do this for you, but by doing it

yourself you avoid possible delay which can affect the liquidation price of your shares. If your broker is a member of the New York Stock Exchange, he will supply the stock power and guarantee it. If he is not a member, he will supply the stock power but you will have to go to the bank to get it guaranteed. Always send liquidation requests by registered mail, return receipt requested. That way, you will have proof of when the bank received your request. They can't claim that it never arrived or arrived late. Look at the date on the return receipt and compare that with the mailing date on the envelope in which you receive the check (do not go by the date on the check because they frequently hold it a few days). If they have not remitted within the seven-day statutory period, demand interest at the prime rate for every day they are late. So that the regulatory authorities will know who is not conforming to the requirements of the Investment Company Act of 1940, send a copy of your letter demanding interest to Division of Corporate Regulation, Securities and Exchange Commission, 500 North Capitol Avenue, Washington, D.C.

Incidentally, the signature guarantee serves no useful purpose and is simply a nuisance. If people who guarantee signatures were aware of the terrible legal responsibility they take on, there would be no one left to make such guarantees. When a bank officer guarantees your signature, he is not just guaranteeing that you are John Smith—he is also guaranteeing that you have the *right* to sign. If a dishonest person comes into possession of a stock certificate worth $50,000 and registered in the name of "John Smith," he could put $100 into a bank checking account in that name—and turn up a few days later with the stock certificate, asking that his signature be guaranteed. The bank man who opened the account for him a few days earlier remembers him as "John Smith" and cheerfully guarantees the signature. He probably does not know that he has just guaranteed that the thief had the *right* to sign the certificate and thus sell the shares. The bank is on the hook for the $50,000.

*If you own a no-load fund:*

Read carefully all that I have just explained because you are going to have to do all the work yourself. You will not be able to accomplish a telephone liquidation; only an investment dealer can do that. If you have a share certificate, mail it along with a guaranteed stock power to the fund's custodian bank with a letter saying: "Enclosed find certificate No. ———— for ———— shares of ABC Fund registered in the name of the undersigned. Kindly liquidate the shares and remit a check for the proceeds to me within the statutory period." If you have unissued shares, write the custodian bank a letter similar to that which I have indicated above for load funds, and be sure you enclose the stock power, obtainable without charge or obligation from almost any commercial bank or broker.

However, there is no guarantee that following all the requirements will ensure smooth redemption. Observing that her $50,000 investment in the Johnston Mutual Fund had declined 15 percent in the seven weeks she had owned it, Mrs. W. B. D—— decided to liquidate. Since her shares were all unissued and in the possession of the Bankers Trust Company, the fund's custodian and agent, Mrs. D—— on Tuesday, April 14, 1970, sent that bank a properly signed and authenticated stock power together with a letter requesting redemption. Sent by certified mail, the letter was delivered four days later, on Friday, April 17 (Mrs. D—— lives an hour's drive from the bank). Since the Investment Company Act of 1940 specifically provides that shares presented for redemption shall be liquidated as of the next closing of the New York Stock Exchange after delivery to the fund or its agent, this shareholder was entitled to redemption at Friday's closing price. In clear contravention of the Act, and in the face of a sharply falling market, the bank held the request for six days and then mailed it to the fund. Upon receipt of it, the fund held it for two days and then repurchased the shares, mailing the investor a check on Monday, April 27, for $1,400 less than the shares were worth on the day on which, according to law, they should have been liquidated. When the shareholder demanded that the fund make good the loss she had suffered at its hands, one of its senior officers cut her short and told her that if she had any complaint, to file it with the S.E.C. And we all know what good that would do! Let the buyer beware.

If you have urgent need for money while the market is down, postpone redemption of your fund shares by putting them up as collateral for a bank loan until the market has recovered.

# Chapter 16

# DISTRIBUTIONS AND THEIR
# TAX LIABILITY

Sums distributed to shareholders by a mutual fund fall into three categories. Dividends received from stocks owned by the fund and interest received from bonds are called *ordinary income*. Most funds distribute this quarterly, except growth funds which may pay it out only once a year. These funds do not collect much in dividends from the kind of growth securities they invest in, you will remember, so they do not have a great deal to pay out, and they can cut down on the expenses involved in apportioning dividends among the shareholders by making such distributions only once each year.

The second type of mutual fund payout is called a *capital gains distribution*. Whenever a fund sells one of the securities in its portfolio, any profit involved must be set aside in a "realized profit account." If the fund sells something at a loss, it can draw upon the realized profits account to make up the loss. At the end of its fiscal year, it distributes to each shareholder his proportionate share of the sums remaining in the realized profit account.

The third form of mutual fund payout is a distribution from *capital surplus*. This is a simple device for deluding the shareholder and confusing the record books. A payment of capital surplus is simply a distribution of a part of the fund's principal. It is like having $1,000 in a savings account paying 5 percent interest. At the end of the year, you go to the bank and draw your $50.00 interest plus another $25.00 out of your principal. The $25.00 is "capital surplus"—your own money. You do not have to pay any tax when you spend your own principal, so the capital surplus distribution made by the mutual fund is tax free. Of course, when you draw the extra $25.00 out of your savings account, you know you are drawing out and spending some of your principal, whereas not one shareholder in a thousand understands that that is what he is doing when he is paid a capital surplus.

The distribution of capital surplus is designed to keep shareholders happy in a lean year. If a fund has been regularly paying dividends and distributions totaling $1.00 per year, and it runs into a lean year and such distributions total only 75 cents, it may well peel off another 25 cents of surplus. The shareholder's purchasing power, and incidentally his loyalty to the fund, remains undiminished, and the record books will show no embarrassing drop in the amount of annual distributions per share. There are disadvantages, of course. On December 30, 1969, one large balanced fund paid out $7.5 million of capital surplus. In anticipation of the payout, the managers had to keep that amount of cash sitting idle. If they did not have the cash on hand, they would have to sell some securities to raise it. Selling securities involves brokerage commissions—and the commissions on $7.5 million are substantial. Selling also involves realizing a profit on certain of the securities, a profit which is passed on to the shareholders in the form of an increased tax liability. There was a lot of expensive bookkeeping involved in making such a distribution to more than 300,000 shareholders, few, if any, of whom need or want this kind of financial pablum. There is no justification for this kind of deception. It should be prohibited.

Let us assume that you and I each own a share of the ABC Fund which pays dividends quarterly as of the last day of March, June, September, and December. You bought your share on January 2, while I bought mine on March 27. The fund announces that on April 10, it will pay a quarterly dividend of $1.00 per share to each person who owned a share at the close of business on March 30. We each owned a share, and so we are each going to receive identically the same $1.00 dividend. A mutual fund must pay the same dividend per share to all shareholders.

But that is hardly fair, considering that you will have

had your money working for a full three months while mine will have worked for only three days. Should you not be entitled to a larger dividend? Funds have a way of adjusting this inequality. From day to day the fund establishes the proportionate interest which each owner of a share has in the whole portfolio. During the current quarter, it has been accumulating all ordinary income in a cash account, and it next determines the proportionate interest of each share in that cash account. When you bought your share on January 2, the quarter was just beginning and there was no money in the income account, so all that you paid for your share of the fund was its proportionate interest in the value of all of the portfolio securities. But as the quarter progressed, income accumulated. When I decided to buy my one share on March 27, the fund first determined the proportionate interest of each share in the whole portfolio. Then it checked the income account and found that there was enough cash accumulated in it to pay each shareholder 99 cents. Because they were issuing to me a share which a few days later must be paid the same dividend as all other shares—a dividend to which I obviously would not be entitled because my money hadn't been working for a full three months as yours has—they added 99 cents to the cost of the share they were selling me. True, I will receive the same $1.00 dividend as you, but 99 cents of it will be my own money coming back to me. The remaining 1 cent will be my share of the earnings of the fund for the three days my money actually worked. If I had decided to make my investment in the fund on February 15 when there was, say, 50 cents per share of income accumulated, that's the amount the fund would have added to my cost for the share. In that case, when I received the $1.00 dividend in April, 50 cents would have been my own money coming back to me and the other 50 cents would have been my share of the income from February 15 to March 30. After the payment of any kind of distribution by a mutual fund, the quoted value—and the quoted price—of a share immediately drop by *exactly* the amount of the distribution. My Johnnie-come-lately purchase in March did not really do me any good, then, because my share immediately dropped in price by the amount of the distribution.

If I bought my share on March 27 and receive my $1.00 dividend on April 10, I know that 99 cents of it is not a dividend at all, and the fund knows that the 99 cents is not a dividend, but Uncle Sam doesn't seem to know it. He requires the fund to send the tax authorities a report that it has paid me a $1.00 dividend, and insists that I report the entire dollar as income and pay a tax upon it.

House funds can be another tax liability. In addition to the funds they offer to the public, successful fund managers or sponsors commonly maintain a house fund. The house fund is private; only the insiders own its

shares. If the fund proves successful, a public offering is made. Some management groups will operate several such house funds and "go public" with the one that shows the best record. Officially, the Securities and Exchange Commission has banned bar charts of performance that include results prior to the public offering. The Commission's fumbling "blow hot, blow cold" regulation permits exceptions, however.

The problem with the house fund is that its private success is necessarily reflected in a substantial unrealized appreciation in the value of its assets. The public who buy in acquire a share in the tax liability attached to that unrealized appreciation without acquiring any actual profit to themselves.

If, shortly after it opens its doors to the public, the fund's managers dispose of holdings that show substantial profits, the profits will be distributed pro rata to all shareholders. The fund's net asset value, which is now reduced by the amount of the distribution, may not have increased at all since the public offering and there is therefore no real profit to the shareholder. But the capital gains distribution he has received is nevertheless fully taxable.

Opposite are two charts recently published as a part of the sales literature of Ivest Fund and Colonial Equities Fund, both of which should know better. The Ivest chart starts nearly three years before the fund began public sale. An investment of $10,000 on the date the fund started was worth about $26,000 on the going-public date. Obviously, there was a lot of accumulated unrealized appreciation, the tax liability for which Ivest insiders generously shared with the unsuspecting new investors in the fund. The Colonial Equities chart is a lulu. It starts toward the end of 1952, three and a half years before the fund became a registered investment company. The shares were not available to the public until November 7, 1966, over ten years later, by which time 25 percent of the asset value represented unrealized appreciation. These reports were filed with the Securities and Exchange Commission, which apparently found nothing improper in their use.

Fund sponsors should be prohibited from thus saddling the public with the tax on their private profits. It should be a requirement that all accumulated profits be realized by the insider shareholders before the fund goes public. The financial statement on the opening date of the public offering should show cost and market value as the same figure.

The new shareholders will participate in any subsequent appreciation and any subsequent tax will be on profit *they* enjoyed, not simply on someone else's.

One advantage of getting into a genuinely new fund starting from scratch with cash is that one eliminates the problem of sharing other people's tax liability. A disadvantage, of course, is that the fund has no perform-

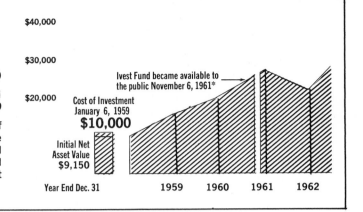

## THE IVEST FUND INVESTMENT RECORD

### An illustration (excerpted by the author) of an assumed $10,000 investment: Jan. 6, 1959

*The record for the period prior to August 29, 1961, is that of Professional Investors, predecessor to the Fund, which was a private investment association with substantially the same management and objectives as the Fund, but was managed without compensation and was not subject to the provisions of the Investment Company Act of 1940.

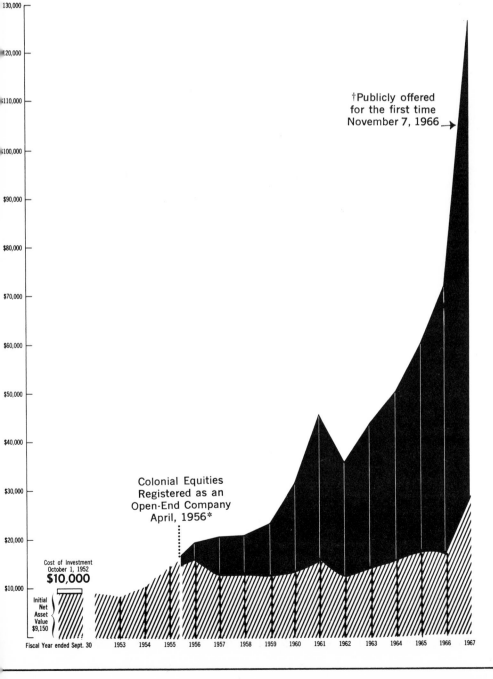

†Publicly offered
for the first time
November 7, 1966 →

Colonial Equities
Registered as an
Open-End Company
April, 1956*

Cost of Investment
October 1, 1952
**$10,000**

## COLONIAL EQUITIES INVESTMENT RECORD

An illustration of an assumed $10,000 investment: October 1, 1952.

*Prior to April, 1956, the Fund operated as a private investment association with substantially the same management and objectives as the Fund, but was managed without compensation and was not subject to the provisions of the Investment Company Act of 1940.

†Author's notation, which was not included in the original illustration.

ance record. It is bought on the basis of faith and hope, possibly on the strength of investor confidence in the managers, which may in turn be based on their previous performance with another fund. However, a successful record of management of an earlier fund offers no assurance that the record will be repeated with a new fund.

Few mutual fund buyers understand or appreciate the extent of the tax liability that may attach to the purchase of shares of any established fund, not just to a house fund being opened to the public. This is particularly true when there has been a sustained upward movement of the market, and the problem tends to be more significant in the case of conservative funds which invest for the long haul and minimize portfolio turnover. Their long-term holdings provide a greater likelihood of substantial capital appreciation. Performance fund managers are a nervous lot about their profits. If they have one, frequently they are inclined to sell the holding and nail down the profit lest it slip away. A performance fund invests for the short haul and is more prone to paying capital gains distributions, then. This is particularly true of those operators who have arranged for their incentive fee to be a percentage of the fund's realized profits.

The tax liability unnecessarily imposed on all shareholders by such practices is a definite disadvantage which should be considered as a material fact in considering the fund's performance. The investor's concern is with the net results to him. Given two funds with exactly equal performance records, he should favor the one that does not churn its portfolio to produce an impressive capital gains payout record or to enhance its own fees. An alert S.E.C. would have stopped such operators cold. A practice that encourages managers to sell out securities on which they have substantial profits in order to fatten their fee is inequitable.

The Securities and Exchange Commission and the National Association of Securities Dealers have declared it improper for a broker-dealer to knowingly sell shares of a mutual fund by recommending to the prospective buyer that he purchase just before the record date of an upcoming dividend or capital gains distribution.

Just as it is wrong for an investment dealer knowingly to disadvantage the share buyer in this matter of taxable dividends, it is equally wrong for him to do it unknowingly. Such a wrong lies not in the dealer's knowledge or lack of knowledge of the fund's scheduled distribution but rather in the imposition upon the buyer of an unnecessary and unjustified tax liability.

Fortunately, the great majority of investment dealers make an effort to avoid saddling the customer with such tax liability. They take careful note of announcements of scheduled distributions and advise customers to time purchases to avoid the tax on a profit that is not a profit.

Procedures that have the effect of shifting tax liability from one person or group to another are not uncommon: one person is burdened with a liability while another is relieved of it. The tax liability attendant on a purchase just prior to an ex-dividend date has no such redeeming grace. It is a tax liability created out of nothing, and its imposition lightens no one's tax burden.

However vigilant the investment dealer may be in alerting himself to planned distributions, many dealers are frustrated in such efforts by the procedures adopted by some funds for giving public notice of dividend declarations. To cite an example: my firm made repeated fruitless telephone inquiries of Shareholders Management Company in an effort to ascertain when it would be paying the annual income and capital gains distributions on one of its funds. Our first knowledge of such distribution came when we observed that the price had dropped unaccountably. We wrote asking that in the future we be given some sort of notification of intended distributions.

The company replied that "the Board of Directors voted on the afternoon of January 15th to declare a dividend payable to shareholders of record on January 17th. A press release stating that this action had been taken was issued on the morning of the 16th." By "issued," they meant that they mailed out a notice addressed to financial editors. With nearly 1,100 registered investment companies, financial editors do not always regard the payment of a dividend or distribution by one of them as earth-shaking news, and the fact of the imminent dividend does not come to the attention of the investment dealer. In this instance, it would have been impossible for a dealer placing an order on January 16 to know that the fund was going ex-dividend the very next day.

The sponsor's letter concluded with the somewhat arrogant statement that its "course of conduct . . . provides dissemination of information regarding fund dividends and distributions sufficient to meet the needs of the investing public."

It is not sufficient. It is not in the public interest that investment dealers be kept in ignorance of upcoming distributions with the result that they unknowingly operate in violation of Commission regulations.

Incidentally, an investor in a high tax bracket and contemplating redemption of shares who wishes to effect such redemption prior to the ex-dividend date and thus convert his heavily taxed income dividend into a lower-taxed long-term capital gain, should be privileged to do so. He is clearly entitled to timely notice of the projected dividend payment.

Increasingly, growth type funds are electing to pay income dividends once each year. The accumulation tends to make the dividend larger and the potential unjustified tax liability greater, not to mention the disadvantage involved where such income distributions are automatically reinvested at the asked price, which includes a sales charge. Capital gains distributions equal to 25 percent or more of the net asset value per share are not uncommon. A system that permits a fund to impose an unjustified tax on 25 percent of one's investment a few days after one has made it is obviously in need of overhauling.

To illustrate the impact of these taxable distributions we have been discussing, consider the following facts concerning Fidelity Capital Fund:

| Beginning the year | Net asset value per share | Capital gains distribution during the year | % of net asset value distributed |
|---|---|---|---|
| 1965 | $11.42 | $2.64 | 23 |
| 1966 | 14.22 | 2.10 | 15 |
| 1967 | 12.47 | 1.44 | 12 |
| 1968 | 14.82 | .88 | 6 |

An investor who bought $10,000 worth of Fidelity Capital Fund on January 2, 1965, would have paid an 8 percent sales charge. Immediately after he bought them, his shares would have been worth $9,200. Within four weeks, he would have been paid a capital gains distribution of $2,127, not a cent of which represented profit to him. The net asset value of each of his 805.8 shares immediately dropped $2.64. If he paid the standard 25 percent capital gains tax, he lost $531 to Uncle Sam by reason of his receipt of this distribution of "realized profit" which was not a profit at all so far as he was concerned. That $531 was 5.31 percent of his investment in the fund. He obviously decided that it was worth paying 8 percent to get into the fund. Had he been aware of it ahead of time, would he have concluded that it was worth paying a total of 13.31 percent to get in? That was his real sales charge in this instance.

So that the investor may be aware of the exact extent of the potential tax liability represented by the unrealized appreciation in the portfolio of a fund in which he may be considering investing, there follows a compilation disclosing the ratio of unrealized appreciation to total portfolio assets of some leading funds for year-end 1969.

This listing is not intended to suggest that you should not buy Chemical Fund (52.2%), Wall Street Investing (49%), or Massachusetts Investors Growth Stock Fund (44%). What I am saying is that the substantial tax liability reflected in these high unrealized appreciation ratios is one factor that should be considered when choosing a fund.

---

| | | | |
|---|---|---|---|
| Aberdeen Fund | 8% | Hartwell & Campbell Fund | 7 |
| Affiliated Fund | 6.4 | Investment Company of America | 2.5 |
| American Express Investment Co. | 10 | Investment Trust of Boston | 22 |
| Axe-Houghton Fund B | 37 | Investors Mutual | 1.4 |
| Boston Common Stock Fund | 26 | Investors Stock Fund | 6.9 |
| Boston Fund | 97 | Johnston Mutual Fund | 21 |
| Broad Street Investing | 24 | Keystone K–2 Growth Fund | 5 |
| Bullock Fund | 11 | Keystone S–1 High Grade Common | 3 |
| Canadian Fund | 45 | Keystone S–4 Low Priced Common | 10 |
| Century Shares Trust | 43 | Knickerbocker Fund | 25 |
| Chase Fund of Boston | 1.7 | Knickerbocker Growth Fund | 19 |
| Chemical Fund | 52.2 | Manhattan Fund | 4 |
| Dividend Shares | 45 | Massachusetts Investors Growth | 44 |
| Dreyfus Fund | 9 | Massachusetts Investors Trust | 46 |
| Eaton & Howard Balanced Fund | 27.8 | National Dividend Series | 6.6 |
| Eaton & Howard Stock Fund | 26 | National Growth Series | 8.3 |
| Energy Fund | 7.6 | National Income Series | 1 |
| Fidelity Fund | 5.4 | National Investors | 41 |
| Financial Industrial Fund | 2.3 | National Stock Series | 12 |
| Founders Mutual Fund | 35 | One William Street Fund | 26 |
| Fundamental Investors | 10 | Philadelphia Fund | 18 |
| Group Common Stock Fund | 2.1 | Pioneer Fund | 7 |
| Growth Industry Shares | 29 | T. Rowe Price Growth Fund | 19 |
| Guardian Mutual Fund | 2.5 | Rowe Price New Horizons Fund | 25 |

| | | | |
|---|---|---|---|
| Puritan Fund | 5 | Supervised Investors Growth Stock | 2.1 |
| George Putnam Fund | 6 | Technology Fund | 5.9 |
| Putnam Growth Fund | 2.5 | United Accumulative Fund | 3 |
| Putnam Investors Fund | 26 | United Income Fund | 18.5 |
| Security Equity Fund | 4 | United Science Fund | 8 |
| Selected American Shares | 5 | Wall Street Investing Company | 49 |
| Sigma Shares | 9 | Windsor Fund | 4.7 |
| Stein Roe & Farnham Balanced Fund | 6.4 | Wisconsin Fund | 12.9 |

The following list covers state taxation of mutual fund capital gains distributions. However, such tax rulings are subject to change or reinterpretation.

### State Taxation of Capital Gains Distribution

| State | Taxed as taken in cash | Taxed as taken in stock | Balance check on distribution taken in stock |
|---|---|---|---|
| Alabama | Income | Income | Income |
| Alaska | Capital gain | Capital gain | Capital gain |
| Arizona | Income | Income | Income |
| Arkansas | Income | Income | Income |
| California | Income | Income | Income |
| Colorado | Capital gain | Capital gain | Capital gain |
| Connecticut | Capital gain | Capital gain | Capital gain |
| Delaware | Income | Income | Income |
| District of Columbia | Income | Income | Income |
| Florida | Not taxed | Not taxed | Not taxed |
| Georgia | Capital gain | Capital gain | Capital gain |
| Hawaii | Capital gain | Capital gain | Capital gain |
| Idaho | Capital gain | Capital gain | Capital gain |
| Illinois | Income | Income | Income |
| Indiana | Capital gain | Capital gain | Capital gain |
| Iowa | Capital gain | Capital gain | Capital gain |
| Kansas | Capital gain | Capital gain | Capital gain |
| Kentucky | Capital gain | Capital gain | Capital gain |
| Louisiana | Income | Income | Income |
| Maine | Capital gain | Capital gain | Capital gain |
| Maryland | Capital gain | Capital gain | Capital gain |
| Massachusetts | Income | Not taxed | Income |
| Michigan | Income | Capital gain | Income |
| Minnesota | Capital gain | Capital gain | Capital gain |
| Mississippi | Income | Income | Income |
| Missouri | Capital gain | Capital gain | Capital gain |
| Montana | Capital gain | Capital gain | Capital gain |
| Nebraska | Capital gain | Capital gain | Capital gain |
| Nevada | Not taxed | Not taxed | Not taxed |
| New Hampshire | Not taxed | Not taxed | Not taxed |
| New Jersey | Not taxed | Not taxed | Not taxed |
| New Mexico | Capital gain | Capital gain | Capital gain |
| New York | Capital gain | Capital gain | Capital gain |
| North Carolina | Income | Income | Income |
| North Dakota | Capital gain | Capital gain | Capital gain |
| Ohio | Not taxed | Not taxed | Not taxed |

## State Taxation of Capital Gains Distribution

| State | Taxed as taken in cash | Taxed as taken in stock | Balance check on distribution taken in stock |
|---|---|---|---|
| Oklahoma | Income | Income | Income |
| Oregon | Capital gain | Capital gain | Capital gain |
| Pennsylvania | Not taxed | Not taxed | Not taxed |
| Rhode Island | Capital gain | Capital gain | Capital gain |
| South Carolina | Capital gain | Capital gain | Capital gain |
| South Dakota | Not taxed | Not taxed | Not taxed |
| Tennessee | Income | Income | Income |
| Texas | Not taxed | Not taxed | Not taxed |
| Utah | Income | Income | Income |
| Vermont | Capital gain | Capital gain | Capital gain |
| Virginia | Income | Income | Income |
| Washington | Not taxed | Not taxed | Not taxed |
| West Virginia | Capital gain | Capital gain | Capital gain |
| Wisconsin | Income | Income | Income |
| Wyoming | Not taxed | Not taxed | Not taxed |

# Chapter 17

# LAWSUITS AGAINST FUNDS

In recent years a great many lawsuits have been brought against mutual funds, their sponsors, and their managers, and I have yet to hear of a plaintiff losing such a suit. This record is significant: while anyone can bring a suit, proving one's case is quite another matter, and the logical assumption is that the charges had a solid basis in fact. Of course, some suits constitute barratry—legal actions instituted for the enrichment of the attorneys who bring them, with only incidental benefits, if any, to the shareholders. It is these and other such suits I wish to discuss.

While it is one thing to bring an action disclosing corruption, it is quite another to harass sponsors with nuisance suits. Any litigation involving a fund must be reported in its prospectus. Obviously, it does not help sell shares when the prospectus records a suit for fraud against the fund or its sponsors. No one stops to study the nature of the litigation. A shareholder has sued the fund, and that is all anyone needs to know to decide that the particular fund is not for him.

Some suits, though successful, serve no useful purpose. Old conservative Wellington Fund brought out a new growth fund called the Wellington Equity Fund. With an investment of a few hundred dollars in Wellington Fund, someone filed suit complaining that the name Wellington belonged to the shareholders of the original Wellington Fund, and that the new fund had no right to it. After long, costly litigation, Wellington's sponsor was ordered by a court to discontinue the use of the name on its growth fund, which was renamed Windsor Fund. What are the mental processes of the judicial mind that could render such a decision?

The commonest type of legal action is brought by some obscure shareholder with fewer than $500 of recently purchased shares and a brother-in-law who is a lawyer. The suit charges the fund with collecting excessive management fees. A lot of fund management fees are excessive, particularly with funds that have grown huge but have made no effort to scale down their fees. I have never known a fund charged with excessive management fees to win a suit. They always settle, if only to end the embarrassing litigation that must be reported in their prospectus. The point is, they do reduce their fees, and that is good for the shareholders.

A plaintiff named Kaufman has filed an action, still to be litigated, naming sixty-five different mutual funds, charging them with exacting excessive management compensation. Actually, Kaufman owns only one or two of the funds. It is difficult to understand the basis for his action against funds that have none of his money in their possession and therefore could not have disadvantaged him in any way.

Some people buy mutual funds with the deliberate intention of bringing a suit against them. A lawyer will study a fund operation and find some technicality upon which he can base a suit. Then he looks around for someone who owns some shares of that fund.

While many members of the Bar engage in this type of litigation, two or three giants strike terror into the hearts of fund sponsors. However, all of them fight over the spoils like jackals snarling over a carcass. Often enough, a lawyer conceiving of a cause of action that may or may not benefit the shareholders—but which will produce a fee for him, if only in settlement of it as a nuisance—unwittingly creates legal predators. Immediately the first suit is filed, the jackal pack moves in on the first attorney, threatening to go into court with a similar claim and have the case taken away from him on the grounds that one of the others is better qualified to press the action on behalf of the shareholders. It ends with the most powerful man selling off shares in the "take"—5 percent to this one, 10 percent to that one, and so on. The other partners then gracefully withdraw, hugging their equity in the action. All too frequently, the shareholders get little actual benefit out of these actions, but the counselors wax fat on the legal fees paid by the sponsors or the fund on order of the judge hearing the case.

Considering the sanctimonious talk we hear about the legal profession's canons of ethics, isn't all this enough to make honest people sick all over the carpet?

Many suits involve the charge that funds have improperly channeled the fund's brokerage business to certain persons with some resultant benefit to the fund sponsor. The usual charge is that the fund requires brokers with whom it places securities orders for the fund portfolio to split their commission with the investment dealer who originated the purchase of the fund shares in the first place. If the broker who executes the order does not split the commission, he ends up with the whole thing. The fund does not get it any cheaper. Actually, he doesn't do too much work to get it: the fund telephones him and places an order for 25,000 shares of ABC common. He writes a "buy" ticket, drops it into the hopper and goes to lunch. When the Stock Exchange closed in midafternoon, he leaves. The work he has done is vastly different from that of the dealer's mutual fund salesman who had to sit around the kitchen table with Ma and Pa at 9:30 at night, explaining about mutual funds and perhaps taking a small order. The mutual fund dealer, competing with other dealers for the services of that salesman, gives him as high a commission as he can afford. Many times the so-called "reciprocal commissions" which resulted from the commission splitting arranged by the mutual fund made the difference between a profitable and a nonprofitable operation for the dealer.

Of course, there can be abuses. If the dealer allows his men to sell only the shares of funds that require brokerage commission splitting, the customer does not get an unbiased recommendation from among all available funds and is unaware that he is being deliberately limited in his choice to funds that make the reciprocal commission payoff. Also there is the danger of a fund churning its portfolio to generate that steady flow of commisisons to be split with the dealers who sell its shares.

Unfortunately, in a distressingly large number of suits,

it has been discovered that the split commissions did not flow to the dealers who sold the fund's shares. They went to the fund's sponsors or managers through some sort of under-the-counter deal, the money being passed along until it reached the people who placed the orders in the first place. That is dishonest. If the funds can figure out a way to get some of the brokerage costs back, the money should inure to the benefit of the fund shareholders.

I have instituted several shareholders' derivative suits or class actions against funds whose sponsors or managers I have caught with their hands in the till in one way or another. In each case, I was a substantial shareholder of long standing. In most such cases, I have sold out all but a token holding of the fund's shares. If I think they are crooked, I'm certainly not going to leave my money in their custody. Any damages I might collect from the malefactors will be paid into the fund to benefit all shareholders, and though the benefit to any one shareholder, myself particularly, will be minuscule, collectively it should amount to quite a bundle. If these characters get their knuckles rapped hard, they will begin to realize that it is someone else's money in their care and that it is not up for grabs.

In the Congressional hearings on the subject of possible changes in mutual fund legislation, a powerful element within the fund industry suggested that action against funds should be left to the Securities and Exchange Commission, and that shareholders should not be permitted to sue directly unless they owned at least 10 percent of the fund's outstanding shares. Congressman John E. Moss and his colleagues on the House Interstate and Foreign Commerce subcommittee lowered the boom on that one and it died a quick death.

Heaven help us if we had to wait for the Securities and Exchange Commission to take action to protect us. I have seen countless letters from people who complained to the Commission about violations of the securities laws and were told to go hire a lawyer. I am beginning to wonder what the people at the Commission are being paid to do.

# Chapter 18

# THE MATES STORY

We were jammed into a tiny booth in a small, crowded luncheonette in midtown New York. Fred Mates put down his sandwich.

"I'd like to convince you, if I can, that I'm not a crook," he said.

"The evidence is pretty overwhelming, but go ahead," I replied.

We had spent the morning on opposite sides of a long table, surrounded by a battery of nine lawyers. As an owner of shares in the Mates Investment Fund, Inc., I had instituted a shareholder's derivative action against Mates, his management firm, the directors of his fund and an associate broker-dealer firm, charging them with the improper purchase and valuation of restricted securities as well as other assorted improprieties in the administration of the fund. That morning's session was to give the attorneys for the defendants the requested opportunity to question me on the substance of my charges. When we had adjourned at noon, Fred Mates approached and asked me to have lunch with him. I had readily agreed, and we walked around the block until we found a small sandwich shop.

Mates told me of his "impossible dream." He wanted to bring competent investment management to the little people of modest means, he explained. He had not meant to do anything wrong, and he was sure that he had not. A quiet-spoken, pleasant-looking man, he has a way of looking at you sadly, as if to say, "Why are you doing this to me?"

Why *was* I doing it to him?

On February 7, 1968, as president of the Mates Investment Fund, Inc., he wrote his shareholders:

> In recent months, there has been a tendency among several mutual funds to take positions via "investment letter" directly from the issuing companies or principal stockholders. This limits the liquidity of these positions since the shares so purchased must be registered with the Securities and Exchange Commission or held for a period of time before they can be resold to the public. Since "investment letter" stock is generally available at a substantial discount from market, mutual funds which engage in this sort of activity can show quite remarkable results over the shorter term. Although we would not hesitate to step off the beaten path in search of unusual investment values, we believe that deliberately locking oneself into a position delegates too much of management's responsibilities to the vagaries of the market. Thus, you may be pleased to know that there is nothing in our portfolio that we could not sell immediately if we so choose.

Mates continued to mail the letter to new shareholders in his fund through May 1968. Despite the representations in the letter, between April 15, 1968, and July 23, 1968, Mates acquired for the fund substantial amounts of various issues of restricted securities. Six of those issues (Bell Television, Inc., Longchamps, Inc., Process Plants Corp., Zimmer Homes, Inc., Omega Equities Corp., and Giffen Industries, Inc), which had an aggregate cost of $3,610,000, were assigned a value of $7,161,250 when first placed in the fund's pricing sheets for the purpose of determining the net asset value of the shares. Four of the six securities were valued at the market price for unrestricted securities of the same issuer and class. Two, shares of stock of Omega Equities Corporation and Giffen Industries, Inc., were valued at what amounted to a small constant dollar discount from the fluctuating market price for the corresponding unrestricted shares.

In his letter to shareholders commenting on the impropriety of just such a course of action, Mates had noted that "mutual funds which engage in this sort of activity can show quite remarkable results over the shorter term." By June 1968, Mates was beginning to show "quite remarkable results." That well-publicized spectacular performance brought in a torrent of investor money with which the fund's bookkeeping and administrative facilities could not cope, and it was obliged to discontinue the sale of new shares. While the fund's announcement gave the impression that the suspension was voluntary, Mates explained to me that it was on orders of the S.E.C. The Commission required Mates to review all sales and redemptions to confirm that they had been executed at the proper price. This had nothing to do with the overvaluation of the letter stock; it involved simply bookkeeping errors. The review turned up hundreds of discrepancies. Where investors had been overcharged, Mates was required to refund the overcharge with interest. Where investors had purchased shares at prices that were too low, Mates was required to pay the difference into the fund. Similarly, with redemptions Mates was obliged to make additional payments with interest to people who had been paid too little upon redemption or to reimburse the fund where investors had received too much when they redeemed.

At about the same time, the fund borrowed more than $7,000,000 from two banks and collateralized the loans with the fund's entire portfolio. The borrowed money was used in part to purchase the restricted securities and in addition to satisfy fund shareholders who presented their shares for redemption. At no time during this period was any disclosure made to the fund's shareholders or to the investing public in general of the fund's acquisition of the restricted securities or of its phony valuation procedures. Letters sent to the fund's shareholders in August and September 1968 made no mention of these facts or of the fund's borrowing of over $7,000,000. During the April–December 1968 period, Mates gave at least three press interviews in which he referred to the market performance of his fund, but made no reference whatever to the restricted securities. A story carried in *The New York Times* on July 28, 1968, reported that the fund had appreciated more than 100 percent during the period from August 1967 to July 28, 1968. Mates continued through November 1968 to value his restricted holdings as if they were unrestricted, except for the Omega and Giffen shares, which were carried at small dollar discounts from the market price for unrestricted shares. As of November 26, 1968, the six issues of restricted securities were carried in the fund's portfolio at a value of $13,459,000, more than $10,000,000 in excess of their cost. As of that date, the fund claimed unrealized appreciation in its portfolio amounting to $13,600,000—and more than $10,000,000 of that figure was directly traceable to the unwarranted valuation of its letter stocks.

On November 18, 1968, the fund's independent auditors, produced certification of the fund's financial statements as of May 31, 1968. On November 20, 1968, Mates and the fund were sued by certain individuals who alleged violations of the securities laws in connection with the fund's acquisition of certain other securities. As a result of the ensuing publicity, the fund's independent accountants on November 21, 1968, withdrew their certification of the fund's financial statement as of May 31, 1968. Thereafter, Mates informed the accountants for the first time of the substantial acquisitions of restricted securities subsequent to May 31, 1968. The accountants resigned. On December 19, 1968, the fund's board of directors lowered the value of the restricted securities to $11,576,085, or $3,223,165 below the market price of corresponding unrestricted shares. The Investment Company Act of 1940 requires that in determining net asset value, "securities for which market quotations are readily available" must be valued at current market value while other securities and assets must be valued at "fair value as determined in good faith by the board of directors." Readily available market quotations mean reports of current public transactions or current public offers. No current public transactions or current public offers can exist in the case of restricted securities. Accordingly, their values must be determined in good faith by the board of directors. *In the case of the Mates Fund, during the period from April through August 1968, the fund's board of directors did not even purport to value the fund's holdings of restricted securities.* In August 1968 the directors apparently were advised of Mates's valuation methods and made no objections. Mates continued through November 1969 to value his restricted holdings at the market price for unrestricted securities or at a small discount from such prices.

On July 8, 1968, Mates had agreed to purchase 300,000 restricted shares of Omega for $3.25 per share, reflecting a discount of about 46 percent from the current market price of approximately $6.00 per share for the unrestricted stock. However, the fund did not include these shares in its portfolio valuation sheets for ten days, or until July 18, 1968, when it valued them at $5.75 per share, the market price for the unrestricted securities having risen by that date to $8.12. On May 31, 1968, the fund had agreed to purchase 36,000 restricted shares of Giffen at $30.00 per share *at a time when the market price for the unrestricted stock was only $23.00 per share.* However, the fund did not value the Giffen stock for portfolio purposes until July 23, 1968, when the market value of the unrestricted stock had climbed to $58.00, at which time the restricted stock was assigned a value of $49.00 per share. Why was Mates willing to pay more than the market value of the Giffen stock? Was there a deliberately planned scheme to manipulate the price of the free stock upward to justify the inflation of the price of the restricted shares? The curious pattern of *delay* in first valuing the restricted securities after they had been purchased was typical of the fund's operations. It had the effect of creating the impression that the fund's appreciation was being achieved over a shorter period of time and thus distorted the public's understanding of Mates's skill as a manager.

On the historic day—December 20, 1968—the S.E.C. suspended trading in Omega, you will remember that more than 20 percent of the fund was invested in it and an additional 22 percent was in other restricted securities. Mates was trapped. The man who earlier that year had written to his shareholders that he did not believe in locking himself into a position that delegated too much of management's responsibilities to the vagaries of the market had done exactly that. Mates had telephoned the S.E.C. and, you will recall, had obtained its hasty approval of his fund's suspension of redemptions.

In order to place the fund in a more liquid position to enable it to pay off the huge bank loans and to provide cash to accommodate shareholders requesting redemption, Mates, following the fund's suspension of redemptions, desperately began unloading its holdings. *The New York Times* noted reports that the fund was "peddling" many of its securities at huge reductions in price, while *Newsweek* speculated on the manner in which professional traders, knowing what securities the fund had available for sale and of the urgency involved in their disposal, could take short positions—which would have the effect of further depressing their prices.

Mates found buyers for a number of restricted securities but only at prices substantially below those at which they had been carried in the portfolio. For example, on December 31, 1968, Mates sold his Giffen shares for $41.00 per share, only about two thirds of the market price of unrestricted shares. (Remember, he had paid 33 percent *above* the market price when he bought it.) On December 30, he sold the Longchamps, Inc., stock, which he had carried in his portfolio on December 19 at $37.00 per share, for $12.00 less than that figure.

When Fred Mates had been required to suspend sale of his fund's shares in June, he hit upon a temporary solution to the problem of what to do with all the money that was being offered to him. He organized Mates Financial Services, an investment advisory firm. In the next five months, he accepted more than $17 million from 717 individuals with glowing promises that he would invest it with the same spectacular results that had marked his fund's operations. On December 24, 1968, four days after his suspension of fund redemptions, I telephoned Mates and questioned him about his operations. He acknowledged that many of his private accounts had been invested in unrestricted shares of Omega Equities and that he had got all of them out of

the stock before trading in it was suspended. I concluded that having purchased the Omega letter stock for the fund, he had then used the money in the private accounts to trade in the free stock with the objective of running its price up to justify concurrent increased valuation of the letter stock to the point where he was valuing it at approximately ten times what he had paid for it. He got his private accounts out with a tidy profit. It was the fund shareholders who were left holding the bag with the restricted stock. They sat helplessly by, watching the market decline steadily while they were unable to break out of the fund.

The trading for the fund and for the 717 individual accounts generated a substantial volume of brokerage business. It would have been obviously improper for Mates to openly demand of the brokers with whom he placed the securities business that they give him a kickback. Instead, the Mates Financial Services produced an inconsequential "market letter" which it sold to brokers for a monthly subscription price of $5,000, later reduced to $3,000. All concerned knew that in consideration of the "subscription," the broker involved would receive a substantial volume of securities transactions. Just as "a rose by any other name would smell as sweet," so a kickback by any other name was just as profitable. Mr. Mates took in over $90,000 in "subscriptions," despite the fact that a brochure distributed to prospective clients stated that his advisory firm was not a broker and collected no commissions on clients' accounts. As the S.E.C. put it: "These arrangements enabled Mates to derive undisclosed personal benefits . . . which were inconsistent with his fiduciary relationship with his advisory clients. These actions were violative of the anti-fraud and anti-manipulative provisions of the Securities Exchange Act and the Investment Advisers Act."

The fund's auditors having resigned, Mates appointed another nationally known firm. That company resigned, too, after only eight weeks. In April 1969, Mates distributed to shareholders an annual report prepared and certified by Price, Waterhouse and Co., which disclosed the status of the fund as of a date almost one year earlier, long before Price, Waterhouse had become its auditors and prior to its purchase of letter stock. In his notice of the annual meeting of shareholders held on July 20, 1969, Mates gave a very confusing explanation of his purchases and valuation of letter stock. In some instances, he quoted the valuation discount in dollars, while in others he quoted it in percentages. (Valuing something at a discount of $1.25 from the $5.00 market price of its free counterpart reflects a 25 percent discount. But when the free stock has been moved upward to $35.00 per share, and you are still carrying your restricted stock at the same $1.25 discount from market, you are discounting it only 3½ percent.)

A great many of these facts were reported in one financial journal or another. In the circumstances, it was to be expected that if the Securities and Exchange Commission did not put Fred Mates out of business, the shareholders of the Mates Investment Fund would the minute they got a chance to redeem.

On July 20, 1969, the annual meeting of shareholders took place, not in New York, where the fund and its custodian bank were headquartered, but in Wilmington, Delaware. The agenda included the election of directors and the approval of a renewal of the management contract with Fred Mates. The shareholders gathered in person and by proxy—shareholders who had been lied to and cheated and locked into the fund during seven months of a sharply falling market. Now, at last they would have a chance to speak their minds.

They did. In an incredible display of mass masochism, 70 percent of them voted to reelect Mates and his associates as directors and to renew the investment management contract with him.

In its May 2, 1970, issue, *Life* magazine presented a glamorized study of Fred Mates. A triumph of unobjective reporting, the seven-page article unaccountably glossed over the facts of Mates's transgressions and pictured him as an investment genius, a superman whose mutual fund had racked up, in the second half of 1969, the "best performance record of almost any money manager in the U.S." The fact is that in the twelve-month period immediately preceding publication of the *Life* article, the Mates Investment Fund ranked 337 among 414 funds rated—which put it in the bottom 20 percent. *Life*'s panegyric leaves the magazine with a heavy responsibility.

I listened thoughtfully to Fred Mates that day in the restaurant in New York. He did not convince *me*.

# Chapter 19

# THE WINFIELD STORY

For many years, Winfield Growth Fund, Inc., was operated by a San Francisco investment adviser under his own name, during which time it compiled an undistinguished record as a balanced fund.

The present management took over in 1957 and changed Winfield to a growth fund. In the bull market of 1967 and 1968, the fund did extremely well, showing a gain of 101 percent in 1967 and 16.4 percent in 1968. Management skill? No, just jiggery-pokery with the books.

From their own admission, we know that they held restricted stock in mid-1967. Their purchases continued. On January 17, 1968, the fund purchased 87,500 shares of International Chemical and Nuclear Corporation at $40.00 per share for a total cost of $3,500,000, a 44.4 percent discount from the current market value of International's unrestricted stock. Five and a half months later, it carried the shares in its June 30, 1968, report to shareholders at $8,050,000—or 100 percent of the market value which the shares would have had if they had been unrestricted. Winfield's June 30 report to the Securities and Exchange Commission disclosed both the cost and the valuation placed upon the securities, and the Commission said nothing.

On June 29, 1968, Winfield purchased 40,000 shares of Volt Technical at $65.00 per share, the total cost being $2,600,000. *Twenty-four hours later,* it carried the shares in its June 30 report to shareholders at $4,320,000. It had purchased the shares at a 40.4 percent discount from market, and immediately valued them at market. These facts were fully disclosed in the fund's June 30 report to the Securities and Exchange Commission.

On May 28, 1968, the fund bought 20,000 shares of 3i-Information Interscience Incorporated at $12.00 per share, a discount of 53.9 percent from market. On June 24, 1968, it purchased another 10,000 shares at a 76.9 percent discount from market. Curiously, neither of these purchases appeared in the fund's June 30, 1968, report to shareholders, but the facts were reported in the fund's June 30 N-1-R report to the Securities and Exchange Commission. This showed that the securities purchased during the previous month for $360,000 had quadrupled in value to $1,440,000, a patent violation of the "fair market value" rule. Still the Commission said nothing.

Winfield's forged genius brought thousands of new investors into the fund, while its doctored valuations inflated the management fee. As a result, every person who bought Winfield Fund during a two-and-one-half-year period beginning in mid-1967 grossly overpaid. Those who redeemed got back too much.

An honest mistake? Valuations in good faith? Simply a difference of opinion of what constitutes a fair price? Certainly not! When Winfield's portfolio managers negotiated a purchase of Volt Technical stock at $65.00 per share, at a 40.4 percent discount from the current market price, they were not stealing the securities. The officers of the issuer were intimately familiar with every facet of their stock's value, and when they agreed to sell 40,000 shares at the reduced price, they knew exactly what they were doing. If they had released the stock for less than it was actually worth, they might well have been faced with a stockholder's suit charging them with a wasting of company assets. They and the Winfield portfolio managers haggled over the price and finally agreed that an unregistered share of the company's stock was worth $65.00. In the circumstances, what possible justification could there be for Winfield's valuation of the stock at $108 just twenty-four hours later?

The current prospectus of Winfield Fund contains this historical note: "During the period from July 1, 1967, to August 1968, restricted securities held in the Fund's portfolio were valued by Messrs. Meid and Wiskemann at the market price of unrestricted securities of the same class, if any. In September, 1968, the Fund's Board of Directors, after reviewing various methods for valuing restricted securities, determined that restricted securities, taken as a group, thereafter should be valued at a uniform formula discount of 12% from the market price of unrestricted securities of the same class and not be considered as securities for which market prices are readily available."'

The restricted securities now in the Winfield portfolio were purchased at an average discount of 37.7 percent from the current market price. The directors now value those securities at a uniform 12 percent discount from market, apparently under the impression that thereby they are making an honest woman of Winfield. I am afraid that I don't agree. They should cut another 25 percent off their valuations. They are still grossly over-valuing the restricted holdings. The mere fact that the sleeping giants at 500 North Capitol Avenue in Washington let them get away with it is not justification enough.

According to the Investment Company Act of 1940 a registered mutual fund may not own more than 10 percent of the stock of any one corporation. Winfield's purchase of 87,500 restricted shares of International Chemical and Nuclear Corporation (later split 2 for 1) constituted 12 percent of the outstanding common stock of the issuer. Winfield Fund remained in violation of the Act for fifteen months, or until April 15, 1969, when the issuer registered a block of additional stock, which brought Winfield's holdings down to less than 10 percent.

Early in February 1969, I sat down with the New York Regional Administrator of the S.E.C. and his aides and laid before them the facts I had discovered concerning Winfield's operations. In addition, on February 17, 1969, on behalf of two shareholders a suit was instituted against Winfield Fund by a New York attorney to whom my own attorney had confided the facts of my information against Winfield. To my charges against the fund for letter stock improprieties, the lawyer added others he had uncovered, which involved the secret channeling of brokerage business back to the sponsors and managers.

Without admitting any wrongdoing, the defendants agreed with the plaintiffs that the fund suffered damages of approximately $1 million. A settlement of $500,000, or 50 cent on the dollar, was worked out in December, 1969. This will take the form of a remission of a part of the management fee over a four-year period. I don't need to tell you that getting $500,000 over a four-year period is not the same as getting $500,000 in one lump sum. Indeed, discounted at the present prime rate, it is really a settlement of only $415,000.

This settlement was approved by Judge Edward C. McLean in a New York District Federal Court. I ob-

jected vigorously. As a shareholder in Winfield Fund, I had intervened in the suit to protest that it was not proper to settle a million dollar claim for half that amount. It was clearly established in the course of the proceedings that $921,000 of brokerage commissions had been improperly diverted to the sponsor and investment adviser of the fund. The managers further acknowledged that Winfield Fund had suffered a loss of $280,000 by reason of payments to redeeming shareholders based upon valuations of restricted securities at market instead of at the 12 percent discount established later as a regular valuation formula. Actually, the discount was one third of what it should have been. (We already noted that since such securities were purchased at a discount averaging 37.7 percent from market, they should at least have been consistent and valued them at all future times at the same discount, not at the 12 percent figure arbitrarily set by the sponsor.) Accordingly the restricted stock loss should have been set at $840,000. Combined with the $921,000 brokerage claim, the total damages thus became $1,761,000. The discounted settlement of $415,000 represented a settlement of less than 25 cents on the dollar, I contended. If a bank is robbed and the guilty parties are caught, they are not allowed to keep 75 percent of the loot. The return of 25 percent of what has been stolen is not an equitable treatment of the depositors of the bank. If the damages were $1.76 million in the Winfield case, that is the figure that should be used in arriving at a settlement. It is unthinkable that wrongdoers should be allowed to continue to hold onto and enjoy the fruits of their dishonesty.

Most previous suits against funds had involved excessive management fees. There was no wrongdoing involved—shareholders had been aware of the management fee schedule when they entered the fund and had accepted it. Subsequently, encouraged by lawyers, they had brought suits seeking to have the fees reduced. Such suits generally stated an amount of alleged damages sustained by reason of the exorbitant fees, and commonly such suits were settled for sums approximately 25 percent to 50 percent of the claimed damages. The Winfield matter was not of that type. It was not charged that too much had been taken but rather that the sums involved should never have been taken at all. It was not appropriate that the formula of a settlement of 25 percent to 50 percent of the claim should be found acceptable, I argued before the court.

My arguments were all in vain. Judge McLean approved the settlement under which the fund would benefit by a remission of a part of the management fees over the next four years. Winfield Fund collected $25,000 at the start and waited for the rest.

But then the inexplicable Judge McLean ordered *the fund* to pay the plaintiff's counsel a fee of $95,500 in two installments, half then and half in January 1971. To recover over a period of four years $500,000 of the $1,761,000 which had been improperly taken from them, the shareholders of the fund were required to pay out $95,500 within the first year! I argued that the shareholders should not be compelled to pay fees predicated upon the creation of a fund for their benefit until enough of the fund created had been received to pay the fees. The shareholders should not be out of pocket at any point in time. It was to no avail. In all likelihood, the fees for defending the officers and directors of the fund against the charges of wrongdoing were also charged to the fund and were thus an expense to the shareholders.

The fee for plaintiff's counsel must be paid by today's shareholders, but many of them would have no hope of participating in the recovery. Many shareholders, myself included, would obviously be disenchanted with a management that would engage in such shenanigans, and would want no part of it over the next four years. Once out of the fund, these shareholders would receive no benefit whatever from the management fee remissions over the next four years.

The cunningly contrived Winfield settlement was so worded as to preclude any other derivative action by a shareholder to obtain more equitable redress. However, there still is open to shareholders a class action to recover for the letter stock overvaluations which resulted in incoming shareholders paying too much for their shares.

It had taken ten months after my meeting with the Commission's New York Regional Administrator on my charges against Winfield for the Commission to institute an action against Winfield, which was based on my information. The long delay was significant: during that period, many more people were abused by the fund's accounting peccadillos.

Judge McLean, who approved this inequitable settlement, does not seem sympathetic to the interests of fund shareholders. In the case of my shareholders' derivative action against Enterprise Fund, which we will pursue in the following chapter, he acceded to the sponsor's request that the litigation be transferred from New York to Los Angeles. This required the employment of a whole new set of attorneys to press the action there. At about the same time, Vance, Sanders & Co., of Boston, sponsors and distributors of a number of prominent funds, had asked that a suit against them charging excessive management fees and improper allocation of brokerage be transferred from New York to Boston for their convenience. But this time another federal judge in New York ruled that New York was the financial center of the country and that many of the fund shareholders in the Vance, Sanders case were located in the area and that the suit should therefore be heard there. Judge McLean, on the other hand, had played along with the Enterprise effort to make it difficult for the shareholders to press their action against Enterprise Fund. More recently, McLean sat in judgment in a suit against Dreyfus Fund where excessive management fees were charged. Although Dreyfus's assets had grown to $2.26 billion, the management fee remained at .5 percent. The plaintiff shareholders and the Securities and Exchange Commission both asked that the court require Dreyfus management to reduce its fee proportionately as the fund size increased. Judge McLean approved an incredible "settlement": he reduced the management fee to .492 percent.

In connection with Judge McLean's decision' in the Dreyfus Fund, it would be interesting to know whether he required the shareholders also to pay a substantial fee to the plaintiff's attorney, as well as to absorb the cost of the fund's defense against the charges. Dreyfus Fund has declined to clarify this point.

I advise anyone contemplating the purchase of Winfield Growth Fund to read the prospectus very carefully.

# Chapter 20

# THE ENTERPRISE STORY

In April 1967, Shareholders Management Company of Los Angeles retained me to conduct a public estate-planning forum in the Shrine Auditorium in that city before an audience of nearly 5,000 people. The company executives were very hospitable and the evening appeared to be a success—it was 1:00 A.M. before I left the auditorium.

That was my introduction to Shareholders Management. The company was sponsoring and managing three mutual funds—Convertible Securities Fund (now known as Harbor Fund), Fletcher Fund, and Enterprise Fund—and its officers drew my attention particularly to the impressive performance record of the latter two. I took note of their investment policies and, having watched their performance for five or six months, decided to invest some of my own money and to direct some of the assets of clients into the two funds. It appeared to be working out well: Enterprise Fund finished 1967 as the No. 1 performing fund in the country, up 116.3 percent, while Fletcher Fund was close behind with a total overall gain of 103.4 percent. Late in 1967, Fletcher Fund reached its preset goal of $100 million of assets and discontinued sales. In early April of 1968, Shareholders Management made a ten-day offering of a new Fletcher Capital Fund. It expected the underwriting to bring in perhaps $35 million but the Enterprise record of the same managers proved a great lure for investors and $177 million worth of shares were sold.

In 1968, Enterprise again performed well, up 43.6 percent, while Fletcher Fund gained only 12.5 percent. Fletcher Capital did far better, up 26 percent in its eight months of operation.

Douglas B. Fletcher and Myron D. Winkler had formed Shareholders Management in 1962, but not until Fred Carr joined the team in 1966 had things begun to move. Carr became portfolio manager of Enterprise and very shortly the fund "took off." His fame grew through 1967 and 1968, and he became the golden boy of American investment managers. As late as May 1969, *Business Week* featured Carr on its cover with a headline, "A Mutual Fund Wizard Builds an Empire." But by then, Carr was in trouble. The bear market had set in at year-end 1968 and Carr's methods began to undergo close scrutiny. Under the microscope, the performance record began to appear something less than genuine.

Carr had come to Enterprise from Kleiner, Bell & Co., a West Coast securities firm with a reputation as wheeler-dealers specializing in private placements. Carr had been research director there, and he had brought his letter stock skills to Enterprise.

In December 1968, after the Mates Investment Fund had suspended redemptions because of its letter stock difficulties, I began looking around to see who else might have traveled the letter stock route. The first place that I looked was Enterprise Fund, confident that I would find no such problems. What I found made me realize that the fund's magnificent performance was an out-and-out fake, contrived largely of discounted letter stock purchases and gross overvaluation of such holdings.

In the files of the Securities and Exchange Commission in Washington I examined the reports filed with the Commission by Enterprise showing its securities purchases during 1967 and 1968. I checked these against the fund's periodic reports to shareholders.

In a *New York Times* interview on January 5, 1969, Fred Carr stated that "letter securities account for no more than 10% of gross assets." I wrote to Shareholders Management and asked for an explanation of its policies with respect to the purchase and valuation of letter stock. At what discounts had they generally bought letter stock, I asked, and at what discounts did they value such stocks in their portfolio? The company replied that it was not prepared to make such information public. "What do you mean you're not prepared to make such information public?" I demanded. "You have more than a quarter of a million dollars of my money in your Enterprise Fund and Fletcher Capital Fund and I want to know what you're doing with it! I want to know whether or not you're doing the same sort of thing that got Mates into difficulties."

The company became more responsive. On February 4, 1969, Eugene Shutler, Assistant Vice-President of Shareholders Management Company, wrote:

> It has been and continues to be our policy to limit the portion of the assets of Enterprise Fund and Fletcher Capital Fund invested in private placement to not more than 10% of each of the Funds' total assets at the time of purchase, and all such holdings, in the aggregate . . . do not at present comprise more than 10% of the portfolio of either Fund.
>
> In the pricing of securities obtained by means of a private placement, please read and consider page 11 of the enclosed prospectus of SMC Investment Corporation, which we manage. There is also enclosed a letter from Fred Carr to the staff of the Securities and Exchange Commission, which further sets forth our policies on valuing such securities. These policies are in effect for all funds which we manage.

Mr. Shutler's referred-to letter by Mr. Carr was addressed to Theodore Alcaide ("Dear Ted") of the Division of Corporate Regulation, Securities and Exchange Commission, and, as Mr. Shutler noted, it concerned the investment policies of SMC Investment Corporation, a closed-end investment company managed by Shareholders Management Corporation with the avowed investment policy of putting most of its money into restricted securities. However, that type of security is a perfectly proper investment for a closed-end company which issues a block of shares at the outset of its operations—and never is called upon to redeem them. As we have seen earlier, such shares trade in the open market at a price determined by the law of supply and demand and by the public's evaluation of the skill of the management. The net asset value of the company's shares is not determined each business day as is the case with the shares of an open-end mutual fund. No representation is made to the buyer that the shares are worth anything at all, much less that they are worth exactly what he has paid for them.

Despite the quite different nature of SMC Investment Corporation as a closed-end investment company, Shareholders Management went to great lengths in its prospectus to place purchasers on notice that it was the company's intention to invest heavily in restricted secu-

rities and to warn them of the hazards of such investment. But neither Enterprise Fund nor Fletcher Capital Fund in their prospectuses had made any such disclosure.

Mr. Carr's letter said in part:

> We propose to value restricted securities . . . at an amount equal to the market value of the non-restricted securities reduced by the same percentage discount as reflected in the purchase price of the restricted securities at the time agreement was reached for the purchase.

Mr. Carr therefore was on record with the S.E.C. that restricted securities would be valued by SMC Investment Corporation at the same discount from market at which they had been purchased, and Mr. Shutler had confirmed that the same valuation policies "are in effect for all funds which we manage." The date of his letter was February 4, 1969, when he said that restricted securities did not comprise more than 10 percent of the portfolio of either Enterprise Fund or Fletcher Capital.

On March 3, 1969, Douglas Fletcher wrote a letter "To Our Friends In The Securities Business," stating Shareholders Management Company's position of a 10 percent restriction on letter stock, and establishing such investments as of that date for Enterprise Fund at 8.8 percent. He also explained that "some private placements have been carried on the books at lesser or greater discounts than those prevailing at the time of purchase, depending upon the circumstances of the particular issue involved."

The 1969 edition of Arthur Wiesenberger's *Investment Companies,* the "bible" of the mutual fund industry, reported that on December 31, 1968, Enterprise had $123.1 million, or 12.9 percent of its assets, in twenty-eight restricted securities. But had Carr not reported to *The New York Times* on January 5 that they never went over 10 percent? And what of Shutler's February 4 statement that they "do not at present comprise more than 10 percent," or Fletcher's March 3 letter declaring that Enterprise had 8.8 percent in restricted stock and never went above 10 percent? Wiesenberger reported that Enterprise Fund had 50 percent more in letter stock than Fletcher acknowledged and 29 percent more than Shutler, Carr, and Fletcher said was their top limit.

In what light should one review these blatantly contradictory statements?

Here are some examples of their holdings and the assigned valuations:

In 1967, Enterprise Fund purchased 60,000 shares of Shinn Industries, a Los Angeles engineering firm, at $10.00 per share. The holding appeared in the 1967 year-end report to shareholders at $18.11, a discount of 10 percent from market. Shareholders Management Company also managed the Douglas Fund for Bernard Cornfeld, then head of the Geneva-based Investors Overseas Services. At the same time that it was buying the Shinn Industries shares for its own Enterprise Fund, it bought an additional 40,000 shares at $10.00 per share for the Douglas Fund, but at year-end 1967, it valued Cornfeld's Shinn stock at only $15.90, a 20 percent discount from market. The Enterprise record was public. Padding the figures brought new investors flocking into the fund with resultant fame and fortune for Doug Fletcher and Fred Carr. No one knew that Shareholders was managing Cornfeld's Douglas Fund. Besides, Cornfeld was looking over their shoulder, so the Shinn stock was valued more conservatively in that fund. The Securities and Exchange Commission received and examined both reports and found nothing amiss.

On December 22, 1967, Enterprise bought 21,000 shares of Larson Industries for $2,101,000, or $100 per share. Five business days later, in its December 31, 1967, report, it valued those 21,000 shares at $2,473,000, or $118 per share. The 18 percent increase in value in those five days was certainly a splendid gain, considering that Enterprise Fund as a whole went up only 2.4 percent in that period.

On the same December 22, 1967, the fund purchased 80,000 shares of AITS, Inc., for $2,081,000. Those shares appeared in the December 31, 1967, report five business days later at $2,718,000. The $637,000 markup was equal to 30.6 percent. The shares were valued only 5.6 percent below the $2,880,000 market value of that number of unrestricted shares. On December 31, 1967, they valued the stock at 94.4 percent of market; on June 30, 1968, they valued the same stock at 88.8 percent of market; and on September 30, 1968, they valued it at 89.7 percent of market. This is a classic example of how letter stock was *not* valued at the same discount from market at which they had purchased it, notwithstanding Carr's and Shutler's official assurances.

On May 1, 1967, Enterprise bought 100,000 shares of Texas American Oil Company for $552,382. In its June 30 report, sixty days later, the stock was valued at $762,968, a 38 percent increase. During that period, Enterprise Fund as a whole went up 14 percent.

On March 27, 1967, Enterprise bought $316,000 worth of Bell Electronics 6 percent convertible debentures. In the March 31 report, four days later, the Bell holdings were valued at $444,744, a four-day gain of 40 percent.

On June 28, 1967, Enterprise bought 50,000 shares of Wellington Electronics for $743,000, or 14.86 per share. Forty-eight hours later, according to the fund's report to shareholders, it owned 53,500 shares valued at $1,263,938, or $23.62 per share—a 59 percent gain

in price. I was not able to account for the odd 3,500 shares on the last entry. It would be interesting to explore whether or not those 3,500 shares were in fact unrestricted shares bought in the open market during the two days as part of a deliberate scheme to run up the price of the free stock to justify the unconscionable increase in the valuation of the restricted stockholding.

The fund filed a report with the Securities and Exchange Commission disclosing that on June 28, 1967, it had purchased 40,000 shares of TBS Computer for $380,000. Curiously, in its June 30, 1967, report to shareholders, the TBS Computer stock did not appear.

Financial reports to shareholders are required to disclose not only the names and amounts of securities held on a specific date but must also specifically identify in a separate listing all companies added or eliminated during the period since the last report. The December 31, 1968, report of Enterprise Fund disclosed holdings of $1,167,750 of Shinn Industries and $2,473,800 of Larson Industries preferred. Neither of these showed up in the mid-1969 report to shareholders, but also did not appear among the portfolio eliminations.

Similarly, a $449,500 common stock holding and a $299,700 preferred stock holding of Macrodyne-Chatillon Corporation appeared in the mid-1969 report for the first time, but were not included in the list of portfolio additions.

When I drew these discrepancies to the attention of the Securities and Exchange Commission, the Commission replied with a perfunctory "Thank you for your letter."

I supplied the Securities and Exchange Commission's Division of Corporate Regulation with all these facts of Enterprise Fund's gross overvaluation of its letter stock holdings. I pointed out that the overvaluation had substantially increased the management fees being collected by Shareholders Management, a procedure which was simply outrageous. I drew attention to the fact that as a result of the overvaluation, the public was being misled into buying huge quantities of the fund's shares in the belief that the managers were far better than they actually were. Because the shares were being overvalued, these people were paying more per share than they should be—or, stated another way, they weren't receiving as many shares as they should have been for the money they were investing. I urged that the Commission halt sales of Enterprise Fund until an audit could be made to determine the extent of the inequities.

Once again, the Commission acknowledged receipt of the information and did nothing.

Someone had to do *something,* so on February 11, 1969, I filed the earlier-mentioned shareholder's derivative suit against Enterprise Fund charging that without making any disclosure in its prospectus of its intention to do so, Enterprise had more than a hundred million dollars of its shareholders' money invested in securities for which no public market existed, and that it had grossly overvalued these securities—all to the sponsor's gain.

Three different divisions of the S.E.C. asked for a copy of the complaint against Enterprise, and I supplied them.

Meanwhile, the people who had invested in the fund had still another problem: shareholder accounting. Every mutual fund is required by law to have its assets in the custody of a bank but most funds delegate to that bank the responsibility for all shareholder accounting. As custodian of Fletcher Fund and Enterprise Fund, the Bank of America in Los Angeles had handled ("mishandled" would be a better word) all shareholder accounting prior to May 1, 1968. Here is an example of how they executed their responsibility: I requested the redemption of shares of Fletcher Fund I owned, which had a value of $58,000. In due course, I received a check for the $58,000 and a new confirmation which indicated that instead of canceling the shares I owned, the bank had added a like number. One week later, I received a second check for $58,000. Having started out with $58,000 worth of Fletcher Fund, I ended up with $116,000 in cash and twice as many shares as I had at the start. I considered briefly retiring from business and spending the rest of my life redeeming shares of Fletcher Fund. Amused, I wondered how long it would take the fund and the bank to discover the huge mistake, and I waited expectantly for the excited telephone call which I was sure would come, asking me to return the overpayment.

It never came. "Is it possible," I asked myself, "for a mutual fund to lose such a large sum and not have it discovered? Isn't there a system of checks and balances that must turn up the deficiency?"

It *was* possible for them to lose the money, and there was no system of checks and balances. I telephoned Inge Johnston, a Shareholders Management executive, and made an appointment to fly to Los Angeles to review with him the whole accounting mess, which, it was to become increasingly clear, enveloped Enterprise and its sister funds. When I arrived, Mr. Johnston was not to be found. In his absence, I talked with Vice-President Vincent McGuinness. When I disclosed to him the overpayment that had been made to me, he shrugged it off, saying that it was the bank's worry.

In the months that followed, it became ever more apparent that while Shareholders Management Company spared no expense in getting dealers to put new customers on its books, once those customers had handed over their money the sponsor completely lost interest in them. I discovered that my own firm's experience was duplicated with other investment firms around the country. We would invest a client's money in Enterprise Fund and pay for the shares—and that would be the last we would ever hear of it. Complaints to the sponsor that the shareholder had never been credited with the shares, or had been credited with the wrong number of shares, or had never received a certificate or had not received dividends to which he was entitled—all these went unheeded by Shareholders Management. The most they would provide was a scanty printed card confirming that the complaint had been received and had been referred to the custodian bank.

Mr. McGuinness then disclosed to me that the company had fired the Bank of America as custodian. Later, executives of the bank advised me that it was they who had fired Enterprise Fund. I do not know which to believe, for each had a pretty well established credibility gap. In any case, on May 1, 1968, the Bank of America turned all of the Enterprise Fund records over to the State Street Bank and Trust Company of Boston, the fund's new custodian. It was quite a package. It included twenty thousand complaint letters from Enterprise shareholders. McGuinness told me that these were general complaints about the share total not being right, that a certificate had not been issued, that an address or tax number was wrong, etc. But a leading financial editor told me that his investigation disclosed that there were twenty thousand letters from people who had bought and paid for shares of Enterprise Fund—*but for whom no account had ever been opened.*

The fund did not even know how many of its shares were outstanding. A friend, an officer at the State Street Bank, confided to me that share certificates were regularly being presented for redemption by persons of whom the bank had no record. The certificates were valid, though, and the bank redeemed the shares.

If Enterprise Fund did not know about all of those outstanding certificates of which its custodian bank had no record, if it did not know exactly how many of its shares were in the hands of investors, how could it arrive at an accurate daily valuation of its shares?

The announced net asset value per share was far too high, which made the fund's performance record look even better. Meanwhile, all new investors who bought at the inaccurate net asset value (plus a sales charge) were overpaying and those who redeemed were paid too much. Surviving shareholders were left holding the bag.

On March 17, 1969, Enterprise Fund held its annual meeting in the auditorium of the State Street Bank and Trust Company in Boston. It had been preceded by a costly three weeks of intensive canvassing of shareholders by letter, telephone, and in person—all at shareholder expense—to generate sufficient proxies to provide a quorum. Originally scheduled for 11:00 A.M., the meeting had to be adjourned until 2:30 P.M. for lack of a quorum. Though the fund put forth a maximum effort in the interim, combing the metropolitan Boston area to scrape up additional proxies, it failed to obtain enough to provide the quorum and the meeting was adjourned for two weeks.

The period before adjournment in the morning did present an opportunity for some of those present to question the fund officers and directors, and many investors and investment dealers availed themselves of that opportunity. The essence of the complaints was that the State Street Bank and Trust Company had displayed an arrogant disregard of the rights of the shareholders, while the sponsor, once it had sold the shares, cared not a whit whether the purchaser ever received what he had paid for. One investment dealer denounced the sponsor from the floor as displaying a callous disinterest in shareholders the like of which he had not seen in all his years in the investment business.

At the meeting, I tried unsuccessfully to have the management explain how it arrived at certain of the valuations of its investments. Both the chairman, Douglas Fletcher, and the portfolio manager, Larry Rader, declined to answer the questions.

I also drew the chairman's attention to a provision in the prospectus under which I had bought my shares to the effect that a purchaser might elect to have his dividends and capital gains distributions automatically reinvested or, alternatively, he could have them paid in cash. This is a choice common to practically all funds. But Enterprise went a fantastic step further. It offered each shareholder who elected to take his dividends and distributions in cash the right to return it within fifteen days of the payment date with a request that it be reinvested in additional shares at the price prevailing on the record date. In 1965, for example, the shareholder could have returned his dividend check on March 3 (when the net asset value was $9.72) and requested reinvestment at the $9.09 price prevailing on the earlier record date. He was thus permitted to buy shares at 6.6 percent discount from the prevailing net asset value—at the expense of the other shareholders.

Similarly, in 1966, a shareholder could have returned his dividend check on March 1 (when the net asset value was $13.63) and had it reinvested at the $12.67 price prevailing on the record date, a 7.1 percent discount, again at the expense of the other shareholders.

In 1967, the shareholder could have returned his check on March 1 (when the price was $14.96) and had it reinvested at the $13.21 price prevailing on the record date. At the expense of the other shareholders, he could thus have purchased shares at an 11.75 percent discount.

I asked the chairman to explain this inequitable arrangement. He indicated that he did not know that it existed. Since he claimed to know nothing about it, it was impossible to obtain from him any estimate of the loss which the provision had imposed upon the shareholders. The provision has now been dropped from the prospectus, but the fund is contractually bound to continue the privilege to all purchasers who bought their shares under the old prospectus.

All during 1967–1968, Enterprise shareholders were greatly disadvantaged by the fund's procedures for filling orders. The unfair practice of "forward pricing" was then sanctioned by the S.E.C. Shares were valued twice each day—at 1:00 P.M. and again when the market closed at 3:30 P.M., each valuation becoming effective one hour later. Under the "forward pricing" scheme, an investment dealer could always purchase shares at the last computed price. For example: Enterprise would compute its net asset value and new asked price at the close on Monday and that price was effective from 4:30 P.M. on that day until 2:00 P.M. on Tuesday. If the market boiled up in the morning, a dealer would know that the revalued 2:00 P.M. price for shares would be higher, and he could place new orders for shares until 2:00 P.M., guaranteeing the purchasers an immediate increase in value. In effect, the fund was selling shares for less than they were worth, the instant profit to the new shareholder being wrung from the old shareholders. In a sharply rising market, many dealers would get on the telephone to their customers and alert them to the fact that they could get an order in for them on this very favorable basis.

This abuse was widespread in the fund industry, but Enterprise made it worse by its improper order procedures. When the dealer called to place an order at 1:45 P.M on Tuesday at Monday's closing price, the fund's order room quite frequently advised him that it was busy and would call him back. Sometimes it would not return his call until Wednesday afternoon; at other times, he heard nothing more from the fund and had to call again. By the time his order was recorded, there had been three or four price changes in Enterprise Fund. Whether the orders were actually received from the customer on Tuesday, Wednesday, or Thursday, did not matter—all were accepted by the fund at Monday's closing price. Most customers knew nothing about the inequity of this arrangement. They just knew that somehow they were being permitted to buy shares at a price below the current asked price. No one ever asked: "If to get me into the fund they will do this to the old shareholders, what might they do to *me* once I become a shareholder?"

Some dealers have called back several days after their initial call to order shares, and the fund cheerfully accepted their backdated orders. Sprinkled in among the orders thus accepted by the fund were some from dealers who had made no earlier call. The fund's order room apparently kept no record of calls and simply accepted without argument the dealer's claim that he had attempted to place the order earlier. It is impossible to estimate how many thousands of dollars were lost to fund shareholders by this improper system for selling the fund's shares.

At the meeting on March 17, I asked Chairman Fletcher publicly: "Has the Securities and Exchange Commission at any time raised with you the question of the propriety of your operations in the area of restricted stocks?" Mr. Fletcher consulted with his colleagues and answered flatly, "No."

I pressed him further, saying, "Do we understand you correctly, Mr. Chairman? Are you saying that at no time has the S.E.C. questioned your practices with respect to letter stocks?" The answer: "That is correct."

Over a period of a year and a half, I had supplied the Securities and Exchange Commission's Division of Corporate Regulation with all of these facts as I uncovered them. It also had evidence that the fund's bookkeeping was in a state of chaos. In addition to my complaints, the Division was deluged with complaints filed directly with it by shareholders. Finally, the Commission had by this time the grace of several months to mull over the significant effects of the Mates disaster. During that period, restricted securities were a major subject of discussion in financial circles and in the press.

Yet the Commission did nothing—absolutely nothing. In those three months, it was not interested enough in the subject to check the complaints against Enterprise to learn if they were well founded.

On June 13, 1969, a seminar was held in Los Angeles on the subject of securities regulation, with special emphasis upon problems of disclosure. The chairman of the seminar was Alan B. Levenson, Senior Vice-President of Enterprise Fund. The featured speakers were Securities and Exchange Commissioner Francis M. Wheat and the Commission's Regional Administrator in San Francisco, Arthur Pennekamp. Prior to the conference, I wrote to Commissioner Wheat expressing the view that it was improper for two high Commission officials to be appearing on the platform with, and flatteringly introduced by, a senior officer of a company that was the subject of a bulging file of formal complaints and a shareholders' derivative suit charging out-and-out dishonesty and violation of the securities laws. I pointed out that Commissioner Wheat was scheduled to speak on the subject of adequate disclosure—precisely what Mr. Levenson's company had not provided its investors. Commissioner Wheat's appearance on the platform, I observed, constituted a monumental conflict of interest which could only compromise the Commission's application of the securities laws to Enterprise Fund. Commissioner Wheat rejected my suggestion that he withdraw. He and Mr. Pennekamp appeared publicly with

the very man whose acts they were supposed to be judging.

The Commission's curious unwillingness to enforce the law so far as Enterprise Fund was concerned puzzled me—*until I discovered five ex-S.E.C. lawyers on the Enterprise payroll:* Levenson was Executive Assistant Director of the Commission's Division of Corporation Finance until he resigned in January 1969 to become Executive Vice-President of Shareholders Management Company. Alan R. Gordon was former Chief Counsel of the Division of Corporate Regulation, its second most powerful man, and now Senior Vice-President of Shareholders Management. Three other ex-Commission men occupy less exalted posts at Shareholders.

In addition to these men, Herbert E. Milstein, now Chief Enforcement Attorney of the Division of Corporate Regulation, and Milstein's predecessor, David M. Butowsky, share the responsibility for the Commission's inaction.

Syndicated columnist Bill Doyle reported in June 1969:

> Back in March, a spokesman for the Shareholders Management told this newspaper that restricted stocks used to be valued at discount of 10% "or more" from the market prices of freely transferable stocks of the same corporations. Dacey's chapter and verse recitals, of course, dispute the statements from the Shareholders Management man. The management company spokesman did add that "after discussions with the Securities and Exchange Commission, Enterprise and other funds in the group now carry restricted stocks at the same discounts at which they were purchased."
>
> A suspicious mind might just come up with the idea that Enterprise was able to do well with stated performance by marking up values of restricted stocks—before the SEC got into the act. Since holding those "discussions" with the Federal agency, Enterprise hasn't been able to show run-ups in share value.

Fred Carr had in the meantime climbed from portfolio manager of Enterprise alone to a position of eminence, succeeding Douglas Fletcher as president of Shareholders Management Company when Fletcher moved up to the chairmanship of the board. But in 1969's disastrous market, Carr had lost his magic touch. The fund was in trouble. Late in November 1969, Carr resigned saying that it was matter of conscience. He did not indicate whether it was his own or someone else's conscience that was bothering him.

On December 6, 1969, at the invitation of Congressman Moss, I appeared before his House Interstate and

Foreign Commerce Subcommittee considering mutual fund legislation. There, I reported publicly for the first time the facts I had uncovered about Enterprise Fund and the Commission's failure to enforce the law. The following day, the committee summoned Hamer H. Budge, S.E.C. Chairman, to testify.

Within six weeks, the then Chief Enforcement Attorney of the Division of Corporate Regulation, David M. Butowsky, "resigned" and the Commission filed suit against Enterprise Fund in federal court in Los Angeles, echoing the charges I had made that the fund was maintaining inadequate books and records. The Commission's complaint asserted that the books of the State Street Bank and Trust Company showed an existing outstanding share total "approximately" 388,000 greater than that used by the company in computing its daily net asset value. In addition, more than 853,000 shares, either purchases or redemptions, had never been posted to the shareholders' accounts by the custodian bank.

The word "approximately" in the Commission's complaint reflected its inability to unravel the mess sufficiently to determine exactly how many shares actually existed. To determine the amount of the discrepancy accurately would require an accounting job of monumental proportions and cost. Charging that the fund did not know exactly how many of its shares were outstanding and, accordingly, could not determine the value of a share for purposes of establishing the sales price, the Commission asked the court to issue an injunction against the sale of new shares of Enterprise until bookkeeping order had been established. On February 27, 1970, the court issued such an injunction, still in force, requiring Enterprise Fund to suspend sales.

Immediately upon the issuance of the injunction against Enterprise, I drew the Commission's attention to the fact that, by the same token, the fund could not determine the value of a share for purposes of liquidation, and I urged the Commission to require the fund to suspend redemptions until it knew exactly what a share was worth. Until such time as the discrepancy ceased to be "approximate" and was known exactly, it was impossible to properly value the shares for redemption purposes. The Commission affected not to see that and allowed redemptions to continue.

It was obvious that the shares were being valued at too high a price, that those shareholders who were redeeming were being paid too much, and that all of this would be at the expense of the surviving shareholders. I talked with a leading financial editor who told me that his information was that the fund was being flooded with redemption orders and that it was having to sell off some of its better securities to raise the cash to cover the redemptions, leaving the less desirable holdings for the surviving share owners.

Vincent McGuinness, Shareholders' vice-president in charge of sales, was reported in Switzerland beyond reach of a subpoena and with a $600,000 settlement from Douglas Fletcher in his pocket. In March 1970, Myron K. Winkler, who with Douglas Fletcher had organized Shareholders Management Company in 1962, resigned as vice-president and director. Late in April, Alan B. Levenson resigned his vice-presidency, citing "personal reasons," as had Fred Carr earlier. *The Los Angeles Times* ran a critical appraisal of its position that sounded like an obituary; an Eastern financial journal disclosed the inner workings of the operations between Carr and the controlling group at Kleiner, Bell and Company; and reports circulated that Enterprise redemptions had skyrocketed. Shareholders Management was coming apart at the seams. Its stock sagged from 28 to 3½. Fletcher's paper loss was $40 million.

The fund received demands running into the hundreds from people who asked for their money back on the grounds that (1) it had failed to adequately disclose its intention to buy letter stocks, (2) it had grossly overvalued such stocks, and (3) it had allowed its bookkeeping to fall into a state of chaos. Swamped, the fund's legal counsel, O'Melveny and Myers, of Los Angeles, was reduced to sending out printed letters denying any wrongdoing and refusing rescission. All who bought Enterprise after June 30, 1967, have a loss, and are entitled to demand their money back, with interest. If all the valid claims for rescission were to be asserted, I estimate the liability at something over $150 million. Even if it were less it would still be enormous and beyond the capacity of Shareholders Management to pay. Shareholders Management Company has no such funds to pay. Such an enormous potential legal liability raises a serious question of the management's ability to meet its contractual obligations under its contract with the fund (e.g., it is committed to provide quarters for the fund, and pursuant to that commitment has executed a lease of premises which involves the payment of several million dollars over a period of years). It also has substantial potential liability under three legal actions pending against it.

Where Enterprise Fund goes from here is anybody's guess. On May 13, 1970, it was revealed that Alan B. Levenson had returned to the S.E.C. to head the Division of Corporation Finance, where once he was No. 2 man. In January, the Commission had brought suit against the company of which Levenson was executive vice-president, charging violations of the securities laws. Fifteen weeks later, it appointed Levenson to head one of its five major divisions. What a farce securities regulation has become in America!

# Chapter 21

# THE DACEY COMPOSITE FUND

In an earlier chapter on contractual plans, I explained that most funds have a built-in obsolescence. If a fund is long established and has remained small, it is likely that its performance has been consistently mediocre. If the performance had been superior, the fund would have attracted many investors and would have grown to important size. I noted, too, that not infrequently, an influx of new money into a successful fund exceeds the capacity of the managers to employ it productively and the fund becomes unwieldy. Sometimes a smart portfolio manager is lured away. In other instances, his techniques become dated; in changing times, he does not change with the times, he does not roll with the economic punch. For any one of many reasons, then, a fund can cease to be a good investment.

Twenty years ago, at a time when all of my assets were invested in Wellington Fund, I established a bank trust account into which I arranged for the fund shares and the proceeds of my life insurance to pass at my death. The bank would be the bookkeeper, watchdog, and disbursing agent, but Wellington Fund would manage the combined account. I obtained the traditional advantages of bank trusteeship, but I eliminated its two occasional disadvantages: incompetence by small banks or neglect by large competent ones. The arrangement seemed so practical that I began telling clients about it and before long many hundreds of such bank trust accounts were established. The idea spread, and the mutual fund and banking industries came to refer to this type of account as a "Dacey Trust."

Wellington Fund performed well from its inception in 1928 until the sharp market decline of 1962, when it went down less than just about anything else. But with the general recovery, interest rates began to rise and Wellington's huge portfolio of mature bonds became a very unfashionable medium of investment. The Philadelphia-based fund never recovered, which was a great tragedy because the mutual fund industry has never known a finer, more conscientious group of men.

As a professional investor, I watched Wellington's floundering in the period 1962–1965 with increasing dismay. I met a number of times with the fund's investment committee, to whom investment success, like Hoover's prosperity, was always just around the corner. Finally, despairing of the hoped-for recovery, I sold out my shares and amended my own trust to provide that the bank invest the money in Fidelity Trend and Puritan. These two members of the Fidelity Group of funds in Boston had been performing very well. The choice proved satisfactory; as noted earlier, Fidelity Trend Fund was the 1965 champ, up 57 percent, which brought in over $1 billion of new money in the next twenty-four months. Fidelity, you will remember, ended 1967 with eighty-four other funds outperforming it. The following year, it did even less well. I transferred to Enterprise Fund, and made an appropriate amendment to my trust to make Enterprise the medium of investment after I was gone. I need not remind you what a mess Fletcher, Winkler, and Carr made of that fund! It was then that I said to myself, "I can keep going back to the bank as long as I live, changing funds as they cease to be good performers, but who's going to do it after I'm gone? What I need is a fund that will *stay good*. What the hundreds of people who have set up trusts of this type need is a fund that will not become obsolete."

Why not a "fund of funds," I thought, a mutual fund which simply invests its assets in a cross section of the best-performing mutual funds? Given unlimited research facilities and the capacity for making computer-based studies of comparative performance trends among all funds, it could spot worthy young candidates for investment while keeping an eye out for signs of fatigue on the part of large, well-established funds. Having once invested in such a fund, a shareholder would never need to change, for any needed change would take place continuously and automatically within the composite fund itself.

One could with complete confidence establish a trust, with instructions to the trustee to invest on a permanent basis in such a composite fund, with reasonable expectation that it would represent a cross section of the best funds today, and that five years, ten years, twenty-five years from now, it would represent a cross section of the best funds in those years.

If such a composite fund were a no-load fund, it could result in substantial savings to investors over the costs of purchasing individual funds. In choosing investments for the composite fund, its managers would give prime consideration to performance, not to the sales charge involved. If a choice narrowed down to two funds which appeared to be equal in performance, one a load fund and the other a no-load, the composite fund managers would select for investment the one without a sales charge. However, since such a composite fund would be investing large amounts of money and would be entitled to the maximum discount on the sales charge, in all probability most of the sales charges it paid would approximate only 1 percent, rather than the 8½ percent the investor would pay were he investing on his own. By having the composite fund register with the Securities and Exchange Commission as a broker-dealer, its purchases of load funds for its own account would result in the return to it of a "dealer allowance" of at least 75 percent of the sales charge. The net sales charge it would be paying on load funds therefore would be only about one fourth of 1 percent. I estimate that load funds might constitute perhaps 30 to 35 percent of its portfolio holdings, with the balance being no-load funds. Thus, while the investor in the composite fund would indirectly be paying the sales charges that the fund itself paid, such charges would be minuscule so far as he was concerned and a vast reduction from the 8½ percent he would be paying to invest on his own.

Most mutual funds are corporations. By setting up the composite fund in the form of a trust, additional important benefits could be gained for the shareholder. Each participant could enter into his own individual inter vivos trust instrument with the trustees of the composite fund, and the instrument could provide that upon his death the trustees would make such disposition of his share of the investment fund as he had directed. These assets, passing under a trust, would be completely exempt from probate and would be turned over to the named beneficiaries without delay, expense, or publicity. A shareholder could name the fund to receive the proceeds of his life insurance at his death, and these would be added to his lifetime estate accumulation, with the income and/or principal thereafter paid to the beneficiary he has named.

The composite fund could accept cash for deposit,

or it could accept shares of other mutual funds. If the funds were among those which the managers of the composite fund considered suitable as an investment for their fund, they could retain them in the portfolio and issue to the investor shares of the composite fund having an equal value. If the shares tendered were considered unsuitable, they could be liquidated and the proceeds reinvested in one of the sixteen portfolio funds. To the extent that the composite fund received tenders of shares of load funds, for which it would otherwise have had to pay a small sales charge to acquire, the "trade-in" arrangement would be beneficial to all of the participants.

Such a composite fund seemed to be the answer to the problem of my own trust account. By the same token, it could be of enormous benefit to every layman who lacked the experience and research facilities required to maintain a mutual fund investment among the best-established funds.

On August 26, 1968, I filed with the Securities and Exchange Commission a registration statement covering the Dacey Composite Fund, a mutual fund embodying all of the advantages I have just described. At this writing, the registration is still awaiting clearance. About two months after filing and while I was absent abroad, the registration was returned stuffed into an envelope with no letter of transmittal or other explanation. When I returned to the country, I called the Commission and discussed it with them. They insisted that it be filed in a different form. On December 26, 1968, I hand-carried it to Washington and personally refiled it. When I telephoned a month later to inquire as to its progress through the registration procedures, no one could give me any information. They would "check on it." Another month passed, and there came a telephone call from a Commission lawyer reporting that my registration could not be found. Would I please file another one? I did. Three weeks later came another telephone call from the Commission advising me that half of the refiled registration was not to be found. Would I refile the missing half? I did, although I must confess that by this time I had grown somewhat impatient at the Commission's unbusinesslike way of doing things, and I observed to the caller that there was a lot of work involved in a registration statement and that it was my feeling that the work and the $2,000 filing fee required to be paid entitled an applicant to fair consideration—and my application seemed not to be receiving such fair consideration.

Two weeks later, another call from the Commission reported that an insufficient number of copies had been filed. I picked up the regulations and read them to the caller. Eight copies of the registration under the 1933 Act and three copies of the registration under the 1940 Act were required according to the regulations issued by the Commission. "I don't care what the regulations say," replied the Division attorney. "We require fourteen copies of everything, and your registration cannot be considered until we have the fourteen copies."

Finally, in July 1969, I received the Division's "letter of comment" in which it set forth those things in the prospectus to which it took exception. It wanted no discussion of inflation and the necessity for investment as a hedge against it. It wanted no discussion on investment in general. A very brief quotation from a world-famous economist was "superfluous" and, besides, they had never heard of the economist. Absolutely no photographs of the trustees would be permitted, nor any illustrations to make the booklet more attractive and therefore more readable. In vain did I lay before them the prospectuses of Dreyfus, Oppenheimer, and other funds which contained all of these things. "The Commission's thinking on this changes from week to week," I was told, "and this week, it's no pictures, no illustrations."

A key feature of the Dacey Composite Fund was its administration by five individual trustees not only during the lifetime of the shareholder but, if he chose to have it, after he was gone as well. He could, for example, have the income alone paid to his spouse, with the principal distributed among their children after she was gone. In a word, the Dacey Composite Fund would provide exactly the same trust facilities a local trust company would provide and at substantially lower cost. The trust assets would at all times be in a fund which represented a cross section of the finest investment managements currently available. But the Commission threw cold water on this concept. It insisted, for example, that the trust beneficiaries annually "reelect" the trustees. A trustee's first responsibility is to preserve an estate entrusted to him. Not infrequently, he finds himself at odds with beneficiaries bent upon dissipating the assets of a trust. Under the Commission's approach, the trustee who refused to allow profligate heirs to exhaust a trust would find himself voted out of office to be succeeded by someone more amenable to their demands. Under such circumstances, the trusteeship would become a farce. Trying to anticipate every contingency, I wrote into the trust instrument a provision that if at some time in the future it seemed desirable to both the trustees and the shareholders for a corporate trustee to succeed the individual trustees, it could be done. But the S.E.C. refused to allow a corporate trustee to serve in place of the individual trustees.

Another benefit of the fund that appeared to cause the Commission lawyers great concern was the avoidance of probate, which it provided by reason of its status as an inter vivos trust. I recalled how the American Bar Association had found *How to Avoid Probate* unpalatable because it disclosed how, among others, widows and orphans might obtain the estates that were rightfully theirs without having to pay ransom to the Bar. The Commission's attorneys now did everything they could to knock out the fund's probate exemption, requiring that we advise every person desiring to invest in the fund that he consult a lawyer first, that the simple act of naming a beneficiary was fraught with legal peril, etc. People buy life insurance policies every day and name beneficiaries, and the insurance companies do not advise them to see a lawyer first.

The Commission told me that it would be necessary to apply for exemptions from two provisions of the Investment Company Act of 1940. In August 1969, I filed application for such exemptions. The regulations provide that when application is made for such an exemption, the Commission will promptly issue a public notice of the application and set a date thirty days later for a hearing. At the end of that period, anyone wishing to be heard in opposition to the application will be given an opportunity to voice his objections. If no objections are offered, the Commission can grant the exemptions forthwith. In my case, after waiting for the month without ever seeing any notice of a hearing, I called the office of the Commission secretary and was told that they had no knowledge of any such application. Six months later, I wrote to the Commission and asked what had become of my applications for exemption. I received a curt acknowledgment that the application had been received. That was all. Neither application was ever acted upon.

Following is a list of mutual funds whose applications for registration became effective in 1969, showing how many months each took to clear.

| Fund | Months |
|---|---|
| First Investors Discovery Fund | 2 |
| Fiduciary Growth Associates | 2½ |
| Mutual Fund for Investing in U.S. Government Securities | 3¾ |
| Union Capital | 4 |
| Berger-Kent Special | 4½ |
| BLC Growth Fund | 4½ |
| BLC Income Fund | 4½ |
| IDS Progressive | 4½ |
| Fund of the Southwest | 4¾ |
| Tudor Hedge Fund | 5 |
| Transamerica Investors | 6 |
| Chase Capital | 6 |
| New York Venture | 6½ |
| Pace Fund | 6½ |
| Pension Capital Growth | 6¾ |
| Berkeley Dean Special | 7 |
| Davidge | 7 |
| J. Hancock Growth | 7 |
| J. Hancock Signature | 7 |

| | |
|---|---|
| Boston Mutual Equity | 7 |
| Dreyfus Leverage | 7¼ |
| Drexel Hedge | 7¾ |
| Westwood Fund | 8¼ |
| United Vanguard | 8½ |
| Spectra Fund | 8¾ |
| Putnam Voyager | 8¾ |
| Fund for Mutual Depositors | 9 |
| Financial Venture Fund | 9½ |
| Paul Bunyan Fund | 9½ |
| Summit Capital Fund | 9¾ |
| Ohio Farmers Growth | 9¾ |
| Nicholas Strong Fund | 10¼ |
| Incentive Fund | 10¼ |
| Torrence Equity Fund | 10¾ |
| Gateway Fund | 10¾ |
| Downtown Fund | 11¾ |

Obviously it does not have to take two years for a fund to clear. Among those that took only four and one half months from filing to public sale is IDS Progressive Fund, sponsored by a company that included Richard M. Nixon as a director until he became President. While IDS was in registration, Chairman Hamer Budge of the Securities and Exchange Commission, who was appointed by Mr. Nixon, was revealed to be negotiating with the fund sponsor for a top post on its staff. Senator Proxmire had called him in and asked him to explain this small violation of federal law.

During this period, I was advised by a knowledgeable attorney that if I hired an ex-S.E.C. attorney for a fee of $25,000, he would "walk" my registration through the Commission in short order. I declined the suggestion. When one pays a registration fee of several thousand dollars, that should be enough to ensure honest consideration. The S.E.C. seems to be a revolving door between law school and a lucrative practice as an "attorney specializing in S.E.C. matters," which is simply a euphemism for influence peddling.

Weary of the struggle, I confided to Manuel Cohen, a former chairman of the Securities and Exchange Commission, that I had decided to withdraw my fund with a public statement of why I was doing so. Mr. Cohen urged me not to withdraw it, assuring me that it was a worthwhile project, that it was in the public interest, and that if I pressed ahead, I would prevail.

No doubt my concurrent negotiations with the Division of Corporate Regulation and the Division's Enforcement Department concerning the activities of a dozen or so funds, chiefly Enterprise, did not endear me to the Commission. But even this did not forewarn me of what was yet to come!

Two or three days after I had filed my revised registration statement on December 26, 1968, the fact of the refiling was reported in the financial media and within a few days many letters began coming in asking for information about the new fund. One such letter was typical:

> Dear Sir:
> Please send me a prospectus on your proposed mutual fund. Am I to understand that you will not be buying shares of stock of listed companies on the exchanges but instead only be investing in existing mutual fund companies?
> Very truly yours,
> Peter J. Z———

The batch of letters dismayed me somewhat, principally because they asked questions that deserved to be answered. I had been out of the country on a diplomatic mission to the Middle East which had me shuttling back and forth between Cairo and Jerusalem for more than a month and I was far behind in my work. The flow of letters—more than 50,000, altogether—from people who had read *How to Avoid Probate* had trickled down to about thirty per day, but these had accumulated during my absence. Finally, all else had been put aside while I spent three weeks working on the fund registration, and this, too, put me far behind.

In the circumstances, I viewed the influx of inquiries about the fund with consternation. "Am I going to have to answer each one of these inquiries with a personal letter?" I asked myself. The normal practice in the investment business would be to throw all such inquiries into a box until a prospectus was printed, and then send a copy of it to each inquirer. I did not know how many months would pass before we had a prospectus, though. These people had been kind enough to write asking for information about my fund, and ordinary business courtesy entitled them to an answer to their questions. After all, my fund had some peculiar characteristics. If it was not what they had in mind, they should know it as soon as possible so that they would waste no time waiting for it. I decided that the thing to do was to quickly make up a form letter which could serve to answer most of the inquiries we had received. The girl assigned to opening the mail was instructed to send a copy of the form letter to each person who wrote about the fund and then to file his inquiry away. No other individual in our firm, executive or clerical, saw the inquiries. No further contact was had with those to whom letters were sent. But it was to become the beginning of an ominous event.

I continued my correspondence with David M. Butowsky, Chief Enforcement Attorney of the Division of Corporate Regulation at the Commission, and Herbert E. Milstein, Assistant Chief Enforcement Attorney. It was clear to me that they planned to do nothing to protect the Enterprise Fund shareholders. On May 26, 1969, I wrote Mr. Milstein:

You *know* that the accounts of thousands of Enterprise Fund shareholders are being handled in an incompetent fashion. You *know* that there are thousands of complaints on file.

Why are you doing nothing about it? Why do you allow these people to continue to violate the Investment Company Act of 1940? Does the fact that Mr. Alan B. Levenson was an S.E.C. attorney charged with enforcement until January 1969 and is now a vice-president of Shareholders Management Company, sponsor of Enterprise Fund, have anything to do with your failure to enforce the law?

You *know* that they have failed to maintain adequate books and records, and that certificates, of the existence of which the custodian bank has no record, are daily being presented for redemption. Why have you not required them to discontinue sales of new shares until they have placed their back office in order?

On April 30, 1969, a client of this firm requested redemption of $85,000 worth of Enterprise Fund. More than three weeks have passed and he has heard nothing. The bank has just acknowledged to us on the telephone that it cannot even *find* his request.

While all this is going on, you sit sphinxlike and motionless, with hands folded in prayerful meditation, monotonously repeating over and over like a broken record, "We are glad to receive any information you care to give us. We cannot, of course, disclose the results of our investigation, if any. We are glad to receive any information you care to give us, etc., etc., etc."

I'll give you some information: *You are not doing your job.*

The scheduled appearance in Los Angeles (home of Shareholders Management Company) on June 13th of Commissioner Wheat and San Francisco Regional Administrator Pennekamp as featured speakers on a program run by this same vice-president of Shareholders Management Company (who instead of investigating the company while with your Commission was apparently quietly preparing to become its vice-president) further compromises your Commission's position with respect to the formal complaints against Shareholders Management Company now before it.

Your Commission *knows* that Enterprise Fund up-valued its investment letter stock as much as 59 percent within forty-eight hours of its purchase, but you've done nothing about it. You *know* that purchasers paid artificially inflated prices for Enterprise shares, but you've done

nothing to halt the practice. Responsibility for the whole ugly "investment letter stock" mess, which has given the mutual fund industry the greatest black eye in its history, rests solely upon your Commission's shoulders. It certainly ranks as the greatest "goof" in the history of securities regulation in this country, but fearful of your terrible wrath, nobody seems to have had the guts to stand up and tell you so.

There is a serious question in my mind as to whether or not in the light of all this fumbling and conflict of interest, a taxpayer/shareholder is not entitled to bring a suit charging you with gross dereliction of duty.

On July 8, 1969, Milstein wrote me that he had been in touch with Enterprise Fund and had been "assured that everything is in order." I did not regard this as adequate regulation and I informed him that I was going to refer the matter to the Senate Banking Committee. A few days later, two S.E.C. representatives from the Boston regional office presented themselves at my place of business, explaining that they were there at the telephoned request of the enforcement attorneys in Washington, with instructions to go through my files and make a complete audit of my books. It was obvious that anyone who threatens the Enforcement Division with a Senate investigation does so at his peril. If a federal regulatory agency can conduct its operation in this Gestapo-like fashion, we are but one step from the midnight knock on the door.

The S.E.C. men acknowledged that my books were in perfect order. In the course of ransacking my files, they came upon the form letter I had sent out to those who had inquired about my fund, and carried it away with them. A few days later, they telephoned asking for a list of the names of all those persons to whom it had been sent. I bundled up all the inquiries and sent them off to them.

Shortly thereafter, I received a telephone call from a man in California who had been among those inquiring about the Dacey Composite Fund and who now reported that he had received a call from someone who identified himself as an "enforcement attorney" with the Securities and Exchange Commission in Washington. The Washington caller framed questions and reframed them in what the California man regarded as an obvious attempt to twist and distort the answers he was giving. Over and over again, the Washington caller asked if it were not true that the initial contact had originated with us. Over and over again, the California man emphasized that he had read of the filing of the fund's registration in a financial journal and had written for information. The persistence and slanted attitude of the caller so aggravated the man that he ended by doubting the genuineness of the call. He hung up and called the Commission's San Francisco regional office, asking the staff if they knew the identity and purpose of the mysterious caller. They assured him that they knew nothing of the matter.

A few days later, a vice-president of my firm took a telephone call from a man who refused to give his name but who said, "I understand that your fund is in trouble. What's it all about?"

These acts by the enforcement attorneys were not simply improper—they were illegal. The Dacey Composite Fund was in no trouble of any kind and such statements by the Commission's staff were slanderous and deliberately calculated to damage my reputation. When you tell a government employee that you are going to disclose his shortcomings to a Senate committee, you do not expect to receive a birthday card from him. On the other hand, you do not expect him to slander you or to marshal all of the forces of his public office to try to get something on you.

On December 6, 1969, I appeared as a witness at Congressman Moss's subcommittee hearings on possible new legislation affecting mutual funds. There I gave the facts I had unearthed about Enterprise Fund and the S.E.C. failure to regulate it.

It was these hearings, mentioned earlier in connection with Enterprise Fund, that brought about the embarrassment of S.E.C. Chairman Budge and which were followed by the departure of Chief Enforcement Attorney Butowsky, as well as the Commission suit against Enterprise. Milstein moved up to fill Butowsky's shoes.

On December 20, 1969, I received a subpoena from the Commission charging me with using the "instruments of transportation to carry or transmit prospectuses which failed to meet the requirements of the Securities Act of 1933." I had employed "devices, schemes and artifices to defraud." I had "engaged in transactions which operated as a fraud upon purchasers." Since I had not sent out any prospectuses, had not engaged in any "devices," "schemes," or "artifices" and had not sold anyone a single share of my fund, it was all pretty inexplicable.

On January 5 and 13, 1970, hearings on the S.E.C. charges against me took place in Washington. The Commission designated them as "private proceedings" and barred the press. Mr. Milstein represented the Division, I represented myself. Since no shares of the Dacey Composite Fund had ever been sold, I asked the Division if it was prepared to enter evidence in support of its charge that sales had been made. Mr. Milstein acknowledged that he had no such evidence. Was the Division prepared to withdraw the charge? No, it was not. I pointed out to the hearing examiner that the charge had obviously been brought recklessly and without any evidence that it was true. I asked that in the circumstances, it be stricken from the complaint. Mr. Milstein declined

to allow it to be stricken. I then asked that the Division identify for me the "prospectus" which it had charged me with sending. It declined to do so. What "schemes" had been employed, what "artifices"? Who had been defrauded? The Division declined to answer any of these questions or provide any information. I took the witness chair in my own defense and invited the Commission to question me. Mr. Milstein pressed to the attack. How many children did I have? What were their names? Their ages? Were any of them married? When was my eldest daughter married? To whom? While I had long questioned Mr. Milstein's integrity in the administration of his assigned duties, this was the first time that I realized that he had other more serious problems. As he pressed forward with his questioning, wondering looks were exchanged around the room. Finally, the hearing examiner himself halted the questioning and inquired gently of Mr. Milstein what it was that he was trying to bring out. Mr. Milstein's somewhat incoherent explanation failed to satisfy the examiner who directed him to drop that line of questioning and get on with the charges.

Later, I asked Mr. Milstein to take the witness stand. I sat alone at a table on one side of the room, while a long row of Commission attorneys sat at a table opposite me. Each time I asked Milstein a question, one of them would spring to his feet to object. Finally, however, I managed to get in a series of questions. Suddenly, Milstein lost control of himself, screaming at me at the top of his voice. The hearing examiner told him sternly to compose himself, that he would not tolerate any further outbursts. The Enforcement Attorney wiped his brow and looked about him. I thought of a wounded animal at bay and began to feel sorry for him. I abandoned the questioning. The hearing ended shortly thereafter.

Mr. Milstein asked the hearing examiner to find me guilty of fraud and to suspend me and my company from business for three months. A few weeks earlier, the Commission had found Merrill Lynch and the First National City Bank of New York guilty of selling shares of an unregistered investment company. More than one thousand people had been sold a total of $35 million worth of the shares. In that case, Mr. Milstein had not asked that anyone be suspended. After all, no one involved had accused him of not doing his job. I had not sold anyone anything, but I *had* charged him with betraying his trust. He insisted that I be suspended for three months. What he sought, of course, was to publicly disgrace his tormentor. I had leveled charges against him that he was unable to answer. He fell back upon a desperate attempt to disgrace me. Would it work?

The hearing examiner ruled that the offending letter was technically a prospectus and as such constituted an "inadvertent violation" of the Securities Act. The letters were "not part of a sales campaign, but responses to unsolicited inquiries, and there were no sales of the fund shares actually effected. The form letters did not in specific terms offer fund shares." Holding that "there was no intent to evade the regulatory provisions of the Act," he ruled that "it does not appear appropriate in the public interest to impose ninety-day suspensions as proposed by the Division. Under the circumstances, and in view of the indicated excellent reputation that Dacey enjoys in as well as outside the financial community, censure will suffice."

Some days later, the Commission went to unusual lengths in issuing a public news release, including causing it to appear on the Dow-Jones ticker, reporting that I had been censured for violations of the securities laws. Although it acknowledged that I had sold nothing, it made no reference to the other qualifying statements in the Decision: I had asked no one to buy anything; I had simply written a letter thanking people for their interest and saying that I would send them a prospectus when one was available.

That the action had not been instituted in the public interest but was rooted in a spirit of animosity and revenge and was intended to punish me for public criticism of the failure of the Enforcement Division to carry out its assigned tasks is obvious. It is frightening to discover that the police facilities of the Commission can be thus misused by personnel in pursuit of a private vendetta against a critic of their misfeasance.

I had sharply criticized the operations of Enterprise Fund. The Senior Vice-President of Enterprise Fund, Alan R. Gordon, was the former chief counsel of the Commission's Division of Corporate Regulation. The Division of Corporate Regulation was the office that charged me with "fraud" for having written a form letter thanking people for their inquiries and saying that I would send them a prospectus when one became available. At secret hearings, from which the press and public were barred, I was found guilty. The Commission's publicity department went to extreme lengths to publicize the finding.

The Dacey Composite Fund is not available to the public. Smothered beneath a noxious blanket of a corrupt bureaucracy, it may never see the light of day. Of course, I *could* hire an ex-S.E.C. official to see to its registration.

# Chapter 22

# THE SECURITIES AND EXCHANGE COMMISSION

The organization, administration, and distribution of mutual funds is controlled by the Securities Act of 1933, the Securities Exchange Act of 1934, and the Investment Company Act of 1940. In addition, mutual fund managements are subject to registration under the Investment Advisers Act of 1940.

The Securities and Exchange Commission is charged with the administration of all of these laws.

During the studies which preceded the drafting of the Investment Company Act of 1940 more than thirty years ago, I was invited by the Commission to offer my views on certain aspects of the investment company industry. On numerous occasions since, I have volunteered comment upon some practice that seemed undesirable, and at times the Commission's staff solicited my views either on a stand it proposed to take or an effective way of dealing with a problem then before it.

The point I am making is that I have always been on the side of the Commission. Any differences that ever existed invariably stemmed from my feeling that the Commission should be stricter in its enforcement of the securities laws.

All that has changed—because the Commission has changed. The quality of its administration of the securities laws has deteriorated sadly. I am not sure that I can put my finger on the date that the deterioration began. I recall that awhile ago I became aware of a seriously improper practice in the contractual plan field. I wrote the Commission, detailing my findings and having heard nothing for six months, wrote again asking if my first letter had ever come to anyone's attention. Two months later, a reply came, explaining that they were investigating the matter and would be in touch with me shortly. Nine months later, I received a telephone call from an individual who identified himself as a "special counsel" in the Division of Corporate Regulation. Apol-

ogizing, he explained that one of the top officials had recently resigned and his successor had discovered my correspondence in the bottom drawer of the departed official's desk. It struck me that it was a rather lax way of dealing with complaints of securities violations. I began to wonder about the Commission.

Some years ago, under the direction of the Securities and Exchange Commission, a joint committee of the Congress—the Temporary National Economic Committee—had conducted an exhaustive study of important aspects of the life insurance business. More recently, the Commission had had occasion to become concerned about the proliferation of stock life insurance companies organized by promoters who knew nothing at all about the life insurance business. Their only interest was in foisting upon the public stock that was worthless or soon to become worthless. Senator Edward M. Kennedy informed me that the Commission had written to him saying:

> We have had many problems in connection with insurance company stocks. Many of these issues and the sales techniques involved in their distribution appear to involve abuses and possible violations of the Securities Act or the Securities Exchange Act which require extensive investigation.

Within some fifteen years past, approximately 1,600 new life insurance companies had been formed, more than 40 percent of which have since gone out of business or merged with other companies in a salvage operation. On one occasion, the Securities and Exchange Commission suspended trading in the stock of a life company on the grounds that its capital and surplus had been impaired. I wrote to the Commission applauding the action it had taken to protect investors but asking what action was being taken to protect the policyholders who, in a sense, were also investors in the company. If the company's capital and surplus were impaired, I inquired on behalf of the policyholders, why was it being allowed to continue to offer its financial contracts to the public? Investors recognize that they are taking a risk but policyholders are led to believe that they are participating in a riskless medium. I was puzzled that a company should be permitted to send out its agents to solicit new customers when there was a serious question as to whether or not it was in a position to meet its obligations under its old contracts. The S.E.C. apparently did not have an answer, for I received no response.

During his administration, I had written to President Lyndon B. Johnson reciting a long list of widespread abuses in the life insurance industry and urging him to cause an investigation to be made of the industry. Various governmental agencies were approached by a representative of Mr. Johnson to discover what they might know about the problems I had cited. The Securities and Exchange Commission was one of the agencies whose views were solicited. But when the President's emissary inquired as to the validity of my charges of wholesale fraud in the life insurance industry, including my report of widespread sale of junk stock in fly-by-night insurance companies, the Commission responded that it was "not qualified to judge nor in any position to know whether the life insurance industry was so conducting its operations as to cause concern for the best interests of the policyholders." This was very peculiar coming from the federal agency that had conducted the historic TNEC investigation of the life insurance industry and had reported that wholesale fraud had been found. It was then, I think, that my confidence in the Commission's competence began to leach away.

The peculiarity of the S.E.C. mentality was seen recently in its handling of Merrill Lynch's association with Douglas Aircraft. In the preparation and underwriting of a bond issue, Merrill Lynch became privy to information concerning the company's finances, including the fact of a sharp drop in earnings which, when it became public knowledge, would inevitably result in a substantial price decline for the company's stock. With a fine disregard for principle, Merrill Lynch passed the word to some of its important customers, including a dozen mutual funds. The fund managers promptly dumped their Douglas holdings. (To give you some idea of the hazards facing the small investor who depends on the advice of his broker, consider the fact that while Merrill Lynch was tipping off its fund clients to sell out their holdings of Douglas stock, some of the firm's salesmen around the country were selling Douglas stock to small investors.) When word of these proceedings reached the S.E.C., it brought suit against Merrill Lynch and against each of the fund managers. The latter, it claimed, had acted on "inside information."

Why a suit against the fund managers? Doesn't one hire an investment manager for his professional knowledge of investments, because he knows when to buy and when to sell? And how does he know all this? Is it not by keeping his ear to the ground and maintaining a financial seismometer that records distant shock waves not discernible to the unskilled layman? If having hired someone to manage my money, I discovered after some untoward financial event that my manager knew in advance of it and did nothing to protect me from it, I would fire him on the spot. But the S.E.C. would denounce him as a rascal for doing his best to protect my invested dollars. The blabbermouths at Merrill Lynch who violated a client's confidence should get what is coming to them, but it is ridiculous for the S.E.C. to sue the fundmen for doing what came naturally.

The fact is that the Commission pursues actions selected by its public relations experts as most likely to bring it favorable publicity.

A brace of Commission officials can always be found on the panels of seminars, which are the phenomenon of our time. The Practicing Law Institute and Corporate Seminars, Inc., each runs a continuing series of one-, two-, or three-day meetings on a wide range of financial subjects. The "faculty" for such seminars consists of knowledgeable individuals who can speak with authority on their subject. An S.E.C. man can usually be found pontificating on his specialty. Registration fees for these affairs run from $150 for a one-day conference up to $500 for a three-day session. It is like a traveling Chautauqua—the same panel appears this week in New York, next week in Chicago, the following week in Las Vegas, and closes out the tour in San Francisco. It may be very profitable for the Commission officials, but who is tending the store? Write to the Commission for information or guidance and they lose your letter or leave it in a desk drawer where it is found shortly after they have retired to a cushy lifetime job with one of the mutual funds they have been regulating. That is the current formula: "first we regulate them, then we join them." The only way one can get information is by attending a forum privately sponsored for profit. If Chairman Budge would require his staff to be at their desks more regularly instead of moonlighting around the country, he would not have to make his periodic appearance before congressional hearings to wring his hands over the budgetary limitations placed upon his department, which limitations he claims make it impossible to carry on the enforcement activities he feels are necessary.

It appears to me that the S.E.C. enforces what might be called "selective regulation." Late in 1969, for example, the Commission filed a suit against the Value Line Special Situations Fund, its sponsor, Arnold Bernhard & Company, and against Mr. Bernhard and his son, the two principal officers of the company, charging them with failure to maintain adequate books and records. Actually, the Value Line people themselves brought their bookkeeping problems to the Commission's attention. If it had remained for the Commission to find it out, it would still be a secret. The firm had retained the Investment Companies Service Corporation of Boston to handle its shareholder accounting. This is a service bureau subsidiary of the Keystone group of mutual funds. I had discussed the shareholder accounting of the Dacey Composite Fund with ICSC. Stringing broad "a's" in a row like pearls in a necklace, they explained that their fee would be breathtakingly large "because, you see, we know exactly what has to be done and how to do it correctly so that the client experiences no problems whatever." Despite their self-assurance, the Bernhards reported that these people made a mess of the Value Line accounting and brought the wrath of the Commission down upon the sponsor. I have personal knowledge of the problems the Bernhards faced and I can testify that they were not one tenth those of Enterprise Fund. In bringing the Value Line action, the Commission accused the Bernhards of personal responsibility for the bookkeeping inadequacies. In the Enterprise suit, which the Commission finally was forced to bring after public disclosure of its failure to enforce the law, none of the ex-S.E.C. officials who were running the fund were mentioned. The "graduates" were all handled with kid gloves by their alma mater, while the Bernhards got the back of the Commission's hand.

The Commission required the Value Line people to surrender 190,820 shares of the Special Situations Fund having a value of $1,250,000 to "protect shareholders in the Fund against any adverse effects of a then existing discrepancy between the share total shown in the Fund's capital shares account and the apparent total credited to shareholders' accounts." In the case of the Commission's suit against Enterprise Fund, the bookkeeping discrepancy was 388,000 shares having a current value in excess of $3,000,000, but Shareholders Management was not required by the Commission to post any such "bond." It is this kind of discriminatory enforcement of the law which has shaken the public's confidence in the integrity of the Securities and Exchange Commission.

In January 1970, syndicated columnist Jack Anderson reported that "brokers who handle stock transactions are so poorly regulated that they have been getting away with law violations. This column has turned up evidence, including official documents labeled 'confidential,' that the securities market is policed by most reluctant regulators. The Securities and Exchange Commission, set up to protect the public, has been slow to act.

Doctor A. M. D. _____, an Enterprise shareholder, wrote to the Commission on July 15, 1969:

Gentlemen:

I have made purchases of shares of Enterprise Fund upon the dates and in the amounts shown below:

| Date | Amount |
|------|--------|
| Dec. 25, 1968 | $85,937.63 |
| Jan. 14, 1969 | 1,538.97 |
| Jan. 20, 1969 | 699.39 |
| Feb. 7, 1969 | 250.00 |
| Mar. 5, 1969 | 500.00 |

Since buying my shares, I have discovered that the Fund has made substantial investments in letter stock which is restricted as to resale. The prospectus which I examined prior to making my investment did not disclose the fact that it was the Fund's policy and intention to purchase stock which was not readily marketable, nor did the Fund's financial statement identify any holdings as being restricted as to resale. All such holdings were identified only as private placements which I submit did not adequately disclose their true nature. Had I been aware that it was the Fund's policy to invest in securities which were legally disabled, and that without disclosing that policy it had invested more than one hundred million dollars of the shareholders' money in such securities, the value of which could not be readily determined, I would not have invested a penny in it, because among other things there would be no way of determining whether the per share price charged me was the proper one.

It now appears from newspaper accounts of the Fund's activities, that having purchased the restricted securities without adequate disclosure, it improperly valued them, contrary to the representation in the prospectus that it would value its securities in good faith.

I have examined a prospectus of SMC Investment Corporation, an investment company under the same management and sponsorship as Enterprise Fund. It devoted substantial space to disclosure of the Fund's intention to buy restricted stocks and gave careful warning of the problems and possible hazards inherent in the purchase of such securities. Yet the prospectus upon which I relied made no such disclosure and gave no such warnings with respect to Enterprise Fund which has in fact invested a far greater amount in restricted securities than SMC Investment Corporation.

I now intend to request rescission. I request

that your Commission examine the enclosed prospectus which was given to me to enable me to form a judgment as to whether or not the Fund's policies and objectives met my needs and desires, and the financial statement given me with that prospectus. After such examination, I ask that you advise me whether in the light of the known facts concerning the Fund's actual policy and practice with respect to restricted stocks, the prospectus and financial statement fully meet the adequate disclosure requirements of the Securities Act of 1933 and the Investment Company Act of 1940.

> Very truly yours,
> A. M. D———

In its reply, the Commission said:

> As you may be aware, the statutes under which the Commission functions do not allow us to aid investors in pursuing their individual rights which have been given to them by the federal securities laws. In this connection, you may wish to consult an attorney concerning any possible rights you may have under the Investment Company Act and the other securities laws relating to the problems which you have raised in your letter. In addition, I might note that it would seem particularly inappropriate for the staff of the Commission to comment on an informal basis to your inquiries which appear to raise the very issues being currently litigated in a private shareholder's lawsuit brought by Mr. Norman F. Dacey against the Enterprise Fund.
>
> The views which you have expressed in your letter are of great interest to the Commission and its staff. You may be assured that these views will be carefully considered and weighed in our attempts to deal with the problems raised by fund purchases of restricted securities.
>
> Sincerely,
> Herbert E. Milstein
> Assistant Chief Enforcement Attorney

The Securities and Exchange Commission is a governmental agency charged with administration of the securities laws. Those laws specify that there shall be adequate disclosure of a company's investment policies in its prospectus. This investor wrote asking this public agency to look at the prospectus that was given him, to look at what the company had done with his money, and tell him whether or not the prospectus did, in fact, make adequate disclosure. Mind you, he did not ask the Commission to get his money back for him. He simply asked if the prospectus met the requirements of the law.

And what did this public agency, staffed by men who are being paid a good salary to protect just such citizen-investors, do? It told him to go hire a lawyer.

The next time you are mugged on a dark street, don't call a cop. Hire a lawyer.

If you catch a sneak thief with his hand in your pocket, don't call the police department. Call the bar association.

Of course, Doctor D——— had asked the Commission a very embarrassing question. He had sent along the prospectus that had been given him when he bought the shares and which the Commission's Division of Corporate Regulation had approved, and he had asked the Commission whether or not, in the light of the fund's purchase of $115 million worth of restricted securities, the prospectus had made adequate disclosure of the fund's investment policy with respect to such securities.

Adequate disclosure? It made *no* disclosure! But if the Commission acknowledged to Doctor D——— that the prospectus it had approved was inadequate, it would look pretty silly, wouldn't it? So the Commission wriggled out of the question by telling the good doctor to hire a lawyer if he thought that the investment laws were violated.

If the Securities and Exchange Commission is to do the job for which it was organized, it desperately needs rehabilitation.

# Chapter 23

# BUY TERM AND INVEST
# THE DIFFERENCE

Millions of Americans have been led to believe that the life insurance policies they own constitute a form of investment. Since it is quite likely that you are one of those misled millions, let us examine the subject.

Life insurance is a wonderful thing. There is just no substitute for it. But it is probably the most abused economic instrument in America.

That abuse is born of a widespread misunderstanding of the real purpose of life insurance: to provide protection. Now, before you say, "Oh, everyone knows that's the purpose of life insurance," let me assure you that everyone does not know it, or knowing it, does not remember it when he is ready to buy.

You buy life insurance to pay off the mortgage or to educate your children or to retire at age sixty-five. Give a modern life insurance salesman half a chance and he will have life insurance doing everything but sweeping your kitchen.

Life insurance was never intended to do those things. It was intended to provide you with an estate if you do not live long enough to accumulate one yourself.

When you insure your home or your car, you give the insurance company just the cost of the protection. You would never think of handing the company an extra hundred dollars to hold for you with the understanding that it was to be returned at a future date. If you want a savings account you open it with a savings bank, not with an insurance company.

When you buy life insurance, you are insuring your future income against your dying before you have had time to earn it. It will help you to understand the problem and to select your insurance wisely if you will bear in mind the two basic principles that apply to all insurance. The first is that we insure risks. Risk implies the possibility of loss. If the loss is inevitable, there is no risk and insurance is impractical, if not impossible.

Death is certain to occur; therefore nobody will insure you against death. You can, however, insure against death within a certain period of time.

The second fundamental principle of insurance is that we insure only economic, as distinguished from sentimental, values. How much economic value is there in your earned income after age sixty-five? None, if you retire. You may have investment income but this will continue even after you retire. It will not be lost; therefore you need not insure it. If you will earn no more income, there is nothing to insure. Unless it is for some special purpose, then, life insurance should be planned to terminate at age sixty-five.

Protection is what you need, the same kind of protection that is given by the insurance you buy on your house and your car. Give the company just the cost of protecting you, and not another penny. Remember, it is an insurance company and not a savings bank. This is essential for every individual to understand because life insurance companies encourage you to regard them as both a savings bank and an insurance company.

There are two types of life insurance: term insurance (which is pure protection) and all other kinds. All other kinds consist of some combination of term insurance plus a savings account maturing at some date in the future. "Whole life," "ordinary life," "straight life"—all different names for the same thing—consist of term insurance plus a savings account that matures at age 100 (age 96 on older policies). "Twenty payment life" and "thirty payment life" are similar except that instead of paying until you die (or until the policy matures at age 100) you crowd the lifetime of premiums into the first twenty or thirty years. That way, if you die at seventy-five, the company does not lose all the premiums you would have paid if you had lived to age 100—you obligingly prepaid them.

Obviously, the chances of your living until maturity of the policy at age 100 are pretty slim, actually about one in 903,000.

Policies that provide for the savings account to mature early enough to offer the purchaser some reasonable hope of living long enough to get his savings account back are called "endowment policies." Policies sold to educate children are fifteen- or seventeen-year endowments: term insurance plus a savings account that matures when your youngster is ready for college. Retirement income policies consist of term insurance plus a savings account that matures at age sixty or sixty-five, and is automatically applied to the purchase of an annuity.

No one will quarrel with the idea of providing protection for your family while at the same time accumulating a fund for some such purpose as education or retirement. The incredible thing about this "package" of protection-plus-a-savings account offered by the insurance companies is that, if you die, the company keeps your savings account.

Let us illustrate: you have a $1,000 twenty-year endowment—actually a twenty-year term insurance—policy plus a savings account that matures for $1,000 at the end of that time. The savings account is called "the cash value." Each year, when you pay the premium you give the company the cost of the protection—and some extra dollars to be put away for you until the end of the twenty years. You have had the policy fifteen years. Your savings account with the company has accumulated to $675. That is your money, the accumulation of extra dollars that you need never have given the company in the first place.

You die. The company pays your beneficiary the $1,000 face amount of the policy (the "protection" for which you gave them a premium this year) and they keep your $675 savings account! The only way you can get that savings account back is by living right up to the very last day of the twenty years. If you die in the nineteenth year, when the savings account has grown to $950, the company will pay the $1,000 of insurance—and keep your $950 savings account. Stated another way, in the nineteenth year, you have a $50.00 insurance policy plus a $950 savings account.

Or, consider that ordinary life policy you own. Each year until you are age 100, you give the company the cost of the protection plus some extra dollars to be salted away in the savings account. To actually collect that savings account, you must stick around—and keep paying premiums—until your hundredth birthday. If you die before that, even one day before it, the company will pay the insurance for which you gave them a premium ·that year—and they will pocket your savings account.

Seriously now, would you go down to a bank and open a savings account with the understanding that if you died before age 100, the bank could keep your money? You would not? Why, then, do you do it with the insurance company?

If you own a retirement income policy, read no further—unless your blood has a very high boiling point. These policies, beginning at age sixty-five, generally provide a retirement income of $10.00 per month for each $1,000 of insurance. If you were sixty-five today and wanted an insurance company to pay you $10.00 per month for life, ten years certain, you would have to give them about $1,350. If that retirement income policy of yours guarantees you $10.00 per month at age sixty-five, it has got to have a cash value of $1,350 on that date. Therefore, on this type of policy the cash value builds up much faster. On an endowment it need only accumulate to $1,000 by maturity, but on your retirement income policy it has to grow to $1,350. The face of the policy states that if you die, the company will pay the face amount "or the cash value, whichever is the greater." As far back as age fifty-two or fifty-five, the cash value of your policy may have reached $1,000. From then on, if you die the company will pay your family the cash value. Come to think of it, you could get the cash value without dying. What are you paying them a premium each year for? You don't have a penny of actual "life insurance protection" in force. All those last years of the policy, the company rides free, collecting premiums but taking no risk whatever.

Whenever you need to use some of the money you've accumulated in your savings account with the insurance company, you may borrow it back at twice the interest rate at which you are lending it to them. If like the insurance company, a savings bank offered you 2½ percent interest and suggested that if you needed the money at any time it would lend it back to you at 5 percent interest, you would leave immediately taking your money with you. "Imagine their offering to lend me back my own money for twice what I'm lending it to them!" you would exclaim. Again, if you would not think of doing it with a savings bank, why do you do it with an insurance company?

If you become aware of the inequity of this loan arrangement and inform the insurance company that you will not borrow back your own money, that you will just take the savings account out altogether, the company will say, "If you do, we'll cancel your protection." You must take either the loan value or the cash value; if you take the latter, they cancel your policy.

You would be much better off if you just bought term insurance in the first place and put the difference in premium in the savings bank. By any given date in the future, you would accumulate more in your savings account, because insurance companies pay out 15 percent of everything you pay in in your lifetime just for selling the policy, including 15 percent of the savings account.

If you buy term insurance and put the difference in the savings bank, the bank will not pay anyone for selling you a savings account. You will accumulate more "savings account," and, if you die, your family will have all the term insurance plus all the money in the savings bank. You will be better off if you live, and your family will be better off if you die.

There are two types of term insurance: "level term" and "decreasing term." On each, the premium remains the same during the entire period the contract is to run. With a level term policy, the amount of insurance protection provided by the company remains constant throughout the lifetime of the contract. With a decreasing term policy, the amount of insurance steadily reduces until, in the last few years, it is a small fraction of the original face amount. With decreasing term the company's risk reduces steadily, which fact is reflected in the premium, making this type much cheaper than level term insurance. The period of time covered by either level or decreasing term can be one, five, ten, fifteen, or twenty years, or until you are sixty-five or seventy years of age. The best buy is decreasing term to age sixty-five or seventy.

Actually, you are accustomed to buying term insurance on your house or your automobile. You give the insurance company just the cost of the protection. There is no "cash value" to such policies.

Insurance men have long insisted that life insurance is a good "investment" and have loaded up the American breadwinner with endowment policies, limited payment life policies, and whole life policies. The high premium endowments and limited payment policies are now pretty much discredited, and it has become increasingly difficult for insurance men to find suckers who will buy them. As for whole life, the lads with the rate books still insist it is the only insurance to buy, and they denounce term insurance as "temporary" protection.

We can squelch this argument once and for all.

Let us assume that you are a male aged forty, and that you are considering the purchase of a $75,000 nonparticipating whole life policy with a premium waiver clause for disability. It requires an annual premium of $1701.75 and has a guaranteed cash value of $35,175 at age sixty-five.

Consider, instead, the purchase of a $100,000 nonparticipating "decreasing term to age seventy" policy with an annual premium of $432.50 and no cash value at age sixty-five (rates are those of Bankers Security Life of New York). The obvious premium saving is $1,269.25 per year.

Deposit the premium saving in a savings bank paying 5 percent, and at age sixty-five you will have $60,577 in the bank versus the $35,175 cash value "guaranteed" by the whole life policy. If the purpose of insurance is to provide protection, isn't a policy that provides 33⅓

percent more protection for only one quarter of the outlay the better policy?

Since insurance men talk a lot about the "safety" of life insurance, it is worth noting that the term insurance/savings bank package is every bit as safe as the whole life policy. Indeed, the savings account is insured while life insurance companies are not, and hundreds of them have failed.

But why be satisfied to inter your money in a savings account when we have already agreed on the importance of putting it to work where it will stand a fighting chance against inflation?

Dig out your insurance policies tonight and look up the table headed "cash value." That is your savings account. That is what the insurance company will inherit if you die tomorrow. Even if you live long enough to get it back, inflation will have melted away its real value.

Let us assume it is a $10,000 policy with a $7,000 cash value. You do not have to be very smart to figure out that if you cancel that $10,000 policy and put the $7,000 cash value into a mutual fund, and go out and buy $3,000 of term insurance, your family will have the same $10,000 total if you die—and you will be paying the premium for only $3,000 of insurance instead of $10,000.

Of course, if you are a financial jellyfish who cannot save any money unless the insurance company takes it away from you, you had better stick with the insurance. But you should at least realize the high price you are paying for your weakness.

The following pages reveal the actual results of investing the $1,269.25 you saved each year, from age forty to sixty-five, in any one of the existing mutual funds that have been in operation for twenty-five years or more. For funds that make a sales charge, the results shown are net *after* the sales charge; most such funds now have rights of accumulation which should result in reduced sales charges on similar plans established in the future.

Turn to the first chart, that of Aberdeen Fund. The first figure in column three discloses that $1,269 was invested that year (1944). Column four reveals that ordinary income dividends of $52.00 were paid during that year. These were reinvested and the total investment in 1944 thus became $1,321 (column six). At year's-end, the initial investment of $1,269 had a value of $1,327 (column seven) while the $52.00 of reinvested dividends were worth $55.00 (column ten). The total value of the investment plan at the end of 1944 was $1,382 (column eleven) and this, added to the $100,000 of term insurance constituted a death estate totaling $101,382. As indicated in the footnote at the bottom of the page, there were no capital gains distributions made by the fund in either of the first two years, and thus there was no year-end value shown for such distributions (column eight).

Look next at the year 1948. Column three confirms that the annual investments to date totaled $6,346. The ordinary income dividend paid that year was $459 (column four), such dividends totaling $1,076 for the five years (column five). Combined, the out-of-pocket investments (column three) and the reinvested dividends during the five years (column five) totaled $7,422 (column six). At the end of the year, the accumulated payments of $6,346 (column three) had a value of $4,962 (column seven). The $1,076 of accumulated reinvested dividends (column five) were worth $930 (column ten). In the footnote, we see that Aberdeen paid capital gains distributions of $422 in 1946 and $88 in 1948. Column eight discloses that the $510 cumulative total of such distributions had a 1948 year-end value of $446. You will note that on many of the charts, column eight reveals instances where year-end values are reduced from the previous year, simply reflecting a market decline during that particular year. The footnote indicates that the capital gains distributions actually paid by Aberdeen Fund during the twenty-five years totaled $38,533, while the value of such reinvested distributions at the end of the period totaled $51,084 (column eight). Incidentally, what may appear to be minor discrepancies in the final totals results from the dropping of cents in all the figures, although these have been taken into account in making computations. For example, the indicated premium saving of $1,269 annually was in fact $1,269.25 but all computations were based upon the latter figure.

A composite chart at the end of the fund charts summarizes their individual performances. In the individual charts, the figures disclose that an out-of-pocket investment of $31,731 ($1,269 each year for twenty-five years) in the best-performing fund, Keystone S-4, produced a liquidation value of $375,515. A similar investment in the poorest-performing fund, Scudder, Stevens & Clark Balanced Fund, produced a liquidation value of $96,950. The composite figures disclose an average liquidation value for all the funds of $180,955.

As you will see from the records, it is the combination of money and time that works the miracle. To illustrate the importance of time, look at Fundamental Investors in which $31,731 was put aside at the rate of $1,269 per year for twenty-five years. This grew to $180,160. Now, consider this startling fact: if you had begun the $1,269 per year investment of your premium savings ten years earlier, at age thirty, by sixty-five your total out-of-pocket investment of $44,423 would have grown to an incredible $606,719!

# ILLUSTRATIONS OF ASSUMED ANNUAL INVESTMENTS OF $1,269 FOR TWENTY-FIVE YEARS FROM 1944 TO 1968

# ABERDEEN FUND

Illustration of assumed annual investments of $1,269 for twenty-five years from 1944 to 1968. All dividends and distributions reinvested.

This tabulation covers an illustration of an assumed investment of $1,269 annually on January 1 of each year from 1944 through 1968. This was a period in which stock prices fluctuated widely because of changing business and economic conditions, and were significantly higher at the end of the period than at the beginning. Thus, these results should not be considered as a representation of the dividend income or capital gain or loss that may be realized from an investment made in the fund today. A program of the type illustrated does not assure a profit nor protect against depreciation in declining markets.

| | | COST OF SHARES | | | | VALUE OF SHARES | | | | |
|---|---|---|---|---|---|---|---|---|---|---|
| YEAR ENDING DEC. 31 | AGE | CUMULATIVE ANNUAL INVEST- MENTS | ANNUAL INCOME DIVIDENDS REIN- VESTED | CUMULA- TIVE COST OF SHARES PURCHASED WITH DIVIDENDS | TOTAL COST (INCLUDES REIN- VESTED DIVIDENDS) | ACQUIRED THROUGH ANNUAL INVEST- MENTS | ACCEPTED AS CAPITAL GAINS DIS- TRIBUTIONS (CUMU- LATIVE) | SUB- TOTAL | PURCHASED THROUGH REINVEST- MENT OF INCOME (CUMULATIVE) | TOTAL VALUE |
| 1944 | 41 | $ 1,269 | $ 52 | $ 52 | $ 1,321 | $ 1,327 | $ 0 | $ 1,327 | $ 55 | $ 1,382 |
| 1945 | 42 | 2,538 | 103 | 155 | 2,694 | 3,173 | 0 | 3,173 | 184 | 3,357 |
| 1946 | 43 | 3,807 | 161 | 316 | 4,124 | 3,442 | 422 | 3,864 | 284 | 4,148 |
| 1947 | 44 | 5,077 | 301 | 617 | 5,694 | 4,376 | 401 | 4,777 | 573 | 5,350 |
| 1948 | 45 | 6,346 | 459 | 1,076 | 7,422 | 4,962 | 446 | 5,408 | 930 | 6,338 |
| 1949 | 46 | 7,615 | 559 | 1,635 | 9,251 | 6,301 | 459 | 6,760 | 1,570 | 8,330 |
| 1950 | 47 | 8,884 | 713 | 2,348 | 11,233 | 8,724 | 537 | 9,261 | 2,601 | 11,862 |
| 1951 | 48 | 10,154 | 720 | 3,068 | 13,222 | 10,719 | 796 | 11,515 | 3,571 | 15,086 |
| 1952 | 49 | 11,423 | 697 | 3,765 | 15,188 | 12,408 | 1,415 | 13,823 | 4,435 | 18,258 |
| 1953 | 50 | 12,692 | 734 | 4,499 | 17,192 | 13,064 | 1,573 | 14,637 | 5,024 | 19,661 |
| 1954 | 51 | 13,961 | 821 | 5,320 | 19,282 | 19,365 | 3,745 | 23,110 | 7,751 | 30,861 |
| 1955 | 52 | 15,231 | 870 | 6,190 | 21,421 | 24,326 | 5,359 | 29,685 | 10,103 | 39,788 |
| 1956 | 53 | 16,500 | 852 | 7,042 | 23,542 | 28,629 | 6,771 | 35,400 | 12,209 | 47,609 |
| 1957 | 54 | 17,769 | 1,021 | 8,063 | 25,833 | 26,157 | 6,749 | 32,906 | 11,654 | 44,560 |
| 1958 | 55 | 19,038 | 1,120 | 9,183 | 28,222 | 36,805 | 10,081 | 46,886 | 16,958 | 63,844 |
| 1959 | 56 | 20,308 | 841 | 10,024 | 30,332 | 44,033 | 13,019 | 57,052 | 20,548 | 77,600 |
| 1960 | 57 | 21,577 | 1,483 | 11,507 | 33,084 | 42,784 | 13,503 | 56,287 | 20,974 | 77,261 |
| 1961 | 58 | 22,846 | 1,184 | 12,691 | 35,538 | 51,166 | 17,275 | 68,441 | 25,632 | 94,073 |
| 1962 | 59 | 24,115 | 1,391 | 14,082 | 38,198 | 43,043 | 15,139 | 58,182 | 22,508 | 80,690 |
| 1963 | 60 | 25,385 | 1,494 | 15,576 | 40,961 | 51,789 | 18,976 | 70,765 | 27,958 | 98,723 |
| 1964 | 61 | 26,654 | 1,597 | 17,173 | 43,827 | 57,160 | 21,964 | 79,124 | 31,803 | 110,927 |
| 1965 | 62 | 27,923 | 1,887 | 19,060 | 46,984 | 67,589 | 28,444 | 96,033 | 38,903 | 134,936 |
| 1966 | 63 | 29,192 | 2,153 | 21,213 | 50,406 | 61,393 | 27,231 | 88,624 | 36,831 | 125,455 |
| 1967 | 64 | 30,462 | 2,242 | 23,455 | 53,917 | 73,097 | 38,150 | 111,247 | 45,312 | 156,559 |
| 1968 | 65 | 31,731 | 1,623 | 25,078 | 56,809 | 74,258 | 51,084 | 125,342 | 46,954 | 172,296 |

The total cost figures represent the cumulative total of yearly investments of $1,269 plus the cumulative amount of income dividends reinvested, and include the sales charge of $8\frac{1}{2}\%$ on all shares so purchased, as described in the prospectus. No adjustment has been made for any income taxes payable by shareholders on security distributions and dividends reinvested in shares. The dollar amounts of security profits distributions taken in shares were:

| 1944 | 0 | 1948 | 88 | 1952 | 577 | 1956 | 738 | 1960 | 1,173 | 1964 | 1,480 | 1968 | 13,349 |
|---|---|---|---|---|---|---|---|---|---|---|---|---|---|
| 1945 | 0 | 1949 | 0 | 1953 | 213 | 1957 | 845 | 1961 | 1,562 | 1965 | 2,862 | Total: | $38,533 |
| 1946 | 422 | 1950 | 0 | 1954 | 1,530 | 1958 | 999 | 1962 | 934 | 1966 | 1,844 | | |
| 1947 | 0 | 1951 | 212 | 1955 | 877 | 1959 | 1,321 | 1963 | 1,218 | 1967 | 6,289 | | |

| LIVING ESTATE | | | DEATH ESTATE | | | |
|---|---|---|---|---|---|---|
| "Buying Term and Investing the Difference" | Buying Whole Life | | "Buying Term and Investing the Difference" | | | Buying Whole Life |
| TOTAL VALUE OF SHARES | CASH VALUE | AGE ↓ | TOTAL VALUE OF SHARES | + DECREASING TERM INSURANCE | = TOTAL DEATH ESTATE | FACE VALUE |
| $ 1,382 | $ 0 | 41 | $ 1,382 | $100,000 | $101,382 | $75,000 |
| 3,357 | 225 | 42 | 3,357 | 95,000 | 98,357 | 75,000 |
| 4,148 | 1,575 | 43 | 4,148 | 90,000 | 94,148 | 75,000 |
| 5,350 | 3,000 | 44 | 5,350 | 85,000 | 90,350 | 75,000 |
| 6,338 | 4,425 | 45 | 6,338 | 80,000 | 86,338 | 75,000 |
| 8,330 | 5,925 | 46 | 8,330 | 75,000 | 83,330 | 75,000 |
| 11,862 | 7,425 | 47 | 11,862 | 70,000 | 81,862 | 75,000 |
| 15,086 | 8,925 | 48 | 15,086 | 65,000 | 80,086 | 75,000 |
| 18,258 | 10,425 | 49 | 18,258 | 60,000 | 78,258 | 75,000 |
| 19,661 | 11,925 | 50 | 19,661 | 55,000 | 74,661 | 75,000 |
| 30,861 | 13,500 | 51 | 30,861 | 50,000 | 80,861 | 75,000 |
| 39,788 | 15,000 | 52 | 39,788 | 46,250 | 86,038 | 75,000 |
| 47,609 | 16,575 | 53 | 47,609 | 42,500 | 90,109 | 75,000 |
| 44,560 | 18,150 | 54 | 44,560 | 38,750 | 83,310 | 75,000 |
| 63,844 | 19,725 | 55 | 63,844 | 35,000 | 98,844 | 75,000 |
| 77,600 | 21,300 | 56 | 77,600 | 31,250 | 108,850 | 75,000 |
| 77,261 | 22,950 | 57 | 77,261 | 28,750 | 106,011 | 75,000 |
| 94,073 | 24,525 | 58 | 94,073 | 26,250 | 120,323 | 75,000 |
| 80,690 | 26,100 | 59 | 80,690 | 23,750 | 104,440 | 75,000 |
| 98,723 | 27,750 | 60 | 98,723 | 21,250 | 119,973 | 75,000 |
| 110,927 | 29,250 | 61 | 110,927 | 18,750 | 129,677 | 75,000 |
| 134,936 | 30,750 | 62 | 134,936 | 17,500 | 152,436 | 75,000 |
| 125,455 | 32,175 | 63 | 125,455 | 16,250 | 141,705 | 75,000 |
| 156,559 | 33,675 | 64 | 156,559 | 15,000 | 171,559 | 75,000 |
| 172,296 | 35,175 | 65 | 172,296 | 14,400 | 186,696 | 75,000 |

Whether you
**lived** or **died**
you would have been better off
"Buying Term and Investing the Difference"

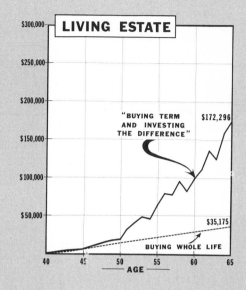

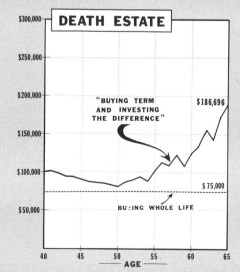

141

# AFFILIATED FUND

Illustration of assumed annual investments of $1,269 for twenty-five years from 1944 to 1968. All dividends and distributions reinvested.

This tabulation covers an illustration of an assumed investment of $1,269 annually on January 1 of each year from 1944 through 1968. This was a period in which stock prices fluctuated widely because of changing business and economic conditions, and were significantly higher at the end of the period than at the beginning. Thus, these results should not be considered as a representation of the dividend income or capital gain or loss that may be realized from an investment made in the fund today. A program of the type illustrated does not assure a profit nor protect against depreciation in declining markets.

| | | COST OF SHARES | | | | VALUE OF SHARES | | | | |
|---|---|---|---|---|---|---|---|---|---|---|
| YEAR ENDING DEC. 31 | AGE | CUMULATIVE ANNUAL INVESTMENTS | ANNUAL INCOME DIVIDENDS REINVESTED | CUMULATIVE COST OF SHARES PURCHASED WITH DIVIDENDS | TOTAL COST (INCLUDES REINVESTED DIVIDENDS) | ACQUIRED THROUGH ANNUAL INVESTMENTS | ACCEPTED AS CAPITAL GAINS DISTRIBUTIONS (CUMULATIVE) | SUBTOTAL | PURCHASED THROUGH REINVESTMENT OF INCOME (CUMULATIVE) | TOTAL VALUE |
| 1944 | 41 | $ 1,269 | $ 33 | $ 33 | $ 1,302 | $ 1,468 | $ 68 | $ 1,536 | $ 32 | $ 1,568 |
| 1945 | 42 | 2,538 | 78 | 111 | 2,650 | 4,280 | 330 | 4,610 | 152 | 4,762 |
| 1946 | 43 | 3,807 | 91 | 202 | 4,010 | 3,882 | 997 | 4,879 | 166 | 5,045 |
| 1947 | 44 | 5,077 | 270 | 473 | 5,550 | 4,396 | 1,357 | 5,755 | 382 | 6,137 |
| 1948 | 45 | 6,346 | 422 | 896 | 7,242 | 5,076 | 1,452 | 6,528 | 713 | 7,241 |
| 1949 | 46 | 7,615 | 653 | 1,550 | 9,166 | 7,128 | 1,656 | 8,784 | 1,507 | 10,291 |
| 1950 | 47 | 8,884 | 664 | 2,214 | 11,099 | 9,168 | 2,577 | 11,745 | 2,341 | 14,086 |
| 1951 | 48 | 10,154 | 1,061 | 3,276 | 13,430 | 10,564 | 4,110 | 14,674 | 3,385 | 18,059 |
| 1952 | 49 | 11,423 | 908 | 4,184 | 15,607 | 12,453 | 4,890 | 17,343 | 4,461 | 21,804 |
| 1953 | 50 | 12,692 | 1,020 | 5,204 | 17,897 | 13,060 | 5,021 | 18,081 | 5,221 | 23,302 |
| 1954 | 51 | 13,961 | 1,196 | 6,401 | 20,363 | 17,088 | 7,649 | 24,737 | 7,431 | 32,168 |
| 1955 | 52 | 15,231 | 1,355 | 7,756 | 22,987 | 18,764 | 9,738 | 28,502 | 8,885 | 37,387 |
| 1956 | 53 | 16,500 | 1,521 | 9,278 | 25,778 | 19,338 | 11,144 | 30,482 | 9,980 | 40,462 |
| 1957 | 54 | 17,769 | 1,692 | 10,970 | 28,740 | 18,953 | 11,796 | 30,749 | 10,706 | 41,455 |
| 1958 | 55 | 19,038 | 1,871 | 12,841 | 31,880 | 26,937 | 17,829 | 44,768 | 16,196 | 60,964 |
| 1959 | 56 | 20,308 | 1,953 | 14,795 | 35,103 | 29,369 | 21,924 | 51,293 | 18,691 | 69,984 |
| 1960 | 57 | 21,577 | 2,335 | 17,130 | 38,707 | 29,930 | 24,688 | 54,618 | 20,525 | 75,143 |
| 1961 | 58 | 22,846 | 2,442 | 19,572 | 42,419 | 36,536 | 32,677 | 69,213 | 26,382 | 95,595 |
| 1962 | 59 | 24,115 | 2,759 | 22,331 | 46,447 | 32,104 | 31,765 | 63,869 | 25,049 | 88,918 |
| 1963 | 60 | 25,385 | 3.007 | 25,338 | 50,723 | 37,001 | 39,347 | 76,350 | 30,603 | 106,953 |
| 1964 | 61 | 26,654 | 3,658 | 28,995 | 55,649 | 41,502 | 47,844 | 89,346 | 36,594 | 125,940 |
| 1965 | 62 | 27,923 | 4,262 | 33,258 | 61,182 | 44,314 | 56,460 | 100,774 | 41,938 | 142,712 |
| 1966 | 63 | 29,192 | 5,140 | 38,398 | 67,591 | 38,911 | 55,878 | 94,789 | 40,309 | 135,098 |
| 1967 | 64 | 30,462 | 5,716 | 44,114 | 74,576 | 44,262 | 74,130 | 118,392 | 49,535 | 167,927 |
| 1968 | 65 | 31,731 | 6,422 | 50,536 | 82,267 | 48,312 | 92,775 | 141,087 | 58,673 | 199,760 |

The total cost figures represent the cumulative total of yearly investments of $1,269 plus the cumulative amount of income dividends reinvested, and include the sales charge of 7½% on all shares so purchased, as described in the prospectus. No adjustment has been made for any income taxes payable by shareholders on security distributions and dividends reinvested in shares. The dollar amounts of security profits distributions taken in shares were:

| | | | | | | | | | | | | |
|---|---|---|---|---|---|---|---|---|---|---|---|---|
| 1944 | 67 | 1948 | 225 | 1952 | 494 | 1956 | 1,721 | 1960 | 3,017 | 1964 | 5,141 | 1968 | 13,747 |
| 1945 | 190 | 1949 | 0 | 1953 | 325 | 1957 | 1,476 | 1961 | 3,709 | 1965 | 6,735 | Total: $75,635 |
| 1946 | 718 | 1950 | 709 | 1954 | 1,508 | 1958 | 1,958 | 1962 | 3,678 | 1966 | 7,534 |
| 1947 | 481 | 1951 | 1,493 | 1955 | 1,824 | 1959 | 3,182 | 1963 | 4,010 | 1967 | 11,693 |

| LIVING ESTATE | | | | DEATH ESTATE | | | |
|---|---|---|---|---|---|---|---|
| "Buying Term and Investing the Difference" | Buying Whole Life | AGE | | "Buying Term and Investing the Difference" | | | Buying Whole Life |
| TOTAL VALUE OF SHARES | CASH VALUE | | TOTAL VALUE OF SHARES | + DECREASING TERM INSURANCE | = TOTAL DEATH ESTATE | FACE VALUE |
| $ 1,568 | $ 0 | 41 | $ 1,568 | $100,000 | $101,568 | $75,000 |
| 4,762 | 225 | 42 | 4,762 | 95,000 | 99,762 | 75,000 |
| 5,045 | 1,575 | 43 | 5,045 | 90,000 | 95,045 | 75,000 |
| 6,137 | 3,000 | 44 | 6,137 | 85,000 | 91,137 | 75,000 |
| 7,241 | 4,425 | 45 | 7,241 | 80,000 | 87,241 | 75,000 |
| 10,291 | 5,925 | 46 | 10,291 | 75,000 | 85,291 | 75,000 |
| 14,086 | 7,425 | 47 | 14,086 | 70,000 | 84,086 | 75,000 |
| 18,059 | 8,925 | 48 | 18,059 | 65,000 | 83,059 | 75,000 |
| 21,804 | 10,425 | 49 | 21,804 | 60,000 | 81,804 | 75,000 |
| 23,302 | 11,925 | 50 | 23,302 | 55,000 | 78,302 | 75,000 |
| 32,168 | 13,500 | 51 | 32,168 | 50,000 | 82,168 | 75,000 |
| 37,387 | 15,000 | 52 | 37,387 | 46,250 | 83,637 | 75,000 |
| 40,462 | 16,575 | 53 | 40,462 | 42,500 | 82,962 | 75,000 |
| 41,455 | 18,150 | 54 | 41,455 | 38,750 | 80,205 | 75,000 |
| 60,964 | 19,725 | 55 | 60,964 | 35,000 | 95,964 | 75,000 |
| 69,984 | 21,300 | 56 | 69,984 | 31,250 | 101,234 | 75,000 |
| 75,143 | 22,950 | 57 | 75,143 | 28,750 | 103,893 | 75,000 |
| 95,595 | 24,525 | 58 | 95,595 | 26,250 | 121,845 | 75,000 |
| 88,918 | 26,100 | 59 | 88,918 | 23,750 | 112,668 | 75,000 |
| 106,953 | 27,750 | 60 | 106,953 | 21,250 | 128,203 | 75,000 |
| 125,940 | 29,250 | 61 | 125,940 | 18,750 | 144,690 | 75,000 |
| 142,712 | 30,750 | 62 | 142,712 | 17,500 | 160,212 | 75,000 |
| 135,098 | 32,175 | 63 | 135,098 | 16,250 | 151,348 | 75,000 |
| 167,927 | 33,675 | 64 | 167,927 | 15,000 | 182,927 | 75,000 |
| 199,760 | 35,175 | 65 | 199,760 | 14,400 | 214,160 | 75,000 |

Whether you
**lived** or **died**
you would have been better off
"Buying Term and Investing the Difference"

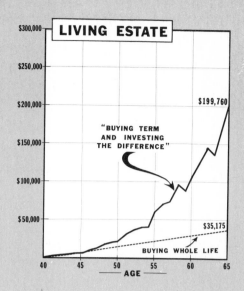

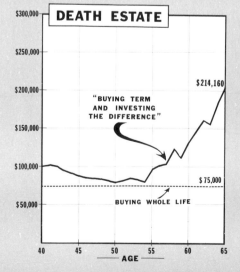

143

# AMERICAN BUSINESS SHARES

Illustration of assumed annual investments of $1,269 for twenty-five years from 1944 to 1968. All dividends and distributions reinvested.

This tabulation covers an illustration of an assumed investment of $1,269 annually on January 1 of each year from 1944 through 1968. This was a period in which stock prices fluctuated widely because of changing business and economic conditions, and were significantly higher at the end of the period than at the beginning. Thus, these results should not be considered as a representation of the dividend income or capital gain or loss that may be realized from an investment made in the fund today. A program of the type illustrated does not assure a profit nor protect against depreciation in declining markets.

| | | COST OF SHARES | | | | VALUE OF SHARES | | | | |
|---|---|---|---|---|---|---|---|---|---|---|
| YEAR ENDING DEC. 31 | AGE | CUMULATIVE ANNUAL INVEST-MENTS | ANNUAL INCOME DIVIDENDS REIN-VESTED | CUMULA-TIVE COST OF SHARES PURCHASED WITH DIVIDENDS | TOTAL COST (INCLUDES REIN-VESTED DIVIDENDS) | ACQUIRED THROUGH ANNUAL INVEST-MENTS | ACCEPTED AS CAPITAL GAINS DIS-TRIBUTIONS (CUMU-LATIVE) | SUB-TOTAL | PURCHASED THROUGH REINVEST-MENT OF INCOME (CUMULATIVE) | TOTAL VALUE |
| 1944 | 41 | $ 1,269 | $ 44 | $ 44 | $ 1,313 | $ 1,362 | $ 54 | $ 1,416 | $ 42 | $ 1,458 |
| 1945 | 42 | 2,538 | 100 | 143 | 2,682 | 3,290 | 202 | 3,492 | 160 | 3,652 |
| 1946 | 43 | 3,807 | 123 | 267 | 4,074 | 3,685 | 455 | 4,140 | 227 | 4,367 |
| 1947 | 44 | 5,077 | 234 | 502 | 5,579 | 4,538 | 578 | 5,116 | 425 | 5,541 |
| 1948 | 45 | 6,346 | 314 | 816 | 7,163 | 5,486 | 665 | 6,151 | 691 | 6,842 |
| 1949 | 46 | 7,615 | 402 | 1,218 | 8,834 | 7,096 | 709 | 7,805 | 1,135 | 8,940 |
| 1950 | 47 | 8,884 | 461 | 1,680 | 10,565 | 8,566 | 1,292 | 9,858 | 1,610 | 11,468 |
| 1951 | 48 | 10,154 | 492 | 2,172 | 12,327 | 9,546 | 1,990 | 11,536 | 2,024 | 13,560 |
| 1952 | 49 | 11,423 | 557 | 2,730 | 14,154 | 10,991 | 2,478 | 13,469 | 2,600 | 16,069 |
| 1953 | 50 | 12,692 | 646 | 3,377 | 16,070 | 11,985 | 2,440 | 14,425 | 3,167 | 17,592 |
| 1954 | 51 | 13,961 | 762 | 4,140 | 18,102 | 13,786 | 4,793 | 18,579 | 4,003 | 22,582 |
| 1955 | 52 | 15,231 | 863 | 5,003 | 20,234 | 14,639 | 6,012 | 20,651 | 4,692 | 25,343 |
| 1956 | 53 | 16,500 | 952 | 5,955 | 22,456 | 14,537 | 6,128 | 20,665 | 5,146 | 25,811 |
| 1957 | 54 | 17,769 | 1,091 | 7,047 | 24,817 | 15,504 | 6,046 | 21,550 | 6,098 | 27,648 |
| 1958 | 55 | 19,038 | 1,220 | 8,267 | 27,306 | 19,151 | 7,594 | 26,745 | 8,193 | 34,938 |
| 1959 | 56 | 20,308 | 1,308 | 9,576 | 29,884 | 19,798 | 9,943 | 29,741 | 9,146 | 38,887 |
| 1960 | 57 | 21,577 | 1,466 | 11,043 | 32,621 | 21,174 | 11,763 | 32,937 | 10,608 | 43,545 |
| 1961 | 58 | 22,846 | 1,592 | 12,635 | 35,483 | 24,909 | 16,290 | 41,199 | 13,284 | 54,483 |
| 1962 | 59 | 24,115 | 1,717 | 14,352 | 38,468 | 21,502 | 20,087 | 41,589 | 12,366 | 53,955 |
| 1963 | 60 | 25,385 | 1,992 | 16,344 | 41,730 | 24,032 | 24,112 | 48,144 | 14,923 | 63,067 |
| 1964 | 61 | 26,654 | 2,189 | 18,534 | 45,189 | 26,257 | 27,063 | 53,320 | 17,560 | 70,880 |
| 1965 | 62 | 27,923 | 2,444 | 20,978 | 48,903 | 26,979 | 29,786 | 56,765 | 19,493 | 76,258 |
| 1966 | 63 | 29,192 | 2,908 | 23,887 | 53,081 | 23,910 | 32,268 | 56,178 | 18,939 | 75,117 |
| 1967 | 64 | 30,462 | 3,489 | 27,377 | 57,840 | 24,307 | 39,180 | 63,487 | 21,295 | 84,782 |
| 1968 | 65 | 31,731 | 3,932 | 31,310 | 63,042 | 26,961 | 46,575 | 73,536 | 26,202 | 99,738 |

The total cost figures represent the cumulative total of yearly investments of $1,269 plus the cumulative amount of income dividends reinvested, and include the sales charge of 7½% on all shares so purchased, as described in the prospectus. No adjustment has been made for any income taxes payable by shareholders on security distributions and dividends reinvested in shares. The dollar amounts of security profits distributions taken in shares were:

| | | | | | | | | | | | |
|---|---|---|---|---|---|---|---|---|---|---|---|
| 1944 | 51 | 1948 | 109 | 1952 | 421 | 1956 | 603 | 1960 | 1,696 | 1964 | 1,946 | 1968 | 5,198 |
| 1945 | 125 | 1949 | 0 | 1953 | 0 | 1957 | 0 | 1961 | 3,185 | 1965 | 3,147 | Total: $49,016 |
| 1946 | 273 | 1950 | 536 | 1954 | 2,190 | 1958 | 644 | 1962 | 6,634 | 1966 | 6,910 | |
| 1947 | 154 | 1951 | 709 | 1955 | 1,321 | 1959 | 2,539 | 1963 | 2,805 | 1967 | 7,820 | |

# LIVING ESTATE

| "Buying Term and Investing the Difference" TOTAL VALUE OF SHARES | Buying Whole Life CASH VALUE | AGE | "Buying Term and Investing the Difference" TOTAL VALUE OF SHARES | + DECREASING TERM INSURANCE | = TOTAL DEATH ESTATE | Buying Whole Life FACE VALUE |
|---|---|---|---|---|---|---|
| $ 1,458 | $ 0 | 41 | $ 1,458 | $100,000 | $101,458 | $75,000 |
| 3,652 | 225 | 42 | 3,652 | 95,000 | 98,652 | 75,000 |
| 4,367 | 1,575 | 43 | 4,367 | 90,000 | 94,367 | 75,000 |
| 5,541 | 3,000 | 44 | 5,541 | 85,000 | 90,541 | 75,000 |
| 6,842 | 4,425 | 45 | 6,842 | 80,000 | 86,842 | 75,000 |
| 8,940 | 5,925 | 46 | 8,940 | 75,000 | 83,940 | 75,000 |
| 11,468 | 7,425 | 47 | 11,468 | 70,000 | 81,468 | 75,000 |
| 13,560 | 8,925 | 48 | 13,560 | 65,000 | 78,560 | 75,000 |
| 16,069 | 10,425 | 49 | 16,069 | 60,000 | 76,069 | 75,000 |
| 17,592 | 11,925 | 50 | 17,592 | 55,000 | 72,592 | 75,000 |
| 22,582 | 13,500 | 51 | 22,582 | 50,000 | 72,582 | 75,000 |
| 25,343 | 15,000 | 52 | 25,343 | 46,250 | 71,593 | 75,000 |
| 25,811 | 16,575 | 53 | 25,811 | 42,500 | 68,311 | 75,000 |
| 27,648 | 18,150 | 54 | 27,648 | 38,750 | 66,398 | 75,000 |
| 34,938 | 19,725 | 55 | 34,938 | 35,000 | 69,938 | 75,000 |
| 38,887 | 21,300 | 56 | 38,887 | 31,250 | 70,137 | 75,000 |
| 43,545 | 22,950 | 57 | 43,545 | 28,750 | 72,295 | 75,000 |
| 54,483 | 24,525 | 58 | 54,483 | 26,250 | 80,733 | 75,000 |
| 53,955 | 26,100 | 59 | 53,955 | 23,750 | 77,705 | 75,000 |
| 63,067 | 27,750 | 60 | 63,067 | 21,250 | 84,317 | 75,000 |
| 70,880 | 29,250 | 61 | 70,880 | 18,750 | 89,630 | 75,000 |
| 76,258 | 30,750 | 62 | 76,258 | 17,500 | 93,758 | 75,000 |
| 75,117 | 32,175 | 63 | 75,117 | 16,250 | 91,367 | 75,000 |
| 84,782 | 33,675 | 64 | 84,782 | 15,000 | 99,782 | 75,000 |
| 99,738 | 35,175 | 65 | 99,738 | 14,400 | 114,138 | 75,000 |

(The right-hand columns belong under the heading **DEATH ESTATE**.)

Whether you
**lived** or **died**
you would have been better off
"Buying Term and Investing the Difference"

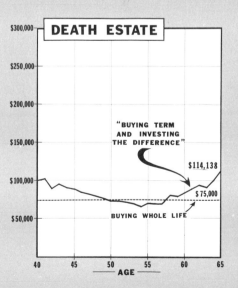

**LIVING ESTATE**

"BUYING TERM AND INVESTING THE DIFFERENCE" — $99,738

BUYING WHOLE LIFE — $35,175

**DEATH ESTATE**

"BUYING TERM AND INVESTING THE DIFFERENCE" — $114,138

BUYING WHOLE LIFE — $75,000

# ANCHOR INCOME FUND

Illustration of assumed annual investments of $1,269 for twenty-five years from 1944 to 1968. All dividends and distributions reinvested.

This tabulation covers an illustration of an assumed investment of $1,269 annually on January 1 of each year from 1944 through 1968. This was a period in which stock prices fluctuated widely because of changing business and economic conditions, and were significantly higher at the end of the period than at the beginning. Thus, these results should not be considered as a representation of the dividend income or capital gain or loss that may be realized from an investment made in the fund today. A program of the type illustrated does not assure a profit nor protect against depreciation in declining markets.

| | | COST OF SHARES | | | | VALUE OF SHARES | | | | |
|---|---|---|---|---|---|---|---|---|---|---|
| YEAR ENDING DEC. 31 | AGE | CUMULATIVE ANNUAL INVEST- MENTS | ANNUAL INCOME DIVIDENDS REIN- VESTED | CUMULA- TIVE COST OF SHARES PURCHASED WITH DIVIDENDS | TOTAL COST (INCLUDES REIN- VESTED DIVIDENDS) | ACQUIRED THROUGH ANNUAL INVEST- MENTS | ACCEPTED AS CAPITAL GAINS DIS- TRIBUTIONS (CUMU- LATIVE) | SUB- TOTAL | PURCHASED THROUGH REINVEST- MENT OF INCOME (CUMULATIVE) | TOTAL VALUE |
| 1944 | 41 | $ 1,269 | $ 0 | $ 0 | $ 1,269 | $ 1,182 | $ 0 | $ 1,182 | $ 0 | $ 1,182 |
| 1945 | 42 | 2,538 | 147 | 147 | 2,686 | 2,848 | 62 | 2,910 | 148 | 3,058 |
| 1946 | 43 | 3,807 | 198 | 345 | 4,153 | 3,442 | 167 | 3,609 | 293 | 3,902 |
| 1947 | 44 | 5,077 | 313 | 658 | 5,735 | 4,119 | 149 | 4,268 | 544 | 4,812 |
| 1948 | 45 | 6,346 | 418 | 1,076 | 7,422 | 5,052 | 143 | 5,195 | 890 | 6,085 |
| 1949 | 46 | 7,615 | 465 | 1,540 | 9,156 | 6,773 | 155 | 6,928 | 1,438 | 8,366 |
| 1950 | 47 | 8,884 | 631 | 2,171 | 11,056 | 9,292 | 182 | 9,474 | 2,313 | 11,787 |
| 1951 | 48 | 10,154 | 800 | 2,971 | 13,125 | 10,465 | 700 | 11,165 | 3,048 | 14,213 |
| 1952 | 49 | 11,423 | 864 | 3,835 | 15,258 | 12,388 | 1,103 | 13,491 | 4,078 | 17,569 |
| 1953 | 50 | 12,692 | 986 | 4,822 | 17,515 | 12,688 | 1,119 | 13,807 | 4,711 | 18,518 |
| 1954 | 51 | 13,961 | 1,167 | 5,988 | 19,950 | 18,698 | 2,727 | 21,425 | 7,597 | 29,022 |
| 1955 | 52 | 15,231 | 1,391 | 7,379 | 22,610 | 21,044 | 4,499 | 25,543 | 9,333 | 34,876 |
| 1956 | 53 | 16,500 | 1,566 | 8,946 | 25,446 | 21,616 | 5,970 | 27,586 | 10,459 | 38,045 |
| 1957 | 54 | 17,769 | 1,753 | 10,698 | 28,468 | 18,369 | 5,712 | 24,081 | 9,841 | 33,922 |
| 1958 | 55 | 19,038 | 1,898 | 12,596 | 31,635 | 24,228 | 8,307 | 32,535 | 14,129 | 46,664 |
| 1959 | 56 | 20,308 | 1,755 | 14,351 | 34,659 | 25,103 | 9,900 | 35,003 | 15,509 | 50,512 |
| 1960 | 57 | 21,577 | 2,007 | 16,358 | 37,935 | 25,206 | 11,347 | 36,553 | 16,741 | 53,294 |
| 1961 | 58 | 22,846 | 2,202 | 18,560 | 41,407 | 29,480 | 14,622 | 44,102 | 20,779 | 64,881 |
| 1962 | 59 | 24,115 | 2,389 | 20,949 | 45,065 | 27,434 | 15,107 | 42,541 | 20,760 | 63,301 |
| 1963 | 60 | 25,385 | 2,605 | 23,554 | 48,939 | 29,782 | 18,162 | 47,944 | 23,980 | 71,924 |
| 1964 | 61 | 26,654 | 2,834 | 26,388 | 53,042 | 32,757 | 21,910 | 54,667 | 27,971 | 82,638 |
| 1965 | 62 | 27,923 | 3,068 | 29,456 | 57,380 | 35,839 | 26,353 | 62,192 | 32,434 | 94,626 |
| 1966 | 63 | 29,192 | 3,414 | 32,870 | 62,063 | 31,782 | 26,045 | 57,827 | 30,700 | 88,527 |
| 1967 | 64 | 30,462 | 3,724 | 36,594 | 67,056 | 37,469 | 33,371 | 70,840 | 38,340 | 109,180 |
| 1968 | 65 | 31,731 | 3,969 | 40,563 | 72,294 | 40,592 | 39,352 | 79,944 | 44,034 | 123,978 |

The total cost figures represent the cumulative total of yearly investments of $1,269 plus the cumulative amount of income dividends reinvested, and include the sales charge of 8¾% on all shares so purchased, as described in the prospectus. No adjustment has been made for any income taxes payable by shareholders on security distributions and dividends reinvested in shares. The dollar amounts of security profits distributions taken in shares were:

| | | | | | | | | | | | | | |
|---|---|---|---|---|---|---|---|---|---|---|---|---|---|
| 1944 | 0 | 1948 | 0 | 1952 | 347 | 1956 | 1,604 | 1960 | 1,787 | 1964 | 2,682 | 1968 | 4,279 |
| 1945 | 60 | 1949 | 0 | 1953 | 84 | 1957 | 901 | 1961 | 1,955 | 1965 | 3,174 | Total: | $34,565 |
| 1946 | 115 | 1950 | 0 | 1954 | 1,124 | 1958 | 1,199 | 1962 | 1,984 | 1966 | 3,342 | | |
| 1947 | 0 | 1951 | 506 | 1955 | 1,603 | 1959 | 1,682 | 1963 | 2,391 | 1967 | 3,746 | | |

## LIVING ESTATE / DEATH ESTATE

| LIVING ESTATE | | | DEATH ESTATE | | | |
|---|---|---|---|---|---|---|
| "Buying Term and Investing the Difference" | Buying Whole Life | AGE ↓ | "Buying Term and Investing the Difference" | | | Buying Whole Life |
| TOTAL VALUE OF SHARES | CASH VALUE | | TOTAL VALUE OF SHARES + | DECREASING TERM INSURANCE = | TOTAL DEATH ESTATE | FACE VALUE |
| $ 1,182 | $ 0 | 41 | $ 1,182 | $100,000 | $101,182 | $75,000 |
| 3,058 | 225 | 42 | 3,058 | 95,000 | 98,058 | 75,000 |
| 3,902 | 1,575 | 43 | 3,902 | 90,000 | 93,902 | 75,000 |
| 4,812 | 3,000 | 44 | 4,812 | 85,000 | 89,812 | 75,000 |
| 6,085 | 4,425 | 45 | 6,085 | 80,000 | 86,085 | 75,000 |
| 8,366 | 5,925 | 46 | 8,366 | 75,000 | 83,366 | 75,000 |
| 11,787 | 7,425 | 47 | 11,787 | 70,000 | 81,787 | 75,000 |
| 14,213 | 8,925 | 48 | 14,213 | 65,000 | 79,213 | 75,000 |
| 17,569 | 10,425 | 49 | 17,569 | 60,000 | 77,569 | 75,000 |
| 18,518 | 11,925 | 50 | 18,518 | 55,000 | 73,518 | 75,000 |
| 29,022 | 13,500 | 51 | 29,022 | 50,000 | 79,022 | 75,000 |
| 34,876 | 15,000 | 52 | 34,876 | 46,250 | 81,126 | 75,000 |
| 38,045 | 16,575 | 53 | 38,045 | 42,500 | 80,545 | 75,000 |
| 33,922 | 18,150 | 54 | 33,922 | 38,750 | 72,672 | 75,000 |
| 46,664 | 19,725 | 55 | 46,664 | 35,000 | 81,664 | 75,000 |
| 50,512 | 21,300 | 56 | 50,512 | 31,250 | 81,762 | 75,000 |
| 53,294 | 22,950 | 57 | 53,294 | 28,750 | 82,044 | 75,000 |
| 64,881 | 24,525 | 58 | 64,881 | 26,250 | 91,131 | 75,000 |
| 63,301 | 26,100 | 59 | 63,301 | 23,750 | 87,051 | 75,000 |
| 71,924 | 27,750 | 60 | 71,924 | 21,250 | 93,174 | 75,000 |
| 82,638 | 29,250 | 61 | 82,638 | 18,750 | 101,388 | 75,000 |
| 94,626 | 30,750 | 62 | 94,626 | 17,500 | 112,126 | 75,000 |
| 88,527 | 32,175 | 63 | 88,527 | 16,250 | 104,777 | 75,000 |
| 109,180 | 33,675 | 64 | 109,180 | 15,000 | 124,180 | 75,000 |
| 123,978 | 35,175 | 65 | 123,978 | 14,400 | 138,378 | 75,000 |

Whether you
**lived** or **died**
you would have been better off
"Buying Term and Investing the Difference"

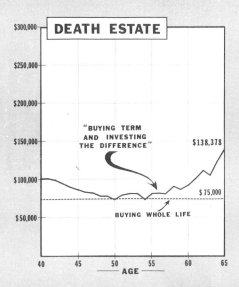

LIVING ESTATE

"BUYING TERM AND INVESTING THE DIFFERENCE" $123,978

$35,175 BUYING WHOLE LIFE

DEATH ESTATE

"BUYING TERM AND INVESTING THE DIFFERENCE" $138,378

$75,000 BUYING WHOLE LIFE

# ASSOCIATED FUND TRUST

Illustration of assumed annual investments of $1,269 for twenty-five years from 1944 to 1968. All dividends and distributions reinvested.

This tabulation covers an illustration of an assumed investment of $1,269 annually on January 1 of each year from 1944 through 1968. This was a period in which stock prices fluctuated widely because of changing business and economic conditions, and were significantly higher at the end of the period than at the beginning. Thus, these results should not be considered as a representation of the dividend income or capital gain or loss that may be realized from an investment made in the fund today. A program of the type illustrated does not assure a profit nor protect against depreciation in declining markets.

| | | COST OF SHARES | | | | VALUE OF SHARES | | | | |
|---|---|---|---|---|---|---|---|---|---|---|
| YEAR ENDING DEC. 31 | AGE | CUMULATIVE ANNUAL INVESTMENTS | ANNUAL INCOME DIVIDENDS REINVESTED | CUMULATIVE COST OF SHARES PURCHASED WITH DIVIDENDS | TOTAL COST (INCLUDES REINVESTED DIVIDENDS) | ACQUIRED THROUGH ANNUAL INVESTMENTS | ACCEPTED AS CAPITAL GAINS DISTRIBUTIONS (CUMULATIVE) | SUBTOTAL | PURCHASED THROUGH REINVESTMENT OF INCOME (CUMULATIVE) | TOTAL VALUE |
| 1944 | 41 | $ 1,269 | $ 87 | $ 87 | $ 1,356 | $ 1,405 | $ 57 | $ 1,462 | $ 92 | $ 1,554 |
| 1945 | 42 | 2,538 | 122 | 209 | 2,748 | 3,250 | 244 | 3,494 | 252 | 3,746 |
| 1946 | 43 | 3,807 | 193 | 402 | 4,210 | 3,660 | 424 | 4,084 | 388 | 4,472 |
| 1947 | 44 | 5,077 | 302 | 704 | 5,781 | 4,500 | 611 | 5,111 | 668 | 5,779 |
| 1948 | 45 | 6,346 | 414 | 1,118 | 7,464 | 5,339 | 670 | 6,009 | 1,026 | 7,035 |
| 1949 | 46 | 7,615 | 488 | 1,606 | 9,222 | 6,807 | 917 | 7,724 | 1,590 | 9,314 |
| 1950 | 47 | 8,884 | 625 | 2,231 | 11,116 | 8,689 | 1,223 | 9,912 | 2,384 | 12,296 |
| 1951 | 48 | 10,154 | 717 | 2,948 | 13,102 | 10,015 | 1,707 | 11,722 | 3,140 | 14,862 |
| 1952 | 49 | 11,423 | 743 | 3,691 | 15,114 | 11,439 | 2,165 | 13,604 | 3,970 | 17,574 |
| 1953 | 50 | 12,692 | 802 | 4,493 | 17,186 | 11,764 | 2,528 | 14,292 | 4,499 | 18,791 |
| 1954 | 51 | 13,961 | 977 | 5,470 | 19,432 | 16,618 | 3,960 | 20,578 | 6,882 | 27,460 |
| 1955 | 52 | 15,231 | 1,279 | 6,749 | 21,980 | 19,620 | 5,222 | 24,842 | 8,914 | 33,756 |
| 1956 | 53 | 16,500 | 1,454 | 8,203 | 24,703 | 21,025 | 6,691 | 27,716 | 10,539 | 38,255 |
| 1957 | 54 | 17,769 | 1,653 | 9,856 | 27,626 | 17,515 | 6,665 | 24,180 | 9,811 | 33,991 |
| 1958 | 55 | 19,038 | 1,682 | 11,538 | 30,577 | 23,914 | 10,447 | 34,361 | 14,428 | 48,789 |
| 1959 | 56 | 20,308 | 1,770 | 13,308 | 33,616 | 25,558 | 12,726 | 38,284 | 16,474 | 54,758 |
| 1960 | 57 | 21,577 | 1,957 | 15,265 | 36,842 | 24,268 | 13,669 | 37,937 | 16,931 | 54,868 |
| 1961 | 58 | 22,846 | 1,994 | 17,259 | 40,106 | 29,108 | 18,088 | 47,196 | 21,432 | 68,628 |
| 1962 | 59 | 24,115 | 2,236 | 19,495 | 43,611 | 25,756 | 28,077 | 43,833 | 20,476 | 64,309 |
| 1963 | 60 | 25,385 | 2,256 | 21,751 | 47,136 | 28,799 | 21,883 | 50,682 | 24,171 | 74,853 |
| 1964 | 61 | 26,654 | 2,636 | 24,387 | 41,041 | 32,459 | 26,564 | 59,023 | 28,876 | 87,899 |
| 1965 | 62 | 27,923 | 3,191 | 27,578 | 55,502 | 36,844 | 32,159 | 69,003 | 34,994 | 103,997 |
| 1966 | 63 | 29,192 | 3,120 | 30,698 | 59,891 | 27,935 | 34,794 | 62,729 | 28,625 | 91,354 |
| 1967 | 64 | 30,462 | 4,724 | 35,422 | 65,884 | 34,031 | 48,497 | 82,528 | 38,132 | 120,660 |
| 1968 | 65 | 31,731 | 4,992 | 40,414 | 72,145 | 37,468 | 62,209 | 99,677 | 45,753 | 145,430 |

The total cost figures represent the cumulative total of yearly investments of $1,269 plus the cumulative amount of income dividends reinvested, and include the sales charge of 8½% on all shares so purchased, as described in the prospectus. No adjustment has been made for any income taxes payable by shareholders on security distributions and dividends reinvested in shares. The dollar amounts of security profits distributions taken in shares were:

| | | | | | | | | | | | | | |
|---|---|---|---|---|---|---|---|---|---|---|---|---|---|
| 1944 | 55 | 1948 | 99 | 1952 | 409 | 1956 | 1,383 | 1960 | 2,048 | 1964 | 2,819 | 1968 | 10,704 |
| 1945 | 157 | 1949 | 200 | 1953 | 514 | 1957 | 1,520 | 1961 | 2,352 | 1965 | 2,926 | Total: | $56,279 |
| 1946 | 238 | 1950 | 212 | 1954 | 620 | 1958 | 1,744 | 1962 | 2,637 | 1966 | 11,875 | | |
| 1947 | 210 | 1951 | 469 | 1955 | 812 | 1959 | 2,048 | 1963 | 2,538 | 1967 | 7,690 | | |

## LIVING ESTATE

| "Buying Term and Investing the Difference" | Buying Whole Life |
| --- | --- |
| TOTAL VALUE OF SHARES | CASH VALUE |

## DEATH ESTATE

| "Buying Term and Investing the Difference" | | | Buying Whole Life |
| --- | --- | --- | --- |
| TOTAL VALUE OF SHARES + | DECREASING TERM INSURANCE = | TOTAL DEATH ESTATE | FACE VALUE |

| TOTAL VALUE OF SHARES | CASH VALUE | AGE | TOTAL VALUE OF SHARES | + DECREASING TERM INSURANCE | = TOTAL DEATH ESTATE | FACE VALUE |
| --- | --- | --- | --- | --- | --- | --- |
| $ 1,554 | $ 0 | 41 | $ 1,554 | $100,000 | $101,554 | $75,000 |
| 3,746 | 225 | 42 | 3,746 | 95,000 | 98,746 | 75,000 |
| 4,472 | 1,575 | 43 | 4,472 | 90,000 | 94,472 | 75,000 |
| 5,779 | 3,000 | 44 | 5,779 | 85,000 | 90,779 | 75,000 |
| 7,035 | 4,425 | 45 | 7,035 | 80,000 | 87,035 | 75,000 |
| 9,314 | 5,925 | 46 | 9,314 | 75,000 | 84,314 | 75,000 |
| 12,296 | 7,425 | 47 | 12,296 | 70,000 | 82,296 | 75,000 |
| 14,862 | 8,925 | 48 | 14,862 | 65,000 | 79,862 | 75,000 |
| 17,574 | 10,425 | 49 | 17,574 | 60,000 | 77,574 | 75,000 |
| 18,791 | 11,925 | 50 | 18,791 | 55,000 | 73,791 | 75,000 |
| 27,460 | 13,500 | 51 | 27,460 | 50,000 | 77,460 | 75,000 |
| 33,756 | 15,000 | 52 | 33,756 | 46,250 | 80,006 | 75,000 |
| 38,255 | 16,575 | 53 | 38,255 | 42,500 | 80,755 | 75,000 |
| 33,991 | 18,150 | 54 | 33,991 | 38,750 | 72,741 | 75,000 |
| 48,789 | 19,725 | 55 | 48,789 | 35,000 | 83,789 | 75,000 |
| 54,758 | 21,300 | 56 | 54,758 | 31,250 | 86,008 | 75,000 |
| 54,868 | 22,950 | 57 | 54,868 | 28,750 | 83,618 | 75,000 |
| 68,628 | 24,525 | 58 | 68,628 | 26,250 | 94,878 | 75,000 |
| 64,309 | 26,100 | 59 | 64,309 | 23,750 | 88,059 | 75,000 |
| 74,853 | 27,750 | 60 | 74,853 | 21,250 | 96,103 | 75,000 |
| 87,899 | 29,250 | 61 | 87,899 | 18,750 | 106,649 | 75,000 |
| 103,997 | 30,750 | 62 | 103,997 | 17,500 | 121,497 | 75,000 |
| 91,354 | 32,175 | 63 | 91,354 | 16,250 | 107,604 | 75,000 |
| 120,660 | 33,675 | 64 | 120,660 | 15,000 | 135,660 | 75,000 |
| 145,430 | 35,175 | 65 | 145,430 | 14,400 | 159,830 | 75,000 |

Whether you
**lived** or **died**
you would have been better off
"Buying Term and Investing the Difference"

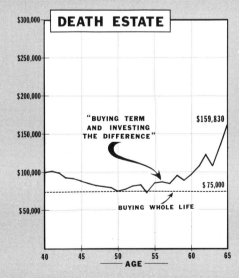

### LIVING ESTATE

"BUYING TERM AND INVESTING THE DIFFERENCE" — $145,430
BUYING WHOLE LIFE — $35,175

### DEATH ESTATE

"BUYING TERM AND INVESTING THE DIFFERENCE" — $159,830
BUYING WHOLE LIFE — $75,000

# AXE–HOUGHTON FUND A

Illustration of assumed annual investments of $1,269 for twenty-five years from 1944 to 1968. All dividends and distributions reinvested.

This tabulation covers an illustration of an assumed investment of $1,269 annually on January 1 of each year from 1944 through 1968. This was a period in which stock prices fluctuated widely because of changing business and economic conditions, and were significantly higher at the end of the period than at the beginning. Thus, these results should not be considered as a representation of the dividend income or capital gain or loss that may be realized from an investment made in the fund today. A program of the type illustrated does not assure a profit nor protect against depreciation in declining markets.

| | | COST OF SHARES | | | | VALUE OF SHARES | | | | |
|---|---|---|---|---|---|---|---|---|---|---|
| YEAR ENDING DEC. 31 | AGE | CUMULATIVE ANNUAL INVEST-MENTS | ANNUAL INCOME DIVIDENDS REIN-VESTED | CUMULA-TIVE COST OF SHARES PURCHASED WITH DIVIDENDS | TOTAL COST (INCLUDES REIN-VESTED DIVIDENDS) | ACQUIRED THROUGH ANNUAL INVEST-MENTS | ACCEPTED AS CAPITAL GAINS DIS-TRIBUTIONS (CUMU-LATIVE) | SUB-TOTAL | PURCHASED THROUGH REINVEST-MENT OF INCOME (CUMULATIVE) | TOTAL VALUE |
| 1944 | 41 | $ 1,269 | $ 51 | $ 51 | $ 1,320 | $ 1,348 | $ 46 | $ 1,394 | $ 53 | $ 1,447 |
| 1945 | 42 | 2,538 | 55 | 106 | 2,645 | 3,130 | 238 | 3,368 | 126 | 3,494 |
| 1946 | 43 | 3,807 | 145 | 251 | 4,059 | 3,544 | 370 | 3,914 | 241 | 4,155 |
| 1947 | 44 | 5,077 | 233 | 484 | 5,561 | 4,564 | 480 | 5,044 | 471 | 5,515 |
| 1948 | 45 | 6,346 | 338 | 822 | 7,168 | 5,348 | 559 | 5,907 | 759 | 6,666 |
| 1949 | 46 | 7,615 | 366 | 1,188 | 8,804 | 7,170 | 716 | 7,886 | 1,249 | 9,135 |
| 1950 | 47 | 8,884 | 574 | 1,762 | 10,647 | 10,619 | 1,241 | 11,860 | 2,226 | 14,086 |
| 1951 | 48 | 10,154 | 572 | 2,334 | 12,488 | 12,196 | 2,008 | 14,204 | 2,873 | 17,077 |
| 1952 | 49 | 11,423 | 550 | 2,884 | 14,307 | 13,284 | 3,153 | 16,437 | 3,422 | 19,859 |
| 1953 | 50 | 12,692 | 683 | 3,567 | 16,260 | 13,388 | 3,723 | 17,111 | 3,843 | 20,954 |
| 1954 | 51 | 13,961 | 749 | 4,316 | 18,278 | 18,053 | 5,890 | 23,943 | 5,594 | 29,537 |
| 1955 | 52 | 15,231 | 845 | 5,161 | 20,392 | 20,353 | 7,893 | 28,246 | 6,772 | 35,018 |
| 1956 | 53 | 16,500 | 966 | 6,127 | 22,627 | 19,798 | 9,691 | 29,489 | 7,144 | 36,633 |
| 1957 | 54 | 17,769 | 1,169 | 7,296 | 25,066 | 17,800 | 9,743 | 27,543 | 7,114 | 34,657 |
| 1958 | 55 | 19,038 | 1,295 | 8,590 | 27,629 | 22,498 | 13,429 | 35,927 | 9,886 | 45,813 |
| 1959 | 56 | 20,308 | 1,264 | 9,854 | 30,162 | 23,541 | 15,905 | 39,446 | 11,042 | 50,488 |
| 1960 | 57 | 21,577 | 1,544 | 11,398 | 32,975 | 22,957 | 17,973 | 40,930 | 11,806 | 52,736 |
| 1961 | 58 | 22,846 | 1,885 | 13,283 | 36,130 | 25,965 | 21,702 | 47,667 | 14,575 | 62,242 |
| 1962 | 59 | 24,115 | 1,867 | 15,150 | 39,266 | 24,294 | 20,965 | 45,259 | 14,913 | 60,172 |
| 1963 | 60 | 25,385 | 1,965 | 17,115 | 42,500 | 28,941 | 25,063 | 54,004 | 18,936 | 72,940 |
| 1964 | 61 | 26,654 | 2,224 | 19,339 | 45,993 | 33,466 | 30,510 | 63,976 | 23,353 | 87,329 |
| 1965 | 62 | 27,923 | 2,409 | 21,748 | 49,672 | 37,837 | 39,687 | 77,524 | 28,065 | 105,589 |
| 1966 | 63 | 29,192 | 2,535 | 24,284 | 53,477 | 35,143 | 43,472 | 78,615 | 27,753 | 106,368 |
| 1967 | 64 | 30,462 | 2,812 | 27,095 | 57,557 | 52,094 | 75,475 | 127,569 | 43,061 | 170,630 |
| 1968 | 65 | 31,731 | 2,568 | 29,663 | 61,394 | 57,756 | 98,103 | 155,859 | 49,522 | 205,381 |

The total cost figures represent the cumulative total of yearly investments of $1,269 plus the cumulative amount of income dividends reinvested, and include the sales charge of **8%** on all shares so purchased, as described in the prospectus. No adjustment has been made for any income taxes payable by shareholders on security distributions and dividends reinvested in shares. The dollar amounts of security profits distributions taken in shares were:

| | | | | | | | | | | | | | |
|---|---|---|---|---|---|---|---|---|---|---|---|---|---|
| 1944 | 45 | 1948 | 120 | 1952 | 1,123 | 1956 | 2,437 | 1960 | 3,180 | 1964 | 2,640 | 1968 | 15,329 |
| 1945 | 174 | 1949 | 93 | 1953 | 815 | 1957 | 1,588 | 1961 | 2,333 | 1965 | 6,111 | Total: | $66,441 |
| 1946 | 187 | 1950 | 319 | 1954 | 1,194 | 1958 | 1,784 | 1962 | 1,573 | 1966 | 7,867 | | |
| 1947 | 120 | 1951 | 704 | 1955 | 1,622 | 1959 | 2,553 | 1963 | 1,241 | 1967 | 11,289 | | |

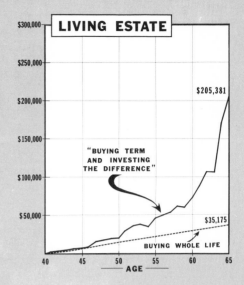

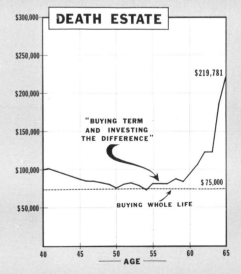

## LIVING ESTATE

| "Buying Term and Investing the Difference" | Buying Whole Life |
| --- | --- |
| TOTAL VALUE OF SHARES | CASH VALUE |

## DEATH ESTATE

| "Buying Term and Investing the Difference" | | | Buying Whole Life |
| --- | --- | --- | --- |
| TOTAL VALUE OF SHARES + | DECREASING TERM INSURANCE = | TOTAL DEATH ESTATE | FACE VALUE |

| LIVING ESTATE — TOTAL VALUE OF SHARES | LIVING ESTATE — CASH VALUE | AGE | TOTAL VALUE OF SHARES | + DECREASING TERM INSURANCE | = TOTAL DEATH ESTATE | FACE VALUE |
| --- | --- | --- | --- | --- | --- | --- |
| $ 1,447 | $ 0 | 41 | $ 1,447 | $100,000 | $101,447 | $75,000 |
| 3,494 | 225 | 42 | 3,494 | 95,000 | 98,494 | 75,000 |
| 4,155 | 1,575 | 43 | 4,155 | 90,000 | 94,155 | 75,000 |
| 5,515 | 3,000 | 44 | 5,515 | 85,000 | 90,515 | 75,000 |
| 6,666 | 4,425 | 45 | 6,666 | 80,000 | 86,666 | 75,000 |
| 9,135 | 5,925 | 46 | 9,135 | 75,000 | 84,135 | 75,000 |
| 14,086 | 7,425 | 47 | 14,086 | 70,000 | 84,086 | 75,000 |
| 17,077 | 8,925 | 48 | 17,077 | 65,000 | 82,077 | 75,000 |
| 19,859 | 10,425 | 49 | 19,859 | 60,000 | 79,859 | 75,000 |
| 20,954 | 11,925 | 50 | 20,954 | 55,000 | 75,954 | 75,000 |
| 29,537 | 13,500 | 51 | 29,537 | 50,000 | 79,537 | 75,000 |
| 35,018 | 15,000 | 52 | 35,018 | 46,250 | 81,268 | 75,000 |
| 36,633 | 16,575 | 53 | 36,633 | 42,500 | 79,133 | 75,000 |
| 34,657 | 18,150 | 54 | 34,657 | 38,750 | 73,407 | 75,000 |
| 45,813 | 19,725 | 55 | 45,813 | 35,000 | 80,813 | 75,000 |
| 50,488 | 21,300 | 56 | 50,488 | 31,250 | 81,738 | 75,000 |
| 52,736 | 22,950 | 57 | 52,736 | 28,750 | 81,486 | 75,000 |
| 62,242 | 24,525 | 58 | 62,242 | 26,250 | 88,492 | 75,000 |
| 60,172 | 26,100 | 59 | 60,172 | 23,750 | 83,922 | 75,000 |
| 72,940 | 27,750 | 60 | 72,940 | 21,250 | 94,190 | 75,000 |
| 87,329 | 29,250 | 61 | 87,329 | 18,750 | 106,079 | 75,000 |
| 105,589 | 30,750 | 62 | 105,589 | 17,500 | 123,089 | 75,000 |
| 106,368 | 32,175 | 63 | 106,368 | 16,250 | 122,618 | 75,000 |
| 170,630 | 33,675 | 64 | 170,630 | 15,000 | 185,630 | 75,000 |
| 205,381 | 35,175 | 65 | 205,381 | 14,400 | 219,781 | 75,000 |

Whether you
**lived** or **died**
you would have been better off
"Buying Term and Investing the Difference"

151

# AXE–HOUGHTON FUND B

Illustration of assumed annual investments of $1,269 for twenty-five years from 1944 to 1968. All dividends and distributions reinvested.

This tabulation covers an illustration of an assumed investment of $1,269 annually on January 1 of each year from 1944 through 1968. This was a period in which stock prices fluctuated widely because of changing business and economic conditions, and were significantly higher at the end of the period than at the beginning. Thus, these results should not be considered as a representation of the dividend income or capital gain or loss that may be realized from an investment made in the fund today. A program of the type illustrated does not assure a profit nor protect against depreciation in declining markets.

| | | COST OF SHARES | | | | VALUE OF SHARES | | | | |
|---|---|---|---|---|---|---|---|---|---|---|
| YEAR ENDING DEC. 31 | AGE | CUMULATIVE ANNUAL INVEST-MENTS | ANNUAL INCOME DIVIDENDS REIN-VESTED | CUMULA-TIVE COST OF SHARES PURCHASED WITH DIVIDENDS | TOTAL COST (INCLUDES REIN-VESTED DIVIDENDS) | ACQUIRED THROUGH ANNUAL INVEST-MENTS | ACCEPTED AS CAPITAL GAINS DIS-TRIBUTIONS (CUMU-LATIVE) | SUB-TOTAL | PURCHASED THROUGH REINVEST-MENT OF INCOME (CUMULATIVE) | TOTAL VALUE |
| 1944 | 41 | $ 1,269 | $ 33 | $ 33 | $ 1,302 | $ 1,383 | $ 50 | $ 1,433 | $ 35 | $ 1,468 |
| 1945 | 42 | 2,538 | 65 | 98 | 2,637 | 3,273 | 209 | 3,482 | 116 | 3,598 |
| 1946 | 43 | 3,807 | 94 | 192 | 4,000 | 3,729 | 343 | 4,072 | 185 | 4,257 |
| 1947 | 44 | 5,077 | 233 | 426 | 5,503 | 4,630 | 440 | 5,070 | 408 | 5,478 |
| 1948 | 45 | 6,346 | 222 | 648 | 6,995 | 5,429 | 621 | 6,050 | 594 | 6,644 |
| 1949 | 46 | 7,615 | 238 | 887 | 8,503 | 6,974 | 886 | 7,860 | 889 | 8,749 |
| 1950 | 47 | 8,884 | 452 | 1,340 | 10,224 | 9,399 | 1,268 | 10,667 | 1,530 | 12,197 |
| 1951 | 48 | 10,154 | 629 | 1,969 | 12,124 | 11,118 | 1,705 | 12,823 | 2,245 | 15,068 |
| 1952 | 49 | 11,423 | 680 | 2,650 | 14,074 | 12,914 | 2,288 | 15,202 | 3,073 | 18,275 |
| 1953 | 50 | 12,692 | 775 | 3,426 | 16,119 | 13,264 | 2,585 | 15,849 | 3,661 | 19,510 |
| 1954 | 51 | 13,961 | 993 | 4,359 | 18,321 | 18,930 | 4,047 | 22,977 | 5,905 | 28,882 |
| 1955 | 52 | 15,231 | 1,017 | 5,377 | 20,608 | 21,529 | 5,588 | 27,117 | 7,375 | 34,492 |
| 1956 | 53 | 16,500 | 1,081 | 6,458 | 22,959 | 21,781 | 7,381 | 29,162 | 8,121 | 37,283 |
| 1957 | 54 | 17,769 | 1,351 | 7,810 | 25,580 | 19,091 | 7,395 | 26,486 | 7,943 | 34,429 |
| 1958 | 55 | 19,038 | 1,448 | 9,258 | 28,297 | 25,436 | 10,980 | 36,417 | 11,621 | 48,038 |
| 1959 | 56 | 20,308 | 1,411 | 10,669 | 30,978 | 26,982 | 13,126 | 40,108 | 13,170 | 53,278 |
| 1960 | 57 | 21,577 | 1,547 | 12,217 | 33,795 | 27,196 | 14,054 | 41,250 | 14,301 | 55,551 |
| 1961 | 58 | 22,846 | 1,596 | 13,813 | 36,661 | 32,681 | 18,460 | 51,141 | 18,151 | 69,292 |
| 1962 | 59 | 24,115 | 1,743 | 15,556 | 39,673 | 29,024 | 17,980 | 47,004 | 17,323 | 64,327 |
| 1963 | 60 | 25,385 | 2,023 | 17,580 | 42,966 | 33,808 | 21,771 | 55,579 | 21,495 | 77,074 |
| 1964 | 61 | 26,654 | 2,428 | 20,009 | 46,664 | 37,649 | 26,076 | 63,725 | 25,616 | 89,341 |
| 1965 | 62 | 27,923 | 2,994 | 23,003 | 50,928 | 42,084 | 32,535 | 74,619 | 30,990 | 105,609 |
| 1966 | 63 | 29,192 | 3,479 | 26,483 | 55,676 | 36,697 | 34,532 | 71,229 | 29,450 | 100,679 |
| 1967 | 64 | 30,462 | 3,766 | 30,249 | 60,712 | 45,796 | 49,924 | 95,720 | 39,527 | 135,247 |
| 1968 | 65 | 31,731 | 4,170 | 34,420 | 66,151 | 49,234 | 61,089 | 110,323 | 45,779 | 156,102 |

The total cost figures represent the cumulative total of yearly investments of $1,269 plus the cumulative amount of income dividends reinvested, and include the sales charge of **8%** on all shares so purchased, as described in the prospectus. No adjustment has been made for any income taxes payable by shareholders on security distributions and dividends reinvested in shares. The dollar amounts of security profits distributions taken in shares were:

| | | | | | | | | | | | | | |
|---|---|---|---|---|---|---|---|---|---|---|---|---|---|
| 1944 | 48 | 1948 | 227 | 1952 | 460 | 1956 | 2,002 | 1960 | 1,299 | 1964 | 2,621 | 1968 | 8,557 |
| 1945 | 125 | 1949 | 213 | 1953 | 419 | 1957 | 1,268 | 1961 | 2,170 | 1965 | 4,052 | Total: | $47,957 |
| 1946 | 199 | 1950 | 225 | 1954 | 592 | 1958 | 1,578 | 1962 | 2,176 | 1966 | 6,790 | | |
| 1947 | 114 | 1951 | 360 | 1955 | 1,175 | 1959 | 1,908 | 1963 | 1,638 | 1967 | 7,741 | | |

| LIVING ESTATE | | | DEATH ESTATE | | | |
|---|---|---|---|---|---|---|
| "Buying Term and Investing the Difference" | Buying Whole Life | AGE | "Buying Term and Investing the Difference" | Buying Whole Life | | |
| TOTAL VALUE OF SHARES | CASH VALUE | | TOTAL VALUE OF SHARES + DECREASING TERM INSURANCE | = TOTAL DEATH ESTATE | FACE VALUE | |
| $ 1,468 | $ 0 | 41 | $ 1,468 | $100,000 | $101,468 | $75,000 |
| 3,598 | 225 | 42 | 3,598 | 95,000 | 98,598 | 75,000 |
| 4,257 | 1,575 | 43 | 4,257 | 90,000 | 94,257 | 75,000 |
| 5,478 | 3,000 | 44 | 5,478 | 85,000 | 90,478 | 75,000 |
| 6,644 | 4,425 | 45 | 6,644 | 80,000 | 86,644 | 75,000 |
| 8,749 | 5,925 | 46 | 8,749 | 75,000 | 83,749 | 75,000 |
| 12,197 | 7,425 | 47 | 12,197 | 70,000 | 82,197 | 75,000 |
| 15,068 | 8,925 | 48 | 15,068 | 65,000 | 80,068 | 75,000 |
| 18,275 | 10,425 | 49 | 18,275 | 60,000 | 78,275 | 75,000 |
| 19,510 | 11,925 | 50 | 19,510 | 55,000 | 74,510 | 75,000 |
| 28,882 | 13,500 | 51 | 28,882 | 50,000 | 78,882 | 75,000 |
| 34,492 | 15,000 | 52 | 34,492 | 46,250 | 80,742 | 75,000 |
| 37,283 | 16,575 | 53 | 37,283 | 42,500 | 79,783 | 75,000 |
| 34,429 | 18,150 | 54 | 34,429 | 38,750 | 73,179 | 75,000 |
| 48,038 | 19,725 | 55 | 48,038 | 35,000 | 83,038 | 75,000 |
| 53,278 | 21,300 | 56 | 53,278 | 31,250 | 84,528 | 75,000 |
| 55,551 | 22,950 | 57 | 55,551 | 28,750 | 84,301 | 75,000 |
| 69,292 | 24,525 | 58 | 69,292 | 26,250 | 95,542 | 75,000 |
| 64,327 | 26,100 | 59 | 64,327 | 23,750 | 88,077 | 75,000 |
| 77,074 | 27,750 | 60 | 77,074 | 21,250 | 98,324 | 75,000 |
| 89,341 | 29,250 | 61 | 89,341 | 18,750 | 108,091 | 75,000 |
| 105,609 | 30,750 | 62 | 105,609 | 17,500 | 123,109 | 75,000 |
| 100,679 | 32,175 | 63 | 100,679 | 16,250 | 116,929 | 75,000 |
| 135,247 | 33,675 | 64 | 135,247 | 15,000 | 150,247 | 75,000 |
| 156,102 | 35,175 | 65 | 156,102 | 14,400 | 170,502 | 75,000 |

Whether you
**lived** or **died**
you would have been better off
"Buying Term and Investing the Difference"

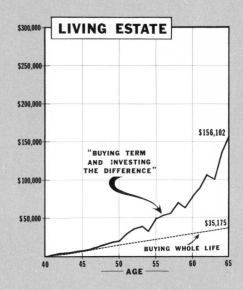

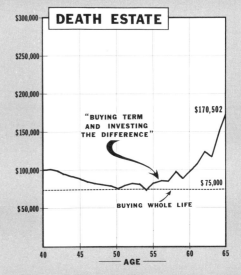

# AXE–HOUGHTON STOCK FUND

Illustration of assumed annual investments of $1,269 for twenty-five years from 1944 to 1968. All dividends and distributions reinvested.

This tabulation covers an illustration of an assumed investment of $1,269 annually on January 1 of each year from 1944 through 1968. This was a period in which stock prices fluctuated widely because of changing business and economic conditions, and were significantly higher at the end of the period than at the beginning. Thus, these results should not be considered as a representation of the dividend income or capital gain or loss that may be realized from an investment made in the fund today. A program of the type illustrated does not assure a profit nor protect against depreciation in declining markets.

| | | COST OF SHARES | | | | VALUE OF SHARES | | | | |
|---|---|---|---|---|---|---|---|---|---|---|
| YEAR ENDING DEC. 31 | AGE | CUMULATIVE ANNUAL INVEST-MENTS | ANNUAL INCOME DIVIDENDS REIN-VESTED | CUMULA-TIVE COST OF SHARES PURCHASED WITH DIVIDENDS | TOTAL COST (INCLUDES REIN-VESTED DIVIDENDS) | ACQUIRED THROUGH ANNUAL INVEST-MENTS | ACCEPTED AS CAPITAL GAINS DIS-TRIBUTIONS (CUMU-LATIVE) | SUB-TOTAL | PURCHASED THROUGH REINVEST-MENT OF INCOME (CUMULATIVE) | TOTAL VALUE |
| 1944 | 41 | $ 1,269 | $ 15 | $ 15 | $ 1,284 | $ 1,294 | $ 64 | $ 1,358 | $ 16 | $ 1,374 |
| 1945 | 42 | 2,538 | 98 | 25 | 2,564 | 3,387 | 260 | 3,647 | 36 | 3,683 |
| 1946 | 43 | 3,807 | 98 | 34 | 3,842 | 3,513 | 427 | 3,940 | 35 | 3,975 |
| 1947 | 44 | 5,077 | 41 | 76 | 5,154 | 3,769 | 622 | 4,391 | 69 | 4,460 |
| 1948 | 45 | 6,346 | 38 | 115 | 6,461 | 3,966 | 853 | 4,819 | 91 | 4,910 |
| 1949 | 46 | 7,615 | 324 | 439 | 8,055 | 4,986 | 1,121 | 6,107 | 434 | 6,541 |
| 1950 | 47 | 8,884 | 583 | 1,022 | 9,907 | 7,607 | 1,453 | 9,060 | 1,185 | 10,245 |
| 1951 | 48 | 10,154 | 462 | 1,485 | 11,640 | 9,001 | 2,042 | 11,043 | 1,679 | 12,722 |
| 1952 | 49 | 11,423 | 546 | 2,032 | 13,456 | 10,489 | 2,762 | 13,251 | 2,287 | 15,538 |
| 1953 | 50 | 12,692 | 670 | 2,710 | 15,404 | 10,813 | 2,846 | 13,659 | 2,788 | 16,447 |
| 1954 | 51 | 13,961 | 729 | 3,439 | 17,401 | 15,438 | 4,485 | 19,923 | 4,438 | 24,361 |
| 1955 | 52 | 15,231 | 821 | 4,261 | 19,493 | 17,510 | 6,139 | 23,649 | 5,524 | 29,173 |
| 1956 | 53 | 16,500 | 785 | 5,046 | 21,547 | 17,052 | 7,398 | 24,450 | 5,799 | 30,249 |
| 1957 | 54 | 17,769 | 872 | 5,919 | 23,690 | 16,190 | 7,477 | 23,667 | 5,974 | 29,641 |
| 1958 | 55 | 19,038 | 1,045 | 6,964 | 26,004 | 22,379 | 10,834 | 33,213 | 8,917 | 42,130 |
| 1959 | 56 | 20,308 | 930 | 7,894 | 28,203 | 23,709 | 13,919 | 37,628 | 9,855 | 47,483 |
| 1960 | 57 | 21,577 | 1,082 | 8,977 | 30,556 | 21,833 | 16,158 | 37,991 | 9,722 | 47,713 |
| 1961 | 58 | 22,846 | 1,234 | 10,212 | 33,060 | 23,485 | 20,974 | 44,459 | 11,147 | 55,606 |
| 1962 | 59 | 24,115 | 1,062 | 11,274 | 35,391 | 22,326 | 20,589 | 42,915 | 11,203 | 54,118 |
| 1963 | 60 | 25,385 | 1,453 | 12,728 | 38,114 | 26,949 | 25,253 | 52,202 | 14,280 | 66,492 |
| 1964 | 61 | 26,654 | 1,377 | 14,105 | 40,761 | 32,571 | 33,995 | 66,566 | 17,989 | 84,555 |
| 1965 | 62 | 27,923 | 1,428 | 15,534 | 43,459 | 39,966 | 54,659 | 94,625 | 22,977 | 117,602 |
| 1966 | 63 | 29,192 | 883 | 16,418 | 45,612 | 38,862 | 58,347 | 97,204 | 22,486 | 119,690 |
| 1967 | 64 | 30,462 | 472 | 16,890 | 47,353 | 64,115 | 110,976 | 175,091 | 36,494 | 211,585 |
| 1968 | 65 | 31,731 | 2,071 | 18,962 | 50,695 | 69,549 | 131,084 | 200,633 | 40,900 | 241,533 |

The total cost figures represent the cumulative total of yearly investments of $1,269 plus the cumulative amount of income dividends reinvested, and include the sales charge of 8½% on all shares so purchased, as described in the prospectus. No adjustment has been made for any income taxes payable by shareholders on security distributions and dividends reinvested in shares. The dollar amounts of security profits distributions taken in shares were:

| | | | | | | | | | | | | | |
|---|---|---|---|---|---|---|---|---|---|---|---|---|---|
| 1944 | 58 * | 1948 | 408 * | 1952 | 648 | 1956 | 1,843 | 1960 | 4,005 | 1964 | 4,697 | 1968 | 12,997 |
| 1945 | 132 * | 1949 | 253 * | 1953 | 280 | 1957 | 952 | 1961 | 4,584 | 1965 | 13,938 | Total: | $79,856 |
| 1946 | 266 * | 1950 | 66 | 1954 | 732 | 1958 | 1,159 | 1962 | 1,661 | 1966 | 7,065 | | |
| 1947 | 284 * | 1951 | 545 | 1955 | 1.372 | 1959 | 3,034 | 1963 | 1,629 | 1967 | 17,248 | | |

\* From 1944 through 1949, before Axe-Houghton Stock Fund came under the management of E. W. Axe & Co., Inc., the present investment adviser, the distributions shown under security profits distributions in the footnote were paid from the Fund's Capital Surplus Account, not from net realized securities profits. The value of the additional shares accepted in payment of such distributions from 1944 through 1949 is included in the above table under the columns "Accepted as Capital Gains Distributions (Cumulative)" and "Total Value." (E. W. Axe & Co., Inc., assumed the management of Axe-Houghton Stock Fund, Inc. on March 15, 1950. Before this date the Fund was under other management not connected with E. W. Axe & Co., Inc.)

# LIVING ESTATE / DEATH ESTATE

| LIVING ESTATE | | AGE | DEATH ESTATE | | | |
|---|---|---|---|---|---|---|
| "Buying Term and Investing the Difference" | Buying Whole Life | | "Buying Term and Investing the Difference" | Buying Whole Life | | |
| TOTAL VALUE OF SHARES | CASH VALUE | | TOTAL VALUE OF SHARES | + DECREASING TERM INSURANCE | = TOTAL DEATH ESTATE | FACE VALUE |
| $ 1,374 | $ 0 | 41 | $ 1,374 | $100,000 | $101,374 | $75,000 |
| 3,683 | 225 | 42 | 3,683 | 95,000 | 98,683 | 75,000 |
| 3,975 | 1,575 | 43 | 3,975 | 90,000 | 93,975 | 75,000 |
| 4,460 | 3,000 | 44 | 4,460 | 85,000 | 89,460 | 75,000 |
| 4,910 | 4,425 | 45 | 4,910 | 80,000 | 84,910 | 75,000 |
| 6,541 | 5,925 | 46 | 6,541 | 75,000 | 81,541 | 75,000 |
| 10,245 | 7,425 | 47 | 10,245 | 70,000 | 80,245 | 75,000 |
| 12,722 | 8,925 | 48 | 12,722 | 65,000 | 77,722 | 75,000 |
| 15,538 | 10,425 | 49 | 15,538 | 60,000 | 75,538 | 75,000 |
| 16,447 | 11,925 | 50 | 16,447 | 55,000 | 71,447 | 75,000 |
| 24,361 | 13,500 | 51 | 24,361 | 50,000 | 74,361 | 75,000 |
| 29,173 | 15,000 | 52 | 29,173 | 46,250 | 75,423 | 75,000 |
| 30,249 | 16,575 | 53 | 30,249 | 42,500 | 72,749 | 75,000 |
| 29,641 | 18,150 | 54 | 29,641 | 38,750 | 68,391 | 75,000 |
| 42,130 | 19,725 | 55 | 42,130 | 35,000 | 77,130 | 75,000 |
| 47,483 | 21,300 | 56 | 47,483 | 31,250 | 78,733 | 75,000 |
| 47,713 | 22,950 | 57 | 47,713 | 28,750 | 76,463 | 75,000 |
| 55,606 | 24,525 | 58 | 55,606 | 26,250 | 81,856 | 75,000 |
| 54,118 | 26,100 | 59 | 54,118 | 23,750 | 77,868 | 75,000 |
| 66,492 | 27,750 | 60 | 66,492 | 21,250 | 87,742 | 75,000 |
| 84,555 | 29,250 | 61 | 84,555 | 18,750 | 103,305 | 75,000 |
| 117,602 | 30,750 | 62 | 117,602 | 17,500 | 135,102 | 75,000 |
| 119,690 | 32,175 | 63 | 119,690 | 16,250 | 135,940 | 75,000 |
| 211,585 | 33,675 | 64 | 211,585 | 15,000 | 226,585 | 75,000 |
| 241,533 | 35,175 | 65 | 241,533 | 14,400 | 255,933 | 75,000 |

Whether you **lived** or **died** you would have been better off "Buying Term and Investing the Difference"

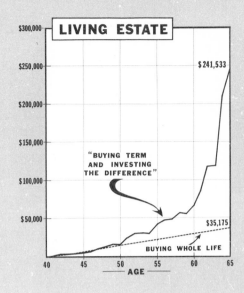

LIVING ESTATE

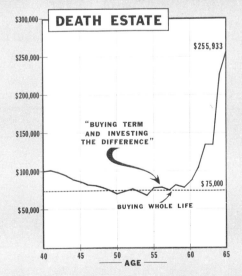

DEATH ESTATE

# BOSTON FOUNDATION FUND

Illustration of assumed annual investments of $1,269 for twenty-five years from 1944 to 1968. All dividends and distributions reinvested.

This tabulation covers an illustration of an assumed investment of $1,269 annually on January 1 of each year from 1944 through 1968. This was a period in which stock prices fluctuated widely because of changing business and economic conditions, and were significantly higher at the end of the period than at the beginning. Thus, these results should not be considered as a representation of the dividend income or capital gain or loss that may be realized from an investment made in the fund today. A program of the type illustrated does not assure a profit nor protect against depreciation in declining markets.

| | | COST OF SHARES | | | | VALUE OF SHARES | | | | |
|---|---|---|---|---|---|---|---|---|---|---|
| YEAR ENDING DEC. 31 | AGE | CUMULATIVE ANNUAL INVEST-MENTS | ANNUAL INCOME DIVIDENDS REIN-VESTED | CUMULA-TIVE COST OF SHARES PURCHASED WITH DIVIDENDS | TOTAL COST (INCLUDES REIN-VESTED DIVIDENDS) | ACQUIRED THROUGH ANNUAL INVEST-MENTS | ACCEPTED AS CAPITAL GAINS DIS-TRIBUTIONS (CUMU-LATIVE) | SUB-TOTAL | PURCHASED THROUGH REINVEST-MENT OF INCOME (CUMULATIVE) | TOTAL VALUE |
| 1944 | 41 | $ 1,269 | $ 29 | $ 29 | $ 1,298 | $ 1,262 | $ 13 | $ 1,275 | $ 31 | $ 1,306 |
| 1945 | 42 | 2,538 | 63 | 92 | 2,631 | 2,922 | 88 | 3,010 | 105 | 3,115 |
| 1946 | 43 | 3,807 | 94 | 186 | 3,994 | 3,925 | 177 | 4,102 | 195 | 4,297 |
| 1947 | 44 | 5,077 | 157 | 343 | 5,420 | 4,674 | 263 | 4,937 | 334 | 5,271 |
| 1948 | 45 | 6,346 | 216 | 559 | 6,905 | 5,657 | 397 | 6,054 | 536 | 6,590 |
| 1949 | 46 | 7,615 | 213 | 772 | 8,388 | 7,550 | 745 | 8,295 | 819 | 9,114 |
| 1950 | 47 | 8,884 | 313 | 1,085 | 9,970 | 9,645 | 1,181 | 10,826 | 1,233 | 12,059 |
| 1951 | 48 | 10,154 | 214 | 1,299 | 11,453 | 11,107 | 2,227 | 13,334 | 1,478 | 14,812 |
| 1952 | 49 | 11,423 | 366 | 1,665 | 13,088 | 12,072 | 3,282 | 15,354 | 1,815 | 17,169 |
| 1953 | 50 | 12,692 | 405 | 2,070 | 14,763 | 12,613 | 3,757 | 16,370 | 2,146 | 18,516 |
| 1954 | 51 | 13,961 | 412 | 2,482 | 16,444 | 17,218 | 6,264 | 23,482 | 3,130 | 26,612 |
| 1955 | 52 | 15,231 | 437 | 2,919 | 18,150 | 20,092 | 8,648 | 28,740 | 3,874 | 32,614 |
| 1956 | 53 | 16,500 | 468 | 3,387 | 19,887 | 20,655 | 10,319 | 30,974 | 4,214 | 35,188 |
| 1957 | 54 | 17,769 | 747 | 4,134 | 21,904 | 19,043 | 10,408 | 29,451 | 4,379 | 33,830 |
| 1958 | 55 | 19,038 | 989 | 5,123 | 24,162 | 23,389 | 13,793 | 37,182 | 6,122 | 43,304 |
| 1959 | 56 | 20,308 | 1,094 | 6,217 | 26,525 | 25,312 | 16,248 | 41,560 | 7,424 | 48,984 |
| 1960 | 57 | 21,577 | 1,183 | 7,400 | 28,977 | 25,493 | 17,675 | 43,168 | 8,330 | 51,498 |
| 1961 | 58 | 22,846 | 1,074 | 8,474 | 31,321 | 29,732 | 22,524 | 52,256 | 10,365 | 62,621 |
| 1962 | 59 | 24,115 | 1,175 | 9,649 | 33,765 | 25,519 | 21,541 | 47,060 | 9,696 | 56,756 |
| 1963 | 60 | 25,385 | 1,805 | 11,454 | 36,839 | 27,516 | 24,807 | 52,323 | 11,799 | 64,122 |
| 1964 | 61 | 26,654 | 2,046 | 13,500 | 40,154 | 29,718 | 28,816 | 58,534 | 14,247 | 72,781 |
| 1965 | 62 | 27,923 | 2,234 | 15,734 | 43,658 | 33,922 | 35,672 | 69,594 | 17,984 | 87,578 |
| 1966 | 63 | 29,192 | 2,685 | 18,419 | 47,612 | 30,766 | 35,550 | 66,316 | 18,340 | 84,656 |
| 1967 | 64 | 30,462 | 3,336 | 21,755 | 52,217 | 35,679 | 46,757 | 82,436 | 23,849 | 106,285 |
| 1968 | 65 | 31,731 | 3,725 | 25,480 | 57,211 | 39,543 | 59,516 | 99,059 | 29,487 | 128,546 |

The total cost figures represent the cumulative total of yearly investments of $1,269 plus the cumulative amount of income dividends reinvested, and include the sales charge of 8½% on all shares so purchased, as described in the prospectus. No adjustment has been made for any income taxes payable by shareholders on security distributions and dividends reinvested in shares. The dollar amounts of security profits distributions taken in shares were:

| | | | | | | | | | | | | | |
|---|---|---|---|---|---|---|---|---|---|---|---|---|---|
| 1944 | 12 | 1948 | 145 | 1952 | 1,090 | 1956 | 1,953 | 1960 | 1,986 | 1964 | 3,114 | 1968 | 9,249 |
| 1945 | 67 | 1949 | 287 | 1953 | 620 | 1957 | 1,495 | 1961 | 2,810 | 1965 | 3,929 | Total: | $52,010 |
| 1946 | 94 | 1950 | 344 | 1954 | 1,500 | 1958 | 1,655 | 1962 | 3,057 | 1966 | 4,406 | | |
| 1947 | 101 | 1951 | 1,009 | 1955 | 1,746 | 1959 | 1,990 | 1963 | 2,590 | 1967 | 6,761 | | |

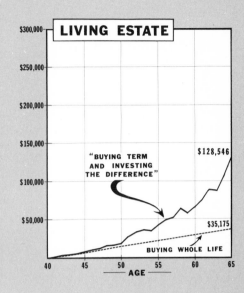

# LIVING ESTATE

# DEATH ESTATE

| LIVING ESTATE — "Buying Term and Investing the Difference" TOTAL VALUE OF SHARES | LIVING ESTATE — Buying Whole Life CASH VALUE | AGE | DEATH ESTATE — "Buying Term and Investing the Difference" TOTAL VALUE OF SHARES | + DECREASING TERM INSURANCE | = TOTAL DEATH ESTATE | DEATH ESTATE — Buying Whole Life FACE VALUE |
|---|---|---|---|---|---|---|
| $ 1,306 | $ 0 | 41 | $ 1,306 | $100,000 | $101,306 | $75,000 |
| 3,115 | 225 | 42 | 3,115 | 95,000 | 98,115 | 75,000 |
| 4,297 | 1,575 | 43 | 4,297 | 90,000 | 94,297 | 75,000 |
| 5,271 | 3,000 | 44 | 5,271 | 85,000 | 90,271 | 75,000 |
| 6,590 | 4,425 | 45 | 6,590 | 80,000 | 86,590 | 75,000 |
| 9,114 | 5,925 | 46 | 9,114 | 75,000 | 84,114 | 75,000 |
| 12,059 | 7,425 | 47 | 12,059 | 70,000 | 82,059 | 75,000 |
| 14,812 | 8,925 | 48 | 14,812 | 65,000 | 79,812 | 75,000 |
| 17,169 | 10,425 | 49 | 17,169 | 60,000 | 77,169 | 75,000 |
| 18,516 | 11,925 | 50 | 18,516 | 55,000 | 73,516 | 75,000 |
| 26,612 | 13,500 | 51 | 26,612 | 50,000 | 76,612 | 75,000 |
| 32,614 | 15,000 | 52 | 32,614 | 46,250 | 78,846 | 75,000 |
| 35,188 | 16,575 | 53 | 35,188 | 42,500 | 77,688 | 75,000 |
| 33,830 | 18,150 | 54 | 33,830 | 38,750 | 72,580 | 75,000 |
| 43,304 | 19,725 | 55 | 43,304 | 35,000 | 78,304 | 75,000 |
| 48,984 | 21,300 | 56 | 48,984 | 31,250 | 80,234 | 75,000 |
| 51,498 | 22,950 | 57 | 51,498 | 28,750 | 80,248 | 75,000 |
| 62,621 | 24,525 | 58 | 62,621 | 26,250 | 88,871 | 75,000 |
| 56,756 | 26,100 | 59 | 56,756 | 23,750 | 80,506 | 75,000 |
| 64,122 | 27,750 | 60 | 64,122 | 21,250 | 85,372 | 75,000 |
| 72,781 | 29,250 | 61 | 72,781 | 18,750 | 91,531 | 75,000 |
| 87,578 | 30,750 | 62 | 87,578 | 17,500 | 105,078 | 75,000 |
| 84,656 | 32,175 | 63 | 84,656 | 16,250 | 100,906 | 75,000 |
| 106,285 | 33,675 | 64 | 106,285 | 15,000 | 121,285 | 75,000 |
| 128,546 | 35,175 | 65 | 128,546 | 14,400 | 142,946 | 75,000 |

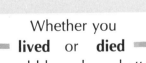

Whether you
**lived** or **died**
you would have been better off
"Buying Term and Investing the Difference"

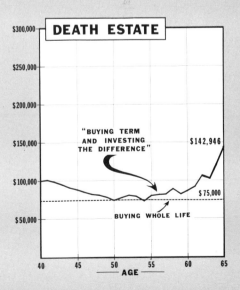

# BOSTON FUND

Illustration of assumed annual investments of $1,269 for twenty-five years from 1944 to 1968. All dividends and distributions reinvested.

This tabulation covers an illustration of an assumed investment of $1,269 annually on January 1 of each year from 1944 through 1968. This was a period in which stock prices fluctuated widely because of changing business and economic conditions, and were significantly higher at the end of the period than at the beginning. Thus, these results should not be considered as a representation of the dividend income or capital gain or loss that may be realized from an investment made in the fund today. A program of the type illustrated does not assure a profit nor protect against depreciation in declining markets.

| | | COST OF SHARES | | | | VALUE OF SHARES | | | | |
|---|---|---|---|---|---|---|---|---|---|---|
| YEAR ENDING DEC. 31 | AGE | CUMULATIVE ANNUAL INVEST-MENTS | ANNUAL INCOME DIVIDENDS REIN-VESTED | CUMULA-TIVE COST OF SHARES PURCHASED WITH DIVIDENDS | TOTAL COST (INCLUDES REIN-VESTED DIVIDENDS) | ACQUIRED THROUGH ANNUAL INVEST-MENTS | ACCEPTED AS CAPITAL GAINS DIS-TRIBUTIONS (CUMU-LATIVE) | SUB-TOTAL | PURCHASED THROUGH REINVEST-MENT OF INCOME (CUMULATIVE) | TOTAL VALUE |
| 1944 | 41 | $ 1,269 | $ 45 | $ 45 | $ 1,315 | $ 1,341 | $ 0 | $ 1,341 | $ 46 | $ 1,387 |
| 1945 | 42 | 2,538 | 108 | 142 | 2,681 | 3,288 | 61 | 3,349 | 168 | 3,517 |
| 1946 | 43 | 3,807 | 156 | 281 | 4,089 | 4,073 | 211 | 4,284 | 274 | 4,558 |
| 1947 | 44 | 5,077 | 247 | 502 | 5,579 | 4,539 | 547 | 5,086 | 435 | 5,521 |
| 1948 | 45 | 6,346 | 311 | 780 | 7,126 | 5,506 | 702 | 6,208 | 679 | 6,887 |
| 1949 | 46 | 7,615 | 398 | 1,135 | 8,751 | 7,575 | 796 | 8,371 | 1,137 | 9,508 |
| 1950 | 47 | 8,884 | 520 | 1,600 | 10,484 | 9,167 | 996 | 10,163 | 1,638 | 11,801 |
| 1951 | 48 | 10,154 | 641 | 2,172 | 12,327 | 10,969 | 1,357 | 12,326 | 2,286 | 14,612 |
| 1952 | 49 | 11,423 | 666 | 2,767 | 14,191 | 12,129 | 2,280 | 14,409 | 2,859 | 17,268 |
| 1953 | 50 | 12,692 | 804 | 3,486 | 16,179 | 12,933 | 2,489 | 15,422 | 3,460 | 18,882 |
| 1954 | 51 | 13,961 | 896 | 4,286 | 18,248 | 18,025 | 3,469 | 21,494 | 5,258 | 26,752 |
| 1955 | 52 | 15,231 | 1,003 | 5,182 | 20,414 | 21,374 | 4,558 | 25,932 | 6,730 | 32,662 |
| 1956 | 53 | 16,500 | 1,124 | 6,186 | 22,687 | 22,065 | 5,652 | 27,717 | 7,512 | 35,229 |
| 1957 | 54 | 17,769 | 1,306 | 7,353 | 25,124 | 21,413 | 7,017 | 28,430 | 7,975 | 36,405 |
| 1958 | 55 | 19,038 | 1,557 | 8,744 | 27,783 | 26,713 | 11,029 | 37,742 | 10,893 | 48,635 |
| 1959 | 56 | 20,308 | 1,708 | 10,271 | 30,580 | 27,717 | 12,635 | 40,352 | 12,253 | 52,605 |
| 1960 | 57 | 21,577 | 2,032 | 12,086 | 33,665 | 28,912 | 15,708 | 44,620 | 14,013 | 58,633 |
| 1961 | 58 | 22,846 | 2,184 | 14,037 | 36,885 | 34,500 | 18,816 | 53,316 | 17,933 | 71,249 |
| 1962 | 59 | 24,115 | 2,337 | 16,125 | 40,242 | 32,308 | 19,055 | 51,363 | 18,185 | 69,548 |
| 1963 | 60 | 25,385 | 2,533 | 18,388 | 43,774 | 35,640 | 21,343 | 56,983 | 21,491 | 78,474 |
| 1964 | 61 | 26,654 | 2,820 | 20,908 | 47,563 | 40,089 | 24,583 | 64,672 | 25,820 | 90,492 |
| 1965 | 62 | 27,923 | 3,163 | 23,734 | 51,659 | 40,443 | 26,925 | 67,368 | 27,905 | 95,273 |
| 1966 | 63 | 29,192 | 3,573 | 26,944 | 56,137 | 35,434 | 24,885 | 60,319 | 26,635 | 86,954 |
| 1967 | 64 | 30,462 | 3,924 | 30,449 | 60,912 | 36,841 | 27,482 | 64,323 | 30,026 | 94,349 |
| 1968 | 65 | 31,731 | 4,034 | 34,053 | 65,786 | 40,068 | 31,525 | 71,593 | 35,125 | 106,718 |

The total cost figures represent the cumulative total of yearly investments of $1,269 plus the cumulative amount of income dividends reinvested, and include the sales charge of 8½% on all shares so purchased, as described in the prospectus. No adjustment has been made for any income taxes payable by shareholders on security distributions and dividends reinvested in shares. The dollar amounts of security profits distributions taken in shares were:

| | | | | | | | | | | | | | |
|---|---|---|---|---|---|---|---|---|---|---|---|---|---|
| 1944 | 0 | 1948 | 168 | 1952 | 881 | 1956 | 1,151 | 1960 | 2,782 | 1964 | 1,212 | 1968 | 2,330 |
| 1945 | 45 | 1949 | 0 | 1953 | 266 | 1957 | 1,798 | 1961 | 705 | 1965 | 2,818 | Total: | $27,543 |
| 1946 | 168 | 1950 | 147 | 1954 | 229 | 1958 | 2,212 | 1962 | 2,091 | 1966 | 2,199 | | |
| 1947 | 377 | 1951 | 285 | 1955 | 612 | 1959 | 1,616 | 1963 | 993 | 1967 | 2,458 | | |

# LIVING ESTATE | DEATH ESTATE

| LIVING ESTATE "Buying Term and Investing the Difference" — TOTAL VALUE OF SHARES | LIVING ESTATE Buying Whole Life — CASH VALUE | AGE | DEATH ESTATE "Buying Term and Investing the Difference" — TOTAL VALUE OF SHARES | + DECREASING TERM INSURANCE | = TOTAL DEATH ESTATE | Buying Whole Life — FACE VALUE |
|---|---|---|---|---|---|---|
| $ 1,387 | $ 0 | 41 | $ 1,387 | $100,000 | $101,387 | $75,000 |
| 3,517 | 225 | 42 | 3,517 | 95,000 | 98,517 | 75,000 |
| 4,558 | 1,575 | 43 | 4,558 | 90,000 | 94,558 | 75,000 |
| 5,521 | 3,000 | 44 | 5,521 | 85,000 | 90,521 | 75,000 |
| 6,887 | 4,425 | 45 | 6,887 | 80,000 | 86,887 | 75,000 |
| 9,508 | 5,925 | 46 | 9,508 | 75,000 | 84,508 | 75,000 |
| 11,801 | 7,425 | 47 | 11,801 | 70,000 | 81,801 | 75,000 |
| 14,612 | 8,925 | 48 | 14,612 | 65,000 | 79,612 | 75,000 |
| 17,268 | 10,425 | 49 | 17,268 | 60,000 | 77,268 | 75,000 |
| 18,882 | 11,925 | 50 | 18,882 | 55,000 | 73,882 | 75,000 |
| 26,752 | 13,500 | 51 | 26,752 | 50,000 | 76,752 | 75,000 |
| 32,662 | 15,000 | 52 | 32,662 | 46,250 | 78,912 | 75,000 |
| 35,229 | 16,575 | 53 | 35,229 | 42,500 | 77,729 | 75,000 |
| 36,405 | 18,150 | 54 | 36,405 | 38,750 | 75,155 | 75,000 |
| 48,635 | 19,725 | 55 | 48,635 | 35,000 | 83,635 | 75,000 |
| 52,605 | 21,300 | 56 | 52,605 | 31,250 | 83,855 | 75,000 |
| 58,633 | 22,950 | 57 | 58,633 | 28,750 | 87,383 | 75,000 |
| 71,249 | 24,525 | 58 | 71,249 | 26,250 | 97,499 | 75,000 |
| 69,548 | 26,100 | 59 | 69,548 | 23,750 | 93,298 | 75,000 |
| 78,474 | 27,750 | 60 | 78,474 | 21,250 | 99,724 | 75,000 |
| 90,492 | 29,250 | 61 | 90,492 | 18,750 | 109,242 | 75,000 |
| 95,273 | 30,750 | 62 | 95,273 | 17,500 | 112,773 | 75,000 |
| 86,954 | 32,175 | 63 | 86,954 | 16,250 | 103,204 | 75,000 |
| 94,349 | 33,675 | 64 | 94,349 | 15,000 | 109,349 | 75,000 |
| 106,718 | 35,175 | 65 | 106,718 | 14,400 | 121,118 | 75,000 |

Whether you
**lived** or **died**
you would have been better off
"Buying Term and Investing the Difference"

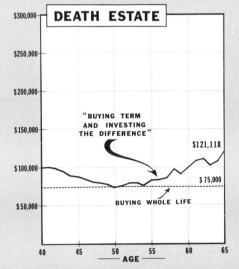

LIVING ESTATE

"BUYING TERM AND INVESTING THE DIFFERENCE" $106,718

$35,175

BUYING WHOLE LIFE

DEATH ESTATE

"BUYING TERM AND INVESTING THE DIFFERENCE" $121,118

$75,000

BUYING WHOLE LIFE

# BROAD STREET INVESTING

Illustration of assumed annual investments of $1,269 for twenty-five years from 1944 to 1968. All dividends and distributions reinvested.

This tabulation covers an illustration of an assumed investment of $1,269 annually on January 1 of each year from 1944 through 1968. This was a period in which stock prices fluctuated widely because of changing business and economic conditions, and were significantly higher at the end of the period than at the beginning. Thus, these results should not be considered as a representation of the dividend income or capital gain or loss that may be realized from an investment made in the fund today. A program of the type illustrated does not assure a profit nor protect against depreciation in declining markets.

| | | COST OF SHARES | | | | VALUE OF SHARES | | | | |
|---|---|---|---|---|---|---|---|---|---|---|
| YEAR ENDING DEC. 31 | AGE | CUMULATIVE ANNUAL INVEST-MENTS | ANNUAL INCOME DIVIDENDS REIN-VESTED | CUMULA-TIVE COST OF SHARES PURCHASED WITH DIVIDENDS | TOTAL COST (INCLUDES REIN-VESTED DIVIDENDS) | ACQUIRED THROUGH ANNUAL INVEST-MENTS | ACCEPTED AS CAPITAL GAINS DIS-TRIBUTIONS (CUMU-LATIVE) | SUB-TOTAL | PURCHASED THROUGH REINVEST-MENT OF INCOME (CUMULATIVE) | TOTAL VALUE |
| 1944 | 41 | $ 1,269 | $ 54 | $ 54 | $ 1,323 | $ 1,370 | $ 11 | $ 1,381 | $ 53 | $ 1,434 |
| 1945 | 42 | 2,538 | 103 | 157 | 2,696 | 3,366 | 121 | 3,487 | 177 | 3,664 |
| 1946 | 43 | 3,807 | 174 | 331 | 4,139 | 4,024 | 442 | 4,466 | 303 | 4,769 |
| 1947 | 44 | 5,077 | 265 | 596 | 5,673 | 4,712 | 575 | 5,287 | 513 | 5,800 |
| 1948 | 45 | 6,346 | 361 | 957 | 7,303 | 5,338 | 762 | 6,100 | 779 | 6,879 |
| 1949 | 46 | 7,615 | 489 | 1,446 | 9,062 | 7,251 | 846 | 8,097 | 1,355 | 9,452 |
| 1950 | 47 | 8,884 | 718 | 2,164 | 11,049 | 9,690 | 1,343 | 11,033 | 2,261 | 13,294 |
| 1951 | 48 | 10,154 | 846 | 3,010 | 13,164 | 12,246 | 2,091 | 14,337 | 3,352 | 17,689 |
| 1952 | 49 | 11,423 | 977 | 3,987 | 15,410 | 14,200 | 2,626 | 16,826 | 4,468 | 21,294 |
| 1953 | 50 | 12,692 | 1,122 | 5,109 | 17,802 | 14,625 | 2,969 | 17,594 | 5,300 | 22,894 |
| 1954 | 51 | 13,961 | 1,317 | 6,426 | 20,388 | 21,259 | 4,912 | 26,171 | 8,484 | 34,655 |
| 1955 | 52 | 15,231 | 1,527 | 7,953 | 23,184 | 24,982 | 6,867 | 31,849 | 10,883 | 42,732 |
| 1956 | 53 | 16,500 | 1,762 | 9,715 | 26,215 | 26,331 | 9,081 | 35,412 | 12,547 | 47,959 |
| 1957 | 54 | 17,769 | 1,984 | 11,699 | 29,469 | 24,792 | 9,263 | 34,055 | 13,059 | 47,114 |
| 1958 | 55 | 19,038 | 2,188 | 13,887 | 32,926 | 33,424 | 13,621 | 47,055 | 19,034 | 66,079 |
| 1959 | 56 | 20,308 | 2,362 | 16,249 | 36,557 | 35,291 | 15,202 | 50,493 | 21,607 | 72,100 |
| 1960 | 57 | 21,577 | 2,525 | 18,774 | 40,351 | 34,657 | 16,261 | 50,918 | 22,906 | 73,824 |
| 1961 | 58 | 22,846 | 2,715 | 21,489 | 44,336 | 42,544 | 21,702 | 64,246 | 29,790 | 94,036 |
| 1962 | 59 | 24,115 | 2,906 | 24,395 | 48,511 | 38,597 | 20,982 | 59,579 | 29,074 | 88,653 |
| 1963 | 60 | 25,385 | 3,174 | 27,569 | 52,954 | 44,531 | 25,526 | 70,057 | 35,554 | 105,611 |
| 1964 | 61 | 26,654 | 3,592 | 31,161 | 57,815 | 50,170 | 31,334 | 81,504 | 42,373 | 123,877 |
| 1965 | 62 | 27,923 | 3,992 | 35,153 | 63,077 | 53,167 | 36,652 | 89,819 | 47,622 | 137,441 |
| 1966 | 63 | 29,192 | 4,278 | 39,431 | 68,672 | 45,889 | 36,792 | 82,681 | 44,007 | 126,688 |
| 1967 | 64 | 30,462 | 4,577 | 44,008 | 74,470 | 50,400 | 49,651 | 100,051 | 51,230 | 151,281 |
| 1968 | 65 | 31,731 | 4,784 | 48,792 | 80,523 | 57,739 | 55,581 | 113,320 | 62,146 | 175,466 |

The total cost figures represent the cumulative total of yearly investments of $1,269 plus the cumulative amount of income dividends reinvested, and include the sales charge of $7\frac{1}{2}\%$ on all shares so purchased, as described in the prospectus. No adjustment has been made for any income taxes payable by shareholders on security distributions and dividends reinvested in shares. The dollar amounts of security profits distributions taken in shares were:

| | | | | | | | | | | | | | |
|---|---|---|---|---|---|---|---|---|---|---|---|---|---|
| 1944 | 11 | 1948 | 240 | 1952 | 405 | 1956 | 2,134 | 1960 | 1,739 | 1964 | 3,322 | 1968 | 0 |
| 1945 | 108 | 1949 | 0 | 1953 | 468 | 1957 | 1,085 | 1961 | 2,428 | 1965 | 4,187 | Total: | $42,361 |
| 1946 | 331 | 1950 | 356 | 1954 | 888 | 1958 | 1,634 | 1962 | 1,802 | 1966 | 5,796 | | |
| 1947 | 168 | 1951 | 569 | 1955 | 1,392 | 1959 | 1,301 | 1963 | 1,992 | 1967 | 10,005 | | |

| LIVING ESTATE | | AGE | DEATH ESTATE | | | |
|---|---|---|---|---|---|---|
| "Buying Term and Investing the Difference" TOTAL VALUE OF SHARES | Buying Whole Life CASH VALUE | | TOTAL VALUE OF SHARES + | DECREASING TERM INSURANCE = | TOTAL DEATH ESTATE | Buying Whole Life FACE VALUE |
| $ 1,434 | $ 0 | 41 | $ 1,434 | $100,000 | $101,434 | $75,000 |
| 3,664 | 225 | 42 | 3,664 | 95,000 | 98,664 | 75,000 |
| 4,769 | 1,575 | 43 | 4,769 | 90,000 | 94,769 | 75,000 |
| 5,800 | 3,000 | 44 | 5,800 | 85,000 | 90,800 | 75,000 |
| 6,879 | 4,425 | 45 | 6,879 | 80,000 | 86,879 | 75,000 |
| 9,452 | 5,925 | 46 | 9,452 | 75,000 | 84,452 | 75,000 |
| 13,294 | 7,425 | 47 | 13,294 | 70,000 | 83,294 | 75,000 |
| 17,689 | 8,925 | 48 | 17,689 | 65,000 | 82,689 | 75,000 |
| 21,294 | 10,425 | 49 | 21,294 | 60,000 | 81,294 | 75,000 |
| 22,894 | 11,925 | 50 | 22,894 | 55,000 | 77,894 | 75,000 |
| 34,655 | 13,500 | 51 | 34,655 | 50,000 | 84,655 | 75,000 |
| 42,732 | 15,000 | 52 | 42,732 | 46,250 | 88,982 | 75,000 |
| 47,959 | 16,575 | 53 | 47,959 | 42,500 | 90,459 | 75,000 |
| 47,114 | 18,150 | 54 | 47,114 | 38,750 | 85,864 | 75,000 |
| 66,079 | 19,725 | 55 | 66,079 | 35,000 | 101,079 | 75,000 |
| 72,100 | 21,300 | 56 | 72,100 | 31,250 | 103,350 | 75,000 |
| 73,824 | 22,950 | 57 | 73,824 | 28,750 | 102,574 | 75,000 |
| 94,036 | 24,525 | 58 | 94,036 | 26,250 | 120,286 | 75,000 |
| 88,653 | 26,100 | 59 | 88,653 | 23,750 | 112,403 | 75,000 |
| 105,611 | 27,750 | 60 | 105,611 | 21,250 | 126,861 | 75,000 |
| 123,877 | 29,250 | 61 | 123,877 | 18,750 | 142,627 | 75,000 |
| 137,441 | 30,750 | 62 | 137,441 | 17,500 | 154,941 | 75,000 |
| 126,688 | 32,175 | 63 | 126,688 | 16,250 | 142,938 | 75,000 |
| 151,281 | 33,675 | 64 | 151,281 | 15,000 | 166,281 | 75,000 |
| 175,466 | 35,175 | 65 | 175,466 | 14,400 | 189,866 | 75,000 |

Whether you
**lived** or **died**
you would have been better off
"Buying Term and Investing the Difference"

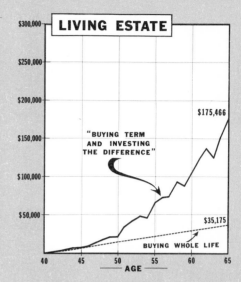

LIVING ESTATE

"BUYING TERM AND INVESTING THE DIFFERENCE" — $175,466

BUYING WHOLE LIFE — $35,175

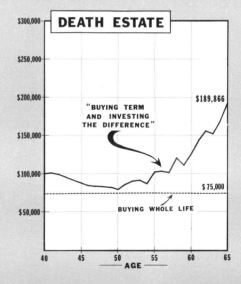

DEATH ESTATE

"BUYING TERM AND INVESTING THE DIFFERENCE" — $189,866

BUYING WHOLE LIFE — $75,000

# BULLOCK FUND

Illustration of assumed annual investments of $1,269 for twenty-five years from 1944 to 1968. All dividends and distributions reinvested.

This tabulation covers an illustration of an assumed investment of $1,269 annually on January 1 of each year from 1944 through 1968. This was a period in which stock prices fluctuated widely because of changing business and economic conditions, and were significantly higher at the end of the period than at the beginning. Thus, these results should not be considered as a representation of the dividend income or capital gain or loss that may be realized from an investment made in the fund today. A program of the type illustrated does not assure a profit nor protect against depreciation in declining markets.

| | | COST OF SHARES | | | | VALUE OF SHARES | | | | |
|---|---|---|---|---|---|---|---|---|---|---|
| YEAR ENDING DEC. 31 | AGE | CUMULATIVE ANNUAL INVEST-MENTS | ANNUAL INCOME DIVIDENDS REIN-VESTED | CUMULA-TIVE COST OF SHARES PURCHASED WITH DIVIDENDS | TOTAL COST (INCLUDES REIN-VESTED DIVIDENDS) | ACQUIRED THROUGH ANNUAL INVEST-MENTS | ACCEPTED AS CAPITAL GAINS DIS-TRIBUTIONS (CUMU-LATIVE) | SUB-TOTAL | PURCHASED THROUGH REINVEST-MENT OF INCOME (CUMULATIVE) | TOTAL VALUE |
| 1944 | 41 | $ 1,269 | $ 44 | $ 44 | $ 1,314 | $ 1,345 | $ 5 | $ 1,350 | $ 44 | $ 1,394 |
| 1945 | 42 | 2,538 | 89 | 134 | 2,673 | 3,284 | 175 | 3,459 | 152 | 3,611 |
| 1946 | 43 | 3,807 | 111 | 246 | 4,053 | 3,718 | 447 | 4,165 | 221 | 4,386 |
| 1947 | 44 | 5,077 | 186 | 432 | 5,509 | 4,597 | 543 | 5,140 | 382 | 5,522 |
| 1948 | 45 | 6,346 | 326 | 759 | 7,106 | 5,319 | 608 | 5,927 | 641 | 6,568 |
| 1949 | 46 | 7,615 | 450 | 1,209 | 8,825 | 7,529 | 746 | 8,275 | 1,217 | 9,492 |
| 1950 | 47 | 8,884 | 619 | 1,828 | 10,713 | 10,308 | 1,291 | 11,599 | 2,047 | 13,646 |
| 1951 | 48 | 10,154 | 806 | 2,635 | 12,789 | 12,042 | 2,175 | 14,217 | 2,874 | 17,091 |
| 1952 | 49 | 11,423 | 883 | 3,519 | 14,943 | 14,099 | 2,868 | 16,967 | 3,919 | 20,886 |
| 1953 | 50 | 12,692 | 970 | 4,489 | 17,182 | 14,027 | 3,292 | 17,319 | 4,477 | 21,796 |
| 1954 | 51 | 13,961 | 1,077 | 5,566 | 19,528 | 21,176 | 5,806 | 26,982 | 7,403 | 34,385 |
| 1955 | 52 | 15,231 | 1,180 | 6,746 | 21,978 | 25,681 | 8,293 | 33,974 | 9,659 | 43,633 |
| 1956 | 53 | 16,500 | 1,464 | 8,211 | 24,712 | 28,360 | 11,039 | 39,399 | 11,568 | 50,967 |
| 1957 | 54 | 17,769 | 1,612 | 9,823 | 27,594 | 23,985 | 11,638 | 35,623 | 10,679 | 46,302 |
| 1958 | 55 | 19,038 | 1,670 | 11,494 | 30,534 | 31,936 | 17,665 | 49,601 | 15,292 | 64,893 |
| 1959 | 56 | 20,308 | 1,826 | 13,320 | 33,629 | 32,739 | 21,067 | 53,806 | 16,744 | 70,550 |
| 1960 | 57 | 21,577 | 2,061 | 15,381 | 36,959 | 31,424 | 23,327 | 54,751 | 17,406 | 72,157 |
| 1961 | 58 | 22,846 | 2,208 | 17,590 | 40,437 | 37,916 | 31,645 | 69,561 | 22,292 | 91,853 |
| 1962 | 59 | 24,115 | 2,606 | 20,197 | 44,313 | 32,704 | 30,426 | 63,130 | 20,965 | 84,095 |
| 1963 | 60 | 25,385 | 2,639 | 22,836 | 48,222 | 38,233 | 38,655 | 76,888 | 26,139 | 103,027 |
| 1964 | 61 | 26,654 | 3,008 | 25,845 | 52,499 | 42,726 | 46,725 | 89,451 | 31,115 | 120,566 |
| 1965 | 62 | 27,923 | 3,405 | 29,249 | 57,174 | 47,086 | 55,723 | 102,809 | 36,598 | 139,407 |
| 1966 | 63 | 29,192 | 4,026 | 33,276 | 62,467 | 41,370 | 54,699 | 96,069 | 34,912 | 130,981 |
| 1967 | 64 | 30,462 | 4,314 | 37,590 | 68,053 | 48,081 | 70,481 | 118,562 | 43,510 | 162,072 |
| 1968 | 65 | 31,731 | 4,280 | 41,870 | 73,603 | 53,267 | 85,720 | 138,987 | 51,149 | 190,136 |

The total cost figures represent the cumulative total of yearly investments of $1,269 plus the cumulative amount of income dividends reinvested, and include the sales charge of 8⅔% on all shares so purchased, as described in the prospectus. No adjustment has been made for any income taxes payable by shareholders on security distributions and dividends reinvested in shares. The dollar amounts of security profits distributions taken in shares were:

| | | | | | | | | | | | | | |
|---|---|---|---|---|---|---|---|---|---|---|---|---|---|
| 1944 | 4 | 1948 | 100 | 1952 | 502 | 1956 | 2,216 | 1960 | 3,565 | 1964 | 4,827 | 1968 | 9,282 |
| 1945 | 163 | 1949 | 37 | 1953 | 642 | 1957 | 2,648 | 1961 | 4,402 | 1965 | 5,446 | Total: | $66,842 |
| 1946 | 284 | 1950 | 393 | 1954 | 1,100 | 1958 | 2,742 | 1962 | 3,625 | 1966 | 6,768 | | |
| 1947 | 118 | 1951 | 783 | 1955 | 1,517 | 1959 | 3,491 | 1963 | 4,181 | 1967 | 8,006 | | |

## LIVING ESTATE

| "Buying Term and Investing the Difference" | Buying Whole Life |
|---|---|
| TOTAL VALUE OF SHARES | CASH VALUE |

## DEATH ESTATE

| "Buying Term and Investing the Difference" | | Buying Whole Life |
|---|---|---|
| TOTAL VALUE OF SHARES + DECREASING TERM INSURANCE = TOTAL DEATH ESTATE | | FACE VALUE |

| TOTAL VALUE OF SHARES | CASH VALUE | AGE | TOTAL VALUE OF SHARES | DECREASING TERM INSURANCE | TOTAL DEATH ESTATE | FACE VALUE |
|---|---|---|---|---|---|---|
| $ 1,394 | $ 0 | 41 | $ 1,394 | $100,000 | $101,394 | $75,000 |
| 3,611 | 225 | 42 | 3,611 | 95,000 | 98,611 | 75,000 |
| 4,386 | 1,575 | 43 | 4,386 | 90,000 | 94,386 | 75,000 |
| 5,522 | 3,000 | 44 | 5,522 | 85,000 | 90,522 | 75,000 |
| 6,568 | 4,425 | 45 | 6,568 | 80,000 | 86,568 | 75,000 |
| 9,492 | 5,925 | 46 | 9,492 | 75,000 | 84,492 | 75,000 |
| 13,646 | 7,425 | 47 | 13,646 | 70,000 | 83,646 | 75,000 |
| 17,091 | 8,925 | 48 | 17,091 | 65,000 | 82,091 | 75,000 |
| 20,886 | 10,425 | 49 | 20,886 | 60,000 | 80,886 | 75,000 |
| 21,796 | 11,925 | 50 | 21,796 | 55,000 | 76,796 | 75,000 |
| 34,385 | 13,500 | 51 | 34,385 | 50,000 | 84,385 | 75,000 |
| 43,633 | 15,000 | 52 | 43,633 | 46,250 | 89,883 | 75,000 |
| 50,967 | 16,575 | 53 | 50,967 | 42,500 | 93,467 | 75,000 |
| 46,302 | 18,150 | 54 | 46,302 | 38,750 | 85,052 | 75,000 |
| 64,893 | 19,725 | 55 | 64,893 | 35,000 | 99,893 | 75,000 |
| 70,550 | 21,300 | 56 | 70,550 | 31,250 | 101,800 | 75,000 |
| 72,157 | 22,950 | 57 | 72,157 | 28,750 | 100,907 | 75,000 |
| 91,853 | 24,525 | 58 | 91,853 | 26,250 | 118,103 | 75,000 |
| 84,095 | 26,100 | 59 | 84,095 | 23,750 | 107,845 | 75,000 |
| 103,027 | 27,750 | 60 | 103,027 | 21,250 | 124,277 | 75,000 |
| 120,566 | 29,250 | 61 | 120,566 | 18,750 | 139,316 | 75,000 |
| 139,407 | 30,750 | 62 | 139,407 | 17,500 | 156,907 | 75,000 |
| 130,981 | 32,175 | 63 | 130,981 | 16,250 | 147,231 | 75,000 |
| 162,072 | 33,675 | 64 | 162,072 | 15,000 | 177,072 | 75,000 |
| 190,136 | 35,175 | 65 | 190,136 | 14,400 | 204,536 | 75,000 |

Whether you **lived** or **died**
you would have been better off
"Buying Term and Investing the Difference"

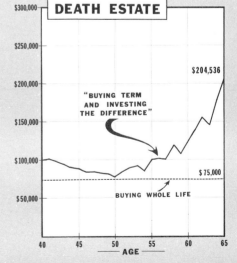

**LIVING ESTATE**

"BUYING TERM AND INVESTING THE DIFFERENCE" — $190,136
BUYING WHOLE LIFE — $35,175

**DEATH ESTATE**

"BUYING TERM AND INVESTING THE DIFFERENCE" — $204,536
BUYING WHOLE LIFE — $75,000

# CENTURY SHARES TRUST

Illustration of assumed annual investments of $1,269 for twenty-five years from 1944 to 1968. All dividends and distributions reinvested.

This tabulation covers an illustration of an assumed investment of $1,269 annually on January 1 of each year from 1944 through 1968. This was a period in which stock prices fluctuated widely because of changing business and economic conditions, and were significantly higher at the end of the period than at the beginning. Thus, these results should not be considered as a representation of the dividend income or capital gain or loss that may be realized from an investment made in the fund today. A program of the type illustrated does not assure a profit nor protect against depreciation in declining markets.

| | | COST OF SHARES | | | | VALUE OF SHARES | | | | |
|---|---|---|---|---|---|---|---|---|---|---|
| YEAR ENDING DEC. 31 | AGE | CUMULATIVE ANNUAL INVESTMENTS | ANNUAL INCOME DIVIDENDS REINVESTED | CUMULATIVE COST OF SHARES PURCHASED WITH DIVIDENDS | TOTAL COST (INCLUDES REINVESTED DIVIDENDS) | ACQUIRED THROUGH ANNUAL INVESTMENTS | ACCEPTED AS CAPITAL GAINS DISTRIBUTIONS (CUMULATIVE) | SUBTOTAL | PURCHASED THROUGH REINVESTMENT OF INCOME (CUMULATIVE) | TOTAL VALUE |
| 1944 | 41 | $ 1,269 | $ 40 | $ 40 | $ 1,309 | $ 1,260 | $ 0 | $ 1,260 | $ 40 | $ 1,300 |
| 1945 | 42 | 2,538 | 80 | 120 | 2,659 | 2,812 | 18 | 2,830 | 128 | 2,958 |
| 1946 | 43 | 3,807 | 120 | 241 | 4,048 | 3,484 | 72 | 3,556 | 211 | 3,767 |
| 1947 | 44 | 5,077 | 165 | 406 | 5,483 | 4,324 | 114 | 4,438 | 346 | 4,784 |
| 1948 | 45 | 6,346 | 252 | 659 | 7,006 | 6,027 | 176 | 6,203 | 632 | 6,835 |
| 1949 | 46 | 7,615 | 283 | 942 | 8,558 | 8,378 | 311 | 8,689 | 1,028 | 9,717 |
| 1950 | 47 | 8,884 | 410 | 1,353 | 10,238 | 10,055 | 437 | 10,492 | 1,475 | 11,967 |
| 1951 | 48 | 10,154 | 475 | 1,828 | 11,983 | 11,623 | 586 | 12,209 | 1,973 | 14,182 |
| 1952 | 49 | 11,423 | 507 | 2,336 | 13,760 | 15,675 | 877 | 16,552 | 2,935 | 19,487 |
| 1953 | 50 | 12,692 | 595 | 2,931 | 15,624 | 17,540 | 914 | 18,454 | 3,650 | 22,104 |
| 1954 | 51 | 13,961 | 678 | 3,610 | 17,572 | 27,500 | 1,850 | 29,350 | 6,117 | 35,467 |
| 1955 | 52 | 15,231 | 747 | 4,358 | 19,589 | 30,179 | 2,955 | 33,134 | 7,118 | 40,252 |
| 1956 | 53 | 16,500 | 874 | 5,232 | 21,733 | 26,315 | 3,629 | 29,944 | 6,773 | 36,717 |
| 1957 | 54 | 17,769 | 937 | 6,169 | 23,940 | 25,769 | 4,662 | 30,431 | 7,154 | 37,585 |
| 1958 | 55 | 19,038 | 998 | 7,168 | 26,207 | 36,620 | 7,953 | 44,573 | 10,816 | 55,389 |
| 1959 | 56 | 20,308 | 1,036 | 8,204 | 28,513 | 38,333 | 9,071 | 47,404 | 11,978 | 59,382 |
| 1960 | 57 | 21,577 | 1,105 | 9,310 | 30,888 | 41,155 | 11,209 | 52,364 | 13,599 | 65,963 |
| 1961 | 58 | 22,846 | 1,191 | 10,501 | 33,349 | 63,113 | 21,001 | 84,114 | 21,535 | 105,649 |
| 1962 | 59 | 24,115 | 1,186 | 11,688 | 35,804 | 57,099 | 21,927 | 79,026 | 20,318 | 99,344 |
| 1963 | 60 | 25,385 | 1,228 | 12,916 | 38,302 | 68,332 | 27,058 | 95,390 | 25,028 | 120,418 |
| 1964 | 61 | 26,654 | 1,269 | 14,186 | 40,841 | 68,547 | 28,469 | 97,016 | 25,814 | 122,830 |
| 1965 | 62 | 27,923 | 1,402 | 15,588 | 43,513 | 65,441 | 29,072 | 94,513 | 25,538 | 120,051 |
| 1966 | 63 | 29,192 | 1,558 | 17,147 | 46,340 | 51,984 | 25,251 | 77,235 | 21,370 | 98,605 |
| 1967 | 64 | 30,462 | 1,779 | 18,926 | 49,389 | 46,270 | 24,333 | 70,603 | 20,179 | 90,782 |
| 1968 | 65 | 31,731 | 2,086 | 21,012 | 52,745 | 64,072 | 36,726 | 100,798 | 29,347 | 130,145 |

The total cost figures represent the cumulative total of yearly investments of $1,269 plus the cumulative amount of income dividends reinvested, and include the sales charge of 8½% on all shares so purchased, as described in the prospectus. No adjustment has been made for any income taxes payable by shareholders on security distributions and dividends reinvested in shares. The dollar amounts of security profits distributions taken in shares were:

| | | | | | | | | | | | | | |
|---|---|---|---|---|---|---|---|---|---|---|---|---|---|
| 1944 | 0 | 1948 | 53 | 1952 | 153 | 1956 | 1,293 | 1960 | 1,655 | 1964 | 1,816 | 1968 | 2,842 |
| 1945 | 21 | 1949 | 115 | 1953 | 0 | 1957 | 1,339 | 1961 | 2,777 | 1965 | 2,448 | Total: | $28,608 |
| 1946 | 59 | 1950 | 119 | 1954 | 343 | 1958 | 1,180 | 1962 | 3,324 | 1966 | 3,145 | | |
| 1947 | 50 | 1951 | 143 | 1955 | 910 | 1959 | 985 | 1963 | 1,148 | 1967 | 2,690 | | |

## LIVING ESTATE | | DEATH ESTATE

| "Buying Term and Investing the Difference" TOTAL VALUE OF SHARES | Buying Whole Life CASH VALUE | AGE | "Buying Term and Investing the Difference" TOTAL VALUE OF SHARES | + DECREASING TERM INSURANCE | = TOTAL DEATH ESTATE | Buying Whole Life FACE VALUE |
|---|---|---|---|---|---|---|
| $ 1,300 | $ 0 | 41 | $ 1,300 | $100,000 | $101,300 | $75,000 |
| 2,958 | 225 | 42 | 2,958 | 95,000 | 97,958 | 75,000 |
| 3,767 | 1,575 | 43 | 3,767 | 90,000 | 93,767 | 75,000 |
| 4,784 | 3,000 | 44 | 4,784 | 85,000 | 89,784 | 75,000 |
| 6,835 | 4,425 | 45 | 6,835 | 80,000 | 86,835 | 75,000 |
| 9,717 | 5,925 | 46 | 9,717 | 75,000 | 84,717 | 75,000 |
| 11,967 | 7,425 | 47 | 11,967 | 70,000 | 81,967 | 75,000 |
| 14,182 | 8,925 | 48 | 14,182 | 65,000 | 79,182 | 75,000 |
| 19,487 | 10,425 | 49 | 19,487 | 60,000 | 79,487 | 75,000 |
| 22,104 | 11,925 | 50 | 22,104 | 55,000 | 77,104 | 75,000 |
| 35,467 | 13,500 | 51 | 35,467 | 50,000 | 85,467 | 75,000 |
| 40,252 | 15,000 | 52 | 40,252 | 46,250 | 86,502 | 75,000 |
| 36,717 | 16,575 | 53 | 36,717 | 42,500 | 79,217 | 75,000 |
| 37,585 | 18,150 | 54 | 37,585 | 38,750 | 76,335 | 75,000 |
| 55,389 | 19,725 | 55 | 55,389 | 35,000 | 90,389 | 75,000 |
| 59,382 | 21,300 | 56 | 59,382 | 31,250 | 90,632 | 75,000 |
| 65,963 | 22,950 | 57 | 65,963 | 28,750 | 94,713 | 75,000 |
| 105,649 | 24,525 | 58 | 105,649 | 26,250 | 131,899 | 75,000 |
| 99,344 | 26,100 | 59 | 99,344 | 23,750 | 123,093 | 75,000 |
| 120,418 | 27,750 | 60 | 120,418 | 21,250 | 141,668 | 75,000 |
| 122,830 | 29,250 | 61 | 122,830 | 18,750 | 141,580 | 75,000 |
| 120,051 | 30,750 | 62 | 120,051 | 17,500 | 137,551 | 75,000 |
| 98,605 | 32,175 | 63 | 98,605 | 16,250 | 114,855 | 75,000 |
| 95,782 | 33,675 | 64 | 95,782 | 15,000 | 105,782 | 75,000 |
| 130,145 | 35,175 | 65 | 130,145 | 14,400 | 144,545 | 75,000 |

Whether you
**lived** or **died**
you would have been better off
"Buying Term and Investing the Difference"

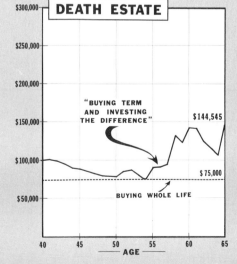

# CHEMICAL FUND

Illustration of assumed annual investments of $1,269 for twenty-five years from 1944 to 1968. All dividends and distributions reinvested.

This tabulation covers an illustration of an assumed investment of $1,269 annually on January 1 of each year from 1944 through 1968. This was a period in which stock prices fluctuated widely because of changing business and economic conditions, and were significantly higher at the end of the period than at the beginning. Thus, these results should not be considered as a representation of the dividend income or capital gain or loss that may be realized from an investment made in the fund today. A program of the type illustrated does not assure a profit nor protect against depreciation in declining markets.

| | | COST OF SHARES | | | | VALUE OF SHARES | | | | |
|---|---|---|---|---|---|---|---|---|---|---|
| YEAR ENDING DEC. 31 | AGE | CUMULATIVE ANNUAL INVEST-MENTS | ANNUAL INCOME DIVIDENDS REIN-VESTED | CUMULA-TIVE COST OF SHARES PURCHASED WITH DIVIDENDS | TOTAL COST (INCLUDES REIN-VESTED DIVIDENDS) | ACQUIRED THROUGH ANNUAL INVEST-MENTS | ACCEPTED AS CAPITAL GAINS DIS-TRIBUTIONS (CUMU-LATIVE) | SUB-TOTAL | PURCHASED THROUGH REINVEST-MENT OF INCOME (CUMULATIVE) | TOTAL VALUE |
| 1944 | 41 | $ 1,269 | $ 36 | $ 36 | $ 1,306 | $ 1,230 | $ 0 | $ 1,230 | $ 36 | $ 1,266 |
| 1945 | 42 | 2,538 | 77 | 114 | 2,653 | 3,144 | 22 | 3,166 | 136 | 3,302 |
| 1946 | 43 | 3,807 | 141 | 255 | 4,063 | 4,961 | 125 | 5,086 | 297 | 5,383 |
| 1947 | 44 | 5,077 | 208 | 463 | 5,540 | 5,579 | 230 | 5,809 | 480 | 6,289 |
| 1948 | 45 | 6,346 | 256 | 720 | 7,066 | 6,228 | 318 | 6,546 | 686 | 7,232 |
| 1949 | 46 | 7,615 | 362 | 1,082 | 8,699 | 8,709 | 505 | 9,214 | 1,203 | 10,417 |
| 1950 | 47 | 8,884 | 542 | 1,625 | 10,509 | 12,407 | 888 | 13,295 | 2,107 | 15,402 |
| 1951 | 48 | 10,154 | 533 | 2,158 | 12,312 | 16,066 | 2,525 | 18,591 | 3,025 | 21,616 |
| 1952 | 49 | 11,423 | 620 | 2,778 | 14,203 | 15,744 | 3,358 | 19,102 | 3,380 | 22,482 |
| 1953 | 50 | 12,692 | 729 | 3,507 | 16,200 | 16,275 | 3,482 | 19,757 | 4,002 | 23,759 |
| 1954 | 51 | 13,961 | 861 | 4,368 | 18,330 | 23,872 | 6,047 | 29,919 | 6,430 | 36,349 |
| 1955 | 52 | 15,231 | 986 | 5,355 | 20,586 | 29,762 | 9,031 | 38,793 | 8,681 | 47,474 |
| 1956 | 53 | 16,500 | 1,167 | 6,522 | 23,023 | 31,009 | 10,902 | 41,911 | 9,807 | 51,718 |
| 1957 | 54 | 17,769 | 1,333 | 7,856 | 25,627 | 30,208 | 12,087 | 42,295 | 10,459 | 52,754 |
| 1958 | 55 | 19,038 | 1,503 | 9,360 | 28,399 | 41,473 | 18,114 | 59,587 | 15,516 | 75,103 |
| 1959 | 56 | 20,308 | 1,624 | 10,984 | 31,293 | 49,846 | 24,066 | 73,912 | 19,808 | 93,720 |
| 1960 | 57 | 21,577 | 1,728 | 12,713 | 34,291 | 48,506 | 25,702 | 74,208 | 20,572 | 94,780 |
| 1961 | 58 | 22,846 | 1,638 | 14,351 | 37,199 | 55,711 | 34,265 | 89,976 | 24,694 | 114,670 |
| 1962 | 59 | 24,115 | 1,790 | 16,141 | 40,258 | 46,908 | 28,928 | 75,836 | 22,211 | 98,047 |
| 1963 | 60 | 25,385 | 1,907 | 18,049 | 43,435 | 59,617 | 39,362 | 98,979 | 29,610 | 128,589 |
| 1964 | 61 | 26,654 | 2,216 | 20,265 | 46,921 | 65,905 | 47,948 | 113,853 | 34,313 | 148,166 |
| 1965 | 62 | 27,923 | 2,625 | 22,891 | 50,816 | 81,143 | 65,090 | 146,233 | 44,284 | 190,517 |
| 1966 | 63 | 29,192 | 3,134 | 26,026 | 55,218 | 76,214 | 67,822 | 144,036 | 44,013 | 188,049 |
| 1967 | 64 | 30,462 | 3,526 | 29,552 | 60,015 | 96,145 | 93,072 | 189,217 | 58,288 | 247,505 |
| 1968 | 65 | 31,731 | 3,663 | 33,216 | 64,949 | 96,865 | 105,943 | 202,808 | 61,615 | 264,423 |

The total cost figures represent the cumulative total of yearly investments of $1,269 plus the cumulative amount of income dividends reinvested, and include the sales charge of $8\frac{1}{2}\%$ on all shares so purchased, as described in the prospectus. No adjustment has been made for any income taxes payable by shareholders on security distributions and dividends reinvested in shares. The dollar amounts of security profits distributions taken in shares were:

| | | | | | | | | | | | | | |
|---|---|---|---|---|---|---|---|---|---|---|---|---|---|
| 1944 | 0 | 1948 | 104 | 1952 | 1,043 | 1956 | 1,873 | 1960 | 2,774 | 1964 | 5,129 | 1968 | 13,680 |
| 1945 | 21 | 1949 | 142 | 1953 | 273 | 1957 | 1,880 | 1961 | 5,540 | 1965 | 7,148 | Total: | $68,498 |
| 1946 | 99 | 1950 | 277 | 1954 | 1,256 | 1958 | 2,116 | 1962 | 664 | 1966 | 7,708 | | |
| 1947 | 116 | 1951 | 1,416 | 1955 | 1,817 | 1959 | 2,877 | 1963 | 3,444 | 1967 | 7,101 | | |

# LIVING ESTATE

| | "Buying Term and Investing the Difference" | Buying Whole Life |
|---|---|---|
| | TOTAL VALUE OF SHARES | CASH VALUE |

# DEATH ESTATE

| | "Buying Term and Investing the Difference" | | | Buying Whole Life |
|---|---|---|---|---|

| AGE | TOTAL VALUE OF SHARES (Living) | CASH VALUE | TOTAL VALUE OF SHARES | + DECREASING TERM INSURANCE | = TOTAL DEATH ESTATE | FACE VALUE |
|---|---|---|---|---|---|---|
| 41 | $ 1,266 | $ 0 | $ 1,266 | $100,000 | $101,266 | $75,000 |
| 42 | 3,302 | 225 | 3,302 | 95,000 | 98,302 | 75,000 |
| 43 | 5,383 | 1,575 | 5,383 | 90,000 | 95,383 | 75,000 |
| 44 | 6,289 | 3,000 | 6,289 | 85,000 | 91,289 | 75,000 |
| 45 | 7,232 | 4,425 | 7,232 | 80,000 | 87,232 | 75,000 |
| 46 | 10,417 | 5,925 | 10,417 | 75,000 | 85,417 | 75,000 |
| 47 | 15,402 | 7,425 | 15,402 | 70,000 | 85,402 | 75,000 |
| 48 | 21,616 | 8,925 | 21,616 | 65,000 | 86,616 | 75,000 |
| 49 | 22,482 | 10,425 | 22,482 | 60,000 | 82,482 | 75,000 |
| 50 | 23,759 | 11,925 | 23,759 | 55,000 | 78,759 | 75,000 |
| 51 | 36,349 | 13,500 | 36,349 | 50,000 | 86,349 | 75,000 |
| 52 | 47,474 | 15,000 | 47,474 | 46,250 | 93,724 | 75,000 |
| 53 | 51,718 | 16,575 | 51,718 | 42,500 | 94,218 | 75,000 |
| 54 | 52,754 | 18,150 | 52,754 | 38,750 | 91,504 | 75,000 |
| 55 | 75,103 | 19,725 | 75,103 | 35,000 | 110,103 | 75,000 |
| 56 | 93,720 | 21,300 | 93,720 | 31,250 | 124,970 | 75,000 |
| 57 | 94,780 | 22,950 | 94,780 | 28,750 | 123,530 | 75,000 |
| 58 | 114,670 | 24,525 | 114,670 | 26,250 | 140,920 | 75,000 |
| 59 | 98,047 | 26,100 | 98,047 | 23,750 | 121,797 | 75,000 |
| 60 | 128,589 | 27,750 | 128,589 | 21,250 | 149,839 | 75,000 |
| 61 | 148,166 | 29,250 | 148,166 | 18,750 | 166,916 | 75,000 |
| 62 | 190,517 | 30,750 | 190,517 | 17,500 | 208,017 | 75,000 |
| 63 | 188,049 | 32,175 | 188,049 | 16,250 | 204,299 | 75,000 |
| 64 | 247,505 | 33,675 | 247,505 | 15,000 | 262,505 | 75,000 |
| 65 | 264,423 | 35,175 | 264,423 | 14,400 | 278,823 | 75,000 |

Whether you
**lived** or **died**
you would have been better off
"Buying Term and Investing the Difference"

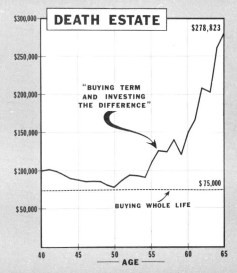

**LIVING ESTATE**

$264,423

"BUYING TERM AND INVESTING THE DIFFERENCE"

$35,175 — BUYING WHOLE LIFE

AGE 40 45 50 55 60 65

**DEATH ESTATE**

$278,823

"BUYING TERM AND INVESTING THE DIFFERENCE"

$75,000 — BUYING WHOLE LIFE

AGE 40 45 50 55 60 65

# COMMONWEALTH INVESTMENT CO.

Illustration of assumed annual investments of $1,269 for twenty-five years from 1944 to 1968. All dividends and distributions reinvested.

This tabulation covers an illustration of an assumed investment of $1,269 annually on January 1 of each year from 1944 through 1968. This was a period in which stock prices fluctuated widely because of changing business and economic conditions, and were significantly higher at the end of the period than at the beginning. Thus, these results should not be considered as a representation of the dividend income or capital gain or loss that may be realized from an investment made in the fund today. A program of the type illustrated does not assure a profit nor protect against depreciation in declining markets.

| | | COST OF SHARES | | | | VALUE OF SHARES | | | | |
|---|---|---|---|---|---|---|---|---|---|---|
| YEAR ENDING DEC. 31 | AGE | CUMULATIVE ANNUAL INVEST-MENTS | ANNUAL INCOME DIVIDENDS REIN-VESTED | CUMULA-TIVE COST OF SHARES PURCHASED WITH DIVIDENDS | TOTAL COST (INCLUDES REIN-VESTED DIVIDENDS) | ACQUIRED THROUGH ANNUAL INVEST-MENTS | ACCEPTED AS CAPITAL GAINS DIS-TRIBUTIONS (CUMU-LATIVE) | SUB-TOTAL | PURCHASED THROUGH REINVEST-MENT OF INCOME (CUMULATIVE) | TOTAL VALUE |
| 1944 | 41 | $ 1,269 | $ 44 | $ 44 | $ 1,313 | $ 1,344 | $ 8 | $ 1,352 | $ 48 | $ 1,400 |
| 1945 | 42 | 2,538 | 80 | 124 | 2,663 | 3,078 | 195 | 3,273 | 148 | 3,421 |
| 1946 | 43 | 3,807 | 105 | 229 | 4,037 | 3,897 | 377 | 4,274 | 237 | 4,511 |
| 1947 | 44 | 5,077 | 183 | 412 | 5,489 | 4,836 | 471 | 5,307 | 412 | 5,719 |
| 1948 | 45 | 6,346 | 282 | 694 | 7,040 | 5,615 | 529 | 6,144 | 656 | 6,800 |
| 1949 | 46 | 7,615 | 378 | 1,072 | 8,688 | 7,314 | 655 | 7,969 | 1,112 | 9,081 |
| 1950 | 47 | 8,884 | 522 | 1,594 | 10,479 | 9,499 | 919 | 10,418 | 1,803 | 12,221 |
| 1951 | 48 | 10,154 | 616 | 2,210 | 12,364 | 11,374 | 1,377 | 12,751 | 2,548 | 15,299 |
| 1952 | 49 | 11,423 | 700 | 2,910 | 14,333 | 12,865 | 1,751 | 14,616 | 3,327 | 17,943 |
| 1953 | 50 | 12,692 | 776 | 3,686 | 16,379 | 13,247 | 1,982 | 15,229 | 3,915 | 19,144 |
| 1954 | 51 | 13,961 | 872 | 4,558 | 18,520 | 18,341 | 2,995 | 21,336 | 5,955 | 27,291 |
| 1955 | 52 | 15,231 | 993 | 5,551 | 20,782 | 21,305 | 4,362 | 25,667 | 7,521 | 33,188 |
| 1956 | 53 | 16,500 | 1,133 | 6,684 | 23,184 | 22,102 | 5,438 | 27,540 | 8,506 | 36,046 |
| 1957 | 54 | 17,769 | 1,334 | 8,017 | 25,787 | 20,261 | 5,594 | 25,855 | 8,622 | 34,477 |
| 1958 | 55 | 19,038 | 1,329 | 9,347 | 28,386 | 26,278 | 8,128 | 34,406 | 12,047 | 46,453 |
| 1959 | 56 | 20,308 | 1,442 | 10,789 | 31,097 | 27,411 | 9,792 | 37,203 | 13,443 | 50,646 |
| 1960 | 57 | 21,577 | 1,625 | 12,414 | 33,991 | 28,071 | 10,730 | 38,801 | 14,851 | 53,652 |
| 1961 | 58 | 22,846 | 1,806 | 14,220 | 37,067 | 32,213 | 13,308 | 45,521 | 18,174 | 63,695 |
| 1962 | 59 | 24,115 | 1,941 | 16,162 | 40,278 | 29,618 | 13,089 | 42,707 | 18,036 | 60,743 |
| 1963 | 60 | 25,385 | 2,088 | 18,249 | 43,634 | 32,666 | 15,619 | 48,285 | 21,216 | 69,501 |
| 1964 | 61 | 26,654 | 2,317 | 20,567 | 47,221 | 35,472 | 19,339 | 54,811 | 24,545 | 79,356 |
| 1965 | 62 | 27,923 | 2,518 | 23,085 | 51,009 | 38,156 | 23,756 | 61,912 | 28,081 | 89,993 |
| 1966 | 63 | 29,192 | 2,737 | 25,822 | 55,015 | 34,211 | 23,641 | 57,852 | 27,063 | 84,915 |
| 1967 | 64 | 30,462 | 2,971 | 28,792 | 59,254 | 39,294 | 31,015 | 70,309 | 33,025 | 103,334 |
| 1968 | 65 | 31,731 | 3,451 | 32,244 | 63,975 | 41,348 | 38,744 | 80,092 | 37,167 | 117,259 |

The total cost figures represent the cumulative total of yearly investments of $1,269 plus the cumulative amount of income dividends reinvested, and include the sales charge of **8½%** on all shares so purchased, as described in the prospectus. No adjustment has been made for any income taxes payable by shareholders on security distributions and dividends reinvested in shares. The dollar amounts of security profits distributions taken in shares were:

| | | | | | | | | | | | | | |
|---|---|---|---|---|---|---|---|---|---|---|---|---|---|
| 1944 | 8 | 1948 | 89 | 1952 | 332 | 1956 | 1,144 | 1960 | 1,105 | 1964 | 2,953 | 1968 | 7,037 |
| 1945 | 185 | 1949 | 82 | 1953 | 334 | 1957 | 884 | 1961 | 1,484 | 1965 | 3,606 | Total: | $35,192 |
| 1946 | 200 | 1950 | 173 | 1954 | 439 | 1958 | 1,204 | 1962 | 1,278 | 1966 | 2,971 | | |
| 1947 | 110 | 1951 | 387 | 1955 | 1,069 | 1959 | 1,670 | 1963 | 1,717 | 1967 | 4,731 | | |

| LIVING ESTATE — "Buying Term and Investing the Difference" — TOTAL VALUE OF SHARES | LIVING ESTATE — Buying Whole Life — CASH VALUE | AGE | DEATH ESTATE — "Buying Term and Investing the Difference" — TOTAL VALUE OF SHARES | + DECREASING TERM INSURANCE | = TOTAL DEATH ESTATE | DEATH ESTATE — Buying Whole Life — FACE VALUE |
|---|---|---|---|---|---|---|
| $ 1,400 | $ 0 | 41 | $ 1,400 | $100,000 | $101,400 | $75,000 |
| 3,421 | 225 | 42 | 3,421 | 95,000 | 98,421 | 75,000 |
| 4,511 | 1,575 | 43 | 4,511 | 90,000 | 94,511 | 75,000 |
| 5,719 | 3,000 | 44 | 5,719 | 85,000 | 90,719 | 75,000 |
| 6,800 | 4,425 | 45 | 6,800 | 80,000 | 86,800 | 75,000 |
| 9,081 | 5,925 | 46 | 9,081 | 75,000 | 84,081 | 75,000 |
| 12,221 | 7,425 | 47 | 12,221 | 70,000 | 82,221 | 75,000 |
| 15,299 | 8,925 | 48 | 15,299 | 65,000 | 80,299 | 75,000 |
| 17,943 | 10,425 | 49 | 17,943 | 60,000 | 77,943 | 75,000 |
| 19,144 | 11,925 | 50 | 19,144 | 55,000 | 74,144 | 75,000 |
| 27,291 | 13,500 | 51 | 27,291 | 50,000 | 77,291 | 75,000 |
| 33,188 | 15,000 | 52 | 33,188 | 46,250 | 79,438 | 75,000 |
| 36,046 | 16,575 | 53 | 36,046 | 42,500 | 78,546 | 75,000 |
| 34,477 | 18,150 | 54 | 34,477 | 38,750 | 73,227 | 75,000 |
| 46,453 | 19,725 | 55 | 46,453 | 35,000 | 81,453 | 75,000 |
| 50,646 | 21,300 | 56 | 50,646 | 31,250 | 81,896 | 75,000 |
| 53,652 | 22,950 | 57 | 53,652 | 28,750 | 82,402 | 75,000 |
| 63,695 | 24,525 | 58 | 63,695 | 26,250 | 89,945 | 75,000 |
| 60,743 | 26,100 | 59 | 60,743 | 23,750 | 84,493 | 75,000 |
| 69,501 | 27,750 | 60 | 69,501 | 21,250 | 90,751 | 75,000 |
| 79,356 | 29,250 | 61 | 79,356 | 18,750 | 98,106 | 75,000 |
| 89,993 | 30,750 | 62 | 89,993 | 17,500 | 107,493 | 75,000 |
| 84,915 | 32,175 | 63 | 84,915 | 16,250 | 101,165 | 75,000 |
| 103,334 | 33,675 | 64 | 103,334 | 15,000 | 118,334 | 75,000 |
| 117,259 | 35,175 | 65 | 117,259 | 14,400 | 131,659 | 75,000 |

Whether you **lived** or **died** you would have been better off "Buying Term and Investing the Difference"

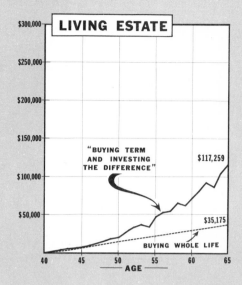

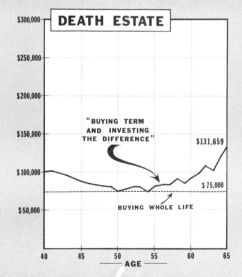

169

# DELAWARE FUND

Illustration of assumed annual investments of $1,269 for twenty-five years from 1944 to 1968. All dividends and distributions reinvested.

This tabulation covers an illustration of an assumed investment of $1,269 annually on January 1 of each year from 1944 through 1968. This was a period in which stock prices fluctuated widely because of changing business and economic conditions, and were significantly higher at the end of the period than at the beginning. Thus, these results should not be considered as a representation of the dividend income or capital gain or loss that may be realized from an investment made in the fund today. A program of the type illustrated does not assure a profit nor protect against depreciation in declining markets.

| | | COST OF SHARES | | | | VALUE OF SHARES | | | | |
|---|---|---|---|---|---|---|---|---|---|---|
| YEAR ENDING DEC. 31 | AGE | CUMULATIVE ANNUAL INVEST-MENTS | ANNUAL INCOME DIVIDENDS REIN-VESTED | CUMULA-TIVE COST OF SHARES PURCHASED WITH DIVIDENDS | TOTAL COST (INCLUDES REIN-VESTED DIVIDENDS) | ACQUIRED THROUGH ANNUAL INVEST-MENTS | ACCEPTED AS CAPITAL GAINS DIS-TRIBUTIONS (CUMU-LATIVE) | SUB-TOTAL | PURCHASED THROUGH REINVEST-MENT OF INCOME (CUMULATIVE) | TOTAL VALUE |
| 1944 | 41 | $ 1,269 | $ 19 | $ 19 | $ 1,288 | $ 1,172 | $ 137 | $ 1,309 | $ 18 | $ 1,327 |
| 1945 | 42 | 2,538 | 49 | 68 | 2,606 | 2,945 | 506 | 3,451 | 74 | 3,525 |
| 1946 | 43 | 3,807 | 73 | 141 | 3,948 | 3,071 | 1,126 | 4,197 | 118 | 4,315 |
| 1947 | 44 | 5,077 | 149 | 290 | 5,367 | 3,748 | 1,232 | 4,980 | 253 | 5,233 |
| 1948 | 45 | 6,346 | 244 | 534 | 6,879 | 4,467 | 1,375 | 5,842 | 456 | 6,298 |
| 1949 | 46 | 7,615 | 273 | 807 | 8,421 | 5,911 | 1,830 | 7,741 | 770 | 8,511 |
| 1950 | 47 | 8,884 | 445 | 1,252 | 10,135 | 7,959 | 2,559 | 10,518 | 1,337 | 11,855 |
| 1951 | 48 | 10,154 | 628 | 1,880 | 12,032 | 9,497 | 3,337 | 12,834 | 2,016 | 14,850 |
| 1952 | 49 | 11,423 | 633 | 2,513 | 13,934 | 10,979 | 4,160 | 15,139 | 2,729 | 17,868 |
| 1953 | 50 | 12,692 | 787 | 3,300 | 15,990 | 11,007 | 4,403 | 15,410 | 3,257 | 18,667 |
| 1954 | 51 | 13,961 | 914 | 4,214 | 18,173 | 16,381 | 7,280 | 23,661 | 5,426 | 29,087 |
| 1955 | 52 | 15,231 | 1,062 | 5,276 | 20,504 | 18,398 | 9,558 | 27,956 | 6,753 | 34,709 |
| 1956 | 53 | 16,500 | 1,250 | 6,526 | 23,023 | 19,542 | 11,659 | 31,201 | 7,979 | 39,180 |
| 1957 | 54 | 17,769 | 1,428 | 7,954 | 25,720 | 16,397 | 10,923 | 27,320 | 7,569 | 34,889 |
| 1958 | 55 | 19,038 | 1,550 | 9,504 | 28,539 | 24,072 | 17,183 | 41,255 | 12,099 | 53,354 |
| 1959 | 56 | 20,308 | 1,425 | 10,929 | 31,233 | 25,870 | 21,356 | 47,226 | 13,827 | 61,053 |
| 1960 | 57 | 21,577 | 1,669 | 12,598 | 34,171 | 24,572 | 22,205 | 46,777 | 14,242 | 61,019 |
| 1961 | 58 | 22,846 | 1,646 | 14,244 | 37,086 | 30,397 | 30,595 | 60,992 | 18,469 | 79,461 |
| 1962 | 59 | 24,115 | 1,507 | 15,751 | 39,862 | 25,127 | 27,185 | 52,312 | 16,270 | 68,582 |
| 1963 | 60 | 25,385 | 1,807 | 17,558 | 42,938 | 28,986 | 34,541 | 63,527 | 19,779 | 83,306 |
| 1964 | 61 | 26,654 | 1,758 | 19,316 | 45,965 | 32,166 | 42,505 | 74,671 | 22,838 | 97,509 |
| 1965 | 62 | 27,923 | 1,923 | 21,239 | 49,157 | 41,938 | 61,201 | 103,139 | 30,890 | 134,029 |
| 1966 | 63 | 29,192 | 2,086 | 23,325 | 52,512 | 40,643 | 66,888 | 107,531 | 31,178 | 138,709 |
| 1967 | 64 | 30,462 | 2,582 | 25,907 | 56,363 | 47,346 | 98,162 | 145,508 | 37,996 | 183,504 |
| 1968 | 65 | 31,731 | 4,474 | 30,381 | 62,106 | 48,831 | 119,901 | 168,732 | 42,896 | 211,628 |

The total cost figures represent the cumulative total of yearly investments of $1,269 plus the cumulative amount of income dividends reinvested, and include the sales charge of 8½% on all shares so purchased, as described in the prospectus. No adjustment has been made for any income taxes payable by shareholders on security distributions and dividends reinvested in shares. The dollar amounts of security profits distributions taken in shares were:

| | | | | | | | | | | | | | |
|---|---|---|---|---|---|---|---|---|---|---|---|---|---|
| 1944 | 138 | 1948 | 265 | 1952 | 704 | 1956 | 2,102 | 1960 | 2,770 | 1964 | 5,756 | 1968 | 20,554 |
| 1945 | 319 | 1949 | 353 | 1953 | 640 | 1957 | 1,780 | 1961 | 4,374 | 1965 | 7,116 | Total: | $95,520 |
| 1946 | 756 | 1950 | 469 | 1954 | 1,255 | 1958 | 2,074 | 1962 | 2,898 | 1966 | 9,071 | | |
| 1947 | 237 | 1951 | 674 | 1955 | 1,905 | 1959 | 3,734 | 1963 | 4,358 | 1967 | 21,218 | | |

| LIVING ESTATE | | AGE | DEATH ESTATE | | | |
| "Buying Term and Investing the Difference" | Buying Whole Life | | "Buying Term and Investing the Difference" | | | Buying Whole Life |
| TOTAL VALUE OF SHARES | CASH VALUE | | TOTAL VALUE OF SHARES | + DECREASING TERM INSURANCE | = TOTAL DEATH ESTATE | FACE VALUE |
|---|---|---|---|---|---|---|
| $ 1,327 | $ 0 | 41 | $ 1,327 | $100,000 | $101,327 | $75,000 |
| 3,525 | 225 | 42 | 3,525 | 95,000 | 98,525 | 75,000 |
| 4,315 | 1,575 | 43 | 4,315 | 90,000 | 94,315 | 75,000 |
| 5,233 | 3,000 | 44 | 5,233 | 85,000 | 90,233 | 75,000 |
| 6,298 | 4,425 | 45 | 6,298 | 80,000 | 86,298 | 75,000 |
| 8,511 | 5,925 | 46 | 8,511 | 75,000 | 83,511 | 75,000 |
| 11,855 | 7,425 | 47 | 11,855 | 70,000 | 81,855 | 75,000 |
| 14,850 | 8,925 | 48 | 14,850 | 65,000 | 79,850 | 75,000 |
| 17,868 | 10,425 | 49 | 17,868 | 60,000 | 77,868 | 75,000 |
| 18,667 | 11,925 | 50 | 18,667 | 55,000 | 73,667 | 75,000 |
| 29,087 | 13,500 | 51 | 29,087 | 50,000 | 79,087 | 75,000 |
| 34,709 | 15,000 | 52 | 34,709 | 46,250 | 80,959 | 75,000 |
| 39,180 | 16,575 | 53 | 39,180 | 42,500 | 81,680 | 75,000 |
| 34,889 | 18,150 | 54 | 34,889 | 38,750 | 73,639 | 75,000 |
| 53,354 | 19,725 | 55 | 53,354 | 35,000 | 88,354 | 75,000 |
| 61,053 | 21,300 | 56 | 61,053 | 31,250 | 92,303 | 75,000 |
| 61,019 | 22,950 | 57 | 61,019 | 28,750 | 89,769 | 75,000 |
| 79,461 | 24,525 | 58 | 79,461 | 26,250 | 105,711 | 75,000 |
| 68,582 | 26,100 | 59 | 68,582 | 23,750 | 92,332 | 75,000 |
| 83,306 | 27,750 | 60 | 83,306 | 21,250 | 104,556 | 75,000 |
| 97,509 | 29,250 | 61 | 97,509 | 18,750 | 116,259 | 75,000 |
| 134,029 | 30,750 | 62 | 134,029 | 17,500 | 151,529 | 75,000 |
| 138,709 | 32,175 | 63 | 138,709 | 16,250 | 154,959 | 75,000 |
| 183,504 | 33,675 | 64 | 183,504 | 15,000 | 198,504 | 75,000 |
| 211,628 | 35,175 | 65 | 211,628 | 14,400 | 226,028 | 75,000 |

Whether you
**lived** or **died**
you would have been better off
"Buying Term and Investing the Difference"

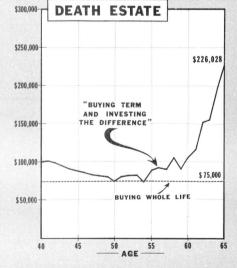

# DIVIDEND SHARES

Illustration of assumed annual investments of $1,269 for twenty-five years from 1944 to 1968. All dividends and distributions reinvested.

This tabulation covers an illustration of an assumed investment of $1,269 annually on January 1 of each year from 1944 through 1968. This was a period in which stock prices fluctuated widely because of changing business and economic conditions, and were significantly higher at the end of the period than at the beginning. Thus, these results should not be considered as a representation of the dividend income or capital gain or loss that may be realized from an investment made in the fund today. A program of the type illustrated does not assure a profit nor protect against depreciation in declining markets.

| | | COST OF SHARES | | | | VALUE OF SHARES | | | | |
|---|---|---|---|---|---|---|---|---|---|---|
| YEAR ENDING DEC. 31 | AGE | CUMULATIVE ANNUAL INVEST- MENTS | ANNUAL INCOME DIVIDENDS REIN- VESTED | CUMULA- TIVE COST OF SHARES PURCHASED WITH DIVIDENDS | TOTAL COST (INCLUDES REIN- VESTED DIVIDENDS) | ACQUIRED THROUGH ANNUAL INVEST- MENTS | ACCEPTED AS CAPITAL GAINS DIS- TRIBUTIONS (CUMU- LATIVE) | SUB- TOTAL | PURCHASED THROUGH REINVEST- MENT OF INCOME (CUMULATIVE) | TOTAL VALUE |
| 1944 | 41 | $ 1,269 | $ 50 | $ 50 | $ 1,319 | $ 1,327 | $ 13 | $ 1,340 | $ 50 | $ 1,390 |
| 1945 | 42 | 2,538 | 92 | 142 | 2,681 | 3,145 | 109 | 3,254 | 165 | 3,419 |
| 1946 | 43 | 3,807 | 127 | 270 | 4,078 | 3,860 | 359 | 4,219 | 254 | 4,473 |
| 1947 | 44 | 5,077 | 212 | 483 | 5,560 | 4,770 | 483 | 5,253 | 437 | 5,690 |
| 1948 | 45 | 6,346 | 295 | 779 | 7,125 | 5,643 | 591 | 6,234 | 676 | 6,910 |
| 1949 | 46 | 7,615 | 435 | 1,215 | 8,831 | 7,613 | 767 | 8,380 | 1,202 | 9,582 |
| 1950 | 47 | 8,884 | 600 | 1,815 | 10,700 | 9,910 | 1,129 | 11,039 | 1,958 | 12,997 |
| 1951 | 48 | 10,154 | 768 | 2,583 | 12,738 | 11,749 | 1,642 | 13,391 | 2,800 | 16,191 |
| 1952 | 49 | 11,423 | 814 | 3,398 | 14,822 | 13,809 | 2,316 | 16,125 | 3,790 | 19,915 |
| 1953 | 50 | 12,692 | 906 | 4,305 | 16,998 | 13,914 | 2,798 | 16,712 | 4,346 | 21,058 |
| 1954 | 51 | 13,961 | 972 | 5,278 | 19,240 | 19,463 | 4,565 | 24,028 | 6,645 | 30,673 |
| 1955 | 52 | 15,231 | 1,131 | 6,410 | 21,641 | 23,373 | 6,420 | 29,793 | 8,643 | 38,436 |
| 1956 | 53 | 16,500 | 1,329 | 7,739 | 24,240 | 24,715 | 7,997 | 32,712 | 9,907 | 42,619 |
| 1957 | 54 | 17,769 | 1,542 | 9,281 | 27,051 | 22,754 | 8,629 | 31,383 | 10,023 | 41,406 |
| 1958 | 55 | 19,038 | 1,615 | 10,896 | 29,936 | 30,384 | 12,659 | 43,043 | 14,408 | 57,451 |
| 1959 | 56 | 20,308 | 1,747 | 12,644 | 32,953 | 31,538 | 14,605 | 46,143 | 15,999 | 62,142 |
| 1960 | 57 | 21,577 | 1,888 | 14,532 | 36,109 | 32,162 | 16,463 | 48,625 | 17,574 | 66,199 |
| 1961 | 58 | 22,846 | 2,039 | 16,572 | 39,420 | 40,328 | 22,615 | 62,943 | 23,284 | 86,227 |
| 1962 | 59 | 24,115 | 2,187 | 18,759 | 42,876 | 35,782 | 22,263 | 58,045 | 22,109 | 80,154 |
| 1963 | 60 | 25,385 | 2,359 | 21,119 | 46,505 | 41,311 | 27,873 | 69,184 | 26,963 | 96,147 |
| 1964 | 61 | 26,654 | 2,734 | 23,853 | 50,507 | 46,105 | 33,645 | 79,750 | 31,806 | 111,556 |
| 1965 | 62 | 27,923 | 3,067 | 26,921 | 54,846 | 48,641 | 38,595 | 87,236 | 35,553 | 122,789 |
| 1966 | 63 | 29,192 | 3,521 | 30,443 | 59,637 | 42,673 | 37,296 | 79,969 | 33,482 | 113,451 |
| 1967 | 64 | 30,462 | 3,801 | 34,244 | 64,708 | 49,589 | 46,761 | 96,350 | 41,439 | 137,789 |
| 1968 | 65 | 31,731 | 4,072 | 38,317 | 70,048 | 54,232 | 55,607 | 109,842 | 48,125 | 157,967 |

The total cost figures represent the cumulative total of yearly investments of $1,269 plus the cumulative amount of income dividends reinvested, and include the sales charge of 8⅔% on all shares so purchased, as described in the prospectus. No adjustment has been made for any income taxes payable by shareholders on security distributions and dividends reinvested in shares. The dollar amounts of security profits distributions taken in shares were:

| | | | | | | | | | | | | | |
|---|---|---|---|---|---|---|---|---|---|---|---|---|---|
| 1944 | 11 | 1948 | 134 | 1952 | 514 | 1956 | 1,477 | 1960 | 1,893 | 1964 | 3,364 | 1968 | 5,553 |
| 1945 | 83 | 1949 | 99 | 1953 | 601 | 1957 | 1,626 | 1961 | 2,497 | 1965 | 3,894 | Total: | $41,864 |
| 1946 | 251 | 1950 | 249 | 1954 | 855 | 1958 | 1,530 | 1962 | 2,434 | 1966 | 3,844 | | |
| 1947 | 142 | 1951 | 425 | 1955 | 1,161 | 1959 | 1,846 | 1963 | 2,887 | 1967 | 4,494 | | |

## LIVING ESTATE

## DEATH ESTATE

| "Buying Term and Investing the Difference" TOTAL VALUE OF SHARES | Buying Whole Life CASH VALUE | AGE | "Buying Term and Investing the Difference" TOTAL VALUE OF SHARES | + DECREASING TERM INSURANCE | = TOTAL DEATH ESTATE | Buying Whole Life FACE VALUE |
|---|---|---|---|---|---|---|
| $ 1,390 | $ 0 | 41 | $ 1,390 | $100,000 | $101,390 | $75,000 |
| 3,419 | 225 | 42 | 3,419 | 95,000 | 98,419 | 75,000 |
| 4,473 | 1,575 | 43 | 4,473 | 90,000 | 94,473 | 75,000 |
| 5,690 | 3,000 | 44 | 5,690 | 85,000 | 90,690 | 75,000 |
| 6,910 | 4,425 | 45 | 6,910 | 80,000 | 86,910 | 75,000 |
| 9,582 | 5,925 | 46 | 9,582 | 75,000 | 84,582 | 75,000 |
| 12,997 | 7,425 | 47 | 12,997 | 70,000 | 82,997 | 75,000 |
| 16,191 | 8,925 | 48 | 16,191 | 65,000 | 81,191 | 75,000 |
| 19,915 | 10,425 | 49 | 19,915 | 60,000 | 79,915 | 75,000 |
| 21,058 | 11,925 | 50 | 21,058 | 55,000 | 76,058 | 75,000 |
| 30,673 | 13,500 | 51 | 30,673 | 50,000 | 80,673 | 75,000 |
| 38,436 | 15,000 | 52 | 38,436 | 46,250 | 84,686 | 75,000 |
| 42,619 | 16,575 | 53 | 42,619 | 42,500 | 85,119 | 75,000 |
| 41,406 | 18,150 | 54 | 41,406 | 38,750 | 80,156 | 75,000 |
| 57,451 | 19,725 | 55 | 57,451 | 35,000 | 92,451 | 75,000 |
| 62,142 | 21,300 | 56 | 62,142 | 31,250 | 93,392 | 75,000 |
| 66,199 | 22,950 | 57 | 66,199 | 28,750 | 94,949 | 75,000 |
| 86,227 | 24,525 | 58 | 86,227 | 26,250 | 112,477 | 75,000 |
| 80,154 | 26,100 | 59 | 80,154 | 23,750 | 103,904 | 75,000 |
| 96,147 | 27,750 | 60 | 96,147 | 21,250 | 117,397 | 75,000 |
| 111,556 | 29,250 | 61 | 111,556 | 18,750 | 130,306 | 75,000 |
| 122,789 | 30,750 | 62 | 122,789 | 17,500 | 140,289 | 75,000 |
| 113,451 | 32,175 | 63 | 113,451 | 16,250 | 129,701 | 75,000 |
| 137,789 | 33,675 | 64 | 137,789 | 15,000 | 152,789 | 75,000 |
| 157,967 | 35,175 | 65 | 157,967 | 14,400 | 172,367 | 75,000 |

Whether you
**lived** or **died**
you would have been better off
"Buying Term and Investing the Difference"

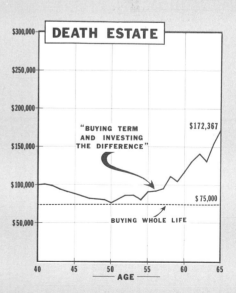

LIVING ESTATE

"BUYING TERM AND INVESTING THE DIFFERENCE" $157,967

BUYING WHOLE LIFE $35,175

AGE

DEATH ESTATE

"BUYING TERM AND INVESTING THE DIFFERENCE" $172,367

$75,000 BUYING WHOLE LIFE

AGE

# EATON & HOWARD BALANCED FUND

Illustration of assumed annual investments of $1,269 for twenty-five years from 1944 to 1968. All dividends and distributions reinvested.

This tabulation covers an illustration of an assumed investment of $1,269 annually on January 1 of each year from 1944 through 1968. This was a period in which stock prices fluctuated widely because of changing business and economic conditions, and were significantly higher at the end of the period than at the beginning. Thus, these results should not be considered as a representation of the dividend income or capital gain or loss that may be realized from an investment made in the fund today. A program of the type illustrated does not assure a profit nor protect against depreciation in declining markets.

| | | COST OF SHARES | | | | VALUE OF SHARES | | | | |
|---|---|---|---|---|---|---|---|---|---|---|
| YEAR ENDING DEC. 31 | AGE | CUMULATIVE ANNUAL INVESTMENTS | ANNUAL INCOME DIVIDENDS REINVESTED | CUMULATIVE COST OF SHARES PURCHASED WITH DIVIDENDS | TOTAL COST (INCLUDES REINVESTED DIVIDENDS) | ACQUIRED THROUGH ANNUAL INVESTMENTS | ACCEPTED AS CAPITAL GAINS DISTRIBUTIONS (CUMULATIVE) | SUBTOTAL | PURCHASED THROUGH REINVESTMENT OF INCOME (CUMULATIVE) | TOTAL VALUE |
| 1944 | 41 | $ 1,269 | $ 48 | $ 48 | $ 1,317 | $ 1,324 | $ 26 | $ 1,350 | $ 47 | $ 1,397 |
| 1945 | 42 | 2,538 | 84 | 133 | 2,672 | 2,867 | 103 | 2,970 | 136 | 3,106 |
| 1946 | 43 | 3,807 | 136 | 269 | 4,077 | 3,852 | 149 | 4,001 | 251 | 4,252 |
| 1947 | 44 | 5,077 | 216 | 486 | 5,563 | 4,679 | 139 | 4,818 | 430 | 5,248 |
| 1948 | 45 | 6,346 | 273 | 759 | 7,105 | 5,818 | 139 | 5,957 | 675 | 6,632 |
| 1949 | 46 | 7,615 | 368 | 1,127 | 8,743 | 8,021 | 159 | 8,180 | 1,133 | 9,313 |
| 1950 | 47 | 8,884 | 486 | 1,613 | 10,498 | 9,912 | 436 | 10,348 | 1,678 | 12,026 |
| 1951 | 48 | 10,154 | 576 | 2,189 | 12,344 | 11,710 | 813 | 12,523 | 2,310 | 14,833 |
| 1952 | 49 | 11,423 | 648 | 2,838 | 14,262 | 13,495 | 1,227 | 14,722 | 3,023 | 17,745 |
| 1953 | 50 | 12,692 | 729 | 3,567 | 16,260 | 14,129 | 1,541 | 15,670 | 3,588 | 19,258 |
| 1954 | 51 | 13,961 | 822 | 4,390 | 18,352 | 19,038 | 2,468 | 21,506 | 5,287 | 26,793 |
| 1955 | 52 | 15,231 | 926 | 5,316 | 20,548 | 22,194 | 3,445 | 25,639 | 6,660 | 32,299 |
| 1956 | 53 | 16,500 | 1,040 | 6,357 | 22,858 | 23,720 | 4,186 | 27,906 | 7,702 | 35,608 |
| 1957 | 54 | 17,769 | 1,178 | 7,535 | 25,306 | 22,485 | 4,487 | 26,972 | 7,976 | 34,948 |
| 1958 | 55 | 19,038 | 1,299 | 8,835 | 27,874 | 28,054 | 6,384 | 34,438 | 10,734 | 45,172 |
| 1959 | 56 | 20,308 | 1,424 | 10,259 | 30,568 | 28,763 | 7,517 | 36,280 | 11,868 | 48,148 |
| 1960 | 57 | 21,577 | 1,627 | 11,887 | 33,465 | 29,612 | 8,120 | 37,732 | 13,261 | 50,993 |
| 1961 | 58 | 22,846 | 1,738 | 13,626 | 36,473 | 34,837 | 11,040 | 45,877 | 16,643 | 62,520 |
| 1962 | 59 | 24,115 | 1,876 | 15,502 | 39,618 | 33,373 | 11,313 | 44,686 | 17,176 | 61,862 |
| 1963 | 60 | 25,385 | 2,014 | 17,516 | 42,902 | 36,477 | 13,641 | 50,118 | 19,985 | 70,103 |
| 1964 | 61 | 26,654 | 2,213 | 19,731 | 46,386 | 39,756 | 16,423 | 56,179 | 23,135 | 79,314 |
| 1965 | 62 | 27,923 | 2,459 | 22,190 | 50,115 | 39,324 | 18,248 | 57,572 | 24,426 | 81,998 |
| 1966 | 63 | 29,192 | 2,796 | 24,986 | 54,180 | 36,303 | 18,721 | 55,024 | 24,412 | 79,436 |
| 1967 | 64 | 30,462 | 3,130 | 28,117 | 58,580 | 36,941 | 22,114 | 59,055 | 26,843 | 85,898 |
| 1968 | 65 | 31,731 | 3,549 | 31,667 | 63,399 | 42,180 | 24,480 | 66,660 | 33,095 | 99,755 |

The total cost figures represent the cumulative total of yearly investments of $1,269 plus the cumulative amount of income dividends reinvested, and include the sales charge of 8½% on all shares so purchased, as described in the prospectus. No adjustment has been made for any income taxes payable by shareholders on security distributions and dividends reinvested in shares. The dollar amounts of security profits distributions taken in shares were:

| | | | | | | | | | | | |
|---|---|---|---|---|---|---|---|---|---|---|---|
| 1944 | 27 | 1948 | 0 | 1952 | 368 | 1956 | 684 | 1960 | 657 | 1964 | 2,016 | 1968 | 0 |
| 1945 | 74 | 1949 | 0 | 1953 | 358 | 1957 | 707 | 1961 | 1,870 | 1965 | 2,465 | Total: $22,031 |
| 1946 | 49 | 1950 | 257 | 1954 | 533 | 1958 | 1,030 | 1962 | 1,061 | 1966 | 2,326 | |
| 1947 | 0 | 1951 | 344 | 1955 | 729 | 1959 | 1,215 | 1963 | 1,669 | 1967 | 3,592 | |

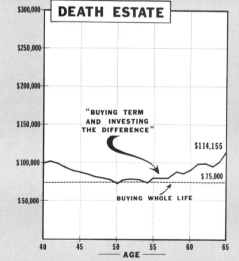

| | LIVING ESTATE | | | DEATH ESTATE | | |
|---|---|---|---|---|---|---|
| | "Buying Term and Investing the Difference" | Buying Whole Life | | "Buying Term and Investing the Difference" | | Buying Whole Life |
| AGE | TOTAL VALUE OF SHARES | CASH VALUE | TOTAL VALUE OF SHARES + | DECREASING TERM INSURANCE = | TOTAL DEATH ESTATE | FACE VALUE |
| 41 | $ 1,397 | $ 0 | $ 1,397 | $100,000 | $101,397 | $75,000 |
| 42 | 3,106 | 225 | 3,106 | 95,000 | 98,106 | 75,000 |
| 43 | 4,252 | 1,575 | 4,252 | 90,000 | 94,252 | 75,000 |
| 44 | 5,248 | 3,000 | 5,248 | 85,000 | 90,248 | 75,000 |
| 45 | 6,632 | 4,425 | 6,632 | 80,000 | 86,632 | 75,000 |
| 46 | 9,313 | 5,925 | 9,313 | 75,000 | 84,313 | 75,000 |
| 47 | 12,026 | 7,425 | 12,026 | 70,000 | 82,026 | 75,000 |
| 48 | 14,833 | 8,925 | 14,833 | 65,000 | 79,833 | 75,000 |
| 49 | 17,745 | 10,425 | 17,745 | 60,000 | 77,745 | 75,000 |
| 50 | 19,258 | 11,925 | 19,258 | 55,000 | 74,258 | 75,000 |
| 51 | 26,793 | 13,500 | 26,793 | 50,000 | 76,793 | 75,000 |
| 52 | 32,299 | 15,000 | 32,299 | 46,250 | 78,549 | 75,000 |
| 53 | 35,608 | 16,575 | 35,608 | 42,500 | 78,108 | 75,000 |
| 54 | 34,948 | 18,150 | 34,948 | 38,750 | 73,698 | 75,000 |
| 55 | 45,172 | 19,725 | 45,172 | 35,000 | 80,172 | 75,000 |
| 56 | 48,148 | 21,300 | 48,148 | 31,250 | 79,398 | 75,000 |
| 57 | 50,993 | 22,950 | 50,993 | 28,750 | 79,743 | 75,000 |
| 58 | 62,520 | 24,525 | 62,520 | 26,250 | 88,770 | 75,000 |
| 59 | 61,862 | 26,100 | 61,862 | 23,750 | 85,612 | 75,000 |
| 60 | 70,103 | 27,750 | 70,103 | 21,250 | 91,353 | 75,000 |
| 61 | 79,314 | 29,250 | 79,314 | 18,750 | 98,064 | 75,000 |
| 62 | 81,998 | 30,750 | 81,998 | 17,500 | 99,498 | 75,000 |
| 63 | 79,436 | 32,175 | 79,436 | 16,250 | 95,686 | 75,000 |
| 64 | 85,898 | 33,675 | 85,898 | 15,000 | 100,898 | 75,000 |
| 65 | 99,755 | 35,175 | 99,755 | 14,400 | 114,155 | 75,000 |

Whether you
**lived** or **died**
you would have been better off
"Buying Term and Investing the Difference"

175

# EATON & HOWARD STOCK FUND

Illustration of assumed annual investments of $1,269 for twenty-five years from 1944 to 1968. All dividends and distributions reinvested.

This tabulation covers an illustration of an assumed investment of $1,269 annually on January 1 of each year from 1944 through 1968. This was a period in which stock prices fluctuated widely because of changing business and economic conditions, and were significantly higher at the end of the period than at the beginning. Thus, these results should not be considered as a representation of the dividend income or capital gain or loss that may be realized from an investment made in the fund today. A program of the type illustrated does not assure a profit nor protect against depreciation in declining markets.

| | | COST OF SHARES | | | | VALUE OF SHARES | | | | |
|---|---|---|---|---|---|---|---|---|---|---|
| YEAR ENDING DEC. 31 | AGE | CUMULATIVE ANNUAL INVESTMENTS | ANNUAL INCOME DIVIDENDS REINVESTED | CUMULATIVE COST OF SHARES PURCHASED WITH DIVIDENDS | TOTAL COST (INCLUDES REINVESTED DIVIDENDS) | ACQUIRED THROUGH ANNUAL INVESTMENTS | ACCEPTED AS CAPITAL GAINS DISTRIBUTIONS (CUMULATIVE) | SUB-TOTAL | PURCHASED THROUGH REINVESTMENT OF INCOME (CUMULATIVE) | TOTAL VALUE |
| 1944 | 41 | $ 1,269 | $ 43 | $ 43 | $ 1,313 | $ 1,378 | $ 13 | $ 1,391 | $ 42 | $ 1,433 |
| 1945 | 42 | 2,538 | 82 | 125 | 2,665 | 2,933 | 243 | 3,176 | 127 | 3,303 |
| 1946 | 43 | 3,807 | 126 | 249 | 4,056 | 3,882 | 373 | 4,255 | 228 | 4,483 |
| 1947 | 44 | 5,077 | 200 | 449 | 5,526 | 4,828 | 356 | 5,184 | 403 | 5,587 |
| 1948 | 45 | 6,346 | 285 | 735 | 7,081 | 6,101 | 363 | 6,464 | 671 | 7,135 |
| 1949 | 46 | 7,615 | 401 | 1,136 | 8,752 | 8,643 | 708 | 9,351 | 1,184 | 10,535 |
| 1950 | 47 | 8,884 | 563 | 1,700 | 10,585 | 10,969 | 1,306 | 12,274 | 1,859 | 14,133 |
| 1951 | 48 | 10,154 | 677 | 2,377 | 12,531 | 13,600 | 1,931 | 15,531 | 2,724 | 18,255 |
| 1952 | 49 | 11,423 | 774 | 3,151 | 14,575 | 15,831 | 2,602 | 18,433 | 3,651 | 22,084 |
| 1953 | 50 | 12,692 | 873 | 4,025 | 16,719 | 16,743 | 2,564 | 19,307 | 4,419 | 23,726 |
| 1954 | 51 | 13,961 | 977 | 5,003 | 18,965 | 25,380 | 4,728 | 30,108 | 7,281 | 37,389 |
| 1955 | 52 | 15,231 | 1,089 | 6,092 | 21,324 | 30,287 | 6,995 | 37,282 | 9,332 | 46,614 |
| 1956 | 53 | 16,500 | 1,307 | 7,400 | 23,901 | 33,450 | 8,319 | 41,769 | 11,125 | 52,894 |
| 1957 | 54 | 17,769 | 1,469 | 8,869 | 26,640 | 30,205 | 7,779 | 37,984 | 10,957 | 48,941 |
| 1958 | 55 | 19,038 | 1,533 | 10,402 | 29,441 | 40,608 | 11,184 | 51,792 | 15,756 | 67,548 |
| 1959 | 56 | 20,308 | 1,651 | 12,053 | 32,362 | 44,273 | 12,767 | 57,040 | 18,253 | 75,293 |
| 1960 | 57 | 21,577 | 1,920 | 13,974 | 35,552 | 44,740 | 13,554 | 58,294 | 19,783 | 78,077 |
| 1961 | 58 | 22,846 | 1,887 | 15,862 | 38,710 | 56,094 | 18,489 | 74,583 | 25,986 | 100,569 |
| 1962 | 59 | 24,115 | 2,053 | 17,916 | 42,032 | 48,583 | 16,732 | 65,315 | 23,975 | 89,290 |
| 1963 | 60 | 25,385 | 2,222 | 20,139 | 45,524 | 56,325 | 20,194 | 76,519 | 29,239 | 105,758 |
| 1964 | 61 | 26,654 | 2,450 | 22,589 | 49,243 | 62,313 | 26,744 | 89,057 | 33,917 | 122,974 |
| 1965 | 62 | 27,923 | 2,886 | 25,476 | 53,401 | 67,918 | 34,451 | 102,369 | 38,999 | 141,368 |
| 1966 | 63 | 29,192 | 3,335 | 28,812 | 58,005 | 61,260 | 35,471 | 96,731 | 37,530 | 134,261 |
| 1967 | 64 | 30,462 | 3,453 | 32,385 | 62,849 | 69,888 | 46,488 | 116,376 | 45,256 | 161,632 |
| 1968 | 65 | 31,731 | 3,563 | 35,949 | 67,680 | 77,919 | 50,976 | 128,895 | 53,093 | 181,988 |

The total cost figures represent the cumulative total of yearly investments of $1,269 plus the cumulative amount of income dividends reinvested, and include the sales charge of 8½% on all shares so purchased, as described in the prospectus. No adjustment has been made for any income taxes payable by shareholders on security distributions and dividends reinvested in shares. The dollar amounts of security profits distributions taken in shares were:

| | | | | | | | | | | | | | |
|---|---|---|---|---|---|---|---|---|---|---|---|---|---|
| 1944 | 142 | 1948 | 0 | 1952 | 518 | 1956 | 869 | 1960 | 936 | 1964 | 4,890 | 1968 | 0 |
| 1945 | 229 | 1949 | 275 | 1953 | 0 | 1957 | 528 | 1961 | 1,965 | 1965 | 5,725 | Total: | $35,558 |
| 1946 | 136 | 1950 | 492 | 1954 | 1,051 | 1958 | 1,067 | 1962 | 1,034 | 1966 | 4,851 | | |
| 1947 | 0 | 1951 | 458 | 1955 | 1,600 | 1959 | 890 | 1963 | 1,226 | 1967 | 6,676 | | |

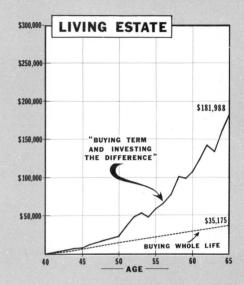

| LIVING ESTATE | | AGE | DEATH ESTATE | | | |
|---|---|---|---|---|---|---|
| "Buying Term and Investing the Difference" | Buying Whole Life | | "Buying Term and Investing the Difference" | | | Buying Whole Life |
| TOTAL VALUE OF SHARES | CASH VALUE | | TOTAL VALUE OF SHARES | + DECREASING TERM INSURANCE | = TOTAL DEATH ESTATE | FACE VALUE |
| $ 1,433 | $ 0 | 41 | $ 1,433 | $100,000 | $101,433 | $75,000 |
| 3,303 | 225 | 42 | 3,303 | 95,000 | 98,303 | 75,000 |
| 4,483 | 1,575 | 43 | 4,483 | 90,000 | 94,483 | 75,000 |
| 5,587 | 3,000 | 44 | 5,587 | 85,000 | 90,587 | 75,000 |
| 7,135 | 4,425 | 45 | 7,135 | 80,000 | 87,135 | 75,000 |
| 10,535 | 5,925 | 46 | 10,535 | 75,000 | 85,535 | 75,000 |
| 14,133 | 7,425 | 47 | 14,133 | 70,000 | 84,133 | 75,000 |
| 18,255 | 8,925 | 48 | 18,255 | 65,000 | 83,255 | 75,000 |
| 22,084 | 10,425 | 49 | 22,084 | 60,000 | 82,084 | 75,000 |
| 23,726 | 11,925 | 50 | 23,726 | 55,000 | 78,726 | 75,000 |
| 37,389 | 13,500 | 51 | 37,389 | 50,000 | 87,389 | 75,000 |
| 46,614 | 15,000 | 52 | 46,614 | 46,250 | 92,864 | 75,000 |
| 52,894 | 16,575 | 53 | 52,894 | 42,500 | 95,394 | 75,000 |
| 48,941 | 18,150 | 54 | 48,941 | 38,750 | 87,691 | 75,000 |
| 67,548 | 19,725 | 55 | 67,548 | 35,000 | 102,548 | 75,000 |
| 75,293 | 21,300 | 56 | 75,293 | 31,250 | 106,543 | 75,000 |
| 78,077 | 22,950 | 57 | 78,077 | 28,750 | 106,827 | 75,000 |
| 100,569 | 24,525 | 58 | 100,569 | 26,250 | 126,819 | 75,000 |
| 89,290 | 26,100 | 59 | 89,290 | 23,750 | 113,040 | 75,000 |
| 105,758 | 27,750 | 60 | 105,758 | 21,250 | 127,008 | 75,000 |
| 122,974 | 29,250 | 61 | 122,974 | 18,750 | 141,724 | 75,000 |
| 141,368 | 30,750 | 62 | 141,368 | 17,500 | 158,868 | 75,000 |
| 134,261 | 32,175 | 63 | 134,261 | 16,250 | 150,511 | 75,000 |
| 161,632 | 33,675 | 64 | 161,632 | 15,000 | 176,632 | 75,000 |
| 181,988 | 35,175 | 65 | 181,988 | 14,400 | 196,388 | 75,000 |

Whether you **lived** or **died** you would have been better off "Buying Term and Investing the Difference"

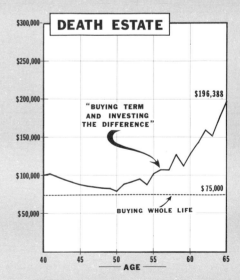

# EQUITY FUND

Illustration of assumed annual investments of $1,269 for twenty-five years from 1944 to 1968. All dividends and distributions reinvested.

This tabulation covers an illustration of an assumed investment of $1,269 annually on January 1 of each year from 1944 through 1968. This was a period in which stock prices fluctuated widely because of changing business and economic conditions, and were significantly higher at the end of the period than at the beginning. Thus, these results should not be considered as a representation of the dividend income or capital gain or loss that may be realized from an investment made in the fund today. A program of the type illustrated does not assure a profit nor protect against depreciation in declining markets.

| | | COST OF SHARES | | | | VALUE OF SHARES | | | | |
|---|---|---|---|---|---|---|---|---|---|---|
| YEAR ENDING DEC. 31 | AGE | CUMULATIVE ANNUAL INVEST-MENTS | ANNUAL INCOME DIVIDENDS REIN-VESTED | CUMULA-TIVE COST OF SHARES PURCHASED WITH DIVIDENDS | TOTAL COST (INCLUDES REIN-VESTED DIVIDENDS) | ACQUIRED THROUGH ANNUAL INVEST-MENTS | ACCEPTED AS CAPITAL GAINS DIS-TRIBUTIONS (CUMU-LATIVE) | SUB-TOTAL | PURCHASED THROUGH REINVEST-MENT OF INCOME (CUMULATIVE) | TOTAL VALUE |
| 1944 | 41 | $ 1,269 | $ 49 | $ 49 | $ 1,319 | $ 1,366 | $ 29 | $ 1,395 | $ 52 | $ 1,447 |
| 1945 | 42 | 2,538 | 43 | 93 | 2,632 | 3,128 | 370 | 3,498 | 113 | 3,611 |
| 1946 | 43 | 3,807 | 128 | 222 | 4,030 | 3,788 | 405 | 4,193 | 221 | 4,414 |
| 1947 | 44 | 5,077 | 228 | 450 | 5,527 | 4,789 | 449 | 5,238 | 448 | 5,686 |
| 1948 | 45 | 6,346 | 357 | 808 | 7,154 | 5,643 | 429 | 6,072 | 770 | 6,842 |
| 1949 | 46 | 7,615 | 441 | 1,254 | 8,870 | 7,323 | 534 | 7,857 | 1,310 | 9,167 |
| 1950 | 47 | 8,884 | 614 | 1,869 | 10,754 | 10,212 | 727 | 10,939 | 2,244 | 13,183 |
| 1951 | 48 | 10,154 | 535 | 2,404 | 12,558 | 12,363 | 1,823 | 14,186 | 2,972 | 17,158 |
| 1952 | 49 | 11,423 | 634 | 3,039 | 14,463 | 14,003 | 2,538 | 16,541 | 3,730 | 20,271 |
| 1953 | 50 | 12,692 | 807 | 3,847 | 16,540 | 14,200 | 2,819 | 17,019 | 4,323 | 21,342 |
| 1954 | 51 | 13,961 | 708 | 4,555 | 18,517 | 19,865 | 5,854 | 25,719 | 6,355 | 32,074 |
| 1955 | 52 | 15,231 | 933 | 5,488 | 20,720 | 21,314 | 8,209 | 29,523 | 7,949 | 37,472 |
| 1956 | 53 | 16,500 | 1,071 | 6,560 | 23,061 | 24,239 | 9,983 | 34,222 | 8,941 | 43,163 |
| 1957 | 54 | 17,769 | 1,247 | 7,808 | 25,578 | 21,624 | 10,075 | 31,699 | 8,723 | 40,422 |
| 1958 | 55 | 19,038 | 1,134 | 8,942 | 27,982 | 29,408 | 15,615 | 45,023 | 12,495 | 57,518 |
| 1959 | 56 | 20,308 | 1,261 | 10,204 | 30,513 | 32,684 | 19,321 | 52,005 | 14,632 | 66,637 |
| 1960 | 57 | 21,577 | 1,521 | 11,726 | 33,304 | 31,880 | 20,519 | 52,399 | 15,300 | 67,699 |
| 1961 | 58 | 22,846 | 1,310 | 13,036 | 35,883 | 41,503 | 29,478 | 70,981 | 20,543 | 91,524 |
| 1962 | 59 | 24,115 | 1,603 | 14,640 | 38,756 | 35,827 | 27,378 | 63,205 | 18,861 | 82,066 |
| 1963 | 60 | 25,385 | 1,937 | 16,577 | 41,963 | 41,402 | 33,879 | 75,281 | 23,047 | 98,328 |
| 1964 | 61 | 26,654 | 2,016 | 18,616 | 45,272 | 47,306 | 42,098 | 89,404 | 27,659 | 117,063 |
| 1965 | 62 | 27,923 | 2,458 | 21,075 | 48,999 | 52,387 | 50,099 | 102,486 | 32,363 | 134,849 |
| 1966 | 63 | 29,192 | 3,398 | 24,473 | 53,667 | 46,241 | 47,736 | 93,977 | 31,243 | 125,220 |
| 1967 | 64 | 30,462 | 3,992 | 28,466 | 58,929 | 53,771 | 62,253 | 116,024 | 39,377 | 155,401 |
| 1968 | 65 | 31,731 | 4,453 | 32,919 | 64,651 | 63,456 | 71,831 | 135,287 | 50,173 | 185,460 |

The total cost figures represent the cumulative total of yearly investments of $1,269 plus the cumulative amount of income dividends reinvested, and include the sales charge of $8\frac{1}{2}\%$ on all shares so purchased, as described in the prospectus. No adjustment has been made for any income taxes payable by shareholders on security distributions and dividends reinvested in shares. The dollar amounts of security profits distributions taken in shares were:

| | | | | | | | | | | | | | |
|---|---|---|---|---|---|---|---|---|---|---|---|---|---|
| 1944 | 26 | 1948 | 3 | 1952 | 636 | 1956 | 1,844 | 1960 | 2,290 | 1964 | 4,420 | 1968 | 0 |
| 1945 | 325 | 1949 | 66 | 1953 | 467 | 1957 | 1,675 | 1961 | 3,665 | 1965 | 4,660 | Total: | $48,824 |
| 1946 | 85 | 1950 | 81 | 1954 | 2,080 | 1958 | 2,417 | 1962 | 2,762 | 1966 | 4,575 | | |
| 1947 | 56 | 1951 | 1,022 | 1955 | 1,707 | 1959 | 2,612 | 1963 | 3,251 | 1967 | 8,099 | | |

# LIVING ESTATE

| "Buying Term and Investing the Difference" | Buying Whole Life | AGE | "Buying Term and Investing the Difference" | | | Buying Whole Life |
|---|---|---|---|---|---|---|
| TOTAL VALUE OF SHARES | CASH VALUE | | TOTAL VALUE OF SHARES + | DECREASING TERM INSURANCE = | TOTAL DEATH ESTATE | FACE VALUE |
| $ 1,447 | $ 0 | 41 | $ 1,447 | $100,000 | $101,447 | $75,000 |
| 3,611 | 225 | 42 | 3,611 | 95,000 | 98,611 | 75,000 |
| 4,414 | 1,575 | 43 | 4,414 | 90,000 | 94,414 | 75,000 |
| 5,686 | 3,000 | 44 | 5,686 | 85,000 | 90,686 | 75,000 |
| 6,842 | 4,425 | 45 | 6,842 | 80,000 | 86,842 | 75,000 |
| 9,167 | 5,925 | 46 | 9,167 | 75,000 | 84,167 | 75,000 |
| 13,183 | 7,425 | 47 | 13,183 | 70,000 | 83,183 | 75,000 |
| 17,158 | 8,925 | 48 | 17,158 | 65,000 | 82,158 | 75,000 |
| 20,271 | 10,425 | 49 | 20,271 | 60,000 | 80,271 | 75,000 |
| 21,342 | 11,925 | 50 | 21,342 | 55,000 | 76,342 | 75,000 |
| 32,074 | 13,500 | 51 | 32,074 | 50,000 | 82,074 | 75,000 |
| 37,472 | 15,000 | 52 | 37,472 | 46,250 | 83,722 | 75,000 |
| 43,163 | 16,575 | 53 | 43,163 | 42,500 | 85,663 | 75,000 |
| 40,422 | 18,150 | 54 | 40,422 | 38,750 | 79,172 | 75,000 |
| 57,518 | 19,725 | 55 | 57,518 | 35,000 | 92,518 | 75,000 |
| 66,637 | 21,300 | 56 | 66,637 | 31,250 | 97,887 | 75,000 |
| 67,699 | 22,950 | 57 | 67,699 | 28,750 | 96,449 | 75,000 |
| 91,524 | 24,525 | 58 | 91,524 | 26,250 | 117,774 | 75,000 |
| 82,066 | 26,100 | 59 | 82,066 | 23,750 | 105,816 | 75,000 |
| 98,328 | 27,750 | 60 | 98,328 | 21,250 | 119,578 | 75,000 |
| 117,063 | 29,250 | 61 | 117,063 | 18,750 | 135,813 | 75,000 |
| 134,849 | 30,750 | 62 | 134,849 | 17,500 | 152,349 | 75,000 |
| 125,220 | 32,175 | 63 | 125,220 | 16,250 | 141,470 | 75,000 |
| 155,401 | 33,675 | 64 | 155,401 | 15,000 | 170,401 | 75,000 |
| 185,460 | 35,175 | 65 | 185,460 | 14,400 | 199,860 | 75,000 |

# DEATH ESTATE

Whether you
**lived** or **died**
you would have been better off
"Buying Term and Investing the Difference"

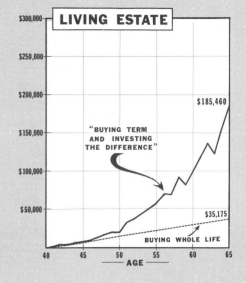

LIVING ESTATE — "BUYING TERM AND INVESTING THE DIFFERENCE" $185,460; BUYING WHOLE LIFE $35,175

DEATH ESTATE — "BUYING TERM AND INVESTING THE DIFFERENCE" $199,860; BUYING WHOLE LIFE $75,000

# FIDELITY FUND

Illustration of assumed annual investments of $1,269 for twenty-five years from 1944 to 1968. All dividends and distributions reinvested.

This tabulation covers an illustration of an assumed investment of $1,269 annually on January 1 of each year from 1944 through 1968. This was a period in which stock prices fluctuated widely because of changing business and economic conditions, and were significantly higher at the end of the period than at the beginning. Thus, these results should not be considered as a representation of the dividend income or capital gain or loss that may be realized from an investment made in the fund today. A program of the type illustrated does not assure a profit nor protect against depreciation in declining markets.

|  |  | COST OF SHARES | | | | VALUE OF SHARES | | | | |
|---|---|---|---|---|---|---|---|---|---|---|
| YEAR ENDING DEC. 31 | AGE | CUMULATIVE ANNUAL INVESTMENTS | ANNUAL INCOME DIVIDENDS REINVESTED | CUMULATIVE COST OF SHARES PURCHASED WITH DIVIDENDS | TOTAL COST (INCLUDES REINVESTED DIVIDENDS) | ACQUIRED THROUGH ANNUAL INVESTMENTS | ACCEPTED AS CAPITAL GAINS DISTRIBUTIONS (CUMULATIVE) | SUBTOTAL | PURCHASED THROUGH REINVESTMENT OF INCOME (CUMULATIVE) | TOTAL VALUE |
| 1944 | 41 | $ 1,269 | $ 47 | $ 47 | $ 1,316 | $ 1,409 | $ 14 | $ 1,423 | $ 47 | $ 1,470 |
| 1945 | 42 | 2,538 | 81 | 128 | 2,667 | 3,243 | 228 | 3,471 | 139 | 3,610 |
| 1946 | 43 | 3,807 | 162 | 291 | 4,098 | 4,038 | 405 | 4,443 | 268 | 4,711 |
| 1947 | 44 | 5,077 | 258 | 549 | 5,626 | 4,939 | 489 | 5,428 | 489 | 5,917 |
| 1948 | 45 | 6,346 | 460 | 1,010 | 7,357 | 5,923 | 474 | 6,397 | 881 | 7,278 |
| 1949 | 46 | 7,615 | 490 | 1,500 | 9,117 | 8,290 | 613 | 8,903 | 1,523 | 10,426 |
| 1950 | 47 | 8,884 | 774 | 2,275 | 11,160 | 11,067 | 1,080 | 12,147 | 2,522 | 14,669 |
| 1951 | 48 | 10,154 | 880 | 3,156 | 13,310 | 13,480 | 1,620 | 15,100 | 3,602 | 18,702 |
| 1952 | 49 | 11,423 | 1,020 | 4,176 | 15,600 | 16,019 | 2,078 | 18,097 | 4,909 | 23,006 |
| 1953 | 50 | 12,692 | 1,176 | 5,353 | 18,046 | 15,721 | 1,952 | 17,673 | 5,560 | 23,233 |
| 1954 | 51 | 13,961 | 1,418 | 6,771 | 20,734 | 25,441 | 3,575 | 29,016 | 9,912 | 38,928 |
| 1955 | 52 | 15,231 | 1,697 | 8,469 | 23,701 | 30,309 | 5,219 | 35,528 | 12,887 | 48,415 |
| 1956 | 53 | 16,500 | 1,877 | 10,347 | 26,848 | 32,152 | 6,643 | 38,794 | 14,905 | 53,699 |
| 1957 | 54 | 17,769 | 1,909 | 12,256 | 30,027 | 25,822 | 6,838 | 32,660 | 13,144 | 45,804 |
| 1958 | 55 | 19,038 | 1,927 | 14,229 | 33,268 | 37,114 | 11,609 | 48,723 | 20,178 | 68,901 |
| 1959 | 56 | 20,308 | 2,014 | 16,270 | 36,579 | 39,913 | 14,588 | 54,501 | 22,959 | 77,460 |
| 1960 | 57 | 21,577 | 2,257 | 18,528 | 40,106 | 38,583 | 16,536 | 55,119 | 23,731 | 78,850 |
| 1961 | 58 | 22,846 | 2,075 | 20,603 | 43,451 | 46,816 | 23,427 | 70,243 | 29,964 | 100,207 |
| 1962 | 59 | 24,115 | 2,464 | 23,068 | 47,184 | 37,918 | 23,831 | 61,749 | 25,991 | 87,740 |
| 1963 | 60 | 25,385 | 2,705 | 25,773 | 51,159 | 45,964 | 31,243 | 77,207 | 33,182 | 110,389 |
| 1964 | 61 | 26,654 | 3,015 | 28,788 | 55,442 | 50,096 | 39,551 | 89,647 | 38,069 | 127,716 |
| 1965 | 62 | 27,923 | 3,251 | 32,040 | 59,965 | 56,723 | 50,240 | 106,963 | 45,335 | 152,298 |
| 1966 | 63 | 29,192 | 3,862 | 35,902 | 65,095 | 51,482 | 55,644 | 107,126 | 43,803 | 150,929 |
| 1967 | 64 | 30,462 | 4,334 | 40,237 | 70,700 | 59,395 | 81,996 | 141,391 | 53,575 | 194,966 |
| 1968 | 65 | 31,731 | 5,331 | 45,568 | 77,299 | 61,773 | 103,715 | 165,488 | 59,768 | 225,256 |

The total cost figures represent the cumulative total of yearly investments of $1,269 plus the cumulative amount of income dividends reinvested, and include the sales charge of 8½% on all shares so purchased, as described in the prospectus. No adjustment has been made for any income taxes payable by shareholders on security distributions and dividends reinvested in shares. The dollar amounts of security profits distributions taken in shares were:

| | | | | | | | | | | | | | |
|---|---|---|---|---|---|---|---|---|---|---|---|---|---|
| 1944 | 13 | 1948 | 0 | 1952 | 296 | 1956 | 1,239 | 1960 | 2,852 | 1964 | 5,741 | 1968 | 17,777 |
| 1945 | 208 | 1949 | 57 | 1953 | 55 | 1957 | 2,104 | 1961 | 3,293 | 1965 | 5,609 | Total: | $81,625 |
| 1946 | 196 | 1950 | 326 | 1954 | 424 | 1958 | 1,600 | 1962 | 6,103 | 1966 | 11,543 | | |
| 1947 | 104 | 1951 | 417 | 1955 | 964 | 1959 | 2,345 | 1963 | 2,721 | 1967 | 15,638 | | |

| LIVING ESTATE | | AGE | DEATH ESTATE | | | | |
|---|---|---|---|---|---|---|---|
| "Buying Term and Investing the Difference" | Buying Whole Life | | "Buying Term and Investing the Difference" | | | | Buying Whole Life |
| TOTAL VALUE OF SHARES | CASH VALUE | AGE | TOTAL VALUE OF SHARES | + DECREASING TERM INSURANCE | = TOTAL DEATH ESTATE | | FACE VALUE |
| $ 1,470 | $ 0 | 41 | $ 1,470 | $100,000 | $101,470 | | $75,000 |
| 3,610 | 225 | 42 | 3,610 | 95,000 | 98,610 | | 75,000 |
| 4,711 | 1,575 | 43 | 4,711 | 90,000 | 94,711 | | 75,000 |
| 5,917 | 3,000 | 44 | 5,917 | 85,000 | 90,917 | | 75,000 |
| 7,278 | 4,425 | 45 | 7,278 | 80,000 | 87,278 | | 75,000 |
| 10,426 | 5,925 | 46 | 10,426 | 75,000 | 85,426 | | 75,000 |
| 14,669 | 7,425 | 47 | 14,669 | 70,000 | 84,669 | | 75,000 |
| 18,702 | 8,925 | 48 | 18,702 | 65,000 | 83,702 | | 75,000 |
| 23,006 | 10,425 | 49 | 23,006 | 60,000 | 83,006 | | 75,000 |
| 23,233 | 11,925 | 50 | 23,233 | 55,000 | 78,233 | | 75,000 |
| 38,928 | 13,500 | 51 | 38,928 | 50,000 | 88,928 | | 75,000 |
| 48,415 | 15,000 | 52 | 48,415 | 46,250 | 94,665 | | 75,000 |
| 53,699 | 16,575 | 53 | 53,699 | 42,500 | 96,199 | | 75,000 |
| 45,804 | 18,150 | 54 | 45,804 | 38,750 | 84,554 | | 75,000 |
| 68,901 | 19,725 | 55 | 68,901 | 35,000 | 103,901 | | 75,000 |
| 77,460 | 21,300 | 56 | 77,460 | 31,250 | 108,710 | | 75,000 |
| 78,850 | 22,950 | 57 | 78,850 | 28,750 | 107,600 | | 75,000 |
| 100,207 | 24,525 | 58 | 100,207 | 26,250 | 126,457 | | 75,000 |
| 87,740 | 26,100 | 59 | 87,740 | 23,750 | 111,490 | | 75,000 |
| 110,389 | 27,750 | 60 | 110,389 | 21,250 | 131,639 | | 75,000 |
| 127,716 | 29,250 | 61 | 127,716 | 18,750 | 146,466 | | 75,000 |
| 152,298 | 30,750 | 62 | 152,298 | 17,500 | 169,798 | | 75,000 |
| 150,929 | 32,175 | 63 | 150,929 | 16,250 | 167,179 | | 75,000 |
| 194,966 | 33,675 | 64 | 194,966 | 15,000 | 209,966 | | 75,000 |
| 225,256 | 35,175 | 65 | 225,256 | 14,400 | 239,656 | | 75,000 |

Whether you **lived** or **died** you would have been better off "Buying Term and Investing the Difference"

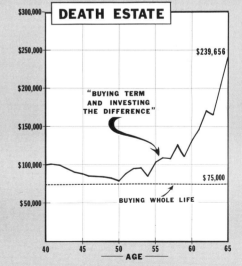

LIVING ESTATE

$300,000 — $250,000 — $200,000 — $150,000 — $100,000 — $50,000

"BUYING TERM AND INVESTING THE DIFFERENCE" — $225,256

BUYING WHOLE LIFE — $35,175

AGE — 40 45 50 55 60 65

DEATH ESTATE

$300,000 — $250,000 — $200,000 — $150,000 — $100,000 — $50,000

"BUYING TERM AND INVESTING THE DIFFERENCE" — $239,656

BUYING WHOLE LIFE — $75,000

AGE — 40 45 50 55 60 65

# FINANCIAL INDUSTRIAL FUND

Illustration of assumed annual investments of $1,269 for twenty-five years from 1944 to 1968. All dividends and distributions reinvested.

This tabulation covers an illustration of an assumed investment of $1,269 annually on January 1 of each year from 1944 through 1968. This was a period in which stock prices fluctuated widely because of changing business and economic conditions, and were significantly higher at the end of the period than at the beginning. Thus, these results should not be considered as a representation of the dividend income or capital gain or loss that may be realized from an investment made in the fund today. A program of the type illustrated does not assure a profit nor protect against depreciation in declining markets.

| | | COST OF SHARES | | | | VALUE OF SHARES | | | | |
|---|---|---|---|---|---|---|---|---|---|---|
| YEAR ENDING DEC. 31 | AGE | CUMULATIVE ANNUAL INVESTMENTS | ANNUAL INCOME DIVIDENDS REINVESTED | CUMULATIVE COST OF SHARES PURCHASED WITH DIVIDENDS | TOTAL COST (INCLUDES REINVESTED DIVIDENDS) | ACQUIRED THROUGH ANNUAL INVESTMENTS | ACCEPTED AS CAPITAL GAINS DISTRIBUTIONS (CUMULATIVE) | SUB-TOTAL | PURCHASED THROUGH REINVESTMENT OF INCOME (CUMULATIVE) | TOTAL VALUE |
| 1944 | 41 | $ 1,269 | $ 47 | $ 47 | $ 1,316 | $ 1,271 | $ 18 | $ 1,289 | $ 48 | $ 1,337 |
| 1945 | 42 | 2,538 | 82 | 129 | 2,667 | 3,126 | 99 | 3,225 | 152 | 3,377 |
| 1946 | 43 | 3,807 | 982 | 227 | 4,035 | 3,502 | 236 | 3,738 | 214 | 3,952 |
| 1947 | 44 | 5,077 | 150 | 377 | 5,455 | 4,405 | 385 | 4,790 | 352 | 5,142 |
| 1948 | 45 | 6,346 | 297 | 675 | 7,022 | 5,131 | 437 | 5,568 | 605 | 6,173 |
| 1949 | 46 | 7,615 | 392 | 1,067 | 8,683 | 6,971 | 554 | 7,525 | 1,107 | 8,632 |
| 1950 | 47 | 8,884 | 532 | 1,600 | 10,484 | 9,874 | 988 | 10,862 | 1,940 | 12,802 |
| 1951 | 48 | 10,154 | 846 | 2,446 | 12,600 | 12,080 | 1,366 | 13,446 | 2,987 | 16,433 |
| 1952 | 49 | 11,423 | 810 | 3,256 | 14,680 | 13,906 | 1,967 | 15,873 | 3,979 | 19,852 |
| 1953 | 50 | 12,692 | 922 | 4,179 | 16,872 | 13,513 | 2,375 | 15,888 | 4,480 | 20,368 |
| 1954 | 51 | 13,961 | 1,055 | 5,234 | 19,196 | 21,317 | 4,542 | 25,859 | 7,782 | 33,641 |
| 1955 | 52 | 15,231 | 1,223 | 6,457 | 21,689 | 25,539 | 6,908 | 32,447 | 10,127 | 42,574 |
| 1956 | 53 | 16,500 | 1,467 | 7,925 | 24,426 | 26,749 | 8,877 | 35,626 | 11,591 | 47,217 |
| 1957 | 54 | 17,769 | 1,741 | 9,667 | 27,437 | 21,387 | 7,953 | 29,340 | 10,346 | 39,686 |
| 1958 | 55 | 19,038 | 1,500 | 11,167 | 30,206 | 30,584 | 11,658 | 42,242 | 15,772 | 58,014 |
| 1959 | 56 | 20,308 | 1,607 | 12,774 | 33,083 | 34,828 | 15,122 | 49,950 | 18,948 | 68,898 |
| 1960 | 57 | 21,577 | 1,684 | 14,458 | 36,035 | 33,299 | 15,801 | 49,100 | 19,228 | 68,328 |
| 1961 | 58 | 22,846 | 1,699 | 16,158 | 39,005 | 41,358 | 20,947 | 62,305 | 24,812 | 87,117 |
| 1962 | 59 | 24,115 | 1,749 | 17,907 | 42,023 | 33,586 | 18,272 | 51,858 | 21,320 | 73,178 |
| 1963 | 60 | 25,385 | 1,921 | 19,829 | 45,214 | 38,750 | 22,115 | 60,865 | 25,715 | 86,580 |
| 1964 | 61 | 26,654 | 2,143 | 21,972 | 48,627 | 44,582 | 28,181 | 72,763 | 30,891 | 103,654 |
| 1965 | 62 | 27,923 | 2,446 | 24,418 | 52,343 | 52,346 | 36,868 | 89,214 | 37,927 | 127,141 |
| 1966 | 63 | 29,192 | 2,769 | 27,187 | 56,381 | 47,404 | 38,988 | 86,392 | 36,247 | 122,639 |
| 1967 | 64 | 30,462 | 3,060 | 30,248 | 60,710 | 54,375 | 54,613 | 108,988 | 43,700 | 152,688 |
| 1968 | 65 | 31,731 | 3,419 | 33,667 | 65,398 | 55,528 | 70,671 | 126,199 | 47,176 | 173,375 |

The total cost figures represent the cumulative total of yearly investments of $1,269 plus the cumulative amount of income dividends reinvested, and include the sales charge of 8½% on all shares so purchased, as described in the prospectus. No adjustment has been made for any income taxes payable by shareholders on security distributions and dividends reinvested in shares. The dollar amounts of security profits distributions taken in shares were:

| | | | | | | | | | | | | | |
|---|---|---|---|---|---|---|---|---|---|---|---|---|---|
| 1944 | 16 | 1948 | 88 | 1952 | 493 | 1956 | 1,957 | 1960 | 1,725 | 1964 | 3,413 | 1968 | 14,819 |
| 1945 | 68 | 1949 | 62 | 1953 | 561 | 1957 | 1,363 | 1961 | 1,947 | 1965 | 4,299 | Total: | $57,548 |
| 1946 | 182 | 1950 | 276 | 1954 | 914 | 1958 | 765 | 1962 | 1,635 | 1966 | 5,818 | | |
| 1947 | 159 | 1951 | 287 | 1955 | 1,721 | 1959 | 2,220 | 1963 | 1,765 | 1967 | 10,995 | | |

# LIVING ESTATE

| "Buying Term and Investing the Difference" | Buying Whole Life |
|---|---|
| TOTAL VALUE OF SHARES | CASH VALUE |

# DEATH ESTATE

| "Buying Term and Investing the Difference" | | | Buying Whole Life |
|---|---|---|---|
| TOTAL VALUE OF SHARES | + DECREASING TERM INSURANCE | = TOTAL DEATH ESTATE | FACE VALUE |

| LIVING — TOTAL VALUE OF SHARES | LIVING — CASH VALUE | AGE | DEATH — TOTAL VALUE OF SHARES | + DECREASING TERM INSURANCE | = TOTAL DEATH ESTATE | FACE VALUE |
|---|---|---|---|---|---|---|
| $ 1,337 | $ 0 | 41 | $ 1,337 | $100,000 | $101,337 | $75,000 |
| 3,377 | 225 | 42 | 3,377 | 95,000 | 98,377 | 75,000 |
| 3,952 | 1,575 | 43 | 3,952 | 90,000 | 93,952 | 75,000 |
| 5,142 | 3,000 | 44 | 5,142 | 85,000 | 90,142 | 75,000 |
| 6,173 | 4,425 | 45 | 6,173 | 80,000 | 86,173 | 75,000 |
| 8,632 | 5,925 | 46 | 8,632 | 75,000 | 83,632 | 75,000 |
| 12,802 | 7,425 | 47 | 12,802 | 70,000 | 82,802 | 75,000 |
| 16,433 | 8,925 | 48 | 16,433 | 65,000 | 81,433 | 75,000 |
| 19,852 | 10,425 | 49 | 19,852 | 60,000 | 79,852 | 75,000 |
| 20,368 | 11,925 | 50 | 20,368 | 55,000 | 75,368 | 75,000 |
| 33,641 | 13,500 | 51 | 33,641 | 50,000 | 83,641 | 75,000 |
| 42,574 | 15,000 | 52 | 42,574 | 46,250 | 88,824 | 75,000 |
| 47,217 | 16,575 | 53 | 47,217 | 42,500 | 89,717 | 75,000 |
| 39,686 | 18,150 | 54 | 39,686 | 38,750 | 78,436 | 75,000 |
| 58,014 | 19,725 | 55 | 58,014 | 35,000 | 93,014 | 75,000 |
| 68,898 | 21,300 | 56 | 68,898 | 31,250 | 100,148 | 75,000 |
| 68,328 | 22,950 | 57 | 68,328 | 28,750 | 97,078 | 75,000 |
| 87,117 | 24,525 | 58 | 87,117 | 26,250 | 113,367 | 75,000 |
| 73,178 | 26,100 | 59 | 73,178 | 23,750 | 96,928 | 75,000 |
| 86,580 | 27,750 | 60 | 86,580 | 21,250 | 107,830 | 75,000 |
| 103,654 | 29,250 | 61 | 103,654 | 18,750 | 122,404 | 75,000 |
| 127,141 | 30,750 | 62 | 127,141 | 17,500 | 144,641 | 75,000 |
| 122,639 | 32,175 | 63 | 122,639 | 16,250 | 138,889 | 75,000 |
| 152,688 | 33,675 | 64 | 152,688 | 15,000 | 167,688 | 75,000 |
| 173,375 | 35,175 | 65 | 173,375 | 14,400 | 187,775 | 75,000 |

Whether you
**lived**  or  **died**
you would have been better off
"Buying Term and Investing the Difference"

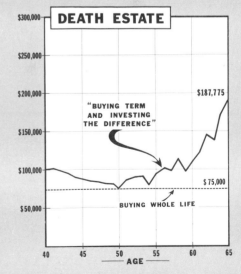

LIVING ESTATE

$173,375

"BUYING TERM AND INVESTING THE DIFFERENCE"

$35,175

BUYING WHOLE LIFE

DEATH ESTATE

$187,775

"BUYING TERM AND INVESTING THE DIFFERENCE"

$75,000

BUYING WHOLE LIFE

# FIRST INVESTORS FUND

---

Illustration of assumed annual investments of $1,269 for twenty-five years from 1944 to 1968. All dividends and distributions reinvested.

---

This tabulation covers an illustration of an assumed investment of $1,269 annually on January 1 of each year from 1944 through 1968. This was a period in which stock prices fluctuated widely because of changing business and economic conditions, and were significantly higher at the end of the period than at the beginning. Thus, these results should not be considered as a representation of the dividend income or capital gain or loss that may be realized from an investment made in the fund today. A program of the type illustrated does not assure a profit nor protect against depreciation in declining markets.

| | | COST OF SHARES | | | | VALUE OF SHARES | | | | |
|---|---|---|---|---|---|---|---|---|---|---|
| YEAR ENDING DEC. 31 | AGE | CUMULATIVE ANNUAL INVEST-MENTS | ANNUAL INCOME DIVIDENDS REIN-VESTED | CUMULA-TIVE COST OF SHARES PURCHASED WITH DIVIDENDS | TOTAL COST (INCLUDES REIN-VESTED DIVIDENDS) | ACQUIRED THROUGH ANNUAL INVEST-MENTS | ACCEPTED AS CAPITAL GAINS DIS-TRIBUTIONS (CUMU-LATIVE) | SUB-TOTAL | PURCHASED THROUGH REINVEST-MENT OF INCOME (CUMULATIVE) | TOTAL VALUE |
| 1944 | 41 | $ 1,269 | $ 39 | $ 39 | $ 1,308 | $ 1,357 | $ 7 | $ 1,364 | $ 42 | $ 1,406 |
| 1945 | 42 | 2,538 | 96 | 135 | 2,674 | 3,361 | 10 | 3,372 | 158 | 3,530 |
| 1946 | 43 | 3,807 | 117 | 252 | 4,060 | 3,954 | 9 | 3,963 | 246 | 4,209 |
| 1947 | 44 | 5,077 | 209 | 462 | 5,539 | 4,888 | 8 | 4,896 | 447 | 5,343 |
| 1948 | 45 | 6,346 | 248 | 711 | 7,057 | 5,611 | 241 | 5,852 | 646 | 6,498 |
| 1949 | 46 | 7,615 | 349 | 1,060 | 8,676 | 7,606 | 381 | 7,987 | 1,089 | 9,076 |
| 1950 | 47 | 8,884 | 331 | 1,391 | 10,276 | 9,408 | 1,044 | 10,452 | 1,510 | 11,962 |
| 1951 | 48 | 10,154 | 387 | 1,779 | 11,934 | 11,138 | 1,866 | 13,004 | 1,980 | 14,984 |
| 1952 | 49 | 11,423 | 418 | 2,197 | 13,621 | 12,245 | 2,576 | 14,821 | 2,394 | 17,215 |
| 1953 | 50 | 12,692 | 547 | 2,745 | 15,438 | 12,599 | 2,838 | 15,437 | 2,797 | 18,234 |
| 1954 | 51 | 13,961 | 677 | 3,422 | 17,384 | 16,997 | 4,343 | 21,340 | 4,217 | 25,557 |
| 1955 | 52 | 15,231 | 781 | 4,204 | 19,435 | 18,945 | 5,665 | 24,610 | 5,200 | 29,810 |
| 1956 | 53 | 16,500 | 1,071 | 5,275 | 21,776 | 19,585 | 6,748 | 26,333 | 6,116 | 32,449 |
| 1957 | 54 | 17,769 | 1,050 | 6,326 | 24,096 | 17,800 | 6,733 | 24,533 | 6,209 | 30,742 |
| 1958 | 55 | 19,038 | 1,278 | 7,604 | 26,643 | 23,240 | 9,260 | 32,500 | 9,037 | 41,537 |
| 1959 | 56 | 20,308 | 1,322 | 8,926 | 29,235 | 24,100 | 10,278 | 34,378 | 10,235 | 44,613 |
| 1960 | 57 | 21,577 | 1,408 | 10,335 | 31,914 | 23,597 | 10,589 | 34,186 | 10,995 | 45,181 |
| 1961 | 58 | 22,846 | 1,517 | 11,853 | 34,701 | 28,653 | 13,844 | 42,497 | 14,278 | 56,775 |
| 1962 | 59 | 24,115 | 1,474 | 13,328 | 37,444 | 24,468 | 12,129 | 36,597 | 13,151 | 49,748 |
| 1963 | 60 | 25,385 | 1,460 | 14,788 | 40,174 | 28,268 | 14,909 | 43,177 | 16,000 | 59,177 |
| 1964 | 61 | 26,654 | 1,567 | 16,356 | 43,011 | 31,089 | 17,982 | 49,071 | 18,468 | 67,539 |
| 1965 | 62 | 27,923 | 1,756 | 18,112 | 46,037 | 35,793 | 22,705 | 58,498 | 22,343 | 80,841 |
| 1966 | 63 | 29,192 | 1,997 | 20,110 | 49,304 | 33,087 | 22,549 | 55,636 | 21,900 | 77,536 |
| 1967 | 64 | 30,462 | 2,179 | 22,290 | 52,753 | 36,523 | 28,007 | 64,530 | 25,484 | 90,014 |
| 1968 | 65 | 31,731 | 2,198 | 24,488 | 56,221 | 35,707 | 40,870 | 76,577 | 26,222 | 102,799 |

The total cost figures represent the cumulative total of yearly investments of $1,269 plus the cumulative amount of income dividends reinvested, and include the sales charge of 8¾% on all shares so purchased, as described in the prospectus. No adjustment has been made for any income taxes payable by shareholders on security distributions and dividends reinvested in shares. The dollar amounts of security profits distributions taken in shares were:

| | | | | | | | | | | | | | |
|---|---|---|---|---|---|---|---|---|---|---|---|---|---|
| 1944 | 0 | 1948 | 235 | 1952 | 708 | 1956 | 1,226 | 1960 | 931 | 1964 | 2,228 | 1968 | 14,330 |
| 1945 | 0 | 1949 | 109 | 1953 | 416 | 1957 | 963 | 1961 | 1,544 | 1965 | 2,742 | Total: | $39,229 |
| 1946 | 0 | 1950 | 623 | 1954 | 761 | 1958 | 951 | 1962 | 779 | 1966 | 2,215 | | |
| 1947 | 0 | 1951 | 755 | 1955 | 1,111 | 1959 | 1,104 | 1963 | 1,543 | 1967 | 3,955 | | |

## LIVING ESTATE

| "Buying Term and Investing the Difference" — TOTAL VALUE OF SHARES | Buying Whole Life — CASH VALUE |
|---|---|

## DEATH ESTATE

| "Buying Term and Investing the Difference" — TOTAL VALUE OF SHARES | + DECREASING TERM INSURANCE | = TOTAL DEATH ESTATE | Buying Whole Life — FACE VALUE |
|---|---|---|---|

| LIVING ESTATE – TOTAL VALUE OF SHARES | LIVING ESTATE – CASH VALUE | AGE | DEATH ESTATE – TOTAL VALUE OF SHARES | + DECREASING TERM INSURANCE | = TOTAL DEATH ESTATE | FACE VALUE |
|---|---|---|---|---|---|---|
| $ 1,406 | $ 0 | 41 | $ 1,406 | $100,000 | $101,406 | $75,000 |
| 3,530 | 225 | 42 | 3,530 | 95,000 | 98,530 | 75,000 |
| 4,209 | 1,575 | 43 | 4,209 | 90,000 | 94,209 | 75,000 |
| 5,343 | 3,000 | 44 | 5,343 | 85,000 | 90,343 | 75,000 |
| 6,498 | 4,425 | 45 | 6,498 | 80,000 | 86,498 | 75,000 |
| 9,076 | 5,925 | 46 | 9,076 | 75,000 | 84,076 | 75,000 |
| 11,962 | 7,425 | 47 | 11,962 | 70,000 | 81,962 | 75,000 |
| 14,984 | 8,925 | 48 | 14,984 | 65,000 | 79,984 | 75,000 |
| 17,215 | 10,425 | 49 | 17,215 | 60,000 | 77,215 | 75,000 |
| 18,234 | 11,925 | 50 | 18,234 | 55,000 | 73,234 | 75,000 |
| 25,557 | 13,500 | 51 | 25,557 | 50,000 | 75,557 | 75,000 |
| 29,810 | 15,000 | 52 | 29,810 | 46,250 | 76,060 | 75,000 |
| 32,449 | 16,575 | 53 | 32,449 | 42,500 | 74,949 | 75,000 |
| 30,742 | 18,150 | 54 | 30,742 | 38,750 | 69,492 | 75,000 |
| 41,537 | 19,725 | 55 | 41,537 | 35,000 | 76,537 | 75,000 |
| 44,613 | 21,300 | 56 | 44,613 | 31,250 | 75,863 | 75,000 |
| 45,181 | 22,950 | 57 | 45,181 | 28,750 | 73,931 | 75,000 |
| 56,775 | 24,525 | 58 | 56,775 | 26,250 | 83,025 | 75,000 |
| 49,748 | 26,100 | 59 | 49,748 | 23,750 | 73,498 | 75,000 |
| 59,177 | 27,750 | 60 | 59,177 | 21,250 | 80,427 | 75,000 |
| 67,539 | 29,250 | 61 | 67,539 | 18,750 | 86,289 | 75,000 |
| 80,841 | 30,750 | 62 | 80,841 | 17,500 | 98,341 | 75,000 |
| 77,536 | 32,175 | 63 | 77,536 | 16,250 | 93,787 | 75,000 |
| 99,014 | 33,675 | 64 | 90,014 | 15,000 | 105,014 | 75,000 |
| 102,799 | 35,175 | 65 | 102,799 | 14,400 | 117,199 | 75,000 |

Whether you **lived** or **died** you would have been better off "Buying Term and Investing the Difference"

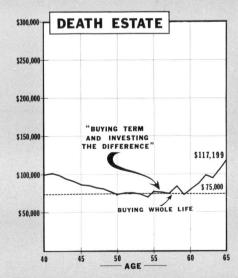

LIVING ESTATE

"BUYING TERM AND INVESTING THE DIFFERENCE" $102,799

$35,175 — BUYING WHOLE LIFE

DEATH ESTATE

"BUYING TERM AND INVESTING THE DIFFERENCE" $117,199

$75,000 — BUYING WHOLE LIFE

# FOUNDERS MUTUAL FUND

Illustration of assumed annual investments of $1,269 for twenty-five years from 1944 to 1968. All dividends and distributions reinvested.

This tabulation covers an illustration of an assumed investment of $1,269 annually on January 1 of each year from 1944 through 1968. This was a period in which stock prices fluctuated widely because of changing business and economic conditions, and were significantly higher at the end of the period than at the beginning. Thus, these results should not be considered as a representation of the dividend income or capital gain or loss that may be realized from an investment made in the fund today. A program of the type illustrated does not assure a profit nor protect against depreciation in declining markets.

| | | COST OF SHARES | | | | VALUE OF SHARES | | | | |
|---|---|---|---|---|---|---|---|---|---|---|
| YEAR ENDING DEC. 31 | AGE | CUMULATIVE ANNUAL INVESTMENTS | ANNUAL INCOME DIVIDENDS REINVESTED | CUMULATIVE COST OF SHARES PURCHASED WITH DIVIDENDS | TOTAL COST (INCLUDES REINVESTED DIVIDENDS) | ACQUIRED THROUGH ANNUAL INVESTMENTS | ACCEPTED AS CAPITAL GAINS DISTRIBUTIONS (CUMULATIVE) | SUBTOTAL | PURCHASED THROUGH REINVESTMENT OF INCOME (CUMULATIVE) | TOTAL VALUE |
| 1944 | 41 | $ 1,269 | $ 43 | $ 43 | $ 1,312 | $ 1,278 | $ 0 | $ 1,279 | $ 46 | $ 1,325 |
| 1945 | 42 | 2,538 | 78 | 122 | 2,660 | 3,129 | 0 | 3,130 | 151 | 3,281 |
| 1946 | 43 | 3,807 | 117 | 239 | 4,047 | 4,028 | 0 | 4,028 | 259 | 4,287 |
| 1947 | 44 | 5,077 | 196 | 436 | 5,513 | 5,219 | 8 | 5,227 | 472 | 5,699 |
| 1948 | 45 | 6,346 | 295 | 731 | 7,078 | 6,156 | 8 | 6,164 | 760 | 6,924 |
| 1949 | 46 | 7,615 | 422 | 1,154 | 8,770 | 8,160 | 11 | 8,171 | 1,325 | 9,496 |
| 1950 | 47 | 8,884 | 559 | 1,713 | 10,598 | 11,439 | 74 | 11,513 | 2,270 | 13,783 |
| 1951 | 48 | 10,154 | 1,004 | 2,717 | 12,872 | 14,049 | 86 | 14,135 | 3,601 | 17,736 |
| 1952 | 49 | 11,423 | 821 | 3,538 | 14,962 | 16,493 | 93 | 16,586 | 4,784 | 21,370 |
| 1953 | 50 | 12,692 | 902 | 4,441 | 17,134 | 16,693 | 91 | 16,782 | 5,448 | 22,230 |
| 1954 | 51 | 13,961 | 1,042 | 5,483 | 19,446 | 26,178 | 208 | 26,386 | 9,239 | 35,625 |
| 1955 | 52 | 15,231 | 1,125 | 6,608 | 21,840 | 33,859 | 285 | 34,144 | 12,691 | 46,835 |
| 1956 | 53 | 16,500 | 1,376 | 7,985 | 24,486 | 37,387 | 369 | 37,756 | 14,939 | 52,695 |
| 1957 | 54 | 17,769 | 1,348 | 9,333 | 27,104 | 33,717 | 574 | 34,291 | 14,139 | 48,430 |
| 1958 | 55 | 19,038 | 1,727 | 11,061 | 30,101 | 49,921 | 1,169 | 51,090 | 22,063 | 73,153 |
| 1959 | 56 | 20,308 | 1,666 | 12,727 | 33,036 | 57,538 | 1,317 | 58,855 | 26,600 | 85,455 |
| 1960 | 57 | 21,577 | 1,882 | 14,609 | 36,187 | 56,908 | 1,277 | 58,185 | 27,736 | 85,921 |
| 1961 | 58 | 22,846 | 2,006 | 16,616 | 39,463 | 70,705 | 1,812 | 72,517 | 35,675 | 108,192 |
| 1962 | 59 | 24,115 | 2,315 | 18,932 | 43,048 | 60,554 | 1,526 | 62,080 | 32,365 | 94,445 |
| 1963 | 60 | 25,385 | 2,647 | 21,579 | 46,965 | 74,749 | 2,041 | 76,790 | 41,912 | 118,702 |
| 1964 | 61 | 26,654 | 3,865 | 25,445 | 52,099 | 87,902 | 2,649 | 90,551 | 52,636 | 143,187 |
| 1965 | 62 | 27,923 | 3,915 | 29,361 | 57,285 | 100,756 | 3,106 | 103,863 | 63,740 | 167,603 |
| 1966 | 63 | 29,192 | 4,702 | 34,063 | 63,257 | 85,105 | 2,948 | 88,053 | 57,351 | 145,404 |
| 1967 | 64 | 30,462 | 4,956 | 39,020 | 69,483 | 103,308 | 4,477 | 107,785 | 73,069 | 180,854 |
| 1968 | 65 | 31,731 | 5,438 | 44,458 | 76,190 | 111,125 | 5,084 | 116,209 | 83,439 | 199,648 |

The total cost figures represent the cumulative total of yearly investments of $1,269 plus the cumulative amount of income dividends reinvested, and include the sales charge of **8½%** on all shares so purchased, as described in the prospectus. No adjustment has been made for any income taxes payable by shareholders on security distributions and dividends reinvested in shares. The dollar amounts of security profits distributions taken in shares were:

| | | | | | | | | | | | | | |
|---|---|---|---|---|---|---|---|---|---|---|---|---|---|
| 1944 | 0 | 1948 | 0 | 1952 | .09 | 1956 | 65 | 1960 | 0 | 1964 | 273 | 1968 | 304 |
| 1945 | 0 | 1949 | 2 | 1953 | .21 | 1957 | 98 | 1961 | 24 | 1965 | 99 | Total: | $1,180 |
| 1946 | 0 | 1950 | 54 | 1954 | 65 | 1958 | 16 | 1962 | 0 | 1966 | 34 | | |
| 1947 | 7 | 1951 | 2 | 1955 | 26 | 1959 | 0 | 1963 | 18 | 1967 | 93 | | |

| LIVING ESTATE "Buying Term and Investing the Difference" TOTAL VALUE OF SHARES | LIVING ESTATE Buying Whole Life CASH VALUE | AGE | DEATH ESTATE "Buying Term and Investing the Difference" TOTAL VALUE OF SHARES | + DECREASING TERM INSURANCE | = TOTAL DEATH ESTATE | DEATH ESTATE Buying Whole Life FACE VALUE |
|---|---|---|---|---|---|---|
| $ 1,325 | $ 0 | 41 | $ 1,325 | $100,000 | $101,325 | $75,000 |
| 3,281 | 225 | 42 | 3,281 | 95,000 | 98,281 | 75,000 |
| 4,287 | 1,575 | 43 | 4,287 | 90,000 | 94,287 | 75,000 |
| 5,699 | 3,000 | 44 | 5,699 | 85,000 | 90,699 | 75,000 |
| 6,924 | 4,425 | 45 | 6,924 | 80,000 | 86,924 | 75,000 |
| 9,496 | 5,925 | 46 | 9,496 | 75,000 | 84,496 | 75,000 |
| 13,783 | 7,425 | 47 | 13,783 | 70,000 | 83,783 | 75,000 |
| 17,736 | 8,925 | 48 | 17,736 | 65,000 | 82,736 | 75,000 |
| 21,370 | 10,425 | 49 | 21,370 | 60,000 | 81,370 | 75,000 |
| 22,230 | 11,925 | 50 | 22,230 | 55,000 | 77,230 | 75,000 |
| 35,625 | 13,500 | 51 | 35,625 | 50,000 | 85,625 | 75,000 |
| 46,835 | 15,000 | 52 | 46,835 | 46,250 | 93,085 | 75,000 |
| 52,695 | 16,575 | 53 | 52,695 | 42,500 | 95,195 | 75,000 |
| 48,430 | 18,150 | 54 | 48,430 | 38,750 | 87,180 | 75,000 |
| 73,153 | 19,725 | 55 | 73,153 | 35,000 | 108,153 | 75,000 |
| 85,455 | 21,300 | 56 | 85,455 | 31,250 | 116,705 | 75,000 |
| 85,921 | 22,950 | 57 | 85,921 | 28,750 | 114,671 | 75,000 |
| 108,192 | 24,525 | 58 | 108,192 | 26,250 | 134,442 | 75,000 |
| 94,445 | 26,100 | 59 | 94,445 | 23,750 | 118,195 | 75,000 |
| 118,702 | 27,750 | 60 | 118,702 | 21,250 | 139,952 | 75,000 |
| 143,187 | 29,250 | 61 | 143,187 | 18,750 | 161,937 | 75,000 |
| 167,603 | 30,750 | 62 | 167,603 | 17,500 | 185,103 | 75,000 |
| 145,404 | 32,175 | 63 | 145,404 | 16,250 | 161,654 | 75,000 |
| 180,854 | 33,675 | 64 | 180,854 | 15,000 | 196,854 | 75,000 |
| 199,648 | 35,175 | 65 | 199,648 | 14,400 | 214,048 | 75,000 |

Whether you
**lived** or **died**
you would have been better off
"Buying Term and Investing the Difference"

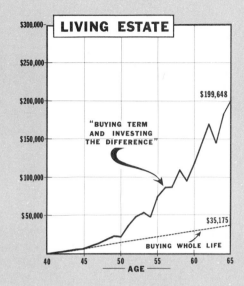

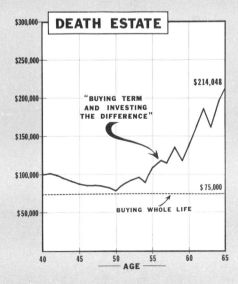

# FUNDAMENTAL INVESTORS

Illustration of assumed annual investments of $1,269 for twenty-five years from 1944 to 1968. All dividends and distributions reinvested.

This tabulation covers an illustration of an assumed investment of $1,269 annually on January 1 of each year from 1944 through 1968. This was a period in which stock prices fluctuated widely because of changing business and economic conditions, and were significantly higher at the end of the period than at the beginning. Thus, these results should not be considered as a representation of the dividend income or capital gain or loss that may be realized from an investment made in the fund today. A program of the type illustrated does not assure a profit nor protect against depreciation in declining markets.

|  |  | COST OF SHARES | | | | VALUE OF SHARES | | | | |
| YEAR ENDING DEC. 31 | AGE | CUMULATIVE ANNUAL INVESTMENTS | ANNUAL INCOME DIVIDENDS REINVESTED | CUMULATIVE COST OF SHARES PURCHASED WITH DIVIDENDS | TOTAL COST (INCLUDES REINVESTED DIVIDENDS) | ACQUIRED THROUGH ANNUAL INVESTMENTS | ACCEPTED AS CAPITAL GAINS DISTRIBUTIONS (CUMULATIVE) | SUBTOTAL | PURCHASED THROUGH REINVESTMENT OF INCOME (CUMULATIVE) | TOTAL VALUE |
|---|---|---|---|---|---|---|---|---|---|---|
| 1944 | 41 | $ 1,269 | $ 37 | $ 37 | $ 1,307 | $ 1,376 | $ 30 | $ 1,406 | $ 37 | $ 1,443 |
| 1945 | 42 | 2,538 | 73 | 110 | 2,649 | 3,431 | 213 | 3,644 | 127 | 3,771 |
| 1946 | 43 | 3,807 | 77 | 188 | 3,996 | 3,879 | 439 | 4,318 | 167 | 4,485 |
| 1947 | 44 | 5,077 | 199 | 387 | 5,464 | 4,872 | 500 | 5,372 | 347 | 5,719 |
| 1948 | 45 | 6,346 | 360 | 747 | 7,094 | 5,815 | 505 | 6,320 | 653 | 6,973 |
| 1949 | 46 | 7,615 | 426 | 1,173 | 8,790 | 7,906 | 631 | 8,537 | 1,168 | 9,705 |
| 1950 | 47 | 8,884 | 629 | 1,803 | 10,688 | 10,723 | 956 | 11,679 | 1,981 | 13,660 |
| 1951 | 48 | 10,154 | 810 | 2,614 | 12,768 | 13,155 | 1,521 | 14,676 | 2,946 | 17,622 |
| 1952 | 49 | 11,423 | 878 | 3,492 | 14,916 | 15,074 | 2,064 | 17,138 | 3,928 | 21,066 |
| 1953 | 50 | 12,692 | 997 | 4,490 | 17,183 | 15,003 | 2,010 | 17,013 | 4,560 | 21,573 |
| 1954 | 51 | 13,961 | 1,126 | 5,616 | 19,578 | 22,908 | 4,053 | 26,961 | 7,672 | 34,633 |
| 1955 | 52 | 15,231 | 1,314 | 6,930 | 22,162 | 27,836 | 6,328 | 34,164 | 10,113 | 44,277 |
| 1956 | 53 | 16,500 | 1,500 | 8,431 | 24,932 | 30,713 | 8,577 | 39,290 | 12,057 | 51,347 |
| 1957 | 54 | 17,769 | 1,642 | 10,117 | 27,888 | 25,790 | 7,966 | 33,756 | 11,125 | 44,881 |
| 1958 | 55 | 19,038 | 1,651 | 11,769 | 30,808 | 36,762 | 12,288 | 49,050 | 16,950 | 66,000 |
| 1959 | 56 | 20,308 | 1,705 | 13,475 | 33,783 | 40,158 | 14,810 | 54,968 | 19,510 | 74,478 |
| 1960 | 57 | 21,577 | 1,814 | 15,289 | 36,867 | 38,151 | 15,994 | 54,145 | 19,674 | 73,819 |
| 1961 | 58 | 22,846 | 1,988 | 17,278 | 40,126 | 47,025 | 21,933 | 68,958 | 25,365 | 94,323 |
| 1962 | 59 | 24,115 | 2,164 | 19,443 | 43,559 | 40,384 | 20,578 | 60,962 | 23,212 | 84,174 |
| 1963 | 60 | 25,385 | 2,356 | 21,799 | 47,185 | 46,656 | 26,145 | 72,801 | 28,260 | 101,061 |
| 1964 | 61 | 26,654 | 2,562 | 24,362 | 51,017 | 53,229 | 32,828 | 86,057 | 33,840 | 119,897 |
| 1965 | 62 | 27,923 | 2,780 | 27,142 | 55,067 | 61,055 | 42,835 | 103,890 | 40,637 | 144,527 |
| 1966 | 63 | 29,192 | 3,038 | 30,180 | 59,374 | 50,774 | 47,040 | 97,814 | 35,607 | 133,421 |
| 1967 | 64 | 30,462 | 3,308 | 33,489 | 63,952 | 59,435 | 65,939 | 125,374 | 43,762 | 169,136 |
| 1968 | 65 | 31,731 | 3,660 | 37,149 | 68,882 | 58,588 | 75,996 | 134,585 | 45,576 | 180,161 |

The total cost figures represent the cumulative total of yearly investments of $1,269 plus the cumulative amount of income dividends reinvested, and include the sales charge of 8¾% on all shares so purchased, as described in the prospectus. No adjustment has been made for any income taxes payable by shareholders on security distributions and dividends reinvested in shares. The dollar amounts of security profits distributions taken in shares were:

| 1944 | 30 | 1948 | 23 | 1952 | 453 | 1956 | 1,855 | 1960 | 2,321 | 1964 | 3,737 | 1968 | 12,149 |
|---|---|---|---|---|---|---|---|---|---|---|---|---|---|
| 1945 | 174 | 1949 | 58 | 1953 | 102 | 1957 | 1,016 | 1961 | 2,826 | 1965 | 5,958 | Total: | $67,060 |
| 1946 | 259 | 1950 | 209 | 1954 | 1,154 | 1958 | 1,415 | 1962 | 2,198 | 1966 | 12,075 | | |
| 1947 | 75 | 1951 | 457 | 1955 | 1,637 | 1959 | 1,803 | 1963 | 3,024 | 1967 | 12,052 | | |

## LIVING ESTATE

| "Buying Term and Investing the Difference" | Buying Whole Life |
|---|---|
| TOTAL VALUE OF SHARES | CASH VALUE |
| $ 1,443 | $ 0 |
| 3,771 | 225 |
| 4,485 | 1,575 |
| 5,719 | 3,000 |
| 6,973 | 4,425 |
| 9,705 | 5,925 |
| 13,660 | 7,425 |
| 17,622 | 8,925 |
| 21,066 | 10,425 |
| 21,573 | 11,925 |
| 34,633 | 13,500 |
| 44,277 | 15,000 |
| 51,347 | 16,575 |
| 44,881 | 18,150 |
| 66,000 | 19,725 |
| 74,478 | 21,300 |
| 73,819 | 22,950 |
| 94,323 | 24,525 |
| 84,174 | 26,100 |
| 101,061 | 27,750 |
| 119,897 | 29,250 |
| 144,527 | 30,750 |
| 133,421 | 32,175 |
| 169,136 | 33,675 |
| 180,161 | 35,175 |

## DEATH ESTATE

| AGE | "Buying Term and Investing the Difference" TOTAL VALUE OF SHARES | + DECREASING TERM INSURANCE | = TOTAL DEATH ESTATE | Buying Whole Life FACE VALUE |
|---|---|---|---|---|
| 41 | $ 1,443 | $100,000 | $101,443 | $75,000 |
| 42 | 3,771 | 95,000 | 98,771 | 75,000 |
| 43 | 4,485 | 90,000 | 94,485 | 75,000 |
| 44 | 5,719 | 85,000 | 90,719 | 75,000 |
| 45 | 6,973 | 80,000 | 86,973 | 75,000 |
| 46 | 9,705 | 75,000 | 84,705 | 75,000 |
| 47 | 13,660 | 70,000 | 83,660 | 75,000 |
| 48 | 17,622 | 65,000 | 82,622 | 75,000 |
| 49 | 21,066 | 60,000 | 81,066 | 75,000 |
| 50 | 21,573 | 55,000 | 76,573 | 75,000 |
| 51 | 34,633 | 50,000 | 84,633 | 75,000 |
| 52 | 44,277 | 46,250 | 90,527 | 75,000 |
| 53 | 51,347 | 42,500 | 93,847 | 75,000 |
| 54 | 44,881 | 38,750 | 83,631 | 75,000 |
| 55 | 66,000 | 35,000 | 101,000 | 75,000 |
| 56 | 74,478 | 31,250 | 105,728 | 75,000 |
| 57 | 73,819 | 28,750 | 102,569 | 75,000 |
| 58 | 94,323 | 26,250 | 120,573 | 75,000 |
| 59 | 84,174 | 23,750 | 107,924 | 75,000 |
| 60 | 101,061 | 21,250 | 122,311 | 75,000 |
| 61 | 119,897 | 18,750 | 138,647 | 75,000 |
| 62 | 144,527 | 17,500 | 162,027 | 75,000 |
| 63 | 133,421 | 16,250 | 149,671 | 75,000 |
| 64 | 169,136 | 15,000 | 184,136 | 75,000 |
| 65 | 180,161 | 14,400 | 194,561 | 75,000 |

Whether you
**lived** or **died**
you would have been better off
"Buying Term and Investing the Difference"

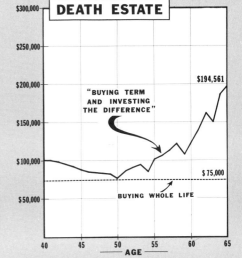

LIVING ESTATE

$300,000 — $250,000 — $200,000 — $150,000 — $100,000 — $50,000

$180,161

"BUYING TERM AND INVESTING THE DIFFERENCE"

$35,175

BUYING WHOLE LIFE

AGE 40 45 50 55 60 65

DEATH ESTATE

$300,000 — $250,000 — $200,000 — $150,000 — $100,000 — $50,000

$194,561

"BUYING TERM AND INVESTING THE DIFFERENCE"

$75,000

BUYING WHOLE LIFE

AGE 40 45 50 55 60 65

# GROUP SECURITIES — COMMON STOCK FUND

Illustration of assumed annual investments of $1,269 for twenty-five years from 1944 to 1968. All dividends and distributions reinvested.

This tabulation covers an illustration of an assumed investment of $1,269 annually on January 1 of each year from 1944 through 1968. This was a period in which stock prices fluctuated widely because of changing business and economic conditions, and were significantly higher at the end of the period than at the beginning. Thus, these results should not be considered as a representation of the dividend income or capital gain or loss that may be realized from an investment made in the fund today. A program of the type illustrated does not assure a profit nor protect against depreciation in declining markets.

| | | COST OF SHARES | | | | VALUE OF SHARES | | | | |
|---|---|---|---|---|---|---|---|---|---|---|
| YEAR ENDING DEC. 31 | AGE | CUMULATIVE ANNUAL INVEST-MENTS | ANNUAL INCOME DIVIDENDS REIN-VESTED | CUMULA-TIVE COST OF SHARES PURCHASED WITH DIVIDENDS | TOTAL COST (INCLUDES REIN-VESTED DIVIDENDS) | ACQUIRED THROUGH ANNUAL INVEST-MENTS | ACCEPTED AS CAPITAL GAINS DIS-TRIBUTIONS (CUMU-LATIVE) | SUB-TOTAL | PURCHASED THROUGH REINVEST-MENT OF INCOME (CUMULATIVE) | TOTAL VALUE |
| 1944 | 41 | $ 1,269 | $ 49 | $ 49 | $ 1,318 | $ 1,231 | $ 23 | $ 1,254 | $ 50 | $ 1,304 |
| 1945 | 42 | 2,538 | 83 | 133 | 2,672 | 3,124 | 140 | 3,264 | 159 | 3,423 |
| 1946 | 43 | 3,807 | 125 | 258 | 4,065 | 3,338 | 372 | 3,710 | 225 | 3,935 |
| 1947 | 44 | 5,077 | 215 | 473 | 5,550 | 4,598 | 491 | 5,089 | 459 | 5,548 |
| 1948 | 45 | 6,346 | 319 | 793 | 7,140 | 4,900 | 476 | 5,376 | 687 | 6,063 |
| 1949 | 46 | 7,615 | 443 | 1,236 | 8,852 | 6,805 | 533 | 7,338 | 1,264 | 8,602 |
| 1950 | 47 | 8,884 | 693 | 1,929 | 10,814 | 9,327 | 623 | 9,950 | 2,237 | 12,187 |
| 1951 | 48 | 10,154 | 874 | 2,804 | 12,958 | 10,941 | 704 | 11,645 | 3,226 | 14,871 |
| 1952 | 49 | 11,423 | 927 | 3,731 | 15,155 | 12,998 | 899 | 13,897 | 4,450 | 18,347 |
| 1953 | 50 | 12,692 | 1,093 | 4,825 | 17,518 | 13,054 | 961 | 14,015 | 5,176 | 19,191 |
| 1954 | 51 | 13,961 | 1,235 | 6,060 | 20,022 | 19,615 | 1,679 | 21,294 | 8,622 | 29,916 |
| 1955 | 52 | 15,231 | 1,415 | 7,475 | 22,707 | 21,591 | 5,316 | 26,907 | 10,375 | 37,282 |
| 1956 | 53 | 16,500 | 1,783 | 9,259 | 25,760 | 21,796 | 7,429 | 29,225 | 11,663 | 40,888 |
| 1957 | 54 | 17,769 | 2,002 | 11,261 | 29,031 | 19,443 | 7,995 | 27,438 | 11,710 | 39,148 |
| 1958 | 55 | 19,038 | 2,223 | 13,484 | 32,524 | 27,326 | 11,704 | 39,030 | 18,043 | 57,073 |
| 1959 | 56 | 20,308 | 2,366 | 15,851 | 36,160 | 27,866 | 14,272 | 42,138 | 19,905 | 62,043 |
| 1960 | 57 | 21,577 | 2,681 | 18,532 | 40,110 | 27,745 | 15,031 | 42,776 | 21,742 | 64,518 |
| 1961 | 58 | 22,846 | 2,797 | 21,329 | 44,177 | 34,076 | 22,472 | 56,548 | 28,466 | 85,014 |
| 1962 | 59 | 24,115 | 2,992 | 24,322 | 48,439 | 29,356 | 20,575 | 49,931 | 26,634 | 76,565 |
| 1963 | 60 | 25,385 | 3,240 | 27,563 | 52,949 | 34,227 | 25,956 | 60,183 | 33,189 | 93,372 |
| 1964 | 61 | 26,654 | 3,582 | 31,145 | 57,801 | 38,584 | 32,091 | 70,675 | 39,808 | 110,483 |
| 1965 | 62 | 27,923 | 4,033 | 35,179 | 63,104 | 41,766 | 38,510 | 80,276 | 45,923 | 126,199 |
| 1966 | 63 | 29,192 | 4,806 | 39,985 | 69,179 | 35,417 | 36,758 | 72,175 | 42,222 | 114,397 |
| 1967 | 64 | 30,462 | 5,289 | 45,276 | 75,739 | 39,576 | 45,732 | 85,308 | 50,853 | 136,161 |
| 1968 | 65 | 31,731 | 5,707 | 50,983 | 82,715 | 45,640 | 59,225 | 104,865 | 63,202 | 168,067 |

The total cost figures represent the cumulative total of yearly investments of $1,269 plus the cumulative amount of income dividends reinvested, and include the sales charge of 8½% on all shares so purchased, as described in the prospectus. No adjustment has been made for any income taxes payable by shareholders on security distributions and dividends reinvested in shares. The dollar amounts of security profits distributions taken in shares were:

| | | | | | | | | | | | | | |
|---|---|---|---|---|---|---|---|---|---|---|---|---|---|
| 1944 | 22 | 1948 | 66 | 1952 | 138 | 1956 | 2,304 | 1960 | 1,335 | 1964 | 3,918 | 1968 | 7,654 |
| 1945 | 107 | 1949 | 0 | 1953 | 134 | 1957 | 1,696 | 1961 | 4,727 | 1965 | 4,710 | Total: | $50,181 |
| 1946 | 264 | 1950 | 0 | 1954 | 327 | 1958 | 1,066 | 1962 | 1,734 | 1966 | 5,044 | | |
| 1947 | 106 | 1951 | 51 | 1955 | 3,455 | 1959 | 2,768 | 1963 | 2,815 | 1967 | 5,740 | | |

## LIVING ESTATE

| "Buying Term and Investing the Difference" — TOTAL VALUE OF SHARES | Buying Whole Life — CASH VALUE |
|---|---|
| $ 1,304 | $ 0 |
| 3,423 | 225 |
| 3,935 | 1,575 |
| 5,548 | 3,000 |
| 6,063 | 4,425 |
| 8,602 | 5,925 |
| 12,187 | 7,425 |
| 14,871 | 8,925 |
| 18,347 | 10,425 |
| 19,191 | 11,925 |
| 29,916 | 13,500 |
| 37,282 | 15,000 |
| 40,888 | 16,575 |
| 39,148 | 18,150 |
| 57,073 | 19,725 |
| 62,043 | 21,300 |
| 64,518 | 22,950 |
| 85,014 | 24,525 |
| 76,565 | 26,100 |
| 93,372 | 27,750 |
| 110,483 | 29,250 |
| 126,199 | 30,750 |
| 114,397 | 32,175 |
| 136,161 | 33,675 |
| 168,067 | 35,175 |

## AGE / DEATH ESTATE

| AGE | "Buying Term and Investing the Difference" — TOTAL VALUE OF SHARES | + DECREASING TERM INSURANCE | = TOTAL DEATH ESTATE | Buying Whole Life — FACE VALUE |
|---|---|---|---|---|
| 41 | $ 1,304 | $100,000 | $101,304 | $75,000 |
| 42 | 3,423 | 95,000 | 98,423 | 75,000 |
| 43 | 3,935 | 90,000 | 93,935 | 75,000 |
| 44 | 5,548 | 85,000 | 90,548 | 75,000 |
| 45 | 6,063 | 80,000 | 86,063 | 75,000 |
| 46 | 8,602 | 75,000 | 83,602 | 75,000 |
| 47 | 12,187 | 70,000 | 82,187 | 75,000 |
| 48 | 14,871 | 65,000 | 79,871 | 75,000 |
| 49 | 18,347 | 60,000 | 78,347 | 75,000 |
| 50 | 19,191 | 55,000 | 74,191 | 75,000 |
| 51 | 29,916 | 50,000 | 79,916 | 75,000 |
| 52 | 37,282 | 46,250 | 83,532 | 75,000 |
| 53 | 40,888 | 42,500 | 83,388 | 75,000 |
| 54 | 39,148 | 38,750 | 77,898 | 75,000 |
| 55 | 57,073 | 35,000 | 92,073 | 75,000 |
| 56 | 62,043 | 31,250 | 93,293 | 75,000 |
| 57 | 64,518 | 28,750 | 93,268 | 75,000 |
| 58 | 85,014 | 26,250 | 111,264 | 75,000 |
| 59 | 76,565 | 23,750 | 100,315 | 75,000 |
| 60 | 93,372 | 21,250 | 114,622 | 75,000 |
| 61 | 110,483 | 18,750 | 129,233 | 75,000 |
| 62 | 126,199 | 17,500 | 143,699 | 75,000 |
| 63 | 114,397 | 16,250 | 130,647 | 75,000 |
| 64 | 136,161 | 15,000 | 151,161 | 75,000 |
| 65 | 168,067 | 14,400 | 182,467 | 75,000 |

Whether you
**lived** or **died**
you would have been better off
"Buying Term and Investing the Difference"

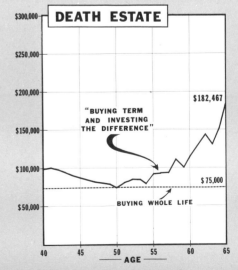

LIVING ESTATE

"BUYING TERM AND INVESTING THE DIFFERENCE"  $168,067

BUYING WHOLE LIFE  $35,175

DEATH ESTATE

"BUYING TERM AND INVESTING THE DIFFERENCE"  $182,467

BUYING WHOLE LIFE  $75,000

# INVESTMENT COMPANY OF AMERICA

Illustration of assumed annual investments of $1,269 for twenty-five years from 1944 to 1968. All dividends and distributions reinvested.

This tabulation covers an illustration of an assumed investment of $1,269 annually on January 1 of each year from 1944 through 1968. This was a period in which stock prices fluctuated widely because of changing business and economic conditions, and were significantly higher at the end of the period than at the beginning. Thus, these results should not be considered as a representation of the dividend income or capital gain or loss that may be realized from an investment made in the fund today. A program of the type illustrated does not assure a profit nor protect against depreciation in declining markets.

| | | COST OF SHARES | | | | VALUE OF SHARES | | | | |
|---|---|---|---|---|---|---|---|---|---|---|
| YEAR ENDING DEC. 31 | AGE | CUMULATIVE ANNUAL INVESTMENTS | ANNUAL INCOME DIVIDENDS REINVESTED | CUMULATIVE COST OF SHARES PURCHASED WITH DIVIDENDS | TOTAL COST (INCLUDES REINVESTED DIVIDENDS) | ACQUIRED THROUGH ANNUAL INVESTMENTS | ACCEPTED AS CAPITAL GAINS DISTRIBUTIONS (CUMULATIVE) | SUB-TOTAL | PURCHASED THROUGH REINVESTMENT OF INCOME (CUMULATIVE) | TOTAL VALUE |
| 1944 | 41 | $ 1,269 | $ 42 | $ 42 | $ 1,311 | $ 1,338 | $ 51 | $ 1,389 | $ 43 | $ 1,432 |
| 1945 | 42 | 2,538 | 71 | 113 | 2,651 | 3,109 | 310 | 3,419 | 130 | 3,549 |
| 1946 | 43 | 3,807 | 140 | 253 | 4,061 | 3,784 | 572 | 4,356 | 246 | 4,602 |
| 1947 | 44 | 5,077 | 245 | 498 | 5,575 | 4,551 | 792 | 5,343 | 468 | 5,811 |
| 1948 | 45 | 6,346 | 322 | 819 | 7,165 | 5,313 | 953 | 6,266 | 742 | 7,008 |
| 1949 | 46 | 7,615 | 373 | 1,192 | 8,808 | 6,526 | 1,271 | 7,797 | 1,136 | 8,933 |
| 1950 | 47 | 8,884 | 498 | 1,689 | 10,574 | 8,540 | 1,773 | 10,313 | 1,782 | 12,095 |
| 1951 | 48 | 10,154 | 587 | 2,276 | 12,430 | 10,512 | 2,598 | 13,110 | 2,525 | 15,635 |
| 1952 | 49 | 11,423 | 658 | 2,934 | 14,357 | 12,046 | 3,492 | 15,538 | 3,266 | 18,804 |
| 1953 | 50 | 12,692 | 791 | 3,725 | 16,418 | 12,393 | 3,806 | 16,199 | 3,858 | 20,057 |
| 1954 | 51 | 13,961 | 875 | 4,599 | 18,561 | 19,533 | 7,038 | 26,571 | 6,555 | 33,126 |
| 1955 | 52 | 15,231 | 1,106 | 5,705 | 20,936 | 23,404 | 11,045 | 34,449 | 8,552 | 43,001 |
| 1956 | 53 | 16,500 | 1,244 | 6,949 | 23,449 | 24,590 | 14,546 | 39,136 | 9,775 | 48,911 |
| 1957 | 54 | 17,769 | 1,413 | 8,362 | 26,132 | 20,699 | 14,304 | 35,003 | 9,120 | 44,123 |
| 1958 | 55 | 19,038 | 1,525 | 9,887 | 28,926 | 29,619 | 21,839 | 51,458 | 14,101 | 65,559 |
| 1959 | 56 | 20,308 | 1,663 | 11,550 | 31,858 | 32,040 | 27,800 | 59,840 | 16,348 | 76,188 |
| 1960 | 57 | 21,577 | 1,958 | 13,508 | 35,085 | 31,897 | 31,244 | 63,141 | 17,718 | 80,859 |
| 1961 | 58 | 22,846 | 2,046 | 15,554 | 38,401 | 37,694 | 40,948 | 78,642 | 22,310 | 100,952 |
| 1962 | 59 | 24,115 | 2,252 | 17,806 | 41,922 | 31,490 | 36,730 | 68,220 | 20,375 | 88,595 |
| 1963 | 60 | 25,385 | 2,407 | 20,213 | 45,598 | 37,502 | 46,875 | 84,378 | 25,916 | 110,294 |
| 1964 | 61 | 26,654 | 2,707 | 22,920 | 49,574 | 41,431 | 57,706 | 99,137 | 30,442 | 129,579 |
| 1965 | 62 | 27,923 | 3,089 | 26,010 | 53,934 | 49,629 | 77,541 | 127,170 | 38,792 | 165,962 |
| 1966 | 63 | 29,192 | 3,985 | 29,994 | 59,187 | 46,425 | 82,978 | 129,403 | 39,365 | 168,768 |
| 1967 | 64 | 30,462 | 4,748 | 34,742 | 65,204 | 56,995 | 110,046 | 167,041 | 51,983 | 219,024 |
| 1968 | 65 | 31,731 | 5,883 | 40,625 | 72,356 | 63,348 | 131,290 | 194,638 | 62,911 | 257,549 |

The total cost figures represent the cumulative total of yearly investments of $1,269 plus the cumulative amount of income dividends reinvested, and include the sales charge of 8½% on all shares so purchased, as described in the prospectus. No adjustment has been made for any income taxes payable by shareholders on security distributions and dividends reinvested in shares. The dollar amounts of security profits distributions taken in shares were:

| | | | | | | | | | | | | | |
|---|---|---|---|---|---|---|---|---|---|---|---|---|---|
| 1944 | 50 | 1948 | 217 | 1952 | 826 | 1956 | 3,511 | 1960 | 4,354 | 1964 | 7,421 | 1968 | 9,310 |
| 1945 | 244 | 1949 | 308 | 1953 | 534 | 1957 | 2,724 | 1961 | 5,233 | 1965 | 9,977 | Total: | $89,745 |
| 1946 | 304 | 1950 | 356 | 1954 | 1,525 | 1958 | 2,265 | 1962 | 3,973 | 1966 | 12,816 | | |
| 1947 | 268 | 1951 | 668 | 1955 | 2,973 | 1959 | 5,003 | 1963 | 4,544 | 1967 | 10,341 | | |

| LIVING ESTATE | | AGE | DEATH ESTATE | | | | |
|---|---|---|---|---|---|---|---|
| "Buying Term and Investing the Difference" TOTAL VALUE OF SHARES | Buying Whole Life CASH VALUE | | "Buying Term and Investing the Difference" TOTAL VALUE OF SHARES | + DECREASING TERM INSURANCE | = TOTAL DEATH ESTATE | Buying Whole Life FACE VALUE | |
| $ 1,432 | $ 0 | 41 | $ 1,432 | $100,000 | $101,432 | $75,000 |
| 3,549 | 225 | 42 | 3,549 | 95,000 | 98,549 | 75,000 |
| 4,602 | 1,575 | 43 | 4,602 | 90,000 | 94,602 | 75,000 |
| 5,811 | 3,000 | 44 | 5,811 | 85,000 | 90,811 | 75,000 |
| 7,008 | 4,425 | 45 | 7,008 | 80,000 | 87,008 | 75,000 |
| 8,933 | 5,925 | 46 | 8,933 | 75,000 | 83,933 | 75,000 |
| 12,095 | 7,425 | 47 | 12,095 | 70,000 | 82,095 | 75,000 |
| 15,635 | 8,925 | 48 | 15,635 | 65,000 | 80,635 | 75,000 |
| 18,804 | 10,425 | 49 | 18,804 | 60,000 | 78,804 | 75,000 |
| 20,057 | 11,925 | 50 | 20,057 | 55,000 | 75,057 | 75,000 |
| 33,126 | 13,500 | 51 | 33,126 | 50,000 | 83,126 | 75,000 |
| 43,001 | 15,000 | 52 | 43,001 | 46,250 | 89,251 | 75,000 |
| 48,911 | 16,575 | 53 | 48,911 | 42,500 | 91,411 | 75,000 |
| 44,123 | 18,150 | 54 | 44,123 | 38,750 | 82,873 | 75,000 |
| 65,559 | 19,725 | 55 | 65,559 | 35,000 | 100,559 | 75,000 |
| 76,188 | 21,300 | 56 | 76,188 | 31,250 | 107,438 | 75,000 |
| 80,859 | 22,950 | 57 | 80,859 | 28,750 | 109,609 | 75,000 |
| 100,952 | 24,525 | 58 | 100,952 | 26,250 | 127,202 | 75,000 |
| 88,595 | 26,100 | 59 | 88,595 | 23,750 | 112,345 | 75,000 |
| 110,294 | 27,750 | 60 | 110,294 | 21,250 | 131,544 | 75,000 |
| 129,579 | 29,250 | 61 | 129,579 | 18,750 | 148,329 | 75,000 |
| 165,962 | 30,750 | 62 | 165,962 | 17,500 | 183,462 | 75,000 |
| 168,768 | 32,175 | 63 | 168,768 | 16,250 | 185,018 | 75,000 |
| 219,024 | 33,675 | 64 | 219,024 | 15,000 | 234,024 | 75,000 |
| 257,549 | 35,175 | 65 | 257,549 | 14,400 | 271,949 | 75,000 |

Whether you **lived** or **died**
you would have been better off
"Buying Term and Investing the Difference"

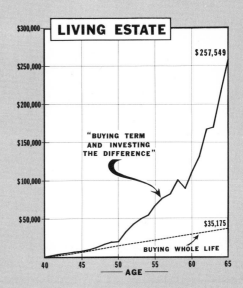

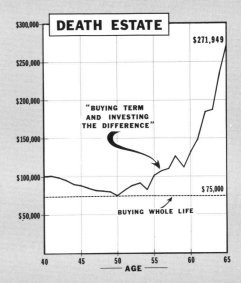

# INVESTORS MUTUAL

Illustration of assumed annual investments of $1,269 for twenty-five years from 1944 to 1968. All dividends and distributions reinvested.

This tabulation covers an illustration of an assumed investment of $1,269 annually on January 1 of each year from 1944 through 1968. This was a period in which stock prices fluctuated widely because of changing business and economic conditions, and were significantly higher at the end of the period than at the beginning. Thus, these results should not be considered as a representation of the dividend income or capital gain or loss that may be realized from an investment made in the fund today. A program of the type illustrated does not assure a profit nor protect against depreciation in declining markets.

| | | COST OF SHARES | | | | VALUE OF SHARES | | | | |
|---|---|---|---|---|---|---|---|---|---|---|
| YEAR ENDING DEC. 31 | AGE | CUMULATIVE ANNUAL INVEST-MENTS | ANNUAL INCOME DIVIDENDS REIN-VESTED | CUMULA-TIVE COST OF SHARES PURCHASED WITH DIVIDENDS | TOTAL COST (INCLUDES REIN-VESTED DIVIDENDS) | ACQUIRED THROUGH ANNUAL INVEST-MENTS | ACCEPTED AS CAPITAL GAINS DIS-TRIBUTIONS (CUMU-LATIVE) | SUB-TOTAL | PURCHASED THROUGH REINVEST-MENT OF INCOME (CUMULATIVE) | TOTAL VALUE |
| 1944 | 41 | $ 1,269 | $ 50 | $ 50 | $ 1,319 | $ 1,308 | $ 44 | $ 1,352 | $ 52 | $ 1,404 |
| 1945 | 42 | 2,538 | 98 | 148 | 2,687 | 2,924 | 120 | 3,044 | 166 | 3,210 |
| 1946 | 43 | 3,807 | 139 | 288 | 4,096 | 3,837 | 313 | 4,150 | 289 | 4,439 |
| 1947 | 44 | 5,077 | 215 | 503 | 5,580 | 4,638 | 356 | 4,994 | 479 | 5,473 |
| 1948 | 45 | 6,346 | 297 | 800 | 7,146 | 5,531 | 444 | 5,975 | 739 | 6,714 |
| 1949 | 46 | 7,615 | 413 | 1,212 | 8,828 | 7,380 | 546 | 7,926 | 1,253 | 9,179 |
| 1950 | 47 | 8,884 | 487 | 1,699 | 10,584 | 9,237 | 700 | 9,937 | 1,856 | 11,793 |
| 1951 | 48 | 10,154 | 631 | 2,330 | 12,484 | 10,891 | 1,047 | 11,938 | 2,577 | 14,515 |
| 1952 | 49 | 11,423 | 710 | 3,040 | 14,463 | 12,672 | 1,363 | 14,035 | 3,438 | 17,473 |
| 1953 | 50 | 12,692 | 817 | 3,857 | 16,550 | 13,321 | 1,522 | 14,843 | 4,132 | 18,975 |
| 1954 | 51 | 13,961 | 945 | 4,802 | 18,764 | 17,914 | 2,200 | 20,114 | 6,119 | 26,233 |
| 1955 | 52 | 15,231 | 1,064 | 5,866 | 21,097 | 20,421 | 2,879 | 23,300 | 7,631 | 30,931 |
| 1956 | 53 | 16,500 | 1,289 | 7,155 | 23,655 | 21,436 | 3,399 | 24,835 | 8,834 | 33,669 |
| 1957 | 54 | 17,769 | 1,400 | 8,555 | 26,325 | 20,406 | 3,362 | 23,768 | 9,282 | 33,050 |
| 1958 | 55 | 19,038 | 1,526 | 10,081 | 29,120 | 27,046 | 4,756 | 31,802 | 13,283 | 45,085 |
| 1959 | 56 | 20,308 | 1,601 | 11,683 | 31,991 | 28,680 | 5,898 | 34,578 | 15,097 | 49,675 |
| 1960 | 57 | 21,577 | 1,789 | 13,472 | 35,049 | 29,790 | 6,282 | 36,072 | 16,888 | 52,960 |
| 1961 | 58 | 22,846 | 1,937 | 15,409 | 38,256 | 35,053 | 7,995 | 43,048 | 21,111 | 64,159 |
| 1962 | 59 | 24,115 | 2,150 | 17,559 | 41,675 | 32,448 | 9,244 | 41,692 | 21,057 | 62,749 |
| 1963 | 60 | 25,385 | 2,371 | 19,930 | 45,315 | 36,462 | 11,248 | 47,710 | 25,219 | 72,929 |
| 1964 | 61 | 26,654 | 2,677 | 22,606 | 49,260 | 39,959 | 13,509 | 53,468 | 29,455 | 82,923 |
| 1965 | 62 | 27,923 | 3,025 | 25,631 | 53,555 | 41,094 | 15,484 | 56,578 | 32,424 | 89,002 |
| 1966 | 63 | 29,192 | 3,289 | 28,919 | 58,112 | 36,838 | 14,803 | 51,641 | 31,423 | 83,064 |
| 1967 | 64 | 30,462 | 3,432 | 32,352 | 62,814 | 40,356 | 17,777 | 58,133 | 36,751 | 94,884 |
| 1968 | 65 | 31,731 | 3,614 | 35,966 | 67,697 | 41,139 | 22,185 | 63,324 | 39,989 | 103,313 |

The total cost figures represent the cumulative total of yearly investments of $1,269 plus the cumulative amount of income dividends reinvested, and include the sales charge of  8%  on all shares so purchased, as described in the prospectus. No adjustment has been made for any income taxes payable by shareholders on security distributions and dividends reinvested in shares. The dollar amounts of security profits distributions taken in shares were:

| | | | | | | | | | | | | |
|---|---|---|---|---|---|---|---|---|---|---|---|---|
| 1944 | 44 | 1948 | 106 | 1952 | 253 | 1956 | 544 | 1960 | 378 | 1964 | 1,569 | 1968 | 4,582 |
| 1945 | 62 | 1949 | 54 | 1953 | 202 | 1957 | 298 | 1961 | 859 | 1965 | 2,002 | Total: $20,513 |
| 1946 | 196 | 1950 | 107 | 1954 | 298 | 1958 | 513 | 1962 | 1,946 | 1966 | 1,274 | |
| 1947 | 68 | 1951 | 314 | 1955 | 512 | 1959 | 1,025 | 1963 | 1,216 | 1967 | 2,091 | |

## LIVING ESTATE

|  | "Buying Term and Investing the Difference" | Buying Whole Life |
| --- | --- | --- |
|  | TOTAL VALUE OF SHARES | CASH VALUE |

## DEATH ESTATE

|  | "Buying Term and Investing the Difference" | | | Buying Whole Life |
| --- | --- | --- | --- | --- |
|  | TOTAL VALUE OF SHARES + | DECREASING TERM INSURANCE = | TOTAL DEATH ESTATE | FACE VALUE |

### Combined table

| LIVING ESTATE — TOTAL VALUE OF SHARES | LIVING ESTATE — CASH VALUE | AGE | DEATH ESTATE — TOTAL VALUE OF SHARES | DECREASING TERM INSURANCE | TOTAL DEATH ESTATE | FACE VALUE |
| --- | --- | --- | --- | --- | --- | --- |
| $ 1,404 | $ 0 | 41 | $ 1,404 | $100,000 | $101,404 | $75,000 |
| 3,210 | 225 | 42 | 3,210 | 95,000 | 98,210 | 75,000 |
| 4,439 | 1,575 | 43 | 4,439 | 90,000 | 94,439 | 75,000 |
| 5,473 | 3,000 | 44 | 5,473 | 85,000 | 90,473 | 75,000 |
| 6,714 | 4,425 | 45 | 6,714 | 80,000 | 86,714 | 75,000 |
| 9,179 | 5,925 | 46 | 9,179 | 75,000 | 84,179 | 75,000 |
| 11,793 | 7,425 | 47 | 11,793 | 70,000 | 81,793 | 75,000 |
| 14,515 | 8,925 | 48 | 14,515 | 65,000 | 79,515 | 75,000 |
| 17,473 | 10,425 | 49 | 17,473 | 60,000 | 77,473 | 75,000 |
| 18,975 | 11,925 | 50 | 18,975 | 55,000 | 73,975 | 75,000 |
| 26,233 | 13,500 | 51 | 26,233 | 50,000 | 76,233 | 75,000 |
| 30,931 | 15,000 | 52 | 30,931 | 46,250 | 77,181 | 75,000 |
| 33,669 | 16,575 | 53 | 33,669 | 42,500 | 76,169 | 75,000 |
| 33,050 | 18,150 | 54 | 33,050 | 38,750 | 71,800 | 75,000 |
| 45,085 | 19,725 | 55 | 45,085 | 35,000 | 80,085 | 75,000 |
| 49,675 | 21,300 | 56 | 49,675 | 31,250 | 80,925 | 75,000 |
| 52,960 | 22,950 | 57 | 52,960 | 28,750 | 81,710 | 75,000 |
| 64,159 | 24,525 | 58 | 64,159 | 26,250 | 90,409 | 75,000 |
| 62,749 | 26,100 | 59 | 62,749 | 23,750 | 86,499 | 75,000 |
| 72,929 | 27,750 | 60 | 72,929 | 21,250 | 94,179 | 75,000 |
| 82,923 | 29,250 | 61 | 82,923 | 18,750 | 101,673 | 75,000 |
| 89,002 | 30,750 | 62 | 89,002 | 17,500 | 106,502 | 75,000 |
| 83,064 | 32,175 | 63 | 83,064 | 16,250 | 99,314 | 75,000 |
| 94,884 | 33,675 | 64 | 94,884 | 15,000 | 109,884 | 75,000 |
| 103,313 | 35,175 | 65 | 103,313 | 14,400 | 117,713 | 75,000 |

Whether you **lived** or **died** you would have been better off "Buying Term and Investing the Difference"

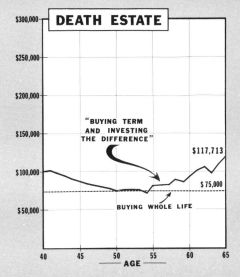

**LIVING ESTATE**

"BUYING TERM AND INVESTING THE DIFFERENCE" — $103,313

BUYING WHOLE LIFE — $35,175

**DEATH ESTATE**

"BUYING TERM AND INVESTING THE DIFFERENCE" — $117,713

BUYING WHOLE LIFE — $75,000

# KEYSTONE K-2

Illustration of assumed annual investments of $1,269 for twenty-five years from 1944 to 1968. All dividends and distributions reinvested.

This tabulation covers an illustration of an assumed investment of $1,269 annually on January 1 of each year from 1944 through 1968. This was a period in which stock prices fluctuated widely because of changing business and economic conditions, and were significantly higher at the end of the period than at the beginning. Thus, these results should not be considered as a representation of the dividend income or capital gain or loss that may be realized from an investment made in the fund today. A program of the type illustrated does not assure a profit nor protect against depreciation in declining markets.

| | | COST OF SHARES | | | | VALUE OF SHARES | | | | |
|---|---|---|---|---|---|---|---|---|---|---|
| YEAR ENDING DEC. 31 | AGE | CUMULATIVE ANNUAL INVEST-MENTS | ANNUAL INCOME DIVIDENDS REIN-VESTED | CUMULA-TIVE COST OF SHARES PURCHASED WITH DIVIDENDS | TOTAL COST (INCLUDES REIN-VESTED DIVIDENDS) | ACQUIRED THROUGH ANNUAL INVEST-MENTS | ACCEPTED AS CAPITAL GAINS DIS-TRIBUTIONS (CUMU-LATIVE) | SUB-TOTAL | PURCHASED THROUGH REINVEST-MENT OF INCOME (CUMULATIVE) | TOTAL VALUE |
| 1944 | 41 | $ 1,269 | $ 48 | $ 48 | $ 1,317 | $ 1,485 | $ 176 | $ 1,661 | $ 47 | $ 1,708 |
| 1945 | 42 | 2,538 | 67 | 115 | 2,654 | 3,326 | 728 | 4,054 | 122 | 4,176 |
| 1946 | 43 | 3,807 | 96 | 212 | 4,020 | 3,395 | 1,069 | 4,464 | 171 | 4,635 |
| 1947 | 44 | 5,077 | 192 | 404 | 5,481 | 4,256 | 1,093 | 5,349 | 340 | 5,689 |
| 1948 | 45 | 6,346 | 297 | 700 | 7,046 | 5,199 | 1,243 | 6,442 | 585 | 7,027 |
| 1949 | 46 | 7,615 | 348 | 1,048 | 8,664 | 7,376 | 1,590 | 8,966 | 1,044 | 10,010 |
| 1950 | 47 | 8,884 | 587 | 1,635 | 10,520 | 9,961 | 2,744 | 12,705 | 1,805 | 14,510 |
| 1951 | 48 | 10,154 | 711 | 2,346 | 12,500 | 11,398 | 3,716 | 15,114 | 2,512 | 17,626 |
| 1952 | 49 | 11,423 | 768 | 3,114 | 14,537 | 12,760 | 4,832 | 17,592 | 3,267 | 20,859 |
| 1953 | 50 | 12,692 | 812 | 3,926 | 16,619 | 11,946 | 6,375 | 18,321 | 3,510 | 21,831 |
| 1954 | 51 | 13,961 | 978 | 4,905 | 18,867 | 17,716 | 10,470 | 28,186 | 5,749 | 33,935 |
| 1955 | 52 | 15,231 | 1,069 | 5,974 | 21,205 | 20,396 | 14,601 | 34,997 | 7,193 | 42,190 |
| 1956 | 53 | 16,500 | 1,222 | 7,196 | 23,696 | 24,030 | 18,124 | 42,154 | 9,221 | 51,375 |
| 1957 | 54 | 17,769 | 1,286 | 8,483 | 26,253 | 18,324 | 15,940 | 34,264 | 7,696 | 41,960 |
| 1958 | 55 | 19,038 | 935 | 9,418 | 28,457 | 28,197 | 24,793 | 52,990 | 12,148 | 65,138 |
| 1959 | 56 | 20,308 | 943 | 10,361 | 30,669 | 32,206 | 30,724 | 62,930 | 14,197 | 77,127 |
| 1960 | 57 | 21,577 | 1,069 | 11,429 | 33,006 | 34,503 | 33,568 | 68,071 | 15,693 | 83,764 |
| 1961 | 58 | 22,846 | 1,008 | 12,437 | 35,284 | 43,079 | 43,335 | 86,414 | 19,862 | 106,276 |
| 1962 | 59 | 24,115 | 1,234 | 13,671 | 37,787 | 34,769 | 35,293 | 70,062 | 16,751 | 86,813 |
| 1963 | 60 | 25,385 | 1,468 | 15,139 | 40,524 | 39,890 | 40,315 | 80,205 | 19,971 | 100,176 |
| 1964 | 61 | 26,654 | 1,332 | 16,471 | 43,125 | 44,049 | 46,484 | 90,533 | 22,666 | 113,199 |
| 1965 | 62 | 27,923 | 1,802 | 18,273 | 46,197 | 52,390 | 68,264 | 120,654 | 27,985 | 148,639 |
| 1966 | 63 | 29,192 | 2,037 | 20,310 | 49,503 | 47,258 | 73,051 | 120,309 | 26,429 | 146,738 |
| 1967 | 64 | 30,462 | 2,278 | 22,588 | 53,050 | 60,731 | 119,757 | 180,488 | 35,365 | 215,853 |
| 1968 | 65 | 31,731 | 1,774 | 24,362 | 56,093 | 56,334 | 138,726 | 195,060 | 33,676 | 228,736 |

The total cost figures represent the cumulative total of yearly investments of $1,269 plus the cumulative amount of income dividends reinvested, and include the sales charge of **8⅓%** on all shares so purchased, as described in the prospectus. No adjustment has been made for any income taxes payable by shareholders on security distributions and dividends reinvested in shares. The dollar amounts of security profits distributions taken in shares were:

| | | | | | | | | | | | | | |
|---|---|---|---|---|---|---|---|---|---|---|---|---|---|
| 1944 | 175 | 1948 | 189 | 1952 | 1,038 | 1956 | 1,730 | 1960 | 1,714 | 1964 | 3,248 | 1968 | 31,411 |
| 1945 | 508 | 1949 | 140 | 1953 | 2,208 | 1957 | 2,920 | 1961 | 2,862 | 1965 | 14,073 | Total: | $116,311 |
| 1946 | 502 | 1950 | 823 | 1954 | 1,733 | 1958 | 1,645 | 1962 | 1,236 | 1966 | 12,719 | | |
| 1947 | 103 | 1951 | 876 | 1955 | 3,194 | 1959 | 3,482 | 1963 | 1,105 | 1967 | 26,677 | | |

| LIVING ESTATE | | AGE | DEATH ESTATE | | | |
|---|---|---|---|---|---|---|
| "Buying Term and Investing the Difference" | Buying Whole Life | | "Buying Term and Investing the Difference" | | Buying Whole Life | |
| TOTAL VALUE OF SHARES | CASH VALUE | | TOTAL VALUE OF SHARES | + DECREASING TERM INSURANCE | = TOTAL DEATH ESTATE | FACE VALUE |
| $ 1,708 | $ 0 | 41 | $ 1,708 | $100,000 | $101,708 | $75,000 |
| 4,176 | 225 | 42 | 4,176 | 95,000 | 99,176 | 75,000 |
| 4,635 | 1,575 | 43 | 4,635 | 90,000 | 94,635 | 75,000 |
| 5,689 | 3,000 | 44 | 5,689 | 85,000 | 90,689 | 75,000 |
| 7,027 | 4,425 | 45 | 7,027 | 80,000 | 87,027 | 75,000 |
| 10,010 | 5,925 | 46 | 10,010 | 75,000 | 85,010 | 75,000 |
| 14,510 | 7,425 | 47 | 14,510 | 70,000 | 84,510 | 75,000 |
| 17,626 | 8,925 | 48 | 17,626 | 65,000 | 82,626 | 75,000 |
| 20,859 | 10,425 | 49 | 20,859 | 60,000 | 80,859 | 75,000 |
| 21,831 | 11,925 | 50 | 21,831 | 55,000 | 76,831 | 75,000 |
| 33,935 | 13,500 | 51 | 33,935 | 50,000 | 83,935 | 75,000 |
| 42,190 | 15,000 | 52 | 42,190 | 46,250 | 88,440 | 75,000 |
| 51,375 | 16,575 | 53 | 51,375 | 42,500 | 93,875 | 75,000 |
| 41,960 | 18,150 | 54 | 41,960 | 38,750 | 80,710 | 75,000 |
| 65,138 | 19,725 | 55 | 65,138 | 35,000 | 100,138 | 75,000 |
| 77,127 | 21,300 | 56 | 77,127 | 31,250 | 108,377 | 75,000 |
| 83,764 | 22,950 | 57 | 83,764 | 28,750 | 112,514 | 75,000 |
| 106,276 | 24,525 | 58 | 106,276 | 26,250 | 132,526 | 75,000 |
| 86,813 | 26,100 | 59 | 86,813 | 23,750 | 110,563 | 75,000 |
| 100,176 | 27,750 | 60 | 100,176 | 21,250 | 121,426 | 75,000 |
| 113,199 | 29,250 | 61 | 113,199 | 18,750 | 131,949 | 75,000 |
| 148,639 | 30,750 | 62 | 148,639 | 17,500 | 166,139 | 75,000 |
| 146,738 | 32,175 | 63 | 146,738 | 16,250 | 162,988 | 75,000 |
| 215,853 | 33,675 | 64 | 215,853 | 15,000 | 230,853 | 75,000 |
| 228,736 | 35,175 | 65 | 228,736 | 14,400 | 243,136 | 75,000 |

Whether you **lived** or **died** you would have been better off "Buying Term and Investing the Difference"

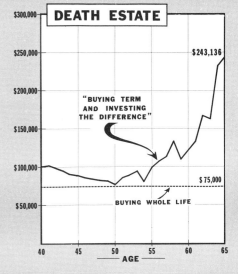

**LIVING ESTATE**

"BUYING TERM AND INVESTING THE DIFFERENCE" — $228,736

BUYING WHOLE LIFE — $35,175

**DEATH ESTATE**

"BUYING TERM AND INVESTING THE DIFFERENCE" — $243,136

BUYING WHOLE LIFE — $75,000

# KEYSTONE S-1

Illustration of assumed annual investments of $1,269 for twenty-five years from 1944 to 1968. All dividends and distributions reinvested.

This tabulation covers an illustration of an assumed investment of $1,269 annually on January 1 of each year from 1944 through 1968. This was a period in which stock prices fluctuated widely because of changing business and economic conditions, and were significantly higher at the end of the period than at the beginning. Thus, these results should not be considered as a representation of the dividend income or capital gain or loss that may be realized from an investment made in the fund today. A program of the type illustrated does not assure a profit nor protect against depreciation in declining markets.

| | | COST OF SHARES | | | | VALUE OF SHARES | | | | |
|---|---|---|---|---|---|---|---|---|---|---|
| YEAR ENDING DEC. 31 | AGE | CUMULATIVE ANNUAL INVEST- MENTS | ANNUAL INCOME DIVIDENDS REIN- VESTED | CUMULA- TIVE COST OF SHARES PURCHASED WITH DIVIDENDS | TOTAL COST (INCLUDES REIN- VESTED DIVIDENDS) | ACQUIRED THROUGH ANNUAL INVEST- MENTS | ACCEPTED AS CAPITAL GAINS DIS- TRIBUTIONS (CUMU- LATIVE) | SUB- TOTAL | PURCHASED THROUGH REINVEST- MENT OF INCOME (CUMULATIVE) | TOTAL VALUE |
| 1944 | 41 | $ 1,269 | $ 50 | $ 50 | $ 1,320 | $ 1,228 | $ 26 | $ 1,254 | $ 50 | $ 1,304 |
| 1945 | 42 | 2,538 | 90 | 141 | 2,680 | 2,891 | 49 | 2,940 | 154 | 3,094 |
| 1946 | 43 | 3,807 | 124 | 265 | 4,073 | 3,435 | 323 | 3,758 | 239 | 3,997 |
| 1947 | 44 | 5,077 | 204 | 469 | 5,547 | 4,609 | 398 | 5,007 | 432 | 5,439 |
| 1948 | 45 | 6,346 | 293 | 763 | 7,110 | 5,609 | 388 | 5,997 | 698 | 6,695 |
| 1949 | 46 | 7,615 | 378 | 1,142 | 8,756 | 7,712 | 441 | 8,153 | 1,202 | 9,355 |
| 1950 | 47 | 8,884 | 566 | 1,709 | 10,593 | 9,616 | 1,204 | 10,820 | 1,874 | 12,694 |
| 1951 | 48 | 10,154 | 700 | 2,409 | 12,563 | 11,703 | 2,374 | 14,077 | 2,701 | 16,778 |
| 1952 | 49 | 11,423 | 781 | 3,191 | 14,615 | 13,514 | 3,468 | 16,982 | 3,606 | 20,588 |
| 1953 | 50 | 12,692 | 859 | 4,050 | 16,744 | 14,064 | 4,339 | 18,403 | 4,275 | 22,679 |
| 1954 | 51 | 13,961 | 1,003 | 5,053 | 19,016 | 20,556 | 7,526 | 28,082 | 6,916 | 34,998 |
| 1955 | 52 | 15,231 | 1,124 | 6,178 | 21,410 | 23,311 | 11,768 | 35,079 | 8,510 | 43,589 |
| 1956 | 53 | 16,500 | 1,405 | 7,584 | 24,085 | 23,505 | 13,875 | 37,380 | 9,446 | 46,826 |
| 1957 | 54 | 17,769 | 1,449 | 9,033 | 26,803 | 21,110 | 14,424 | 35,534 | 9,311 | 44,845 |
| 1958 | 55 | 19,038 | 1,452 | 10,485 | 29,525 | 30,458 | 19,728 | 50,186 | 14,424 | 64,610 |
| 1959 | 56 | 20,308 | 1,481 | 11,967 | 32,275 | 33,222 | 22,939 | 56,161 | 16,570 | 72,731 |
| 1960 | 57 | 21,577 | 1,545 | 13,512 | 35,090 | 35,501 | 23,684 | 59,185 | 18,639 | 77,824 |
| 1961 | 58 | 22,846 | 1,599 | 15,111 | 37,959 | 43,638 | 32,899 | 76,537 | 23,760 | 100,297 |
| 1962 | 59 | 24,115 | 1,767 | 16,879 | 40,995 | 37,619 | 29,946 | 67,565 | 21,531 | 89,096 |
| 1963 | 60 | 25,385 | 2,143 | 19,022 | 44,408 | 43,703 | 35,129 | 78,832 | 26,366 | 105,198 |
| 1964 | 61 | 26,654 | 2,483 | 21,505 | 48,161 | 49,623 | 40,227 | 89,850 | 31,550 | 121,400 |
| 1965 | 62 | 27,923 | 2,505 | 24,011 | 51,936 | 49,462 | 53,696 | 103,158 | 32,970 | 136,128 |
| 1966 | 63 | 29,192 | 2,412 | 26,423 | 55,616 | 41,475 | 59,648 | 101,123 | 29,062 | 130,185 |
| 1967 | 64 | 30,462 | 2,489 | 28,913 | 59,376 | 47,444 | 67,690 | 115,134 | 34,684 | 149,818 |
| 1968 | 65 | 31,731 | 3,110 | 31,923 | 63,655 | 49,405 | 77,325 | 126,724 | 38,057 | 164,781 |

The total cost figures represent the cumulative total of yearly investments of $1,269 plus the cumulative amount of income dividends reinvested, and include the sales charge of 8⅓% on all shares so purchased, as described in the prospectus. No adjustment has been made for any income taxes payable by shareholders on security distributions and dividends reinvested in shares. The dollar amounts of security profits distributions taken in shares were:

| | | | | | | | | | | | | | |
|---|---|---|---|---|---|---|---|---|---|---|---|---|---|
| 1944 | 25 | 1948 | 0 | 1952 | 907 | 1956 | 2,586 | 1960 | 0 | 1964 | 1,314 | 1968 | 8,154 |
| 1945 | 16 | 1949 | 0 | 1953 | 928 | 1957 | 2,766 | 1961 | 4,465 | 1965 | 13,952 | Total: | $63,808 |
| 1946 | 277 | 1950 | 645 | 1954 | 1,391 | 1958 | 0 | 1962 | 2,154 | 1966 | 14,764 | | |
| 1947 | 74 | 1951 | 1,035 | 1955 | 3,539 | 1959 | 2,162 | 1963 | 1,346 | 1967 | 1,308 | | |

| LIVING ESTATE | | | DEATH ESTATE | | | |
| --- | --- | --- | --- | --- | --- | --- |
| "Buying Term and Investing the Difference" | Buying Whole Life | AGE | "Buying Term and Investing the Difference" | Buying Whole Life | | |
| TOTAL VALUE OF SHARES | CASH VALUE | | TOTAL VALUE OF SHARES + | DECREASING TERM INSURANCE = | TOTAL DEATH ESTATE | FACE VALUE |
| $ 1,304 | $ 0 | 41 | $ 1,304 | $100,000 | $101,304 | $75,000 |
| 3,094 | 225 | 42 | 3,094 | 95,000 | 98,094 | 75,000 |
| 3,997 | 1,575 | 43 | 3,997 | 90,000 | 93,997 | 75,000 |
| 5,439 | 3,000 | 44 | 5,439 | 85,000 | 90,439 | 75,000 |
| 6,695 | 4,425 | 45 | 6,695 | 80,000 | 86,695 | 75,000 |
| 9,355 | 5,925 | 46 | 9,355 | 75,000 | 84,355 | 75,000 |
| 12,694 | 7,425 | 47 | 12,694 | 70,000 | 82,694 | 75,000 |
| 16,778 | 8,925 | 48 | 16,778 | 65,000 | 81,778 | 75,000 |
| 20,588 | 10,425 | 49 | 20,588 | 60,000 | 80,588 | 75,000 |
| 22,679 | 11,925 | 50 | 22,679 | 55,000 | 77,679 | 75,000 |
| 34,998 | 13,500 | 51 | 34,998 | 50,000 | 84,998 | 75,000 |
| 43,589 | 15,000 | 52 | 43,589 | 46,250 | 89,839 | 75,000 |
| 46,826 | 16,575 | 53 | 46,826 | 42,500 | 89,326 | 75,000 |
| 44,845 | 18,150 | 54 | 44,845 | 38,750 | 83,595 | 75,000 |
| 64,610 | 19,725 | 55 | 64,610 | 35,000 | 99,610 | 75,000 |
| 72,731 | 21,300 | 56 | 72,731 | 31,250 | 103,981 | 75,000 |
| 77,824 | 22,950 | 57 | 77,824 | 28,750 | 106,574 | 75,000 |
| 100,297 | 24,525 | 58 | 100,297 | 26,250 | 126,547 | 75,000 |
| 89,096 | 26,100 | 59 | 89,096 | 23,750 | 112,846 | 75,000 |
| 105,198 | 27,750 | 60 | 105,198 | 21,250 | 126,448 | 75,000 |
| 121,400 | 29,250 | 61 | 121,400 | 18,750 | 140,150 | 75,000 |
| 136,128 | 30,750 | 62 | 136,128 | 17,500 | 153,628 | 75,000 |
| 130,185 | 32,175 | 63 | 130,185 | 16,250 | 146,435 | 75,000 |
| 149,818 | 33,675 | 64 | 149,818 | 15,000 | 164,818 | 75,000 |
| 164,781 | 35,175 | 65 | 164,781 | 14,400 | 179,181 | 75,000 |

Whether you
**lived** or **died**
you would have been better off
"Buying Term and Investing the Difference"

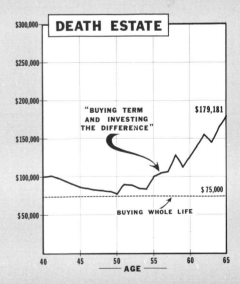

LIVING ESTATE

"BUYING TERM AND INVESTING THE DIFFERENCE" $164,781

BUYING WHOLE LIFE $35,175

DEATH ESTATE

"BUYING TERM AND INVESTING THE DIFFERENCE" $179,181

BUYING WHOLE LIFE $75,000

199

# KEYSTONE S-2

Illustration of assumed annual investments of $1,269 for twenty-five years from 1944 to 1968. All dividends and distributions reinvested.

This tabulation covers an illustration of an assumed investment of $1,269 annually on January 1 of each year from 1944 through 1968. This was a period in which stock prices fluctuated widely because of changing business and economic conditions, and were significantly higher at the end of the period than at the beginning. Thus, these results should not be considered as a representation of the dividend income or capital gain or loss that may be realized from an investment made in the fund today. A program of the type illustrated does not assure a profit nor protect against depreciation in declining markets.

| | | COST OF SHARES | | | | VALUE OF SHARES | | | | |
|---|---|---|---|---|---|---|---|---|---|---|
| YEAR ENDING DEC. 31 | AGE | CUMULATIVE ANNUAL INVEST-MENTS | ANNUAL INCOME DIVIDENDS REIN-VESTED | CUMULA-TIVE COST OF SHARES PURCHASED WITH DIVIDENDS | TOTAL COST (INCLUDES REIN-VESTED DIVIDENDS) | ACQUIRED THROUGH ANNUAL INVEST-MENTS | ACCEPTED AS CAPITAL GAINS DIS-TRIBUTIONS (CUMU-LATIVE) | SUB-TOTAL | PURCHASED THROUGH REINVEST-MENT OF INCOME (CUMULATIVE) | TOTAL VALUE |
| 1944 | 41 | $ 1,269 | $ 72 | $ 72 | $ 1,341 | $ 1,270 | $ 35 | $ 1,305 | $ 74 | $ 1,379 |
| 1945 | 42 | 2,538 | 143 | 215 | 2,754 | 3,080 | 122 | 3,202 | 238 | 3,440 |
| 1946 | 43 | 3,807 | 187 | 402 | 4,210 | 3,548 | 285 | 3,833 | 360 | 4,193 |
| 1947 | 44 | 5,077 | 307 | 709 | 5,786 | 4,419 | 265 | 4,684 | 626 | 5,310 |
| 1948 | 45 | 6,346 | 405 | 1,114 | 7,460 | 5,446 | 259 | 5,705 | 964 | 6,669 |
| 1949 | 46 | 7,615 | 528 | 1,642 | 9,258 | 7,401 | 290 | 7,691 | 1,623 | 9,314 |
| 1950 | 47 | 8,884 | 685 | 2,327 | 11,212 | 9,484 | 398 | 9,882 | 2,481 | 12,363 |
| 1951 | 48 | 10,154 | 831 | 3,158 | 13,312 | 11,407 | 1,324 | 12,731 | 3,439 | 16,170 |
| 1952 | 49 | 11,423 | 944 | 4,102 | 15,525 | 13,287 | 1,742 | 15,029 | 4,572 | 19,601 |
| 1953 | 50 | 12,692 | 1,069 | 5,172 | 17,865 | 13,138 | 2,633 | 15,771 | 5,138 | 20,909 |
| 1954 | 51 | 13,961 | 1,249 | 6,421 | 20,383 | 19,050 | 5,187 | 24,237 | 8,194 | 32,431 |
| 1955 | 52 | 15,231 | 1,423 | 7,844 | 23,075 | 21,502 | 7,749 | 29,251 | 10,074 | 39,325 |
| 1956 | 53 | 16,500 | 1,747 | 9,592 | 26,092 | 21,918 | 11,050 | 32,968 | 11,319 | 44,287 |
| 1957 | 54 | 17,769 | 1,952 | 11,544 | 29,314 | 17,388 | 10,967 | 28,355 | 10,073 | 38,428 |
| 1958 | 55 | 19,038 | 1,986 | 13,530 | 32,569 | 25,668 | 16,552 | 42,220 | 16,043 | 58,263 |
| 1959 | 56 | 20,308 | 2,051 | 15,581 | 35,889 | 26,107 | 21,697 | 47,804 | 17,460 | 65,264 |
| 1960 | 57 | 21,577 | 2,245 | 17,826 | 39,403 | 26,354 | 23,807 | 50,161 | 19,094 | 69,255 |
| 1961 | 58 | 22,846 | 2,460 | 20,286 | 43,133 | 32,550 | 33,627 | 66,177 | 24,937 | 91,114 |
| 1962 | 59 | 24,115 | 2,589 | 22,876 | 46,992 | 28,967 | 29,901 | 58,868 | 23,889 | 82,757 |
| 1963 | 60 | 25,385 | 2,739 | 25,615 | 51,000 | 33,316 | 36,652 | 69,968 | 28,948 | 98,916 |
| 1964 | 61 | 26,654 | 3,295 | 28,910 | 55,564 | 36,817 | 42,302 | 79,119 | 33,961 | 113,080 |
| 1965 | 62 | 27,923 | 3,850 | 32,759 | 60,683 | 38,472 | 56,042 | 94,514 | 37,978 | 132,492 |
| 1966 | 63 | 29,192 | 3,949 | 36,708 | 65,901 | 27,449 | 62,016 | 89,465 | 29,509 | 118,974 |
| 1967 | 64 | 30,462 | 4,126 | 40,834 | 71,296 | 32,825 | 71,149 | 103,974 | 37,683 | 141,657 |
| 1968 | 65 | 31,731 | 4,587 | 45,420 | 77,151 | 39,173 | 89,465 | 128,638 | 47,901 | 176,539 |

The total cost figures represent the cumulative total of yearly investments of $1,269 plus the cumulative amount of income dividends reinvested, and include the sales charge of $8\frac{1}{3}\%$ on all shares so purchased, as described in the prospectus. No adjustment has been made for any income taxes payable by shareholders on security distributions and dividends reinvested in shares. The dollar amounts of security profits distributions taken in shares were:

| | | | | | | | | | | | | | |
|---|---|---|---|---|---|---|---|---|---|---|---|---|---|
| 1944 | 33 | 1948 | 0 | 1952 | 319 | 1956 | 3,391 | 1960 | 2,547 | 1964 | 3,211 | 1968 | 7,272 |
| 1945 | 74 | 1949 | 0 | 1953 | 1,015 | 1957 | 2,759 | 1961 | 5,326 | 1965 | 12,391 | Total: | $75,872 |
| 1946 | 172 | 1950 | 71 | 1954 | 1,447 | 1958 | 1,277 | 1962 | 892 | 1966 | 21,745 | | |
| 1947 | 0 | 1951 | 867 | 1955 | 2,095 | 1959 | 5,412 | 1963 | 3,556 | 1967 | 0 | | |

# LIVING ESTATE

| "Buying Term and Investing the Difference" | Buying Whole Life |
|---|---|

# DEATH ESTATE

| "Buying Term and Investing the Difference" | Buying Whole Life |
|---|---|

| TOTAL VALUE OF SHARES | CASH VALUE | AGE | TOTAL VALUE OF SHARES | + DECREASING TERM INSURANCE | = TOTAL DEATH ESTATE | FACE VALUE |
|---|---|---|---|---|---|---|
| $ 1,379 | $ 0 | 41 | $ 1,379 | $100,000 | $101,379 | $75,000 |
| 3,440 | 225 | 42 | 3,440 | 95,000 | 98,440 | 75,000 |
| 4,193 | 1,575 | 43 | 4,193 | 90,000 | 94,193 | 75,000 |
| 5,310 | 3,000 | 44 | 5,310 | 85,000 | 90,310 | 75,000 |
| 6,669 | 4,425 | 45 | 6,669 | 80,000 | 86,669 | 75,000 |
| 9,314 | 5,925 | 46 | 9,314 | 75,000 | 84,314 | 75,000 |
| 12,363 | 7,425 | 47 | 12,363 | 70,000 | 82,363 | 75,000 |
| 16,170 | 8,925 | 48 | 16,170 | 65,000 | 81,170 | 75,000 |
| 19,601 | 10,425 | 49 | 19,601 | 60,000 | 79,601 | 75,000 |
| 20,909 | 11,925 | 50 | 20,909 | 55,000 | 75,909 | 75,000 |
| 32,431 | 13,500 | 51 | 32,431 | 50,000 | 82,431 | 75,000 |
| 39,325 | 15,000 | 52 | 39,325 | 46,250 | 85,575 | 75,000 |
| 44,287 | 16,575 | 53 | 44,287 | 42,500 | 86,787 | 75,000 |
| 38,428 | 18,150 | 54 | 38,428 | 38,750 | 77,178 | 75,000 |
| 58,263 | 19,725 | 55 | 58,263 | 35,000 | 93,263 | 75,000 |
| 65,264 | 21,300 | 56 | 65,264 | 31,250 | 96,514 | 75,000 |
| 69,255 | 22,950 | 57 | 69,255 | 28,750 | 98,005 | 75,000 |
| 91,114 | 24,525 | 58 | 91,114 | 26,250 | 117,364 | 75,000 |
| 82,757 | 26,100 | 59 | 82,757 | 23,750 | 106,507 | 75,000 |
| 98,916 | 27,750 | 60 | 98,916 | 21,250 | 120,166 | 75,000 |
| 113,080 | 29,250 | 61 | 113,080 | 18,750 | 131,830 | 75,000 |
| 132,492 | 30,750 | 62 | 132,492 | 17,500 | 149,992 | 75,000 |
| 118,974 | 32,175 | 63 | 118,974 | 16,250 | 135,224 | 75,000 |
| 141,657 | 33,675 | 64 | 141,657 | 15,000 | 156,657 | 75,000 |
| 176,539 | 35,175 | 65 | 176,539 | 14,400 | 190,939 | 75,000 |

Whether you
**lived** or **died**
you would have been better off
"Buying Term and Investing the Difference"

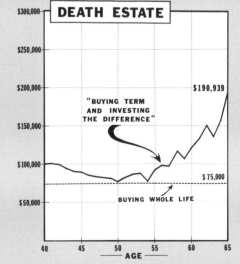

**LIVING ESTATE**

"BUYING TERM AND INVESTING THE DIFFERENCE" — $176,539

BUYING WHOLE LIFE — $35,175

**DEATH ESTATE**

"BUYING TERM AND INVESTING THE DIFFERENCE" — $190,939

BUYING WHOLE LIFE — $75,000

# KEYSTONE S-3

Illustration of assumed annual investments of $1,269 for twenty-five years from 1944 to 1968. All dividends and distributions reinvested.

This tabulation covers an illustration of an assumed investment of $1,269 annually on January 1 of each year from 1944 through 1968. This was a period in which stock prices fluctuated widely because of changing business and economic conditions, and were significantly higher at the end of the period than at the beginning. Thus, these results should not be considered as a representation of the dividend income or capital gain or loss that may be realized from an investment made in the fund today. A program of the type illustrated does not assure a profit nor protect against depreciation in declining markets.

| | | COST OF SHARES | | | | VALUE OF SHARES | | | | |
|---|---|---|---|---|---|---|---|---|---|---|
| YEAR ENDING DEC. 31 | AGE | CUMULATIVE ANNUAL INVEST-MENTS | ANNUAL INCOME DIVIDENDS REIN-VESTED | CUMULA-TIVE COST OF SHARES PURCHASED WITH DIVIDENDS | TOTAL COST (INCLUDES REIN-VESTED DIVIDENDS) | ACQUIRED THROUGH ANNUAL INVEST-MENTS | ACCEPTED AS CAPITAL GAINS DIS-TRIBUTIONS (CUMU-LATIVE) | SUB-TOTAL | PURCHASED THROUGH REINVEST-MENT OF INCOME (CUMULATIVE) | TOTAL VALUE |
| 1944 | 41 | $ 1,269 | $ 83 | $ 83 | $ 1,353 | $ 1,421 | $ 3 | $ 1,424 | $ 90 | $ 1,514 |
| 1945 | 42 | 2,538 | 132 | 216 | 2,755 | 3,424 | 182 | 3,606 | 264 | 3,870 |
| 1946 | 43 | 3,807 | 134 | 351 | 4,158 | 3,564 | 349 | 3,913 | 317 | 4,230 |
| 1947 | 44 | 5,077 | 199 | 550 | 5,627 | 4,828 | 351 | 5,179 | 520 | 5,699 |
| 1948 | 45 | 6,346 | 356 | 906 | 7,253 | 5,456 | 319 | 5,775 | 783 | 6,558 |
| 1949 | 46 | 7,615 | 497 | 1,404 | 9,020 | 7,109 | 343 | 7,452 | 1,355 | 8,807 |
| 1950 | 47 | 8,884 | 597 | 2,002 | 10,886 | 11,183 | 464 | 11,647 | 2,497 | 14,144 |
| 1951 | 48 | 10,154 | 888 | 2,890 | 13,044 | 13,310 | 888 | 14,198 | 3,535 | 17,733 |
| 1952 | 49 | 11,423 | 1,014 | 3,905 | 15,328 | 14,820 | 1,826 | 16,646 | 4,601 | 21,247 |
| 1953 | 50 | 12,692 | 1,125 | 5,030 | 17,724 | 13,904 | 3,009 | 16,913 | 5,051 | 21,964 |
| 1954 | 51 | 13,961 | 1,259 | 6,290 | 20,252 | 23,991 | 7,057 | 31,048 | 9,570 | 40,618 |
| 1955 | 52 | 15,231 | 1,354 | 7,644 | 22,876 | 26,710 | 16,712 | 43,422 | 11,439 | 54,861 |
| 1956 | 53 | 16,500 | 1,666 | 9,311 | 25,812 | 30,724 | 22,210 | 52,934 | 14,222 | 67,156 |
| 1957 | 54 | 17,769 | 1,654 | 10,965 | 28,736 | 21,732 | 19,309 | 41,041 | 10,927 | 51,968 |
| 1958 | 55 | 19,038 | 1,619 | 12,585 | 31,624 | 32,502 | 27,901 | 60,403 | 17,370 | 77,773 |
| 1959 | 56 | 20,308 | 1,464 | 14,049 | 34,358 | 34,763 | 35,139 | 69,902 | 19,314 | 89,216 |
| 1960 | 57 | 21,577 | 1,750 | 15,800 | 37,378 | 32,314 | 33,388 | 65,702 | 19,055 | 84,757 |
| 1961 | 58 | 22,846 | 1,716 | 17,516 | 40,363 | 40,571 | 43,646 | 84,217 | 24,723 | 108,940 |
| 1962 | 59 | 24,115 | 1,884 | 19,400 | 43,516 | 34,223 | 37,209 | 71,432 | 21,991 | 93,423 |
| 1963 | 60 | 25,385 | 1,974 | 21,375 | 46,761 | 41,868 | 46,474 | 88,342 | 27,966 | 116,308 |
| 1964 | 61 | 26,654 | 2,148 | 23,523 | 50,178 | 47,481 | 57,107 | 104,588 | 32,839 | 137,427 |
| 1965 | 62 | 27,923 | 2,790 | 26,313 | 54,238 | 61,491 | 83,554 | 145,045 | 44,476 | 189,521 |
| 1966 | 63 | 29,192 | 3,033 | 29,347 | 58,540 | 50,555 | 101,276 | 151,831 | 38,518 | 190,349 |
| 1967 | 64 | 30,462 | 3,109 | 32,456 | 62,919 | 60,804 | 145,781 | 206,585 | 48,187 | 254,772 |
| 1968 | 65 | 31,731 | 3,788 | 36,245 | 67,977 | 58,675 | 168,847 | 227,525 | 49,100 | 276,625 |

The total cost figures represent the cumulative total of yearly investments of $1,269 plus the cumulative amount of income dividends reinvested, and include the sales charge of 8⅓% on all shares so purchased, as described in the prospectus. No adjustment has been made for any income taxes payable by shareholders on security distributions and dividends reinvested in shares. The dollar amounts of security profits distributions taken in shares were:

| | | | | | | | | | | | | | |
|---|---|---|---|---|---|---|---|---|---|---|---|---|---|
| 1944 | 3 | 1948 | 0 | 1952 | 829 | 1956 | 3,438 | 1960 | 1,633 | 1964 | 5,782 | 1968 | 31,957 |
| 1945 | 164 | 1949 | 0 | 1953 | 1,278 | 1957 | 4,663 | 1961 | 3,049 | 1965 | 9,962 | Total: | $139,749 |
| 1946 | 197 | 1950 | 0 | 1954 | 1,818 | 1958 | 435 | 1962 | 1,260 | 1966 | 29,745 | | |
| 1947 | 0 | 1951 | 386 | 1955 | 8,517 | 1959 | 5,942 | 1963 | 2,350 | 1967 | 26,341 | | |

# LIVING ESTATE

| "Buying Term and Investing the Difference" TOTAL VALUE OF SHARES | Buying Whole Life CASH VALUE | AGE | "Buying Term and Investing the Difference" TOTAL VALUE OF SHARES | + DECREASING TERM INSURANCE | = TOTAL DEATH ESTATE | Buying Whole Life FACE VALUE |
|---|---|---|---|---|---|---|
| $ 1,514 | $ 0 | 41 | $ 1,514 | $100,000 | $101,514 | $75,000 |
| 3,870 | 225 | 42 | 3,870 | 95,000 | 98,870 | 75,000 |
| 4,230 | 1,575 | 43 | 4,230 | 90,000 | 94,230 | 75,000 |
| 5,699 | 3,000 | 44 | 5,699 | 85,000 | 90,699 | 75,000 |
| 6,558 | 4,425 | 45 | 6,558 | 80,000 | 86,558 | 75,000 |
| 8,807 | 5,925 | 46 | 8,807 | 75,000 | 83,807 | 75,000 |
| 14,144 | 7,425 | 47 | 14,144 | 70,000 | 84,144 | 75,000 |
| 17,733 | 8,925 | 48 | 17,733 | 65,000 | 82,733 | 75,000 |
| 21,247 | 10,425 | 49 | 21,247 | 60,000 | 81,247 | 75,000 |
| 21,964 | 11,925 | 50 | 21,964 | 55,000 | 76,964 | 75,000 |
| 40,618 | 13,500 | 51 | 40,618 | 50,000 | 90,618 | 75,000 |
| 54,861 | 15,000 | 52 | 54,861 | 46,250 | 101,111 | 75,000 |
| 67,156 | 16,575 | 53 | 67,156 | 42,500 | 109,656 | 75,000 |
| 51,968 | 18,150 | 54 | 51,968 | 38,750 | 90,718 | 75,000 |
| 77,773 | 19,725 | 55 | 77,773 | 35,000 | 112,773 | 75,000 |
| 89,216 | 21,300 | 56 | 89,216 | 31,250 | 120,466 | 75,000 |
| 84,757 | 22,950 | 57 | 84,757 | 28,750 | 113,507 | 75,000 |
| 108,940 | 24,525 | 58 | 108,940 | 26,250 | 135,190 | 75,000 |
| 93,423 | 26,100 | 59 | 93,423 | 23,750 | 117,173 | 75,000 |
| 116,308 | 27,750 | 60 | 116,308 | 21,250 | 137,558 | 75,000 |
| 137,427 | 29,250 | 61 | 137,427 | 18,750 | 156,177 | 75,000 |
| 189,521 | 30,750 | 62 | 189,521 | 17,500 | 207,021 | 75,000 |
| 190,349 | 32,175 | 63 | 190,349 | 16,250 | 206,599 | 75,000 |
| 254,772 | 33,675 | 64 | 254,772 | 15,000 | 269,772 | 75,000 |
| 276,625 | 35,175 | 65 | 276,625 | 14,400 | 291,025 | 75,000 |

# DEATH ESTATE

Whether you **lived** or **died** you would have been better off "Buying Term and Investing the Difference"

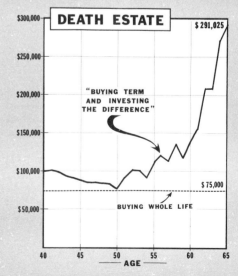

203

# KEYSTONE S-4

Illustration of assumed annual investments of $1,269 for twenty-five years from 1944 to 1968. All dividends and distributions reinvested.

This tabulation covers an illustration of an assumed investment of $1,269 annually on January 1 of each year from 1944 through 1968. This was a period in which stock prices fluctuated widely because of changing business and economic conditions, and were significantly higher at the end of the period than at the beginning. Thus, these results should not be considered as a representation of the dividend income or capital gain or loss that may be realized from an investment made in the fund today. A program of the type illustrated does not assure a profit nor protect against depreciation in declining markets.

| | | COST OF SHARES | | | | VALUE OF SHARES | | | | |
|---|---|---|---|---|---|---|---|---|---|---|
| YEAR ENDING DEC. 31 | AGE | CUMULATIVE ANNUAL INVEST- MENTS | ANNUAL INCOME DIVIDENDS REIN- VESTED | CUMULA- TIVE COST OF SHARES PURCHASED WITH DIVIDENDS | TOTAL COST (INCLUDES REIN- VESTED DIVIDENDS) | ACQUIRED THROUGH ANNUAL INVEST- MENTS | ACCEPTED AS CAPITAL GAINS DIS- TRIBUTIONS (CUMU- LATIVE) | SUB- TOTAL | PURCHASED THROUGH REINVEST- MENT OF INCOME (CUMULATIVE) | TOTAL VALUE |
| 1944 | 41 | $ 1,269 | $ 50 | $ 50 | $ 1,320 | $ 1,438 | $ 49 | $ 1,487 | $ 48 | $ 1,535 |
| 1945 | 42 | 2,538 | 86 | 137 | 2,676 | 3,846 | 521 | 4,367 | 161 | 4,528 |
| 1946 | 43 | 3,807 | 54 | 192 | 4,000 | 3,003 | 983 | 3,986 | 142 | 4,128 |
| 1947 | 44 | 5,077 | 112 | 304 | 5,381 | 3,956 | 918 | 4,874 | 235 | 5,109 |
| 1948 | 45 | 6,346 | 296 | 601 | 6,947 | 4,979 | 893 | 5,872 | 485 | 6,357 |
| 1949 | 46 | 7,615 | 456 | 1,057 | 8,674 | 6,634 | 965 | 7,599 | 991 | 8,590 |
| 1950 | 47 | 8,884 | 652 | 1,709 | 10,594 | 10,844 | 1,344 | 12,188 | 2,050 | 14,238 |
| 1951 | 48 | 10,154 | 807 | 2,517 | 12,671 | 12,317 | 2,889 | 15,206 | 2,876 | 18,082 |
| 1952 | 49 | 11,423 | 598 | 3,116 | 14,540 | 15,084 | 4,818 | 19,902 | 3,794 | 23,696 |
| 1953 | 50 | 12,692 | 678 | 3,794 | 16,487 | 13,021 | 6,561 | 19,582 | 3,648 | 23,230 |
| 1954 | 51 | 13,961 | 797 | 4,592 | 18,554 | 21,343 | 12,027 | 33,370 | 6,321 | 39,691 |
| 1955 | 52 | 15,231 | 1,150 | 5,742 | 20,974 | 23,622 | 20,469 | 44,091 | 7,711 | 51,802 |
| 1956 | 53 | 16,500 | 1,343 | 7,086 | 23,587 | 25,799 | 26,341 | 52,140 | 9,275 | 61,415 |
| 1957 | 54 | 17,769 | 1,283 | 8,370 | 26,140 | 17,674 | 23,491 | 41,165 | 7,083 | 48,248 |
| 1958 | 55 | 19,038 | 1,223 | 9,593 | 28,632 | 33,490 | 41,770 | 75,260 | 13,929 | 89,189 |
| 1959 | 56 | 20,308 | 1,311 | 10,904 | 31,213 | 41,077 | 57,944 | 99,021 | 17,750 | 116,771 |
| 1960 | 57 | 21,577 | 1,839 | 12,744 | 34,322 | 38,935 | 55,920 | 94,855 | 18,025 | 112,880 |
| 1961 | 58 | 22,846 | 2,125 | 14,869 | 37,717 | 49,413 | 73,890 | 123,303 | 24,177 | 147,480 |
| 1962 | 59 | 24,115 | 2,037 | 16,907 | 41,024 | 37,588 | 56,868 | 94,456 | 19,937 | 114,393 |
| 1963 | 60 | 25,385 | 2,109 | 19,016 | 44,402 | 43,779 | 64,253 | 108,032 | 24,496 | 132,528 |
| 1964 | 61 | 26,654 | 2,777 | 21,794 | 48,449 | 53,408 | 76,366 | 129,774 | 31,749 | 161,523 |
| 1965 | 62 | 27,923 | 2,525 | 24,320 | 52,245 | 70,295 | 98,374 | 168,669 | 43,473 | 212,142 |
| 1966 | 63 | 29,192 | 2,682 | 27,003 | 56,196 | 58,793 | 101,627 | 160,420 | 38,117 | 198,537 |
| 1967 | 64 | 30,462 | 1,533 | 28,584 | 59,047 | 85,120 | 191,463 | 276,583 | 55,687 | 332,270 |
| 1968 | 65 | 31,731 | 856 | 29,441 | 61,173 | 81,955 | 239,824 | 321,783 | 53,732 | 375,515 |

The total cost figures represent the cumulative total of yearly investments of $1,269 plus the cumulative amount of income dividends reinvested, and include the sales charge of $8\frac{1}{3}\%$ on all shares so purchased, as described in the prospectus. No adjustment has been made for any income taxes payable by shareholders on security distributions and dividends reinvested in shares. The dollar amounts of security profits distributions taken in shares were:

| | | | | | | | | | | | | | |
|---|---|---|---|---|---|---|---|---|---|---|---|---|---|
| 1944 | 47 | 1948 | 0 | 1952 | 1,433 | 1956 | 4,901 | 1960 | 2,586 | 1964 | 0 | 1968 | 54,429 |
| 1945 | 356 | 1949 | 0 | 1953 | 2,846 | 1957 | 8,533 | 1961 | 4,883 | 1965 | 0 | Total: | $163,090 |
| 1946 | 944 | 1950 | 0 | 1954 | 1,660 | 1958 | 0 | 1962 | 1,721 | 1966 | 22,419 | | |
| 1947 | 0 | 1951 | 1,342 | 1955 | 7,440 | 1959 | 7,829 | 1963 | 0 | 1967 | 39,721 | | |

# LIVING ESTATE

| "Buying Term and Investing the Difference" TOTAL VALUE OF SHARES | Buying Whole Life CASH VALUE | AGE |
|---|---|---|
| $ 1,535 | $ 0 | 41 |
| 4,528 | 225 | 42 |
| 4,128 | 1,575 | 43 |
| 5,109 | 3,000 | 44 |
| 6,357 | 4,425 | 45 |
| 8,590 | 5,925 | 46 |
| 14,238 | 7,425 | 47 |
| 18,082 | 8,925 | 48 |
| 23,696 | 10,425 | 49 |
| 23,230 | 11,925 | 50 |
| 39,691 | 13,500 | 51 |
| 51,802 | 15,000 | 52 |
| 61,415 | 16,575 | 53 |
| 48,248 | 18,150 | 54 |
| 89,189 | 19,725 | 55 |
| 116,771 | 21,300 | 56 |
| 112,880 | 22,950 | 57 |
| 147,480 | 24,525 | 58 |
| 114,393 | 26,100 | 59 |
| 132,528 | 27,750 | 60 |
| 161,523 | 29,250 | 61 |
| 212,142 | 30,750 | 62 |
| 198,537 | 32,175 | 63 |
| 332,270 | 33,675 | 64 |
| 375,515 | 35,175 | 65 |

# DEATH ESTATE

| AGE | "Buying Term and Investing the Difference" TOTAL VALUE OF SHARES | + DECREASING TERM INSURANCE | = TOTAL DEATH ESTATE | Buying Whole Life FACE VALUE |
|---|---|---|---|---|
| 41 | $ 1,535 | $100,000 | $101,535 | $75,000 |
| 42 | 4,528 | 95,000 | 99,528 | 75,000 |
| 43 | 4,128 | 90,000 | 94,128 | 75,000 |
| 44 | 5,109 | 85,000 | 90,109 | 75,000 |
| 45 | 6,357 | 80,000 | 86,357 | 75,000 |
| 46 | 8,590 | 75,000 | 83,590 | 75,000 |
| 47 | 14,238 | 70,000 | 84,238 | 75,000 |
| 48 | 18,082 | 65,000 | 83,082 | 75,000 |
| 49 | 23,696 | 60,000 | 83,696 | 75,000 |
| 50 | 23,230 | 55,000 | 78,230 | 75,000 |
| 51 | 39,691 | 50,000 | 89,691 | 75,000 |
| 52 | 51,802 | 46,250 | 98,052 | 75,000 |
| 53 | 61,415 | 42,500 | 103,915 | 75,000 |
| 54 | 48,248 | 38,750 | 86,998 | 75,000 |
| 55 | 89,189 | 35,000 | 124,189 | 75,000 |
| 56 | 116,771 | 31,250 | 148,021 | 75,000 |
| 57 | 112,880 | 28,750 | 141,630 | 75,000 |
| 58 | 147,480 | 26,250 | 173,730 | 75,000 |
| 59 | 114,393 | 23,750 | 138,143 | 75,000 |
| 60 | 132,528 | 21,250 | 153,778 | 75,000 |
| 61 | 161,523 | 18,750 | 180,273 | 75,000 |
| 62 | 212,142 | 17,500 | 229,642 | 75,000 |
| 63 | 198,537 | 16,250 | 214,787 | 75,000 |
| 64 | 332,270 | 15,000 | 347,270 | 75,000 |
| 65 | 375,515 | 14,400 | 389,915 | 75,000 |

Whether you **lived** or **died** you would have been better off "Buying Term and Investing the Difference"

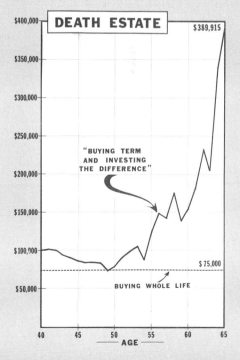

LIVING ESTATE
$375,515
"BUYING TERM AND INVESTING THE DIFFERENCE"
$35,175
BUYING WHOLE LIFE

DEATH ESTATE
$389,915
"BUYING TERM AND INVESTING THE DIFFERENCE"
$75,000
BUYING WHOLE LIFE

# MASSACHUSETTS INVESTORS GROWTH STOCK

Illustration of assumed annual investments of $1,269 for twenty-five years from 1944 to 1968. All dividends and distributions reinvested.

This tabulation covers an illustration of an assumed investment of $1,269 annually on January 1 of each year from 1944 through 1968. This was a period in which stock prices fluctuated widely because of changing business and economic conditions, and were significantly higher at the end of the period than at the beginning. Thus, these results should not be considered as a representation of the dividend income or capital gain or loss that may be realized from an investment made in the fund today. A program of the type illustrated does not assure a profit nor protect against depreciation in declining markets.

|  |  | COST OF SHARES | | | | | VALUE OF SHARES | | | | |
|---|---|---|---|---|---|---|---|---|---|---|---|
| YEAR ENDING DEC. 31 | AGE | CUMULATIVE ANNUAL INVEST-MENTS | ANNUAL INCOME DIVIDENDS REIN-VESTED | CUMULA-TIVE COST OF SHARES PURCHASED WITH DIVIDENDS | TOTAL COST (INCLUDES REIN-VESTED DIVIDENDS) | ACQUIRED THROUGH ANNUAL INVEST-MENTS | ACCEPTED AS CAPITAL GAINS DIS-TRIBUTIONS (CUMU-LATIVE) | SUB-TOTAL | PURCHASED THROUGH REINVEST-MENT OF INCOME (CUMULATIVE) | TOTAL VALUE |
| 1944 | 41 | $ 1,269 | $ 51 | $ 51 | $ 1,321 | $ 1,382 | $ 0 | $ 1,382 | $ 51 | $ 1,433 |
| 1945 | 42 | 2,538 | 111 | 163 | 2,702 | 3,385 | 41 | 3,426 | 186 | 3,612 |
| 1946 | 43 | 3,807 | 153 | 317 | 4,124 | 3,360 | 812 | 4,172 | 253 | 4,425 |
| 1947 | 44 | 5,077 | 200 | 517 | 5,594 | 4,504 | 809 | 5,313 | 440 | 5,753 |
| 1948 | 45 | 6,346 | 322 | 839 | 7,186 | 5,469 | 782 | 6,251 | 709 | 6,960 |
| 1949 | 46 | 7,615 | 400 | 1,240 | 8,856 | 7,524 | 887 | 8,411 | 1,201 | 9,612 |
| 1950 | 47 | 8,884 | 527 | 1,767 | 10,652 | 10,673 | 1,647 | 12,320 | 1,986 | 14,306 |
| 1951 | 48 | 10,154 | 479 | 2,246 | 12,401 | 13,845 | 2,883 | 16,728 | 2,775 | 19,503 |
| 1952 | 49 | 11,423 | 600 | 2,847 | 14,271 | 15,056 | 3,324 | 18,380 | 3,343 | 21,723 |
| 1953 | 50 | 12,692 | 660 | 3,507 | 16,200 | 15,017 | 3,441 | 18,458 | 3,700 | 22,158 |
| 1954 | 51 | 13,961 | 751 | 4,258 | 18,220 | 23,987 | 5,894 | 29,881 | 6,298 | 36,179 |
| 1955 | 52 | 15,231 | 887 | 5,145 | 20,377 | 28,789 | 9,395 | 38,184 | 8,036 | 46,220 |
| 1956 | 53 | 16,500 | 1,048 | 6,194 | 22,695 | 33,305 | 13,001 | 46,306 | 9,893 | 56,199 |
| 1957 | 54 | 17,769 | 1,142 | 7,337 | 25,108 | 28,948 | 12,015 | 40,963 | 9,236 | 50,199 |
| 1958 | 55 | 19,038 | 1,216 | 8,554 | 27,593 | 43,748 | 18,121 | 61,869 | 14,752 | 76,621 |
| 1959 | 56 | 20,308 | 1,266 | 9,821 | 30,129 | 49,899 | 22,348 | 72,247 | 17,596 | 89,843 |
| 1960 | 57 | 21,577 | 1,411 | 11,410 | 32,988 | 53,827 | 24,777 | 78,604 | 20,074 | 98,678 |
| 1961 | 58 | 22,846 | 1,519 | 12,930 | 35,777 | 66,368 | 33,081 | 99,449 | 25,661 | 125,110 |
| 1962 | 59 | 24,115 | 1,704 | 14,634 | 38,751 | 54,181 | 27,919 | 82,100 | 22,172 | 104,272 |
| 1963 | 60 | 25,385 | 1,889 | 16,524 | 41,910 | 63,174 | 34,680 | 97,851 | 27,076 | 124,927 |
| 1964 | 61 | 26,654 | 2,162 | 18,686 | 45,341 | 68,937 | 38,680 | 107,617 | 31,008 | 138,625 |
| 1965 | 62 | 27,923 | 2,486 | 21,172 | 49,097 | 84,677 | 50,054 | 134,731 | 39,933 | 174,664 |
| 1966 | 63 | 29,192 | 2,783 | 23,957 | 53,150 | 83,072 | 54,245 | 137,317 | 41,142 | 178,459 |
| 1967 | 64 | 30,462 | 3,126 | 27,082 | 57,545 | 104,991 | 72,469 | 177,460 | 54,212 | 231,672 |
| 1968 | 65 | 31,731 | 3,268 | 30,351 | 62,084 | 104,936 | 75,114 | 180,050 | 56,686 | 236,736 |

The total cost figures represent the cumulative total of yearly investments of $1,269 plus the cumulative amount of income dividends reinvested, and include the sales charge of 8½% on all shares so purchased, as described in the prospectus. No adjustment has been made for any income taxes payable by shareholders on security distributions and dividends reinvested in shares. The dollar amounts of security profits distributions taken in shares were:

| | | | | | | | | | | | | | |
|---|---|---|---|---|---|---|---|---|---|---|---|---|---|
| 1944 | 0 | 1948 | 0 | 1952 | 406 | 1956 | 2,514 | 1960 | 1,151 | 1964 | 1,519 | 1968 | 3,608 |
| 1945 | 45 | 1949 | 0 | 1953 | 334 | 1957 | 1,149 | 1961 | 3,252 | 1965 | 3,302 | Total: | $40,318 |
| 1946 | 745 | 1950 | 521 | 1954 | 800 | 1958 | 642 | 1962 | 1,394 | 1966 | 5,726 | | |
| 1947 | 0 | 1951 | 913 | 1955 | 2,633 | 1959 | 2,183 | 1963 | 2,755 | 1967 | 4,726 | | |

| LIVING ESTATE | | | DEATH ESTATE | | | |
|---|---|---|---|---|---|---|
| "Buying Term and Investing the Difference" | Buying Whole Life | | "Buying Term and Investing the Difference" | | | Buying Whole Life |
| TOTAL VALUE OF SHARES | CASH VALUE | AGE | TOTAL VALUE OF SHARES + | DECREASING TERM INSURANCE | = TOTAL DEATH ESTATE | FACE VALUE |
| $ 1,433 | $ 0 | 41 | $ 1,433 | $100,000 | $101,433 | $75,000 |
| 3,612 | 225 | 42 | 3,612 | 95,000 | 98,612 | 75,000 |
| 4,425 | 1,575 | 43 | 4,425 | 90,000 | 94,425 | 75,000 |
| 5,753 | 3,000 | 44 | 5,753 | 85,000 | 90,753 | 75,000 |
| 6,960 | 4,425 | 45 | 6,960 | 80,000 | 86,690 | 75,000 |
| 9,612 | 5,925 | 46 | 9,612 | 75,000 | 84,612 | 75,000 |
| 14,306 | 7,425 | 47 | 14,306 | 70,000 | 84,306 | 75,000 |
| 19,503 | 8,925 | 48 | 19,503 | 65,000 | 84,503 | 75,000 |
| 21,723 | 10,425 | 49 | 21,723 | 60,000 | 81,723 | 75,000 |
| 22,158 | 11,925 | 50 | 22,158 | 55,000 | 77,158 | 75,000 |
| 36,179 | 13,500 | 51 | 36,179 | 50,000 | 86,179 | 75,000 |
| 46,220 | 15,000 | 52 | 46,220 | 46,250 | 92,470 | 75,000 |
| 56,199 | 16,575 | 53 | 56,199 | 42,500 | 98,699 | 75,000 |
| 50,199 | 18,150 | 54 | 50,199 | 38,750 | 88,949 | 75,000 |
| 76,621 | 19,725 | 55 | 76,621 | 35,000 | 111,621 | 75,000 |
| 89,843 | 21,300 | 56 | 89,843 | 31,250 | 121,093 | 75,000 |
| 98,678 | 22,950 | 57 | 98,678 | 28,750 | 127,428 | 75,000 |
| 125,110 | 24,525 | 58 | 125,110 | 26,250 | 151,360 | 75,000 |
| 104,272 | 26,100 | 59 | 104,272 | 23,750 | 128,022 | 75,000 |
| 124,927 | 27,750 | 60 | 124,927 | 21,250 | 146,177 | 75,000 |
| 138,625 | 29,250 | 61 | 138,625 | 18,750 | 157,375 | 75,000 |
| 174,664 | 30,750 | 62 | 174,664 | 17,500 | 192,164 | 75,000 |
| 178,459 | 32,175 | 63 | 178,459 | 16,250 | 194,709 | 75,000 |
| 231,672 | 33,675 | 64 | 231,672 | 15,000 | 246,672 | 75,000 |
| 236,736 | 35,175 | 65 | 236,736 | 14,400 | 251,136 | 75,000 |

Whether you
**lived** or **died**
you would have been better off
"Buying Term and Investing the Difference"

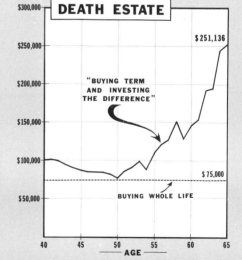

**LIVING ESTATE**
$300,000 — $250,000 — $200,000 — $150,000 — $100,000 — $50,000
$236,736
"BUYING TERM AND INVESTING THE DIFFERENCE"
$35,175
BUYING WHOLE LIFE
AGE 40 45 50 55 60 65

**DEATH ESTATE**
$300,000 — $250,000 — $200,000 — $150,000 — $100,000 — $50,000
$251,136
"BUYING TERM AND INVESTING THE DIFFERENCE"
$75,000
BUYING WHOLE LIFE
AGE 40 45 50 55 60 65

# MASSACHUSETTS INVESTORS TRUST

Illustration of assumed annual investments of $1,269 for twenty-five years from 1944 to 1968. All dividends and distributions reinvested.

This tabulation covers an illustration of an assumed investment of $1,269 annually on January 1 of each year from 1944 through 1968. This was a period in which stock prices fluctuated widely because of changing business and economic conditions, and were significantly higher at the end of the period than at the beginning. Thus, these results should not be considered as a representation of the dividend income or capital gain or loss that may be realized from an investment made in the fund today. A program of the type illustrated does not assure a profit nor protect against depreciation in declining markets.

| | | COST OF SHARES | | | | VALUE OF SHARES | | | | |
|---|---|---|---|---|---|---|---|---|---|---|
| YEAR ENDING DEC. 31 | AGE | CUMULATIVE ANNUAL INVEST-MENTS | ANNUAL INCOME DIVIDENDS REIN-VESTED | CUMULA-TIVE COST OF SHARES PURCHASED WITH DIVIDENDS | TOTAL COST (INCLUDES REIN-VESTED DIVIDENDS) | ACQUIRED THROUGH ANNUAL INVEST-MENTS | ACCEPTED AS CAPITAL GAINS DIS-TRIBUTIONS (CUMU-LATIVE) | SUB-TOTAL | PURCHASED THROUGH REINVEST-MENT OF INCOME (CUMULATIVE) | TOTAL VALUE |
| 1944 | 41 | $ 1,269 | $ 56 | $ 56 | $ 1,324 | $ 1,344 | $ 0 | $ 1,344 | $ 53 | $ 1,397 |
| 1945 | 42 | 2,538 | 111 | 167 | 2,707 | 3,143 | 56 | 3,199 | 178 | 3,377 |
| 1946 | 43 | 3,807 | 172 | 340 | 4,148 | 3,816 | 169 | 3,985 | 305 | 4,290 |
| 1947 | 44 | 5,077 | 261 | 602 | 5,679 | 4,852 | 166 | 5,018 | 535 | 5,553 |
| 1948 | 45 | 6,346 | 370 | 979 | 7,325 | 5,755 | 157 | 5,912 | 842 | 6,754 |
| 1949 | 46 | 7,615 | 472 | 1,451 | 9,068 | 7,885 | 179 | 8,064 | 1,427 | 9,491 |
| 1950 | 47 | 8,884 | 699 | 2,151 | 11,036 | 10,876 | 216 | 11,092 | 2,413 | 13,505 |
| 1951 | 48 | 10,154 | 824 | 2,975 | 13,130 | 13,677 | 778 | 14,455 | 3,513 | 17,968 |
| 1952 | 49 | 11,423 | 952 | 3,928 | 15,352 | 16,031 | 1,136 | 17,167 | 4,707 | 21,874 |
| 1953 | 50 | 12,692 | 1,067 | 4,995 | 17,689 | 16,443 | 1,087 | 17,530 | 5,505 | 23,035 |
| 1954 | 51 | 13,961 | 1,298 | 6,294 | 20,256 | 25,231 | 2,367 | 27,598 | 9,240 | 36,838 |
| 1955 | 52 | 15,231 | 1,581 | 7,875 | 23,106 | 30,966 | 3,967 | 34,933 | 12,339 | 47,272 |
| 1956 | 53 | 16,500 | 1,806 | 9,681 | 26,182 | 34,132 | 4,861 | 38,993 | 14,753 | 53,746 |
| 1957 | 54 | 17,769 | 1,960 | 11,641 | 29,412 | 29,497 | 4,898 | 34,395 | 13,957 | 48,352 |
| 1958 | 55 | 19,038 | 2,104 | 13,652 | 32,691 | 42,109 | 7,333 | 49,442 | 21,262 | 70,704 |
| 1959 | 56 | 20,308 | 2,174 | 15,826 | 36,135 | 45,182 | 8,873 | 54,055 | 24,202 | 78,257 |
| 1960 | 57 | 21,577 | 2,420 | 18,247 | 39,825 | 43,785 | 9,555 | 53,340 | 25,156 | 78,496 |
| 1961 | 58 | 22,846 | 2,380 | 20,626 | 43,474 | 53,069 | 14,979 | 68,048 | 31,918 | 99,966 |
| 1962 | 59 | 24,115 | 2,631 | 23,257 | 47,374 | 46,455 | 14,987 | 61,442 | 29,807 | 91,249 |
| 1963 | 60 | 25,385 | 2,941 | 26,198 | 51,584 | 54,515 | 19,332 | 73,847 | 36,859 | 110,706 |
| 1964 | 61 | 26,654 | 3,331 | 29,530 | 56,185 | 62,211 | 22,955 | 85,166 | 44,246 | 129,412 |
| 1965 | 62 | 27,923 | 3,791 | 33,322 | 61,247 | 65,753 | 28,533 | 94,286 | 49,372 | 143,658 |
| 1966 | 63 | 29,192 | 4,221 | 37,543 | 66,736 | 57,150 | 30,355 | 87,505 | 45,784 | 133,289 |
| 1967 | 64 | 30,462 | 4,497 | 42,040 | 72,503 | 63,833 | 43,215 | 107,048 | 54,084 | 161,132 |
| 1968 | 65 | 31,731 | 4,349 | 46,440 | 78,172 | 65,506 | 54,960 | 120,461 | 58,373 | 178,834 |

The total cost figures represent the cumulative total of yearly investments of $1,269 plus the cumulative amount of income dividends reinvested, and include the sales charge of **8½%** on all shares so purchased, as described in the prospectus. No adjustment has been made for any income taxes payable by shareholders on security distributions and dividends reinvested in shares. The dollar amounts of security profits distributions taken in shares were:

| | | | | | | | | | | | | | |
|---|---|---|---|---|---|---|---|---|---|---|---|---|---|
| 1944 | 0 | 1948 | 0 | 1952 | 281 | 1956 | 639 | 1960 | 1,173 | 1964 | 1,353 | 1968 | 11,406 |
| 1945 | 56 | 1949 | 0 | 1953 | 0 | 1957 | 831 | 1961 | 3,713 | 1965 | 4,715 | Total: | $48,725 |
| 1946 | 110 | 1950 | 0 | 1954 | 675 | 1958 | 629 | 1962 | 2,075 | 1966 | 5,985 | | |
| 1947 | 0 | 1951 | 500 | 1955 | 1,179 | 1959 | 1,215 | 1963 | 2,205 | 1967 | 9,985 | | |

## LIVING ESTATE

| "Buying Term and Investing the Difference" TOTAL VALUE OF SHARES | Buying Whole Life CASH VALUE |
|---|---|

## DEATH ESTATE

| "Buying Term and Investing the Difference" TOTAL VALUE OF SHARES | + DECREASING TERM INSURANCE | = TOTAL DEATH ESTATE | Buying Whole Life FACE VALUE |
|---|---|---|---|

| LIVING ESTATE — TOTAL VALUE OF SHARES | CASH VALUE | AGE | TOTAL VALUE OF SHARES | + DECREASING TERM INSURANCE | = TOTAL DEATH ESTATE | FACE VALUE |
|---|---|---|---|---|---|---|
| $ 1,397 | $ 0 | 41 | $ 1,397 | $100,000 | $101,397 | $75,000 |
| 3,377 | 225 | 42 | 3,377 | 95,000 | 98,377 | 75,000 |
| 4,290 | 1,575 | 43 | 4,290 | 90,000 | 94,290 | 75,000 |
| 5,553 | 3,000 | 44 | 5,553 | 85,000 | 90,553 | 75,000 |
| 6,754 | 4,425 | 45 | 6,754 | 80,000 | 86,754 | 75,000 |
| 9,491 | 5,925 | 46 | 9,491 | 75,000 | 84,491 | 75,000 |
| 13,505 | 7,425 | 47 | 13,505 | 70,000 | 83,505 | 75,000 |
| 17,968 | 8,925 | 48 | 17,968 | 65,000 | 82,968 | 75,000 |
| 21,874 | 10,425 | 49 | 21,874 | 60,000 | 81,874 | 75,000 |
| 23,035 | 11,925 | 50 | 23,035 | 55,000 | 78,035 | 75,000 |
| 36,838 | 13,500 | 51 | 36,838 | 50,000 | 86,838 | 75,000 |
| 47,272 | 15,000 | 52 | 47,272 | 46,250 | 93,522 | 75,000 |
| 53,746 | 16,575 | 53 | 53,746 | 42,500 | 96,240 | 75,000 |
| 48,352 | 18,150 | 54 | 48,352 | 38,750 | 87,102 | 75,000 |
| 70,704 | 19,725 | 55 | 70,704 | 35,000 | 105,704 | 75,000 |
| 78,257 | 21,300 | 56 | 78,257 | 31,250 | 109,507 | 75,000 |
| 78,496 | 22,950 | 57 | 78,496 | 28,750 | 107,246 | 75,000 |
| 99,966 | 24,525 | 58 | 99,966 | 26,250 | 126,216 | 75,000 |
| 91,249 | 26,100 | 59 | 91,249 | 23,750 | 114,999 | 75,000 |
| 110,706 | 27,750 | 60 | 110,706 | 21,250 | 131,956 | 75,000 |
| 129,412 | 29,250 | 61 | 129,412 | 18,750 | 148,162 | 75,000 |
| 143,658 | 30,750 | 62 | 143,658 | 17,500 | 161,158 | 75,000 |
| 133,289 | 32,175 | 63 | 133,289 | 16,250 | 149,539 | 75,000 |
| 161,132 | 33,675 | 64 | 161,132 | 15,000 | 176,132 | 75,000 |
| 178,834 | 35,175 | 65 | 178,834 | 14,400 | 193,234 | 75,000 |

Whether you
**lived** or **died**
you would have been better off
"Buying Term and Investing the Difference"

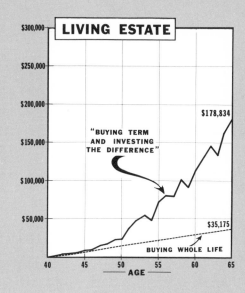

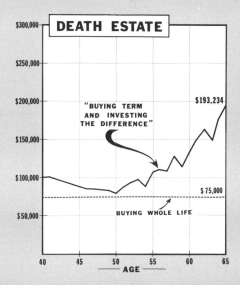

# NATIONAL SECURITIES—GROWTH STOCKS

Illustration of assumed annual investments of $1,269 for twenty-five years from 1944 to 1968. All dividends and distributions reinvested.

This tabulation covers an illustration of an assumed investment of $1,269 annually on January 1 of each year from 1944 through 1968. This was a period in which stock prices fluctuated widely because of changing business and economic conditions, and were significantly higher at the end of the period than at the beginning. Thus, these results should not be considered as a representation of the dividend income or capital gain or loss that may be realized from an investment made in the fund today. A program of the type illustrated does not assure a profit nor protect against depreciation in declining markets.

| | | COST OF SHARES | | | | VALUE OF SHARES | | | | |
|---|---|---|---|---|---|---|---|---|---|---|
| YEAR ENDING DEC. 31 | AGE | CUMULATIVE ANNUAL INVEST-MENTS | ANNUAL INCOME DIVIDENDS REIN-VESTED | CUMULA-TIVE COST OF SHARES PURCHASED WITH DIVIDENDS | TOTAL COST (INCLUDES REIN-VESTED DIVIDENDS) | ACQUIRED THROUGH ANNUAL INVEST-MENTS | ACCEPTED AS CAPITAL GAINS DIS-TRIBUTIONS (CUMU-LATIVE) | SUB-TOTAL | PURCHASED THROUGH REINVEST-MENT OF INCOME (CUMULATIVE) | TOTAL VALUE |
| 1944 | 41 | $ 1,269 | $ 5 | $ 5 | $ 1,274 | $ 1,236 | $ 0 | $ 1,236 | $ 5 | $ 1,241 |
| 1945 | 42 | 2,538 | 56 | 61 | 2,600 | 3,452 | 118 | 3,570 | 73 | 3,643 |
| 1946 | 43 | 3,807 | 80 | 142 | 3,949 | 3,295 | 187 | 3,482 | 113 | 3,595 |
| 1947 | 44 | 5,077 | 144 | 286 | 5,363 | 3,973 | 166 | 4,139 | 235 | 4,374 |
| 1948 | 45 | 6,346 | 261 | 548 | 6,895 | 4,871 | 199 | 5,070 | 456 | 5,526 |
| 1949 | 46 | 7,615 | 310 | 859 | 8,475 | 6,336 | 264 | 6,600 | 803 | 7,403 |
| 1950 | 47 | 8,884 | 476 | 1,335 | 10,220 | 10,088 | 354 | 10,442 | 1,589 | 12,031 |
| 1951 | 48 | 10,154 | 672 | 2,008 | 12,162 | 13,668 | 430 | 14,098 | 2,600 | 16,698 |
| 1952 | 49 | 11,423 | 784 | 2,792 | 14,216 | 15,837 | 459 | 16,296 | 3,550 | 19,846 |
| 1953 | 50 | 12,692 | 863 | 3,655 | 16,349 | 16,515 | 446 | 16,961 | 4,259 | 21,220 |
| 1954 | 51 | 13,961 | 938 | 4,594 | 18,556 | 26,839 | 1,605 | 28,444 | 7,536 | 35,980 |
| 1955 | 52 | 15,231 | 950 | 5,545 | 20,776 | 31,671 | 2,887 | 34,558 | 9,451 | 44,009 |
| 1956 | 53 | 16,500 | 1,077 | 6,622 | 23,123 | 35,767 | 4,608 | 40,375 | 11,312 | 51,687 |
| 1957 | 54 | 17,769 | 1,093 | 7,716 | 25,486 | 29,633 | 6,136 | 35,769 | 9,948 | 45,717 |
| 1958 | 55 | 19,038 | 1,173 | 8,890 | 27,929 | 43,159 | 9,476 | 52,635 | 15,236 | 67,871 |
| 1959 | 56 | 20,308 | 1,148 | 10,038 | 30,347 | 53,963 | 13,803 | 67,766 | 19,684 | 87,450 |
| 1960 | 57 | 21,577 | 1,208 | 11,247 | 32,825 | 54,083 | 15,749 | 69,832 | 20,450 | 90,282 |
| 1961 | 58 | 22,846 | 1,053 | 12,300 | 35,148 | 62,244 | 19,956 | 82,200 | 24,019 | 106,219 |
| 1962 | 59 | 24,115 | 1,113 | 13,413 | 37,529 | 48,573 | 18,561 | 67,134 | 19,401 | 86,535 |
| 1963 | 60 | 25,385 | 1,314 | 14,727 | 40,113 | 54,883 | 25,102 | 79,985 | 22,666 | 102,651 |
| 1964 | 61 | 26,654 | 1,404 | 16,132 | 42,787 | 59,040 | 31,169 | 90,209 | 25,181 | 115,390 |
| 1965 | 62 | 27,923 | 1,639 | 17,771 | 45,696 | 70,722 | 42,995 | 113,717 | 31,224 | 144,941 |
| 1966 | 63 | 29,192 | 2,199 | 19,971 | 49,164 | 66,641 | 46,736 | 113,377 | 30,944 | 144,321 |
| 1967 | 64 | 30,462 | 3,716 | 23,687 | 54,150 | 85,701 | 75,404 | 161,105 | 42,724 | 203,829 |
| 1968 | 65 | 31,731 | 4,475 | 28,163 | 59,896 | 84,514 | 102,452 | 186,965 | 45,716 | 232,681 |

The total cost figures represent the cumulative total of yearly investments of $1,269 plus the cumulative amount of income dividends reinvested, and include the sales charge of **8½%** on all shares so purchased, as described in the prospectus. No adjustment has been made for any income taxes payable by shareholders on security distributions and dividends reinvested in shares. The dollar amounts of security profits distributions taken in shares were:

| | | | | | | | | | | | | | |
|---|---|---|---|---|---|---|---|---|---|---|---|---|---|
| 1944 | 0 | 1948 | 46 | 1952 | 0 | 1956 | 1,428 | 1960 | 2,071 | 1964 | 4,699 | 1968 | 26,171 |
| 1945 | 92 | 1949 | 46 | 1953 | 0 | 1957 | 2,827 | 1961 | 2,178 | 1965 | 5,534 | Total: | $78,653 |
| 1946 | 134 | 1950 | 0 | 1954 | 687 | 1958 | 625 | 1962 | 3,784 | 1966 | 7,310 | | |
| 1947 | 0 | 1951 | 0 | 1955 | 980 | 1959 | 1,965 | 1963 | 4,152 | 1967 | 13,924 | | |

| LIVING ESTATE | | | DEATH ESTATE | | | |
| "Buying Term and Investing the Difference" | Buying Whole Life | AGE ↓ | "Buying Term and Investing the Difference" | Buying Whole Life | | |
| TOTAL VALUE OF SHARES | CASH VALUE | | TOTAL VALUE OF SHARES | + DECREASING TERM INSURANCE | = TOTAL DEATH ESTATE | FACE VALUE |
|---|---|---|---|---|---|---|
| $ 1,241 | $ 0 | 41 | $ 1,241 | $100,000 | $101,241 | $75,000 |
| 3,643 | 225 | 42 | 3,643 | 95,000 | 98,643 | 75,000 |
| 3,595 | 1,575 | 43 | 3,595 | 90,000 | 93,595 | 75,000 |
| 4,374 | 3,000 | 44 | 4,374 | 85,000 | 89,374 | 75,000 |
| 5,526 | 4,425 | 45 | 5,526 | 80,000 | 85,526 | 75,000 |
| 7,403 | 5,925 | 46 | 7,403 | 75,000 | 82,403 | 75,000 |
| 12,031 | 7,425 | 47 | 12,031 | 70,000 | 82,031 | 75,000 |
| 16,698 | 8,925 | 48 | 16,698 | 65,000 | 81,698 | 75,000 |
| 19,846 | 10,425 | 49 | 19,846 | 60,000 | 79,846 | 75,000 |
| 21,220 | 11,925 | 50 | 21,220 | 55,000 | 76,220 | 75,000 |
| 35,980 | 13,500 | 51 | 35,980 | 50,000 | 85,980 | 75,000 |
| 44,009 | 15,000 | 52 | 44,009 | 46,250 | 90,259 | 75,000 |
| 51,687 | 16,575 | 53 | 51,687 | 42,500 | 94,187 | 75,000 |
| 45,717 | 18,150 | 54 | 45,717 | 38,750 | 84,467 | 75,000 |
| 67,871 | 19,725 | 55 | 67,871 | 35,000 | 102,871 | 75,000 |
| 87,450 | 21,300 | 56 | 87,450 | 31,250 | 118,700 | 75,000 |
| 90,282 | 22,950 | 57 | 90,282 | 28,750 | 119,032 | 75,000 |
| 106,219 | 24,525 | 58 | 106,219 | 26,250 | 132,469 | 75,000 |
| 86,535 | 26,100 | 59 | 86,535 | 23,750 | 110,285 | 75,000 |
| 102,651 | 27,750 | 60 | 102,651 | 21,250 | 123,901 | 75,000 |
| 115,390 | 29,250 | 61 | 115,390 | 18,750 | 134,140 | 75,000 |
| 144,941 | 30,750 | 62 | 144,941 | 17,500 | 162,441 | 75,000 |
| 144,321 | 32,175 | 63 | 144,321 | 16,250 | 160,571 | 75,000 |
| 203,829 | 33,675 | 64 | 203,829 | 15,000 | 218,829 | 75,000 |
| 232,681 | 35,175 | 65 | 232,681 | 14,400 | 247,081 | 75,000 |

Whether you
**lived** or **died**
you would have been better off
"Buying Term and Investing the Difference"

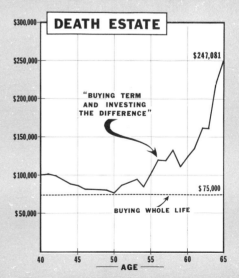

LIVING ESTATE

$232,681

"BUYING TERM AND INVESTING THE DIFFERENCE"

$35,175

BUYING WHOLE LIFE

AGE

DEATH ESTATE

$247,081

"BUYING TERM AND INVESTING THE DIFFERENCE"

$75,000

BUYING WHOLE LIFE

AGE

211

# NATIONAL INVESTORS CORP.

Illustration of assumed annual investments of $1,269 for twenty-five years from 1944 to 1968. All dividends and distributions reinvested.

This tabulation covers an illustration of an assumed investment of $1,269 annually on January 1 of each year from 1944 through 1968. This was a period in which stock prices fluctuated widely because of changing business and economic conditions, and were significantly higher at the end of the period than at the beginning. Thus, these results should not be considered as a representation of the dividend income or capital gain or loss that may be realized from an investment made in the fund today. A program of the type illustrated does not assure a profit nor protect against depreciation in declining markets.

| | | COST OF SHARES | | | | VALUE OF SHARES | | | | |
|---|---|---|---|---|---|---|---|---|---|---|
| YEAR ENDING DEC. 31 | AGE | CUMULATIVE ANNUAL INVEST- MENTS | ANNUAL INCOME DIVIDENDS REIN- VESTED | CUMULA- TIVE COST OF SHARES PURCHASED WITH DIVIDENDS | TOTAL COST (INCLUDES REIN- VESTED DIVIDENDS) | ACQUIRED THROUGH ANNUAL INVEST- MENTS | ACCEPTED AS CAPITAL GAINS DIS- TRIBUTIONS (CUMU- LATIVE) | SUB- TOTAL | PURCHASED THROUGH REINVEST- MENT OF INCOME (CUMULATIVE) | TOTAL VALUE |
| 1944 | 41 | $ 1,269 | $ 44 | $ 44 | $ 1,313 | $ 1,428 | $ 8 | $ 1,436 | $ 42 | $ 1,478 |
| 1945 | 42 | 2,538 | 81 | 125 | 2,664 | 3,776 | 138 | 3,914 | 148 | 4,062 |
| 1946 | 43 | 3,807 | 133 | 258 | 4,066 | 4,451 | 310 | 4,761 | 248 | 5,009 |
| 1947 | 44 | 5,077 | 228 | 486 | 5,563 | 4,960 | 449 | 5,409 | 424 | 5,833 |
| 1948 | 45 | 6,346 | 309 | 796 | 7,141 | 5,178 | 732 | 5,910 | 628 | 6,538 |
| 1949 | 46 | 7,615 | 396 | 1,191 | 8,807 | 7,592 | 993 | 8,585 | 1,148 | 9,733 |
| 1950 | 47 | 8,884 | 598 | 1,789 | 10,674 | 9,998 | 1,749 | 11,747 | 1,892 | 13,639 |
| 1951 | 48 | 10,154 | 654 | 2,443 | 12,597 | 12,793 | 3,297 | 16,090 | 2,770 | 18,860 |
| 1952 | 49 | 11,423 | 689 | 3,132 | 14,555 | 13,822 | 3,959 | 17,781 | 3,388 | 21,169 |
| 1953 | 50 | 12,692 | 796 | 3,928 | 16,621 | 14,420 | 4,429 | 18,849 | 4,014 | 22,863 |
| 1954 | 51 | 13,961 | 888 | 4,816 | 18,778 | 21,916 | 7,459 | 29,375 | 6,571 | 35,946 |
| 1955 | 52 | 15,231 | 1,065 | 5,881 | 21,112 | 25,322 | 10,696 | 36,018 | 8,192 | 44,210 |
| 1956 | 53 | 16,500 | 1,263 | 7,144 | 23,644 | 28,827 | 14,498 | 43,325 | 10,068 | 53,393 |
| 1957 | 54 | 17,769 | 1,396 | 8,540 | 26,310 | 26,236 | 14,576 | 40,812 | 9,973 | 50,785 |
| 1958 | 55 | 19,038 | 1,520 | 10,060 | 29,099 | 37,675 | 23,860 | 61,535 | 15,303 | 76,838 |
| 1959 | 56 | 20,308 | 1,590 | 11,650 | 31,958 | 43,961 | 29,034 | 72,995 | 18,848 | 91,843 |
| 1960 | 57 | 21,577 | 1,745 | 13,395 | 34,972 | 48,439 | 33,956 | 82,395 | 21,898 | 104,293 |
| 1961 | 58 | 22,846 | 1,840 | 15,235 | 38,082 | 58,176 | 41,690 | 99,866 | 27,394 | 127,260 |
| 1962 | 59 | 24,115 | 2,143 | 17,378 | 41,494 | 48,764 | 35,402 | 84,166 | 24,644 | 108,810 |
| 1963 | 60 | 25,385 | 2,311 | 19,689 | 45,074 | 57,475 | 42,858 | 100,333 | 30,558 | 130,891 |
| 1964 | 61 | 26,654 | 2,744 | 22,433 | 49,087 | 62,983 | 48,691 | 111,674 | 35,372 | 147,046 |
| 1965 | 62 | 27,923 | 3,130 | 25,563 | 53,487 | 76,112 | 61,119 | 137,231 | 45,101 | 182,332 |
| 1966 | 63 | 29,192 | 3,264 | 28,827 | 58,020 | 73,374 | 61,626 | 135,000 | 45,734 | 180,734 |
| 1967 | 64 | 30,462 | 3,692 | 32,519 | 62,981 | 92,407 | 86,641 | 179,048 | 60,172 | 239,220 |
| 1968 | 65 | 31,731 | 3,935 | 36,454 | 68,185 | 99,814 | 92,403 | 192,217 | 67,822 | 260,039 |

The total cost figures represent the cumulative total of yearly investments of $1,269 plus the cumulative amount of income dividends reinvested, and include the sales charge of $7\frac{1}{2}\%$ on all shares so purchased, as described in the prospectus. No adjustment has been made for any income taxes payable by shareholders on security distributions and dividends reinvested in shares. The dollar amounts of security profits distributions taken in shares were:

| | | | | | | | | | | | | | |
|---|---|---|---|---|---|---|---|---|---|---|---|---|---|
| 1944 | 9 | 1948 | 349 | 1952 | 680 | 1956 | 2,797 | 1960 | 2,668 | 1964 | 2,671 | 1968 | 0 |
| 1945 | 128 | 1949 | 130 | 1953 | 618 | 1957 | 1,970 | 1961 | 1,919 | 1965 | 3,317 | Total: | $45,573 |
| 1946 | 182 | 1950 | 592 | 1954 | 1,188 | 1958 | 3,677 | 1962 | 1,153 | 1966 | 3,548 | | |
| 1947 | 171 | 1951 | 1,263 | 1955 | 2,489 | 1959 | 2,001 | 1963 | 2,080 | 1967 | 9,973 | | |

| LIVING ESTATE | | | DEATH ESTATE | | | |
|---|---|---|---|---|---|---|
| "Buying Term and Investing the Difference" | Buying Whole Life | | "Buying Term and Investing the Difference" | | | Buying Whole Life |
| TOTAL VALUE OF SHARES | CASH VALUE | AGE | TOTAL VALUE OF SHARES | + DECREASING TERM INSURANCE | = TOTAL DEATH ESTATE | FACE VALUE |
| $ 1,478 | $ 0 | 41 | $ 1,478 | $100,000 | $101,478 | $75,000 |
| 4,062 | 225 | 42 | 4,062 | 95,000 | 99,062 | 75,000 |
| 5,009 | 1,575 | 43 | 5,009 | 90,000 | 95,009 | 75,000 |
| 5,833 | 3,000 | 44 | 5,833 | 85,000 | 90,833 | 75,000 |
| 6,538 | 4,425 | 45 | 6,538 | 80,000 | 86,538 | 75,000 |
| 9,733 | 5,925 | 46 | 9,733 | 75,000 | 84,733 | 75,000 |
| 13,639 | 7,425 | 47 | 13,639 | 70,000 | 83,639 | 75,000 |
| 18,860 | 8,925 | 48 | 18,860 | 65,000 | 83,860 | 75,000 |
| 21,169 | 10,425 | 49 | 21,169 | 60,000 | 81,169 | 75,000 |
| 22,863 | 11,925 | 50 | 22,863 | 55,000 | 77,863 | 75,000 |
| 35,946 | 13,500 | 51 | 35,946 | 50,000 | 85,946 | 75,000 |
| 44,210 | 15,000 | 52 | 44,210 | 46,250 | 90,460 | 75,000 |
| 53,393 | 16,575 | 53 | 53,393 | 42,500 | 95,893 | 75,000 |
| 50,785 | 18,150 | 54 | 50,785 | 38,750 | 89,508 | 75,000 |
| 76,838 | 19,725 | 55 | 76,838 | 35,000 | 111,838 | 75,000 |
| 91,843 | 21,300 | 56 | 91,843 | 31,250 | 123,093 | 75,000 |
| 104,293 | 22,950 | 57 | 104,293 | 28,750 | 133,043 | 75,000 |
| 127,260 | 24,525 | 58 | 127,260 | 26,250 | 153,510 | 75,000 |
| 108,810 | 26,100 | 59 | 108,810 | 23,750 | 132,560 | 75,000 |
| 130,891 | 27,750 | 60 | 130,891 | 21,250 | 152,141 | 75,000 |
| 147,046 | 29,250 | 61 | 147,046 | 18,750 | 165,796 | 75,000 |
| 182,332 | 30,750 | 62 | 182,332 | 17,500 | 199,832 | 75,000 |
| 180,734 | 32,175 | 63 | 180,734 | 16,250 | 196,984 | 75,000 |
| 239,220 | 33,675 | 64 | 239,220 | 15,000 | 254,220 | 75,000 |
| 260,039 | 35,175 | 65 | 260,039 | 14,400 | 274,439 | 75,000 |

Whether you
**lived** or **died**
you would have been better off
"Buying Term and Investing the Difference"

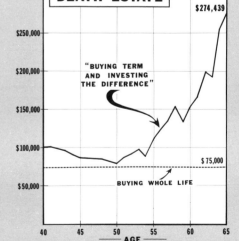

213

# NATIONAL SECURITIES—STOCK SERIES

Illustration of assumed annual investments of $1,269 for twenty-five years from 1944 to 1968. All dividends and distributions reinvested.

This tabulation covers an illustration of an assumed investment of $1,269 annually on January 1 of each year from 1944 through 1968. This was a period in which stock prices fluctuated widely because of changing business and economic conditions, and were significantly higher at the end of the period than at the beginning. Thus, these results should not be considered as a representation of the dividend income or capital gain or loss that may be realized from an investment made in the fund today. A program of the type illustrated does not assure a profit nor protect against depreciation in declining markets.

| | | COST OF SHARES | | | | VALUE OF SHARES | | | | |
|---|---|---|---|---|---|---|---|---|---|---|
| YEAR ENDING DEC. 31 | AGE | CUMULATIVE ANNUAL INVEST-MENTS | ANNUAL INCOME DIVIDENDS REIN-VESTED | CUMULA-TIVE COST OF SHARES PURCHASED WITH DIVIDENDS | TOTAL COST (INCLUDES REIN-VESTED DIVIDENDS) | ACQUIRED THROUGH ANNUAL INVEST-MENTS | ACCEPTED AS CAPITAL GAINS DIS-TRIBUTIONS (CUMU-LATIVE) | SUB-TOTAL | PURCHASED THROUGH REINVEST-MENT OF INCOME (CUMULATIVE) | TOTAL VALUE |
| 1944 | 41 | $ 1,269 | $ 18 | $ 18 | $ 1,288 | $ 1,242 | $ 0 | $ 1,242 | $ 18 | $ 1,260 |
| 1945 | 42 | 2,538 | 162 | 181 | 2,720 | 3,093 | 106 | 3,199 | 208 | 3,407 |
| 1946 | 43 | 3,807 | 233 | 414 | 4,222 | 3,315 | 156 | 3,471 | 337 | 3,808 |
| 1947 | 44 | 5,077 | 368 | 783 | 5,860 | 4,013 | 162 | 4,175 | 635 | 4,810 |
| 1948 | 45 | 6,346 | 489 | 1,273 | 7,619 | 4,772 | 183 | 4,955 | 1,007 | 5,962 |
| 1949 | 46 | 7,615 | 619 | 1,892 | 9,508 | 5,800 | 265 | 6,065 | 1,592 | 7,657 |
| 1950 | 47 | 8,884 | 707 | 2,599 | 11,484 | 8,571 | 417 | 8,988 | 2,709 | 11,697 |
| 1951 | 48 | 10,154 | 962 | 3,561 | 13,715 | 10,165 | 900 | 11,065 | 3,721 | 14,786 |
| 1952 | 49 | 11,423 | 1,115 | 4,677 | 16,101 | 11,215 | 2,066 | 13,281 | 4,762 | 18,043 |
| 1953 | 50 | 12,692 | 1,261 | 5,939 | 18,632 | 10,212 | 2,294 | 12,506 | 4,995 | 17,501 |
| 1954 | 51 | 13,961 | 1,462 | 7,401 | 21,363 | 17,289 | 3,803 | 21,092 | 9,317 | 30,409 |
| 1955 | 52 | 15,231 | 1,716 | 9,118 | 24,349 | 21,461 | 5,299 | 26,760 | 12,572 | 39,332 |
| 1956 | 53 | 16,500 | 1,999 | 11,117 | 27,618 | 23,594 | 6,929 | 30,523 | 15,036 | 45,559 |
| 1957 | 54 | 17,769 | 2,350 | 13,468 | 31,238 | 17,479 | 6,620 | 24,099 | 12,408 | 36,507 |
| 1958 | 55 | 19,038 | 2,428 | 15,896 | 34,935 | 24,683 | 10,802 | 35,485 | 19,074 | 54,559 |
| 1959 | 56 | 20,308 | 2,348 | 18,245 | 38,553 | 26,714 | 13,070 | 39,784 | 21,881 | 61,665 |
| 1960 | 57 | 21,577 | 2,723 | 20,968 | 42,547 | 24,246 | 13,469 | 37,715 | 21,489 | 59,204 |
| 1961 | 58 | 22,846 | 2,836 | 23,805 | 46,653 | 29,834 | 18,323 | 48,157 | 27,932 | 76,089 |
| 1962 | 59 | 24,115 | 3,006 | 26,811 | 50,928 | 25,341 | 17,322 | 42,663 | 25,474 | 68,137 |
| 1963 | 60 | 25,385 | 2,917 | 29,729 | 55,115 | 28,960 | 22,113 | 51,073 | 30,568 | 81,641 |
| 1964 | 61 | 26,654 | 3,188 | 32,918 | 59,573 | 33,047 | 28,104 | 61,151 | 36,572 | 97,723 |
| 1965 | 62 | 27,923 | 3,703 | 36,621 | 64,546 | 36,702 | 34,617 | 71,319 | 42,792 | 114,111 |
| 1966 | 63 | 29,192 | 4,158 | 40,780 | 69,973 | 32,324 | 34,059 | 66,383 | 40,145 | 106,528 |
| 1967 | 64 | 30,462 | 4,693 | 45,474 | 75,937 | 37,543 | 43,782 | 81,325 | 49,410 | 130,735 |
| 1968 | 65 | 31,731 | 5,289 | 50,763 | 82,496 | 45,296 | 58,691 | 103,989 | 63,344 | 167,333 |

The total cost figures represent the cumulative total of yearly investments of $1,269 plus the cumulative amount of income dividends reinvested, and include the sales charge of 8½% on all shares so purchased, as described in the prospectus. No adjustment has been made for any income taxes payable by shareholders on security distributions and dividends reinvested in shares. The dollar amounts of security profits distributions taken in shares were:

| | | | | | | | | | | | | | | |
|---|---|---|---|---|---|---|---|---|---|---|---|---|---|---|
| 1944 | 0 | 1948 | 34 | 1952 | 1,092 | 1956 | 1,349 | 1960 | 2,138 | 1964 | 3,595 | 1968 | 6,103 |
| 1945 | 84 | 1949 | 78 | 1953 | 646 | 1957 | 2,160 | 1961 | 2,359 | 1965 | 4,134 | Total: | $44,907 |
| 1946 | 95 | 1950 | 75 | 1954 | 228 | 1958 | 1,528 | 1962 | 2,655 | 1966 | 5,101 | | |
| 1947 | 21 | 1951 | 449 | 1955 | 762 | 1959 | 1,892 | 1963 | 3,008 | 1967 | 5,321 | | |

| LIVING ESTATE | | | DEATH ESTATE | | | |
|---|---|---|---|---|---|---|
| "Buying Term and Investing the Difference" | Buying Whole Life | AGE | "Buying Term and Investing the Difference" | | | Buying Whole Life |
| TOTAL VALUE OF SHARES | CASH VALUE | | TOTAL VALUE OF SHARES + | DECREASING TERM INSURANCE = | TOTAL DEATH ESTATE | FACE VALUE |
| $ 1,260 | $ 0 | 41 | $ 1,260 | $100,000 | $101,260 | $75,000 |
| 3,407 | 225 | 42 | 3,407 | 95,000 | 98,407 | 75,000 |
| 3,808 | 1,575 | 43 | 3,808 | 90,000 | 93,808 | 75,000 |
| 4,810 | 3,000 | 44 | 4,810 | 85,000 | 89,810 | 75,000 |
| 5,962 | 4,425 | 45 | 5,962 | 80,000 | 85,962 | 75,000 |
| 7,657 | 5,925 | 46 | 7,657 | 75,000 | 82,657 | 75,000 |
| 11,697 | 7,425 | 47 | 11,697 | 70,000 | 81,697 | 75,000 |
| 14,786 | 8,925 | 48 | 14,786 | 65,000 | 79,786 | 75,000 |
| 18,043 | 10,425 | 49 | 18,043 | 60,000 | 78,043 | 75,000 |
| 17,501 | 11,925 | 50 | 17,501 | 55,000 | 72,501 | 75,000 |
| 30,409 | 13,500 | 51 | 30,409 | 50,000 | 80,409 | 75,000 |
| 39,332 | 15,000 | 52 | 39,332 | 46,250 | 85,582 | 75,000 |
| 45,559 | 16,575 | 53 | 45,559 | 42,500 | 88,059 | 75,000 |
| 36,507 | 18,150 | 54 | 36,507 | 38,750 | 75,257 | 75,000 |
| 54,559 | 19,725 | 55 | 54,559 | 35,000 | 89,559 | 75,000 |
| 61,665 | 21,300 | 56 | 61,665 | 31,250 | 92,915 | 75,000 |
| 59,204 | 22,950 | 57 | 59,204 | 28,750 | 87,954 | 75,000 |
| 76,089 | 24,525 | 58 | 76,089 | 26,250 | 102,339 | 75,000 |
| 68,137 | 26,100 | 59 | 68,137 | 23,750 | 91,887 | 75,000 |
| 81,641 | 27,750 | 60 | 81,641 | 21,250 | 102,891 | 75,000 |
| 97,723 | 29,250 | 61 | 97,723 | 18,750 | 116,473 | 75,000 |
| 114,111 | 30,750 | 62 | 114,111 | 17,500 | 131,611 | 75,000 |
| 106,528 | 32,175 | 63 | 106,528 | 16,250 | 122,778 | 75,000 |
| 130,735 | 33,675 | 64 | 130,735 | 15,000 | 145,735 | 75,000 |
| 167,333 | 35,175 | 65 | 167,333 | 14,400 | 181,733 | 75,000 |

Whether you **lived** or **died** you would have been better off "Buying Term and Investing the Difference"

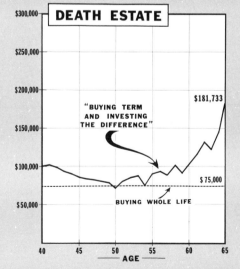

# NATION–WIDE SECURITIES

Illustration of assumed annual investments of $1,269 for twenty-five years from 1944 to 1968. All dividends and distributions reinvested.

This tabulation covers an illustration of an assumed investment of $1,269 annually on January 1 of each year from 1944 through 1968. This was a period in which stock prices fluctuated widely because of changing business and economic conditions, and were significantly higher at the end of the period than at the beginning. Thus, these results should not be considered as a representation of the dividend income or capital gain or loss that may be realized from an investment made in the fund today. A program of the type illustrated does not assure a profit nor protect against depreciation in declining markets.

| | | COST OF SHARES | | | | VALUE OF SHARES | | | | |
|---|---|---|---|---|---|---|---|---|---|---|
| YEAR ENDING DEC. 31 | AGE | CUMULATIVE ANNUAL INVEST- MENTS | ANNUAL INCOME DIVIDENDS REIN- VESTED | CUMULA- TIVE COST OF SHARES PURCHASED WITH DIVIDENDS | TOTAL COST (INCLUDES REIN- VESTED DIVIDENDS) | ACQUIRED THROUGH ANNUAL INVEST- MENTS | ACCEPTED AS CAPITAL GAINS DIS- TRIBUTIONS (CUMU- LATIVE) | SUB- TOTAL | PURCHASED THROUGH REINVEST- MENT OF INCOME (CUMULATIVE) | TOTAL VALUE |
| 1944 | 41 | $ 1,269 | $ 51 | $ 51 | $ 1,321 | $ 1,336 | $ 9 | $ 1,345 | $ 50 | $ 1,395 |
| 1945 | 42 | 2,538 | 99 | 150 | 2,690 | 2,740 | 264 | 3,004 | 148 | 3,152 |
| 1946 | 43 | 3,807 | 139 | 290 | 4,098 | 3,645 | 436 | 4,081 | 261 | 4,342 |
| 1947 | 44 | 5,077 | 194 | 485 | 5,562 | 4,470 | 523 | 4,993 | 417 | 5,410 |
| 1948 | 45 | 6,346 | 323 | 808 | 7,155 | 5,432 | 535 | 5,967 | 691 | 6,658 |
| 1949 | 46 | 7,615 | 418 | 1,226 | 8,842 | 7,238 | 606 | 7,844 | 1,165 | 9,009 |
| 1950 | 47 | 8,884 | 513 | 1,740 | 10,625 | 8,918 | 799 | 9,717 | 1,725 | 11,442 |
| 1951 | 48 | 10,154 | 535 | 2,275 | 12,429 | 10,231 | 1,053 | 11,284 | 2,249 | 13,533 |
| 1952 | 49 | 11,423 | 676 | 2,951 | 14,375 | 12,173 | 1,354 | 13,527 | 3,048 | 16,575 |
| 1953 | 50 | 12,692 | 781 | 3,733 | 16,426 | 12,693 | 1,591 | 14,284 | 3,630 | 17,914 |
| 1954 | 51 | 13,961 | 838 | 4,571 | 18,533 | 16,559 | 2,368 | 18,927 | 5,176 | 24,103 |
| 1955 | 52 | 15,231 | 944 | 5,515 | 20,747 | 18,871 | 3,491 | 22,362 | 6,400 | 28,762 |
| 1956 | 53 | 16,500 | 1,113 | 6,629 | 23,130 | 19,053 | 4,441 | 23,494 | 7,074 | 30,568 |
| 1957 | 54 | 17,769 | 1,306 | 7,935 | 25,705 | 18,910 | 5,405 | 24,315 | 7,787 | 32,102 |
| 1958 | 55 | 19,038 | 1,430 | 9,365 | 28,404 | 23,570 | 7,622 | 31,192 | 10,557 | 41,749 |
| 1959 | 56 | 20,308 | 1,527 | 10,893 | 31,201 | 23,868 | 8,820 | 32,688 | 11,560 | 44,248 |
| 1960 | 57 | 21,577 | 1,724 | 12,617 | 34,195 | 25,658 | 10,636 | 36,294 | 13,523 | 49,817 |
| 1961 | 58 | 22,846 | 1,885 | 14,502 | 37,350 | 30,908 | 14,391 | 45,299 | 17,352 | 62,651 |
| 1962 | 59 | 24,115 | 2,134 | 16,636 | 40,753 | 29,031 | 14,979 | 44,010 | 17,710 | 61,720 |
| 1963 | 60 | 25,385 | 2,351 | 18,988 | 44,374 | 32,215 | 18,049 | 50,264 | 21,075 | 71,339 |
| 1964 | 61 | 26,654 | 2,572 | 21,560 | 48,215 | 35,434 | 21,461 | 56,895 | 24,735 | 81,630 |
| 1965 | 62 | 27,923 | 2,841 | 24,401 | 52,326 | 36,851 | 24,168 | 61,019 | 27,591 | 88,610 |
| 1966 | 63 | 29,192 | 3,218 | 27,619 | 56,813 | 32,901 | 23,706 | 56,607 | 26,781 | 83,388 |
| 1967 | 64 | 30,462 | 3,583 | 31,202 | 61,666 | 34,687 | 26,925 | 61,612 | 30,472 | 92,084 |
| 1968 | 65 | 31,731 | 4,061 | 35,264 | 66,996 | 38,807 | 32,359 | 71,166 | 36,835 | 108,001 |

The total cost figures represent the cumulative total of yearly investments of $1,269 plus the cumulative amount of income dividends reinvested, and include the sales charge of $7\frac{1}{2}\%$ on all shares so purchased, as described in the prospectus. No adjustment has been made for any income taxes payable by shareholders on security distributions and dividends reinvested in shares. The dollar amounts of security profits distributions taken in shares were:

| | | | | | | | | | | | | | |
|---|---|---|---|---|---|---|---|---|---|---|---|---|---|
| 1944 | 8 | 1948 | 30 | 1952 | 218 | 1956 | 1,153 | 1960 | 1,526 | 1964 | 2,244 | 1968 | 3,143 |
| 1945 | 253 | 1949 | 20 | 1953 | 286 | 1957 | 1,261 | 1961 | 2,053 | 1965 | 2,475 | Total: | $28,806 |
| 1946 | 195 | 1950 | 154 | 1954 | 431 | 1958 | 1,170 | 1962 | 1,842 | 1966 | 2,665 | | |
| 1947 | 120 | 1951 | 243 | 1955 | 953 | 1959 | 1,476 | 1963 | 2,067 | 1967 | 2,820 | | |

## LIVING ESTATE

| | |
|---|---|
| "Buying Term and Investing the Difference" | Buying Whole Life |

## DEATH ESTATE

| | |
|---|---|
| "Buying Term and Investing the Difference" | Buying Whole Life |

| TOTAL VALUE OF SHARES | CASH VALUE | AGE | TOTAL VALUE OF SHARES | + DECREASING TERM INSURANCE | = TOTAL DEATH ESTATE | FACE VALUE |
|---|---|---|---|---|---|---|
| $ 1,395 | $ 0 | 41 | $ 1,395 | $100,000 | $101,395 | $75,000 |
| 3,152 | 225 | 42 | 3,152 | 95,000 | 98,152 | 75,000 |
| 4,342 | 1,575 | 43 | 4,342 | 90,000 | 94,342 | 75,000 |
| 5,410 | 3,000 | 44 | 5,410 | 85,000 | 90,410 | 75,000 |
| 6,658 | 4,425 | 45 | 6,658 | 80,000 | 86,658 | 75,000 |
| 9,009 | 5,925 | 46 | 9,009 | 75,000 | 84,009 | 75,000 |
| 11,442 | 7,425 | 47 | 11,442 | 70,000 | 81,442 | 75,000 |
| 13,533 | 8,925 | 48 | 13,533 | 65,000 | 78,353 | 75,000 |
| 16,575 | 10,425 | 49 | 16,575 | 60,000 | 76,575 | 75,000 |
| 17,914 | 11,925 | 50 | 17,914 | 55,000 | 72,914 | 75,000 |
| 24,103 | 13,500 | 51 | 24,103 | 50,000 | 74,103 | 75,000 |
| 28,762 | 15,000 | 52 | 28,762 | 46,250 | 75,012 | 75,000 |
| 30,568 | 16,575 | 53 | 30,568 | 42,500 | 73,068 | 75,000 |
| 32,102 | 18,150 | 54 | 32,102 | 38,750 | 70,762 | 75,000 |
| 41,749 | 19,725 | 55 | 41,749 | 35,000 | 76,749 | 75,000 |
| 44,248 | 21,300 | 56 | 44,248 | 31,250 | 75,498 | 75,000 |
| 49,817 | 22,950 | 57 | 49,817 | 28,750 | 78,567 | 75,000 |
| 62,651 | 24,525 | 58 | 62,651 | 26,250 | 88,901 | 75,000 |
| 61,720 | 26,100 | 59 | 61,720 | 23,750 | 85,470 | 75,000 |
| 71,339 | 27,750 | 60 | 71,339 | 21,250 | 92,589 | 75,000 |
| 81,630 | 29,250 | 61 | 81,630 | 18,750 | 100,380 | 75,000 |
| 88,610 | 30,750 | 62 | 88,610 | 17,500 | 106,110 | 75,000 |
| 83,388 | 32,175 | 63 | 83,388 | 16,250 | 99,638 | 75,000 |
| 92,084 | 33,675 | 64 | 92,084 | 15,000 | 107,084 | 75,000 |
| 108,001 | 35,175 | 65 | 108,001 | 14,400 | 122,401 | 75,000 |

Whether you **lived** or **died** you would have been better off "Buying Term and Investing the Difference"

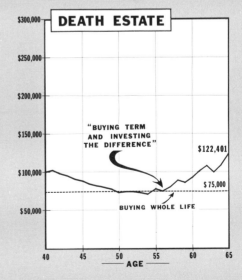

**LIVING ESTATE**

"BUYING TERM AND INVESTING THE DIFFERENCE" $108,001

$35,175 BUYING WHOLE LIFE

**DEATH ESTATE**

"BUYING TERM AND INVESTING THE DIFFERENCE" $122,401

$75,000 BUYING WHOLE LIFE

# PIONEER FUND

Illustration of assumed annual investments of $1,269 for twenty-five years from 1944 to 1968. All dividends and distributions reinvested.

This tabulation covers an illustration of an assumed investment of $1,269 annually on January 1 of each year from 1944 through 1968. This was a period in which stock prices fluctuated widely because of changing business and economic conditions, and were significantly higher at the end of the period than at the beginning. Thus, these results should not be considered as a representation of the dividend income or capital gain or loss that may be realized from an investment made in the fund today. A program of the type illustrated does not assure a profit nor protect against depreciation in declining markets.

| | | COST OF SHARES | | | | VALUE OF SHARES | | | | |
|---|---|---|---|---|---|---|---|---|---|---|
| YEAR ENDING DEC. 31 | AGE | CUMULATIVE ANNUAL INVESTMENTS | ANNUAL INCOME DIVIDENDS REINVESTED | CUMULATIVE COST OF SHARES PURCHASED WITH DIVIDENDS | TOTAL COST (INCLUDES REINVESTED DIVIDENDS) | ACQUIRED THROUGH ANNUAL INVESTMENTS | ACCEPTED AS CAPITAL GAINS DISTRIBUTIONS (CUMULATIVE) | SUBTOTAL | PURCHASED THROUGH REINVESTMENT OF INCOME (CUMULATIVE) | TOTAL VALUE |
| 1944 | 41 | $ 1,269 | $ 86 | $ 86 | $ 1,355 | $ 1,585 | $ 0 | $ 1,585 | $ 85 | $ 1,670 |
| 1945 | 42 | 2,538 | 146 | 232 | 2,771 | 3,967 | 26 | 3,993 | 282 | 4,275 |
| 1946 | 43 | 3,807 | 251 | 483 | 4,291 | 5,549 | 28 | 5,577 | 537 | 6,114 |
| 1947 | 44 | 5,077 | 339 | 822 | 5,899 | 6,466 | 157 | 6,623 | 822 | 7,445 |
| 1948 | 45 | 6,346 | 448 | 1,270 | 7,616 | 7,194 | 278 | 7,472 | 1,168 | 8,640 |
| 1949 | 46 | 7,615 | 507 | 1,777 | 9,393 | 9,023 | 435 | 9,458 | 1,762 | 11,220 |
| 1950 | 47 | 8,884 | 656 | 2,433 | 11,318 | 12,071 | 696 | 12,767 | 2,753 | 15,520 |
| 1951 | 48 | 10,154 | 724 | 3,157 | 13,311 | 14,713 | 1,079 | 15,792 | 3,743 | 19,535 |
| 1952 | 49 | 11,423 | 838 | 3,995 | 15,418 | 16,729 | 1,494 | 18,223 | 4,739 | 22,962 |
| 1953 | 50 | 12,692 | 1,019 | 5,014 | 17,707 | 17,850 | 1,791 | 19,641 | 5,671 | 25,312 |
| 1954 | 51 | 13,961 | 1,196 | 6,210 | 20,172 | 25,107 | 2,769 | 27,876 | 8,743 | 36,619 |
| 1955 | 52 | 15,231 | 1,288 | 7,498 | 22,729 | 29,636 | 4,017 | 33,653 | 11,078 | 44,731 |
| 1956 | 53 | 16,500 | 1,570 | 9,068 | 25,568 | 32,546 | 5,375 | 37,921 | 13,173 | 51,094 |
| 1957 | 54 | 17,769 | 1,756 | 10,824 | 28,594 | 28,987 | 5,802 | 34,789 | 12,743 | 47,532 |
| 1958 | 55 | 19,038 | 1,946 | 12,770 | 31,809 | 40,464 | 9,221 | 49,685 | 19,124 | 68,809 |
| 1959 | 56 | 20,308 | 2,078 | 14,848 | 35,156 | 45,298 | 11,634 | 56,932 | 22,756 | 79,688 |
| 1960 | 57 | 21,577 | 2,299 | 17,147 | 38,724 | 44,942 | 13,185 | 58,127 | 24,130 | 82,257 |
| 1961 | 58 | 22,846 | 2,498 | 19,645 | 42,492 | 53,671 | 19,983 | 73,654 | 30,386 | 104,040 |
| 1962 | 59 | 24,115 | 2,976 | 22,621 | 46,737 | 47,320 | 21,478 | 68,798 | 28,884 | 97,682 |
| 1963 | 60 | 25,385 | 3,298 | 25,919 | 51,304 | 52,077 | 26,951 | 79,028 | 33,994 | 113,022 |
| 1964 | 61 | 26,654 | 3,609 | 29,528 | 56,182 | 56,915 | 34,136 | 91,051 | 39,678 | 130,729 |
| 1965 | 62 | 27,923 | 3,896 | 33,424 | 61,348 | 67,628 | 46,744 | 114,372 | 50,018 | 164,390 |
| 1966 | 63 | 29,192 | 4,343 | 37,767 | 66,960 | 60,146 | 49,860 | 110,006 | 47,464 | 157,470 |
| 1967 | 64 | 30,462 | 4,916 | 42,683 | 73,145 | 78,990 | 73,439 | 152,429 | 65,825 | 218,254 |
| 1968 | 65 | 31,731 | 5,872 | 48,555 | 80,286 | 96,120 | 101,691 | 197,811 | 84,623 | 282,434 |

The total cost figures represent the cumulative total of yearly investments of $1,269 plus the cumulative amount of income dividends reinvested, and include the sales charge of 8½% on all shares so purchased, as described in the prospectus. No adjustment has been made for any income taxes payable by shareholders on security distributions and dividends reinvested in shares. The dollar amounts of security profits distributions taken in shares were:

| | | | | | | | | | | | | | |
|---|---|---|---|---|---|---|---|---|---|---|---|---|---|
| 1944 | 0 | 1948 | 129 | 1952 | 347 | 1956 | 1,084 | 1960 | 1,856 | 1964 | 5,275 | 1968 | 13,699 |
| 1945 | 25 | 1949 | 131 | 1953 | 304 | 1957 | 1,209 | 1961 | 4,690 | 1965 | 6,776 | Total: | $65,902 |
| 1946 | 0 | 1950 | 173 | 1954 | 394 | 1958 | 1,353 | 1962 | 4,178 | 1966 | 8,757 | | |
| 1947 | 131 | 1951 | 306 | 1955 | 879 | 1959 | 1,573 | 1963 | 3,851 | 1967 | 8,782 | | |

## LIVING ESTATE

| "Buying Term and Investing the Difference"<br>TOTAL VALUE OF SHARES | Buying Whole Life<br>CASH VALUE |
|---|---|
| $ 1,670 | $ 0 |
| 4,275 | 225 |
| 6,114 | 1,575 |
| 7,445 | 3,000 |
| 8,640 | 4,425 |
| 11,220 | 5,925 |
| 15,520 | 7,425 |
| 19,535 | 8,925 |
| 22,962 | 10,425 |
| 25,312 | 11,925 |
| 36,619 | 13,500 |
| 44,731 | 15,000 |
| 51,094 | 16,575 |
| 47,532 | 18,150 |
| 68,809 | 19,725 |
| 79,688 | 21,300 |
| 82,257 | 22,950 |
| 104,040 | 24,525 |
| 97,682 | 26,100 |
| 113,022 | 27,750 |
| 130,729 | 29,250 |
| 164,390 | 30,750 |
| 157,470 | 32,175 |
| 218,254 | 33,675 |
| 282,434 | 35,175 |

## DEATH ESTATE

| AGE | "Buying Term and Investing the Difference"<br>TOTAL VALUE OF SHARES | + DECREASING TERM INSURANCE | = TOTAL DEATH ESTATE | Buying Whole Life<br>FACE VALUE |
|---|---|---|---|---|
| 41 | $ 1,670 | $100,000 | $101,670 | $75,000 |
| 42 | 4,275 | 95,000 | 99,275 | 75,000 |
| 43 | 6,114 | 90,000 | 96,114 | 75,000 |
| 44 | 7,445 | 85,000 | 92,445 | 75,000 |
| 45 | 8,640 | 80,000 | 88,640 | 75,000 |
| 46 | 11,220 | 75,000 | 86,220 | 75,000 |
| 47 | 15,520 | 70,000 | 85,520 | 75,000 |
| 48 | 19,535 | 65,000 | 84,535 | 75,000 |
| 49 | 22,962 | 60,000 | 82,962 | 75,000 |
| 50 | 25,312 | 55,000 | 80,312 | 75,000 |
| 51 | 36,619 | 50,000 | 86,619 | 75,000 |
| 52 | 44,731 | 46,250 | 90,981 | 75,000 |
| 53 | 51,094 | 42,500 | 93,594 | 75,000 |
| 54 | 47,532 | 38,750 | 86,282 | 75,000 |
| 55 | 68,809 | 35,000 | 103,809 | 75,000 |
| 56 | 79,688 | 31,250 | 110,938 | 75,000 |
| 57 | 82,257 | 28,750 | 111,007 | 75,000 |
| 58 | 104,040 | 26,250 | 130,290 | 75,000 |
| 59 | 97,682 | 23,750 | 121,432 | 75,000 |
| 60 | 113,022 | 21,250 | 134,272 | 75,000 |
| 61 | 130,729 | 18,750 | 149,479 | 75,000 |
| 62 | 164,390 | 17,500 | 181,890 | 75,000 |
| 63 | 157,470 | 16,250 | 173,720 | 75,000 |
| 64 | 218,254 | 15,000 | 233,254 | 75,000 |
| 65 | 282,434 | 14,400 | 296,834 | 75,000 |

Whether you
**lived** or **died**
you would have been better off
"Buying Term and Investing the Difference"

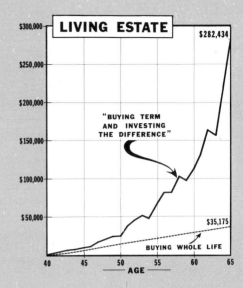

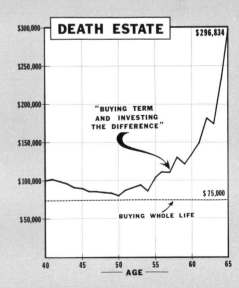

# GEORGE PUTNAM FUND

---

Illustration of assumed annual investments of $1,269 for twenty-five years from 1944 to 1968. All dividends and distributions reinvested.

---

This tabulation covers an illustration of an assumed investment of $1,269 annually on January 1 of each year from 1944 through 1968. This was a period in which stock prices fluctuated widely because of changing business and economic conditions, and were significantly higher at the end of the period than at the beginning. Thus, these results should not be considered as a representation of the dividend income or capital gain or loss that may be realized from an investment made in the fund today. A program of the type illustrated does not assure a profit nor protect against depreciation in declining markets.

| | | COST OF SHARES | | | | VALUE OF SHARES | | | | |
|---|---|---|---|---|---|---|---|---|---|---|
| YEAR ENDING DEC. 31 | AGE | CUMULATIVE ANNUAL INVEST- MENTS | ANNUAL INCOME DIVIDENDS REIN- VESTED | CUMULA- TIVE COST OF SHARES PURCHASED WITH DIVIDENDS | TOTAL COST (INCLUDES REIN- VESTED DIVIDENDS) | ACQUIRED THROUGH ANNUAL INVEST- MENTS | ACCEPTED AS CAPITAL GAINS DIS- TRIBUTIONS (CUMU- LATIVE) | SUB- TOTAL | PURCHASED THROUGH REINVEST- MENT OF INCOME (CUMULATIVE) | TOTAL VALUE |
| 1944 | 41 | $ 1,269 | $ 44 | $ 44 | $ 1,313 | $ 1,314 | $ 23 | $ 1,337 | $ 45 | $ 1,382 |
| 1945 | 42 | 2,538 | 75 | 119 | 2,658 | 2,841 | 91 | 2,932 | 132 | 3,064 |
| 1946 | 43 | 3,807 | 134 | 253 | 4,061 | 3,720 | 155 | 3,875 | 253 | 4,128 |
| 1947 | 44 | 5,077 | 215 | 468 | 5,545 | 4,605 | 205 | 4,810 | 451 | 5,261 |
| 1948 | 45 | 6,346 | 283 | 751 | 7,097 | 5,556 | 270 | 5,826 | 708 | 6,534 |
| 1949 | 46 | 7,615 | 381 | 1,132 | 8,748 | 7,412 | 363 | 7,775 | 1,192 | 8,967 |
| 1950 | 47 | 8,884 | 522 | 1,654 | 10,539 | 9,701 | 486 | 10,187 | 1,901 | 12,088 |
| 1951 | 48 | 10,154 | 575 | 2,229 | 12,383 | 11,441 | 909 | 12,350 | 2,573 | 14,923 |
| 1952 | 49 | 11,423 | 664 | 2,893 | 14,316 | 13,094 | 1,401 | 14,495 | 3,344 | 17,839 |
| 1953 | 50 | 12,692 | 755 | 3,648 | 16,341 | 13,446 | 1,837 | 15,283 | 3,909 | 19,192 |
| 1954 | 51 | 13,961 | 858 | 4,506 | 18,468 | 19,124 | 3,132 | 22,256 | 6,077 | 28,333 |
| 1955 | 52 | 15,231 | 1,013 | 5,519 | 20,750 | 21,997 | 4,557 | 26,554 | 7,599 | 34,153 |
| 1956 | 53 | 16,500 | 1,209 | 6,728 | 23,228 | 22,604 | 5,978 | 28,582 | 8,607 | 37,189 |
| 1957 | 54 | 17,769 | 1,347 | 8,075 | 25,845 | 20,756 | 6,265 | 27,021 | 8,739 | 35,760 |
| 1958 | 55 | 19,038 | 1,446 | 9,521 | 28,560 | 27,538 | 9,450 | 36,988 | 12,597 | 49,585 |
| 1959 | 56 | 20,308 | 1,579 | 11,100 | 31,408 | 30,123 | 11,927 | 42,050 | 14,795 | 56,845 |
| 1960 | 57 | 21,577 | 1,763 | 12,863 | 34,440 | 31,905 | 14,513 | 46,418 | 16,877 | 63,295 |
| 1961 | 58 | 22,846 | 1,920 | 14,783 | 37,630 | 38,741 | 19,741 | 58,482 | 21,699 | 80,181 |
| 1962 | 59 | 24,115 | 2,088 | 16,871 | 40,987 | 33,779 | 17,438 | 51,217 | 20,446 | 71,663 |
| 1963 | 60 | 25,385 | 2,273 | 19,144 | 44,529 | 37,054 | 21,055 | 58,109 | 23,996 | 82,105 |
| 1964 | 61 | 26,654 | 2,540 | 21,684 | 48,338 | 40,027 | 25,125 | 65,152 | 27,706 | 92,858 |
| 1965 | 62 | 27,923 | 2,858 | 24,542 | 52,466 | 43,802 | 30,132 | 73,934 | 32,430 | 106,364 |
| 1966 | 63 | 29,192 | 3,175 | 27,717 | 53,910 | 40,036 | 31,372 | 71,408 | 32,019 | 103,427 |
| 1967 | 64 | 30,462 | 3,455 | 31,172 | 61,634 | 45,613 | 39,678 | 85,291 | 39,050 | 124,341 |
| 1968 | 65 | 31,731 | 3,836 | 35,008 | 66,739 | 46,828 | 49,089 | 95,917 | 43,063 | 138,980 |

The total cost figures represent the cumulative total of yearly investments of $1,269 plus the cumulative amount of income dividends reinvested, and include the sales charge of 8½% on all shares so purchased, as described in the prospectus. No adjustment has been made for any income taxes payable by shareholders on security distributions and dividends reinvested in shares. The dollar amounts of security profits distributions taken in shares were:

| | | | | | | | | | | | | | |
|---|---|---|---|---|---|---|---|---|---|---|---|---|---|
| 1944 | 22 | 1948 | 72 | 1952 | 449 | 1956 | 1,505 | 1960 | 2,280 | 1964 | 2,937 | 1968 | 8,070 |
| 1945 | 63 | 1949 | 62 | 1953 | 513 | 1957 | 1,075 | 1961 | 2,795 | 1965 | 3,225 | Total: | $41,730 |
| 1946 | 70 | 1950 | 74 | 1954 | 698 | 1958 | 1,535 | 1962 | 811 | 1966 | 4,920 | | |
| 1947 | 60 | 1951 | 395 | 1955 | 1,155 | 1959 | 1,976 | 1963 | 2,420 | 1967 | 4,548 | | |

# LIVING ESTATE

| "Buying Term and Investing the Difference" | Buying Whole Life |
| --- | --- |
| TOTAL VALUE OF SHARES | CASH VALUE |

# DEATH ESTATE

| "Buying Term and Investing the Difference" | | | Buying Whole Life |
| --- | --- | --- | --- |
| TOTAL VALUE OF SHARES + | DECREASING TERM INSURANCE = | TOTAL DEATH ESTATE | FACE VALUE |

## Combined table

| LIVING ESTATE — TOTAL VALUE OF SHARES | LIVING ESTATE — CASH VALUE | AGE | DEATH ESTATE — TOTAL VALUE OF SHARES | + DECREASING TERM INSURANCE | = TOTAL DEATH ESTATE | FACE VALUE |
| ---: | ---: | :---: | ---: | ---: | ---: | ---: |
| $ 1,382 | $ 0 | 41 | $ 1,382 | $100,000 | $101,382 | $75,000 |
| 3,064 | 225 | 42 | 3,064 | 95,000 | 98,064 | 75,000 |
| 4,128 | 1,575 | 43 | 4,128 | 90,000 | 94,128 | 75,000 |
| 5,261 | 3,000 | 44 | 5,261 | 85,000 | 90,261 | 75,000 |
| 6,534 | 4,425 | 45 | 6,534 | 80,000 | 86,534 | 75,000 |
| 8,967 | 5,925 | 46 | 8,967 | 75,000 | 83,967 | 75,000 |
| 12,088 | 7,425 | 47 | 12,088 | 70,000 | 82,088 | 75,000 |
| 14,923 | 8,925 | 48 | 14,923 | 65,000 | 79,923 | 75,000 |
| 17,839 | 10,425 | 49 | 17,839 | 60,000 | 77,839 | 75,000 |
| 19,192 | 11,925 | 50 | 19,192 | 55,000 | 74,192 | 75,000 |
| 28,333 | 13,500 | 51 | 28,333 | 50,000 | 78,333 | 75,000 |
| 34,153 | 15,000 | 52 | 34,153 | 46,250 | 80,403 | 75,000 |
| 37,189 | 16,575 | 53 | 37,189 | 42,500 | 79,689 | 75,000 |
| 35,760 | 18,150 | 54 | 35,760 | 38,750 | 74,510 | 75,000 |
| 49,585 | 19,725 | 55 | 49,585 | 35,000 | 84,585 | 75,000 |
| 56,845 | 21,300 | 56 | 56,845 | 31,250 | 88,095 | 75,000 |
| 63,295 | 22,950 | 57 | 63,295 | 28,750 | 92,045 | 75,000 |
| 80,181 | 24,525 | 58 | 80,181 | 26,250 | 106,431 | 75,000 |
| 71,663 | 26,100 | 59 | 71,663 | 23,750 | 95,413 | 75,000 |
| 82,105 | 27,750 | 60 | 82,105 | 21,250 | 103,355 | 75,000 |
| 92,858 | 29,250 | 61 | 92,858 | 18,750 | 111,608 | 75,000 |
| 106,364 | 30,750 | 62 | 106,364 | 17,500 | 123,864 | 75,000 |
| 103,427 | 32,175 | 63 | 103,427 | 16,250 | 119,677 | 75,000 |
| 124,341 | 33,675 | 64 | 124,341 | 15,000 | 139,341 | 75,000 |
| 138,980 | 35,175 | 65 | 138,980 | 14,400 | 153,380 | 75,000 |

Whether you
**lived** or **died**
you would have been better off
"Buying Term and Investing the Difference"

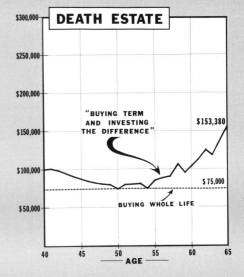

**LIVING ESTATE**

"BUYING TERM AND INVESTING THE DIFFERENCE" — $138,980

BUYING WHOLE LIFE — $35,175

**DEATH ESTATE**

"BUYING TERM AND INVESTING THE DIFFERENCE" — $153,380

BUYING WHOLE LIFE — $75,000

# PUTNAM INVESTORS FUND

Illustration of assumed annual investments of $1,269 for twenty-five years from 1944 to 1968. All dividends and distributions reinvested.

This tabulation covers an illustration of an assumed investment of $1,269 annually on January 1 of each year from 1944 through 1968. This was a period in which stock prices fluctuated widely because of changing business and economic conditions, and were significantly higher at the end of the period than at the beginning. Thus, these results should not be considered as a representation of the dividend income or capital gain or loss that may be realized from an investment made in the fund today. A program of the type illustrated does not assure a profit nor protect against depreciation in declining markets.

| | | COST OF SHARES | | | | VALUE OF SHARES | | | | |
|---|---|---|---|---|---|---|---|---|---|---|
| YEAR ENDING DEC. 31 | AGE | CUMULATIVE ANNUAL INVESTMENTS | ANNUAL INCOME DIVIDENDS REINVESTED | CUMULATIVE COST OF SHARES PURCHASED WITH DIVIDENDS | TOTAL COST (INCLUDES REINVESTED DIVIDENDS) | ACQUIRED THROUGH ANNUAL INVESTMENTS | ACCEPTED AS CAPITAL GAINS DISTRIBUTIONS (CUMULATIVE) | SUBTOTAL | PURCHASED THROUGH REINVESTMENT OF INCOME (CUMULATIVE) | TOTAL VALUE |
| 1944 | 41 | $ 1,269 | $ 52 | $ 52 | $ 1,321 | $ 1,395 | $ 65 | $ 1,460 | $ 50 | $ 1,510 |
| 1945 | 42 | 2,538 | 97 | 149 | 2,688 | 3,311 | 431 | 3,742 | 157 | 3,899 |
| 1946 | 43 | 3,807 | 139 | 288 | 4,096 | 3,428 | 543 | 3,971 | 237 | 4,208 |
| 1947 | 44 | 5,077 | 267 | 555 | 5,632 | 4,201 | 555 | 4,756 | 458 | 5,214 |
| 1948 | 45 | 6,346 | 403 | 958 | 7,304 | 4,937 | 511 | 5,448 | 766 | 6,214 |
| 1949 | 46 | 7,615 | 499 | 1,457 | 9,073 | 6,834 | 571 | 7,405 | 1,352 | 8,757 |
| 1950 | 47 | 8,884 | 649 | 2,106 | 10,991 | 10,396 | 1,166 | 11,562 | 2,392 | 13,954 |
| 1951 | 48 | 10,154 | 749 | 2,855 | 13,009 | 12,893 | 1,866 | 14,759 | 3,339 | 18,098 |
| 1952 | 49 | 11,423 | 783 | 3,638 | 15,061 | 14,931 | 2,644 | 17,575 | 4,279 | 21,854 |
| 1953 | 50 | 12,692 | 850 | 4,488 | 17,181 | 14,673 | 2,418 | 17,091 | 4,679 | 21,770 |
| 1954 | 51 | 13,961 | 985 | 5,473 | 19,435 | 24,037 | 4,469 | 28,506 | 8,226 | 36,732 |
| 1955 | 52 | 15,231 | 1,179 | 6,652 | 21,883 | 30,617 | 6,209 | 36,826 | 11,131 | 47,957 |
| 1956 | 53 | 16,500 | 1,439 | 8,091 | 24,591 | 33,042 | 9,696 | 42,738 | 12,891 | 55,629 |
| 1957 | 54 | 17,769 | 1,520 | 9,611 | 27,381 | 24,244 | 8,838 | 33,082 | 10,293 | 43,375 |
| 1958 | 55 | 19,038 | 1,263 | 10,874 | 29,913 | 35,019 | 14,615 | 49,634 | 15,607 | 65,241 |
| 1959 | 56 | 20,308 | 1,318 | 12,192 | 32,500 | 37,808 | 19,499 | 57,307 | 17,552 | 74,859 |
| 1960 | 57 | 21,577 | 1,471 | 13,663 | 35,240 | 32,452 | 21,197 | 53,649 | 15,948 | 69,597 |
| 1961 | 58 | 22,846 | 1,470 | 15,133 | 37,980 | 35,377 | 28,575 | 63,952 | 18,123 | 82,075 |
| 1962 | 59 | 24,115 | 1,603 | 16,736 | 40,852 | 27,888 | 25,376 | 53,264 | 15,292 | 68,556 |
| 1963 | 60 | 25,385 | 1,721 | 18,457 | 43,842 | 31,792 | 30,352 | 62,144 | 18,370 | 80,514 |
| 1964 | 61 | 26,654 | 1,862 | 20,319 | 46,973 | 34,772 | 35,878 | 70,650 | 21,100 | 91,750 |
| 1965 | 62 | 27,923 | 2,022 | 22,341 | 50,265 | 37,646 | 42,643 | 80,289 | 24,046 | 104,335 |
| 1966 | 63 | 29,192 | 2,234 | 24,575 | 53,768 | 34,723 | 44,943 | 79,666 | 23,519 | 103,185 |
| 1967 | 64 | 30,462 | 2,407 | 26,982 | 57,444 | 43,327 | 61,772 | 105,099 | 30,812 | 135,911 |
| 1968 | 65 | 31,731 | 2,104 | 29,086 | 60,817 | 44,975 | 77,070 | 122,045 | 33,241 | 155,286 |

The total cost figures represent the cumulative total of yearly investments of $1,269 plus the cumulative amount of income dividends reinvested, and include the sales charge of 8½% on all shares so purchased, as described in the prospectus. No adjustment has been made for any income taxes payable by shareholders on security distributions and dividends reinvested in shares. The dollar amounts of security profits distributions taken in shares were:

| | | | | | | | | | | | | | |
|---|---|---|---|---|---|---|---|---|---|---|---|---|---|
| 1944 | 63 | 1948 | 0 | 1952 | 644 | 1956 | 2,862 | 1960 | 5,266 | 1964 | 3,649 | 1968 | 12,294 |
| 1945 | 348 | 1949 | 0 | 1953 | 13 | 1957 | 2,585 | 1961 | 5,641 | 1965 | 4,652 | Total: | $66,044 |
| 1946 | 208 | 1950 | 411 | 1954 | 531 | 1958 | 1,712 | 1962 | 4,237 | 1966 | 7,240 | | |
| 1947 | 58 | 1951 | 562 | 1955 | 637 | 1959 | 3,909 | 1963 | 2,375 | 1967 | 6,147 | | |

# LIVING ESTATE

| "Buying Term and Investing the Difference"<br>TOTAL VALUE OF SHARES | Buying Whole Life<br>CASH VALUE |
|---|---|

# DEATH ESTATE

| "Buying Term and Investing the Difference"<br>TOTAL VALUE OF SHARES | DECREASING TERM INSURANCE | TOTAL DEATH ESTATE | Buying Whole Life<br>FACE VALUE |
|---|---|---|---|

| LIVING: TOTAL VALUE OF SHARES | LIVING: CASH VALUE | AGE | DEATH: TOTAL VALUE OF SHARES | + DECREASING TERM INSURANCE | = TOTAL DEATH ESTATE | FACE VALUE |
|---|---|---|---|---|---|---|
| $ 1,510 | $ 0 | 41 | $ 1,510 | $100,000 | $101,510 | $75,000 |
| 3,899 | 225 | 42 | 3,899 | 95,000 | 98,899 | 75,000 |
| 4,208 | 1,575 | 43 | 4,208 | 90,000 | 94,208 | 75,000 |
| 5,214 | 3,000 | 44 | 5,214 | 85,000 | 90,214 | 75,000 |
| 6,214 | 4,425 | 45 | 6,214 | 80,000 | 86,214 | 75,000 |
| 8,757 | 5,925 | 46 | 8,757 | 75,000 | 83,757 | 75,000 |
| 13,954 | 7,425 | 47 | 13,954 | 70,000 | 83,954 | 75,000 |
| 18,098 | 8,925 | 48 | 18,098 | 65,000 | 83,098 | 75,000 |
| 21,854 | 10,425 | 49 | 21,854 | 60,000 | 81,854 | 75,000 |
| 21,770 | 11,925 | 50 | 21,770 | 55,000 | 76,770 | 75,000 |
| 36,732 | 13,500 | 51 | 36,732 | 50,000 | 86,732 | 75,000 |
| 47,957 | 15,000 | 52 | 47,957 | 46,250 | 94,207 | 75,000 |
| 55,629 | 16,575 | 53 | 55,629 | 42,500 | 98,129 | 75,000 |
| 43,375 | 18,150 | 54 | 43,375 | 38,750 | 82,125 | 75,000 |
| 65,241 | 19,725 | 55 | 65,241 | 35,000 | 100,241 | 75,000 |
| 74,859 | 21,300 | 56 | 74,859 | 31,250 | 106,109 | 75,000 |
| 69,597 | 22,950 | 57 | 69,597 | 28,750 | 98,347 | 75,000 |
| 82,075 | 24,525 | 58 | 82,075 | 26,250 | 108,325 | 75,000 |
| 68,556 | 26,100 | 59 | 68,556 | 23,750 | 92,306 | 75,000 |
| 80,514 | 27,750 | 60 | 80,514 | 21,250 | 101,764 | 75,000 |
| 91,750 | 29,250 | 61 | 91,750 | 18,750 | 110,500 | 75,000 |
| 104,335 | 30,750 | 62 | 104,335 | 17,500 | 121,835 | 75,000 |
| 103,185 | 32,175 | 63 | 103,185 | 16,250 | 119,435 | 75,000 |
| 135,911 | 33,675 | 64 | 135,911 | 15,000 | 150,911 | 75,000 |
| 155,286 | 35,175 | 65 | 155,286 | 14,400 | 169,686 | 75,000 |

Whether you
**lived** or **died**
you would have been better off
"Buying Term and Investing the Difference"

LIVING ESTATE

"BUYING TERM AND INVESTING THE DIFFERENCE" $155,286

$35,175 BUYING WHOLE LIFE

DEATH ESTATE

"BUYING TERM AND INVESTING THE DIFFERENCE" $169,686

$75,000 BUYING WHOLE LIFE

# SCUDDER, STEVENS & CLARK BALANCED FUND

Illustration of assumed annual investments of $1,269 for twenty-five years from 1944 to 1968. All dividends and distributions reinvested.

This tabulation covers an illustration of an assumed investment of $1,269 annually on January 1 of each year from 1944 through 1968. This was a period in which stock prices fluctuated widely because of changing business and economic conditions, and were significantly higher at the end of the period than at the beginning. Thus, these results should not be considered as a representation of the dividend income or capital gain or loss that may be realized from an investment made in the fund today. A program of the type illustrated does not assure a profit nor protect against depreciation in declining markets.

| | | COST OF SHARES | | | | VALUE OF SHARES | | | | |
|---|---|---|---|---|---|---|---|---|---|---|
| YEAR ENDING DEC. 31 | AGE | CUMULATIVE ANNUAL INVEST-MENTS | ANNUAL INCOME DIVIDENDS REIN-VESTED | CUMULA-TIVE COST OF SHARES PURCHASED WITH DIVIDENDS | TOTAL COST (INCLUDES REIN-VESTED DIVIDENDS) | ACQUIRED THROUGH ANNUAL INVEST-MENTS | ACCEPTED AS CAPITAL GAINS DIS-TRIBUTIONS (CUMU-LATIVE) | SUB-TOTAL | PURCHASED THROUGH REINVEST-MENT OF INCOME (CUMULATIVE) | TOTAL VALUE |
| 1944 | 41 | $ 1,269 | $ 43 | $ 43 | $ 1,312 | $ 1,367 | $ 10 | $ 1,377 | $ 45 | $ 1,422 |
| 1945 | 42 | 2,538 | 85 | 128 | 2,666 | 3,013 | 139 | 3,152 | 140 | 3,292 |
| 1946 | 43 | 3,807 | 126 | 254 | 4,061 | 4,114 | 231 | 4,345 | 257 | 4,602 |
| 1947 | 44 | 5,077 | 169 | 423 | 5,499 | 5,021 | 354 | 5,375 | 406 | 5,781 |
| 1948 | 45 | 6,346 | 231 | 654 | 6,999 | 6,045 | 428 | 6,473 | 617 | 7,090 |
| 1949 | 46 | 7,615 | 286 | 940 | 8,554 | 7,968 | 614 | 8,582 | 978 | 9,560 |
| 1950 | 47 | 8,884 | 339 | 1,279 | 10,162 | 10,009 | 1,021 | 11,030 | 1,413 | 12,443 |
| 1951 | 48 | 10,154 | 396 | 1,675 | 11,827 | 11,487 | 1,539 | 13,026 | 1,838 | 14,864 |
| 1952 | 49 | 11,423 | 550 | 2,225 | 13,646 | 13,042 | 1,863 | 14,905 | 2,434 | 17,339 |
| 1953 | 50 | 12,692 | 607 | 2,832 | 15,522 | 13,820 | 2,111 | 15,931 | 2,964 | 18,895 |
| 1954 | 51 | 13,961 | 725 | 3,557 | 17,516 | 18,502 | 3,112 | 21,614 | 4,420 | 26,034 |
| 1955 | 52 | 15,231 | 832 | 4,389 | 19,617 | 20,753 | 4,488 | 25,241 | 5,471 | 30,712 |
| 1956 | 53 | 16,500 | 965 | 5,354 | 21,851 | 21,775 | 5,847 | 27,622 | 6,348 | 33,970 |
| 1957 | 54 | 17,769 | 1,136 | 6,490 | 24,256 | 20,076 | 5,368 | 25,444 | 6,588 | 32,032 |
| 1958 | 55 | 19,038 | 1,233 | 7,723 | 26,758 | 26,497 | 7,571 | 34,068 | 9,533 | 43,601 |
| 1959 | 56 | 20,308 | 1,311 | 9,034 | 29,338 | 27,473 | 9,676 | 37,149 | 10,714 | 47,863 |
| 1960 | 57 | 21,577 | 1,479 | 10,513 | 32,086 | 27,539 | 10,871 | 38,410 | 11,757 | 50,167 |
| 1961 | 58 | 22,846 | 1,614 | 12,127 | 34,969 | 32,376 | 14,656 | 47,032 | 14,836 | 61,868 |
| 1962 | 59 | 24,115 | 1,733 | 13,860 | 37,971 | 29,620 | 15,714 | 45,334 | 14,764 | 60,098 |
| 1963 | 60 | 25,385 | 1,913 | 15,773 | 41,153 | 32,120 | 20,882 | 53,002 | 17,232 | 70,234 |
| 1964 | 61 | 26,654 | 2,104 | 17,877 | 44,526 | 35,840 | 24,751 | 60,591 | 20,612 | 81,203 |
| 1965 | 62 | 27,923 | 2,302 | 20,179 | 48,097 | 37,465 | 28,853 | 66,318 | 23,109 | 89,427 |
| 1966 | 63 | 29,192 | 2,555 | 22,734 | 51,921 | 34,075 | 25,384 | 59,459 | 22,838 | 82,297 |
| 1967 | 64 | 30,462 | 2,471 | 25,205 | 55,661 | 35,115 | 29,538 | 64,653 | 25,081 | 89,734 |
| 1968 | 65 | 31,731 | 2,580 | 27,785 | 59,510 | 35,409 | 34,534 | 69,943 | 27,007 | 96,950 |

The total cost figures represent the cumulative total of yearly investments of $1,269 plus the cumulative amount of income dividends reinvested, and include NO sales charge on shares so purchased, as described in the prospectus. No adjustment has been made for any income taxes payable by shareholders on security distributions and dividends reinvested in shares. The dollar amounts of security profits distributions taken in shares were:

| | | | | | | | | | | | | | |
|---|---|---|---|---|---|---|---|---|---|---|---|---|---|
| 1944 | 10 | 1948 | 88 | 1952 | 289 | 1956 | 1,389 | 1960 | 1,545 | 1964 | 2,355 | 1968 | 5,557 |
| 1945 | 128 | 1949 | 145 | 1953 | 313 | 1957 | 282 | 1961 | 2,456 | 1965 | 3,816 | Total: | $35,638 |
| 1946 | 95 | 1950 | 343 | 1954 | 512 | 1958 | 874 | 1962 | 2,781 | 1966 | 0 | | |
| 1947 | 136 | 1951 | 500 | 1955 | 1,210 | 1959 | 2,150 | 1963 | 4,482 | 1967 | 4,182 | | |

## LIVING ESTATE

| "Buying Term and Investing the Difference" | Buying Whole Life |
|---|---|
| TOTAL VALUE OF SHARES | CASH VALUE |

## DEATH ESTATE

| "Buying Term and Investing the Difference" | | | Buying Whole Life |
|---|---|---|---|
| TOTAL VALUE OF SHARES | + DECREASING TERM INSURANCE | = TOTAL DEATH ESTATE | FACE VALUE |

| LIVING ESTATE — TOTAL VALUE OF SHARES | LIVING ESTATE — CASH VALUE | AGE | DEATH ESTATE — TOTAL VALUE OF SHARES | + DECREASING TERM INSURANCE | = TOTAL DEATH ESTATE | FACE VALUE |
|---|---|---|---|---|---|---|
| $ 1,422 | $ 0 | 41 | $ 1,422 | $100,000 | $101,422 | $75,000 |
| 3,292 | 225 | 42 | 3,292 | 95,000 | 98,292 | 75,000 |
| 4,602 | 1,575 | 43 | 4,602 | 90,000 | 94,602 | 75,000 |
| 5,781 | 3,000 | 44 | 5,781 | 85,000 | 90,781 | 75,000 |
| 7,090 | 4,425 | 45 | 7,090 | 80,000 | 87,090 | 75,000 |
| 9,560 | 5,925 | 46 | 9,560 | 75,000 | 84,560 | 75,000 |
| 12,443 | 7,425 | 47 | 12,443 | 70,000 | 82,443 | 75,000 |
| 14,864 | 8,925 | 48 | 14,864 | 65,000 | 79,864 | 75,000 |
| 17,339 | 10,425 | 49 | 17,339 | 60,000 | 77,339 | 75,000 |
| 18,895 | 11,925 | 50 | 18,895 | 55,000 | 73,895 | 75,000 |
| 26,034 | 13,500 | 51 | 26,034 | 50,000 | 76,034 | 75,000 |
| 30,712 | 15,000 | 52 | 30,712 | 46,250 | 76,962 | 75,000 |
| 33,970 | 16,575 | 53 | 33,970 | 42,500 | 76,470 | 75,000 |
| 32,032 | 18,150 | 54 | 32,032 | 38,750 | 70,782 | 75,000 |
| 43,601 | 19,725 | 55 | 43,601 | 35,000 | 78,601 | 75,000 |
| 47,863 | 21,300 | 56 | 47,863 | 31,250 | 79,113 | 75,000 |
| 50,167 | 22,950 | 57 | 50,167 | 28,750 | 78,917 | 75,000 |
| 61,868 | 24,525 | 58 | 61,868 | 26,250 | 88,118 | 75,000 |
| 60,098 | 26,100 | 59 | 60,098 | 23,750 | 83,848 | 75,000 |
| 70,234 | 27,750 | 60 | 70,234 | 21,250 | 91,484 | 75,000 |
| 81,203 | 29,250 | 61 | 81,203 | 18,750 | 99,953 | 75,000 |
| 89,427 | 30,750 | 62 | 89,427 | 17,500 | 106,927 | 75,000 |
| 82,297 | 32,175 | 63 | 82,297 | 16,250 | 98,547 | 75,000 |
| 89,734 | 33,675 | 64 | 89,734 | 15,000 | 104,734 | 75,000 |
| 96,950 | 35,175 | 65 | 96,950 | 14,400 | 111,350 | 75,000 |

Whether you
**lived** or **died**
you would have been better off
"Buying Term and Investing the Difference"

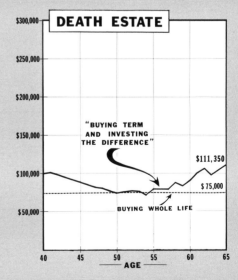

### LIVING ESTATE

"BUYING TERM AND INVESTING THE DIFFERENCE" — $96,950
$35,175
BUYING WHOLE LIFE

### DEATH ESTATE

"BUYING TERM AND INVESTING THE DIFFERENCE" — $111,350
$75,000
BUYING WHOLE LIFE

# SELECTED AMERICAN SHARES

Illustration of assumed annual investments of $1,269 for twenty-five years from 1944 to 1968. All dividends and distributions reinvested.

This tabulation covers an illustration of an assumed investment of $1,269 annually on January 1 of each year from 1944 through 1968. This was a period in which stock prices fluctuated widely because of changing business and economic conditions, and were significantly higher at the end of the period than at the beginning. Thus, these results should not be considered as a representation of the dividend income or capital gain or loss that may be realized from an investment made in the fund today. A program of the type illustrated does not assure a profit nor protect against depreciation in declining markets.

| | | COST OF SHARES | | | | VALUE OF SHARES | | | | |
|---|---|---|---|---|---|---|---|---|---|---|
| YEAR ENDING DEC. 31 | AGE | CUMULATIVE ANNUAL INVEST- MENTS | ANNUAL INCOME DIVIDENDS REIN- VESTED | CUMULA- TIVE COST OF SHARES PURCHASED WITH DIVIDENDS | TOTAL COST (INCLUDES REIN- VESTED DIVIDENDS) | ACQUIRED THROUGH ANNUAL INVEST- MENTS | ACCEPTED AS CAPITAL GAINS DIS- TRIBUTIONS (CUMU- LATIVE) | SUB- TOTAL | PURCHASED THROUGH REINVEST- MENT OF INCOME (CUMULATIVE) | TOTAL VALUE |
| 1944 | 41 | $ 1,269 | $ 58 | $ 58 | $ 1,327 | $ 1,348 | $ 19 | $ 1,367 | $ 53 | $ 1,420 |
| 1945 | 42 | 2,538 | 92 | 150 | 2,689 | 3,326 | 170 | 3,496 | 154 | 3,650 |
| 1946 | 43 | 3,807 | 122 | 272 | 4,080 | 3,815 | 591 | 4,406 | 223 | 4,629 |
| 1947 | 44 | 5,077 | 209 | 481 | 5,558 | 4,646 | 658 | 5,304 | 388 | 5,692 |
| 1948 | 45 | 6,346 | 350 | 831 | 7,177 | 5,357 | 606 | 5,963 | 642 | 6,605 |
| 1949 | 46 | 7,615 | 447 | 1,278 | 8,894 | 6,972 | 647 | 7,619 | 1,088 | 8,707 |
| 1950 | 47 | 8,884 | 673 | 1,951 | 10,836 | 9,622 | 951 | 10,573 | 1,894 | 12,467 |
| 1951 | 48 | 10,154 | 697 | 2,648 | 12,802 | 11,518 | 1,847 | 13,365 | 2,612 | 15,977 |
| 1952 | 49 | 11,423 | 782 | 3,430 | 14,853 | 13,086 | 2,741 | 15,827 | 3,375 | 19,202 |
| 1953 | 50 | 12,692 | 857 | 4,287 | 16,980 | 13,127 | 3,195 | 16,322 | 3,840 | 20,162 |
| 1954 | 51 | 13,961 | 973 | 5,260 | 19,222 | 19,724 | 4,406 | 24,130 | 6,218 | 30,348 |
| 1955 | 52 | 15,231 | 759 | 6,019 | 21,250 | 23,171 | 7,050 | 30,221 | 7,592 | 37,813 |
| 1956 | 53 | 16,500 | 1,285 | 7,304 | 23,804 | 24,815 | 9,850 | 34,665 | 8,886 | 43,551 |
| 1957 | 54 | 17,769 | 1,485 | 8,786 | 26,559 | 19,624 | 10,951 | 30,575 | 7,843 | 38,418 |
| 1958 | 55 | 19,038 | 1,666 | 10,455 | 29,494 | 27,935 | 16,593 | 44,528 | 12,295 | 56,823 |
| 1959 | 56 | 20,308 | 1,600 | 12,055 | 32,363 | 29,661 | 19,656 | 49,317 | 13,928 | 63,245 |
| 1960 | 57 | 21,577 | 1,701 | 13,756 | 35,333 | 27,625 | 21,277 | 48,902 | 14,024 | 62,926 |
| 1961 | 58 | 22,846 | 1,702 | 15,458 | 38,305 | 33,685 | 27,105 | 60,790 | 17,966 | 78,756 |
| 1962 | 59 | 24,115 | 1,846 | 17,304 | 41,420 | 29,044 | 25,988 | 55,032 | 16,609 | 71,641 |
| 1963 | 60 | 25,385 | 1,986 | 19,290 | 44,675 | 34,410 | 32,002 | 66,412 | 20,731 | 87,143 |
| 1964 | 61 | 26,654 | 2,128 | 21,418 | 48,072 | 37,911 | 37,562 | 75,473 | 23,960 | 99,433 |
| 1965 | 62 | 27,923 | 2,302 | 23,720 | 51,644 | 45,517 | 49,891 | 95,408 | 30,223 | 125,631 |
| 1966 | 63 | 29,192 | 2,514 | 26,234 | 55,427 | 41,716 | 51,946 | 93,662 | 29,105 | 122,767 |
| 1967 | 64 | 30,462 | 2,782 | 29,016 | 59,478 | 49,600 | 71,637 | 121,237 | 36,284 | 157,521 |
| 1968 | 65 | 31,731 | 3,128 | 32,144 | 63,875 | 48,042 | 83,048 | 131,090 | 37,198 | 168,288 |

The total cost figures represent the cumulative total of yearly investments of $1,269 plus the cumulative amount of income dividends reinvested, and include the sales charge of 7½% on all shares so purchased, as described in the prospectus. No adjustment has been made for any income taxes payable by shareholders on security distributions and dividends reinvested in shares. The dollar amounts of security profits distributions taken in shares were:

| | | | | | | | | | | | | | |
|---|---|---|---|---|---|---|---|---|---|---|---|---|---|
| 1944 | 20 | 1948 | 0 | 1952 | 828 | 1956 | 2,417 | 1960 | 3,735 | 1964 | 3,179 | 1968 | 14,219 |
| 1945 | 157 | 1949 | 0 | 1953 | 672 | 1957 | 4,148 | 1961 | 1,867 | 1965 | 5,054 | Total: | $66,551 |
| 1946 | 439 | 1950 | 198 | 1954 | 0 | 1958 | 1,360 | 1962 | 3,761 | 1966 | 7,758 | | |
| 1947 | 115 | 1951 | 823 | 1955 | 1,776 | 1959 | 2,569 | 1963 | 2,097 | 1967 | 9,359 | | |

## LIVING ESTATE

| "Buying Term and Investing the Difference" TOTAL VALUE OF SHARES | Buying Whole Life CASH VALUE |
| --- | --- |

## DEATH ESTATE

| "Buying Term and Investing the Difference" | | | Buying Whole Life |

| AGE | LIVING ESTATE "Buying Term..." TOTAL VALUE OF SHARES | LIVING ESTATE Buying Whole Life CASH VALUE | DEATH ESTATE TOTAL VALUE OF SHARES | + DECREASING TERM INSURANCE | = TOTAL DEATH ESTATE | Buying Whole Life FACE VALUE |
| --- | --- | --- | --- | --- | --- | --- |
| 41 | $ 1,420 | $ 0 | $ 1,420 | $100,000 | $101,420 | $75,000 |
| 42 | 3,650 | 225 | 3,650 | 95,000 | 98,650 | 75,000 |
| 43 | 4,629 | 1,575 | 4,629 | 90,000 | 94,629 | 75,000 |
| 44 | 5,692 | 3,000 | 5,692 | 85,000 | 90,692 | 75,000 |
| 45 | 6,605 | 4,425 | 6,605 | 80,000 | 86,605 | 75,000 |
| 46 | 8,707 | 5,925 | 8,707 | 75,000 | 83,707 | 75,000 |
| 47 | 12,467 | 7,425 | 12,467 | 70,000 | 82,467 | 75,000 |
| 48 | 15,977 | 8,925 | 15,977 | 65,000 | 80,977 | 75,000 |
| 49 | 19,202 | 10,425 | 19,202 | 60,000 | 79,202 | 75,000 |
| 50 | 20,162 | 11,925 | 20,162 | 55,000 | 75,162 | 75,000 |
| 51 | 30,348 | 13,500 | 30,348 | 50,000 | 80,348 | 75,000 |
| 52 | 37,813 | 15,000 | 37,813 | 46,250 | 84,063 | 75,000 |
| 53 | 43,551 | 16,575 | 43,551 | 42,500 | 86,051 | 75,000 |
| 54 | 38,418 | 18,150 | 38,418 | 38,750 | 77,168 | 75,000 |
| 55 | 56,823 | 19,725 | 56,823 | 35,000 | 91,823 | 75,000 |
| 56 | 63,245 | 21,300 | 63,245 | 31,250 | 94,495 | 75,000 |
| 57 | 62,926 | 22,950 | 62,926 | 28,750 | 91,676 | 75,000 |
| 58 | 78,756 | 24,525 | 78,756 | 26,250 | 105,006 | 75,000 |
| 59 | 71,641 | 26,100 | 71,641 | 23,750 | 95,391 | 75,000 |
| 60 | 87,143 | 27,750 | 87,143 | 21,250 | 108,393 | 75,000 |
| 61 | 99,433 | 29,250 | 99,433 | 18,750 | 118,183 | 75,000 |
| 62 | 125,631 | 30,750 | 125,631 | 17,500 | 143,131 | 75,000 |
| 63 | 122,767 | 32,175 | 122,767 | 16,250 | 139,017 | 75,000 |
| 64 | 157,521 | 33,675 | 157,521 | 15,000 | 172,521 | 75,000 |
| 65 | 168,288 | 35,175 | 168,288 | 14,400 | 182,688 | 75,000 |

Whether you
**lived** or **died**
you would have been better off
"Buying Term and Investing the Difference"

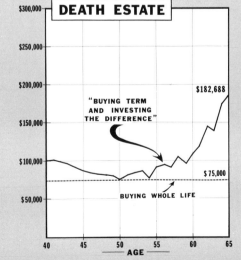

LIVING ESTATE
"BUYING TERM AND INVESTING THE DIFFERENCE" — $168,288
BUYING WHOLE LIFE — $35,175

DEATH ESTATE
"BUYING TERM AND INVESTING THE DIFFERENCE" — $182,688
BUYING WHOLE LIFE — $75,000

# UNITED ACCUMULATIVE FUND

Illustration of assumed annual investments of $1,269 for twenty-five years from 1944 to 1968. All dividends and distributions reinvested.

This tabulation covers an illustration of an assumed investment of $1,269 annually on January 1 of each year from 1944 through 1968. This was a period in which stock prices fluctuated widely because of changing business and economic conditions, and were significantly higher at the end of the period than at the beginning. Thus, these results should not be considered as a representation of the dividend income or capital gain or loss that may be realized from an investment made in the fund today. A program of the type illustrated does not assure a profit nor protect against depreciation in declining markets.

| | | COST OF SHARES | | | | VALUE OF SHARES | | | | |
|---|---|---|---|---|---|---|---|---|---|---|
| YEAR ENDING DEC. 31 | AGE | CUMULATIVE ANNUAL INVEST-MENTS | ANNUAL INCOME DIVIDENDS REIN-VESTED | CUMULA-TIVE COST OF SHARES PURCHASED WITH DIVIDENDS | TOTAL COST (INCLUDES REIN-VESTED DIVIDENDS) | ACQUIRED THROUGH ANNUAL INVEST-MENTS | ACCEPTED AS CAPITAL GAINS DIS-TRIBUTIONS (CUMU-LATIVE) | SUB-TOTAL | PURCHASED THROUGH REINVEST-MENT OF INCOME (CUMULATIVE) | TOTAL VALUE |
| 1944 | 41 | $ 1,269 | $ 55 | $ 55 | $ 1,324 | $ 1,336 | $ 22 | $ 1,358 | $ 55 | $ 1,413 |
| 1945 | 42 | 2,538 | 84 | 140 | 2,678 | 2,938 | 318 | 3,256 | 150 | 3,406 |
| 1946 | 43 | 3,807 | 127 | 267 | 4,074 | 3,516 | 603 | 4,119 | 256 | 4,375 |
| 1947 | 44 | 5,077 | 120 | 387 | 5,464 | 4,285 | 960 | 5,245 | 354 | 5,599 |
| 1948 | 45 | 6,346 | 451 | 839 | 7,185 | 4,857 | 904 | 5,761 | 769 | 6,530 |
| 1949 | 46 | 7,615 | 458 | 1,297 | 8,913 | 6,363 | 1,264 | 7,627 | 1,274 | 8,901 |
| 1950 | 47 | 8,884 | 661 | 2,137 | 11,022 | 8,649 | 1,673 | 10,322 | 2,349 | 12,671 |
| 1951 | 48 | 10,154 | 942 | 3,080 | 13,234 | 10,736 | 2,085 | 12,821 | 3,521 | 16,342 |
| 1952 | 49 | 11,423 | 854 | 3,937 | 15,361 | 12,431 | 2,562 | 14,993 | 4,550 | 19,543 |
| 1953 | 50 | 12,692 | 970 | 4,907 | 17,600 | 12,869 | 2,768 | 15,637 | 5,270 | 20,907 |
| 1954 | 51 | 13,961 | 1,110 | 6,018 | 19,980 | 21,635 | 5,045 | 26,680 | 9,290 | 35,970 |
| 1955 | 52 | 15,231 | 1,535 | 7,553 | 22,785 | 26,567 | 6,978 | 33,545 | 12,373 | 45,918 |
| 1956 | 53 | 16,500 | 1,538 | 9,093 | 25,593 | 29,644 | 9,237 | 38,881 | 14,783 | 53,664 |
| 1957 | 54 | 17,769 | 1,723 | 10,816 | 28,587 | 24,160 | 8,899 | 33,059 | 13,345 | 46,404 |
| 1958 | 55 | 19,038 | 2,011 | 12,829 | 31,869 | 33,076 | 13,070 | 46,146 | 19,468 | 65,614 |
| 1959 | 56 | 20,308 | 2,106 | 14,935 | 35,244 | 37,361 | 15,981 | 53,342 | 23,364 | 76,706 |
| 1960 | 57 | 21,577 | 2,311 | 17,247 | 38,825 | 37,559 | 17,244 | 54,803 | 25,119 | 79,922 |
| 1961 | 58 | 22,846 | 2,468 | 19,716 | 42,564 | 47,718 | 22,991 | 70,709 | 33,409 | 104,118 |
| 1962 | 59 | 24,115 | 2,601 | 22,318 | 46,434 | 41,443 | 21,215 | 62,658 | 30,940 | 93,598 |
| 1963 | 60 | 25,385 | 2,761 | 25,079 | 50,465 | 48,289 | 25,899 | 74,188 | 37,885 | 112,073 |
| 1964 | 61 | 26,654 | 3,141 | 28,220 | 54,876 | 55,439 | 30,925 | 86,364 | 45,574 | 131,938 |
| 1965 | 62 | 27,923 | 3,534 | 31,755 | 59,679 | 62,554 | 36,297 | 98,851 | 53,952 | 152,803 |
| 1966 | 63 | 29,192 | 3,699 | 35,454 | 64,648 | 56,886 | 36,556 | 93,442 | 51,934 | 145,376 |
| 1967 | 64 | 30,462 | 3,747 | 39,202 | 69,665 | 60,497 | 46,511 | 107,008 | 57,941 | 164,949 |
| 1968 | 65 | 31,731 | 2,534 | 41,736 | 73,469 | 61,586 | 55,612 | 117,198 | 60,301 | 177,499 |

The total cost figures represent the cumulative total of yearly investments of $1,269 plus the cumulative amount of income dividends reinvested, and include the sales charge of **8½%** on all shares so purchased, as described in the prospectus. No adjustment has been made for any income taxes payable by shareholders on security distributions and dividends reinvested in shares. The dollar amounts of security profits distributions taken in shares were:

| | | | | | | | | | | | | | |
|---|---|---|---|---|---|---|---|---|---|---|---|---|---|
| 1944 | 22 | 1948 | 47 | 1952 | 377 | 1956 | 1,758 | 1960 | 1,642 | 1964 | 1,914 | 1968 | 9,285 |
| 1945 | 290 | 1949 | 305 | 1953 | 344 | 1957 | 1,627 | 1961 | 1,753 | 1965 | 2,087 | Total: | $42,468 |
| 1946 | 304 | 1950 | 209 | 1954 | 739 | 1958 | 1,429 | 1962 | 1,710 | 1966 | 3,446 | | |
| 1947 | 403 | 1951 | 251 | 1955 | 1,090 | 1959 | 1,707 | 1963 | 1,816 | 1967 | 8,923 | | |

| LIVING ESTATE | | | DEATH ESTATE | | | |
|---|---|---|---|---|---|---|
| "Buying Term and Investing the Difference" | Buying Whole Life | | "Buying Term and Investing the Difference" | | | Buying Whole Life |
| TOTAL VALUE OF SHARES | CASH VALUE | AGE | TOTAL VALUE OF SHARES | + DECREASING TERM INSURANCE | = TOTAL DEATH ESTATE | FACE VALUE |
| $ 1,413 | $ 0 | 41 | $ 1,413 | $100,000 | $101,413 | $75,000 |
| 3,406 | 225 | 42 | 3,406 | 95,000 | 98,406 | 75,000 |
| 4,375 | 1,575 | 43 | 4,375 | 90,000 | 94,375 | 75,000 |
| 5,599 | 3,000 | 44 | 5,599 | 85,000 | 90,599 | 75,000 |
| 6,530 | 4,425 | 45 | 6,530 | 80,000 | 86,530 | 75,000 |
| 8,901 | 5,925 | 46 | 8,901 | 75,000 | 83,901 | 75,000 |
| 12,671 | 7,425 | 47 | 12,671 | 70,000 | 82,671 | 75,000 |
| 16,342 | 8,925 | 48 | 16,342 | 65,000 | 81,342 | 75,000 |
| 19,543 | 10,425 | 49 | 19,543 | 60,000 | 79,543 | 75,000 |
| 20,907 | 11,925 | 50 | 20,907 | 55,000 | 75,907 | 75,000 |
| 35,970 | 13,500 | 51 | 35,970 | 50,000 | 85,970 | 75,000 |
| 45,918 | 15,000 | 52 | 45,918 | 46,250 | 92,168 | 75,000 |
| 53,664 | 16,575 | 53 | 53,664 | 42,500 | 96,164 | 75,000 |
| 46,404 | 18,150 | 54 | 46,404 | 38,750 | 85,154 | 75,000 |
| 65,614 | 19,725 | 55 | 65,614 | 35,000 | 100,614 | 75,000 |
| 76,706 | 21,300 | 56 | 76,706 | 31,250 | 107,956 | 75,000 |
| 79,922 | 22,950 | 57 | 79,922 | 28,750 | 108,672 | 75,000 |
| 104,118 | 24,525 | 58 | 104,118 | 26,250 | 130,368 | 75,000 |
| 93,598 | 26,100 | 59 | 93,598 | 23,750 | 117,348 | 75,000 |
| 112,073 | 27,750 | 60 | 112,073 | 21,250 | 133,323 | 75,000 |
| 131,938 | 29,250 | 61 | 131,938 | 18,750 | 150,688 | 75,000 |
| 152,803 | 30,750 | 62 | 152,803 | 17,500 | 170,303 | 75,000 |
| 145,376 | 32,175 | 63 | 145,376 | 16,250 | 161,626 | 75,000 |
| 164,949 | 33,675 | 64 | 164,949 | 15,000 | 179,949 | 75,000 |
| 177,499 | 35,175 | 65 | 177,499 | 14,400 | 191,899 | 75,000 |

Whether you
**lived** or **died**
you would have been better off
"Buying Term and Investing the Difference"

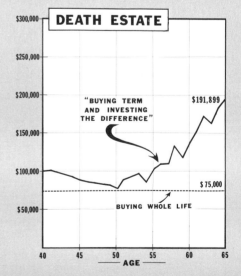

**LIVING ESTATE**

"BUYING TERM AND INVESTING THE DIFFERENCE" — $177,499

BUYING WHOLE LIFE — $35,175

**DEATH ESTATE**

"BUYING TERM AND INVESTING THE DIFFERENCE" — $191,899

BUYING WHOLE LIFE — $75,000

229

# UNITED INCOME FUND

Illustration of assumed annual investments of $1,269 for twenty-five years from 1944 to 1968. All dividends and distributions reinvested.

This tabulation covers an illustration of an assumed investment of $1,269 annually on January 1 of each year from 1944 through 1968. This was a period in which stock prices fluctuated widely because of changing business and economic conditions, and were significantly higher at the end of the period than at the beginning. Thus, these results should not be considered as a representation of the dividend income or capital gain or loss that may be realized from an investment made in the fund today. A program of the type illustrated does not assure a profit nor protect against depreciation in declining markets.

| | | COST OF SHARES | | | | VALUE OF SHARES | | | | |
|---|---|---|---|---|---|---|---|---|---|---|
| YEAR ENDING DEC. 31 | AGE | CUMULATIVE ANNUAL INVEST- MENTS | ANNUAL INCOME DIVIDENDS REIN- VESTED | CUMULA- TIVE COST OF SHARES PURCHASED WITH DIVIDENDS | TOTAL COST (INCLUDES REIN- VESTED DIVIDENDS) | ACQUIRED THROUGH ANNUAL INVEST- MENTS | ACCEPTED AS CAPITAL GAINS DIS- TRIBUTIONS (CUMU- LATIVE) | SUB- TOTAL | PURCHASED THROUGH REINVEST- MENT OF INCOME (CUMULATIVE) | TOTAL VALUE |
| 1944 | 41 | $ 1,269 | $ 52 | $ 52 | $ 1,322 | $ 1,313 | $ 48 | $ 1,361 | $ 55 | $ 1,416 |
| 1945 | 42 | 2,538 | 86 | 139 | 2,678 | 3,029 | 306 | 3,335 | 160 | 3,495 |
| 1946 | 43 | 3,807 | 201 | 341 | 4,149 | 3,582 | 524 | 4,106 | 327 | 4,433 |
| 1947 | 44 | 5,077 | 231 | 573 | 5,650 | 4,277 | 793 | 5,070 | 526 | 5,596 |
| 1948 | 45 | 6,346 | 461 | 1,035 | 7,382 | 4,955 | 823 | 5,778 | 908 | 6,686 |
| 1949 | 46 | 7,615 | 590 | 1,626 | 9,243 | 6,667 | 935 | 7,602 | 1,637 | 9,239 |
| 1950 | 47 | 8,884 | 704 | 2,331 | 11,217 | 8,959 | 1,294 | 10,253 | 2,631 | 12,884 |
| 1951 | 48 | 10,154 | 765 | 3,098 | 13,252 | 10,950 | 1,859 | 12,809 | 3,628 | 16,437 |
| 1952 | 49 | 11,423 | 840 | 3,939 | 15,362 | 12,757 | 2,458 | 15,215 | 4,685 | 19,900 |
| 1953 | 50 | 12,692 | 1,072 | 5,012 | 17,705 | 13,104 | 2,756 | 15,860 | 5,492 | 21,352 |
| 1954 | 51 | 13,961 | 1,137 | 6,151 | 20,113 | 20,818 | 4,807 | 25,625 | 9,339 | 35,964 |
| 1955 | 52 | 15,231 | 1,458 | 7,609 | 22,840 | 24,777 | 6,479 | 31,256 | 12,040 | 43,296 |
| 1956 | 53 | 16,500 | 1,818 | 9,428 | 25,928 | 26,697 | 8,066 | 34,763 | 14,201 | 48,964 |
| 1957 | 54 | 17,769 | 1,951 | 11,379 | 29,149 | 22,510 | 8,068 | 30,578 | 13,275 | 43,853 |
| 1958 | 55 | 19,038 | 1,944 | 13,325 | 32,364 | 31,105 | 12,644 | 43,749 | 19,572 | 63,321 |
| 1959 | 56 | 20,308 | 2,117 | 15,442 | 35,751 | 33,098 | 15,362 | 48,460 | 22,197 | 70,657 |
| 1960 | 57 | 21,577 | 2,291 | 17,733 | 39,312 | 33,674 | 17,734 | 51,408 | 24,201 | 75,609 |
| 1961 | 58 | 22,846 | 2,415 | 20,150 | 42,997 | 42,741 | 24,615 | 67,356 | 32,221 | 99,577 |
| 1962 | 59 | 24,115 | 2,668 | 22,820 | 46,936 | 36,897 | 23,650 | 60,547 | 29,763 | 90,310 |
| 1963 | 60 | 25,385 | 2,880 | 25,701 | 51,087 | 41,874 | 29,325 | 71,199 | 35,637 | 106,836 |
| 1964 | 61 | 26,654 | 3,087 | 28,788 | 55,444 | 47,895 | 36,255 | 84,150 | 42,806 | 126,956 |
| 1965 | 62 | 27,923 | 3,478 | 32,266 | 60,191 | 52,219 | 42,734 | 94,953 | 49,132 | 144,085 |
| 1966 | 63 | 29,192 | 3,710 | 35,978 | 65,171 | 46,658 | 42,397 | 89,055 | 46,586 | 135,641 |
| 1967 | 64 | 30,462 | 3,671 | 39,649 | 70,113 | 55,603 | 55,837 | 111,440 | 57,954 | 169,394 |
| 1968 | 65 | 31,731 | 3,485 | 43,136 | 74,867 | 61,670 | 68,551 | 130,221 | 66,555 | 196,776 |

The total cost figures represent the cumulative total of yearly investments of $1,269 plus the cumulative amount of income dividends reinvested, and include the sales charge of $8\frac{1}{2}\%$ on all shares so purchased, as described in the prospectus. No adjustment has been made for any income taxes payable by shareholders on security distributions and dividends reinvested in shares. The dollar amounts of security profits distributions taken in shares were:

| | | | | | | | | | | | | | |
|---|---|---|---|---|---|---|---|---|---|---|---|---|---|
| 1944 | 47 | 1948 | 100 | 1952 | 493 | 1956 | 1,383 | 1960 | 2,591 | 1964 | 3,641 | 1968 | 7,688 |
| 1945 | 232 | 1949 | 36 | 1953 | 443 | 1957 | 1,561 | 1961 | 2,872 | 1965 | 4,065 | Total: | $50,171 |
| 1946 | 286 | 1950 | 220 | 1954 | 770 | 1958 | 1,961 | 1962 | 2,996 | 1966 | 5,045 | | |
| 1947 | 326 | 1951 | 452 | 1955 | 1,054 | 1959 | 2,374 | 1963 | 3,233 | 1967 | 6,302 | | |

| LIVING ESTATE | | AGE | DEATH ESTATE | | | |
|---|---|---|---|---|---|---|
| "Buying Term and Investing the Difference" | Buying Whole Life | | "Buying Term and Investing the Difference" | Buying Whole Life | | |
| TOTAL VALUE OF SHARES | CASH VALUE | | TOTAL VALUE OF SHARES | + DECREASING TERM INSURANCE | = TOTAL DEATH ESTATE | FACE VALUE |
| $ 1,416 | $ 0 | 41 | $ 1,416 | $100,000 | $101,416 | $75,000 |
| 3,495 | 225 | 42 | 3,495 | 95,000 | 98,495 | 75,000 |
| 4,433 | 1,575 | 43 | 4,433 | 90,000 | 94,433 | 75,000 |
| 5,596 | 3,000 | 44 | 5,596 | 85,000 | 90,596 | 75,000 |
| 6,686 | 4,425 | 45 | 6,686 | 80,000 | 86,686 | 75,000 |
| 9,239 | 5,925 | 46 | 9,239 | 75,000 | 84,239 | 75,000 |
| 12,884 | 7,425 | 47 | 12,884 | 70,000 | 82,884 | 75,000 |
| 16,437 | 8,925 | 48 | 16,437 | 65,000 | 81,437 | 75,000 |
| 19,900 | 10,425 | 49 | 19,900 | 60,000 | 79,900 | 75,000 |
| 21,352 | 11,925 | 50 | 21,352 | 55,000 | 76,352 | 75,000 |
| 35,964 | 13,500 | 51 | 35,964 | 50,000 | 85,964 | 75,000 |
| 43,296 | 15,000 | 52 | 43,296 | 46,250 | 89,546 | 75,000 |
| 48,964 | 16,575 | 53 | 48,964 | 42,500 | 91,464 | 75,000 |
| 43,853 | 18,150 | 54 | 43,853 | 38,750 | 82,603 | 75,000 |
| 63,321 | 19,725 | 55 | 63,321 | 35,000 | 98,321 | 75,000 |
| 70,657 | 21,300 | 56 | 70,657 | 31,250 | 101,907 | 75,000 |
| 75,609 | 22,950 | 57 | 75,609 | 28,750 | 104,359 | 75,000 |
| 99,577 | 24,525 | 58 | 99,577 | 26,250 | 125,827 | 75,000 |
| 90,310 | 26,100 | 59 | 90,310 | 23,750 | 114,060 | 75,000 |
| 106,836 | 27,750 | 60 | 106,836 | 21,250 | 128,086 | 75,000 |
| 126,956 | 29,250 | 61 | 126,956 | 18,750 | 145,706 | 75,000 |
| 144,085 | 30,750 | 62 | 144,085 | 17,500 | 161,585 | 75,000 |
| 135,641 | 32,175 | 63 | 135,641 | 16,250 | 151,891 | 75,000 |
| 169,394 | 33,675 | 64 | 169,394 | 15,000 | 184,394 | 75,000 |
| 196,776 | 35,175 | 65 | 196,776 | 14,400 | 211,176 | 75,000 |

Whether you
**lived** or **died**
you would have been better off
"Buying Term and Investing the Difference"

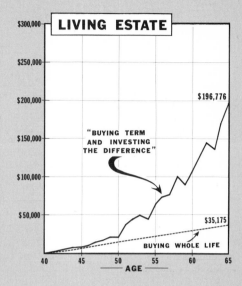

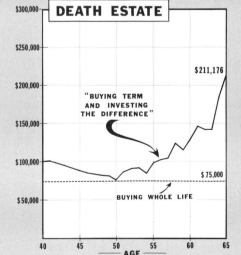

# WELLINGTON FUND

Illustration of assumed annual investments of $1,269 for twenty-five years from 1944 to 1968. All dividends and distributions reinvested.

This tabulation covers an illustration of an assumed investment of $1,269 annually on January 1 of each year from 1944 through 1968. This was a period in which stock prices fluctuated widely because of changing business and economic conditions, and were significantly higher at the end of the period than at the beginning. Thus, these results should not be considered as a representation of the dividend income or capital gain or loss that may be realized from an investment made in the fund today. A program of the type illustrated does not assure a profit nor protect against depreciation in declining markets.

| | | COST OF SHARES | | | | VALUE OF SHARES | | | | |
|---|---|---|---|---|---|---|---|---|---|---|
| YEAR ENDING DEC. 31 | AGE | CUMULATIVE ANNUAL INVEST-MENTS | ANNUAL INCOME DIVIDENDS REIN-VESTED | CUMULA-TIVE COST OF SHARES PURCHASED WITH DIVIDENDS | TOTAL COST (INCLUDES REIN-VESTED DIVIDENDS) | ACQUIRED THROUGH ANNUAL INVEST-MENTS | ACCEPTED AS CAPITAL GAINS DIS-TRIBUTIONS (CUMU-LATIVE) | SUB-TOTAL | PURCHASED THROUGH REINVEST-MENT OF INCOME (CUMULATIVE) | TOTAL VALUE |
| 1944 | 41 | $ 1,269 | $ 44 | $ 44 | $ 1,314 | $ 1,297 | $ 43 | $ 1,340 | $ 46 | $ 1,386 |
| 1945 | 42 | 2,538 | 75 | 120 | 2,659 | 2,806 | 197 | 3,003 | 133 | 3,136 |
| 1946 | 43 | 3,807 | 107 | 227 | 4,035 | 3,619 | 353 | 3,972 | 224 | 4,196 |
| 1947 | 44 | 5,077 | 173 | 401 | 5,478 | 4,356 | 445 | 4,801 | 370 | 5,171 |
| 1948 | 45 | 6,346 | 251 | 652 | 6,998 | 5,399 | 570 | 5,969 | 609 | 6,578 |
| 1949 | 46 | 7,615 | 377 | 1,029 | 8,645 | 7,212 | 737 | 7,949 | 1,068 | 9,017 |
| 1950 | 47 | 8,884 | 462 | 1,491 | 10,376 | 8,898 | 964 | 9,862 | 1,617 | 11,479 |
| 1951 | 48 | 10,154 | 541 | 2,033 | 12,187 | 10,588 | 1,363 | 11,951 | 2,252 | 14,203 |
| 1952 | 49 | 11,423 | 623 | 2,656 | 14,080 | 12,255 | 1,820 | 14,075 | 2,985 | 17,060 |
| 1953 | 50 | 12,692 | 708 | 3,365 | 16,058 | 12,837 | 2,155 | 14,992 | 3,573 | 18,565 |
| 1954 | 51 | 13,961 | 821 | 4,186 | 18,148 | 17,236 | 3,310 | 20,546 | 5,299 | 25,845 |
| 1955 | 52 | 15,231 | 967 | 5,154 | 20,385 | 19,908 | 4,575 | 24,483 | 6,717 | 31,200 |
| 1956 | 53 | 16,500 | 1,095 | 6,249 | 22,750 | 20,563 | 5,595 | 26,158 | 7,614 | 33,772 |
| 1957 | 54 | 17,769 | 1,253 | 7,502 | 25,273 | 19,333 | 6,163 | 25,496 | 7,936 | 33,432 |
| 1958 | 55 | 19,038 | 1,365 | 8,867 | 27,907 | 24,607 | 8,822 | 33,429 | 11,013 | 44,442 |
| 1959 | 56 | 20,308 | 1,529 | 10,397 | 30,706 | 26,271 | 10,616 | 36,887 | 12,756 | 49,643 |
| 1960 | 57 | 21,577 | 1,709 | 12,106 | 33,684 | 26,927 | 12,249 | 39,176 | 14,758 | 53,434 |
| 1961 | 58 | 22,846 | 1,868 | 13,974 | 36,822 | 31,405 | 15,717 | 47,122 | 17,821 | 64,943 |
| 1962 | 59 | 24,115 | 1,982 | 15,957 | 40,073 | 28,959 | 15,904 | 44,863 | 17,813 | 62,676 |
| 1963 | 60 | 25,385 | 2,128 | 18,085 | 43,471 | 31,583 | 19,028 | 50,611 | 20,821 | 71,432 |
| 1964 | 61 | 26,654 | 2,383 | 20,469 | 47,125 | 34,011 | 22,442 | 56,453 | 24,017 | 80,470 |
| 1965 | 62 | 27,923 | 2,635 | 23,105 | 51,030 | 34,704 | 25,083 | 59,787 | 26,286 | 86,073 |
| 1966 | 63 | 29,192 | 2,979 | 26,084 | 55,278 | 31,296 | 24,325 | 55,623 | 25,846 | 81,469 |
| 1967 | 64 | 30,462 | 3,168 | 29,253 | 59,716 | 32,760 | 27,416 | 60,176 | 29,191 | 89,367 |
| 1968 | 65 | 31,731 | 3,158 | 32,411 | 64,144 | 34,258 | 30,773 | 65,031 | 32,670 | 97,701 |

The total cost figures represent the cumulative total of yearly investments of $1,269 plus the cumulative amount of income dividends reinvested, and include the sales charge of 8½% on all shares so purchased, as described in the prospectus. No adjustment has been made for any income taxes payable by shareholders on security distributions and dividends reinvested in shares. The dollar amounts of security profits distributions taken in shares were:

| | | | | | | | | | | | | | |
|---|---|---|---|---|---|---|---|---|---|---|---|---|---|
| 1944 | 42 | 1948 | 136 | 1952 | 394 | 1956 | 1,120 | 1960 | 1,765 | 1964 | 2,665 | 1968 | 3,006 |
| 1945 | 146 | 1949 | 108 | 1953 | 413 | 1957 | 1,186 | 1961 | 2,047 | 1965 | 2,939 | Total: | $30,862 |
| 1946 | 177 | 1950 | 175 | 1954 | 638 | 1958 | 1,382 | 1962 | 1,917 | 1966 | 2,409 | | |
| 1947 | 125 | 1951 | 342 | 1955 | 988 | 1959 | 1,615 | 1963 | 2,317 | 1967 | 2,810 | | |

| LIVING ESTATE | | | DEATH ESTATE | | | |
|---|---|---|---|---|---|---|
| "Buying Term and Investing the Difference" | Buying Whole Life | | "Buying Term and Investing the Difference" | Buying Whole Life | | |
| TOTAL VALUE OF SHARES | CASH VALUE | AGE | TOTAL VALUE OF SHARES | + DECREASING TERM INSURANCE | = TOTAL DEATH ESTATE | FACE VALUE |
| $ 1,386 | $ 0 | 41 | $ 1,386 | $100,000 | $101,386 | $75,000 |
| 3,136 | 225 | 42 | 3,136 | 95,000 | 98,136 | 75,000 |
| 4,196 | 1,575 | 43 | 4,196 | 90,000 | 94,196 | 75,000 |
| 5,171 | 3,000 | 44 | 5,171 | 85,000 | 90,171 | 75,000 |
| 6,578 | 4,425 | 45 | 6,578 | 80,000 | 86,578 | 75,000 |
| 9,017 | 5,925 | 46 | 9,017 | 75,000 | 84,017 | 75,000 |
| 11,479 | 7,425 | 47 | 11,479 | 70,000 | 81,479 | 75,000 |
| 14,203 | 8,925 | 48 | 14,203 | 65,000 | 79,203 | 75,000 |
| 17,060 | 10,425 | 49 | 17,060 | 60,000 | 77,060 | 75,000 |
| 18,565 | 11,925 | 50 | 18,565 | 55,000 | 73,565 | 75,000 |
| 25,845 | 13,500 | 51 | 25,845 | 50,000 | 75,845 | 75,000 |
| 31,200 | 15,000 | 52 | 31,200 | 46,250 | 77,450 | 75,000 |
| 33,772 | 16,575 | 53 | 33,772 | 42,500 | 76,272 | 75,000 |
| 33,432 | 18,150 | 54 | 33,432 | 38,750 | 72,182 | 75,000 |
| 44,442 | 19,725 | 55 | 44,442 | 35,000 | 79,442 | 75,000 |
| 49,643 | 21,300 | 56 | 49,643 | 31,250 | 80,893 | 75,000 |
| 53,434 | 22,950 | 57 | 53,434 | 28,750 | 82,184 | 75,000 |
| 64,943 | 24,525 | 58 | 64,943 | 26,250 | 91,193 | 75,000 |
| 62,676 | 26,100 | 59 | 62,676 | 23,750 | 86,426 | 75,000 |
| 71,432 | 27,750 | 60 | 71,432 | 21,250 | 92,682 | 75,000 |
| 80,470 | 29,250 | 61 | 80,470 | 18,750 | 99,220 | 75,000 |
| 86,073 | 30,750 | 62 | 86,073 | 17,500 | 103,573 | 75,000 |
| 81,469 | 32,175 | 63 | 81,469 | 16,250 | 97,719 | 75,000 |
| 89,367 | 33,675 | 64 | 89,367 | 15,000 | 104,367 | 75,000 |
| 97,701 | 35,175 | 65 | 97,701 | 14,400 | 112,101 | 75,000 |

Whether you **lived** or **died** you would have been better off "Buying Term and Investing the Difference"

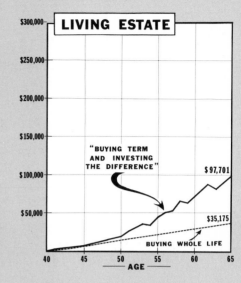

LIVING ESTATE

"BUYING TERM AND INVESTING THE DIFFERENCE" — $97,701

$35,175 — BUYING WHOLE LIFE

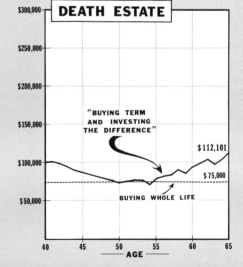

DEATH ESTATE

"BUYING TERM AND INVESTING THE DIFFERENCE" — $112,101

$75,000 — BUYING WHOLE LIFE

# WINFIELD GROWTH FUND

Illustration of assumed annual investments of $1,269 for twenty-five years from 1944 to 1968. All dividends and distributions reinvested.

This tabulation covers an illustration of an assumed investment of $1,269 annually on January 1 of each year from 1944 through 1968. This was a period in which stock prices fluctuated widely because of changing business and economic conditions, and were significantly higher at the end of the period than at the beginning. Thus, these results should not be considered as a representation of the dividend income or capital gain or loss that may be realized from an investment made in the fund today. A program of the type illustrated does not assure a profit nor protect against depreciation in declining markets.

| | | COST OF SHARES | | | | VALUE OF SHARES | | | | |
|---|---|---|---|---|---|---|---|---|---|---|
| YEAR ENDING DEC. 31 | AGE | CUMULATIVE ANNUAL INVEST-MENTS | ANNUAL INCOME DIVIDENDS REIN-VESTED | CUMULA-TIVE COST OF SHARES PURCHASED WITH DIVIDENDS | TOTAL COST (INCLUDES REIN-VESTED DIVIDENDS) | ACQUIRED THROUGH ANNUAL INVEST-MENTS | ACCEPTED AS CAPITAL GAINS DIS-TRIBUTIONS (CUMU-LATIVE) | SUB-TOTAL | PURCHASED THROUGH REINVEST-MENT OF INCOME (CUMULATIVE) | TOTAL VALUE |
| 1944 | 41 | $ 1,269 | $ 0 | $ 0 | $ 1,269 | $ 1,116 | $ 229 | $ 1,345 | $ 0 | $ 1,345 |
| 1945 | 42 | 2,538 | 0 | 0 | 2,538 | 2,123 | 885 | 3,008 | 0 | 3,008 |
| 1946 | 43 | 3,807 | 0 | 0 | 3,807 | 2,511 | 1,540 | 4,051 | 0 | 4,051 |
| 1947 | 44 | 5,077 | 0 | 0 | 5,077 | 3,360 | 1,756 | 5,116 | 0 | 5,116 |
| 1948 | 45 | 6,346 | 140 | 139 | 6,483 | 4,217 | 1,793 | 6,010 | 123 | 6,133 |
| 1949 | 46 | 7,615 | 213 | 353 | 7,969 | 6,085 | 2,273 | 8,358 | 343 | 8,701 |
| 1950 | 47 | 8,884 | 113 | 467 | 9,352 | 7,774 | 3,229 | 11,003 | 474 | 11,477 |
| 1951 | 48 | 10,154 | 217 | 684 | 10,839 | 8,593 | 4,633 | 13,226 | 639 | 13,865 |
| 1952 | 49 | 11,423 | 235 | 921 | 12,345 | 9,539 | 5,135 | 14,674 | 842 | 15,516 |
| 1953 | 50 | 12,692 | 387 | 1,309 | 14,002 | 9,880 | 5,492 | 15,372 | 1,131 | 16,503 |
| 1954 | 51 | 13,961 | 834 | 2,144 | 16,106 | 13,839 | 7,081 | 20,920 | 2,329 | 23,249 |
| 1955 | 52 | 15,231 | 829 | 2,974 | 18,205 | 16,478 | 8,930 | 25,408 | 3,384 | 28,792 |
| 1956 | 53 | 16,500 | 999 | 3,974 | 20,474 | 16,709 | 10,609 | 27,318 | 4,117 | 31,435 |
| 1957 | 54 | 17,769 | 1,049 | 5,024 | 22,795 | 13,900 | 10,579 | 24,479 | 4,047 | 28,526 |
| 1958 | 55 | 19,038 | 1,113 | 6,138 | 25,177 | 19,807 | 16,034 | 35,841 | 6,563 | 42,404 |
| 1959 | 56 | 20,308 | 496 | 6,635 | 26,944 | 24,185 | 21,492 | 45,677 | 8,059 | 53,736 |
| 1960 | 57 | 21,577 | 450 | 7,086 | 28,664 | 26,269 | 25,294 | 51,563 | 8,801 | 60,364 |
| 1961 | 58 | 22,846 | 388 | 7,476 | 30,322 | 37,432 | 37,088 | 74,520 | 12,419 | 86,939 |
| 1962 | 59 | 24,115 | 102 | 7,580 | 31,696 | 30,041 | 30,746 | 60,787 | 9,767 | 70,554 |
| 1963 | 60 | 25,385 | 423 | 8,003 | 33,389 | 36,669 | 37,017 | 73,680 | 11,880 | 85,560 |
| 1964 | 61 | 26,654 | 445 | 8,450 | 35,105 | 39,083 | 42,111 | 81,194 | 12,678 | 93,872 |
| 1965 | 62 | 27,923 | 1,102 | 9,553 | 37,477 | 49,559 | 60,340 | 109,899 | 16,777 | 126,676 |
| 1966 | 63 | 29,192 | 695 | 10,249 | 39,443 | 40,134 | 70,690 | 110,824 | 13,878 | 124,702 |
| 1967 | 64 | 30,462 | 186 | 10,435 | 40,898 | 74,241 | 152,788 | 227,029 | 25,164 | 252,193 |
| 1968 | 65 | 31,731 | 0 | 10,435 | 42,168 | 85,124 | 181,337 | 266,461 | 28,396 | 294,857 |

The total cost figures represent the cumulative total of yearly investments of $1,269 plus the cumulative amount of income dividends reinvested, and include the sales charge of 8½% on all shares so purchased, as described in the prospectus. No adjustment has been made for any income taxes payable by shareholders on security distributions and dividends reinvested in shares. The dollar amounts of security profits distributions taken in shares were:

| | | | | | | | | | | | | | |
|---|---|---|---|---|---|---|---|---|---|---|---|---|---|
| 1944 | 228 | 1948 | 167 | 1952 | 608 | 1956 | 2,154 | 1960 | 2,798 | 1964 | 3,830 | 1968 | 7,374 |
| 1945 | 692 | 1949 | 208 | 1953 | 769 | 1957 | 2,839 | 1961 | 2,223 | 1965 | 6,646 | Total: | $91,260 |
| 1946 | 926 | 1950 | 759 | 1954 | 175 | 1958 | 1,796 | 1962 | 2,221 | 1966 | 26,410 | | |
| 1947 | 351 | 1951 | 1,524 | 1955 | 1,081 | 1959 | 2,815 | 1963 | 843 | 1967 | 21,823 | | |

# LIVING ESTATE

| "Buying Term and Investing the Difference" | Buying Whole Life | AGE | "Buying Term and Investing the Difference" | | | Buying Whole Life |
|---|---|---|---|---|---|---|
| TOTAL VALUE OF SHARES | CASH VALUE | | TOTAL VALUE OF SHARES + | DECREASING TERM INSURANCE = | TOTAL DEATH ESTATE | FACE VALUE |
| $ 1,345 | $ 0 | 41 | $ 1,345 | $100,000 | $101,345 | $75,000 |
| 3,008 | 225 | 42 | 3,008 | 95,000 | 98,008 | 75,000 |
| 4,051 | 1,575 | 43 | 4,051 | 90,000 | 94,051 | 75,000 |
| 5,116 | 3,000 | 44 | 5,116 | 85,000 | 90,116 | 75,000 |
| 6,133 | 4,425 | 45 | 6,133 | 80,000 | 86,133 | 75,000 |
| 8,701 | 5,925 | 46 | 8,701 | 75,000 | 83,701 | 75,000 |
| 11,477 | 7,425 | 47 | 11,477 | 70,000 | 81,477 | 75,000 |
| 13,865 | 8,925 | 48 | 13,865 | 65,000 | 78,865 | 75,000 |
| 15,516 | 10,425 | 49 | 15,516 | 60,000 | 75,516 | 75,000 |
| 16,503 | 11,925 | 50 | 16,503 | 55,000 | 71,503 | 75,000 |
| 23,249 | 13,500 | 51 | 23,249 | 50,000 | 73,249 | 75,000 |
| 28,792 | 15,000 | 52 | 28,792 | 46,250 | 75,042 | 75,000 |
| 31,435 | 16,575 | 53 | 31,435 | 42,500 | 73,935 | 75,000 |
| 28,526 | 18,150 | 54 | 28,526 | 38,750 | 67,276 | 75,000 |
| 42,404 | 19,725 | 55 | 42,404 | 35,000 | 77,404 | 75,000 |
| 53,736 | 21,300 | 56 | 53,736 | 31,250 | 84,986 | 75,000 |
| 60,364 | 22,950 | 57 | 60,364 | 28,750 | 89,114 | 75,000 |
| 86,939 | 24,525 | 58 | 86,939 | 26,250 | 113,189 | 75,000 |
| 70,554 | 26,100 | 59 | 70,554 | 23,750 | 94,304 | 75,000 |
| 85,560 | 27,750 | 60 | 85,560 | 21,250 | 106,810 | 75,000 |
| 93,872 | 29,250 | 61 | 93,872 | 18,750 | 112,622 | 75,000 |
| 126,676 | 30,750 | 62 | 126,676 | 17,500 | 144,176 | 75,000 |
| 124,702 | 32,175 | 63 | 124,702 | 16,250 | 140,952 | 75,000 |
| 252,193 | 33,675 | 64 | 252,193 | 15,000 | 267,193 | 75,000 |
| 294,857 | 35,175 | 65 | 294,857 | 14,400 | 309,257 | 75,000 |

Column header for the right table: **DEATH ESTATE**

Whether you
**lived** or **died**
you would have been better off
"Buying Term and Investing the Difference"

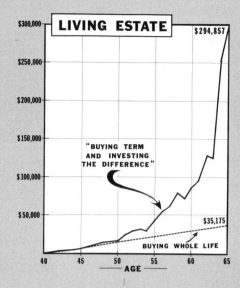

LIVING ESTATE — $294,857
"BUYING TERM AND INVESTING THE DIFFERENCE"
$35,175 — BUYING WHOLE LIFE

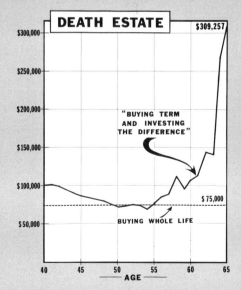

DEATH ESTATE — $309,257
"BUYING TERM AND INVESTING THE DIFFERENCE"
$75,000 — BUYING WHOLE LIFE

# WISCONSIN FUND

Illustration of assumed annual investments of $1,269 for twenty-five years from 1944 to 1968. All dividends and distributions reinvested.

This tabulation covers an illustration of an assumed investment of $1,269 annually on January 1 of each year from 1944 through 1968. This was a period in which stock prices fluctuated widely because of changing business and economic conditions, and were significantly higher at the end of the period than at the beginning. Thus, these results should not be considered as a representation of the dividend income or capital gain or loss that may be realized from an investment made in the fund today. A program of the type illustrated does not assure a profit nor protect against depreciation in declining markets.

| | | COST OF SHARES | | | | VALUE OF SHARES | | | | |
|---|---|---|---|---|---|---|---|---|---|---|
| YEAR ENDING DEC. 31 | AGE | CUMULATIVE ANNUAL INVEST- MENTS | ANNUAL INCOME DIVIDENDS REIN- VESTED | CUMULA- TIVE COST OF SHARES PURCHASED WITH DIVIDENDS | TOTAL COST (INCLUDES REIN- VESTED DIVIDENDS) | ACQUIRED THROUGH ANNUAL INVEST- MENTS | ACCEPTED AS CAPITAL GAINS DIS- TRIBUTIONS (CUMU- LATIVE) | SUB- TOTAL | PURCHASED THROUGH REINVEST- MENT OF INCOME (CUMULATIVE) | TOTAL VALUE |
| 1944 | 41 | $ 1,269 | $ 62 | $ 62 | $ 1,331 | $ 1,400 | $ 0 | $ 1,400 | $ 59 | $ 1,459 |
| 1945 | 42 | 2,538 | 64 | 126 | 2,665 | 3,252 | 279 | 3,531 | 138 | 3,669 |
| 1946 | 43 | 3,807 | 63 | 189 | 3,997 | 3,839 | 694 | 4,533 | 173 | 4,706 |
| 1947 | 44 | 5,077 | 130 | 319 | 5,396 | 4,452 | 825 | 5,277 | 271 | 5,548 |
| 1948 | 45 | 6,346 | 143 | 462 | 6,808 | 5,142 | 1,041 | 6,183 | 377 | 6,560 |
| 1949 | 46 | 7,615 | 338 | 800 | 8,416 | 7,095 | 1,398 | 8,493 | 752 | 9,245 |
| 1950 | 47 | 8,884 | 400 | 1,200 | 10,085 | 8,751 | 1,816 | 10,567 | 1,195 | 11,762 |
| 1951 | 48 | 10,154 | 537 | 1,737 | 11,891 | 10,599 | 2,540 | 13,139 | 1,771 | 14,910 |
| 1952 | 49 | 11,423 | 704 | 2,441 | 13,864 | 12,042 | 3,081 | 15,123 | 2,466 | 17,589 |
| 1953 | 50 | 12,692 | 712 | 3,153 | 15,846 | 12,522 | 3,547 | 16,069 | 2,982 | 19,051 |
| 1954 | 51 | 13,961 | 910 | 4,063 | 18,025 | 17,534 | 5,331 | 22,865 | 4,720 | 27,585 |
| 1955 | 52 | 15,231 | 1,064 | 5,127 | 20,358 | 21,037 | 5,998 | 27,035 | 6,313 | 33,348 |
| 1956 | 53 | 16,500 | 1,295 | 6,422 | 22,922 | 20,603 | 8,216 | 28,819 | 7,030 | 35,849 |
| 1957 | 54 | 17,769 | 1,381 | 7,803 | 25,573 | 18,191 | 8,450 | 26,641 | 7,095 | 33,736 |
| 1958 | 55 | 19,038 | 1,349 | 9,152 | 28,191 | 25,248 | 11,911 | 37,159 | 10,594 | 47,753 |
| 1959 | 56 | 20,308 | 1,362 | 10,514 | 30,822 | 28,598 | 13,971 | 42,569 | 12,746 | 55,315 |
| 1960 | 57 | 21,577 | 1,469 | 11,983 | 33,562 | 30,226 | 15,974 | 46,200 | 14,407 | 60,607 |
| 1961 | 58 | 22,846 | 1,578 | 13,561 | 36,408 | 38,484 | 21,928 | 60,412 | 19,181 | 79,593 |
| 1962 | 59 | 24,115 | 1,726 | 15,287 | 39,403 | 32,383 | 21,582 | 53,965 | 17,325 | 71,290 |
| 1963 | 60 | 25,385 | 1,866 | 17,153 | 42,538 | 36,482 | 26,629 | 63,111 | 20,582 | 83,693 |
| 1964 | 61 | 26,654 | 2,017 | 19,170 | 45,824 | 39,983 | 32,299 | 72,282 | 23,745 | 96,027 |
| 1965 | 62 | 27,923 | 2,044 | 21,214 | 49,138 | 44,645 | 40,071 | 84,716 | 27,744 | 112,460 |
| 1966 | 63 | 29,192 | 2,366 | 23,580 | 52,773 | 40,305 | 40,715 | 81,020 | 26,580 | 107,600 |
| 1967 | 64 | 30,462 | 2,381 | 25,961 | 56,423 | 48,801 | 53,265 | 102,066 | 33,487 | 135,553 |
| 1968 | 65 | 31,731 | 2,806 | 28,767 | 60,498 | 49,430 | 63,053 | 112,483 | 35,845 | 148,328 |

The total cost figures represent the cumulative total of yearly investments of $1,269 plus the cumulative amount of income dividends reinvested, and include the sales charge of 8½% on all shares so purchased, as described in the prospectus. No adjustment has been made for any income taxes payable by shareholders on security distributions and dividends reinvested in shares. The dollar amounts of security profits distributions taken in shares were:

| | | | | | | | | | | | | | |
|---|---|---|---|---|---|---|---|---|---|---|---|---|---|
| 1944 | 0 | 1948 | 295 | 1952 | 475 | 1956 | 2,600 | 1960 | 1,666 | 1964 | 3,695 | 1968 | 9,674 |
| 1945 | 273 | 1949 | 214 | 1953 | 631 | 1957 | 1,775 | 1961 | 1,889 | 1965 | 4,500 | Total: | $49,174 |
| 1946 | 446 | 1950 | 318 | 1954 | 766 | 1958 | 686 | 1962 | 4,134 | 1966 | 5,966 | | |
| 1947 | 211 | 1951 | 578 | 1955 | 0 | 1959 | 987 | 1963 | 2,876 | 1967 | 4,519 | | |

# LIVING ESTATE / DEATH ESTATE

| LIVING ESTATE — "Buying Term and Investing the Difference" TOTAL VALUE OF SHARES | LIVING ESTATE — Buying Whole Life CASH VALUE | AGE | DEATH ESTATE — "Buying Term and Investing the Difference" TOTAL VALUE OF SHARES | + DECREASING TERM INSURANCE | = TOTAL DEATH ESTATE | Buying Whole Life FACE VALUE |
|---|---|---|---|---|---|---|
| $ 1,459 | $ 0 | 41 | $ 1,459 | $100,000 | $101,459 | $75,000 |
| 3,669 | 225 | 42 | 3,669 | 95,000 | 98,669 | 75,000 |
| 4,706 | 1,575 | 43 | 4,706 | 90,000 | 94,706 | 75,000 |
| 5,548 | 3,000 | 44 | 5,548 | 85,000 | 90,548 | 75,000 |
| 6,560 | 4,425 | 45 | 6,560 | 80,000 | 86,560 | 75,000 |
| 9,245 | 5,925 | 46 | 9,245 | 75,000 | 84,245 | 75,000 |
| 11,762 | 7,425 | 47 | 11,762 | 70,000 | 81,762 | 75,000 |
| 14,910 | 8,925 | 48 | 14,910 | 65,000 | 79,910 | 75,000 |
| 17,589 | 10,425 | 49 | 17,589 | 60,000 | 77,589 | 75,000 |
| 19,051 | 11,925 | 50 | 19,051 | 55,000 | 74,051 | 75,000 |
| 27,585 | 13,500 | 51 | 27,585 | 50,000 | 77,585 | 75,000 |
| 33,348 | 15,000 | 52 | 33,348 | 46,250 | 79,598 | 75,000 |
| 35,849 | 16,575 | 53 | 35,849 | 42,500 | 78,349 | 75,000 |
| 33,736 | 18,150 | 54 | 33,736 | 38,750 | 72,486 | 75,000 |
| 47,753 | 19,725 | 55 | 47,753 | 35,000 | 82,753 | 75,000 |
| 55,315 | 21,300 | 56 | 55,315 | 31,250 | 86,565 | 75,000 |
| 60,607 | 22,950 | 57 | 60,607 | 28,750 | 89,357 | 75,000 |
| 79,593 | 24,525 | 58 | 79,593 | 26,250 | 105,843 | 75,000 |
| 71,290 | 26,100 | 59 | 71,290 | 23,750 | 95,040 | 75,000 |
| 83,693 | 27,750 | 60 | 83,693 | 21,250 | 104,943 | 75,000 |
| 96,027 | 29,250 | 61 | 96,027 | 18,750 | 114,777 | 75,000 |
| 112,460 | 30,750 | 62 | 112,460 | 17,500 | 129,960 | 75,000 |
| 107,600 | 32,175 | 63 | 107,600 | 16,250 | 123,850 | 75,000 |
| 135,553 | 33,675 | 64 | 135,553 | 15,000 | 150,553 | 75,000 |
| 148,328 | 35,175 | 65 | 148,328 | 14,400 | 162,728 | 75,000 |

Whether you **lived** or **died** you would have been better off "Buying Term and Investing the Difference"

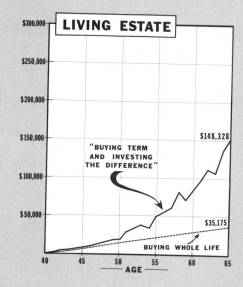

LIVING ESTATE

"BUYING TERM AND INVESTING THE DIFFERENCE" — $148,328

BUYING WHOLE LIFE — $35,175

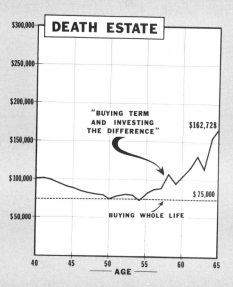

DEATH ESTATE

"BUYING TERM AND INVESTING THE DIFFERENCE" — $162,728

BUYING WHOLE LIFE — $75,000

## AVERAGE OF ALL 49 FUNDS

### LIVING ESTATE

| "Buying Term and Investing the Difference" | Buying Whole Life |
|---|---|
| TOTAL VALUE OF SHARES | CASH VALUE |

### DEATH ESTATE

| "Buying Term and Investing the Difference" | | | Buying Whole Life |
|---|---|---|---|
| TOTAL VALUE OF SHARES + | DECREASING TERM INSURANCE = | TOTAL DEATH ESTATE | FACE VALUE |

| LIVING: TOTAL VALUE OF SHARES | LIVING: CASH VALUE | AGE | DEATH: TOTAL VALUE OF SHARES | DEATH: DECREASING TERM INSURANCE | DEATH: TOTAL DEATH ESTATE | FACE VALUE |
|---|---|---|---|---|---|---|
| $ 1,354 | $ 0 | 41 | $ 1,354 | $100,000 | $101,354 | $75,000 |
| 3,529 | 225 | 42 | 3,529 | 95,000 | 98,529 | 75,000 |
| 4,380 | 1,575 | 43 | 4,380 | 90,000 | 94,380 | 75,000 |
| 5,500 | 3,000 | 44 | 5,500 | 85,000 | 90,500 | 75,000 |
| 6,659 | 4,425 | 45 | 6,659 | 80,000 | 86,659 | 75,000 |
| 9,161 | 5,925 | 46 | 9,161 | 75,000 | 84,161 | 75,000 |
| 12,793 | 7,425 | 47 | 12,793 | 70,000 | 82,793 | 75,000 |
| 16,217 | 8,925 | 48 | 16,217 | 65,000 | 81,217 | 75,000 |
| 19,392 | 10,425 | 49 | 19,392 | 60,000 | 79,392 | 75,000 |
| 20,547 | 11,925 | 50 | 20,547 | 55,000 | 75,547 | 75,000 |
| 31,589 | 13,500 | 51 | 31,589 | 50,000 | 81,589 | 75,000 |
| 39,072 | 15,000 | 52 | 39,072 | 46,250 | 85,322 | 75,000 |
| 43,874 | 16,575 | 53 | 43,874 | 42,500 | 86,374 | 75,000 |
| 40,151 | 18,150 | 54 | 40,151 | 38,750 | 78,901 | 75,000 |
| 57,925 | 19,725 | 55 | 57,925 | 35,000 | 92,925 | 75,000 |
| 65,000 | 21,300 | 56 | 65,000 | 31,250 | 96,250 | 75,000 |
| 68,826 | 22,950 | 57 | 68,826 | 28,750 | 97,576 | 75,000 |
| 87,329 | 24,525 | 58 | 87,329 | 26,250 | 113,579 | 75,000 |
| 78,192 | 26,100 | 59 | 78,192 | 23,750 | 101,942 | 75,000 |
| 93,384 | 27,750 | 60 | 93,384 | 21,250 | 114,634 | 75,000 |
| 108,014 | 29,250 | 61 | 108,014 | 18,750 | 126,764 | 75,000 |
| 128,361 | 30,750 | 62 | 128,361 | 17,500 | 145,861 | 75,000 |
| 122,567 | 32,175 | 63 | 122,567 | 16,250 | 138,817 | 75,000 |
| 158,458 | 33,675 | 64 | 158,458 | 15,000 | 173,458 | 75,000 |
| 180,955 | 35,175 | 65 | 180,955 | 14,400 | 195,355 | 75,000 |

Whether you **lived** or **died** you would have been better off "Buying Term and Investing the Difference"

LIVING ESTATE

"BUYING TERM AND INVESTING THE DIFFERENCE" $180,955

$35,175 BUYING WHOLE LIFE

DEATH ESTATE

"BUYING TERM AND INVESTING THE DIFFERENCE" $195,355

$75,000 BUYING WHOLE LIFE

## Funding

As a counterpoint to buying term and investing the difference, you may be offered "funding."

When the life insurance men began moving into the mutual fund industry, as "dually licensed" salesmen, they devised the funding arrangement. Treasury regulations prohibited investment dealers from arranging loans for the purchase of mutual fund shares, thus proscribing insurance men from arranging for the policyholders to borrow against the cash value of their life insurance policies. As soon as the insurance men had started selling funds, they tried to chuck the cash value insurance overboard in pursuit of mutual fund sales. The insurance companies promptly threatened to excommunicate them if they caused the policies to be cash-surrendered and the proceeds invested in funds. The industry did not mind so much the insurance men arranging for policyholders simply to borrow the cash values. After all, the policyholders were lending the money to the companies at 2½ percent or 3 percent, so the companies were quite willing to let them borrow their own money at 5 percent. But the dually licensed salesmen discovered that they could not arrange the policy loans without violating Treasury regulations.

This led them to design funding, which gives the whole process a reverse twist: you buy mutual fund shares and put them up as collateral for a loan to pay the premium on the life insurance policy which the "dual-y" also sells you. The theory is that if you have $1,000, you do not have to divide it by putting, say, $700 in fund shares and $300 toward a life insurance premium. Instead, you invest the whole $1,000 in fund shares, and put them up as collateral for a loan to pay the insurance premium. In a word, you are introducing an element of leveraging into your estate planning. That is a good idea. Examining the interest rate you are asked to pay on the loan, you simply decide whether you are likely to make more than that investing your money in a mutual fund instead of tying it up in a life insurance premium. Generally, you can do better investing it.

The fly in the ointment is that the promoters of funding generally refuse to sell you term insurance in connection with the scheme. As the prospectus puts it: "The basic life insurance contract recommended for the programs is an individual ordinary or whole life policy."

The funding company generally has two subsidiaries. One is a broker-dealer, the other is a life insurance company. In setting up the program, it makes a commission on both the fund share sale and on the life insurance. The company makes more on a cash value policy, and the salesman is paid more for selling it. This extra profit to them comes out of the customer's pocket.

Do not enter into the plan unless you can buy decreasing term insurance. Also, check the rates for the coverage they offer with those of competing companies. In the prospectus of one such company the charge for whole life insurance at age thirty-five is $20.00 per year per $1,000. At thirty-five you can buy decreasing term insurance to age seventy for $3.12 per year per $1,000. This gives you an idea of the extra costs of a funding program, which is not simply a few dollars a year difference in premium. If the purpose of insurance is to give your family protection, and you can afford $500, does it make sense to give your family $25,000 of protection via the funding company's cash value policy when you can buy a $160,000 decreasing term policy for the same premium outlay? What would be the real cost to your family if you bought the funding company's cash value policy and died soon after?

Before buying a funding program, carefully read the part of the prospectus that states that the company can withdraw from the scheme whenever it chooses. The premium loans are on a demand or short-term basis and the company can terminate the arrangement. Consider that if the collateral should shrink in value, they would unquestionably require you to reduce your indebtedness. Alternatively, they would sell enough of your fund holdings at that low point in the market to pay off what you owe.

Be careful of funding.

# Chapter 24

# MUTUAL FUNDS VS.
# THE LIFE INSURANCE INDUSTRY

In 1974, the mutual fund industry will celebrate its fiftieth birthday—if it still exists as an industry on that date.

I say "if" because if present trends continue, by then the fund industry will have become the tail on the life insurance dog. That will be a real tragedy.

The American people owe a very great debt to the mutual fund industry—particularly the thousands of broker-dealers and their sales representatives who have been selling fund shares at retail for the past three decades or more. Those retail salespeople were just about the only source of correct information about life insurance available to the public. I am not saying that they were unbiased. It just happened that their best interests and those of their prospective clients coincided, and so their clients became the beneficiaries of some very good advice. The fundmen early became aware that not only did they have to sell their prospects on the desirability of mutual fund investment, but they also had to point out to the prospect where he could get the money to invest. Mutual funds were not just "good" —they were "better" than something else. The fundmen began pointing out what it was that funds were better than, and life insurance became their chief target. Generations of Americans had known no mediums of accumulation other than life insurance and savings accounts. Savings accounts were easy to explain away. Life insurance, with its element of protection, was a little more involved. Thousands of fundmen became truly expert on the subject of life insurance. They did not sell it; they simply explained to their investment prospects how it could best be used. There was no commission for them in a clients' purchase of insurance, so the fundmen saw to it that the clients got the most for their insurance dollar—leaving as much as possible for the fundmen to put to work in investment.

For some time organizations such as Mutual Fund Services in Naugatuck, Connecticut, have distributed to fund people a wide variety of educational materials on the subject of insurance. One such folder, titled "To the Great Northern Insurance Company I Bequeath the Cash Value of My Life Insurance Policies," is said to have sold well over $1 billion worth of mutual fund shares.

The life insurance industry viewed this counseling by fund people successively with disdain, with annoyance, with alarm, and finally with resignation. Unable to refute the arguments, the insurance companies took another tack. They argued that the fund salesman was spending a lot of time giving advice for which he was not being paid. Why send the client somewhere else to buy the term insurance? Why not sell it himself? A very great number of fund salesmen accepted the invitation to become "dually licensed" to sell both insurance and mutual funds. Having wangled them onto the payroll and given them a taste of the honey of commission checks, the companies then slyly explained that, of course, if the insurance policies they had sold so far had been whole life or twenty-payment life, the commissions would be many times larger. Perhaps in the future, they might wish to offer the more profitable types of policies, etc., etc. Alas, the bulk of the fundmen were corrupted. They stopped advising clients to "buy term and invest the difference" and began selling cash value policies just like the insurance men. This was a tremendous loss to the public.

Over the years, though, the obvious greater profitability of mutual funds led people to abandon endowments, retirement income policies, and other high-priced types of insurance, and the insurers' share of the total savings in the United States fell from 42 percent in 1950 to 20 percent in 1969. The Prudential first broke the solid ranks of the insurance industry by seeking to make available a "variable annuity" whose benefits at retirement age would reflect the success of the company in employing the premium in equity investment. The opposition to it from within and without the industry made it obvious that it was a long, slow solution to the industry's problem of successfully combating the mutual funds.

Next, one or two insurance companies made arrangements with no-load funds for package sales with their policies. Then three life companies bought control of the management companies of small funds. Now, the move by life companies into the fund industry has become a stampede. More than 16 percent of the assets of the mutual fund industry are now under the control of life insurance companies.

One by one, the important companies in the fund business are selling out to the insurance industry. A recent casualty was the old and highly respected Putnam group of eight funds in Boston which dates back to 1937. Melvin L. Gold, a consulting actuary and Fellow of the American Society of Actuaries, writing in *Best's* [Insurance] *Review* noted: "Life insurance companies missed the opportunity to dominate the fund business at a fraction of the price they are paying today." Nevertheless, they appear determined to dominate it.

Hugh Johnson & Company Inc. (*Johnson's Charts*), a Buffalo member firm of the New York Stock Exchange has for many years published a small booklet called *Your* TOMORROW. The booklet is sold to mutual fund dealers and salesmen for distribution to their fund prospects and customers. Each issue contains two or three articles dramatizing the use of mutual funds and reciting their investment advantages, and frequently includes articles giving guidance in the proper use of life insurance, that is, stressing the importance of buying low-cost term insurance rather than the high-cost cash value life insurance so dear to the hearts of life insurance executives and so profitable for the life insurance salesman.

On the following page is an extract from a sample copy of the magazine sent out in April 1970 to mutual fund people—now including thousands of new, dually licensed life insurance men. Note the unwholesome influence that the entry of insurance men into the mutual fund field has had on the editorial policy of the magazine.

The insurance companies have not given up the battle against term insurance. It is just that if most of the people who sell mutual funds are under the direct or indirect supervision of life companies, those companies can effectively discourage the sale of the low-cost protection from which they profit least. Just as they do not give their own salesmen credit for term insurance sales

in the periodic sales contests to honor "good old J. B., our president," and pay the salesmen reduced commissions for such sales, so they will by similar pressure effectively discourage term insurance sales by their dually licensed representatives.

In the previous chapter, the results of buying term and investing the difference in a long-established company, Loomis-Sayles Mutual Fund, could not be shown because the New England Mutual Life Insurance Company had bought control of the fund's management company and refused to provide figures showing how much more profitable it would have been to have bought term insurance and invested the difference in the fund.

Mutual life insurance companies supposedly were organized to provide life insurance protection *at cost*. They are insurance cooperatives, not profit-making enterprises. However, we have seen how without any notice to—much less approval of—their policyholders they have waded into the mutual fund business, their purpose being to recapture what they have lost in recent years to investment men. There is no justification for their move into funds any more than they could justify the opening of a broker-dealer department or affiliate to sell stocks and bonds.

While the mutual fund industry has always compensated its sales force on a commission basis from the sales charges—under no circumstances could the assets of a fund be drawn upon to pay for sales efforts—it has not been so for the mutual life insurance companies, which pay generous salaries and drawing accounts. Instead of paying out the profits to the policyholders to give them life insurance at cost, the company managements sequester such profits in huge surplus accounts, greatly in excess of what is required legally. Their excuse is that these extra reserves are needed against either the possibility of an unfavorable mortality experience due to an epidemic or to an unexpected decline in the company's investment earnings in an economic depression. The surpluses have been carried to ridiculous lengths and the policyholders have been deprived of billions in profits. In recent years, these companies have engaged in a free-swinging battle for business, marked by huge increases in salesmen's compensation. It now costs the industry $135 to $200 to put $100 in new premiums on the books. Obviously, if it collects $100 and pays out $135, the difference has to come from somewhere. It comes from surplus.

The life insurance industry pays its men a salary during their three-to-five year training period. Thereafter, they are on a drawing account seldom less than $12,000 per year. Invading the fund business, the mutual life companies will pay their dually licensed representatives a salary or drawing account to sell funds. Where will this money come from? From the sur-

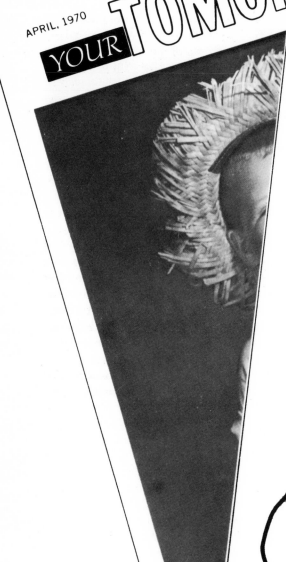

APRIL, 1970

# YOUR TOMORROW

## What is YOUR TOMORROW?

This is a sample copy of *Your* TOMORROW magazine, a monthly publication designed to help you sell more mutual funds to both customers and prospects. All articles are approved by the N. A. S. D. as well as by all states which require it.

Many representatives send *Your* TOMORROW to their customers every month. They tell us that these customers are often stimulated to buy more funds by *Your* TOMORROW articles. *Your* TOMORROW is also an ideal prospecting tool.

This entire page is reserved for your advertisement. Most dealers use a short message, followed by the firm name, address and phone number. Each salesman can individualize his copies with a rubber stamp.

Quantities of 200 or more are sent to you each month for distribution. You can mail them out first class for 6 cents. No envelope is needed. Merely write the person's name and address on the back cover.

Why not use this prestige mailing piece every month? No long-term contract is required. You may cancel at any time with 90-days' notice.

*Attention:* LIFE INSURANCE AGENTS

You will be relieved to learn that we have made a major change in our policy concerning cash value life insurance. Henceforth, *Your* TOMORROW will no longer be critical of your product. You can start now to use *Your* TOMORROW to increase your mutual fund business and have no fear that your life insurance customers will be disturbed by what they read in our magazine.

JOHN SLATTER
*Editor*

plus, which legally belongs to the life insurance policy-holders—that faceless throng who never approved the company's venture into the mutual fund business and who don't even know they are in it.

Among the major life insurance companies now in the fund business at the expense of their policyholders are the Berkshire Mutual Life, Boston Mutual Life, Fidelity Mutual Life, John Hancock Mutual Life, Mutual Life of New York, New England Mutual Life, New York Life, Northwestern Mutual Life, Phoenix Mutual Life, Provident Mutual Life, Prudential, and State Mutual Life.

If I owned a policy in any of these companies, I would bring a policyholder's derivative suit, charging it with the gross misuse of the fiduciary funds in its care. These ambitious people, who hold office by reason of a vote of less than 1 percent of their policyholders, need to be reminded of whose money it is.

The 450,000 full-time or part-time insurance men in the United States compare with about 175,000 brokers and salesmen licensed to sell funds, including an estimated 80,000 who deal exclusively in the funds and 50,000 insurance agents who are already licensed to sell funds as well.

Obviously, fund sales are going to leap ahead. The question is: How will they be made? The great majority of the life insurance policies in force in this country today were sold through misrepresentation. Not one person in a hundred who buys a life insurance policy knows what he has bought. For generations the life insurance industry has sold its product with oral presentations devised by home-office sales psychologists. Salesmen are taught less of what life insurance is than of how to sell it—by clever "power phrases" to shame a man into buying. The industry appeals to a mixed bag of sales candidates. Since Oregon began requiring applicants for life insurance licenses to be fingerprinted, three to five applicants per day were revealed to have criminal records. States without similar precautions, which routinely process such undesirable recruits, turn them loose to prey upon the public.

The life insurance industry has an intense disdain for regulation. Indeed, the one thing that principally deterred the industry's invasion of the mutual fund field

has been the prospectus. Every person solicited by a fund must be given a written prospectus. It should always have been a requirement for the insurance industry as well. However, nothing so unnerves an insurance executive as the suggestion that his salesmen be obligated to provide a prospective buyer of a life insurance policy with a prospectus setting forth all the material facts. Harry Wade, president of Standard Life of Indiana, summed up that antipathy:

"If the regulation forcing stock [insurance] companies to report on an SEC form goes through, we'll soon have SEC in the mutuals, too: and if we have to live under SEC regulation of our selling methods, I'll sell out and go into the banana business."

The industry appears to need something that the mutual fund product has to offer. Thomas B. Murphy, Vice-Chairman of Boston Mutual Life, in an article for *Best's Review,* May 1970, probing the increasing costs of establishing and maintaining a life insurance sales organization, observed that, unless the increasing costs and decreasing productivity of insurance salesmen can be reversed, "the function will price itself out of the market." Citing the industry's venture into the fund business, he noted that "the acceptability of the mutual fund paves the way for building the client relationships and improving the relative status of the job from that of life insurance salesman to security planner. The service a life insurance agent performs is most often discovered at death. The service a mutual fund salesman performs is discovered when the fund shares appreciate or when income or capital gains dividends are paid, a relatively frequent occurrence. A favorable performance for fund shares would remind the client of the salesman's service."

\*  \*  \*

There was a young lady of Niger
Who smiled as she rode on a tiger
They returned from the ride
With the lady inside
And the smile on the face of the tiger.

Is the mutual fund industry to be the lady of Niger?

# Chapter 25

# WHICH PAPER DO YOU READ?

Investment is not an exact science. There are varying degrees of professional skill and competence, which are reflected in the results.

With the proliferation of funds—there are now more than a thousand registered investment companies, of which about 500 are of consequence—there has been a somewhat similar flowering of statistical services which purport to provide an accurate record of their comparative performance.

The granddaddy of mutual fund statistical services is Arthur Wiesenberger's *Investment Companies,* a volume published annually in May at $40.00 per copy and available in many public libraries. Wiesenberger is at 5 Hanover Square, New York City. This volume is a thorough, complete, and accurate purveyor of mutual fund information. In addition to separate chapters on different aspects of mutual fund operation, it gives detailed information about the annual operation and performance for each fund over the last decade. For mutual fund dealers, Weisenberger provides a quarterly updating of performance figures. A dealer is permitted to show you the book, but he cannot quote the performance figures orally, or in a letter or other written form. He cannot show you the quarterly updated figures unless he shows you the book at the same time.

If all this seems ridiculous, you are correct. It is not the publisher but the Securities and Exchange Commission that restricts the use of the information. The Commission has issued a Statement of Policy which specifies what can or cannot be said about mutual funds. Every mutual fund dealer in the country violates the Statement of Policy every day. He cannot help it. If he writes you a letter in which he says "I think that the ABC Fund is a good investment," he has violated the Statement, which requires that every written communication containing a sales message or appeal intended to influence you to purchase mutual fund shares must be submitted in advance to the Investment Companies Committee of the National Association of Securities Dealers for clearance.

If a mutual fund dealer tells you that the XYZ Fund produced a total overall gain last year of 19 percent, the S.E.C. and the NASD will make his life miserable. While the figure consists of 3 percent ordinary income dividends, 4 percent capital gains distributions, and 12 percent unrealized appreciation, no one of these is significant by itself. It is the total overall gain resulting from an investment that must be taken into account. But, in addition to the restriction requiring the use of the book, the S.E.C. makes it a further violation of the law for a mutual fund dealer to combine them in a single figure.

*Johnson's Charts,* an annual volume published by Hugh Johnson & Company, Inc., gives fund performance information in graph form. Johnson is at the Rand Building, Buffalo, New York. Paraphrasing what the Governor of North Carolina said to the Governor of South Carolina, "It's a long time between editions"; that is the only fault I find with Mr. Johnson's otherwise excellent work.

Another excellent source of information is *FundScope,* a monthly magazine that compares funds statistically from every conceivable angle, with useful and occasionally critical commentary. This is at 1800 Avenue of the Stars, Century City, Los Angeles, California.

The Arthur Lipper Corporation publishes mutual fund performance figures weekly, but while it cheerfully issues them to the newspapers to be quoted, it will not sell them to a layman. He might not want to buy them, anyway, for the cost is $500 per annum. They are at 140 Broadway, New York City.

*The Mutual Fund Buyer's Guide* provides a twice-a-month service for the individual investor. The *Guide* will not only give you the performance figures but will also tell you which funds it considers likely to deliver superior performance.

The United Business Service publishes its *Mutual Fund Selector,* which gives comparative performance figures for a limited list of funds, commentary on fund performance, and vignettes of individual funds. The *Selector* is at 212 Newbury Street in Boston. It is interesting, though some of it may be familiar: I keep finding material in it that I have written for other publications, published here without attribution and without so much as a by-your-leave.

The *Aggressive Growth Funds* report confines its attention to a rather small group of growth funds but the publisher does an excellent job of rooting out information about new small funds, and offers a "recommended list" of likely good performers. They are at P.O. Box 667, Los Altos, California.

The difficulty with all of the above and a dozen smaller statistical and/or advisory services is that no two use the same yardstick, with the result that the performance figures they give can be very conflicting.

Several months ago, I supplied the Securities and Exchange Commission with a detailed analysis of the figures produced by the various services and I suggested that the publication of widely disparate figures could well have the effect of misleading investors. A mutual fund dealer pushing a particular fund might well show you a report by one of the statistical services disclosing that Fund A was up 25 percent for the past twelve months and therefore should be bought in preference to Fund B which is up only 22 percent for the same period. You may accept his figures as authentic and buy from him. But if another dealer whose favorite is Fund B got to you first and showed you the report of a statistical service that indicated that Fund A actually was up only 24 percent for the period while Fund B was up 27 percent, you would undoubtedly go for Fund B.

Your decision depends not only upon the personal preference of the dealer, then, but also upon the figures produced by the particular statistical service he lays before you. The first dealer may advise you to buy Fund A because it was up 25 percent, while the second dealer advises you to buy Fund B because it was up 27 percent. If they are not using the same common denominator in arriving at their conclusions, they serve only to confuse the fund buyer and warp his judgment.

I urged the Commission to establish some standard formula for arriving at mutual fund performance results to end the confusion. I never even got an acknowledgment of my interest.

To illustrate the point, compare these 1969 performance figures for over 150 funds as published by five leading statistical services:

| Fund | Wiesenberger | Lipper | United Bus. Svce. | M.F. Buyer's Guide | FundScope |
|---|---|---|---|---|---|
| Admiralty Income Fund | −19.5% | −20.9% | −20.9% | −22.8% | −20.7% |
| Afuture Fund | −20.7 | −20.7 | * | −23.7 | −15.5 |
| All American Fund | −40.7 | −41.0 | −37.6 | −42.9 | −38.4 |
| AMCAP Fund | − 6.5 | − 5.5 | − 6.3 | − 6.8 | − 6.3 |
| American Business Shares | − 9.7 | −10.4 | − 9.8 | −15.0 | − 9.6 |
| American Enterprise | −25.5 | −25.8 | * | −23.7 | * |
| American Express Capital Fund | −14.5 | −14.6 | −14.5 | −15.9 | −14.4 |
| American Express Stock Fund | −15.7 | −15.8 | −15.3 | −14.5 | −15.2 |
| American Invest. Couns. | −16.4 | * | * | −23.7 | * |
| American National Growth | −13.5 | −13.9 | −13.6 | −14.5 | −13.4 |
| Anchor Capital | −14.0 | −14.0 | −14.1 | −15.4 | −14.0 |
| Anchor Growth | −16.4 | −16.5 | −16.4 | −17.9 | −16.3 |
| Astron Fund | −28.1 | −27.8 | −27.7 | −27.0 | −27.6 |
| Axe-Houghton Fund B | −24.7 | −25.0 | −24.2 | −26.6 | −24.1 |
| Axe Science Corporation | −29.7 | −29.7 | −29.4 | −32.0 | −29.5 |
| Babson (David L.) Investment | + 1.3 | + 1.3 | * | + 0.1 | + 1.3 |
| Beacon Hill Mutual | −10.5 | − 9.5 | * | − 9.5 | − 9.5 |
| Berkshire Capital | * | − 7.8 | * | − 6.9 | * |
| Berkshire Growth | * | − 0.6 | * | + 1.3 | * |
| Blair Fund | − 6.5 | − 6.6 | − 7.3 | −13.5 | − 7.1 |
| Boston Common Stock | + 2.1 | + 2.2 | 0 | − 1.6 | + .2 |
| Boston Fund | − 8.6 | − 9.0 | − 8.4 | −11.0 | − 8.3 |
| Broad Street Investing | − 3.7 | − 3.8 | − 3.7 | −11.6 | − 3.6 |

* Not Rated

| Fund | Wiesenberger | Lipper | United Bus. Svce. | M.F. Buyer's Guide | FundScope |
|---|---|---|---|---|---|
| Bullock Fund | − 6.8% | − 7.1% | − 6.6% | − 8.1% | − 6.6% |
| Cap America | −10.1 | −10.3 | − 9.8 | −12.8 | − 9.8 |
| Capital Shares | −15.7 | −15.8 | * | −16.7 | −15.4 |
| Century Shares | −10.0 | −10.1 | −12.3 | −11.1 | − 9.7 |
| Channing Balanced | −13.2 | −13.4 | −12.6 | −15.3 | −12.5 |
| Channing Common | −15.3 | −15.4 | −14.1 | −17.1 | −13.8 |
| Channing Growth | −27.8 | −27.9 | −24.9 | −31.3 | −24.8 |
| Channing Income | −13.0 | −13.2 | −12.3 | −16.4 | −12.3 |
| Charter Fund | * | − 3.0 | * | − 4.8 | * |
| Chemical Fund | + 5.8 | + 5.9 | + 5.5 | + 4.3 | + 5.7 |
| Colonial Fund | −16.3 | −16.6 | −16.0 | −18.5 | −16.0 |
| Colonial Growth | −16.0 | −16.1 | −14.8 | −15.2 | −14.6 |
| Columbia Growth | − 3.2 | − 3.1 | * | − 2.3 | − 2.9 |
| Combined Securities | −19.3 | −20.1 | * | −25.2 | * |
| Common Stock Fund | − 6.9 | − 6.7 | − 6.7 | −10.0 | − 6.3 |
| Composite Fund | −17.4 | −17.7 | −17.0 | −19.8 | −17.1 |
| Comstock Fund | −18.9 | −19.0 | −17.0 | −17.8 | −18.9 |
| Concord Fund | −31.9 | −33.7 | * | −31.1 | −32.3 |
| Corporate Leaders | −12.6 | −13.3 | −14.8 | −16.1 | −12.5 |
| Dividend Shares | − 4.8 | − 5.1 | − 4.8 | − 6.6 | − 4.6 |
| Eaton & Howard Growth | − 5.4 | − 7.1 | − 6.9 | − 8.5 | − 6.9 |
| Eaton & Howard Stock | −13.6 | −13.7 | −12.7 | −14.6 | −12.7 |
| Eberstadt Fund | − 8.5 | − 8.4 | − 8.3 | − 9.7 | − 8.2 |
| Energy Fund | −14.8 | −14.7 | * | −15.7 | −14.6 |
| Enterprise Fund | −25.9 | −26.0 | −25.0 | −24.3 | −25.0 |
| Equity Growth | −13.1 | −13.2 | −12.1 | −12.0 | −12.1 |
| Everest Income | −26.1 | −26.8 | −24.9 | −28.0 | * |
| Federated Growth | −13.0 | −13.1 | −13.1 | −14.1 | −13.0 |
| Fidelity Capital | −14.0 | −14.3 | −14.0 | −15.6 | −14.0 |
| Fidelity Fund | − 7.4 | − 7.6 | − 7.0 | −18.4 | − 7.1 |
| Fidelity Trend | −12.1 | −12.3 | −11.6 | −19.1 | −11.6 |
| Financial Dynamics | −16.5 | −16.8 | −15.5 | −15.7 | −15.4 |
| Financial Industrial Fund | −14.9 | −15.0 | −14.7 | −16.0 | −14.6 |
| Financial Industrial Income | −16.3 | −16.4 | −15.5 | −25.6 | −16.0 |
| First Investors Stock | −11.5 | −11.8 | −10.7 | −14.1 | −11.8 |
| Fletcher Capital | −31.9 | −33.2 | −31.6 | −35.0 | −32.0 |
| Fletcher Fund | −29.3 | −29.3 | −25.9 | −26.3 | −27.3 |
| Franklin Utilities | −12.0 | −12.4 | −12.0 | −13.7 | −11.6 |
| Freedom Fund | −13.2 | −14.0 | −13.6 | −16.8 | −13.6 |
| Fund of America | −16.5 | −16.5 | −16.5 | −17.2 | −16.5 |
| Fundamental Investors | −12.7 | −12.9 | −12.6 | −13.8 | −12.6 |
| Gibraltar Growth | −13.2 | −13.2 | * | −18.6 | −12.9 |
| Greenfield, Sam | −24.6 | −23.7 | * | −22.4 | * |
| Group Sec.—Common | −12.8 | −13.1 | −12.5 | −15.1 | −12.4 |
| Gryphon Fund | −28.2 | −28.2 | −28.2 | −28.5 | −28.2 |
| Guardian Mutual | − 8.9 | − 9.0 | * | −10.3 | − 8.9 |
| Hamilton Fund | −20.4 | −20.6 | −21.9 | −21.9 | −20.3 |
| Hanover Fund | −12.3 | −13.0 | * | −12.8 | −12.4 |
| Hedge Fund of America | −25.1 | −25.2 | −23.5 | −22.7 | −23.4 |
| Herold Fund | − 6.6 | − 6.7 | * | − 5.3 | − 6.5 |
| IDS New Dimensions | −12.8 | −12.9 | −12.4 | −13.8 | −12.8 |
| Imperial Growth | −18.8 | −18.9 | −18.0 | −17.7 | −18.0 |
| International Investors | −16.1 | −17.0 | * | −17.8 | −16.1 |

* Not Rated

| Fund | Wiesenberger | Lipper | United Bus. Svce. | M.F. Buyer's Guide | FundScope |
|------|--------------|--------|-------------------|--------------------|-----------|
| Investment Co. of America | −10.6% | −10.7% | −10.2% | −11.3% | −10.1% |
| Investment Indicators | −20.7 | −20.7 | * | −19.5 | −20.7 |
| Investment Trust of Boston | − 8.9 | − 9.0 | − 8.6 | − 9.8 | − 8.5 |
| ISI Growth | −18.2 | −18.4 | −18.0 | −20.6 | −17.9 |
| Ivy Fund | −28.8 | −29.2 | * | −27.3 | −27.7 |
| Johnston Mutual | + .5 | + .5 | * | − 3.3 | + .3 |
| Keystone S–1 | − 5.6 | − 5.6 | − 5.8 | − 7.4 | − 5.7 |
| Keystone S–2 | −14.6 | −14.4 | −13.7 | −16.7 | −14.0 |
| Keystone S–4 | −20.5 | −20.8 | −20.7 | −22.2 | −20.7 |
| Lexington Research | − 7.7 | − 7.8 | − 7.1 | − 6.8 | − 7.1 |
| Loomis-Sayles Canadian & International | +11.5 | +11.0 | * | + 9.2 | +11.0 |
| Loomis-Sayles Capital Development | −16.3 | −16.4 | * | −21.5 | −15.4 |
| Loomis-Sayles Mutual | − 7.5 | − 7.7 | * | −14.5 | − 7.3 |
| Manhattan Fund | −10.5 | −10.1 | − 8.5 | −29.0 | − 8.5 |
| Massachusetts Investors Trust | − 4.8 | − 5.0 | − 4.8 | − 6.5 | − 4.7 |
| Mates Fund | −21.7 | −21.8 | * | −24.9 | −22.8 |
| Mathers Fund | − 6.0 | − 5.9 | * | − 4.8 | − 5.3 |
| Medici Fund | − 9.4 | − 9.4 | * | −10.4 | − 9.4 |
| Mediterranean | * | −31.5 | * | −35.1 | −31.3 |
| Moody's Capital | −19.5 | −19.6 | −17.8 | −17.6 | −17.7 |
| Mutual of Omaha Growth | −14.3 | −14.5 | −14.6 | −15.7 | −14.5 |
| Nassau Fund | −12.4 | −12.5 | * | −16.2 | −12.2 |
| National Industries | −21.1 | −21.1 | * | −22.2 | −21.0 |
| National Investors | + 4.4 | + 4.4 | + 4.1 | − .7 | + 4.1 |
| National Securities–Balanced | −13.8 | −14.1 | −13.5 | −15.6 | −13.4 |
| National Securities–Stock | −17.2 | −17.8 | −16.6 | −18.5 | −16.6 |
| NEL Equity | * | − 4.8 | * | − 3.7 | − 4.7 |
| Neuwirth Fund | −17.3 | −17.4 | * | −16.3 | −17.0 |
| New World Fund | −11.4 | −11.5 | * | −12.5 | −11.4 |
| Omega Fund | −18.6 | −18.9 | −18.6 | −20.0 | −18.5 |
| One Hundred Fund | −19.5 | −19.9 | −19.6 | −20.6 | −19.5 |
| One William Street | − 3.9 | − 3.9 | * | − 4.7 | − 3.7 |
| OTC Securities | −10.8 | −11.0 | * | −12.2 | −10.8 |
| Paramount Mutual | − 7.6 | − 8.3 | * | − 9.8 | * |
| Penn Square Mutual | −16.2 | −16.5 | * | −18.0 | −15.2 |
| Pennsylvania Mutual | −26.0 | −26.0 | * | −24.0 | −25.4 |
| Philadelphia Fund | − 3.3 | − 3.2 | − 3.4 | − 4.9 | − 3.3 |
| Pilgrim Fund | −13.7 | −13.7 | −12.7 | −12.6 | −12.6 |
| Pilot Fund | −20.6 | −20.6 | −20.1 | −19.3 | −20.0 |
| Pine Street | −10.0 | −10.0 | * | −12.1 | − 9.8 |
| Pioneer Fund | −15.6 | −15.9 | −17.9 | −18.4 | −15.2 |
| T. Rowe Price Growth Stock | + 3.4 | + 3.7 | * | − .5 | + 3.2 |
| Rowe Price New Horizons | − 6.8 | − 6.8 | * | −11.8 | * |
| Provident Fund for Income | −21.2 | −21.5 | −20.4 | −22.2 | −19.4 |
| Puerto Rican Inv. | * | − 2.4 | * | − 1.6 | − 2.1 |
| Puritan Fund | −14.9 | −15.4 | −14.8 | −18.1 | −14.8 |
| Putnam Equities | −36.9 | −37.0 | −34.8 | −34.4 | −34.8 |
| George Putnam | − 6.6 | − 6.6 | − 6.4 | − 8.7 | − 6.3 |
| Putnam Growth | −13.3 | −13.4 | −13.1 | −14.6 | −13.0 |
| Putnam Vista | −28.7 | −28.7 | −28.7 | −27.7 | −28.6 |
| Republic Technology | −27.4 | −27.4 | −27.4 | −26.2 | −27.4 |
| Revere Fund | −22.1 | −22.0 | −21.5 | −20.8 | −21.4 |
| L. M. Rosenthal | −27.6 | −28.5 | −28.1 | −29.0 | −28.0 |

* Not Rated

| Fund | Wiesenberger | Lipper | United Bus. Svce. | M.F. Buyer's Guide | FundScope |
|---|---|---|---|---|---|
| Salem Fund | −18.1% | −18.5% | −19.0% | −19.8% | −18.1% |
| Schuster Fund | −10.8 | −10.9 | −10.6 | − 9.8 | −10.4 |
| Scudder Special | −18.0 | −18.0 | * | −18.9 | −17.9 |
| Scudder, Stevens & Clark Balanced | − 6.1 | − 6.2 | * | −12.7 | − 5.9 |
| Scudder, Stevens & Clark Common | − 6.7 | − 6.8 | * | −10.2 | − 6.6 |
| Security Equity | −20.3 | −20.3 | −20.3 | −21.4 | −20.2 |
| Security Investment | −16.3 | −16.4 | −16.3 | −19.0 | −16.3 |
| Selected Special Shares | − 9.0 | − 9.0 | − 8.7 | −15.1 | − 8.7 |
| Sherman Dean | −19.1 | −19.3 | * | −16.0 | −18.6 |
| Smith Barney | − 7.3 | − 7.4 | * | − 8.9 | − 7.4 |
| Sovereign Investors | −11.9 | −12.2 | −13.9 | −18.4 | −11.9 |
| Stein Roe & Farnham Balanced | − 7.8 | − 7.8 | * | −14.7 | − 7.4 |
| Stein Roe & Farnham Capital Oppor. | − 6.7 | − 6.7 | * | −19.3 | − 5.8 |
| Stein Roe & Farnham Stock | − 7.5 | − 7.5 | * | −12.7 | − 7.2 |
| Synchro Growth | −11.8 | −12.4 | −15.5 | −14.2 | −11.6 |
| Technivest | * | −11.5 | −11.4 | −10.2 | −11.5 |
| Technology Fund | − 9.3 | − 9.4 | − 8.9 | −10.3 | − 8.9 |
| Transamerica | −28.2 | −28.3 | * | −29.6 | −27.2 |
| Twentieth Century Growth | −24.6 | −24.6 | −22.2 | −32.8 | −22.1 |
| United Accumulative | −11.2 | −11.0 | −11.0 | −12.6 | −11.0 |
| United Income | − 9.2 | − 9.3 | − 9.3 | −11.5 | − 9.3 |
| Value Line Fund | −21.1 | −21.0 | −19.8 | −18.8 | −19.4 |
| Value Line Income | −23.0 | −23.4 | −21.5 | −23.9 | −21.4 |
| Value Line Special Situations | −33.0 | −33.0 | −31.8 | −30.7 | −31.7 |
| Vantage 10/90 | * | + 8.6 | * | +10.1 | + 8.6 |
| Varied Industry Plan | −18.1 | −18.0 | −17.9 | −21.8 | −18.0 |
| Venture Securities | −21.5 | −21.5 | * | −19.9 | −21.1 |
| Washington Mutual | −13.9 | −14.2 | −13.2 | −14.9 | −13.2 |
| Wellington Fund | − 7.7 | − 7.8 | − 7.0 | −11.3 | − 7.6 |
| Western Industrial Shares | −13.6 | −13.6 | −13.5 | −12.9 | −13.4 |
| Whipple Fund | − 9.1 | * | * | −12.1 | * |
| Windsor Fund | − 3.6 | − 3.7 | − 4.4 | − 5.3 | − 3.4 |
| Worth Fund | −39.9 | −40.1 | −30.2 | −56.3 | −30.0 |

* Not Rated

From the foregoing figures, apparently it is not enough to pick the right fund. You have also to pick the right statistical service!

If you owned Berkshire Growth Fund in 1969, be sure you look it up in the *Mutual Fund Buyer's Guide* where you will show a profit of 1.3 percent on it for the year, rather than Lipper where you will have suffered a loss of .6 percent.

If you owned Broad Street Investing Corporation, of course check your results in *FundScope,* where you will only have a loss of 3.6 percent rather than the *Mutual Fund Buyer's Guide*'s 11.6 percent.

If you want to cut your losses in the Blair Fund, throw away the *Mutual Fund Buyer's Guide* (−13.5 percent) and stick with Lipper (−6.6 percent).

United Business Service is for you if you owned Fidelity Fund in 1969. There you lost 7 percent instead of the 18.4 percent you might have lost if you had looked it up in the *Mutual Fund Buyer's Guide*.

If you were one of the few who had not redeemed Manhattan Fund by 1969, steer clear of the *Mutual Fund Buyer's Guide* where Manhattan went down 29 percent. No point in taking a loss unnecessarily. United Business Service (−8.5 percent) or FundScope (−8.5 percent) is a better choice.

If you hold Johnston Mutual, nail down your profit in Wiesenberger or *FundScope*. Do not take a 3.3 percent loss by looking it up in the *Mutual Fund Buyer's Guide;* the same goes for T. Rowe Price Growth Stock Fund. Take your profits in Wiesenberger, *FundScope,* and Lipper and avoid the loss in the *Mutual Fund Buyer's Guide*.

You are pretty unhappy all around if you owned the last one on the list, Worth Fund. You have a 30 percent loss in *FundScope,* a 30 percent loss in the United Business Service, a 39 percent loss in Wiesenberger, a 40 percent loss in Lipper, and a 56 percent loss in the *Mutual Fund Buyer's Guide.*

It's all pretty foolish, isn't it?

The S.E.C. should say to all these services: "It's time we cut out all this funny business with the performance figures. From now on, *this* is the way you compute them."

The only product these statistical services have to sell is accurate reporting. Therefore, it is just possible that some irritated subscriber might sue one of them for misleading him into buying a fund that was not as good as it made it out to be.

Will the *real* No. 1 performing mutual fund please stand up?

# Chapter 26

# AVOIDING PROBATE OF
# MUTUAL FUND SHARES

If you are not careful, probate is what will happen to your mutual fund shares, along with the rest of your estate, after you die.

Probate originated generations ago as a device to protect heirs. It has deteriorated steadily over the years, though, until today that which was intended to protect them has become their greatest enemy. It now exists principally for the enrichment of members of the Bar. Probate costs too much, takes too long, and there is too much publicity attached to it. It costs too much because in most jurisdictions everyone connected with the process works on commission, that is, everyone collects a percentage of the estate. I have records of estates that were entirely consumed by the costs of probating them. In the course of "protecting" the heirs, the probate boys protected them right out of the whole estate. It is quite common for probate costs (lawyer, executor, appraiser, and probate court fees) to take more than 25 percent of an estate. I see no reason why the widows and orphans of America should have to pay ransom for what is rightfully theirs.

There are many probate abuses and they are common to all sections of the country, though they may vary in degree. In one community, the appraiser racket may be particularly bad, with the probate judge appointing his close friends or political henchmen to juicy appraiserships. In another, it may be customary to allow attorneys to charge for "extraordinary services" in connection with the simplest probate procedures they carry out. In still another, lawyers are appointed to highly paid jobs as "special guardians" for children who come into money, over the protests of the children's parents who are quite capable of taking care of the money. The American Bar Association has for many years been working on a Uniform Probate Code which is not intended to eliminate any of the abuses but simply to make them uniform throughout the country. Lawyers will never clean up the probate system because they have a vested interest in its profits.

There is little likelihood, then, that we shall see adequate probate reform in our time. Each person should therefore do what he can to avoid probate by taking advantage of such means as are available to achieve that end.

Many people think that they can avoid probate by registering mutual fund shares in joint tenancy, but such joint ownership frequently creates many more problems than it solves. In the first place, if the joint owners die in a so-called common disaster, the shares will be thrown into probate. Secondly, joint tenancy involves a gift to the other person whose name you place on the shares along with your own. Gifts of any appreciable amount may require the filing of gift tax returns and payment of a gift tax. When one joint owner dies, the federal tax authorities will take the position that the shares were owned completely by that person and are therefore fully taxable as a part of his estate. To avoid the tax on his share, the surviving joint owner must present documentary proof that he contributed one half of the purchase price. A wife who "helped my husband in the business" or who saved up her contribution "out of the house money" doesn't stand a chance. Many transfer agents today will not transfer the jointly owned shares to the survivor without first receiving a tax waiver from the state tax department. In a word, joint ownership can be a headache. Do not, therefore, buy a hundred shares of a mutual fund and register them "John Smith and Mary Smith as joint tenants with right of survivorship." Register fifty shares in each name. That way, if one person dies the only thing that Uncle Sam can talk about for death tax purposes are the shares registered in the name of the person who has died. The other fifty shares are in the clear. Bear in mind that if you register fifty shares in a name other than your own, you will be making that person a gift of the cost of the shares. You can give as many persons as you choose up to $3,000 per year with no requirement that you report it or pay a tax on it. If the other person is your spouse, you can give up to $6,000 in any one year without any tax liability. In addition to the $3,000 "annual exclusion," you have another $30,000 "lifetime exemption." If you give any of this, you do not have to pay any tax but you do have to file a gift tax return. Uncle Sam wants to know when you have used up the exemption, so he keeps close track of your returns reporting such gifts.

Joint tenancy is not the ideal way to avoid probate, then. A much better way is through the use of a revocable inter vivos or "living" trust. This you can establish by executing a simple form of "declaration of trust" in which you state that you are holding the shares in trust for any beneficiary you wish to name. You direct that, upon your death, the successor trustee is to turn the shares over to the beneficiary and terminate the trust. Finally, you appoint as successor trustee "whosoever shall at that time be beneficiary hereunder." In his capacity as successor trustee, the person you have named simply turns the shares over to himself as beneficiary. That is all there is to it. No lawyers, executors, administrators, appraisers, or probate court costs to pay. No two- to five-year delay. No piece in the local paper telling all your business. It is a much nicer way to pass on your estate. All the successor trustee/beneficiary has to do to obtain possession of the shares is to mail the certificate to the transfer agent with a copy of the declaration of trust and a death certificate and request that the shares be reregistered in the new name.

For your convenience in avoiding probate of your mutual fund shares, you will find in the pages that follow four forms of declaration of trust you may use to establish a revocable inter vivos trust to cover such shares. The instruments, identified by a designation in the upper right-hand corner, are as follows:

DT– 9: For naming some one person to receive the shares upon your death;

DT–10: For naming some one person as primary beneficiary and some one other person as contingent beneficiary to receive the shares if the primary beneficiary be not surviving;

DT–11: For naming two or more persons, sharing equally, to receive the shares upon your death;

DT–12: For naming some one person as primary beneficiary, with your children, sharing equally, as contingent beneficiaries to receive the shares upon your death.

Observe carefully the instructions given with each form of declaration of trust. Make certain that you understand how the form should be executed, how the shares should be registered, and what you are to do with the form after you have executed it. Note particularly that Paragraph 7 on each of the forms *should be left blank* unless you have named a minor as beneficiary, in which case you fill in there the name of an adult who can act as trustee for the minor until he or she has attained the age of twenty-one years.

Additional copies of a form may be obtained for $1.00 each by writing to The National Estate Planning Council, 180 Church Street, Naugatuck, Connecticut.

```
┌─────────────────────────────────────────┐
│          DECLARATION OF TRUST            │
│               FOR NAMING                 │
│            ONE BENEFICIARY               │
│               TO RECEIVE                 │
│          MUTUAL FUND SHARES              │
└─────────────────────────────────────────┘
```

Instructions:

On the following pages will be found duplicate copies of a declaration of trust (DT–9) which will be suitable for use in connection with the inter vivos trust arrangement suggested above, where it is desired simply to name some *one* person to receive mutual fund shares upon the death of the owner.

Cross out *"city"* or *"town,"* leaving the appropriate designation of your community.

Enter the name of the beneficiary in the appropriate place in Paragraph 1.

### For shares purchased outright:

If you are buying shares outright, enter the name of the fund in the appropriate place in the instrument. Instruct your mutual fund dealer that the shares are to be registered *"(Your name), Trustee u/d/t dated _____."* Some funds will wish to examine the declaration of trust at the time the shares are issued, so execute both original and duplicate and offer one to the dealer to send along with the registration instructions. In any case, if you ever decide to sell the shares, or if you die and the beneficiary requests their transfer, the fund will ask to see the declaration of trust. It is suggested, therefore, that when the share certificate is issued, the signed declaration of trust be permanently stapled to it. If you make subsequent additional purchases of the same fund, it is not necessary to execute a new declaration of trust each time—simply register the shares exactly as you did your first purchase. If you wish to name a different beneficiary on such subsequent purchases, then you *will* need to execute a new declaration of trust. To avoid confusion, never date two instruments the same date.

If you have a "voluntary plan" or "open account," the fund will hold the shares and no certificate will be issued. It is important, then, that you place the original declaration of trust where you can find it readily if you decide to sell your shares or where the beneficiary can find it if you die.

### For contractual plans:

If you are buying a contractual plan which does not provide a declaration of trust to designate the beneficiary, in the place in the instrument provided for the name of the fund, enter *"(Name of fund) held in (Name of fund) Investment Plan No. _____."* Instruct your mutual fund dealer to send the completed instrument along with the plan application. The plan's custodian bank will fill in the number assigned to your account. With a contractual plan, the beneficiary designation—and therefore the probate exemption—is *not effective* unless and until the instrument is permanently filed with the plan's custodian bank. It isn't absolutely necessary that the instrument be filed at the time the plan is applied for; you can send it in later. If you choose this latter course, be sure to ask for acknowledgment of its receipt. Many banks charge a "late filing fee" of $2.50 if the declaration of trust does not accompany the application.

When your plan certificate is issued, staple the executed duplicate declaration of trust into it for your permanent record and for the information of the beneficiary.

\* \* \*

Whenever there is any possibility of a minor child receiving the property, make certain that you name an adult who can act as trustee for the child. The name of that adult should be inserted in Paragraph 7 of the instrument shown here. Avoid naming as trustee a person not likely to survive until the child has reached age twenty-one.

# Declaration of Trust

of the

WHEREAS, I, **John J. Smith** , State of **Connecticut** ,

Town of **Jonesville** , County of **Fairfax**

am the owner of certain shares of the capital stock of:

**Ajax Mutual Fund**

(Name of Fund)

NOW, THEREFORE, KNOW ALL MEN BY THESE PRESENTS, that I do hereby acknowledge and declare that I hold and will hold said Shares and all right, title and interest in and to said Shares IN TRUST, for the following uses and purposes:

1. To add, or cause to be added, to the corpus of this Trust all income and distributions which may from time to time be received on the said Shares, by causing the same to be invested in additional shares, or if I shall so elect from time to time to pay said income and distributions or cause the same to be paid to myself during my lifetime.

2. To hold said Shares and all right, title and interest therein for the use and benefit of:

_____, of

(Name) **Mary A. Smith    (my niece)**        **Jonesville**        **Connecticut**

City        State

(Address) **750        Porter Street**

Number        Street

Upon my death, unless the beneficiary shall predecease me or unless we both shall die as a result of a common accident or disaster, my Successor Trustee is hereby directed forthwith to transfer said Shares and all right, title and interest in and to said Shares unto the beneficiary absolutely and thereby terminate this trust; _provided_, however, that if the beneficiary hereunder shall then be a minor, the Successor Trustee shall hold the trust assets in continuing trust until such beneficiary attains the age of twenty-one years. Prior to that date, the Successor Trustee may apply or expend any or all of the income or principal for the maintenance, education and support of the minor beneficiary, without the intervention of any guardian and without application to any court. Such payments of income or principal may be made to the parents of such minor or to the person with whom the minor is living without any liability upon the Successor Trustee to see to the application thereof. If such minor survives me but dies before attaining the age of twenty-one years, at his or her death the Successor Trustee shall deliver, pay over, transfer and distribute the trust property to such minor's personal representatives, absolutely.

3. I reserve the right to register any shares held hereunder in the name of a nominee, which nominee may be myself as an individual. The right, power and authority is hereby conferred upon any Successor Trustee hereunder, at any time during the minority of the beneficiary, to invest and reinvest without limitation or restriction, to sell all or any part of the Shares being held, holding either Shares or the proceeds of the sale thereof until the minor beneficiary attains the age of twenty-one years.

4. This Trust is created upon the express understanding that the issuer or custodian of the Shares hereunder shall be under no liability whatsoever to see to its proper administration, and that upon the transfer of the right, title and interest in and to said Shares by any Trustee hereunder, said issuer or custodian shall conclusively treat the transferee as the sole owner of said Shares. In the event that any shares, cash or other property shall be distributable at any time under the terms of said Shares, the said issuer or custodian is fully authorized to pay, deliver and distribute the same to whosoever shall then be trustee hereunder, and shall be under no liability to see to the proper application thereof, provided, however, that as and if I shall elect from time to time to cause dividends and distributions on said Shares to be distributed, rather than reinvested, the issuer or custodian shall be fully authorized to pay such dividends and distributions direct to me individually rather than to me as Trustee hereunder and may continue such payments to me individually unless there shall have been filed with it written notice of my death or incapacity satisfactory to it. The issuer or custodian is authorized to make such distributions under a mutual fund systematic withdrawal plan as have been specified by me or by any Successor Trustee acting hereunder. Until the issuer or custodian shall receive from some person interested in this Trust, written notice of any death or other event upon which the right to receive may depend, the issuer or custodian shall incur no liability for payments made in good faith to persons whose interests shall have been affected by such event. The issuer or custodian shall be protected in acting upon any notice or other instrument or document believed by it to be genuine and to have been signed or presented by the proper party or parties.

... ... upon the revo... ...mination of this ... rust for ... benefit of any person whatsoever.

...nto myself ...

7. In the case of my death or legal incapacity, I hereby nominate and appoint as Successor Trustee hereunder the Beneficiary unless he or she shall be a minor or otherwise legally incapacitated, in either of which events, I hereby nominate and appoint

_____, of

(Name) **Henry P. Adams**        **Jonesville**        **Connecticut**

City        State

(Address) **125        Barnum Street**

Number        Street

and upon his or her failure to act (or should I for any reason fail to designate the person intended to be nominated), then and in either event I nominate and appoint as such Successor Trustee whosoever shall qualify as Executor or Administrator of my estate, as the case may be.

8. This Declaration of Trust shall extend to and be binding upon the heirs, executors, administrators and assigns of the undersigned and upon the successors to the Trustee.

9. This Declaration of Trust shall be construed and enforced in accordance with the laws of the State of **Connecticut**

WHEREAS, I,_____of the

City/Town of_____, County of_____, State of_____,

am the owner of certain shares of the capital stock of:

_____
(Name of Fund)

NOW, THEREFORE, KNOW ALL MEN BY THESE PRESENTS, that I do hereby acknowledge and declare that I hold and will hold said Shares and all right, title and interest in and to said Shares IN TRUST, for the following uses and purposes:

1. To add, or cause to be added, to the corpus of this Trust all income and distributions which may from time to time be received on the said Shares, by causing the same to be invested in additional shares, or if I shall so elect from time to time to pay said income and distributions or cause the same to be paid to myself during my lifetime.

2. To hold said Shares and all right, title and interest therein for the use and benefit of:

(Name)_____, of

(Address)_____.
         Number            Street            City          State

Upon my death, unless the beneficiary shall predecease me or unless we both shall die as a result of a common accident or disaster, my Successor Trustee is hereby directed forthwith to transfer said Shares and all right, title and interest in and to said Shares unto the beneficiary absolutely and thereby terminate this trust; *provided,* however, that if the beneficiary hereunder shall then be a minor, the Successor Trustee shall hold the trust assets in continuing trust until such beneficiary attains the age of twenty-one years. Prior to that date, the Successor Trustee may apply or expend any or all of the income or principal for the maintenance, education and support of the minor beneficiary without the intervention of any guardian and without application to any court. Such payments of income or principal may be made to the parents of such minor or to the person with whom the minor is living without any liability upon the Successor Trustee to see to the application thereof. If such minor survives me but dies before attaining the age of twenty-one years, at his or her death the Successor Trustee shall deliver, pay over, transfer and distribute the trust property to such minor's personal representatives, absolutely.

3. I reserve the right to register any shares held hereunder in the name of a nominee, which nominee may be myself as an individual, or to pledge the shares as collateral for a loan. The right, power and authority is hereby conferred upon any Successor Trustee hereunder, at any time during the minority of the beneficiary, to invest and reinvest without limitation or restriction, to sell all or any part of the Shares being held, holding either Shares or the proceeds of the sale thereof until the minor beneficiary attains the age of twenty-one years.

4. This Trust is created upon the express understanding that the issuer or custodian of the Shares hereunder shall be under no liability whatsoever to see to its proper administration, and that upon the transfer of the right, title and interest in and to said Shares by any Trustee hereunder, said issuer or custodian shall conclusively treat the transferee as the sole owner of said Shares. In the event that any shares, cash or other property shall be distributable at any time under the terms of said Shares, the said issuer or custodian is fully authorized to pay, deliver and distribute the same to whosoever shall then be trustee hereunder, and shall be under no liability to see to the proper application thereof, provided, however, that as and if I shall elect from time to time to cause dividends and distributions on said Shares to be distributed, rather than reinvested, the issuer or custodian shall be fully authorized to pay such dividends and distributions direct to me individually rather than to me as Trustee hereunder and may continue such payments to me individually unless there shall have been filed with it written notice of my death or incapacity satisfactory to it. The issuer or custodian is authorized to make such distributions under a mutual fund systematic withdrawal plan as have been specified by me or by any Successor Trustee acting hereunder. Until the issuer or custodian shall receive from some person interested in this Trust, written notice of any death or other event upon which the right to receive may depend, the issuer or custodian shall incur no liability for payments made in good faith to persons whose interests shall have been affected by such event. The issuer or custodian shall be protected in acting upon any notice or other instrument or document believed by it to be genuine and to have been signed or presented by the proper party or parties.

5. The death during my lifetime, or in a common accident or disaster with me, of the beneficiary designated hereunder shall revoke such designation, and in the former event I reserve the right to designate a new beneficiary. Should I for any reason fail to designate such new beneficiary, this trust shall terminate upon my death and the trust property shall revert to my estate.

6. I hereby reserve unto myself the power and right at any time during my lifetime, before actual distribution to the beneficiary hereunder, to revoke in whole or in part or to amend the Trust hereby created without the necessity of obtaining the consent of the beneficiary and without giving notice to the beneficiary. Any one of the following acts shall be conclusive evidence of such revocation of this Trust:

    (a) The delivery to the issuer or custodian of the Shares by me of written notice that this Trust is revoked in whole or in part;

    (b) The transfer by me of my right, title and interest in and to said Shares;

    (c) The delivery by me to the issuer or custodian of the Shares of written notice of the death of the beneficiary hereunder.

I hereby reserve unto myself the right, upon the revocation or termination of this Trust, to create a new Trust for the benefit of any person whatsoever.

7. In the case of my death or legal incapacity, I hereby nominate and appoint as Successor Trustee hereunder the Beneficiary unless he or she shall be a minor or otherwise legally incapacitated, in either of which events, I hereby nominate and appoint

(Name)_____, of

(Address)_____
          Number          Street          City          State

and upon his or her failure to act (or should I for any reason fail to designate the person intended to be nominated), then and in either event I nominate and appoint as such Successor Trustee whosoever shall qualify as Executor or Administrator of my estate, as the case may be.

8. This Declaration of Trust shall extend to and be binding upon the heirs, executors, administrators and assigns of the undersigned and upon the successors to the Trustee.

9. This Declaration of Trust shall be construed and enforced in accordance with the laws of the State of

_____.

IN WITNESS WHEREOF I have hereunto set my hand and seal this_____day

of_____, 19____.

(sign here)_____L.S.

Witness:  (1)_____

Witness:  (2)_____

STATE OF _____
                            ss:  _____
COUNTY OF _____

On the_____day of_____, nineteen hundred and_____, before

me came_____known to me to be the individual described in, and who executed

the foregoing instrument, and _____ acknowledged that _____ executed the same; and in due form of law acknowledged the foregoing instrument to be _____ act and deed and desired the same might be recorded as such.

WITNESS my hand and notarial seal the day and year aforesaid.

_____
(Notary Seal)                                       Notary Public

```
┌─────────────────────────────────────────┐
│                                           │
│         DECLARATION OF TRUST              │
│              FOR NAMING                    │
│       ONE PRIMARY BENEFICIARY             │
│                 AND                       │
│     ONE CONTINGENT BENEFICIARY            │
│              TO RECEIVE                    │
│        MUTUAL FUND SHARES                 │
│                                           │
└─────────────────────────────────────────┘
```

Instructions:

On the following pages will be found duplicate copies of a declaration of trust (DT–10) which will be suitable for use in connection with the inter vivos trust arrangement suggested above, where it is desired to name some *one* person as primary beneficiary with some *one* other person as contingent beneficiary to receive mutual fund shares if the primary beneficiary does not survive.

Cross out "city" or "town," leaving the appropriate designation of your community.

Enter the names of the beneficiaries in the appropriate places in Paragraph 2.

*For shares purchased outright:*

If you are buying shares outright, enter the name of the fund in the appropriate place in the instrument. Instruct your mutual fund dealer that the shares are to be registered *"(Your Name) Trustee u/d/t dated _____."* Some funds will wish to examine the declaration of trust at the time the shares are issued, so execute both original and duplicate and offer one to the dealer to send along with the registration instructions. In any case, if you ever decide to sell the shares, or if you die and the beneficiary requests their transfer, the fund will ask to see the declaration of trust. It is suggested, therefore, that when the share certificate is issued, the signed declaration of trust be permanently stapled to it. If you make subsequent additional purchases of the same fund, it is not necessary to execute a new declaration of trust each time—simply register the shares exactly as you did your first purchase. If you wish to name a different beneficiary on such subsequent purchases, then you *will* need to execute a new declaration of trust. To avoid confusion, never date two instruments the same date.

If you have a "voluntary plan" or "open account," the fund will hold the shares and no certificate will be issued. It is important, then, that you place the original declaration of trust where you can find it readily if you decide to sell your shares or where the beneficiary can find it if you die.

*For contractual plans:*

If you are buying a contractual plan which does not provide a declaration of trust to designate the beneficiary, in the place in the instrument provided for the name of fund, enter *"(Name of fund) held in (Name of Fund) Investment Plan No. _____."* Instruct your mutual fund dealer to send the completed instrument along with the plan application. The plan's custodian bank will fill in the number assigned to your account. With a contractual plan, the beneficiary designation—and therefore the probate exemption—is *not effective* unless and until it is permanently filed with the plan's custodian bank. It isn't absolutely necessary that the instrument be filed at the time the plan is applied for; you can send it in later. If you choose this latter course, be sure to ask for acknowledgment of its receipt. Many banks charge a "late filing fee" of $2.50 if the declaration of trust does not accompany the application.

When your plan certificate is issued, staple the executed duplicate declaration of trust into it for your permanent record and for the information of the beneficiary.

Whenever there is any possibility of a minor child receiving the property, make certain that you name an adult who can act as trustee for the child. The name of that adult should be inserted in Paragraph 7 of the instrument shown here. Avoid naming as trustee a person not likely to survive until the child has reached age twenty-one.

## Declaration of Trust

_____ of the

WHEREAS, I,_____John J. Smith_____, State of _____Connecticut_____

~~City~~/Town of _____Jonesville_____, County of _____Fairfax_____

am the owner of certain shares of the capital stock of:
_____Ajax Mutual Fund_____
**held in Ajax Mutual Fund Investment Plan No.** _____
(Name of Fund)

NOW, THEREFORE, KNOW ALL MEN BY THESE PRESENTS, that I do hereby acknowledge and declare that I hold and will hold said Shares and all right, title and interest in and to said Shares IN TRUST, for the following uses and purposes:

1. To add, or cause to be added, to the corpus of this Trust all income and distributions which may from time to time be received on the said Shares, by causing the same to be invested in additional shares, or if I shall so elect from time to time to pay said income and distributions or cause the same to be paid to myself during my lifetime.

2. To hold said Shares and all right, title and interest therein for the use and benefit of: _____, of

(Name)_____Mary A. Smith    (my niece)_____ City _____Jonesville_____ State _____Connecticut_____

(Address)_____750_____ Porter Street
          Number              Street

or, if such beneficiary be not surviving, for the use and benefit of _____, of

(Name)_____William B. Connors (my nephew)_____ City _____Jonesville_____ State _____Connecticut_____

(Address)_____250_____ County Street
          Number              Street

Upon my death, unless the beneficiaries shall predecease me or unless we shall die as a result of a common accident or disaster, my Successor Trustee is hereby directed forthwith to transfer said Shares and all right, title and interest in and to said Shares unto the beneficiary absolutely and thereby terminate this Trust; provided, however, that if the beneficiary hereunder shall then be a minor, the Successor Trustee shall hold the trust assets in continuing trust until such beneficiary attains the age of twenty-one years. Prior to that date, the Successor Trustee may apply or expend any or all of the income or principal for the maintenance, education and support of the minor beneficiary without the intervention of any guardian and without application to any court. Such payments of income or principal may be made to the parents of such minor or to the person with whom the minor is living without any liability upon the Successor Trustee to see to the application thereof. If such minor survives me but dies before attaining the age of twenty-one years, at his or her death the Successor Trustee shall deliver, pay over, transfer and distribute the trust property to such minor's personal representatives, absolutely.

3. I reserve the right to register any shares held hereunder in the name of a nominee, which nominee may be myself as an individual. The right, power and authority is hereby conferred upon any Successor Trustee hereunder, at any time during the minority of the beneficiary, to invest and reinvest without limitation or restriction, to sell all or any part of the Shares being held, holding either Shares or the proceeds of the sale thereof until the minor beneficiary attains the age of twenty-one years.

4. This Trust is created upon the express understanding that the issuer or custodian of the Shares hereunder shall be under no liability whatsoever to see to its proper administration, and that upon the transfer of the right, title and interest in and to said Shares by any Trustee hereunder, said issuer or custodian shall conclusively treat the transferee as the sole owner of said Shares. In the event that any shares, cash or other property shall be distributable at any time under the terms of said Shares, the said issuer or custodian is fully authorized to pay, deliver and distribute the same to whosoever shall then be trustee hereunder, and shall be under no liability to see to the proper application thereof, provided, however, that as and if I shall elect from time to time to cause dividends and distributions on said Shares to be distributed, rather than reinvested, the issuer or custodian shall be fully authorized to pay such dividends and distributions direct to me individually rather than to me as Trustee hereunder and may continue such payments to me individually unless there shall have been filed with it written notice of my death or incapacity satisfactory to it. The issuer or custodian is authorized to make such distributions under a mutual fund systematic withdrawal plan as have been specified by me or by any Successor Trustee acting hereunder. Until the issuer or custodian shall receive from some person interested in this Trust, written notice of any death or other event upon which the right to receive may depend, the issuer or custodian shall incur no liability for payments made in good faith to persons whose interests shall have been affected by such event. The issuer or custodian shall be protected in acting upon any notice or other instrument or document believed by it to be genuine and to have been signed or presented by the proper party or parties.

_____ upon the revoca_____

_____ any person whatso_____

7. In the case of my death or legal incapacity, I hereby nominate and appoint as Successor Trustee hereunder whosoever shall at that time be beneficiary unless he or she shall be a minor or otherwise legally incapacitated, in either of which events I hereby nominate and appoint as Successor Trustee: _____, of

(Name)_____Henry P. Adams_____ City _____Jonesville_____ State _____Connecticut_____

(Address)_____125_____ Barnum Street
          Number              Street

and upon his or her failure to act (or should I for any reason fail to designate the person intended to be nominated), then and in either event I nominate and appoint as such Successor Trustee whosoever shall qualify as Executor or Administrator of my estate, as the case may be.

8. This Declaration of Trust shall extend to and be binding upon the heirs, executors, administrators and assigns of the undersigned and upon the successors to the Trustee.

9. This Declaration of Trust shall be construed and enforced in accordance with the laws of the State of _____Connecticut_____

WHEREAS, I,_____of the

City/Town of_____, County of_____, State of_____,

am the owner of certain shares of the capital stock of:

_____
(Name of Fund)

NOW, THEREFORE, KNOW ALL MEN BY THESE PRESENTS, that I do hereby acknowledge and declare that I hold and will hold said Shares and all right, title and interest in and to said Shares IN TRUST, for the following uses and purposes:

1. To add, or cause to be added, to the corpus of this Trust all income and distributions which may from time to time be received on the said Shares, by causing the same to be invested in additional shares, or if I shall so elect from time to time to pay said income and distributions or cause the same to be paid to myself during my lifetime.

2. To hold said Shares and all right, title and interest therein for the use and benefit of:

(Name)_____, of

(Address)_____

      Number          Street          City          State

or, if such beneficiary be not surviving, for the use and benefit of

(Name)_____, of

(Address)_____

      Number          Street          City          State

Upon my death, unless the beneficiaries shall predecease me or unless we shall die as a result of a common accident or disaster, my Successor Trustee is hereby directed forthwith to transfer said Shares and all right, title and interest in and to said Shares unto the beneficiary absolutely and thereby terminate this Trust; provided, however, that if the beneficiary hereunder shall then be a minor, the Successor Trustee shall hold the trust assets in continuing trust until such beneficiary attains the age of twenty-one years. Prior to that date, the Successor Trustee may apply or expend any or all of the income or principal for the maintenance, education and support of the minor beneficiary without the intervention of any guardian and without application to any court. Such payments of income or principal may be made to the parents of such minor or to the person with whom the minor is living without any liability upon the Successor Trustee to see to the application thereof. If such minor survives me but dies before attaining the age of twenty-one years, at his or her death the Successor Trustee shall deliver, pay over, transfer and distribute the trust property to such minor's personal representatives, absolutely.

3. I reserve the right to register any shares held hereunder in the name of a nominee, which nominee may be myself as an individual, or to pledge the shares as collateral for a loan. The right, power and authority is hereby conferred upon any Successor Trustee hereunder, at any time during the minority of the beneficiary, to invest and reinvest without limitation or restriction, to sell all or any part of the Shares being held, holding either Shares or the proceeds of the sale thereof until the minor beneficiary attains the age of twenty-one years.

4. This Trust is created upon the express understanding that the issuer or custodian of the Shares hereunder shall be under no liability whatsoever to see to its proper administration, and that upon the transfer of the right, title and interest in and to said Shares by any Trustee hereunder, said issuer or custodian shall conclusively treat the transferee as the sole owner of said Shares. In the event that any shares, cash or other property shall be distributable at any time under the terms of said Shares, the said issuer or custodian is fully authorized to pay, deliver and distribute the same to whosoever shall then be trustee hereunder, and shall be under no liability to see to the proper application thereof, provided, however, that as and if I shall elect from time to time to cause dividends and distributions on said Shares to be distributed, rather than reinvested, the issuer or custodian shall be fully authorized to pay such dividends and distributions direct to me individually rather than to me as Trustee hereunder and may continue such payments to me individually unless there shall have been filed with it written notice of my death or incapacity satisfactory to it. The issuer or custodian is authorized to make such distributions under a mutual fund systematic withdrawal plan as have been specified by me or by any Successor Trustee acting hereunder. Until the issuer or custodian shall receive from some person interested in this Trust, written notice of any death or other event upon which the right to receive may depend, the issuer or custodian shall incur no liability for payments made in good faith to persons whose interests shall have been affected by such event. The issuer or custodian shall be protected in acting upon any notice or other instrument or document believed by it to be genuine and to have been signed or presented by the proper party or parties.

5. The death during my lifetime, or in a common accident or disaster with me, of any beneficiary designated hereunder shall revoke such designation, and in the former event I reserve the right to designate a new beneficiary. Should I for any reason fail to designate such new beneficiary and should no designated beneficiary be surviving, this Trust shall terminate upon my death and the trust property shall revert to my estate.

6. I hereby reserve unto myself the power and right at any time during my lifetime, before actual distribution to the beneficiary hereunder, to revoke in whole or in part or to amend the Trust hereby created without the necessity of obtaining the consent of the beneficiary and without giving notice to the beneficiary. Any one of the following acts shall be conclusive evidence of such revocation of this Trust:

    (a)  The delivery to the issuer or custodian of the Shares by me of written notice that this Trust is revoked in whole or in part;

    (b)  The transfer by me of my right, title and interest in and to said Shares;

    (c)  The delivery by me to the issuer or custodian of the Shares of written notice of the death of the Beneficiary hereunder.

I hereby reserve unto myself the right, upon the revocation or termination of this Trust, to create a new Trust for the benefit of any person whatsoever.

7. In the case of my death or legal incapacity, I hereby nominate and appoint as Successor Trustee hereunder whosoever shall at that time be beneficiary unless he or she shall be a minor or otherwise legally incapacitated, in either of which events I hereby nominate and appoint as Successor Trustee:

(Name) _____ , of

(Address) _____
           Number              Street              City            State

and upon his or her failure to act (or should I for any reason fail to designate the person intended to be nominated), then and in either event I nominate and appoint as such Successor Trustee whosoever shall qualify as Executor or Administrator of my estate, as the case may be.

8. This Declaration of Trust shall extend to and be binding upon the heirs, executors, administrators and assigns of the undersigned and upon the successors to the Trustee.

9. This Declaration of Trust shall be construed and enforced in accordance with the laws of the State of

_____ .

IN WITNESS WHEREOF I have hereunto set my hand and seal this_____day

of_____, 19_____.

(sign here) _____ L.S.

Witness: (1)_____

Witness: (2)_____

STATE OF _____ ⎫
                                ⎬ ss: _____
COUNTY OF _____ ⎭

On the_____day of_____, nineteen hundred and_____,

before me came_____known to me to be the individual described in, and who

executed the foregoing instrument, and_____ acknowledged that _____ executed the same; and in due form of law acknowledged the foregoing instrument to be _____ act and deed and desired the same might be recorded as such.

WITNESS my hand and notarial seal the day and year aforesaid.

(Notary Seal)                        _____
                                                Notary Public

```
┌─────────────────────────────────────┐
│       DECLARATION OF TRUST           │
│            FOR NAMING                │
│    TWO OR MORE BENEFICIARIES         │
│         SHARING EQUALLY              │
│            TO RECEIVE                 │
│       MUTUAL FUND SHARES             │
└─────────────────────────────────────┘
```

## Instructions:

On the following pages will be found duplicate copies of a declaration of trust (DT–11) which will be suitable for use in connection with the inter vivos trust arrangement suggested above, where it is desired to name several persons, sharing equally, to receive mutual fund shares upon the death of the owner.

Cross out "city" or "town," leaving the appropriate designation of your community.

Enter the names of the beneficiaries in the appropriate place in Paragraph 2. Note that the instrument specifies that the named beneficiaries are to receive *"in equal shares, or the survivor of them/per stirpes."* Now, think carefully: If you have named your three brothers with the understanding that if one brother predeceases you, *his* children will take *his* share, cross out *"or the survivor of them"* and initial it. If that is not what you want— if, for example, you prefer that the share of your deceased brother be divided by your two surviving brothers, cross out *"per stirpes"* and initial it. Remember, you must cross out *"or the survivor of them"* or *"per stirpes"*—one or the other.

### For shares purchased outright:

If you are buying shares outright, enter the name of the fund in the appropriate place in the instrument. Instruct your mutual fund dealer that the shares are to be registered *"(Your Name) Trustee u/d/t dated _____."* Some funds will wish to examine the declaration of trust at the time the shares are issued, so execute both original and duplicate and offer one to the dealer to send along with the registration instructions. In any case, if you ever decide to sell the shares, or if you die and the beneficiary requests their transfer, the fund will ask to see the declaration of trust. It is suggested, therefore, that when the share certificate is issued, the signed declaration of trust be permanently stapled to it. If you make subsequent additional purchases of the same fund, it is not necessary to execute a new declaration of trust each time—simply register the shares exactly as you did your first purchase. If you wish to name a different beneficiary on such subsequent purchases, then you *will* need to execute a new declaration of trust. To avoid confusion, never date two instruments the same date.

If you have a "voluntary plan" or "open account," the fund will hold the shares and no certificate will be issued. It is important, then, that you place the original declaration of trust where you can find it readily if you decide to sell your shares or where the beneficiary can find it if you die.

### For contractual plans:

If you are buying a contractual plan which does not use a declaration of trust to designate the beneficiary, in the place in the instrument provided for the name of the fund, enter *"(Name of fund) held in (Name of fund) Investment Plan No. _____."* Instruct your mutual fund dealer to send the completed instrument along with the plan application. The plan's custodian bank will fill in the number assigned to your account. With a contractual plan, the beneficiary designation— and therefore the probate exemption—is *not effective* unless and until the instrument is permanently filed with the plan's custodian bank. It isn't absolutely necessary that the instrument be filed at the time the plan is applied for; you can send it in later. If you choose this latter course, be sure to ask for acknowledgement of its receipt. Many banks charge a "late filing fee" of $2.50 if the declaration of trust does not accompany the application.

When your plan certificate is issued, staple the executed duplicate declaration of trust into it for your permanent record and for the information of the beneficiary.

Whenever there is any possibility of a minor child receiving the property, make certain that you name an adult who can act as trustee for the child. The name of that adult should be inserted in Paragraph 7 of the instrument shown here. Avoid naming as trustee a person not likely to survive until the child has reached age twenty-one.

# Declaration of Trust

_____ of the _____

WHEREAS, I, ___John J. Smith___, State of ___Connecticut___,

City/Town of ___Jonesville___, County of ___Fairfax___

am the owner of certain shares of the capital stock of:

___Ajax Mutual Fund___

(Name of Fund)

NOW, THEREFORE, KNOW ALL MEN BY THESE PRESENTS, that I do hereby acknowledge and declare that I hold and will hold said Shares and all right, title and interest in and to said Shares IN TRUST, for the following uses and purposes:

1. To add, or cause to be added, to the corpus of this Trust all income and distributions which may from time to time be received on the said Shares, by causing the same to be invested in additional shares, or if I shall so elect from time to time to pay said income and distributions or cause the same to be paid to myself during my lifetime.

2. To hold said Shares and all right, title and interest therein for the use and benefit of the following ~~_____~~ _J.J.S._

___three___ persons, in equal shares, or the survivor of them.

| | |
|---|---|
| Thomas B. Smith | (my brother) |
| William R. Smith | (my brother) |
| Charles M. Smith | (my brother) |

Upon my death, unless all of the beneficiaries shall predecease me or unless we shall die as a result of a common accident or disaster, my Successor Trustee is hereby directed forthwith to transfer said Shares and all right, title and interest in and to said Shares unto the beneficiaries absolutely and thereby terminate this trust; provided, however, that if any beneficiary hereunder shall then be a minor, the Successor Trustee shall hold such beneficiary's share of the trust assets in continuing trust until such beneficiary attains the age of twenty-one years. Prior to that date, the Successor Trustee may apply or expend any or all of the income or principal for the maintenance, education and support of the minor beneficiary without the intervention of any guardian and without application to any court. Such payments of income or principal may be made to the parents of such minor or to the person with whom the minor is living without any liability upon the Successor Trustee to see to the application thereof. If such minor survives me but dies before attaining the age of twenty-one years, at his or her death the Successor Trustee shall deliver, pay over, transfer and distribute the trust property to such minor's personal representatives, absolutely.

3. I reserve the right to register any shares held hereunder in the name of a nominee, which nominee may be myself as an individual. The right, power and authority is hereby conferred upon any Successor Trustee hereunder, at any time during the minority of any beneficiary, to invest and reinvest without limitation or restriction, to sell all or any part of the Shares being held, holding either Shares or the proceeds of the sale thereof until the minor beneficiary attains the age of twenty-one years.

4. This Trust is created upon the express understanding that the issuer or custodian of the Shares hereunder shall be under no liability whatsoever to see to its proper administration, and that upon the transfer of the right, title and interest in and to said Shares by any Trustee hereunder, said issuer or custodian shall conclusively treat the transferee as the sole owner of said Shares. In the event that any shares, cash or other property shall be distributable at any time under the terms of said hereunder, and shall be under no liability to see to the proper application thereof, provided, however, that as and if I shall elect from time to time to cause dividends and distributions on said Shares to be distributed, rather than reinvested, the issuer or custodian shall be fully authorized to pay such dividends and distributions direct to me individually rather than to me as Trustee hereunder and may continue such payments to me individually unless there shall have been filed with it written notice of my death or incapacity satisfactory to it. The issuer or custodian is authorized to make such distributions under a mutual fund systematic withdrawal plan as have been specified by me or by any Successor Trustee acting hereunder. Until the issuer

_____ benefit of any person whatsoever.

7. In the case of my death or legal incapacity, I hereby nominate and appoint as Successor Trustee hereunder the beneficiary first above named unless he or she shall be a minor or otherwise legally incapacitated, in which event I hereby nominate and appoint as Successor Trustee hereunder the beneficiary whose name appears second above. If such beneficiary named second above shall be a minor or legally incompetent, then I nominate and appoint as Successor Trustee:

| | | | |
|---|---|---|---|
| ___Henry P. Adams___ | ___Jonesville___ | ___Connecticut___ | of |
| (Name) | City | State | |
| (Address) ___125___ ___Barnum Street___ | | | |
| Number | Street | | |

8. This Declaration of Trust shall extend to and be binding upon the heirs, executors, administrators and assigns of the undersigned and upon the successors to the Trustee.

9. This Declaration of Trust shall be construed and enforced in accordance with the laws of the State of ___Connecticut___.

WHEREAS, I,_____of the

City/Town of_____, County of_____, State of_____,

am the owner of certain shares of the capital stock of:

_____

(Name of Fund)

NOW, THEREFORE, KNOW ALL MEN BY THESE PRESENTS, that I do hereby acknowledge and declare that I hold and will hold said Shares and all right, title and interest in and to said Shares IN TRUST, for the following uses and purposes:

1. To add, or cause to be added, to the corpus of this Trust all income and distributions which may from time to time be received on the said Shares, by causing the same to be invested in additional shares, or if I shall so elect from time to time to pay said income and distributions or cause the same to be paid to myself during my lifetime.

2. To hold said Shares and all right, title and interest therein for the use and benefit of the following

_____persons, in equal shares, or the survivor of them/per stirpes:

Upon my death, unless all of the beneficiaries shall predecease me or unless we shall die as a result of a common accident or disaster, my Successor Trustee is hereby directed forthwith to transfer said Shares and all right, title and interest in and to said Shares unto the beneficiaries absolutely and thereby terminate this trust; provided, however, that if any beneficiary hereunder shall then be a minor, the Successor Trustee shall hold such beneficiary's share of the trust assets in continuing trust until such beneficiary attains the age of twenty-one years. Prior to that date, the Successor Trustee may apply or expend any or all of the income or principal for the maintenance, education and support of the minor beneficiary without the intervention of any guardian and without application to any court. Such payments of income or principal may be made to the parents of such minor or to the person with whom the minor is living without any liability upon the Successor Trustee to see to the application thereof. If such minor survives me but dies before attaining the age of twenty-one years, at his or her death the Successor Trustee shall deliver, pay over, transfer and distribute the trust property to such minor's personal representatives, absolutely.

3. I reserve the right to register any shares held hereunder in the name of a nominee, which nominee may be myself as an individual, or to pledge the shares as collateral for a loan. The right, power and authority is hereby conferred upon any Successor Trustee hereunder, at any time during the minority of the beneficiary, to invest and reinvest without limitation or restriction, to sell all or any part of the Shares being held, holding either Shares or the proceeds of the sale thereof until the minor beneficiary attains the age of twenty-one years.

4. This Trust is created upon the express understanding that the issuer or custodian of the Shares hereunder shall be under no liability whatsoever to see to its proper administration, and that upon the transfer of the right, title and interest in and to said Shares by any Trustee hereunder, said issuer or custodian shall conclusively treat the transferee as the sole owner of said Shares. In the event that any shares, cash or other property shall be distributable at any time under the terms of said Shares, the said issuer or custodian is fully authorized to pay, deliver and distribute the same to whosoever shall then be trustee hereunder, and shall be under no liability to see to the proper application thereof, provided, however, that as and if I shall elect from time to time to cause dividends and distributions on said Shares to be distributed, rather than reinvested, the issuer or custodian shall be fully authorized to pay such dividends and distributions direct to me individually rather than to me as Trustee hereunder and may continue such payments to me individually unless there shall have been filed with it written notice of my death or incapacity satisfactory to it. The issuer or custodian is authorized to make such distributions under a mutual fund systematic withdrawal plan as have been specified by me or by any Successor Trustee acting hereunder. Until the issuer

or custodian shall receive from some person interested in this Trust, written notice of any death or other event upon which the right to receive may depend, the issuer or custodian shall incur no liability for payments made in good faith to persons whose interests shall have been affected by such event. The issuer or custodian shall be protected in acting upon any notice or other instrument or document believed by it to be genuine and to have been signed or presented by the proper party or parties.

5. The death during my lifetime, or in a common accident or disaster with me, of any beneficiary designated hereunder shall revoke such designation, and in the former event I reserve the right to designate a new beneficiary. Should no designated beneficiary be surviving, this Trust shall terminate upon my death and the trust property shall revert to my estate.

6. I hereby reserve unto myself the power and right at any time during my lifetime, before actual distribution to the beneficiaries hereunder, to revoke in whole or in part or to amend the Trust hereby created without the necessity of obtaining the consent of the beneficiaries and without giving notice to the beneficiaries. Any one of the following acts shall be conclusive evidence of such revocation of this Trust:

    (a) The delivery to the issuer or custodian of the Shares by me of written notice that this Trust is revoked in whole or in part;

    (b) The transfer by me of my right, title and interest in and to said Shares;

    (c) The delivery by me to the issuer or custodian of the Shares of written notice of the death of the Beneficiary hereunder.

I hereby reserve unto myself the right, upon the revocation or termination of this Trust, to create a new Trust for the benefit of any person whatsoever.

7. In the case of my death or legal incapacity, I hereby nominate and appoint as Successor Trustee hereunder the beneficiary first above named unless he or she shall be a minor or otherwise legally incapacitated, in which event I hereby nominate and appoint as Successor Trustee hereunder the beneficiary whose name appears second above. If such beneficiary named second above shall be a minor or legally incompetent, then I nominate and appoint as Successor Trustee:

(Name)_____, of

(Address)_____
         Number         Street         City         State

8. This Declaration of Trust shall extend to and be binding upon the heirs, executors, administrators and assigns of the undersigned and upon the successors to the Trustee.

9. This Declaration of Trust shall be construed and enforced in accordance with the laws of the State of

_____.

IN WITNESS WHEREOF I have hereunto set my hand and seal this_____day

of_____, 19____.

          (sign here)_____L.S.

Witness:  (1)_____

Witness:  (2)_____

STATE OF _____ ⎱
                       ss: _____
COUNTY OF _____ ⎰

On the_____day of_____, nineteen hundred and_____, before

me came_____known to me to be the individual described in, and who executed the foregoing instrument, and _____ acknowledged that _____ executed the same; and in due form of law acknowledged the foregoing instrument to be _____ act and deed and desired the same might be recorded as such.

WITNESS my hand and notarial seal the day and year aforesaid.

(Notary Seal)                     _____
                                                    Notary Public

```
┌─────────────────────────────────────────┐
│          DECLARATION OF TRUST            │
│               FOR NAMING                 │
│     ONE PRIMARY BENEFICIARY WITH         │
│   YOUR CHILDREN, SHARING EQUALLY,        │
│     AS CONTINGENT BENEFICIARIES          │
│               TO RECEIVE                 │
│          MUTUAL FUND SHARES              │
└─────────────────────────────────────────┘
```

Instructions:

On the following pages will be found duplicate copies of a declaration of trust (DT-12) which will be suitable for use in connection with the inter vivos trust arrangement suggested above, where it is desired to name one person (ordinarily, one's spouse) as primary beneficiary, with one's children as contingent beneficiaries to receive mutual fund shares upon the death of the owner.

Cross out *"city"* or *"town,"* leaving the appropriate designation of your community.

Enter the name of the primary beneficiary in the appropriate place in Paragraph 2. Note that the instrument refers to your children as *"natural not/or adopted."* Now, decide: If you have an adopted child and you wish to *include* him, cross out the word "not" in the phrase *"natural not/or adopted"* and initial it. If you wish to *exclude* your adopted child, cross out the word *"or"* in the same phrase and initial it. Remember, you *must* cross out *"not"* or *"or"*—one or the other. Note next that the instrument specifies that your children are to receive *"in equal shares, or the survivor of them/per stirpes."* Now, think carefully: If it is your wish that if one of your children does not survive you, his share will revert to *his* children in equal shares, cross out *"or the survivor of them"* and initial it. If that is *not* what you want—if, for example, you prefer that the share of your deceased child be divided among your surviving children, cross out *"per stirpes"* and initial it. Remember, you must cross out *"or the survivor of them"* or *"per stirpes"*—one or the other.

### For shares purchased outright:

If you are buying shares outright, enter the name of the fund in the appropriate place in the instrument. Instruct your mutual fund dealer that the shares are to be registered *"(Your Name) Trustee u/d/t dated _____."* Some funds will wish to examine the declaration of trust at the time the shares are issued, so execute both original and duplicate and offer one to the dealer to send along with the registration instructions. In any case, if you ever decide to sell the shares, or if you die and the beneficiary requests their transfer, the fund will ask to see the declaration of trust. It is suggested, therefore, that when the share certificate is issued, the signed declaration of trust be permanently stapled to it. If you make subsequent additional purchases of the same fund, it is not necessary to execute a new declaration of trust each time—simply register the shares exactly as you did your first purchase. If you wish to name a different beneficiary on such subsequent purchases, then you *will* need to execute a new declaration of trust. To avoid confusion, never date two instruments the same date.

If you have a "voluntary plan" or "open account," the fund will hold the shares and no certificate will be issued. It is important, then, that you place the original declaration of trust where you can find it readily if you decide to sell your shares or where the beneficiary can find it if you die.

### For contractual plans:

If you are buying a contractual plan which does not use a declaration of trust to designate the beneficiary, in the place in the instrument provided for the name of the fund, enter *"(Name of fund) held in (Name of fund) Investment Plan No. _____."* Instruct your mutual fund dealer to send the completed instrument along with the plan application. The plan's custodian bank will fill in the number assigned to your account. With a contractual plan, the beneficiary designation—and therefore the probate exemption—is *not effective* unless and until it is permanently filed with the plan's custodian bank. It isn't absolutely necessary that the instrument be filed at the time the plan is applied for; you can send it in later. If you choose this latter course, be sure to ask for acknowledgment of its receipt. Many banks charge a "late filing fee" of $2.50 if the declaration of trust does not accompany the application.

When your plan certificate is issued, staple the executed duplicate declaration of trust into it for your permanent record and for the information of the beneficiary.

Whenever there is any possibility of a minor child receiving the property, make certain that you name an adult who can act as trustee for the child. The name of that adult should be inserted in Paragraph 7 of the instrument shown here. Avoid naming as trustee a person not likely to survive until the child has reached age twenty-one.

WHEREAS, I,_____of the

City/Town of_____, County of_____, State of_____,

am the owner of certain shares of the capital stock of:

_____

(Name of Fund)

NOW, THEREFORE, KNOW ALL MEN BY THESE PRESENTS, that I do hereby acknowledge and declare that I hold and will hold said Shares and all right, title and interest in and to said Shares IN TRUST, for the following uses and purposes:

1. To add, or cause to be added, to the corpus of this Trust all income and distributions which may from time to time be received on the said Shares, by causing the same to be invested in additional shares, or if I shall so elect from time to time to pay said income and distributions or cause the same to be paid to myself during my lifetime.

2. To hold said Shares and all right, title and interest therein for the use and benefit of:

(Name)_____, of

(Address)_____
          Number              Street              City            State

(hereinafter referred to as the "First Beneficiary") and upon his or her death prior to the termination of the trust, for the use and benefit of my children, natural not/or adopted, in equal shares, or the survivor of them/per stirpes. Upon my death, unless all of the beneficiaries shall predecease me or unless we shall die as a result of a common accident or disaster, my Successor Trustee is hereby directed forthwith to transfer said Shares and all right, title and interest in and to said Shares unto the beneficiary or beneficiaries absolutely and thereby terminate this trust; _provided,_ however, that if any beneficiary hereunder shall then be a minor, the Successor Trustee shall hold such beneficiary's share of the trust assets in continuing trust until such beneficiary attains the age of twenty-one years. Prior to that date, the Successor Trustee may apply or expend any or all of the income or principal of such minor's share for the maintenance, education and support of the minor beneficiary without the intervention of any guardian and without application to any court. Such payments of income or principal may be made to the parents of such minor or to the person with whom the minor is living without any liability upon the Successor Trustee to see to the application thereof. If such minor survives me but dies before attaining the age of twenty-one years, at his or her death the Successor Trustee shall deliver, pay over, transfer and distribute the trust property to such minor's personal representatives, absolutely.

3. I reserve the right to register any shares held hereunder in the name of a nominee, which nominee may be myself as an individual, or to pledge the shares as collateral for a loan. The right, power and authority is hereby conferred upon any Successor Trustee hereunder, at any time during the minority of the beneficiary, to invest and reinvest without limitation or restriction, to sell all or any part of the Shares being held, holding either Shares or the proceeds of the sale thereof until the minor beneficiary attains the age of twenty-one years.

4. This Trust is created upon the express understanding that the issuer or custodian of the Shares hereunder shall be under no liability whatsoever to see to its proper administration, and that upon the transfer of the right, title and interest in and to said Shares by any Trustee hereunder, said issuer or custodian shall conclusively treat the transferee as the sole owner of said Shares. In the event that any shares, cash or other property shall be distributable at any time under the terms of said Shares, the said issuer or custodian is fully authorized to pay, deliver and distribute the same to whosoever shall then be trustee hereunder, and shall be under no liability to see to the proper application thereof, provided, however, that as and if I shall elect from time to time to cause dividends and distributions on said Shares to be distributed, rather than reinvested, the issuer or custodian shall be fully authorized to pay such dividends and distributions direct to me individually rather than to me as Trustee hereunder and may continue such payments to me individually unless there shall have been filed with it written notice of my death or incapacity satisfactory to it. The issuer or custodian is authorized to make such distributions under a mutual fund systematic withdrawal plan as have been specified by me or by any Successor Trustee acting hereunder. Until the issuer or custodian shall receive from some person interested in this Trust, written notice of any death or other event upon which the right to receive may depend, the issuer or custodian shall incur no liability for payments made in good faith to persons whose interests shall have been affected by such event. The issuer or custodian shall be protected in acting upon any notice or other instrument or document believed by it to be genuine and to have been signed or presented by the proper party or parties.

5. The death during my lifetime, or in a common accident or disaster with me, of any beneficiary designated hereunder shall revoke such designation, and in the former event I reserve the right to designate a new beneficiary. Should no designated beneficiary be surviving, this Trust shall terminate upon my death and the trust property shall revert to my estate.

6. I hereby reserve unto myself the power and right at any time during my lifetime, before actual distribution to the beneficiaries hereunder, to revoke in whole or in part or to amend the Trust hereby created without the necessity of obtaining the consent of the beneficiaries and without giving notice to the beneficiaries. Any one of the following acts shall be conclusive evidence of such revocation of this Trust:

    (a)  The delivery to the issuer or custodian of the Shares by me of written notice that this Trust is revoked in whole or in part;

    (b)  The transfer by me of my right, title and interest in and to said Shares;

    (c)  The delivery by me to the issuer or custodian of the Shares of written notice of the death of the Beneficiary hereunder.

I hereby reserve unto myself the right, upon the revocation or termination of this Trust, to create a new Trust for the benefit of any person whatsoever.

7. In the case of my death or legal incapacity, I hereby nominate and appoint as Successor Trustee hereunder the First Beneficiary unless he or she shall be a minor or otherwise legally incapacitated, in which event I hereby nominate and appoint as Successor Trustee hereunder:

(Name)_____, of

(Address)_____
             Number              Street              City              State

and upon his or her failure or ceasing to act or should I for any reason fail to designate the person above intended to be nominated, then I nominate and appoint as Successor Trustee hereunder whosoever shall qualify as Executor, Administrator or Guardian, as the case may be, of my estate.

8. This Declaration of Trust shall extend to and be binding upon the heirs, executors, administrators and assigns of the undersigned and upon the successors to the Trustee.

9. This Declaration of Trust shall be construed and enforced in accordance with the laws of the State of

_____.

IN WITNESS WHEREOF I have hereunto set my hand and seal this_____day

of_____, 19_____.

                                   (sign here)_____L.S.

Witness: (1)_____

Witness: (2)_____

STATE OF _____⎫

                                  ⎬ ss: _____

COUNTY OF _____⎭

On the_____day of_____, nineteen hundred and_____, before

me came_____known to me to be the individual described in, and who executed

the foregoing instrument, and _____ acknowledged that _____ executed the same; and in due form of law

acknowledged the foregoing instrument to be _____ act and deed and desired the same might be recorded as such.

    WITNESS my hand and notarial seal the day and year aforesaid.

    (Notary Seal)                                   _____

                                                            Notary Public

# EPILOGUE

By disclosing the imperfections of the mutual fund industry I did not intend to deter you from employing the valuable services of funds. My purpose was to give you facts which would enable you to make an informed judgment in selecting a fund.

For those of you who want financial independence by retirement age, or who are now retired but want to preserve what you have accumulated and make it pro-

ductive, I know of no better way of achieving your objective than by employing the professional investment management obtainable through mutual funds.

You now know what to look for and what to avoid. You also know the questions to ask.

Good luck, and may all your problems be long-term capital gains!

# INDEX

## TO THE FIVE MILLION AMERICANS WHO NOW OWN MUTUAL FUNDS— TO THE MILLIONS MORE WHO WILL BUY MUTUAL FUNDS IN THE FUTURE— TO COUNTLESS OTHERS WHO SIMPLY WANT TO BE WELL-INFORMED— THIS BOOK PROVIDES STARTLING FACTS NEVER BEFORE DISCLOSED TO THE PUBLIC!

-----------------------------------------------------------------

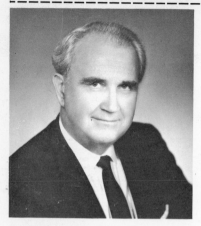

# About the Author

**NORMAN F. DACEY** is America's best-known professional estate planner. In a hundred books and articles, in countless university and law school lectures and public forums, in more than five hundred radio and television broadcasts, he has reached and influenced more people with his philosophy than any other financial planner in history, guiding millions toward the goal of personal financial security. His tremendous best seller HOW TO AVOID PROBATE revolutionized estate planning in America.

The Securities and Exchange Commission has sought his opinion of proposed rules and statutes governing mutual fund operations, while the House Interstate and Foreign Commerce Committee has praised his revealing testimony before it on fund practices. The Senate Antitrust and Monopoly Subcommittee invited him to serve as a special consultant. The Department of Defense has sought his professional assistance. The largest consumer organization in America has retained him as a consultant. The Justice Department has solicited his help. At the invitation of the Air Force, he has delivered a series of lectures at the Air Force Academy. The Episcopal Church in America presented him on a 300-station radio network; the Methodist Church sponsored his appearance in a one-hour nationwide broadcast. CBS radio in Boston, inviting him for a two-hour talk, cancelled succeeding programs and kept him on the air for an unprecedented four hours; CBS radio in Philadelphia gave him six hours of prime time in a single day! His appearances on the Today Show, the Tonight Show and the Alan Burke Show produced the heaviest mail response in their history. The producers of the Mike Douglas Show described the reaction to his five appearances as "tremendous!" Westinghouse Radio twice cancelled scheduled programs to keep him on the air two full hours.

◇

## AUTHORITATIVE!

"If anyone can claim experience with the distribution of mutuals, it is this veteran. To deny his expertise in the mutual fund area is not possible."

*Trusts and Estates* Magazine
January 1970

"Dacey enjoys an excellent reputation in as well as outside the financial community."

U.S. Securities and Exchange Commission
April 1970

"Known wherever mutual funds are sold, he has made many unique contributions to the mutual fund industry over the years, including the first systematic withdrawal plan."

*Investment Dealers' Digest*
January 1970

◇

-----------------------------------------------------------------

## To the Mutual Fund Investor
### Reading This Book Is Like Throwing on a Light Switch in a Pitch-Dark Room!